Lecture Notes in Computer Science   12675

More information about this subseries at http://www.springer.com/series/7410

Nikita Borisov · Claudia Diaz (Eds.)

Financial Cryptography and Data Security

25th International Conference, FC 2021
Virtual Event, March 1–5, 2021
Revised Selected Papers, Part II

 Springer

Editors
Nikita Borisov
University of Illinois at Urbana-Champaign
Urbana, IL, USA

Claudia Diaz
KU Leuven
Leuven, Belgium

ISSN 0302-9743   ISSN 1611-3349 (electronic)
Lecture Notes in Computer Science
ISBN 978-3-662-64330-3   ISBN 978-3-662-64331-0 (eBook)
https://doi.org/10.1007/978-3-662-64331-0

LNCS Sublibrary: SL4 – Security and Cryptology

This Springer imprint is published by the registered company Springer-Verlag GmbH, DE part of Springer Nature
The registered company address is: Heidelberger Platz 3, 14197 Berlin, Germany

Preface

FC 2021, the 25th International Conference on Financial Cryptography and Data Security, was held online during March 1–5, 2021.

We received an all-time record of 223 submissions, of which 6 were desk rejected due to non-compliance with page limits and 217 were considered for review. Of these, 54 were included in the program, 47 as regular papers, four as short papers, and three as Systematization of Knowledge (SoK) papers; a 25% acceptance rate. Revised papers appear in these proceedings.

The review process was double-blind and carried out entirely online via the HotCRP review platform. The review period lasted about 10 weeks, taking place between the end of September and the beginning of December 2020. Papers received four reviews on average. The review period was followed by an online discussion, which was at times extensive—two papers received 27 comments and the median discussion had five comments. After discussion, papers were either accepted, rejected, or conditionally accepted, with a Program Committee (PC) member assigned in the latter case to shepherd the paper and ensure that specific improvements were made. One of the conditionally accepted papers could not be included in the program due to a technical flaw discovered during the shepherding process.

We are grateful to the 127 Program Committee members and 94 external reviewers who reviewed all the submissions and provided thoughtful and constructive feedback, which considerably strengthened the quality of the final program. Two reviewers stood out in terms of the quality of their reviews and were named "Distinguished Reviewers": Zeta Avarikioti and Dionysis Zindros. Additionally, we would like to recognize reviewers whose contributions went above and beyond the expectations of a regular PC member: Joseph Bonneau, Christian Cachin, Jeremy Clark, Juan Garay, Arthur Gervais, Katharina Kohls, Johannes Krupp, Wouter Lueks, Sarah Meiklejohn, Pedro Moreno-Sanchez, Bart Preneel, Marko Vukolić, Riad Wahby, and Ren Zhang. Finally, we would like to recognize three external reviewers for their outstanding service: Christian Badertscher, Ankit Gangwal, and Henning Seidler.

FC 2021 no longer distinguished between two "tracks", one on traditional financial cryptography and another on blockchain research, and instead had a single track with a wide variety of topics including blockchain-related papers. When classifying papers into these two broad categories, we found that 72% of submitted papers were on topics related to blockchain research, while only 55% of accepted papers fell in that category. The accepted papers were organized according to their topic into 12 sessions: Smart Contracts, Anonymity and Privacy in Cryptocurrencies, Secure Multi-party Computation, System and Application Security, Zero-knowledge Proofs, Blockchain Protocols, Payment Channels, Mining, Scaling Blockchains, Authentication and Usability, Measurement, and Cryptography.

Due to the COVID-19 global pandemic, a physical meeting was impossible; instead FC 2021 was held as a four-day online event. Papers were presented in 12 sessions, with a short live presentation followed by a question-and-answer session with the audience.

Authors also recorded a longer paper presentation of 20–30 minutes that is available online, linked from the conference website. In addition to the 12 regular paper sessions, the program included a Rump session, a keynote talk on "Signature and Commitment" by Whitfield Diffie, a keynote Fireside Chat with SEC Commissioner Hester Peirce, a General Assembly, and a social hour at the end of each day. We are grateful to all the session chairs for their service. And we would like to offer special thanks to Kay McKelly and Kevin McCurley for providing and managing the online conference platform. We would also like to thank Sergi Delgado Segura and Rafael Hirschfeld for their service as conference general chairs, and the IFCA directors and Steering Committee for their help organizing the conference during this particularly challenging year.

Finally, we would like to thank the sponsors of the conference for their generous support: our Platinum sponsor Novi; our Gold sponsors Chainalysis and IBM; and our Silver sponsors NTT Research and Protocol Labs.

August 2021

Nikita Borisov
Claudia Diaz

Organization

General Chairs

Sergi Delgado Segura   Talaia Labs, UK
Rafael Hirshfeld   Unipay Technologies, The Netherlands

Program Committee Chairs

Nikita Borisov   University of Illinois at Urbana-Champaign, USA
Claudia Diaz   KU Leuven, Belgium

Steering Committee

Joseph Bonneau   New York University, USA
Rafael Hirshfeld   Unipay Technologies, The Netherlands
Andrew Miller   University of Illinois at Urbana-Champaign, USA
Monica Quaintance   Kadena, USA
Burton Rosenberg   University of Miami, USA

Program Committee

Ittai Abraham   VMware Research, Israel
Gunes Acar   KU Leuven, Belgium
Shashank Agrawal   Western Digital Research, USA
Ross Anderson   University of Cambridge, UK
Elli Androulaki   IBM Research—Zurich, Switzerland
Diego F. Aranha   Aarhus University, Denmark
Man Ho Au   The University of Hong Kong, China
Zeta Avarikioti   ETH Zurich, Switzerland
Erman Ayday   Case Western Reserve University, USA,
     and Bilkent University, Turkey
Foteini Baldimtsi   George Mason University, USA
Shehar Bano   Novi and Facebook, UK
Iddo Bentov   Cornell Tech, USA
Bobby Bhattacharjee   University of Maryland, USA
Alex Biryukov   University of Luxembourg, Luxembourg
Dan Boneh   Stanford University, USA
Joseph Bonneau   New York University, USA
Karima Boudaoud   Université Côte d'Azur, France
Ioana Boureanu   University of Surrey, UK

Xavier Boyen   Queensland University of Technology, Australia
Rainer Böhme   University of Innsbruck, Austria
Jeffrey Burdges   Web 3 Foundation, Switzerland
Benedikt Bünz   Stanford University, USA
Christian Cachin   University of Bern, Switzerland
L. Jean Camp   Indiana University, USA
Srdjan Capkun   ETH Zurich, Switzerland
Pern Hui Chia   Google, USA
Tom Chothia   University of Birmingham, UK
Jeremy Clark   Concordia University, Canada
Shaanan Cohney   University of Pennsylvania, USA,
                                    and University of Melbourne, Australia
George Danezis   University College London and Novi, UK
Sanchari Das   University of Denver, USA
Vensa Daza   Pompeu Fabra University, Spain
Jean Paul Degabriele   TU Darmstadt, Germany
Matteo Dell'Amico   EURECOM, France
Sven Dietrich   City University of New York, USA
Benjamin Edwards   Cyentia Institute, USA
Tariq Elahi   University of Edinburgh, UK
Kaoutar Elkhiyaoui   IBM Research, Switzerland
William Enck   North Carolina State University, USA
Zekeriya Erkin   Delft University of Technology, The Netherlands
Ittay Eyal   Technion, Israel
Antonio Faonio   EURECOM, France
Dario Fiore   IMDEA Software Institute, Spain
Ben Fisch   Stanford University, USA
Simone Fischer-Hübner   Karlstad University, Sweden
Juan Garay   Texas A&M University, USA
Christina Garman   Purdue University, USA
Arthur Gervais   Imperial College London, UK
Esha Ghosh   Microsoft Research, USA
Thomas Gross   Newcastle University, UK
Jens Grossklags   Technical University of Munich, Germany
Feng Hao   University of Warwick, UK
Ethan Heilman   Boston University, USA
Urs Hengartner   University of Waterloo, Canada
Ryan Henry   University of Calgary, Canada
Jori Herrera-Joancomartí   Universitat Autònoma de Barcelona, Spain
Jaap-Henk Hoepman   Radboud University and University of Groeningen,
                                    The Netherlands
Nicholas Hopper   University of Minnesota, USA
Kévin Huguenin   University of Lausanne, Switzerland
Stephanie Hurder   Prysm Group, USA
Alice Hutchings   University of Cambridge, UK
Marc Juarez   University of Southern California, USA

Abhi Shelat	Northeastern University, USA
Jared M. Smith	Oak Ridge National Laboratory, USA
Yonatan Sompolinsky	The Hebrew University of Jerusalem, Israel
Kyle Soska	Carnegie Mellon University, USA
Douglas Stebila	University of Waterloo, Canada
Vanessa Teague	University of Melbourne, Australia
Alin Tomescu	VMware Research, USA
Luke Valenta	Cloudflare Research, USA
Aad van Moorsel	Newcastle University, UK
Marie Vasek	University College London, UK
Pramod Viswanath	University of Illinois at Urbana-Champaign, USA
Artemij Voskobojnikov	University of British Columbia, Canada
Marko Vukolić	IBM Research, Switzerland
Riad S. Wahby	Stanford University, USA
Nick Weaver	International Computer Science Institute, USA
Edgar Wieppl	University of Vienna and SBA Research, Austria
Phillipp Winter	The Tor Project, USA
Jiangshan Yu	Monash University, Australia
Fan Zhang	Chainlink and Duke University, USA
Ren Zhang	Nervos, China
Dionysis Zindros	University of Athens, Greece
Aviv Zohar	The Hebrew University of Jerusalem, Israel

Additional Reviewers

Abramova, Svetlana
Akand, Mamun
Alupotha, Jayamine
Avizheh, Sepideh
Badertscher, Christian
Bag, Samiran
Bagaria, Vivek
Beck, Gabrielle
Bentov, Iddo
Bissias, George
Buhren, Robert
Cascudo, Ignacio
Chatzigiannis, Panagiotis
Choi, Kevin
Das, Sourav
Daveas, Stelios
Diamond, Parker
Elichai, Turkel
Ersoy, Oguzhan
Escudero, Daniel

Farhang, Sadegh
Feher, Daniel
Fietkau, Julian
Fischer, Felix
Fletcher, Christopher
Fröwis, Michael
Gangwal, Ankit
Govinden, Jérôme
Guimarães, Antônio Carlos
Gupta, Abhinav
Haffey, Preston
Haque, Abida
Harishankar, Madhumitha
Humbert, Mathias
Islami, Lejla
Jao, David
Ji, Yan
Karadzic, Vukasin
Karakostas, Dimitris
Karantaidou, Ioanna

Kasper, Daniel
Keller, Patrik
Knapp, Jodie
Kolonelos, Dimitris
Lagorio, Giovanni
Leonardos, Nikos
Li, Tianyu
Linvill, Kirby
Litos, Orfeas
Lorenzo, Martinico
Madhusudan, Akash
Maier, Dominik
Marmolejo Cossío, Francisco
Martinico, Lorenzo
Mazorra, Bruno
McMenamin, Conor
Medley, Liam
Nabi, Mahmudun
Nadahalli, Tejaswi
Navarro-Arribas, Guillermo
Polydouri, Andrianna
Posa, Tibor
Prabhu Kumble, Satwik
Raghuraman, Srinivasan
Ribaudo, Marina
Rovira, Sergi
Sarenche, Roozbeh

Seidler, Henning
Sharifian, Setareh
Shrestha, Nibesh
Silde, Tjerand
Simkin, Mark
Sliwinski, Jakub
Sutton, Michael
Syrmoudis, Emmanuel
Tairi, Erkan
Takahasi, Akira
Terner, Benjamin
Tikhomirov, Sergei
Vadaraj, Srikar
Vitto, Giuseppe
Volkhov, Mikhail
Weber, Brian
Wilsiol, Nils
Wyborski, Shai
Xiang, Zhuolun
Xue, Haiyang
Yang, Rupeng
Zacharakis, Alexandros
Zacharias, Thomas
Zamyatin, Alexei
Zapico, Arantxa
Zhang, Xinyuan

Contents – Part II

Measurement

Cryptography

Contents – Part I

Blockchain Protocols

SoK: Communication Across Distributed Ledgers

Alexei Zamyatin[1,2]([⊠]), Mustafa Al-Bassam[3], Dionysis Zindros[4],
Eleftherios Kokoris-Kogias[5,9], Pedro Moreno-Sanchez[6], Aggelos Kiayias[7,8],
and William J. Knottenbelt[1]

[1] Imperial College London, London, UK
[2] Interlay, Hartlebury, UK
alexei@interlay.io
[3] University College London, London, UK
[4] University of Athens, Athens, Greece
[5] IST Austria, Klosterneuburg, Austria
[6] Novi Research, Tampere, Finland
[7] IMDEA Software Institute, Madrid, Spain
[8] IOHK, Hong kong, China
[9] University of Edinburgh, Edinburgh, UK

Abstract. Since the inception of Bitcoin, a plethora of distributed ledgers differing in design and purpose has been created. While by design, blockchains provide no means to securely communicate with external systems, numerous attempts towards trustless cross-chain communication have been proposed over the years. Today, cross-chain communication (CCC) plays a fundamental role in cryptocurrency exchanges, scalability efforts via sharding, extension of existing systems through sidechains, and bootstrapping of new blockchains. Unfortunately, existing proposals are designed ad-hoc for specific use-cases, making it hard to gain confidence in their correctness and composability. We provide the first systematic exposition of cross-chain communication protocols.

We formalize the underlying research problem and show that CCC is *impossible without a trusted third party*, contrary to common beliefs in the blockchain community. With this result in mind, we develop a framework to design new and evaluate existing CCC protocols, focusing on the inherent trust assumptions thereof, and derive a classification covering the field of cross-chain communication to date. We conclude by discussing open challenges for CCC research and the implications of interoperability on the security and privacy of blockchains.

1 Introduction

Since the introduction of Bitcoin [131] as the first decentralized ledger currency in 2008, the topic of blockchains (or distributed ledgers) has evolved into a well-studied field both in industry and academia. Nevertheless, developments are still largely driven by community effort, resulting in a plethora of blockchain-based digital currencies being created. Taking into account the heterogeneous nature of

© International Financial Cryptography Association 2021
N. Borisov and C. Diaz (Eds.): FC 2021, LNCS 12675, pp. 3–36, 2021.
https://doi.org/10.1007/978-3-662-64331-0_1

these systems in terms of design and purpose, it is unlikely there shall emerge a "coin to rule them all", yielding interoperability an important research problem.

Today, cross-chain communication is found not only in research on cryptocurrency transfers and exchanges [12,13,90,91,165], but is a critical component of scalabilty solutions such as sharding [24,25,27,111,163], feature extensions via sidechains [38,80,107,117], as well as bootstrapping of new systems [99,101,147]. In practice, over \$1bn worth of Bitcoin has been moved to other blockchains [18], and numerous competing interoperability projects, attempting to unite independent systems, have been deployed to practice [14,93,114,145,154,156,158], creating a multi-million dollar industry.

However, in spite of the vast number of use cases and solution attempts, the underlying problem of cross-chain communication has neither been clearly defined, nor have the associated challenges been studied or related to existing research. Early attempts to overview this field offer iterative summaries of mostly community-lead efforts [57,96,143], or focus on a subset of this space, such as atomic swaps [42,129], and support our study. Belchior et al. [39] provide another, more recent, iterative overview of cross-chain projects, yet without clear taxonomy or classification.

This Work. This Systematization of Knowledge (SoK) offers a comprehensive guide for designing protocols bridging the numerous distributed ledgers available today, aiming to facilitate clearer communication between academia, community, and industry. The contributions of this work are thereby twofold:

- We formalize the underlying problem of Correct Cross-Chain Communication (CCC) (Sect. 2), relating CCC to existing research and outlining a generic CCC protocol encompassing existing solutions. We then relate CCC to the Fair Exchange problem and show that contrary to common beliefs in the blockchain community, CCC is *impossible without a trusted third party* (Sect. 3).
- With the impossibility result in mind, we present a framework to design new and evaluate existing CCC protocols, focusing on the inherent trust assumptions thereof (Sects. 4). We apply this framework to classify the field of CCC protocols to date (Sect. 5), highlighting similarities and key differences. Finally, we outline general observations on current developments, provide an outlook on the challenges of CCC research, and discuss the implications of interoperability on the security and privacy of blockchains (Sect. 6).

2   The Cross-Chain Communication Problem

In this section, we relate cross-chain communication to existing research, introduce the model for interconnected distributed ledgers, provide a formal definition of the Correct Cross-Chain Communication (CCC) problem, and sketch the main phases of a generic CCC protocol.

2.1   Historical Background: Distributed Databases

The need for communication among distributed processes is fundamental to any distributed computing algorithm. In databases, to ensure the atomicity of a distributed transaction, an agreement problem must be solved among the set of participating processes. Referred to as the Atomic Commit problem (AC) [46], it requires the processes to agree on a common outcome for the transaction: commit or abort. If there is a strong requirement that every correct process should eventually reach an outcome despite the failure of other processes, the problem is called Non-Blocking Atomic Commit (NB-AC) [37]. Solving this problem enables correct processes to relinquish locks without waiting for crashed processes to recover. As such, we can relate the core ideas of communication across distributed ledgers to NB-AC. The key difference hereby lies within the security model of the interconnected systems. While in classic distributed databases all processes are expected to *adhere to protocol rules* and, in the worst case, may crash, distributed ledgers, where consensus is maintained by a committee, must also consider and handle *Byzantine failures*.

2.2   Distributed Ledger Model

We use the terms *blockchain* and *distributed ledger* as synonyms and introduce some notation, based on [80] with minor alterations.

Ledgers and State Evolution. When speaking of CCC, we consider the interaction between two distributed systems X and Y, which can have distinct consensus participants and may employ different agreement protocols. Thereby, it is assumed the majority[1] of consensus participants in both X and Y are honest, namely, that they follow the designated protocol. The data structures underlying X and Y are *blockchains* (or *chains*), i.e., append-only sequences of blocks, where each block contains a reference to its predecessor(s). We denote a ledger as L (L_x and L_y respectively) and define its *state* as the dynamically evolving sequence of included transactions $\langle TX_1, ..., TX_n \rangle$. We assume that the evolution of the ledger state progresses in discrete *rounds* indexed by natural numbers $r \in \mathbb{N}$. At each round r, a new set of transactions (included in a newly generated block) is written to the ledger L. We use $L^P[r]$ to denote the state of ledger L at round r, i.e., after applying all transactions *written* to the ledger since round $r - 1$, according to the view of some party P. A transaction can be written to L only if it is consistent with the system's consensus rules, given the current ledger state $L^P[r]$. This consistency is left for the particular system to define, and we describe it as a free predicate valid($\cdot$) and we write valid($TX, L_x^P[r]$) to denote that TX is valid under the consensus rules of L_x at round r according to the view of party P. To denote that a transaction TX has been *included* in / successfully written to a ledger L as position r we write $TX \in L^P[r]$. While the ordering of transactions in a block is crucial for their validity, for simplicity, we omit the position of transactions in blocks and assume correct ordering implicitly.

Notion of Time. The state evolution of two distinct ledgers L_x and L_y may progress at different *time* intervals: In the time that L_x progresses *one* round, L_y may, for example, progress *forty* rounds (e.g., as in the case of Bitcoin [131] and

---

[1] In case of Proof-of-Work or Proof-of-Stake blockchains, the majority pertains to computational power [131] or stake [105] respectively.

Ethereum [56]). To correctly capture the ordering of transactions across L_x and L_y, we define a clock function τ which maps a given round on any ledger to the time on a global, synchronized clock $\tau : r \to t$. We assume that the two chains are nevertheless synchronized and that there is no clock drift between them. We use this conversion implicitly in the rest of this paper. For conciseness, we will use the notation $L^P[t]$ to mean the ledger state in the view of party P at the round $r = \tau^{-1}(t)$ which corresponds to time t, namely $L^P[\tau^{-1}(t)]$.

Persistence and Liveness. Each participant P adopts and maintains a local ledger state $L^P[t]$ at time t, i.e., her current view of the ledger. The views of two distinct participants P and Q on the same ledger L may differ at time t (e.g., due to network delay): $L^P[t] \neq L^Q[t]$. However, eventually, all honest parties in the ledger will have the same view. This is captured by the persistence and liveness properties of distributed ledgers [77]:

Definition 1 (Persistence). *Consider two honest parties P, Q of a ledger L and a persistence (or "depth") parameter $k \in \mathbb{N}$. If a transaction TX appears in the ledger of party P at time t, then it will eventually appear in the ledger of party Q at a time $t' > t$ ("stable" transaction). Concretely, for all honest parties P and Q, we have that $\forall t \in \mathbb{N} : \forall t' \geq t + k : L^P[t] \preccurlyeq L^Q[t']$, where $L^P[t] \preccurlyeq L^Q[t']$ denotes that L^P at time t is a (not necessarily proper) prefix of $L^Q[t']$ at time t'.*

As parties will eventually come to agreement about the blocks in their ledgers, we use the notation $L[t]$ to refer to the ledger state at time t shared by all parties; similarly, we use the notation $L[r]$ for the shared view of all parties at round r. This notation is valid when t is at least k time units in the past.

Definition 2 (Liveness). *Consider an honest party P of a ledger L and a liveness delay parameter u. If P attempts to write a transaction TX to its ledger at time $t \in \mathbb{N}$, then TX will appear in its ledger at time t', i.e., $\exists t' \in \mathbb{N} : t' \geq t \wedge TX \in L^P[t']$. The interval $t' - t$ is upper bound by u.*

Transaction Model. A transaction TX, when included, alters the state of a ledger L by defining operations to be executed and agreed upon by consensus participants $P_1, ..., P_n$. The expressiveness of operations is thereby left for the particular system to define, and can range from simple payments to execution of complex programs [159]. For generality, we do not differentiate between specifics transactions models (e.g. UTXO [131] or account-based models [159]).

2.3   Cross-Chain Communication System Model

Consider two independent distributed systems X and Y with underlying ledgers L_x and L_y, as defined in Sect. 2.2. We assume a *closed* system model as in [116] with a process P running on X and a process Q running on Y. A process can influence the state evolution of the underlying system by (i) writing a transaction TX to the underlying ledger L (commit), or (ii) by stopping to interact with the system (abort). We assume that P possesses transaction TX_P, which can be written to L_x, and Q possesses TX_Q, which can be written to L_y. A function *desc* maps a transaction to some "description" which can be compared to an expected description value, e.g., specifying the transaction value and recipient (the description differs from the transaction itself in that it may not, for example, contain any signature). P possesses a description d_Q which characterizes the transaction TX_Q, while Q possesses d_P which characterizes TX_P. Informally, P wants TX_Q to be written to L_y and Q wants TX_P to be written to L_x. Thereby, $d_P = desc(\text{TX}_P)$ implies TX_P is valid in X (at time of CCC execution), as it cannot be written to L_x otherwise (analogous for d_Q).

For the network, we assume no bounds on message delay or deviations between local clocks, unless the individual blockchain protocols require this. We treat failure to communicate as adversarial behavior. We note that, in the anonymous blockchain setting, more synchrony requirements are imposed than in the byzantine setting. Our construction does not impose any *additional* synchrony requirements than the individual ledger protocols. Hence, if P or Q become malicious, we indicate this using boolean "error variables" [78] m_P and m_Q. We assume P and Q know each other's identity and no (trusted) third party is involved in the communication between the two processes.

2.4   Formalization of Correct Cross-Chain Communication

The goal of cross-chain communication can be described as the synchronization of processes P and Q such that Q *writes* TX_Q *to* L_y *if and only if* P *has written* TX_P *to* L_x. Thereby, it must hold that $desc(\text{TX}_P) = d_Q \wedge desc(\text{TX}_Q) = d_P$. The intuition is that TX_P and TX_Q are two transactions which must either both, or neither, be included in L_x and L_y, respectively. For example, they can constitute an exchange of assets which must be completed atomically.

To this end, P must convince Q that it created a transaction TX_P which was included in L_x. Specifically, process Q must verify that at given time t the ledger state $\mathsf{L}_x[t]$ contains TX_P. A cross-chain communication protocol which achieves this goal, i.e., is correct, must hence exhibit the following properties:

Definition 3 (Effectiveness). *If both P and Q behave correctly and TX_P and TX_Q match the expected descriptions (and are valid), then TX_P will be included in L_x and TX_Q will be included in L_y. If either of the transactions are not as expected, then both parties abort.*

$$(desc(\text{TX}_P) = d_Q \wedge desc(\text{TX}_Q) = d_P \wedge m_P = m_Q = \bot \implies \text{TX}_P \in \mathsf{L}_x \wedge \text{TX}_Q \in \mathsf{L}_y)$$
$$\wedge (desc(\text{TX}_P) \neq d_Q \vee desc(\text{TX}_Q) \neq d_P \implies \text{TX}_P \notin \mathsf{L}_x \wedge \text{TX}_Q \notin \mathsf{L}_y)$$

Definition 4 (Atomicity). *There are no outcomes in which P writes TX_P to L_x at time t but Q does not write TX_Q before t', or Q writes TX_Q to L_y at t' but P did not write TX_P to L_x before t.*

$$\neg((\text{TX}_P \in \mathsf{L}_x \wedge \text{TX}_Q \notin \mathsf{L}_y) \vee (\text{TX}_P \notin \mathsf{L}_x \wedge \text{TX}_Q \in \mathsf{L}_y))$$

Definition 5 (Timeliness). *Eventually, a process P that behaves correctly will write a valid transaction TX_P, to its ledger L.*

From Persistence and Liveness of L, it follows that eventually P writes TX_P to L_x and Q becomes aware of and verifies TX_P.

Definition 6 (Correct Cross-Chain Communication (CCC)). *Consider two systems X and Y with ledgers L_x and L_y, each of which has Persistence and Liveness. Consider two processes, P on X and Q on Y, with to-be-synchronized transactions TX_P and TX_Q. Then a correct cross-chain communication protocol is a protocol which achieves $\mathrm{TX}_P \in \mathsf{L}_x \wedge \mathrm{TX}_Q \in \mathsf{L}_y$ and has Effectiveness, Atomicity, and Timeliness.*

Summarizing, Effectiveness and Atomicity are safety properties. Effectiveness determines the outcome if transactions are not as expected or both transaction match descriptions and both processes are behaving correctly. Atomicity globally restricts the outcome to exclude behaviors which place a disadvantage on either process. Timeliness guarantees eventual termination of the protocol, i.e., is a liveness property.

2.5   The Generic CCC Protocol

We now describe the main phases of a Generic CCC Protocol, which can represent the transfer of good, assets or objects, between any two blockchain-based distributed systems X and Y. A visual representation is provided in Fig. 1.

1) Setup. A CCC protocol is parameterized by the involved distributed systems X and Y and the corresponding ledgers L_x and L_y, the involved parties P and Q, the transactions TX_P and TX_Q as well as their descriptions d_P and d_Q. The latter ensure the validity of TX_P and TX_Q and determine the application-level specification of a CCC protocol. For example, in the case of an exchange of digital assets, d_P and d_Q define the asset types, transferred value, time constraints and any additional conditions agreed by parties P and Q. Typically, the setup occurs out-of-band between the involved parties and we hence omit this step hereby.

2) (Pre-)Commit on X. Upon successful setup, a publicly verifiable commitment to execute the CCC protocol is published on X: P writes[2] transaction TX_P to its local ledger L_X^P at time t in round r. Due to Persistence and Liveness of L_x, all honest parties of X will report TX_P as stable ($\mathrm{TX}_P \in \mathsf{L}_x$) in round $r + u_x + k_x$.

3) Verify. The correctness of the commitment on X by P is verified by Q checking (or receiving a proof from P) that (i) $d_P = desc(\mathrm{TX}_P)$ and (ii) $\mathrm{TX}_P \in \mathsf{L}_x$ hold. From Persistence and Liveness of X we know the latter check will succeed at time t' which corresponds to round $r + u_x + k_x$ on X, if P executed correctly.

4a) Commit on Y. Upon successful verification, a publicly verifiable commitment is published on Y: Q writes transaction TX_Q to its local ledger L_Y^Q at time t' in round r' on Y. Due to Persistence and Liveness of L_y, all honest parties of Y will report TX_Q as stable ($\mathrm{TX}_Q \in \mathsf{L}_y$) in round $r' + u_y + k_y$, where u_y is the liveness delay and k_y is the "depth" parameter of Y.

---

[2] In off-chain protocols [85], the commitment can be done by exchanging pre-signed transactions or channel states, which will be written to the ledger at a later point.

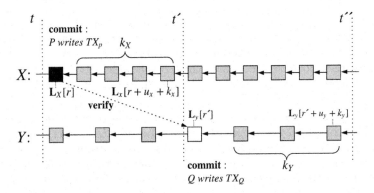

Fig. 1. CCC between X and Y. Process Q writes TX$_Q$ only if P has written TX$_P$. We set exemplary persistence delays for X and Y as $k_X = 4$ and $k_Y = 3$, and liveness delays as $u_x = u_y = 0$. We omit the optional the abort phase.

4b) Abort. If the verification fails and / or Q fails to execute the commitment on Y, a CCC protocol can exhibit an abort step on X, i.e., "reverting" the modifications TX$_P$ made to the state of L$_x$. As blockchains are append-only data structures, reverting requires broadcasting an additional transaction TX$_{P'}$ which resets X to the state before the commitment of TX$_P$.

It is worth noting that some CCC protocols, specifically those facilitating *exchange* of assets, follow a two-phase commit design. In this case, steps 2 and 4a are executed in parallel, followed by the verification and (optional) abort steps on *both* X and Y. A further observation is that a CCC protocol necessarily requires a *conditional state transition* to occur on Y, given a state transition on X. As such, we do *not* consider (oracle) protocols which merely relay data across distributed ledgers [3,52,54,57,153], as CCC protocols by themselves.

3 Impossibility of CCC Without a Trusted Third Party

In this section we show that, in the asynchronous setting, CCC is impossible without a trusted third party by reducing it to the Fair Exchange problem [29,133].

Fair Exchange. On a high level, an exchange between two (or more) parties is considered fair if either both parties receive the item they expect, or neither do [31]. Fair exchange can be considered a sub-problem of fair secure computation [44], and is known to be impossible without a trusted third party [72,73,133,160]. We recall the definition of Fair Exchange the full paper version[3].

3.1 What Is a Trusted Third Party?

Numerous recent works use *a single* distributed ledger such as Bitcoin and Ethereum to construct (optimistic) fair exchange protocols [28,44,70,106,110,

---

[3] The full version of this paper is available at https://eprint.iacr.org/2019/1128.pdf.

112]. They leverage smart contracts (i.e., programs or scripts), the result of which is agreed upon and enforced by consensus participants, to ensure the correctness of the exchange. These protocols thus use the consensus of the distributed ledgers as an abstraction for a trusted third party. If the majority of consensus participants are honest, correct behavior of processes/participants of the fair exchange is enforced – typically, the correct release of a_Q to P if Q received a_P.

A CCC protocol aims to achieve synchronization between *two* such distributed ledgers, both of which are inherently trusted to operate correctly. As we show below, a (possibly additional) TTP can be used to (i) confirm to the consensus participants of Y that TX_P was included in L_x, who in turn enforce the inclusion of TX_Q in L_y; or (ii) directly enforce correct behavior of Q, such that $\text{TX}_Q \in \mathsf{L}_y$.

Similar to the abstraction of TTPs used in fair exchange protocols, in CCC it does not matter how exactly the TTP is implemented, as long as it enforces correct behavior of the participants. Strictly speaking, from the perspective of CCC there is little difference between a TTP consisting of a single individual and a committee where N out of M members must agree to take action (even though a committee is, without question, more resilient against failures) – contrary to the common assumptions made by the blockchain community.

3.2 Relating CCC to Fair Exchange

We proceed to show that Correct Cross-Chain Communication is impossible in the asynchronous setting without a trusted third party (TTP), under the deterministic system model of distributed ledgers, by reducing CCC to Fair Exchange [29,31,133]. We recall, a fair exchange protocol must fulfill three properties: *Effectiveness, (Strong) Fairness* and *Timeliness* [29,133]

Lemma 1. *Let M be a system model. Let C be a protocol which solves* CCC *in M. Then there exists a protocol S which solves Fair Exchange in M.*

Proof (sketch). Consider that the two processes P and Q are parties in a fair exchange. Specifically, P owns an item (or asset) a_P and wishes to exchange it against an item (or asset) a_Q owned by Q. Assume TX_P assigns ownership of a_P to Q and TX_Q transfers ownership of a_Q to P (specified in the "descriptions" d_P of TX_P and d_Q of TX_Q). Then, TX_P must be included in L_x and TX_Q must be included in L_y to correctly execute the exchange. In other words, if $\text{TX}_Q \in \mathsf{L}_y$ and $\text{TX}_P \in \mathsf{L}_x$, then P receives desired a_Q and Q receives desired a_P, i.e., P and Q fairly exchange a_P and a_Q.

We observe the definition of Timeliness in CCC is equivalent to the definition of Timeliness in fair exchange protocols, as defined in [133]. Effectiveness in fair exchange states that if P and Q behave correctly and do not want to abandon the exchange (i.e., $m_P = m_Q = \bot$), and items a_P and a_Q are as expected by Q and P, then at the end of the protocol, P will own the desired a_Q and Q will own the desired a_P [133]. It is easy to see Effectiveness in CCC achieves exactly this property: if P and Q behave correctly and $desc(\text{TX}_P) = d_P$ and $desc(\text{TX}_Q) = d_Q$, i.e., TX_P transfers a_P to Q and TX_Q transfers a_Q to P, then P will write TX_P

to L_y at time t and Q will write TX_Q to L_x before time t'. From Persistence and Liveness of L_x and L_y we know both transactions will eventually be written to the local ledgers of P and Q, consequently all other honest participants of X will report $TX_P \in L_X$ and honest participants of Y will report $TX_Q \in L_Y$. From our model we know that honest participants constitute majorities in both X and Y. Hence, P will receive a_Q and Q will receive a_P.

Strong Fairness in fair exchange states that there is no outcome of the protocol, where P receives a_Q but Q does not receive a_P, or, vice-versa, Q receives a_P but P does not receive a_Q [133]. In our setting, such an outcome is only possible if $TX_P \in L_x \wedge TX_Q \notin L_y$ or $TX_P \notin L_x \wedge TX_Q \in L_y$, which contradicts the Atomicity property of CCC.   □

We construct a protocol for Fair Exchange using CCC in Appendix A. It is now left to show that CCC is defined under the same model as Fair Exchange. The distributed ledger model [77] used in CCC assumes the same asynchronous (explicitly) and deterministic (implicitly) system model (cf. Sect. 2.3) as [76, 133]. Since P and Q by definition can stop participating in the CCC protocol at any time, CCC exhibits the same crash failure model as Fair Exchange [30, 133] (and in turn Consensus [76]). Hence, we conclude:

Theorem 1. *There exists no asynchronous CCC protocol tolerant against misbehaving nodes without a trusted third party.*

Proof. Assume there exists an asynchronous protocol C which solves CCC. Then, due to Lemma 1 there exists a protocol which solves strong fair exchange. As this is a contradiction, there cannot exist such a protocol C.   □

Our result currently holds for the closed model, as in [76, 133]. In the open model, P and Q can be forced to make a decision by the system (or environment), i.e., transactions can be written on their behalf if they crash [111]. In the case of CCC, this means that distributed system Y, or more precisely, the consensus of Y, can write TX_Q to L_y on behalf of Q (if P wrote TX_P to L_x). We observe that the consensus of Y becomes the TTP in this scenario: both P and Q must agree that the consensus of Y enforce correct execution of CCC. In practice, this can be achieved by leveraging smart contracts, similar to blockchain-based fair exchange protocols, e.g. [70]. As such, we can construct a smart contract, the execution of which is enforced by consensus of Y, that will write TX_Q to L_y if P includes TX_P in L_x, i.e., Q is allowed to crash.

However, it remains the question how the consensus participants of Y become aware that $TX_P \in L_x$. In practice, a smart contract, can only perform actions based on some input. As such, before writing TX_Q the contract / consensus of Y must observe and verify that TX_P was included in L_x. A protocol achieving CCC must hence make one of the following assumptions. Either, there exists a TTP that will ensure correct execution of CCC; or the protocol assumes P, or Q, or some other honest, online party (this can again be consensus of Y) will always deliver a proof for $TX_P \in L_x$ to Y within a known, upper bounded delay, i.e., the protocol introduces some form of *synchrony* assumption. As argued in [133], we observe that *introducing a TTP and relying on a synchrony assumption are equivalent*:

Remark 1. When designing a CCC protocol, a choice must be made between introducing a trusted third party, or, equivalently, assuming some synchrony on the network.

The intuition behind this result is as follows. If we assume that process P does not crash and hence submits the necessary proof to the smart contract on Y, and that this message is delivered to the smart contract within a know upper bound, then we can be sure that CCC will occur correctly. Thereby, P intuitively represents its own trusted third party. However, if we cannot make assumptions on when the message will be delivered to the smart contract, as is the case in the asynchronous model, a trusted third party is necessary to determine the outcome of the CCC: the TTP observes $\text{TX}_P \in \mathsf{L}_x$ and informs the smart contract or directly enforces the inclusion of TX_Q in L_y. This illustrates how a TTP can be leveraged to enforce synchrony, i.e., timely delivery of messages, in CCC protocols. While the two models yield equivalent results, the choice between a TTP and network synchrony impacts the implementation details of a CCC protocol.

3.3   Incentives and Rational CCC

Several workarounds to the fair exchange problem, including gradual release mechanisms, optimistic models, and partially fair secure computation [31,44,60, 113], have been suggested in the literature. These workarounds suffer, among others, from a common drawback: they require some form of trusted party that does not collude with the adversary. Further, in case of a adversary-caused abort, honest parties must spend extra efforts to restore fairness, e.g., in the optimistic model the trusted server must be contacted each time fairness is breached.

First suggested in the context of rational exchange protocols [149], the economic dimension of blockchains enabled a shift in this paradigm: Rather than forcing an honest user to invest time and money to achieve fairness, the malicious user is economically punished when breaching fairness and the victim is reimbursed. This has paved the way to design *economically trustless* CCC protocols that follow a game theoretic model under the assumption that actors behave rationally [165]. We remark that malicious/altruistic actors can nevertheless breach CCC properties: even if there is no economic damage to parties P or Q, the correct execution of the communication protocol itself still fails.

4   The CCC Design Framework

With the impossibility result 3 and CCC model (Sect. 2.2) in mind, we now introduce a new framework for creating and evaluating CCC protocols. A generic CCC protocol consists of three main phases: commit (on X), verify (and commit on Y), and an optional abort. The main challenge of designing a CCC protocol is hence to determine the necessary trust model for each phase, from one of the following:

(*i*) relying outright on a TTP, (*ii*) relying on an explicit synchrony assumption, or (*iii*) a hybrid approach, where a TTP is only involved if synchrony is breached. The framework introduced below is structured as follows: for each CCC phase (subsection), we systematize the three possible trust models (TTP, synchrony, hybrid), outlining possible implementations and reasoning about practical consideration. This enables systematic evaluation of existing protocols and, at the same time, acts as a step-by-step guide for creating new CCC schemes.

4.1 (Pre-)Commit Phase

The commit phase(s) of a CCC protocol typically involves the locking and unlocking of assets on chains X and Y, determined by the outcome of the protocol.

Model 1: Trusted Third Party (Coordinators). A *coordinator* is a TTP that is tasked with ensuring correct execution of a CCC protocol. We classify coordinator implementations attending to two criteria: *custody of assets* and *involvement in blockchain consensus*. A coordinator (committee) can thereby be *static* (pre-defined) or *dynamic* (any user can join). And, finally, a CCC protocol can utilize *collateral* to incentivize correct behavior. We first introduce the classification criteria and then detail possible implementations of coordinators.

- *Custody of Assets.* Custody determines with whom the control over assets of (honest) participants resides. We differentiate between *custodians* and *escrows*. *Custodians* receive *unconditional* control over the participant's funds and are thus *trusted* to release them as instructed by the protocol rules. *Escrows* receive control over the participant's funds *conditional* to certain prearranged constraints being fulfilled. Contrary to custodians, escrows can fail to take action, e.g. freeze assets, but cannot commit theft.
- *Involvement in Consensus.* Coordinators can optionally also take part in the blockchain consensus protocol. *Consensus-level* coordinators refer to TTPs that are additionally consensus participants in the underlying chain. This is the case, for example, if the commit step is performed on chain X and enforced directly by the consensus participants of X, e.g. through a smart contract or directly a multi-/threshold signature. *External* coordinators, on the other hand, refer to TTPs which are not represented by the consensus participants of the underlying blockchain. This is the case if (i) the coordinators are external to the chain X, e.g., the consensus participants of chain Y or other parties, or (ii) less than the majority of consensus participants of chain X are involved.
- *Election.* An important distinction to make is between *static*, i.e., unchanged over time (usually permissioned), and *dynamic* coordinator sets. A dynamic coordinator can be chosen by CCC participants for each individual execution, or can be sampled by a pre-defined mechanism, as e.g. studied in [65,108,109, 134] for Proof-of-Work and in [45,64,105,128] for Proof-of-Stake blockchains. We consider CCC protocols where any user can become a coordinator as *unrestricted*, while protocols that require coordinators to be approved by some third party are referred to as *restricted*.

- *Incentives and Collateralization.* Instead of following a *prohibitive* approach, i.e., technically preventing or limiting coordinators from deviating from protocol rules, a CCC protocol can follow a *punishable* approach. That is, ensure misbehavior can be proven and penalized retrospectively. In the latter case, a coordinator will typically be required to lock collateral that can be *slashed* and allocated to (financially) damaged CCC participants.

Coordinator Implementations. We now detail the different coordinator types according to the aforementioned criteria and how they are implemented in practice.

- *External Custodians (Committees).* Instead of relying on the availability and honest behavior of a single external coordinator, trust assumptions can be distributed among a set of N committee members. Decisions require the acknowledgment (e.g. digital signature) of at least $M \leq N$ members, whereby consensus can be achieved via Byzantine Fault Tolerant (BFT) agreement protocols such as PBFT [61,108]. External custodians can be both static or dynamic, and collateralization can be added on involved blockchains to incentivize honest behavior.
- *Consensus-level Custodians (Consensus Committee)* are identical to external custodians, except that they are also responsible for agreeing on the state of the underlying ledger. This model is typically used in blockchain sharding [25,111], where the blockchain X on which the commit step is executed runs a BFT consensus protocol, i.e., there already exists a *static* committee of consensus participants that much be trusted for correctness of CCC (Persistence and Liveness of X). Collateralization of Consensus Custodians is best handled on another blockchain, i.e., where the coordinators have no influence on consensus.
- *External Escrows (Multisignature Contracts).* External Escrows are a special case of External Custodians, where the coordinator is transformed from Custodian to Escrow by means of a *multisignature contract*. Multisignature contracts require signatures of a subset (or majority) of committee members *and* the participant P (e.g., the asset owner), i.e., $P + M, M \leq N$. The committee can thus only execute actions pre-authorized by the participant: it can at most freeze assets, but not commit theft.

Model 2: Synchrony Assumptions (Lock Contracts). An alternative to coordinators consists in relying on synchronous communication between participants and leveraging locking mechanisms which harvest security from cryptographic hardness assumptions. Such protocols are often referred to as *noncustodial*, as they avoid transferring custody over assets to a TTP – failures, in the worst case, result in a permanent lockup of funds without explicit (financial) benefits to a third party. We differentiate between *symmetric* contracts, where identical locks are created on both chains and released atomically, and *asymmetric* contracts where the main protocol logic is hosted on a single chain.

- *Hash Locks (symmetric).* A protocol based on hash locks relies on the *preimage resistance* property of hash functions: participants P and Q transfer assets to each other by means of transactions that must be complemented with the preimage of a hash $h := H(r)$ for a value r chosen by P – the initiator of the protocol – typically uniformly at random [12,13,90,121].

- *Signature-based Locks (symmetric)*. P and Q can transfer assets to each other by means of transactions that require to solve the discrete logarithm problem of a value $Y := g^y$ for a value y, chosen uniformly at random by P (i.e., the initiator of the protocol). The functionality of embedding the discrete logarithm problem in the creation of a digital signature was put forward by the community under the term *adaptor signatures* [135] and formally defined in [32]. In practice, it has been shown that it is possible to implement adaptor signatures leveraging virtually any digital signature scheme [155], including ECDSA and Schnorr which are used for authorization in most blockchains today [48,50,71,122,130,135,150].
- *Timelock Puzzles and Verifiable Delay Functions (symmetric)*. An alternative approach is to construct (cryptographic) challenges, the solution of which will be made public at a predictable time in the future. Thus, P and Q can commit to the cross-chain transfer conditioned on solving one of the aforementioned challenges. Concrete constructions include timelock puzzles and verifiable delay functions. Timelock puzzles [138] build upon inherently sequential functions where the result is only revealed after a predefined number of operations are performed. Verifiable delay functions [48] improve upon timelock puzzles on that the correctness of the result for the challenge is publicly verifiable. This functionality can also be simulated by releasing parts of the preimage of a hash lock interactively bit by bit, until it can be brute forced [43].
- *Smart Contracts (asymmetric)* are programs stored in a ledger which are executed and their result agreed upon by consensus participants [56,59]. As such, trusting in the correct behavior of a smart contract is essentially trusting in the secure operation of the underlying chain, making this a useful construction for (Consensus-level) Escrows. Contrary to Consensus-level Custodians, who must actively follow the CCC protocol and potentially run additional software, with smart contracts, consensus participants are not directly involved in the CCC protocol: an interaction with the CCC smart contract is, by default, treated like any other state transition and no additional software/action is required.

Model 3: Hybrid (Watchtowers). Instead of fully relying on coordinators being available or synchrony assumptions among participants holding, it is possible to employ so called *watchtowers*, i.e., service providers which act as a fallback if CCC participants experience crash failures. We observe strong similarities with optimistic fair exchange protocols [30,31,60]. Specifically, watchtowers take action to enforce the commitment, if one of the parties crashes or synchrony assumptions do not hold, i.e., after a pre-defined timeout [34,36,102,123]. This construction was first introduced and applied to off-chain payment channels [85].

4.2   Verification Phase

The verification phase, during which the commitment on X is verified on Y (or vice-versa), can similarly be executed under different trust models, as detailed in the following. An important distinction concerns the type of verification performed: while most CCC protocols verify the inclusion of a transaction executing the commitment on X, full validation of correctness under X's protocol rules is typically avoided due to the incurred computational overhead. A detailed analysis and taxonomy of different verification techniques is provided in the full paper version (See footnote 3).

Model 1: Trusted Third Party (Coordinators). The simplest approach to cross-chain verification is to rely on a trusted third party (also referred to as *validators* [158]) to handle the verification of the state changes on interlinked chains during CCC execution.

– *External Validators.* A simple approach is to outsource the verification step to a (trusted) third party, external to the verifying ledger (in our case Y), as in [11,154]. The TTP can then be the same as in the commit/abort steps.
– *Consensus Committee / Smart Contracts.* Alternatively, the verification can be handled by the consensus participants of the verifying chain [68,111,118], leveraging the assumption that misbehavior of consensus participants indicates a failure of the chain itself.

Model 2: Synchrony Assumption. Instead of explicitly relying on a TTP, the verification phase can be implemented using:

– *Direct Observation.* Similar to the commit phase of CCC, one can require all participants of a CCC protocol to execute the verification phase individually: i.e., to run (fully validating) nodes in all involved chains. This is often the case in exchange protocols, such as atomic swaps using symmetric locks such as HTLCs [13,90], but also in parent-child settings where one chain by design verifies or validates the other [38,80,117]. This relies on a synchrony assumption, i.e., requires CCC participants to observe commitments and act within a certain time, in order to complete the CCC.
– *Chain Relay Smart Contracts.* The verification process can be encoded in so called *chain relays* [3,57,165] – smart contracts deployed on Y capable of verifying the of state and hence the commitments executed on X. Chain relays resemble cryptocurrency light (or SPV) clients, i.e., store only the bare minimum data to verify the inclusion of transactions in the respective blockchain [103, 120,131]. Accordingly, chain relays can only *verify* that a commitment was executed on X – yet not if it was valid under X's consensus rules. Instead, the "SPV assumption" is applied: if X has Persistence and Liveness, then a commitment (transaction) written to X must be valid [120,131]. To fully *validate* the correctness of a commitment, one must either (i) download the entire state of chain X (infeasible for CCC), or (ii) encode the state of X in succinct proofs of knowledge [40,47,53] (c.f. the full paper version (See footnote 3)).

Model 3: Hybrid. Verificaiton via TTPs and synchrony can be combined:

– *Watchtowers.* Just like in the commit phase, synchrony and TTP assumptions can be combined in the verification phase, such that a CCC protocol initially relies on a synchrony assumption, but can fall back to a TTP (*watchtowers*, c.f Sect. 4.1) to ensure correct termination if messages are not delivered within a per-defined period.

– *Verification Games.* Inversely, *verification games* by default rely on TTPs for verification (mostly for performance improvements) and implement dispute resolution mechanisms as fall-back: users can provide (reactive) fraud proofs [26] or accuse coordinators of misbehavior requiring them to prove correct operation [87,100,151].

4.3   Abort Phase

The abort of a CCC protocol is optional and is encountered typically in exchange protocols. Most other CCC protocols assume that once a commit is executed on X, no abort will be necessary.

Model 1: Trusted Third Party (Coordinators). Similarly to the commit phase, an abort can be handled by a trusted third party and the possible implementations are the same as in Sect. 4.1. If a TTP was introduced in the commit phase, the abort phase will be typically handled by the exact same TTP.

Model 2: Synchrony Assumptions (Timelocks). Alternatively, it is possible to enforce synchrony by introducing timelocks, after the expiry of which the protocol is aborted. Specifically, to ensure that assets are *not locked up indefinitely* in case of a crash failure of a participant or misbehavior of a TTP entrusted with the commit step, all commit techniques can be complimented with *timelocks*: after expiry of the timelock, assets are returned to their original owner. We differentiate between two types of timelocks. *Absolute timelocks* yield a transaction valid only after a certain point in time, defined in by a timestamp or a block (ledger at index i, $L[i]$) located in the future. *Relative timelocks*, on the other hand, condition TX_2 on the existence of another transaction TX_1: TX_2 only becomes valid and can be written to the underlying ledger if TX_1 has already been included and a certain number of blocks (*confirmations* [5]) have passed.

Model 3: Hybrid (Watchtowers). As an additional measure of security, TTPs can be introduced as a fallback to timelocks in case CCC participants experience crash failures, e.g. in form of a watchtower [34,36,102,123] that recovers otherwise potentially lost assets. This is specifically useful in the case of atomic swaps using Hased Timelock Contracts (HTLCs) [2,13,90,136], when either party crashes after the hashlock's secret has been revealed.

5   Classification of Existing CCC Protocols

We now apply the CCC Design Framework introduced in Sect. 4 to classify existing CCC protocols. All CCC protocols observed in practice follow the Generic CCC Protocol model (cf. Sect. 2.5). For each protocol, we hence study and reason about the trust model (TTP, synchrony, hybrid) selected for each phase of the CCC process, and summarize our classification in Table 1. Our analysis thereby focuses on well-documented or deployed protocols - which in turn have seen numerous implementations that are not individually referenced in this paper.

Table 1. Classification of existing of Cross-Chain Communication protocols, in consideration of the selected TTP model (cf. Sect. 4) at each protocol step (commit, verify, abort). Notation for non-binary TTP values: ● uses a TTP, ○ fully relies on synchrony and availability of participants, ◐ hybrid. We also highlight if the TTP (committee) is static or changes dynamically, and whether collateral is utilized to incentivize correct behavior of TTPs. We use the following abbreviations: **EC** for External Custodian, **CC** for Consensus Custodian, **EE** for External Escrow, **SC** for Smart Contract, **EV** for External Validator, **CM** for Consensus Committee, and **DO** for Direct Observation.

Category	Protocol	Commit on chain X — TTP	Dynamic?	Collateral?	Commit Type	Verify & Commit on chain Y — TTP	Verify Type	Abort on chain X (optinal) — TTP	Abort Type
Exchange Protocols — (Atomic Swaps)	Traditional Custodial Exchanges (e.g., [1,43])	●	✗	✗	EC (single, restricted)	●	EV	●	EC (single, restricted)
	A2L [150]	◐	✗	✓	EE (multisig + signature Lock)	○	DO	◐	EE + Timelock
	Arwen [89]	◐	✗	✗	EE (multisig + Hash Lock)	○	DO	◐	EE + Timelock
	Notarized HTLC Atomic Swaps [154]	○	-	-	Hash Lock	●	EV	◐	EE + Timelock
	HTLC Atomic Swaps [13,90,12,154]	○	-	-	Hash Lock	○	DO	○	Timelock
	ECDSA/DLSAG Atomic Swaps [122,130]	○	-	-	Signature Lock	○	DO	○	Timelock
	SPV Atomic Swaps [6,107,165,91]	○	-	-	Standard payment	○	SC(chain relay)	○	Timelock
Exchange Protocols — Cryptocurrency-backed Assets	(Bidirectional) Chain Relays [107,80]	○	-	-	SC	○	SC (chain relay)	-	-
	XCLAIM [165], Dogethereum [152]	●	✓	✓	EC (single, unrestricted)	○	SC (chain relay)	*	-
	tBTC [8]	◐	✗	✓	EC (committee, restricted)	○	SC (chain relay)	*	-
Migration Protocols — Side-chains	Custodial Wrapped Assets (e.g., [11,21,20])	●	✗	✗	EC (single, restricted)	●	EV	●	EC (single, restricted)
	Federated Sidechains/Pegs [38,68,80]	●	✗	✗	EC (consensus of Y)	●	CM	*	-
	RSK [118,117]	●	✗	✗	EC (consensus of Y)	●	CM	*	-
Migration Protocols — Sharding	ATOMIX[111],SBAC[25], Fabric Channels[27]	●	✗	✗	CC (shard X)	●	CM	●	CC (shard X)
	Rapidchain [163]	●	✗	✗	CC (shard X)	●	CM	*	-
	XCMP [55]	●	✗	✗	EC (parent consensus)	●	CM	*	-
Migration Protocols — Boot-strapping	Proof-of-Burn (Federated) [147,101]	○	-	-	SC / Burn address	●	CM	-	-
	Proof-of-Burn (SPV) [101]	○	-	-	SC / Burn address	○	SC (chain relay)	-	-
	Merged Mining/Staking [99,80]	●	✗	✗	CC (consensus of X)	●	CM	-	-

* While not explicitly considered by the protocol, the TTP used for the commitment on X can, at its discretion, abort the CCC protocol manually/out-of-band in case of failure on Y.

In addition to applying the CCC Design Framework, we split existing proposals into two protocol families, based on their design rationale and use case, which have direct implications on the design choices: (i) *exchange* protocols, which synchronize the exchange of assets across two ledgers (Sect. 5.1), and (ii) *migration* protocols, which allow to move an asset or object to a different ledger (Sect. 5.2).

5.1   Exchange Protocols

Exchange protocols synchronize an atomic exchange of digital goods: x on chain X against y on Y. In practice, such protocols implement a *two-phase commit* mechanism, where parties first pre-commit to the exchange and can *explicitly abort* the protocol in case of disagreement or failure during the commit step.

(Pre-)Commit. Trivially, the commit phase can be handled by External Custodians: traditional, centralized exchanges require to deposit (commit) assets with a TTP before trading.

The longest-standing alternative to centralized solutions are atomic swaps via *symmetric locks* which rely on synchrony and cryptographic hardness assumptions. Counterparties P and Q lock (pre-commit) assets in on-chain contracts with identical release conditions on X and Y: spending from one lock releases the other, ensuring Atomicity of CCC. The first and most adopted implementation of symmetric locks are *hashed timelock contracts* (HTLCs) [12,13,90,154], where the same secret (selected by P) is used as pre-image to identical Hash Locks on X and Y. To improve cross-platform compatibility, Hash Locks, which require both chains to support (the same) hash functions, can be replaced with Signature Locks e.g., using ECDSA [122] or group/ring signature schemes [130].

On blockchains which support (near) Turing complete programming languages (e.g., Ethereum [56]) the commitment on X can exhibit more complex locking conditions via smart contracts. In SPV atomic swaps [6,91,107,165], assets of a party P are locked in a smart contract on X which is capable of verifying the state of chain Y (chain relay, cf. Sect. 4.2) - and unlocked only if counterparty Q submits a correct proof for the expected payment (commitment) on Y. The smart contract can be further extended to support collateralization and penalties for misbehaving counterparties (e.g., to mitigate optionally and improve fairness [86,165]).

Both symmetric and SPV atomic swaps suffer from usability challenges impeding adoption: they require users to be online and execute commitments in a timely manner to avoid financial damage (built-in abort mechanisms discussed later). Hybrid protocols seek to combine symmetric locks with TTP models to mitigate usability issues while avoiding full trust in a central provider. In Arwen [89], parties P and Q commit to-be-exchanged assets into on-chain multisignature contracts on X and Y, establishing shared custody with an External Escrow (EE). Trades are executed similar to HTLC swaps, yet utilize the escrow to ensure correct and timely execution. A2L [150] follows a similar multisignature setup but utilizes adaptor signatures [32] to ensure Atomicity of trades: the escrow only forwards P's assets to Q if Q solves a cryptographic challenge, for which Q needs the help of P. Both Arwen and A2L require a complex on-chain setup process (similar to payment channels [136]) and rely on pre-paid fees (Arwen) or collateral (A2L) to protect the escrow from griefing attacks [62] - yielding them inefficient for one-time exchanges.

Verify. Contrary to traditional exchanges, where the custodial (operator) is also responsible for the verification phase, symmetric atomic swap protocols (including Arwen and A2L) require users to *directly observe* all chains involved in the CCC to verify correct execution of the (pre-)commit phase. Notarized atomic swaps (e.g., as in InterLedger [154]) remove the online requirement for users by entrusting an External Validator (EV) e.g., a set of notaries, with the verification of (and timely reaction to) the commitment on X- at the risk of the EV colluding with the a counterparty to commit theft. A more robust approach, implemented in SPV atomic swaps, is the use of *chain relays*: the verification of the commit on X and the correct finalization of the CCC protocol (commit on Y) is executed by a smart contract on Y, enforced by the consensus of Y.

Abort. Exchange CCC protocols typically add timelocks to the release conditions of the commitments of X and Y to ensure an automatic abort of the CCC protocol after a pre-defined delay. This is to prevent indefinite lock-up of assets, should a party crash or misbehave. However, CCC protocols implementing timelocks impose strict online requirements on participants and expose them to race conditions. The initiator P of e.g., a HTLC swap can defraud counterparty Q by recovering assets on X if they remain unclaimed upon expiry of the timelock (e.g., if Q crashed). Some protocols, including A2L and Arwen, partially outsource this responsibility to TTPs [89,150].

5.2 Migration Protocols

Migration protocols temporarily or permanently move digital goods from one blockchain to another. Typically, this is achieved by obtaining a "write lock" on an asset x on chain X, preventing any further updates to x on chain X, and consequently creating a *representation* $y(x)$ on Y. The state of x can only be updated by modifying its "wrapped" version $y(x)$ on $Y-$ comparable to the concept of *mutual exclusion* in concurrency control [67]. The state changes of $y(x)$ will typically be reflected back to chain X by locking or destroying ("burning") $y(x)$ and applying the updates to x when it is unlocked.

Migration protocols only require to execute CCC synchronization across X and Y twice: creating and destroying $y(x)$. The "wrapped" representation $y(x)$ typically exhibits the same properties as "native" assets y, allowing seamless integration with applications on Y. For comparison, Exchange protocols require to setup and execute CCC for *each trade*. The main drawback of Migration protocols is the requirement of giving up custody over x, in the majority of cases to a TTP (cf. Table 1).

In practice, we identify four main use cases for Migration protocols: (i) *cryptocurrency-backed assets* used for transfers across heterogeneous blockchains (e.g., "wrapped" Bitcoin on Ethereum), (ii) communication across homogeneous chains (shards) in *sharded* blockchains, (iii) *sidechains* where a child chain is "pegged" to a parent for feature extensions, and (iv) *bootstrapping* of new blockchains using existing systems.

(Pre-)Commit. The simplest implementation of a Migration protocol (e.g., for cryptocurrency-backed assets) relies on a single, static TTP which receives unrestricted custody over the to-be-migrated assets during the commit phase (External Custodian) – for example, implemented by wBTC [11], a custodial platform for migrating Bitcoin to Ethereum.

Instead of relying on a single TTP, most CCC rely on a TTP committee to improve robustness against failures. Protocols connecting heterogeneous blockchains via cryptocurrency-backed assets, notably tBTC [8], utilize a set of External Custodians (EC). In the tBTC protocol, currently deployed between Bitcoin and Ethereum, ECs construct a jointly controlled deposit public key on X via (ECDSA) threshold signatures [81], to which users send (commit) to-be-migrated assets. The ECs must thereby lock up collateral on Y which is used to reimburse users in case the EC committee commits theft or crashes. At the time of writing, the implemented threshold signature scheme does not support fault attribution, i.e., it impossible to distinguish between honest and malicious committee members when slashing collateral, requiring the EC set to be static and restricted. RenVM [21] aims to replace threshold signatures with distributed key generation via secure multi-party computation [83] but implements a centralized approach at the time of writing.

Sidechains [38,68,80] establish a parent-child relationship between X and Y: the consensus committee of X (Consensus Custodian, CC) or Y (External Custodian, EC) is responsible for handling the correct deposit (commit) of x on X. In practice, implementations follow a similar approach to the heterogeneous setting: users deposit assets x to a public key with shared control among committee members, implemented e.g., via threshold / multisignature [94] schemes. Liquid [38,68], which coined the "sidechain" terminology, maintains an 11-of-15 multisignature, controlled by its consensus participants, to migrate (lock/unlock) Bitcoin to and from the Liquid blockchain. RSK [117,118], a merge-mined [99] Bitcoin sidechain, currently follows the same approach as Liquid but envisions a Bitcoin protocol upgrade enabling miners to vote on migrating assets to RSK.

Similarly, *sharded blockchains*, which consist of a set of homogeneous shard-chains with a homogeneous, shared security model, utilize the consensus committee(s) available within the system for securing cross-shard migrations. While often considered as a separate topic in research, sharded blockchains exhibit built-in CCC protocols [35]: Migrated assets x are locked with the consensus of X (Consensus Custodian, CC) during the commit phase. A novelty compared to heterogeneous systems is the explicit consideration of n-to-m CCC protocols, such as ATOMIX [111], SBAC [25], and Fabric Channels [27], which require an explicit abort step as part of the two-phase commit design.

Recently, a new family of protocols following a permissionless design, was introduced. XCLAIM [165] and Dogethereum [152] allow anyone to become a TTP and accept deposits (commits) of x on X, establishing a dynamic and unrestricted set of coordinators (External Custodians, ECs). The only requirement for registering as an EC is to lock collateral y on Y – the amount of y locked thereby determines the amount of x deposits (and hence minted $y(x)$) an EC can accept. While Dogethereum assumes a constant exchange rate between migrated x (equiv. $y(x)$) and collateral asset y, XCLAIM utilizes a multi-stage over-collateralization scheme to re-balance the economic value of committed x and locked collateral y. To enable ECs to join and leave the system at any point in time, XCLAIM implements a replacement/auction mechanism via cross-chain SPV atomic swaps, where collateral y can be exchanged for committed x held in custody.

In cases where X and Y support smart contracts, specifically chain relays, *bidirectional* chain relays [80,107] can be utilized, enabling non-custodial commitments on X and Y: locking of x and unlocking/minting of $y(x)$ is handled exclusively by smart contracts under the assumption of synchrony.

Proof-of-Burn [101,147] resembles follows a similar design, yet implements a unidirectional protocol: instead of being locked, x is provably destroyed ("burned"), and newly minted as $y(x)$ on Y. As such, Proof-of-Burn is mostly used for bootstrapping of new blockchains. Merged mining [99] was the first CCC protocol deployed in practice (2011 in Namecoin) and is used explicitly for bootstrapping purposes. Miners (stakers) of X can reuse PoW solutions (stake) to progress consensus on Y by including a commitment to Y's state in the ledger of X.

Verify. Migration protocols - with the exception of centralized, custodial services - rely the on consensus of chain Y to correctly verify the commitment on X. We observe two main implementation techniques: (i) under synchrony assumptions by using *chain relay* smart contracts, which cryptographically verify the correctness of the commitment on X, or (ii) by requesting the consensus committee of Y to explicitly sign off on the CCC execution. XCMP [55], a cross-shard protocol, adds an additional verification step: cross-shard transfers are verified by and included in a hierarchically "superior" parent chain – which in turn is verified by the target shard Y before commitment.

Abort. We observe that Migration protocols generally do not implement an explicit abort phase. Instead, they assume that if the commitment on X is executed correctly it will eventually be verified by chain Y, which in turn will result in a correct commitment on Y. An exception hereof are n-to-m transfers in sharded blockchains (e.g., ATOMIX [111] and SBAC [25]) which require an explicit abort phase. Such transfers follow a two-phase-commit protocol: assets on all source shards $X_1, ..., X_n$ are pre-committed and verified on all target shards $Y_1, ..., Y_n$, which in turn execute a pre-commitment. If a single target shard fails to reply with a pre-commitment (within some period), the CCC protocol is aborted on all other source and target shards.

5.3   Insights and General Observations

An interesting, yet expected insight is that performance and usability outweigh security considerations from a user's perspective. Decentralized and non-custodial CCC solution have been proposed as early as 2013 (symmetric swaps [12]) and 2015 (SPV swaps [6]), yet centralized providers remain the dominant cross-chain asset exchange facilitator. The recent rise of decentralized exchanges, which mostly operate within a single chain [9], has boosted the adoption of cryptocurrency-backed assets, although predominantly via custodial approaches: at the time of writing, 99% of "wrapped" Bitcoin on Ethereum has been issued through trusted, custodial services [17].

Decentralized CCC protocols still suffer from practical drawbacks hindering adoption. Symmetric atomic swaps impose strict online requirements on users. SPV atomic swaps, and similarly migration protocols such as XCLAIM and tBTC, make use of chain relays which are only feasible if Y supports smart contracts and the cryptographic primitives used in X. Orthogonal, collateralization, which allows to protect users from financial damage (cf. Sect. 3), incurs high capital requirements and opportunity cost – leading most users to resort to trusted, centralized solutions.

An interesting observation hereby is that sharded systems and sidechains do not necessarily benefit from decentralized CCC protocols. In fact, due to the homogeneous nature of the security models of X and Y in this setting, the use of the consensus committee(s) of X or Y as TTP for CCC does not introduce any additional (external) trust assumptions to the underlying systems.

6   CCC Challenges and Outlook

In this section, we provide an outlook on the (open) problems faced by CCC protocols and possible avenues for future work.

6.1   Heterogeneous Models and Parameters Across Chains

Problems. Different blockchains leverage different system models and parameterizations, which, if not handled correctly by CCC protocols, can lead to protocol failures. For instance, the absence of a global clock across chains requires CCC participants to either agree on a trusted third party as means of synchronization, or to rely on a chain-dependent time definition (e.g., block generation rates [77]) which are often non-deterministic and hence unsafe for strictly time-bound protocols [77,165]. A practical example hereof are race-condition attacks on symmetric exchange protocols such as HTLC atomic swaps, discussed in Sect. 5.

Another consideration are the security models of interconnected chains: while X and Y may exhibit well defined security models, these are typically independent and not easily comparable (with the exception of sharding) – especially when combined within a CCC protocol. For instance, X may rely on PoW and thus assume that adversarial hash rate is bound by $\alpha \leq 33\%$ [74,82,141]. On the other hand, Y may utilize PoS for consensus and similarly assume that the adversary's stake in the system is bound by $\beta \leq 33\%$. While similar at first glance, the cost of accumulating stake [75,79] may be lower than that of accumulating computational power, or vice-versa [51]. Since permissionless ledgers are not Sybil resistant [69], i.e., provide weak identities at best, quantifying adversary strength is challenging even within a single ledger [33]. This task becomes nearly impossible in the cross-chain setting: not only can consensus participants (i) "hop" between different chains [115,127], destabilizing involved systems, but also (ii) be susceptible to bribing attacks executed cross-chain, against which there currently exist no countermeasures [98,125].

Following from different security models, the lack of homogeneous finality guarantees [146] across blockchains poses another challenge for CCC. Consider the following: X accepts a transaction as valid when confirmed by k subsequent blocks e.g., as in PoW blockchains [77]; instead, Y deems transactions valid as soon as they are written to the ledger ($k = 1$, e.g. [22]). A CCC protocol triggers a state transition on Y conditioned on a transaction included in X, however, later an (accidental) fork occurs on X. While the state of X is reverted, this may not be possible on Y according to consensus rules – likely resulting in an inconsistent state on Y and financial damage to users.

Outlook. Considering the plethora of blockchain designs in practice, it is safe to assume a heterogeneous ecosystem for at least the near future. Protocol designers must hence carefully evaluate and consider the specifics of each interlinked chain when implementing CCC schemes: introduction of conservative lower bounds on transaction (commit) finality (hours / days rather than minutes), analysis of computation and communication capabilities of consensus participants, and accounting for peer-to-peer network delays when utilizing a trusted third party as global clock

6.2   Heterogeneous Cryptographic Primitives Across Chains

Problems. Interconnected chains X and Y may rely on different cryptographic schemes, or different instances of the same scheme. CCC protocols, however, often require compatible cryptographic primitives: a CCC protocol between a system X using ECDSA [95] as its digital signature scheme and a system Y using Schnorr [142] is only seamlessly possible if both schemes are instantiated over the same elliptic curve [122]. This is, for example, the reason Ethereum uses the same secp256k1 curve as Bitcoin [10].

Similarly, CCC protocols using Hash Locks, e.g. HTLC swaps, require that the domain of the hash function has the same size in both X and Y– otherwise the protocol is prone to *oversize preimage attacks* [97], i.e., an attack where a transaction cannot be accepted by a chain because the representation of the preimage requires more bits than those previously allocated to store it.

Outlook. A design challenge in CCC protocols is thus the interoperability of chains in terms of (cryptographic) primitives as required in CCC protocols. In cases where interlinked chains implement different elliptic curves, zero-knowledge proofs may provide a workaround, yet at the cost of increased protocol complexity, as well as computation and communication costs [132]. Our observations suggest that this is one of the main reasons for lack of interoperability across current blockchain networks.

6.3   Collateralization and Exchange Rates

Problems. In recent works [8, 107, 152, 165], we observe a trend towards collateralizing coordinators to prevent financial damage to users and incentivize correct behavior of TTPs. Thereby, it is crucial to ensure that the provided collateral has sufficient value to outweigh potential gains from misbehavior. However, in the cross-chain setting, where insured asset and collateral are typically different, collateralized CCC protocols are forced to (i) implement measures against exchange rate fluctuations such as over-collateralization incurring capital inefficiencies for participants, and (ii) rely on (typically centralized) price oracles.

Outlook. Current CCC protocols, if at all, only provide minimal protection against exchange rate fluctuations, such as over-collateralization. An interesting avenue for future research is hence the design of dynamic collateralization e.g., based on the volatility of the locked/collateral assets. Decentralized price oracles already are an active field of research [4, 23, 137, 153, 166], yet as of this writing oracles remain single points of failure in collateralized CCC protocols. Cryptocurrency-backed assets traded on decentralized exchanges, where trading data is available on-chain, may thereby provide a valuable source of information for cross-verification with centralized providers [165].

6.4   Lack of Formal Security Analysis

Problems. While numerous CCC protocols have been deployed and used in practice, handling value transfers worth millions, most lack formal and rigorous security analysis. This lack of formal security guarantees opens the door to possible security threats. For instance, *replay attacks* on state verification, i.e., where proofs are re-submitted multiple times or on multiple chains, can result in failures such as double spending [124] or counterfeited cryptocurrency-backed assets [165]. Another security issue arises with *data availability*. Protocols employing cross-chain verification via chain relays typically rely on timely arrival of proofs and metadata (block headers, transactions, ...). However, if an adversary can withhold this data from the verifying chain [26], such protocols not only become less efficient but potentially vulnerable to double spending and counterfeiting.

Outlook. This state of affairs calls for a rigorous and formal security analysis of existing CCC protocol – least those deployed in practice. In the meantime, ad-hoc solutions to the aforementioned security threats have been discussed in the community. For instance, protections against replay attacks involving the use of sequence numbers, or chains keeping track of previously processed proofs [58, 124, 144]. Similarly, first attempts to mitigate the data availability problem via erasure coding have been suggested in [24, 26, 162] – yet at the cost of protocol complexity and communication overhead

6.5   Lack of Formal Privacy Analysis

Problems. Privacy is a crucial property of financial transactions and hence applies to CCC protocols. Ideally it should not be possible for an observer to determine which two events have been synchronized across chains (e.g., which assets have been exchanged and by whom). Unfortunately, CCC protocols deployed in practice lack formal privacy analysis and numerous privacy issues have already been detected. For instance, recent works [84,121] leverage the fact that the same hash value is used on both chains involved in symmetric HTLC atomic swaps to trivially link exchanged assets and accounts. Other de-anonymization techniques enabled by CCC protocols include miner address clustering via blocks merge-mined across different cryptocurrencies [99], cross-linking of miner and user accounts cross-chain by analyzing of blockchain forks [92,148], and using public exchange datasets to trace cross-ledger trades [161].

Outlook. The academic community has developed formal frameworks that permit rigorous analysis of the privacy properties in the context of exchange protocols [84,88,121,122,150]. First techniques towards privacy-preserving CCC Exchange protocols via asymmetric and unlinkable locking techniques have been studied in [66,121,122,140], yet, at the time of writing, we are not aware of privacy enhancements for the more-widely adopted Migration protocols – an interesting avenue for future research.

6.6   Upcoming Industrial and Research CCC Trends

Interoperability Blockchains. are specialized sharded distributed ledgers which aim to serve as communication layer between other blockchains [14,93, 114,139,145,156,158] and exhibit implementations of existing CCC protocols. Individual shards, which are coordinated via a parent chain running a BFT agreement protocol, connect to and import assets from existing blockchains via Migration CCC protocols, most commonly cryptocurrency-backed assets [7]. A formal treatment of this design, also considering distributed computations, is presented in [119]. Cosmos [114] and Polkadot [158] also implement new standards for (internal) cross-shard communication (IBC [16] and XCMP [55] respectively). As of this writing, the aforementioned systems are under active development, making it difficult to argue about their security, feasibility, and long-term adoption - leaving room for future analysis.

Efficient Light Clients. Cross-chain state verification via chain relays is a fundamental part of robust CCC protocols. While current light/SPV clients suffice for e.g., mobile devices, they often remain infeasible for deployment on top of blockchains for CCC protocols, where storage and bandwidth are priced by the byte. Recent works on sub-linear light clients have achieved first significant theoretical [103,104,120] and practical performance improvements [63,157,164]. In parallel, recent developments in the field of zero-knowledge cryptography [40,47,53] pave the way towards (near)constant verification times and costs for chain relays. First schemes for blockchains with built-in support for such proof systems are put forth in [41,49,126].

Off-Chain Protocols. One of the most actively developed fields in blockchain research are off-chain ("L2") communication networks [85], which aim to improve scalability (and privacy) of distributed ledgers: most transactions are executed off-chain and only channel opening and closure are written to the ledger. The influx of L2 solutions is thereby creating a new field for CCC research: (i) communication across off-chain channels [88,121,122,150], and (ii) communication between off-chain and on-chain networks [15,19]. While similar to conventional CCC protocols, the "off-chain" nature of L2 solutions requires more complex techniques for the verification phase of CCC: intermediate states in off-chain protocols cannot be verified by existing chain relays, which only support verification of on-chain commitments, and must hence resort to cryptographic techniques such as adaptor signatures [32] or succinct proofs of knowledge [40,47,53].

7   Concluding Remarks

Our systematic analysis of cross-chain communication as a new problem in the era of distributed ledgers allows us to relate (mostly) community driven efforts to established academic research in database and distributed systems research. We formalize the cross-chain communication problem and show it cannot be solved without a trusted third party – contrary to the assumptions often made in the blockchain community. Following this result, we introduce a framework for evaluating existing and designing new cross-chain communication protocols, based on the inherent trust assumptions thereof. We then provide a classification and comparative evaluation, taking into account both academic research and the vast number of online resources, allowing us to better understand the similarities and differences between existing cross-chain communication approaches. Finally, by discussing implications and open challenges faced by cross-chain communication protocols, as well as the implications of interoperability on the security and privacy of blockchains, we offer a comprehensive guide for designing protocols, bridging multiple distributed ledgers.

Acknowledgements. We would like express our gratitude to Georgia Avarikioti, Daniel Perez and Dominik Harz for helpful comments and feedback on earlier versions of this manuscript. We also thank Nicholas Stifter, Aljosha Judmayer, Philipp Schindler, Edgar Weippl, and Alistair Stewart for insightful discussions during the early stages of this research. We also wish to thank the anonymous reviewers for their valuable comments that helped improve the presentation of our results.

This research was funded by Bridge 1 858561 SESC; Bridge 1 864738 PR4DLT (all FFG); the Christian Doppler Laboratory for Security and Quality Improvement in the Production System Lifecycle (CDL-SQI); the competence center SBA-K1 funded by COMET; Chaincode Labs through the project SLN: Scalability for the Lightning Network; and by the Austrian Science Fund (FWF) through the Meitner program (project M-2608).

Mustafa Al-Bassam is funded by a scholarship from the Alan Turing Institute. Alexei Zamyatin conducted the early stages of this work during his time at SBA Research, and was supported by a Binance Research Fellowship.

A   Fair Exchange Using CCC

We provide the intuition of how to construct a Fair Exchange protocol using a generic CCC protocol in Algorithm 1. Specifically, P and Q exchange assets a_P and a_Q, if transaction TX_P is written to L_x and transaction TX_Q is written to L_y (cf. Sect. 3.2).

Algorithm 1: Fair Exchange using a generic CCC protocol

Result: $\text{TX}_P \in \mathsf{L}_x \wedge \text{TX}_Q \in \mathsf{L}_y$ (i.e., P has a_P, Q has a_Q) **or**
    $\text{TX}_P \notin \mathsf{L}_x \wedge \text{TX}_Q \notin \mathsf{L}_y$ (i.e., no exchange)
setup(L_x, L_y, TX_P, TX_Q, d_P, d_Q);
if $m_P = \mathsf{false}$ **then**
 | $commit(\text{TX}_P, \mathsf{L}_x)$; // P transfers a_P to Q
end
if $(verify(\text{TX}_P, \mathsf{L}_x, d_P) = \mathsf{true}) \wedge m_Q = \mathsf{false}$ **then**
 | $commit(\text{TX}_Q, \mathsf{L}_y)$; // Q transfers a_Q to P
else
 | $abort(\text{TX}_Q, \mathsf{L}_y)$; // Q does not transfer a_Q to P
end
if $verify(\text{TX}_Q, \mathsf{L}_y, d_Q) = \mathsf{false}$ **then**
 | $abort(\text{TX}_P, \mathsf{L}_x)$; // P recovers a_P
end

Algorithm 2: Commit(TX, L)

---

if $valid(\text{TX}, \mathsf{L})$ **then**
 | Write TX to L;
end

Algorithm 3: Verify(TX, L, d)

---

if $\text{TX} \in \mathsf{L} \wedge desc(\text{TX}) = d$ **then**
 | return true;
end
return false;

Algorithm 4: Abort(TX, L)

---

if $\text{TX} \in \mathsf{L}$ **then**
 | Revert TX; // e.g. using a new transaction
end

References

1. Binance exchange. Online. https://www.binance.com/en. Accessed 19 Sep 2020
2. Bitcoin Wiki: Hashed Time-Lock Contracts. https://en.bitcoin.it/wiki/Hashed_Timelock_Contracts. Accessed 02 Apr 2021
3. Btcrelay. https://github.com/ethereum/btcrelay. Accessed 02 Apr 2021
4. Chainlink: A decentralized oracle network. Online. https://link.smartcontract.com/whitepaper. Accessed 19 Sep 2020
5. Confirmations. https://en.bitcoin.it/wiki/Confirmation. Accessed 02 Apr 2021
6. Ethereum contract allowing ether to be obtained with bitcoin. https://github.com/ethers/EthereumBitcoinSwap. Accessed 02 Apr 2021
7. Polkabtc: Trustless bitcoin on polkadot. Online. https://github.com/interlay/BTC-Parachain. Accessed 19 Sep 2020

8. tbtc: A decentralized redeemable btc-backed erc-20 token. http://docs.keep. network/tbtc/index.pdf. Accessed 02 Apr 2021

9. Top cryptocurrency decentralized exchanges. Online. https://coinmarketcap. com/rankings/exchanges/dex/. Accessed 02 Apr 2021

10. Why does ethereum use secp256k1?

11. Wrapped   bitcoin.   https://www.wbtc.network/assets/wrapped-tokens-whitepaper.pdf. Accessed 02 Apr 2021

12. Alt chains and atomic transfers. bitcointalk.org (2013). https://bitcointalk.org/ index.php?topic=193281.msg2003765#msg2003765. Accessed 02 Apr 2021

13. Atomic swap. Bitcoin Wiki (2013). https://en.bitcoin.it/wiki/Atomic_swap. Accessed 02 Apr 2021

14. Wanchain whitepaper (2017). https://www.wanchain.org/files/Wanchain-Whitepaper-EN-version.pdf. Accessed 02 Apr 2021

15. Submarine swaps service. Online (2018). https://github.com/submarineswaps/ swaps-service. Accessed 02 Apr 2021

16. Inter-blockchain communication protocol (ibc) specification. Online (2019). https://github.com/cosmos/ics/tree/master/ibc. Accessed 02 Apr 2021

17. Bitcoin on ethereum. Online (2020). https://defipulse.com/btc

18. Bitcoin supply on ethereum tops $1b. Coindesk, September 2020. https://www. coindesk.com/bitcoin-supply-on-ethereum-tops-1b

19. Lightning loop. Online (2020). https://github.com/lightninglabs/loop. Accessed 02 Apr 2021

20. Ptokens: How it works. Online (2020). https://ptokens.io/how-it-works. Accessed 19 Sep 2020

21. Renvm. Online (2020). https://renproject.io/renvm. Accessed 19 Sep 2020

22. Abraham, I., Gueta, G., Malkhi, D.: Hot-stuff the linear, optimal-resilience, one-message bft devil (2018). arXiv:1803.05069

23. Adler, J., Berryhill, R., Veneris, A., Poulos, Z., Veira, N., Kastania, A.: Astraea: a decentralized blockchain oracle. In: 2018 IEEE International Conference on Internet Of Things (IThings) and IEEE Green Computing and Communications (GreenCom) and IEEE Cyber, Physical and Social Computing (CPSCom) and IEEE Smart Data (SmartData), pp. 1145–1152. IEEE (2018)

24. Al-Bassam, M.: Lazyledger: A distributed data availability ledger with client-side smart contracts. arXiv preprint arXiv:1905.09274 (2019)

25. Al-Bassam, M., Sonnino, A., Bano, S., Hrycyszyn, D., Danezis, G.: Chainspace: A sharded smart contracts platform. In: 2018 Network and Distributed System Security Symposium (NDSS) (2018)

26. Al-Bassam, M., Sonnino, A., Buterin, V.: Fraud proofs: Maximising light client security and scaling blockchains with dishonest majorities. arXiv preprint arXiv:1809.09044, vol. 160, (2018)

27. Androulaki, E., Cachin, C., De Caro, A., Kokoris-Kogias, E.: Channels: horizontal scaling and confidentiality on permissioned blockchains. In: Lopez, J., Zhou, J., Soriano, M. (eds.) ESORICS 2018. LNCS, vol. 11098, pp. 111–131. Springer, Cham (2018). https://doi.org/10.1007/978-3-319-99073-6_6

28. Andrychowicz, M.: Multiparty computation protocols based on cryptocurrencies (2015). https://depotuw.ceon.pl/bitstream/handle/item/1327/dis.pdf. Accessed 02 Apr 2021

29. Asokan, N.: Fairness in electronic commerce (1998)

30. Asokan, N., Shoup, V., Waidner, M.: Asynchronous protocols for optimistic fair exchange. In: Proceedings 1998 IEEE Symposium on Security and Privacy (Cat. No. 98CB36186), pp. 86–99. IEEE (1998)

31. Asokan, N., Shoup, V., Waidner, M.: Optimistic fair exchange of digital signatures. In: Nyberg, K. (ed.) EUROCRYPT 1998. LNCS, vol. 1403, pp. 591–606. Springer, Heidelberg (1998). https://doi.org/10.1007/BFb0054156
32. Aumayr, L., et al.: Generalized bitcoin-compatible channels. IACR Cryptolology ePrint Arch. 2020, vol. 476 (2020)
33. Avarikioti, G., Käppeli, L., Wang, Y., Wattenhofer, R.: Bitcoin security under temporary dishonest majority. In: 23rd Financial Cryptography and Data Security (FC) (2019)
34. Avarikioti, G., Kogias, E.K., Wattenhofer, R.: Brick: Asynchronous state channels. arXiv preprint arXiv:1905.11360 (2019)
35. Avarikioti, G., Kokoris-Kogias, E., Wattenhofer, R.: Divide and scale: formalization of distributed ledger sharding protocols. arXiv preprint arXiv:1910.10434 (2019)
36. Avarikioti, G., Laufenberg, F., Sliwinski, J., Wang, Y., Wattenhofer, R.: Towards secure and efficient payment channels. arXiv preprint arXiv:1811.12740 (2018)
37. Babaoglu, O., Toueg, S.: Understanding non-blocking atomic commitment. Distributed Systems, pp. 147–168 (1993)
38. Back, A., et al.: Enabling blockchain innovations with pegged sidechains (2014)
39. Belchior, R., Vasconcelos, A., Guerreiro, S., Correia, M.: A survey on blockchain interoperability: past, present, and future trends. arXiv preprint arXiv:2005.14282 (2020)
40. Ben-Sasson, E., Bentov, I., Horesh, Y., Riabzev, M.: Scalable, transparent, and post-quantum secure computational integrity. IACR Cryptology ePrint Archive 2018, vol. 46 (2018)
41. Ben-Sasson, E., Chiesa, A., Spooner, N.: Interactive oracle proofs. In: Hirt, M., Smith, A. (eds.) TCC 2016. LNCS, vol. 9986, pp. 31–60. Springer, Heidelberg (2016). https://doi.org/10.1007/978-3-662-53644-5_2
42. Bennink, P., Gijtenbeek, L.V., Deventer, O.V., Everts, M.: An analysis of atomic swaps on and between ethereum blockchains using smart contracts. Technical report (2018). https://work.delaat.net/rp/2017-2018/p42/report.pdf
43. Bentov, I., et al.: Tesseract: Real-time cryptocurrency exchange using trusted hardware. Cryptology ePrint Archive, Report 2017/1153 (2017). Accessed 04 Dec 2017
44. Bentov, I., Kumaresan, R.: How to use bitcoin to design fair protocols. In: Garay, J.A., Gennaro, R. (eds.) CRYPTO 2014. LNCS, vol. 8617, pp. 421–439. Springer, Heidelberg (2014). https://doi.org/10.1007/978-3-662-44381-1_24
45. Bentov, I., Pass, R., Shi, E.: Snow white: Provably secure proofs of stake (2016). Accessed 08 Nov 2016
46. Bernstein, P.A., Hadzilacos, V., Goodman, N.: Concurrency control and recovery in database systems, vol. 370. Addison-wesley, New York (1987)
47. Bitansky, N., Canetti, R., Chiesa, A., Tromer, E.: From extractable collision resistance to succinct non-interactive arguments of knowledge, and back again. In: Proceedings of the 3rd Innovations in Theoretical Computer Science Conference, pp. 326–349. ACM (2012)
48. Boneh, D., Bonneau, J., Bünz, B., Fisch, B.: Verifiable delay functions. In: CRYPTO (2018)
49. Boneh, D., Bünz, B., Fisch, B.: Batching techniques for accumulators with applications to iops and stateless blockchains. In: Boldyreva, A., Micciancio, D. (eds.) CRYPTO 2019. LNCS, vol. 11692, pp. 561–586. Springer, Cham (2019). https://doi.org/10.1007/978-3-030-26948-7_20

50. Boneh, D., Naor, M.: Timed commitments. In: Bellare, M. (ed.) CRYPTO 2000. LNCS, vol. 1880, pp. 236–254. Springer, Heidelberg (2000). https://doi.org/10.1007/3-540-44598-6_15
51. Bonneau, J.: Why buy when you can rent? bribery attacks on bitcoin consensus. In: BITCOIN '16: Proceedings of the 3rd Workshop on Bitcoin and Blockchain Research, February 2016
52. Bonneau, J., Clark, J., Goldfeder, S.: On bitcoin as a public randomness source (2015). Accessed 25 Act 2015
53. Bünz, B., Bootle, J., Boneh, D., Poelstra, A., Wuille, P., Maxwell, G.: Bulletproofs: Efficient range proofs for confidential transactions (2017). Accessed 10 Nov 2017
54. Bünz, B., Goldfeder, S., Bonneau, J.: Proofs-of-delay and randomness beacons in ethereum (2017)
55. Burdges, J., et al.: Overview of polkadot and its design considerations. arXiv preprint arXiv:2005.13456 (2020)
56. Buterin, V.: Ethereum: A next-generation smart contract and decentralized application platform (2014). Accessed 22 Aug 2016
57. Buterin, V.: Chain interoperability. Technical report (2016). Accessed 25 Mar 2017
58. Buterin, V.: Cross-shard contract yanking. https://ethresear.ch/t/cross-shard-contract-yanking/1450 (2018)
59. Cachin, C.: Architecture of the hyperledger blockchain fabric (2016). Accessed 10 Aug 2016
60. Cachin, C., Camenisch, J.: Optimistic fair secure computation. In: Bellare, M. (ed.) CRYPTO 2000. LNCS, vol. 1880, pp. 93–111. Springer, Heidelberg (2000). https://doi.org/10.1007/3-540-44598-6_6
61. Castro, M., Liskov, B., et al.: Practical byzantine fault tolerance. OSDI **99**, 173–186 (1999)
62. Chesney, T., Coyne, I., Logan, B., Madden, N.: Griefing in virtual worlds: causes, casualties and coping strategies. Inform. Syst. J. **19**(6), 525–548 (2009)
63. Daveas, S., Karantias, K., Kiayias, A., Zindros, D.: A gas-efficient superlight bitcoin client in solidity. In: Proceedings of the 2nd ACM Conference on Advances in Financial Technologies, pp. 132–144 (2020)
64. David, B., Gaži, P., Kiayias, A., Russell, A.: Ouroboros praos: an adaptively-secure, semi-synchronous proof-of-stake blockchain. In: Nielsen, J.B., Rijmen, V. (eds.) EUROCRYPT 2018. LNCS, vol. 10821, pp. 66–98. Springer, Cham (2018). https://doi.org/10.1007/978-3-319-78375-8_3
65. Decker, C., Wattenhofer, R.: Bitcoin transaction malleability and MtGox. In: Kutyłowski, M., Vaidya, J. (eds.) ESORICS 2014. LNCS, vol. 8713, pp. 313–326. Springer, Cham (2014). https://doi.org/10.1007/978-3-319-11212-1_18
66. Deshpande, A., Herlihy, M.: Privacy-preserving cross-chain atomic swaps. In: Bernhard, M., Bracciali, A., Camp, L.J., Matsuo, S., Maurushat, A., Rønne, P.B., Sala, M. (eds.) FC 2020. LNCS, vol. 12063, pp. 540–549. Springer, Cham (2020). https://doi.org/10.1007/978-3-030-54455-3_38
67. Dijkstra, E.W.: Solution of a problem in concurrent programming control. In: Pioneers and Their Contributions to Software Engineering, pp. 289–294. Springer (2001). https://doi.org/10.1007/978-3-642-48354-7_10
68. Dilley, J., Poelstra, A., Wilkins, J., Piekarska, M., Gorlick, B., Friedenbach, M.: Strong federations: An interoperable blockchain solution to centralized third party risks. arXiv preprint arXiv:1612.05491 (2016)

69. Douceur, J.R.: The sybil attack. In: Druschel, P., Kaashoek, F., Rowstron, A. (eds.) IPTPS 2002. LNCS, vol. 2429, pp. 251–260. Springer, Heidelberg (2002). https://doi.org/10.1007/3-540-45748-8_24

70. Dziembowski, S., Eckey, L., Faust, S.: Fairswap: how to fairly exchange digital goods. In: Proceedings of the 2018 ACM SIGSAC Conference on Computer and Communications Security, pp. 967–984. ACM (2018)

71. Egger, C., Moreno-Sanchez, P., Maffei, M.: Atomic multi-channel updates with constant collateral in bitcoin-compatible payment-channel networks. In: CCS (2019)

72. Even, S.: A protocol for signing contracts. Technical report, Computer Science Department, Technion. Presented at CRYPTO'81 (1982)

73. Even, S., Yacobi, Y.: Relations among public key signature systems. Technical report, Computer Science Department, Technion (1980)

74. Eyal, I., Sirer, E.G.: Majority is not enough: Bitcoin mining is vulnerable. In: Financial Cryptography and Data Security, pp. 436–454. Springer (2014)

75. Fanti, G., Kogan, L., Oh, S., Ruan, K., Viswanath, P., Wang, G.: Compounding of wealth in proof-of-stake cryptocurrencies. arXiv preprint arXiv:1809.07468 (2018)

76. Fischer, M.J., Lynch, N.A., Paterson, M.S.: Impossibility of distributed consensus with one faulty process, vol. 32, pp. 374–382. ACM (1985)

77. Garay, J.A., Kiayias, A., Leonardos, N.: The bitcoin backbone protocol with chains of variable difficulty (2016). Accessed 06 Feb 2017

78. Gärtner, F.C.: Specifications for fault tolerance: A comedy of failures (1998)

79. Gaži, P., Kiayias, A., Russell, A.: Stake-bleeding attacks on proof-of-stake blockchains. Cryptology ePrint Archive, Report 2018/248 (2018). Accessed 12 Mar 2018

80. Gazi, P., Kiayias, A., Zindros, D.: Proof-of-stake sidechains. IEEE Security and Privacy, IEEE (2019)

81. Gennaro, R., Goldfeder, S., Narayanan, A.: Threshold-optimal DSA/ECDSA signatures and an application to bitcoin wallet security. In: Manulis, M., Sadeghi, A.-R., Schneider, S. (eds.) ACNS 2016. LNCS, vol. 9696, pp. 156–174. Springer, Cham (2016). https://doi.org/10.1007/978-3-319-39555-5_9

82. Gervais, A., Karame, G.O., Wüst, K., Glykantzis, V., Ritzdorf, H., Capkun, S.: On the security and performance of proof of work blockchains. In: Proceedings of the 2016 ACM SIGSAC, pp. 3–16. ACM (2016)

83. Goldreich, O.: Secure multi-party computation. Manuscript. Preliminary version, vol. 78 (1998)

84. Green, M., Miers, I.: Bolt: Anonymous payment channels for decentralized currencies. Cryptology ePrint Archive, Report 2016/701 (2016). Accessed 07 Aug 2017

85. Gudgeon, L., Moreno-Sanchez, P., Roos, S., McCorry, P., Gervais, A.: Sok: Off the chain transactions. Cryptology ePrint Archive, Report 2019/360 (2019). https://eprint.iacr.org/2019/360

86. Han, R., Lin, H., Yu, J.: On the optionality and fairness of atomic swaps. Cryptology ePrint Archive, Report 2019/896 (2019). https://eprint.iacr.org/2019/896

87. Harz, D., Boman, M.: The scalability of trustless trust. arXiv:1801.09535 (2018). Accessed 31 Jan 2018

88. Heilman, E., Alshenibr, L., Baldimtsi, F., Scafuro, A., Goldberg, S.: Tumblebit: An untrusted bitcoin-compatible anonymous payment hub (2016). Accessed 29 Sep 2017

89. Heilman, E., Lipmann, S., Goldberg, S.: The arwen trading protocols. Whitepaper. https://www.arwen.io/whitepaper.pdf

90. Herlihy, M.: Atomic cross-chain swaps. arXiv:1801.09515 (2018). Accessed 31 Jan 2018
91. Herlihy, M., Liskov, B., Shrira, L.: Cross-chain deals and adversarial commerce. arXiv preprint arXiv:1905.09743 (2019)
92. Hinteregger, A., Haslhofer, B.: An empirical analysis of monero cross-chain traceability. arXiv preprint arXiv:1812.02808 (2018)
93. Hosp, D., Hoenisch, T., Kittiwongsunthorn, P., et al.: Comit-cryptographically-secure off-chain multi-asset instant transaction network. arXiv preprint arXiv:1810.02174 (2018)
94. Itakura, K., Nakamura, K.: A public-key cryptosystem suitable for digital multisignatures. NEC Res. Dev. **71**, 1–8 (1983)
95. Johnson, D., Menezes, A., Vanstone, S.: The elliptic curve digital signature algorithm (ecdsa). Int. J. Inform. Secur. **1**(1), 36–63 (2001)
96. Johnson, S., Robinson, P., Brainard, J.: Sidechains and interoperability. arXiv preprint arXiv:1903.04077 (2019)
97. Jones, J.: abitmore. Optional htlc preimage length and hash160 addition. BSIP 64, blog post. https://github.com/bitshares/bsips/issues/163
98. Judmayer, A., et al.: Pay-to-win: Incentive attacks on proof-of-work cryptocurrencies. Cryptology ePrint Archive, Report 2019/775 (2019). https://eprint.iacr.org/2019/775
99. Judmayer, A., Zamyatin, A., Stifter, N., Voyiatzis, A.G., Weippl, E.: Merged mining: Curse or cure? In: CBT'17: Proceedings of the International Workshop on Cryptocurrencies and Blockchain Technology, September 2017
100. Kalodner, H., Goldfeder, S., Chen, X., Weinberg, S.M., Felten, E.W.: Arbitrum: Scalable, private smart contracts. In: Proceedings of the 27th USENIX Conference on Security Symposium, pp. 1353–1370. USENIX Association (2018)
101. Karantias, K., Kiayias, A., Zindros, D.: Proof-of-burn. In: Bonneau, J., Heninger, N. (eds.) FC 2020. LNCS, vol. 12059, pp. 523–540. Springer, Cham (2020). https://doi.org/10.1007/978-3-030-51280-4_28
102. Khabbazian, M., Nadahalli, T., Wattenhofer, R.: Outpost: A responsive lightweight watchtower (2019)
103. Kiayias, A., Miller, A., Zindros, D.: Non-interactive proofs of proof-of-work. Cryptology ePrint Archive, Report 2017/963 (2017). Accessed 03 Act 2017
104. Kiayias, A., Polydouri, A., Zindros, D.: The Velvet Path to Superlight Blockchain Clients (2020)
105. Kiayias, A., Russell, A., David, B., Oliynykov, R.: Ouroboros: a provably secure proof-of-stake blockchain protocol. In: Katz, J., Shacham, H. (eds.) CRYPTO 2017. LNCS, vol. 10401, pp. 357–388. Springer, Cham (2017). https://doi.org/10.1007/978-3-319-63688-7_12
106. Kiayias, A., Zhou, H.-S., Zikas, V.: Fair and robust multi-party computation using a global transaction ledger. In: Fischlin, M., Coron, J.-S. (eds.) EUROCRYPT 2016. LNCS, vol. 9666, pp. 705–734. Springer, Heidelberg (2016). https://doi.org/10.1007/978-3-662-49896-5_25
107. Kiayias, A., Zindros, D.: Proof-of-work sidechains. In: International Conference on Financial Cryptography and Data Security. Springer (2018)
108. Kogias, E.K., Jovanovic, P., Gailly, N., Khoffi, I., Gasser, L., Ford, B.: Enhancing bitcoin security and performance with strong consistency via collective signing. In: 25th USENIX Security Symposium (USENIX Security 16), Austin, TX, Auguest 2016. USENIX Association
109. Kokoris-Kogias, E.: Robust and scalable consensus for sharded distributed ledgers. Technical report, Cryptology ePrint Archive, Report 2019/676 (2019)

110. Kokoris-Kogias, E., et al.: Calypso: Auditable sharing of private data over blockchains. Technical report, Cryptology ePrint Archive, Report 2018/209 (2018)
111. Kokoris-Kogias, E., Jovanovic, P., Gasser, L., Gailly, N., Syta, E., Ford, B.: Omniledger: A secure, scale-out, decentralized ledger via sharding. In: 2018 IEEE Symposium on Security and Privacy (SP), pp. 583–598. IEEE (2018)
112. Kumaresan, R., Bentov, I.: Amortizing secure computation with penalties. In: Proceedings of the 2016 ACM SIGSAC Conference on Computer and Communications Security, pp. 418–429. ACM (2016)
113. Küpçü, A., Lysyanskaya, A.: Usable optimistic fair exchange. Comput. Netw. **56**(1), 50–63 (2012)
114. Kwon, J., Buchman, E.: Cosmos: A network of distributed ledgers. https://github.com/cosmos/cosmos/blob/master/WHITEPAPER.md (2015)
115. Kwon, Y., Kim, H., Shin, J., Kim, Y.: Bitcoin vs. bitcoin cash: Coexistence or downfall of bitcoin cash? arXiv:1902.11064 (2019)
116. Lamport, L.: A simple approach to specifying concurrent systems. Commun. ACM **32**(1), 32–45 (1989)
117. Lerner, S.: Drivechains, sidechains and hybrid 2-way peg designs. Technical report, Tech. Rep. [Online] (2018)
118. Lerner, S.D.: Rootstock: Bitcoin powered smart contracts. https://docs.rsk.co/RSK_White_Paper-Overview.pdf (2015)
119. Liu, Z., et al.: Hyperservice: Interoperability and programmability across heterogeneous blockchains. arXiv preprint arXiv:1908.09343 (2019)
120. Luu, L., Buenz, B., Zamani, M.: Flyclient super light client for cryptocurrencies. Accessed 17 Apr 2018
121. Malavolta, G., Moreno-Sanchez, P., Kate, A., Maffei, M., Ravi, S.: Concurrency and privacy with payment-channel networks. In: CCS, pp. 455–471 (2017)
122. Malavolta, G., Moreno-Sanchez, P., Schneidewind, C., Kate, A., Maffei, M.: Anonymous multi-hop locks for blockchain scalability and interoperability. In: NDSS (2019)
123. McCorry, P., Bakshi, S., Bentov, I., Miller, A., Meiklejohn, S.: Pisa: Arbitration outsourcing for state channels. IACR Cryptology ePrint Archive 2018, vol. 582 (2018)
124. McCorry, P., Heilman, E., Miller, A.: Atomically trading with roger: Gambling on the success of a hardfork. In: CBT'17: Proceedings of the International Workshop on Cryptocurrencies and Blockchain Technology, September 2017
125. McCorry, P., Hicks, A., Meiklejohn, S.: Smart contracts for bribing miners. In: 5th Workshop on Bitcoin and Blockchain Research, Financial Cryptography and Data Security 18 (FC). Springer (2018)
126. Meckler, I., Shapiro, E.: Coda: Decentralized cryptocurrency at scale. https://cdn.codaprotocol.com/v2/static/coda-whitepaper-05-10-2018-0.pdf (2018)
127. Meshkov, D., Chepurnoy, A., Jansen, M.: Revisiting difficulty control for blockchain systems. Cryptology ePrint Archive, Report 2017/731 (2017). Accessed 03 Aug 2017
128. Micali, S.: Algorand: The efficient and democratic ledger (2016). Accessed 09 Feb 2017
129. Miraz, M., Donald, D.C.: Atomic cross-chain swaps: Development, trajectory and potential of non-monetary digital token swap facilities. Annals of Emerging Technologies in Computing (AETiC), vol. 3 (2019)

130. Moreno-Sanchez, P., Randomrun, D.V.L., Noether, S., Goodell, B., Kate, A.: Dlsag: Non-interactive refund transactions for interoperable payment channels in monero. Cryptology ePrint Archive, Report 2019/595 (2019). https://eprint.iacr.org/2019/595

131. Nakamoto, S.: Bitcoin: A peer-to-peer electronic cash system, December 2008. Accessed 01 Jul 2015

132. Noether, S.: Discrete logarithm equality across groups. Online (2020). https://www.getmonero.org/resources/research-lab/pubs/MRL-0010.pdf

133. Pagnia, H., Gärtner, F.C.: On the impossibility of fair exchange without a trusted third party. Technical report, Technical Report TUD-BS-1999-02, Darmstadt University of Technology (1999)

134. Pass, R., Shi, E.: Hybrid consensus: Scalable permissionless consensus, September 2016. Accessed 17 Act 2016

135. Poelstra, A.: Scriptless scripts. Presentation slides. https://download.wpsoftware.net/bitcoin/wizardry/mw-slides/2017-03-mit-bitcoin-expo/slides.pdf

136. Poon, J., Dryja, T.: The bitcoin lightning network (2016). Accessed 07 Jul 2016

137. Ritzdorf, H., Wüst, K., Gervais, A., Felley, G., et al.: Tls-n: Non-repudiation over tls enabling ubiquitous content signing. In: Network and Distributed System Security Symposium (NDSS) (2018)

138. Rivest, R.L., Shamir, A., Wagner, D.A.: Time-lock puzzles and timed-release crypto (1996)

139. Rocket, T.: Snowflake to avalanche: A novel metastable consensus protocol family for cryptocurrencies (2018). Accessed 4 Dec 2018

140. Rubin, J., Naik, M., Subramanian, N.: Merkelized abstract syntax trees. http://www.mit.edu/jlrubin/public/pdfs/858report.pdf (2014)

141. Sapirshtein, A., Sompolinsky, Y., Zohar, A.: Optimal selfish mining strategies in bitcoin (2015). Accessed 22 Aug 2016

142. Schnorr, C.P.: Efficient signature generation by smart cards. J. Cryptol. **4**(3), 161–174 (1991). https://doi.org/10.1007/BF00196725

143. Siris, V.A., Dimopoulos, D., Fotiou, N., Voulgaris, S., Polyzos, G.C.: Interledger smart contracts for decentralized authorization to constrained things (2019)

144. Sonnino, A., Bano, S., Al-Bassam, M., Danezis, G.: Replay attacks and defenses against cross-shard consensus in sharded distributed ledgers. arXiv preprint arXiv:1901.11218 (2019)

145. Spoke, M., Nuco Engineering Team. Aion: The third-generation blockchain network.   https://aion.network/media/2018/03/aion.network_technical-introduction_en.pdf. Accessed 17 Apr 2018

146. Stewart, A., Kokoris-Kogia, E.: Grandpa: a byzantine finality gadget. arXiv preprint arXiv:2007.01560 (2020)

147. Stewart, I.: Proof of burn (2012). Accessed 10 May 2017

148. Stifter, N., Schindler, P., Judmayer, A., Zamyatin, A., Kern, A., Weippl, E.: Echoes of the past: Recovering blockchain metrics from merged mining. In: Proceedings of the 23nd International Conference on Financial Cryptography and Data Security (FC). Springer (2019)

149. Syverson, P.: Weakly secret bit commitment: applications to lotteries and fair exchange. In: Proceedings 11th IEEE Computer Security Foundations Workshop (Cat. No. 98TB100238), pp. 2–13. IEEE (1998)

150. Tairi, E., Moreno-Sanchez, P., Maffei, M.: A^2l: anonymous atomic locks for scalability and interoperability in payment channel hubs. Cryptology ePrint Archive, Report 2019/589 (2019). https://eprint.iacr.org/2019/589

151. Teutsch, J., Reitwießner, C.: A scalable verification solution for blockchains, March 2017. Accessed 06 Act 2017
152. Teutsch, J., Straka, M., Boneh, D.: Retrofitting a two-way peg between blockchains. Technical report (2018)
153. Teutsch, J.: TrueBit Establishment. On decentralized oracles for data availability (2017)
154. Thomas, S., Schwartz, E.: A protocol for interledger payments. https://interledger.org/interledger.pdf (2015)
155. Thyagarajan, S.A.K., Malavolta, G.: Lockable signatures for blockchains: Scriptless scripts for all signatures. Cryptology ePrint Archive, Report 2020/1613 (2020). https://eprint.iacr.org/2020/1613
156. Verdian, G., Tasca, P., Paterson, C., Mondelli, G.: Quant overledger whitepaper. https://www.quant.network/ (2018)
157. Westerkamp, M., Eberhardt, J.: zkrelay: facilitating sidechains using zksnark-based chain-relays. Contract 1(2), 3 (2020)
158. Wood, G.: Polkadot: Vision for a heterogeneous multi-chain framework. White Paper (2015)
159. Wood, G.: Ethereum: A secure decentralised generalised transaction ledger eip-150 revision (759dccd - 2017-08-07) (2017). Accessed 03 Jan 2018
160. Yao, A.C.-C.: How to generate and exchange secrets. In: 27th Annual Symposium on Foundations of Computer Science (sfcs 1986), pp. 162–167. IEEE (1986)
161. Yousaf, H., Kappos, G., Meiklejohn, S.: Tracing transactions across cryptocurrency ledgers. In: 28th {USENIX} Security Symposium ({USENIX} Security 19), pp. 837–850 (2019)
162. Yu, M., Sahraei, S., Li, S., Avestimehr, S., Kannan, S., Viswanath, P.: Coded merkle tree: Solving data availability attacks in blockchains. arXiv preprint arXiv:1910.01247 (2019)
163. Zamani, M., Movahedi, M., Raykova, M.: Rapidchain: A fast blockchain protocol via full sharding. Cryptology ePrint Archive, Report 2018/460 (2018)
164. Zamyatin, A., Avarikioti, Z., Perez, D., Knottenbelt, W.J.: Txchain: Efficient cryptocurrency light clients via contingent transaction aggregation, September 2020
165. Zamyatin, A., Harz, D., Lind, J., Panayiotou, P., Gervais, A., Knottenbelt, W.: Xclaim: Trustless, interoperable, cryptocurrency-backed assets. IEEE Security and Privacy, IEEE (2019)
166. Zhang, F., Maram, S.K.D., Malvai, S., Goldfeder, H., Juels, A.: Deco: Liberating web data using decentralized oracles for tls. arXiv preprint arXiv:1909.00938 (2019)

Reparo: Publicly Verifiable Layer to Repair Blockchains

Sri Aravinda Krishnan Thyagarajan[1], Adithya Bhat[2(✉)], Bernardo Magri[3,4],
Daniel Tschudi[5], and Aniket Kate[2]

[1] Friedrich-Alexander-Universität Erlangen-Nürnberg, Erlangen, Germany
[2] Purdue University, West Lafayette, USA
bhat24@purdue.edu
[3] Concordium Blockchain Research Center, Aarhus, Denmark
[4] Aarhus University, Aarhus, Denmark
[5] Concordium, Zurich, Switzerland

Abstract. Although blockchains aim for immutability as their core feature, several instances have exposed the harms with perfect immutability. The permanence of illicit content inserted in Bitcoin poses a challenge to law enforcement agencies like Interpol, and millions of dollars were lost in buggy smart contracts in Ethereum. A line of research then spawned on redactable blockchains with the aim of solving the problem of redacting illicit contents from both permissioned and permissionless blockchains. However, all the existing proposals follow the build-new-chain approach for redactions, and *cannot* be integrated with existing running blockchains, such as Bitcoin and Ethereum.

This work demonstrates that the traditional build-new-chain approach for blockchain redactions is not necessary. We present Reparo (In the Harry Potter universe, 'Reparo' is a spell that repairs objects), a publicly verifiable *layer* on top of any blockchain to perform *repairs*, ranging from fixing buggy contracts to removing illicit contents from the chain. We present an efficient instantiation of Reparo over Ethereum (with proof of work based consensus) for repairing smart contract bugs. In this protocol, any Ethereum user may propose a repair and a deliberation process ensues resulting in a decision that complies with the repair policy of the chain and is publicly verifiable. A repair operation (for instance, fixing a bug in a contract) is then performed according to the repair proposal and the state of Ethereum is updated accordingly. Reparo's advantages are multi-fold: (i) Since Reparo follows a layer design, it helps facilitate additional functionalities for Ethereum while maintaining the same provable security guarantees; (ii) Reparo can be easily tailored to different consensus requirements (like proof of stake), does not require heavy cryptographic machinery, and thus, can be integrated with other existing blockchains (such as Bitcoin, Cardano) as well. We evaluate Reparo with Ethereum mainnet and show that the cost of fixing several prominent smart contract bugs is almost negligible. For instance, the cost of repairing the prominent *Parity Multisig wallet* bug with Reparo is as low as 0.00005% of the Ethers that can be retrieved after the fix.

© International Financial Cryptography Association 2021
N. Borisov and C. Diaz (Eds.): FC 2021, LNCS 12675, pp. 37–56, 2021.
https://doi.org/10.1007/978-3-662-64331-0_2

1   Introduction

Blockchain as the underlying technology of cryptocurrencies, such as Bitcoin [26] and Ethereum [33] is an append-only, decentralized ledger equipped with public verifiability and immutability. While immutability in blockchains was always considered attractive, it does come with several issues. Immutability in monetary aspects is quite unforgiving; e.g., the infamous DAO attack [11] exploited a re-entrancy bug in a smart contract resulting in the loss of 3.6 million ETH. In Ethereum alone, other than the DAO bug[1] more than 750K ETH worth more than $150 million [24] (at the time of writing) have been either locked, lost or stolen by malicious attackers or bugs in smart contracts [2,7,17]. In a cryptocurrency with a fixed supply of tokens, stolen or locked tokens pose a huge problem of deflation [13], and even worse, could adversely affect the consensus process on systems based on Proof of Stake (PoS), which Ethereum 2.0 plans to adopt [8,10]. Moreover, writing bug-free software, and therefore smart contracts, seems to be a long-standing hard problem and the situation only worsens when many such buggy contracts are uploaded onto the chain resulting in the loss of hundreds of millions of dollars.

Even much-restricted systems such as Bitcoin suffers from the problem of arbitrary data being inserted in the chain through special transactions,[2] where all miners are required to store and broadcast the data for validation purposes. Several academic and law enforcement groups have studied the problem of illicit content insertion in Bitcoin [20,25,31]. A malicious user can pay a small fee to post illegal and/or harmful content onto the blockchain via these special transactions. Interpol [20] reported the existence of such arbitrary content in the form of illicit materials like child pornography, copyrighted material, sensitive information, etc. on the Bitcoin blockchain. While screening the contents of a transaction before adding it to the blockchain seems to be a straightforward solution, Matzutt et al. [25] showed the infeasibility of this approach while giving a quantitative analysis of already existing contents in the Bitcoin blockchain. Law enforcement agencies [31] are finding it challenging to deal with this problem.

The new General Data Protection Regulation (GDPR) in the European states has thrown the spotlight on the immutability of *personal information* like addresses, transaction values, and timestamps [19]. These issues could adversely affect the adaptability of existing blockchain-based applications, especially for cryptocurrencies if they want to be a credible alternative for fiat currencies.

1.1   Existing Solutions and Their Limitations

Redactable Blockchains. The seminal work of Ateniese et al. [4] was the first to consider the mutability of blockchains. Their redactable Blockchain protocol

---

[1] The DAO bug was fixed in July 16' by introducing an ad-hoc fix that runs DAO transactions differently; resulting in a hard fork, that gave birth to Ethereum Classic.

[2] Arbitrary information is permitted in Bitcoin through OP_RETURN code, that can store up to 80 bytes of arbitrary data on the blockchain.

aims to redact illicit contents from a blockchain using chameleon hash links [21]. However, their protocol requires the miners to run a Multi-Party Computation (MPC) protocol which can be quite prohibitive in large permissionless systems like Bitcoin. Moreover, their protocol requires modifications to the block structure, making it not useful to remove already existing illicit content in the chain of Bitcoin or release frozen Ethers in Ethereum. We refer to this property as *Repairability of Existing Contents (REC)*. Puddu, Dmitrienko and Capkun [28]'s proposal suffers from the same problems, and also, presents the control to modify a transaction to the transaction creator, which is not useful if the creator does not allow the desired modifications. Derler et al. [12] solve the above problem by using attribute-based encryption where the transaction creator lets anyone with the right policy modify the transaction. While they do not require any large-scale MPC among the miners, their protocol lacks public verifiability and requires modifications on how the Merkle roots are computed in the blocks, hence does not guarantee REC for Bitcoin or Ethereum. The recent work of Deuber, Magri and Thyagarajan [14] leverages on-chain voting techniques to reach an agreement on the redaction of contents, thereby adding public verifiability to the redactions. However, their protocol also requires modifications to the block header and therefore does not guarantee REC for current systems. Tezos [18] proposed a PoS protocol that can instantiate any blockchain but does not guarantee REC. While lacking formal security guarantees, it also lacks efficiency for multiple updates. Given that all the aforementioned proposals are *build-new-chain* solutions (no REC) and suffer from other issues as discussed, *none* of them are integrable into existing mainstream permissionless blockchain systems guaranteeing REC[3]. Table 1 summarizes the above discussed limitations. For an extended technical discussion and comparison, we refer the readers to the extended version [30].

Hard Forks. Performing a repair by forking away from a faulty point in the blockchain can lead to a loss of blocks. A hard fork requires miners to update their client software and corresponding mining hardware. Every hard fork brings with it an additional consensus rule in order to validate the whole chain. These additional rules demand additional storage and computational capabilities from clients. Hard forks are also ad-hoc: in Ethereum, DAO was deemed to be a big enough bug to fork the chain, whereas Parity Multisig Wallet was not [17].

Pruning. For repair operations such as redactions or removing old content, there are pruning solutions that locally redact contents [9]. However, the primary purpose of this method is space optimization and there is no consensus on what can be removed or redacted. Therefore, a newly joining full node is still expected to receive all the information on the chain for thorough validation (Fig. 1).

1.2   Our Contributions

In this paper, we contribute in the following ways:

---

[3] In case of permissioned setting, Ateniese et al. [4]'s proposal has been commercially adopted by a large consultancy company [3, 22].

Table 1. Comparison of our work with that of the existing redaction solutions. A cross for *Repairability of Existing Contents (REC)* means the proposal is not useful to redact or modify already inserted contents in blockchain.

Proposals	Stateful repairs	System-scale MPC	REC	Public verifiability
Ateniese et al. [4]	×	Required	×	×
Puddu et al. [28]	×	Required	×	×
Derler et al. [12]	×	Not required	×	×
Deuber et al. [14]	×	Not required	×	✓
Tezos [18]	✓	Not required	×	✓
This work - Reparo	✓	Not required	✓	✓

1. We demonstrate that the conventional *build-new-chain* approach in the literature for redacting contents in a blockchain is unnecessary. We present Reparo, which is a *layered* protocol (in the style of the finality *layer* for blockchains [23]) that can be integrated on top of Ethereum, and one can perform repair operations on its already existing contents (satisfies REC requirement). Specifically, using Reparo one can fix buggy smart contracts, redact illicit data, etc., in Ethereum without requiring a hard fork for every repair performed.

   In the extended version [30], we also generalize our protocol, and give the first generic Reparo protocol that is provably secure and acts as a layer and can easily be integrated on top of *any* existing secure blockchain. Our generic protocol can be adapted to any flavor of consensus (including permissioned systems) without any overhead.

2. We implement our Reparo protocol integrated into Ethereum. As we show in Sect. 4, when importing the latest 26,000 block sub-chain from the Ethereum main network, our baseline implementation has an overhead of just 0.009% when compared to its vanilla counterpart. The choice of Ethereum is motivated by the wide-spread adoption and generality of the Ethereum's functionalities.

   With respect to [14], our instantiation with Reparo has comparable efficiency in terms of time and is significantly better in terms of space efficiency: unlike [14], Reparo does not require an additional values to be stored in every (fresh or repaired) block header.

3. **Practical Implications.** Apart from illicit data redaction in Bitcoin, for Ethereum, a repair involves re-running all the transactions that are affected, thus demanding computation from the network. Therefore, a repair proposal must pay (in gas) an amount proportional to the computation spent by the network to perform the repair. We measure the repair costs of various existing bugs affecting Ethereum today. For concreteness, we demonstrate that the Parity Multi Sig Wallet Bug, which locked over 513K ETH, can be repaired today by paying a little over 0.00094 ETH in gas. Reparo also gives a mechanism to resolve

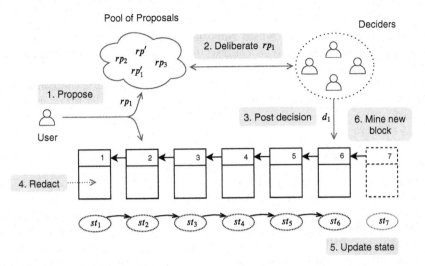

Fig. 1. Step by step description of Reparo in case of performing a redaction. The steps are in gray boxes and highlighted with red color. Here, a block is partitioned into a block header and block body and the block header stores a pointer to the previous block's header. State st_i denotes the state of the chain after block i has been mined.

an issue where users submit a contract creation transaction with no code [15] (due to user errors or buggy wallet code), releasing over 6.53K ETH. Ethereum uses an ad-hoc fix for DAO as it hard-codes a different logic for DAO. Reparo can be used to remove this ad-hoc fix by first repairing DAO code (while the fix is still active) and later removing the ad-hoc fix. Reparo also helps in handling zero-day vulnerabilities and thereby contain the damage. Such mechanism can help a blockchain improve trust and adoption by the users.

Consider situations where users accidentally create contracts with no code in it, it is safe for the user to create a repair transaction with Reparo that adds code to this contract without forking. Users of Reparo enabled blockchains can skip the expensive, cumbersome and often times arbitrary[9] procedures involving a hard fork. Currently, such users *permanently lose* their money.

Reparo can also be used to fix smart contract bugs such as *zero-day vulnerabilities* like the one that was very recently discovered (worth 25K ETH or 9.6M USD) and fixed in an ad-hoc manner [29]. In this sense, Reparo offers consistency and uniformity from Ethereum protocol point of view by eliminating the need for ad-hoc and potentially insecure bug fixes.

2 A Primer on Ethereum

Since we present Reparo as a repair layer on Ethereum, in this section we give a brief background on the Ethereum blockchain protocol. For details about a blockchain protocol in general that will be useful for our generic Reparo protocol, we refer the reader to the extended version [30].

On a high level, Ethereum [33] is a decentralized virtual machine (Ethereum Virtual Machine or EVM), which runs user programs called *smart contracts* upon user's request. Roughly, a contract is a collection of functions and variables, where each function is defined by a sequence of bytecode instructions that operate on some input and the variables associated with the contract. A user interacts with a contract through transactions that calls functions in the contract.

2.1   Ethereum Ledger

Accounts. State in Ethereum is maintained by a collection of account objects (*ACC*). The objects are encoded using RLP (Recursive Length Prefix) format, and a Merkle Patricia trie is built over all the objects. The root of this tree is called the state root (G_{st}). An account consists of (1) an address: hash of the public key, (2) balance (Acc.*bal*): amount of ETH currently owned by the account, (3) nonce (Acc.*nonce*): an incrementing counter used to differentiate states, (4) code hash (Acc.*h*): the hash of the code for this account possibly an empty hash or EVM bytecode for smart contracts), and (5) storage root (Acc.*sr*): the hash of an RLP encoding containing the state of the smart contract (such as data structures owned by the contract).

Transaction. An Ethereum transaction Tx logically[4] consists of (1) a from (`from`) field which is the address that is invoking the transaction, (2) to (`to`) field which is the recipient of the transaction (a smart contract or the recipient of a transfer), (3) a value (`value`) field indicating the amount of ETH dedicated to Tx, and (4) a data (`data`) field which contains encoded bytes used during the execution of the transaction (these are inputs to the smart contracts).

Block. Similar to Bitcoin, Ethereum blocks consist of a header and a body. We describe the relevant[5] fields of the header in Table 2.

State. The G_{st} is updated with every block using a global state transition function $\delta : \{0,1\}^* \times \{0,1\}^* \rightarrow \{0,1\}^*$ which models EVM execution of transactions. It takes as input the state of the accounts in the previous block $G_{st_{i-1}}$ and new transactions included in the current block TX_i and returns the current state of the accounts G_{st_i} in the chain. The output of this function can be thought of as the changing of account objects to G_{st_i} from their previous state $G_{st_{i-1}}$ after applying the new incoming transactions TX_i. These transactions are validated (signature, balance and nonce checks) according to Ethereum rules before applying the state transition. G_{st_i} is analogous to UTXO in Bitcoin and is always derived from the blocks but does not exist as a part of the chain.

---

[4] These are logical fields, derived from other fields. For example, `to` is derived from *v,r,s* which are version and ECDSA signature elements respectively, `value` is derived from *gasprice* * *gas* and so on.

[5] There are other fields like `ommers_hash`, `receipts_root`, `extra_data` in the Ethereum block header.

Table 2. Contents of Ethereum block header.

Value	Description
`parent_hash` (pt)	hash[a] of the previous block header
`state_root` (G_{st})	hash of the root node of the state tree, after all transactions are executed
`tx_root` (G_{tx})	hash of the root node of the tree structure populated with all the transactions TX in the block
`difficulty` (d)	the difficulty of the proof-of-work
`timestamp` (t)	the timestamp of the block
`nonce` (ctr)	value used in proof-of-work

[a] Ethereum uses the 256-bit variant of Keccak/SHA3

Chain Links. Two blocks $\langle s, x, ctr \rangle_{i-1}$ and $\langle s, x, ctr \rangle_i$ are connected by two important links: the hash links pt and the state links G_{st}. The hash link connects the headers by hash, which is embedded in block B_i. The state link is the state root G_{st_i} which is obtained from $G_{st_{i-1}}$ after applying TX_i. It is important to understand this, as we will show later how these links are affected when we repair the state.

3 Repairability in Ethereum

A naïve solution is to perform repairs by simply replacing the buggy contract with a patched contract and recomputing the states until the head of the chain. However, this is not feasible because of three reasons: (i) recomputing the states break the state links as well as the transaction root G_{tx} held in the block header, which now breaks the hash links too, (ii) it is not efficient for a large scale system such as Ethereum where each block contains a lot of stateful computations to perform multiple deep chain repairs, and (iii) light clients are not aware of the state information and only check hash links in the headers, which forces the repair information to be present in the header. This modifies the block structure of the underlying blockchain which needs ad-hoc consensus rules or not allowing repairs of existing contents (no REC).

We present Reparo integration in Ethereum in its current form (PoW based consensus). A pictorial description is given in Fig. 2. Here the blockchain protocol of Ethereum is denoted by Γ and the Reparo integrated protocol is denoted by Γ'. Reparo can handle all repair operations except redaction of content that affects the state of the chain. Below we describe Reparo and how it solves the above mentioned problems.

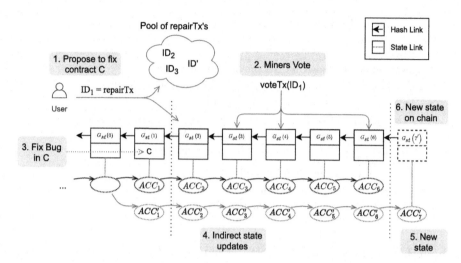

Fig. 2. An overview illustration of how to fix a buggy contract C in block 1 using Reparo in Ethereum. The Reparo layer steps are numbered inside gray boxes and highlighted in red. The voting period lasts for $\ell = 4$ blocks. Proposal ID_1 is approved at block 7.

3.1   Repairing Ethereum Using Reparo

Reparo *Data Structures* We introduce two new data structures in Ethereum: *repair layer* Rdb database and *approved repairs* Adb database[6]. Every block is associated with its own repair layer Rdb database entry that comes into play when the block contents are repaired (directly or indirectly). For repairs that do not statefully impact (removing illicit contents), Rdb of the block contains the old version Tx of the transaction that was repaired to compute G_{tx}. These are data whose changes do not affect the state of accounts, i.e., the new transaction does not break G_{st} of the block. In this case, the hash of the old version of the transaction $H(\text{Tx})$ is stored in the Rdb of the block. In the formal description Fig. 3, we state that the entire set of old transactions and state of accounts is stored in the repair layer. We emphasize that this covers the possibility of many transactions in a block being repaired multiple times.

The *approved repairs* Adb database, stores the repair proposal that was approved by the policy at that time and plays a crucial role during chain validation. The information stored in these data structures do not need any special authentication, as they can be validated using simple hash equality checks: in case of information stored in Rdb, the header of a block stores the corresponding transaction root G_{tx} and state root G_{st}, and in case of Adb, the chain stores the hash of the repair proposal (in the form of votes as explained later).

---

[6] We use the term database because the Ethereum codebase refers to the blockchain as *db* and the state as *statedb*.

The Ethereum protocol consists of a sequence of rounds r. The Ethereum chain is denoted by $\mathcal{C} := (B_1, \ldots, B_r)$.

Initialization. We initialize new databases the repair layer $\mathsf{Rdb_0} \leftarrow$ genesis, and the approved repairs $\mathsf{Adb_0} \leftarrow \emptyset$, set round $r \leftarrow 1$ and an empty list of repair proposals $\mathsf{propPool} \leftarrow \emptyset$.

For each round r, first initialize $\mathsf{Adb}_r \leftarrow \emptyset$, $\mathsf{Rdb}_r \leftarrow \emptyset$ and we describe the following sequence of execution.

Proposal. A node creates a repair proposal $rp_j^* \leftarrow \Gamma'.\mathsf{proposeRepair}(\mathcal{C}, j, TX_j^*)$ for block $B_j, j \in [r-1]$ using transactions TX_j^*. It then broadcasts it to the network.

Update Proposal pool. Collect all repair proposals rp_j^* from the network and add rp_j^* to $\mathsf{propPool}$ iff rp_j^* is valid; otherwise discard rp_j^*.

Repairing the chain. For all repair proposals $rp_j^* := \langle TX_j^* \rangle \in \mathsf{propPool}$, we denote a vote $\mathsf{v}_j \leftarrow \Gamma'.\mathsf{Vt}(\mathcal{C}, rp_j^*)$ and do:
1. If $\Gamma'.\mathsf{chkApproval}(\mathbb{P}, \mathsf{v}_j) = $ approve, then call algorithm $(\mathcal{C}', \mathsf{Rdb}') \leftarrow \Gamma'.\mathsf{repairChain}(\mathcal{C}, \mathsf{Rdb}, rp_j^*)$. Here j-th block in $\mathcal{C}'$ is $\langle \mathsf{header}_j, rp_j^* \rangle$ and subsequent blocks' states are updated accordingly. Then do the following,
   (a) Add TX_j^* to Adb_r and remove rp_j^* from $\mathsf{propPool}$
   (b) set local chain $\mathcal{C} = \mathcal{C}'$ and update $\mathsf{Rdb} = \mathsf{Rdb}'$
2. If $\Gamma'.\mathsf{chkApproval}(\mathbb{P}, \mathsf{v}_j) = $ reject, then remove rp_j^* from $\mathsf{propPool}$
3. If $\Gamma'.\mathsf{chkApproval}(\mathbb{P}, \mathsf{v}_j) = $ voting, then do nothing

Mining a new block. Collect all transactions, denoted by TX from the network for the r-th round and try to build a new block B_r:
1. *(Deliberation process).* For all repair proposals $rp_j^* \in \mathsf{propPool}$ that the node is willing to endorse,
   (a) Parse the proposal $rp_j^* := \langle TX_j^* \rangle$
   (b) Generate $v_j \leftarrow \Gamma'.\mathsf{Vt}(C, s_j^*)$. If $\Gamma'.\mathsf{chkApproval}(\mathbb{P}, \mathsf{v}_j) = $ voting then create a vote transaction voteTx with $\mathsf{voteTx.data} = \mathsf{v}_j$
   (c) Update $TX \leftarrow TX \| \mathsf{voteTx}$
2. *(Determine state transition from the head of the chain).* Repair the chain by applying the repair proposals that are approved: $\forall rp_j^* = TX_j^*$ such that $\Gamma'.\mathsf{chkApproval}(\mathbb{P}, \mathsf{v}_j) = $ approve, where $\mathsf{v}_j \leftarrow \Gamma'.\mathsf{Vt}(\mathcal{C}, rp_j^*)$, set $ACC = \delta(ACC_{r-1}, TX)$.
3. *(Mining).* Extend chain and **Reparo** data structures as follows,
   (a) Perform standard Ethereum mining and set new block $B_r \leftarrow \langle \mathsf{header}, TX \rangle$
   (b) Extend local chain $\mathcal{C} \leftarrow \mathcal{C} \| B_r$, the repair layer $\mathsf{Rdb} \leftarrow \mathsf{Rdb} \| \mathsf{Rdb}_r$ and the approved repairs $\mathsf{Adb} \leftarrow \mathsf{Adb} \| \mathsf{Adb}_r$
   (c) Then broadcast $(\mathcal{C}, \mathsf{Rdb}, \mathsf{Adb})$ to the network

Updating the chain. When a node receives $\mathcal{C}, \mathsf{Rdb},$ and Adb, check if the chain is valid by calling $\Gamma'.\mathsf{validateChain}(\mathcal{C}, \mathsf{Rdb}, \mathsf{Adb}) = 1$. Accept the new chain if the new chain is valid as per Ethereum's fork resolution rule.

Fig. 3. Reparo protocol integration into Ethereum with PoW based consensus and parameterized by policy $\mathbb{P}$ (Ethereum uses Greedy Heaviest Order Sub Tree (GHOST) protocol to rank chains and this is slightly different from the longest chain rule used in Bitcoin)

Proposing Repairs. Any user in Ethereum can request to repair[7] transaction Tx using Γ'.proposeRepair() (refer to the extended version [30]). The user first broadcasts a candidate transaction Tx* to the network. Then, the user sends a repair request transaction `repairTx`. The `to` address field contains a special address REQ_ADDR. REQ_ADDR is a native contract for Reparo. Native contracts are special addresses which are executed outside the EVM by the implementation using normal OS code. The `data` field contains $(H(\text{Tx}), H(\text{Tx}^*))$, where $H(\text{Tx})$ is the hash of the old version (Tx) and $H(\text{Tx}^*)$ is the hash the new version (Tx*). For smart contract bug fixes, Tx was the buggy-contract creation transaction, while Tx* is a similar transaction with the bug fixed. The `repairTx` offers processing fees to the miner to include the transaction into the block and also offer approval fees to the voters of the repair after the policy approval.

Validating Repair Requests. Nodes validate a repair proposal by checking if the proposed new Tx* is a well-formed transaction as per rules of Ethereum (such as correct format, correct signatures, and others) and Tx is in the chain. Proposals are rejected as redundant if they are already in the voting phase.

Repair Policy. A repair proposal is approved by the blockchain users in Reparo with respect to a repair policy $\mathbb{P}$, which is checked using Γ'.chkApproval() (refer to the extended version [30]). Below, we present a candidate repair policy $\mathbb{P}$ for Ethereum:

- The proposal does not propose to modify the address fields or the value field of a transaction.
- The proposal is unambiguously not a double spend attack attempt (needs information from the real world (off-chain information) for confirmation).
- The proposal does not redact or modify votes in the chain.
- The proposal has received more than ρ fraction[8] of votes (>50% of votes) in ℓ consecutive blocks (voting period, that can decided by the system) after the corresponding `repairTx` is included in the chain.

Deliberation by Voting. In the deliberation process, the miners vote for a repair proposal `repairTx` by generating a voting transaction `voteTx` and including that in the block that they propose. This is done using Γ'.Vt(). The `to` field of `voteTx` is a special address VOTE_ADDR of a native contract. The `data` field contains the contents of `data` field of the `repairTx`. Validation consists of checking whether the `repairTx` referred in the `data` field exists and checking that `from` is the author of the block. As per the policy $\mathbb{P}$, when ρ fraction of votes are received in ℓ blocks after `repairTx`, the repair is approved.

Performing Repairs. Upon approval with respect to the policy $\mathbb{P}$, Reparo uses Γ'.repairChain() procedure, where the hash links in the headers are maintained

---

[7] Contracts that have cascading effects such as the uniswap contract [1] cannot be fixed unless an optimization such as state assertion is used.

[8] The probability that a malicious repair proposal is accepted by Reparo is always $< \ell\rho^{\frac{\ell}{2}+1}$, where $\rho < \frac{1}{2}$ is the fraction of byzantine miners. This is negligible for a sufficiently large choice of ℓ.

and the state link at this point is broken. We choose this approach for Ethereum because the light clients in Ethereum only download the headers and after the head of the chain they download the latest state. Full nodes and miners possess maintain the state and know how to build the new state root applying the repair. The old version of the transaction is stored in the repair layer Rdb associated with the block. The candidate transaction is replaced in the new version of the block in the chain. The state of accounts (for this block and the following blocks) is updated according to the repaired transactions.

When updating the state for each block, we ensure that the old blocks containing the old state roots are stored in the corresponding repair layer Rdb. Once the state updates reach the head of the chain, the miner proposes a new block with a state root G_{st} reflecting the repaired state of accounts. The entire set of original transactions and state are stored in the repair layer (allowing the possibility of multiple repairs on the block).

Note that, since a repaired chain always contains the most recent repaired state, performing multiple indirect state updates is efficient as we only apply the transition function over the block's latest contents the state updates.

Block Validation. We give a formal description of block validation algorithm Γ'.validateBlock() (refer to the extended version [30]) which is invoked during the chain validation. The procedure checks if the transactions included in the block are valid as done currently in Ethereum. It then checks if the hash links connect the headers. In case no repair proposal has been approved in this block, the only remaining checks are to see if the state of accounts in the block are correct and if the miner has correct proof of work. If any repair proposals were approved by the policy at this block, the procedure performs these approved repairs on the chain while performing the required state updates for the affected blocks. After all the approved repairs until the block under validation have been applied, the procedure checks if the state of accounts in this block are consistent with the updated states of the previous affected blocks.

Chain Validation for Full Nodes. On receiving a new chain, the chain validation procedure Γ'.validateChain() formally described in the extended version [30] starts validating the blocks from the genesis of the chain. It first switches the block contents with the corresponding transactions and states stored in the repair layer. This results in the chain ($\mathcal{C}_{org}$) with all blocks in its originally mined state. The procedure then validates each block as discussed above using Γ'.validateBlock. This results in performing the repairs (both redactions and other repair operations) as they were performed in sequence. We then obtain a chain in its updated current state and is checked if it is the one that was received.

Chain Validation for Light Clients. Light clients on receiving a chain of headers check proof of work and if all the hash links hold. The client then downloads the latest state G_{st} from the head of the chain from the peers. It then uses the block validation algorithm to maintain the updated state and discards all other blocks, headers and states.

Optimizations. We mention some optimizations that can be applied to improve the repair process.

- *State Assertion*: Instead of recomputing the state, a `repairTx` can propose a state for the affected contract and accounts (in one shot). The protocol can then inject this state if allowed by the policy. This method is inexpensive on-chain as it is without any cascading computation and is useful for users who accidentally locked their funds [15].
- *Defer Deep Repairs*: Since repairing deep blocks also entails recomputing a lot of states, assuming the miners are willing to repair such deep blocks and the contract owner is willing to pay for such costly repairs in gas, we can use a deferred approval based on depth. For a repair at depth d, the state root merges with the main chain after d/c blocks after on-chain approval. The constant c can be chosen empirically based on resources set aside for repairs.

Security Outline. Since the hash function H is modeled as a random oracle (RO), finding a collision on a vote (which is the hash of the ID of the old transaction and the ID of the candidate transaction) is highly improbable. Therefore, when a miner votes for a repair proposal in his newly mined block, no adversary can claim a different repair proposal for the same vote value. Same property of the hash function H also ensures that no adversary can find a different block that hashes to the same hash of an honestly mined block. Therefore an adversary cannot break the integrity of the chain. Together, they imply the *unforgeability* of votes, as if an adversary wishes to vote, he has to mine a block with his vote himself. Assuming majority of the miners are honest in Ethereum, Reparo integration with Ethereum satisfies *editable common prefix* and preserves chain quality and chain growth with respect to repair policy $\mathbb{P}$.

Generalization. Reparo can easily be generalized to perform redactions (removal of illicit content, but does not affect G_{st}). In the extended version [30], we formally describe Reparo for Ethereum but with Proof of Stake (PoS) based consensus. We also give a consensus agnostic version of Reparo that uses interfaces from blockchains and converts it into a repairable blockchain. Reparo can also be generalized into UTXO based blockchains such as Bitcoin and PoS based blockchains such as Cardano.

3.2   Discussion

Notice that Reparo possesses public verifiability of proposals, deliberation and repair operations: Reparo has accountability during and after a deliberation process is over for any repair proposal, referred to as *voting phase accountability* and *victim and new user accountability* [14]. In this section we argue about some crucial features of Reparo that makes it stand apart from the rest of the proposals.

What if Users Decide to Retain Redacted Data? Similar to previous proposals, Reparo does not enforce complete removal of redacted data from a user's local storage. Users can still locally keep redacted data, however, once repaired by Reparo the users are not required by the blockchain protocol to store the redacted information. For instance, in the case of illicit content, this means that the miners who locally keep and broadcast illicit (redacted) data can be prosecuted individually if necessary and the system as a whole is not liable.

Can a Bad Set of Deciders Retroactively Censor Transactions? Similar to censorship of transaction inclusion by miners, it is also possible to "censor" transactions retroactively via the repair operations. However, this can be easily mitigated by requiring multiple decider sets across different deliberation phases to approve a repair operation. Thus, a single bad set of deciders at a given time interval cannot censor. Moreover, contrary to the censorship on transaction inclusion, attempts to censor through repair operations are publicly verifiable as the transaction is already on chain and the network is aware of the deliberation process.

How is Reparo Different from the DAO fix in Ethereum? The hard fork in Ethereum to fix the DAO bug was an ad hoc software patch in the Ethereum client. On the other hand, Reparo is a layer on top of the underlying blockchain system that can handle virtually any kind of repair operations subject to restrictions of the policy.

Using Reparo to Perform Monetary Changes in the State can Cause Inconsistencies? Although Reparo here is described for Ethereum, in Bitcoin, for example, the repair policy could restrict repair operations to be only redaction of auxiliary data that does not affect user's balances. For Ethereum, the policy could allow contract bug fixes that indeed affects monetary balances of user accounts.

4   Experiments in Ethereum

In this section, we report a proof-of-concept implementation of the Reparo protocol on top of Ethereum [32].

We implement two new types of transactions: `repairTx`, and `voteTx`, and measure their performance with respect to a baseline transaction in Ethereum. We also measure the overhead of implementing these special transactions on the Ethereum main network by measuring the time taken to import the *latest* 20 thousand blocks. We measure the time taken to import the blockchain because these introduce overheads for syncing (fully/partially) with the network (see Table 3).

In Ethereum, computation is measured in terms of the gas it needs to run the transaction in the Ethereum Virtual Machine (EVM). Hence, we take a look at the gas costs to repair (by fixing) some popular bugs by computing the transaction dependency graph for the contract creation transaction for these bugs. We estimate the gas cost to re-run all the dependent transactions and provide real-world numbers on the cost of such repairs in Table 4.

Setup and System Configurations. We modify the Go client for Ethereum (`geth`) for our experiments. We use the version `1.9.0-unstable-2388e425` from the official Github repository as the base version. We set the `geth` cache size to

$10,000$ MB and disable the P2P discovery (using the `--nodiscover` flag). The import was done using an export file consisting of blocks from block number $10,903,208$ to $10,929,312$ (latest block as of Sep 25, 2020) created by the export command from a fully synced node.

Our experiments employed the following hardware/software configuration: *CPU*: 24 core, 64-bit, `Intel® Xeon® Silver 4116 CPU` clocked at 2.10 GHz; *RAM*: 128 GB; *OS*: Ubuntu; *Kernel*: 4.15.0-47-generic.

System-Level Optimizations. We employ the following system-level optimizations in our implementation.

1. *Database choice for* Reparo: `geth` implements three types of key-value databases: *Memory Databases* which reside in the system memory, *Cached* and *Uncached Databases* which reside on the disk. The repair layer only stores active requests and the votes for these requests. Hence, a memory database is ideal to implement `repairTx` and `voteTx`.
2. *Native Contracts for* `repairTx`*and* `voteTx`: Native contracts (also referred to as *Pre-compiled* contracts) are client-side implementations of functionalities that are too complex or expensive (in terms of gas) to be implemented inside the EVM. For example, the Ethereum yellow paper [33] uses these native contracts to perform SHA3 and *ecrecover* (a function that returns the address from ECDSA signature values r, s). We use native contracts to support Reparo.
3. *Fast sync and light-client friendliness*: Fast sync is a mode used by the Ethereum clients. In this mode, the clients download the entire chain but only retain the state entries for the recent blocks (pruning). In bandwidth, our implementation only needs to download $|\mathcal{C}| + m$ from full nodes, where m is the number of updates and the final space storage is still $|\mathcal{C}|$ as the nodes can discard the repair layer after syncing.

4.1   Special Transactions: `repairTx`, `voteTx`

Our two special transactions `repairTx`, and `voteTx`, have special `to` addresses `REQ_ADDR = 0x13` and `VOTE_ADDR = 0x14` respectively.

The transactions are always collected in the transaction pool. We modify the transaction pool logic, specifically `validateTx()`. After ensuring well-formedness of inputs, for `repairTx` we check that the `data` field is exactly 64 bytes long and the first 32 bytes correspond to the transaction hash of an existing transaction in the chain. For `voteTx`, we check that the `data` field contains exactly 32 bytes.

The input for `repairTx` consists of hash of the transaction $H(\text{Tx})$ which is to be repaired and the hash of the proposed new transaction $H(\text{Tx}^\star)$. The validation logic ensures that `Tx` exists in the blockchain (repaired blockchain) by adding a new function `isTransactionTrue()`. In the implementation of the native code for this transaction, we add the request to the request memory database, indexed by $ID = H(H(\text{Tx})||H(\text{Tx}^\star))$ and initialize it with 0 votes. This database is created on demand. The footprint of the database is small as we will need to process about $16,384$ repair requests before occupying 1 MB. In contrast, the default

Table 3. Comparison of operations between the modified client and the unmodified client

Operation	Type	Client type	
		Unmodified	Modified
`repairTx`	Time (ms)	–	**76.09**
`voteTx`	Time (ms)	–	**71.89**
Transfer	Time (ms)	71.85	**71.85**
Import	Time (Hours)	2.26	**2.28**
Import	Speed (Mgas/s)	39.70	**39.40**

Table 4. Estimated repair costs (today) using state assertion in Reparo for Ethereum-PoW. K and M stand for Kilo (10^3) and Mega (10^6) multipliers respectively.

Bug	ETH Stuck	Costs of repair	
		Gas	ETH
DAO	3.60 M	3.81 M	0.53
QCX	67.32 K	4.7 M	0.65
Parity	517.34 K	1.95 M	0.27
REXmls	6.67 K	1.69 M	0.23
No Code	6.53 K	438.85 M	0.44

cache memory used by the client ranges from 512 to 4096 MB depending on the client version and is therefore a safe assumption to make.

The input for `voteTx` is the ID described previously. The validation logic ensures that the input is well-formed (of correct length). In the implementation of the native code for this transaction, we check if the request exists in the request memory database. If found, it increments the vote by one. Otherwise, it throws an error and aborts the transaction.

To evaluate the performance overheads of the special transactions on the client (and the network), we compare it with a baseline transfer transaction involving a transfer of ETH between two accounts. The transfer function has the lowest gas requirements ($21,000$). `repairTx` (5.90% overhead) takes 76.09 ms and `voteTx` (0.055% overhead) takes 71.89 ms when compared to a transfer transaction which takes 71.85 ms on an average over 100 iterations. (Refer Table 3.)

4.2 Performing Repairs

In this series of experiments, we analyze the impact of supporting Reparo on client software. For every block, supporting Reparo adds an overhead of checking for approved repairs. If approvals are found, we repair the block body accordingly. In this section, we analyze the read-write overheads to support the repair, the cost of building new states and applying transaction dependencies to repair some real-world bugs (check the extended version [30] for details about these bugs). We use an unedited (clean) chain for our experiments.

Read-Write Costs. In this experiment, we measure the time to update the data of a block. This experiment helps to estimate the I/O overheads of transaction updates in the blockchain. A repair consists of finding a transaction in the blockchain and replacing it with a new transaction. The transaction repair overhead consists of the time taken by a node to read the transaction metadata (block hash, block number and the transaction index in the block) and write the new transaction data. We point the old hash to the new transaction data so that when the hash of the old transaction is accessed, the repaired transaction is furnished by the blockchain. We measure the read and write times for 10,000 random transactions from random blocks in the chain. Random transactions ensure that internal (database, software or operating system) caches do not skew the measurements. The time taken to read the metadata is 649.81 μs and the write operation takes 2.32 ms on average over 100 runs for each of the 10,000 transactions.

Import Costs. In this experiment, we evaluate the time it takes to import the Ethereum chain subset using the modified and unmodified versions of the client to measure the impact of Reparo in everyday performance. The geth client imports blocks in batches. We log the amount of gas (in million gas) in such batches and the time elapsed for the import (and thus compute the speed). We perform 3 iterations on both the modified and unmodified clients. We plot these speeds for the entire import process for the unmodified and modified clients in Fig. 4. As evident from the graph, for most of the parts the modified client is equal to or slightly slower than the unmodified client. This is reasonable in the real world as the slight import delay per block can be accounted for by reducing the gas limit of the block (and thus the computation performed on each block allowing Reparo to utilize the remaining time).

On average, the unmodified client takes 8134.26 seconds to import 26,104 blocks whereas our modified client takes 8213.64 seconds to import the same blocks (Refer to Table 3). This is just 0.98% overhead for a full import of more than 20 thousand blocks. It does not have any significant effect on the block generation, block validation or block propagation as this can be tweaked by reducing the difficulty and/or gas limit of the blocks.

The average amount of gas processed by the unmodified client is 39.70 million gas per second whereas the modified client processes 39.40 million gas per second (Table 3). This 0.76% overhead is due to the hard coding of rules for special transactions whose conditions are checked for every transaction. This overhead does not cause any problems as the average gas limit for an Ethereum block is 10,000,000 (which is under 39 Mgas/s) [5] and both the nodes perform optimally to sync the latest blocks and propagate. Note that this affects the full sync nodes only. Note that the light clients, such as Parity [27] for example, skip verification of states and are thus unaffected.

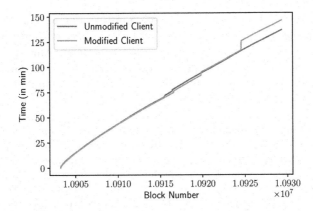

Fig. 4. Batched speed comparison of the modified client and the unmodified client. The modified client has a modified `validateTx` rule, a new function `isTransactionTrue`, and modified structures with flags to detect a dirty (edited chain and blocks).

Repairs. We employ a policy which allows editing any contract call in order to repair the chain. We qualify our previous pessimistic analysis by arguing that most of the repairs have small transaction dependency graphs. This is due to the localization of impact to a few accounts. We bound the number of transactions that need to be re-run to transactions that interact with the contract. This coupled with the fact that we are performing a repair ensures a small transaction dependency graph which significantly reduces the repair costs. Table 4 we highlight the impact of such localizations. We sum the gas in all such transactions to estimate the gas cost of repairs and thus the ETH. Note that we always pay the miners (and hence the network) for the extra computation. We use a gas price of 138 GWei/gas (market price at the time of writing) for our conversions. We refer the interested readers to Appendix A for more details about the bugs and our solutions.

5 Conclusion and Future Work

This work presents Reparo, a secure, systematic way to make any blockchain forget the "forgettable". We present a generic protocol that is adaptable to consensus requirements, and achieves public verifiability and secure chain repairs guaranteeing REC for current mainstream blockchains. We then design and analyze an important application of the protocol in Ethereum to fix contract bugs, and report the implications and feasibility of these repairs for popular contract bugs such as DAO and Parity Multi Sig Wallet. We also provide optimizations that can make the implementation more robust and realizable. We show that, in Ethereum, vulnerabilities, if found, (and existing vulnerabilities) can be immediately isolated to reduce the transaction dependency and repaired efficiently and securely.

In the future, we aim to realize the Reparo protocol on permissioned systems such as Hyperledger. We also intend to study the impact of Reparo on off-chain protocols and whether it can be used to improve them. Among other repair operations, Reparo also offers a means to propose, deliberate and incorporate new features into Bitcoin and Ethereum given the respective communities currently do this in an ad-hoc manner [6,16].

Acknowledgments. We would like to thank Andrew Miller for his valuable comments and constructive feedback. We would also like to thank all the anonymous reviewers for their insightful comments and suggestions to improve the draft.

The first author was supported by the German research foundation (DFG) through the collaborative research center 1223, and by the state of Bavaria at the Nuremberg Campus of Technology (NCT). NCT is a research cooperation between the Friedrich-Alexander-Universität Erlangen-Nürnberg (FAU) and the Technische Hochschule Nürnberg Georg Simon Ohm (THN). This work also has been partially supported by the National Science Foundation under grant CNS-1846316.

A   Prominent Bugs

DAO. This is a re-entrancy bug in the contract that allowed a maliciously crafted call to drain the balance of the contract before it subtracted the balance from the user. We propose to fix this contract by updating all DAO contract creation contracts with the bug fixed code. This is different from the ad-hoc solution employed by Ethereum today. Ethereum hard-coded the address for DAO and executes the contract differently. This ensured that the blockchain should have no transaction dependency because the blockchain already has the state with the contract fixed. This in conjunction with the repair proposal allows an inexpensive repair for DAO even though it has a lot of dependent transactions.

Parity Multisig Wallet Bug. The Parity Mutli Sig Wallet is a library contract that had a bug which had a public constructor that allowed any user to take control of the contract. A user took ownership of the contract and accidentally killed it. We propose to repair this contract by undoing the transaction that killed the contract. The transaction dependency is unaffected as it just resurrects a dead contract. This enables all Parity Multisig Wallet holders to safely recover their funds.

QuadrigaCX (QCX) and REXmls. These contracts have hardcoded wrong addresses in the contract which sent the ICO ETH to an incorrect address (an account that does not exist) thereby permanently locking the coins in those contracts. We propose to repair this bug by proposing a repair transaction with the same code but with the correct address, which can be used to recover and return the lost funds.

No Code Contract. There are 2,986 such contract creation transactions which have money but no code in the creation call. The idea to solve the no code contract problem, is to allow the user to add code to the contract. We give a template of the code in the extended version [30]. The contract allows the user who locked the money in a contract to retrieve the money.

References

1. Adams, H., Zinsmeister, N., Salem, M., Keefer, R., Robinson, D.: Uniswap v3 core (2021)
2. Altabba, M.: Hundreds of millions of dollars locked at ethereum 0x0 address and smart contracts' ..., June 2018. https://medium.com/@maltabba/hundreds-of-millions-of-dollars-locked-at-ethereum-0x0-address-and-smart-contracts-addresses-how-4144dbe3458a. Accessed Mar 2021
3. Ateniese, G., Chiaramonte, M.T., Treat, D., Magri, B., Venturi, D.: Rewritable blockchain, 8 May 2018. US Patent 9,967,096
4. Ateniese, G., Magri, B., Venturi, D., Andrade, E.: Redactable blockchain-or-rewriting history in bitcoin and friends. In: 2017 IEEE European Symposium on Security and Privacy (EuroS&P), pp. 111–126. IEEE (2017)
5. Ethereum average gas limit chart. https://etherscan.io/chart/gaslimit. Accessed 28 July 2019
6. bitcoin/bips: Bitcoin improvement proposals. https://github.com/bitcoin/bips. Accessed 31 July 2019
7. Breidenbach, L., Daian, P., Tramèr, F., Juels, A.: Enter the hydra: towards principled bug bounties and exploit-resistant smart contracts. In: 27th {USENIX} Security Symposium ({USENIX} Security 2018), pp. 1335–1352 (2018)
8. Buterin, V.: ethereum/wiki - proof of stake FAQ. https://github.com/ethereum/wiki/wiki/Proof-of-Stake-FAQ
9. Buterin, V.: State tree pruning. https://blog.ethereum.org/2015/06/26/state-tree-pruning/
10. Buterin, V., Griffith, V.: Casper the friendly finality gadget. arXiv preprint arXiv:1710.09437 (2017)
11. Understanding the DAO attack. https://www.coindesk.com/understanding-dao-hack-journalists
12. Derler, D., Samelin, K., Slamanig, D., Striecks, C.: Fine-grained and controlled rewriting in blockchains: chameleon-hashing gone attribute-based. In: ISOC Network and Distributed System Security Symposium - NDSS 2019. The Internet Society (2019)
13. Deuber, D., Döttling, N., Magri, B., Malavolta, G., Thyagarajan, S.A.K.: Minting mechanisms for blockchain - or - moving from cryptoassets to cryptocurrencies. Cryptology ePrint Archive, Report 2018/1110 (2018). https://eprint.iacr.org/2018/1110
14. Deuber, D., Magri, B., Thyagarajan, S.A.K.: Redactable blockchain in the permissionless setting. In: Proceedings of 2019 IEEE Symposium on Security and Privacy, SP 2019, San Francisco, California, USA, 20–22 May 2019 (2019)
15. Reclaiming of ether in common classes of stuck accounts - issue 156 - ethereum/eips. https://github.com/ethereum/EIPs/issues/156. Accessed 31 July 2019
16. ethereum/eips: The ethereum improvement proposal repository. https://github.com/ethereum/EIPs. Accessed 31 July 2019
17. Major issues resulting in lost or stuck funds. https://github.com/ethereum/wiki/wiki/Major-issues-resulting-in-lost-or-stuck-funds
18. Goodman, L.: Tezos–a self-amending crypto-ledger (2014). https://www.tezos.com/static/papers/whitepaper.pdf
19. Ibáñez, L.D., O'Hara, K., Simperl, E.: On blockchains and the general data protection regulation. In: EU Blockchain Forum and Observatory, pp. 1–13 (2018)

20. Interpol cyber research identifies malware threat to virtual currencies (2015). https://tinyurl.com/y9wfekr6
21. Krawczyk, H., Rabin, T.: Chameleon signatures. In: ISOC Network and Distributed System Security Symposium - NDSS 2000. The Internet Society, February 2000
22. Lumb, R.: Downside of bitcoin: a ledger that can't be corrected (2016). https://tinyurl.com/ydxjlf9e
23. Magri, B., Matt, C., Nielsen, J.B., Tschudi, D.: Afgjort - a semi-synchronous finality layer for blockchains. Cryptology ePrint Archive, Report 2019/504 (2019). https://eprint.iacr.org/2019/504
24. Coinmarketcap. https://coinmarketcap.com
25. Matzutt, R., et al.: A quantitative analysis of the impact of arbitrary blockchain content on bitcoin. In: Meiklejohn, S., Sako, K. (eds.) FC 2018. LNCS, vol. 10957, pp. 420–438. Springer, Heidelberg (2018). https://doi.org/10.1007/978-3-662-58387-6_23
26. Nakamoto, S.: Bitcoin: a peer-to-peer electronic cash system (2008)
27. Getting synced. parity tech documentation. https://wiki.parity.io/Getting-Synced. Accessed 28 July 2019
28. Puddu, I., Dmitrienko, A., Capkun, S.: μchain: how to forget without hard forks. IACR Cryptology ePrint Archive 2017, 106 (2017)
29. Sun, S.: Escaping the dark forest, September 2020. https://samczsun.com/escaping-the-dark-forest/
30. Thyagarajan, S.A.K., Bhat, A., Magri, B., Tschudi, D., Kate, A.: Reparo: publicly verifiable layer to repairblockchains. https://fc21.ifca.ai/papers/119.pdf
31. Tziakouris, G.: Cryptocurrencies–a forensic challenge or opportunity for law enforcement? An interpol perspective. IEEE Secur. Priv. 16(4), 92–94 (2018)
32. Ethereum whitepaper. https://github.com/ethereum/wiki/wiki/White-Paper
33. Wood, G., et al.: Ethereum: a secure decentralised generalised transaction ledger. Ethereum Project Yellow Paper 151, 1–32 (2014)

Short Paper: Debt Representation in UTXO Blockchains

Michael Chiu[1(✉)] and Uroš Kalabić[2]

[1] Department of Computer Science, University of Toronto, Toronto M5S 2E4, Canada
chiu@cs.toronto.edu
[2] Mitsubishi Electric Research Laboratories, Cambridge, MA 02139, USA
kalabic@merl.com

Abstract. We provide a UTXO model of blockchain transactions that is able to represent both credit and debt on the same blockchain. Ordinarily, the UTXO model is solely used to represent credit and the representation of credit and debit together is achieved using the account model because of its support for balances. However, the UTXO model provides superior privacy, safety, and scalability when compared to the account model. In this work, we introduce a UTXO model that has the flexibility of balances with the usual benefits of the UTXO model. This model extends the conventional UTXO model, which represents credits as unmatched outputs, by representing debts as unmatched inputs. We apply our model to solving the problem of transparency in reverse mortgage markets, in which some transparency is necessary for a healthy market but complete transparency leads to adverse outcomes. Here the pseudonymous properties of the UTXO model protect the privacy of loan recipients while still allowing an aggregate view of the loan market. We present a prototype of our implementation in Tendermint and discuss the design and its benefits.

Keywords: Blockchain protocols · Blockchain applications · UTXO · Debt

1 Introduction

There are two main blockchain transaction models: the unspent transaction output (UTXO) model and the account model. UTXOs were introduced in Bitcoin [1] and are predominantly used to represent credits. The UTXO model is stateless; UTXOs represent units of value that must be spent, so any state change within the UTXO model results in old UTXOs being succeeded by new UTXOs. The account model is state-dependent; it implements balances where transactions change the state of the system by keeping a balance [2]. The UTXO model has various advantages over the account model including superior privacy, safety, and scalability, mainly due to the structure of transactions. However, one shortcoming is that it is unable to represent debt.

This work was supported by Mitsubishi Electric Research Laboratories.

N. Borisov and C. Diaz (Eds.): FC 2021, LNCS 12675, pp. 57–64, 2021.
https://doi.org/10.1007/978-3-662-64331-0_3

Debt is an important part of a well-functioning financial system [3] but its opacity within the financial system has been identified as a contributor to the 2008 financial crisis [4]. For this reason, regulatory agencies have recommended increasing transparency in debt markets, such as mortgage markets, in order to prevent build-up of excessive leverage [5]. Nevertheless, it is understood that complete transparency also leads to adverse outcomes like increased price volatility [6].

This work presents a possible solution to the representation of debt on UTXO blockchains. In our design, debt is represented analogously to the way in which credit is represented; where UTXOs represent credit as *unspent transaction outputs*, we represent debt in something akin to *unpaid transaction inputs*, i.e., a debt is a transaction that has not yet been funded. We implement our design in Tendermint [7], a library for state machine replication (SMR), and show how it can be applied to the representation of reverse mortgage transactions on the blockchain. As a practical matter, we note that this work presents a protocol for managing credits and debts in an efficient manner and does not prevent debtholders from abandoning their debt. We expect that this could be done through existing legal frameworks, or through collateralization schemes being pioneered in DeFi technology [8].

The literature has given some consideration to debt representation in the blockchain. One existing approach is the implementation of a debt token and logic to handle debt creation and destruction [9,10]. Another approach uses the blockchain as a shared data layer to record loans [11]. There have been attempts at the representation of debt in a multi-blockchain setting [12], in which debt is represented implicitly by locking tokens on multiple blockchains and not within a single blockchain. Other work has used smart contracts to represent debt [13], but it does not improve the transparency of aggregate debt within the system. Apart from work that represents debt in a blockchain, there is also at least one effort that is moving the home equity loan process onto the blockchain [14], but it does not put mortgage transactions themselves onto the blockchain. To our knowledge, the existing literature has not considered representing debt as unpaid transaction inputs.

The rest of the paper is structured as follows. Section 2 discusses transactions in the UTXO model. Section 3 presents a novel way of representing debt in the UTXO model. Section 4 presents our prototype for representing reverse mortgage transactions on the blockchain. Section 5 is the conclusion.

2 Transactions in the UTXO Model

Transactions are the fundamental data structures in blockchains that represent a state change. In the UTXO model, transactions are generally comprised of transaction inputs, transaction outputs, locktime and other metadata [15].

Transaction outputs are data structures that contain an amount, a locking script and possibly other metadata such as the size of the locking script. Transaction amounts indicate the quantity of value to be transferred. Locking scripts

Fig. 1. Relationship between transactions and UTXOs in the UTXO model

within a transaction output encode the conditions that must be satisfied in order for the amount to be spent.

Transaction inputs contain a transaction hash, an output index, unlocking script, and other metadata. The transaction hash is a hash of the transaction containing the transaction output from where the value is to be drawn; transaction outputs that are not matched to a transaction input therefore are *unspent*. The output index indicates which of the UTXOs in the referenced transaction is to be drawn from. The unlocking script contains the solution to the locking script of the referenced UTXO.

The total amount of UTXOs represent the total amount of available credit in the system. Every node in the blockchain network keeps track of the available UTXOs in memory and this is known as a UTXO pool. When a UTXO is matched with a transaction input, it is no longer considered unspent and is removed from the UTXO pool.

In permissionless UTXO blockchains, the coinbase transaction is used to mint new tokens in the system as rewards for miners. Coinbase transactions have the same fields as regular transactions and are the only transactions in a traditional UTXO model that are allowed to have unmatched transaction inputs. That is, coinbase transactions do not point to an existing UTXO. An overview of how transactions are related to each other in the UTXO model is provided in Fig. 1.

Although the UTXO model is well-suited to the representation of credit, it is unable to represent debt without modification. It is possible to modify a transaction output to hold negative values, but this would require preventing participants with permission to issue debts from sending large, negative amounts to creditors and destroying their equity. It is also possible to represent debt using smart contracts, but such an implementation would be opaque and require additional computation to query the amount of debt issued or owed by a debtor, and it would not allow a straightforward lookup on the blockchain by parsing transactions. Another possible change that could be made to the UTXO model is to simply double the data fields of the transaction so that the duplicate set of fields represent debt tokens. However, not only does this double the size of transactions, it also allows users to send their debts away. We introduce what we believe to be a more elegant solution, detailed in the following.

3   Debt-Enabling UTXO Blockchain

We present a design that enables the representation of debt in a UTXO-based permissioned blockchain. In the design, we represent debts as transactions with unmatched transaction inputs, conforming to the way in which credits are represented using unmatched outputs. To enable this representation, we introduce two new types of transactions: debt transactions and outstanding debt transactions.

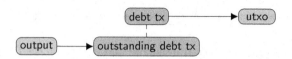

Fig. 2. Debt creation on the blockchain

3.1 Debt Transactions

The first type of transaction is a *debt transaction*. These transactions enable debt to be issued from creditor to debtor. They are similar to coinbase transactions in that they are transactions with unmatched transaction inputs and are only constructed by a subset of network participants. These participants must be given permission to issue debt, and the permissioning model itself can vary. For example, it can be that every trusted participant is able to issue debt, such as in a permissioned network of banks, or that only a subset of trusted participants is able to do so, such as in the case of a single central bank. To this end, special addresses known to the permissioned network protocol, and their corresponding public and private keys, are used to confer the ability to issue debt.

Although similar to coinbase transactions, debt transactions are markedly different in that the transaction input has an actual function. In a debt transaction input, the erstwhile transaction hash field is re-purposed to act as a public key field that records a public key belonging to the creditor; this enables parties involved in the debt issuance to be recorded on the blockchain. The output index is also repurposed and set to, for example, -2 in order to provide a simple flag to check if the transaction is a debt transaction.

The rest is similar to a coinbase transaction in that the debt transaction output is a normal transaction output. Since the transaction output of the debt transaction is a standard UTXO, it is included into the UTXO pool like conventional UTXOs after the debt transaction has been accepted by the network.

The UTXO nature of debt transactions protect the privacy of the debtor since the debt issuance can be split across multiple address, i.e., transaction outputs. The aggregate amount of issued debt remains public and is recorded directly on the blockchain, increasing transparency into the health of the overall system while protecting individual privacy.

3.2 Outstanding Debt Transactions and Debt Pools

Debt transactions are broadcast to the network for inclusion into the blockchain and create UTXOs assigned to the debtor. Debt transactions act as mechanisms to issue debt and are recorded on the blockchain. However, since one needs a mechanism to keep track of outstanding debts and their repayment, we introduce *outstanding debt transactions*, which are created simultaneously with debt transactions, as shown in Fig. 2. Outstanding debt transactions are transactions with unmatched inputs and a transaction output matched with the corresponding debt transaction and the creditor's public key.

After an outstanding debt transaction is created and broadcast to all other nodes, it is inserted into a *debt pool*, which is similar to a UTXO pool, but which holds outstanding debt transactions instead of UTXOs. The debt pool is used to handle debt repayments. An outstanding debt transaction is removed from the debt pool when a debt owner repays the remainder of a debt, i.e., when the outstanding debt transaction's input is matched with a debtor's UTXO containing the funds. Once an outstanding debt transaction has a matched input, it is no different from a normal transaction and is removed from the debt pool and inserted into the transaction pool to be eventually accepted by the network. In the case of partial repayments, we create two new transactions from the original outstanding debt transaction: the first is a normal transaction that records the transfer of value of the repayment amount from the debtor to the creditor; the second is a new outstanding debt transaction with the remaining debt amount, which is similar to the way change transactions are handled in UTXO blockchains. The issuance of two new transactions in the case of repayments ensures that funds allocated to repayment and outstanding debt balances are finalized by the network and not held in debt pools, akin to splitting a UTXO when a transfer of credit is made. Figure 3 illustrates the lifecycle of an outstanding debt transaction.

4   Prototype

We implement a prototype of a UTXO-based blockchain capable of debt representation and apply it to reverse mortgages.[1] Reverse mortgages, also known as home equity loans, allow home owners to use their primary residence as collateral for a loan. The reverse mortgage market is an important source of wealth for many households and borrowing against home equity is a significant percentage of US household leverage [16]. As a significant contributor to the over-leveraging of many households, reverse mortgages are potentially a large source of systemic risk in the financial system and one of the contributing factors to the financial crisis of 2008 [4]. For this reason, there have been many recommendations by regulatory bodies since 2008 that recommend increased transparency in mortgage markets [5]. However, transparency in the current system is difficult because these transactions are private and the relevant data is siloed [17].

A permissioned UTXO blockchain for mortgage transactions offers a solution amenable to all participants since it enables transparency at a system level while preserving individual privacy. Note that an account-based blockchain is unsuitable for this because, unlike UTXO-based transactions, balance-based transactions are unable to provide transaction-level privacy protections for loan recipients. To protect privacy, a loan issuance implemented using a debt transaction can have multiple UTXOs, obfuscating both the possible number of recipients and the total amount issued per recipient. This is in contrast to the account model, where balanced-based transactions reinforce the reuse of balances because they are state-dependent.

---

[1] For code listing, see https://github.com/chiumichael/debtchain.

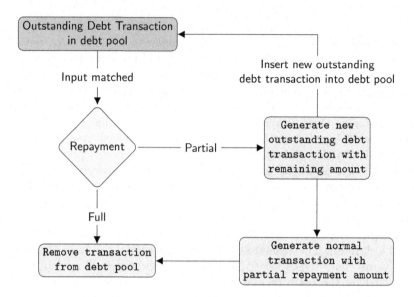

Fig. 3. Lifecycle of an outstanding debt transaction in the debt pool

4.1   System Architecture

Our blockchain prototype is built on top of Tendermint Core[2] [7], an open-source Byzantine fault tolerant (BFT) middleware library for SMR. Tendermint Core provides a consensus mechanism for both permissioned and permissionless BFT blockchains and includes the rotation of the leader after every round, using gossip protocols to communicate with other nodes. Tendermint is comprised of two main components: the Tendermint engine and the ABCI, which is the Tendermint API. The engine handles the consensus and the dissemination of information throughout the network and the ABCI provides an interface for an application to interact with the consensus mechanism. The main benefit of separation of consensus from the application logic is that it allows applications to only consider the local state, not having to explicitly manage synchronization. See Fig. 4 for a schematic.

The first component of our prototype is `pkg/utxi`, a modular library that implements UTXO transactions, along with the debt and outstanding-debt transactions introduced in this work.

The second component implements the blockchain functionality: UTXO and debt pools, and block construction for network acceptance. The memory pools are implemented as in-memory key-value stores using BadgerDB[3] at the application level; they are implemented on top of the ABCI since they rely on the ABCI to receive instructions. Blocks are constructed implicitly; the Merkle root of the hash of the transactions in a block is broadcast to the network for

---

[2] https://github.com/tendermint/tendermint.
[3] https://github.com/dgraph-io/badger.

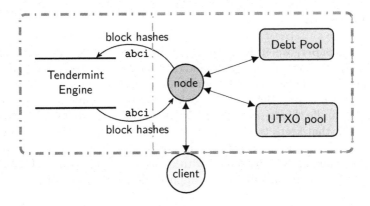

Fig. 4. System level diagram for the prototype, where the blue box contains the back-end components and the red box contains the in-node components (Color figure online)

acceptance. Transactions, within blocks, are stored internally in BadgerDB on top of the ABCI. Tendermint handles the propagation of state changes made by transactions.

The final component is the application node and the client. The application node contains the functionality necessary for a reverse mortgage blockchain such as issuing debt, checking balances, checking the amount of existing debt, among other things, and is implemented on top of the ABCI at the same level of blockchain functionality. The client is a front-end for users to interact with the network and contains user-related functionality such as private key management. There can be many clients connected to a single node, which communicate with the node through HTTP requests.

4.2   Implementation

Home equity loans are implemented as debt transactions. The input of the debt transaction's public key field is interpreted as the issuer and its data field indicates the type of loan.

The backend (Fig. 4; blue box) receives commands from users, through the client (Fig. 4; yellow circle) and the ABCI interface. The two main ABCI interface functions that must be implemented are CheckTx and DeliverTx, which are entry points into the Tendermint engine. Logic for checking the validity of requests is implemented in CheckTx. Logic that changes the state of the application is implemented within or called only from DeliverTx. Since Tendermint handles consensus and the replication of state among nodes, it needs to be able to invoke functions changing state.

When a request to issue debt is sent from a client, a debt transaction is constructed and is broadcast to the network through the DeliverTx function. Simultaneously, the local state of the node is updated and the UTXO pool is updated with the UTXOs belonging to the debtor, while the debt pool is updated with an outstanding debt transaction belonging to the creditor.

5   Conclusion

In this short paper, we introduced a permissioned, UTXO-based blockchain design that is able to represent credit and debt on the same blockchain. The main idea behind the design is that debt can be represented as unmatched transaction inputs in the same way that credits are represented as unmatched transaction outputs. To handle this new construction, we introduced a debt pool, similar to a UTXO pool, that keeps track of debts in the system. A benefit this provides is the ability to keep track of aggregate debt while protecting individual privacy, because one loan can be represented with multiple, pseudonymous UTXOs. We presented a prototype of our design applied to the representation of reverse mortgages.

References

1. Nakamoto, S.: Bitcoin: a peer-to-peer electronic cash system. White Paper (2009)
2. Antonopoulos, A.M., Wood, G.: Mastering Ethereum: Implementing Digital Contracts. O'Reilly, Sebastopol (2018)
3. Holmstrom, B.: Understanding the role of debt in the financial system. BIS Working Paper 479 (2015)
4. Greenlaw, D., et al.: Leveraged losses: lessons from the mortgage market meltdown. In: Proceedings of US Monetary Policy Forum, pp. 8–59 (2008)
5. US Department of the Treasury: Opportunities and challenges in online marketplace lending. White Paper (2016)
6. Pavlov, A., Wachter, S., Zevelev, A.A.: Transparency in the mortgage market. J. Financial Serv. Res. **49**(2–3), 265–280 (2016)
7. Kwon, J.: Tendermint: consensus without mining. White Paper (2014)
8. Werner, S.M., et al.: SoK: Decentralized finance (DeFi). arXiv:2101.08778 (2021)
9. Moy, C., et al.: Systems and methods for distributed ledger-based peer-to-peer lending, US Patent Application 16/040,696, appl. 24 January 2019
10. Wu, C.S., Yu, C.W.: Electronic transaction system and method using a blockchain to store transaction records, US Patent Application 16/492,706, appl. 13 February 2020
11. Dowding, P.F.: Blockchain solutions for financial services and other transactions-based industries, US Patent Application 15/551,065, appl. 6 September 2018
12. Black, M., Liu, T.W., Cai, T.: Atomic loans: cryptocurrency debt instruments. arXiv:1901.05117 (2019)
13. Xie, Y., Holmes, J., Dagher, G.G.: ZeroLender: trustless peer-to-peer Bitcoin lending platform. In: Proceedings of ACM Conference on Data and Application Security and Privacy, pp. 247–258 (2020)
14. Provenance Blockchain: Provenance: Creating the future of finance. White Paper (2019)
15. Antonopoulos, A.M.: Mastering Bitcoin: Unlocking Digital Cryptocurrencies, 2nd edn. O'Reilly, Sebastopol (2017)
16. Mian, A., Sufi, A.: House prices, home equity-based borrowing, and the US household leverage crisis. Am. Econ. Rev. **101**(5), 2132–2156 (2011)
17. Alter, A., Dernaoui, Z.: Non-primary home buyers, shadow banking, and the US housing market. IMF Working Paper 20/174 (2020)

Instant Block Confirmation in the Sleepy Model

Vipul Goyal[1,2], Hanjun Li[1], and Justin Raizes[1(✉)]

[1] Carnegie Mellon University, Pittsburgh, PA, USA
vipul@cmu.edu, jraizes@andrew.cmu.edu
[2] NTT Research, Palo Alto, USA

Abstract. Blockchain protocols suffer from an interesting conundrum: owning stake in the Blockchain doesn't necessarily mean that the party is willing to participate in day to day operations. This leads to large quantities of stake being owned by parties who do not actually participate in the growth of the blockchain, reducing its security. Pass and Shi [23] captured this concern in the *sleepy model*, and subsequent work by Pass et al. [5] extended their results into a full Proof of Stake blockchain protocol which can continue to securely progress even when the majority of parties may be offline. However, their protocol requires 10 or more blocks to be added after a transaction first appears in the ledger for it to be confirmed. On the other hand, existing Byzantine Agreement based blockchain protocols such as Algorand [6,7,14] confirm transactions as soon as they appear in the ledger, but are unable to progress when users are not online when mandated.

The main question we address is:

Do there exist blockchain protocols which can continue to securely progress even when the majority of parties (resp. stake) may be offline, and confirm transactions as soon as they appear in the ledger?

Our main result shows the answer to this question to be "yes". We present a Proof of Stake blockchain protocol which continues to securely progress so long as more than half of the online stake is controlled by honest parties, and instantly confirms transactions upon appearance in the ledger.

1 Introduction

Blockchain protocols provide significant economic and cryptographic implications, by means of the creation and maintenance of a globally agreed-upon log in an environment with low trust. The two most popular variants of blockchain protocols are Proof of Work (PoW) and Proof of Stake (PoS). Proof of Work unfortunately carries expensive hardware requirements and wastes a large amount of energy. Proof of Stake protocols bypass the wastefulness of Proof of Work by

The authors were supported in part by the NSF award 1916939, a gift from Ripple, a DoE NETL award, a JP Morgan Faculty Fellowship, a PNC center for financial services innovation award, and a Cylab seed funding award.

© International Financial Cryptography Association 2021
N. Borisov and C. Diaz (Eds.): FC 2021, LNCS 12675, pp. 65–83, 2021.
https://doi.org/10.1007/978-3-662-64331-0_4

using the amount of stake a user owns in the system as a means for determining whether the user can contribute to its progression.

However, this approach carries the downside of requiring users who own stake in the system to be active in order for the system to securely progress. Since it is more desirable to own stake in the system than it is to actively participate in it (for instance, shareholders rarely want a say in the day-to-day operations of a company), much of the stake present in the system may be owned by inactive users. Current Proof of Stake protocols such as Algorand [6,7,14] are typically unable to effectively deal with this problem, requiring over half of the stake present in the system to be owned by users which are both *active* and honest.

Pass and Shi [23] were the first to address this problem, presenting a protocol which could securely progress even when the majority of stake in the whole system was owned by inactive users, so long as the majority of stake owned by active users was owned by honest users (i.e. the "honest active stake" was over half of the "active" stake). Their protocol was based on the follow-the-longest-chain ideas of Nakamoto [21], which, although revolutionary, bring with them the distinct downside of requiring a block to be "buried" beneath several others before it is confirmed.

On the other hand, Byzantine Agreement-based blockchain protocols allow blocks to be confirmed as soon as they are added to the chain. Unfortunately, it is nontrivial to securely allow progression while the majority of stake may be owned by inactive users and simultaneously scale to millions of users with this style of protocol. Algorand [6,7,14] addresses the latter issue by securely selecting a small committee to run a Byzantine Agreement protocol using a Verifiable Random Function (VRF) [19]. As we will see later, it is difficult to directly extend this committee approach to the heavily inactive setting, which will pose our main challenge.

We present a new blockchain system, using Algorand as a starting point, which allows transactions to be securely added to the ledger *regardless of the amount of stake owned by currently active users*. In comparison, Algorand in its base state cannot progress if even 40% of stake is owned by inactive users. Furthermore, basing the mechanism on Byzantine Agreement *prevents forks*, eliminating the major weakness of Sleepy Consensus [23] and its extension Snow White [5]. While Sleepy Consensus and Snow White require 10 or more blocks to be added after a transaction first appears in the ledger for it to be confirmed, our approach allows transactions to be confirmed *immediately upon appearing in the ledger*.

2   Technical Roadmap

2.1   Starting Point: Algorand

At a high level, in Algorand, a block is added to the chain by randomly selecting a committee, which then runs a Byzantine Agreement protocol to decide on the next block in a consistent manner. Since the probability of being in the committee is proportional to the number of coins a user possesses (users may appear multiple times in the committee if they own multiple coins), is unlikely for a majority corrupt committee to be selected.

Concretely, each coin is associated with a Verifiable Random Function (VRF) [19] for each round, and if its VRF is above some threshold, the owner is granted the right to participate one additional time in the current committee. This threshold is based on the number of coins (amount of stake) in the system, and is set to ensure an average committee size. The larger the actual committee size, the less likely it is to be majority-corrupt, which would allow the adversary to break security. Therefore, Algorand does not allow a committee which is too small to add blocks to the chain.

Unfortunately, in the sleepy model, parties do not know how much stake is online (owned by online users) at any time, so it is not clear how to set the threshold so as to frequently choose a committee large enough for secure progress. Furthermore, since the adversary may control just under half of all online stake and can selectively deliver corrupt messages to subsets of honest parties, it is difficult to even estimate the amount of online stake by using messages from other parties. Therefore, we will need a different approach for selecting a committee.

2.2 Selecting a Committee

To reliably choose a committee which is large enough to be majority honest with high probability, we will build on the idea of using the n parties with the highest VRFs seen as the committee. Though this approach ensures committee sizes are always large enough to make them majority honest with high probability, is obvious that *not all parties are guaranteed to see the same committee*.

In Algorand, players do not necessarily see the full committee, but all honest parties will accept messages from any member of the committee, even if they are received later. In contrast, using our committee selection procedure, the fact that one party accepts a party i as a committee member does *not* imply that another party who receives i's message accepts i as a committee member. For instance, if the adversary controlled 40% of the online stake, we would expect the true list of the top n VRFs to be about 40% corrupt. If the first party receives no corrupt VRFs, its committee will be completely honest. However, a second party receiving all of the corrupt VRFs will replace the lower 40% of the top n honest VRFs with corrupted VRFs. Furthermore, the second party cannot simply extend its committee to include the first party's committee, since it has no way of determining that the first party is not corrupt, and corrupt parties may pretend to see arbitrary committees.

As it is very difficult to entirely patch this flaw and guarantee that all parties see the same committee, we will instead focus our efforts on ensuring that the committees which are seen by various honest parties are "close enough".

2.3 Consensus with Different Committees

Standard Byzantine Agreement protocols rely on all parties knowing the same committee (even if they cannot directly communicate), and break down when this is not the case.

Somewhat surprisingly, we show that the general design of Algorand's binary Byzantine Agreement protocol does work with our committee selection, despite being designed for parties all using the same committee. However, this is not immediately obvious, and there is an additional nuance to iron out: to ensure that parties continue to do the same steps at the same times, parties should not halt at different steps in the Byzantine Agreement protocol. With Algorand's committee selection, when a party halts during an execution of the Byzantine Agreement protocol it is easy to produce a certificate which will convince the other parties to halt. This certificate simply consists of all of the committee messages received during the halting round, and since in Algorand, all parties will always accept the same committee members, parties receiving this certificate will also see a valid halt. However, as discussed previously, with our committee selection, parties *do not necessarily agree* on the committee, and so may reject some of the messages which caused the halting party to halt. To remedy this problem, we will use a binary Byzantine Agreement algorithm from [20] (based on the same design as Algorand's BA), which also has the advantage of reducing our requirements to only $> \frac{1}{2}$ honest online stake (from Algorand's $> \frac{2}{3}$). However, it is also not immediately obvious that the algorithm from [20] works with our committee selection, and we will need to show this formally.

Byzantine Agreement is not the only building block of Algorand which requires consistent views of the committee. Algorand uses a Graded Consensus protocol, which requires consistent views of the committee, to transform binary Byzantine Agreement into multivalued Byzantine Agreement protocol, allowing for *blocks* to be consistently decided on. Informally, Graded Consensus [6,7] allows players to output a value and a grade, indicating how confident they are that all other players output the same value. In the multivalue Byzantine Agreement construction, binary Byzantine Agreement is used to decide on a default value (the empty block), or a variable value, and the non-default value should only be output if some honest party *knows* that all other honest parties are using the same value. Since we ultimately want to decide the next block to add, not the next bit to add, we will also show that the Graded consensus algorithm of [20] with only minor modifications surprisingly still works with our notion of "close enough" committees, despite being designed for the scenario where there is a single committee which all parties accept messages from.

2.4   Summary of Challenges and Theorem Statement

In summary, the challenges we must overcome are:

- Ensuring the committees seen by all honest players are "close enough". The concrete properties we achieve are described in Lemma 1.
- Showing that the binary Byzantine Agreement algorithm from [20] works when parties use different committees which are "close enough".
- Showing that the Graded Consensus protocol from [20] works with minor modifications when parties use different committees which are "close enough".

Theorem 1. *(Informal) If less than half the online stake is adversarially owned, there exists a blockchain protocol in the sleepy model which, with overwhelming probability, does not fork and enters transactions into the ledger at a constant rate on average.*

3   Related Work

Sleepy Consensus. Pass and Shi [23] initiated the study of consensus in the sleepy model, where parties may be either awake or asleep at any given point in time. Upon waking, a previously sleeping user receives both all messages actually sent during the time it was asleep, and some set of adversarially generated messages, intermingled. They showed that it is possible to achieve consensus in this setting if and only if the number of awake honest parties are strictly greater than the number of adversarial parties (which are always awake). However, their protocol requires many blocks to be added before a transaction can be confirmed with high confidence. Snow White [5], a blockchain built using the sleepy consensus protocol, requires 10 additional blocks to be added for 99% confidence when the adversary controls only 16.5% of the online stake. If the adversary controls 30%, the number of blocks required jump to 33, and the authors only note that Snow White is theoretically capable of dealing with 49% corruption, without providing a concrete number of blocks to wait. We aim to achieve immediate confirmation as soon as a transaction appears in the chain, without waiting for additional blocks to be added.

Blockchain Protocols. Both Snow White [5] and Ouroboros Genesis [3] can securely progress in the sleepy model, but requires transaction to be buried below many blocks before being confirmed. Algorand [7] enables immediate confirmation upon a transaction appearing in the chain, but is unable to deal with large quantities of stake being offline. Algorand's method of dealing with offline parties is to allow parties to determine if they will be part of any committees for the next, say, week's worth of blocks. If the user will not be part of a committee for the next week, they can go inactive with good conscience. We wish to treat the more general case where parties *cannot* commit to being active at particular points in time. This may be due to vacations, network interruptions, or simply the user not wanting to participate in the chain's progression. Nevertheless, Algorand forms a strong starting point for our protocol.

Other blockchain protocols include Ouroboros [17], Ouroboros Praos [8], Ouroboros Genesis [3], and the well-known Bitcoin protocol [21]. These all fall into one or more of the categories discussed previously (PoW, long confirmation times, majority online). Thunderella [24] is able to give instant confirmation during the optimistic case of the committee being over $\frac{3}{4}$ honest, but slows down significantly when this is not the case.

Accelerating Meta-solutions.[1] Prism [4] and Parallel Chains [13] give meta-solutions which can be applied to existing solutions to significantly improve

---

[1] We were made aware of these works by helpful reviewers.

transaction throughput and/or confirmation times. In particular, the results of Parallel Chains can be applied to sleepy PoS blockchains such as Snow White and Ouroboros variants, enabling blockchains which progress quickly in the sleepy model. This matches our target application. However, our work additionally contributes to the understanding of how BFT protocols can be adapted to the sleepy setting.

Prism, on the other hand, is specifically for PoW blockchains, and comes with the associated energy waste.

Byzantine Agreement with Unknown Participants. Alchieri et al. [1,2] characterize the possibility of solving Byzantine Agreement when participants do not know all other participants. Their main theorem identifies necessary and sufficient properties for the knowledge graph (defined by the set of parties and which other parties each knows) under which there exists a Byzantine Agreement algorithm robust against an adversary which can corrupt up to t parties.

Though Alchieri et al. provide protocols solving this problem, their results are unfortunately insufficient for our setting. We will additionally require security against an adversary which controls many more corrupt parties than the size of any honest view - the whole set of corrupt players, not just the small fraction of those selected to be committee members. This is in contrast to the adversary considered by Alchieri et al., may only corrupt up to t parties *total*, where all honest views are at least size $2t + 1$.

3.1 Comparison of Confirmation Times and Communication Complexity

Confirmation Times. The time for a transaction to be confirmed in the blockchain depends on both the time to first enter the ledger and the time for it to stabilize in the chain. Our solution entirely eliminates the latter, which can be very large in longest-chain style protocols such as Snow White or Ouroboros. Parallel Chains is able to eliminate that weakness in those protocols, at the cost of increased computation in proportion to the speedup, since parties have to track/participate in multiple blockchains.

Since Algorand is the most similar to our protocol and its performance is well understood by the community, it will form our main comparison point. In both our protocol and Algorand, transactions must be present at block proposal to be included, so transaction confirmation time is at most twice the time for a block to be added. The main contribution to Algorand's block addition time is the number of Byzantine Agreement rounds, the expectation of which is given by the expected number of rounds until an honest leader is elected. In this, our protocol matches Algorand, since we borrow Algorand's leader election. However, due to the complexities of adapting to the sleepy model, the constant time for each Byzantine Agreement round is significantly higher for our protocol. In particular, it takes 4 messages to receive each committee member's message, as opposed to just 1 in Algorand. This leads to our protocol's block addition time being roughly $4x$ Algorand's. Algorand's best case scenario is significantly faster than our protocol's, since it is able to terminate the Byzantine Agreement almost immediately when the next block is proposed by an honest party.

Communication Complexity. One of the major strengths of current PoS blockchain solutions is the subquadratic communication complexity. For a committee size of n and a total number of online users N, current solutions usually achieve a communication complexity of $O(nN)$, or $O(n)$ in the broadcast channel model. Our protocol unfortunately requires a higher communication complexity of $O(N^2)$, or $O(N)$ in the broadcast channel model.

However, future work may be able to mitigate this downside by integrating our protocol as a fallback option to base Algorand. When participation is high, Algorand provides low communication complexity, and during periods of highly sporadic participation, our protocol can be used to provide progress when Algorand would otherwise stall. Using our protocol only when participation is low will also help mitigate the communication complexity slightly, since a lower number of online users incurs a lower communication cost. More work will be required to integrate the two protocols without introducing security issues.

Additionally, the approach of following the highest n VRFs means that after receiving only a few messages, many others become entirely obsolete. Future work may be able to exploit this at the gossip network level by heuristically forwarding only the top n messages seen.

4 Definitions

4.1 Blockchain Execution Model

To allow us to capture the ability of users to be inactive, we adopt the sleepy execution model of Pass and Shi [23], as extended by Bentov et al. [5], with one major difference: we consider a more powerful adversary who can *instantly* corrupt any honest party. In the sleepy model, generally, parties may be either awake or asleep (corrupt parties are assumed to always be awake). The two states differ in that parties may only receive messages when they are awake.

(Weakly) Synchronized Clocks. We assume all player clocks differ by at most a constant at all times. As noted by Pass and Shi [23], the clock offset can be generically transformed into a network delay. Therefore, without loss of generality, we will consider players to have synchronized clocks.

Network Delivery. The adversary is responsible for delivering messages between players. We assume that all messages sent by honest players are received by all awake honest players within Δ time steps, but that the adversary may otherwise delay or reorder messages arbitrarily. It must be emphasized that the adversary can *exactly* control the precise time that an honest player receives a message.

Sleeping players do not receive messages until they wake, whereupon they receive all messages they would have received had they not slept. Note that this may include a polynomial number of adversarially inserted messages, and the ordering of all messages received upon waking may be adversarially chosen.

Corruption Model. Corrupt parties may deviate arbitrarily from protocol (i.e. exhibit Byzantine faults), and are controlled by a probabilistic polynomial time adversary which can see the internal state of corrupt players. At any time, the adversary may instantly corrupt an honest party or cause them to sleep until a future time. However, the adversary is not capable of seeing a message, corrupting the sending party, then erasing the message from the network.

At any time, the adversary may spawn new corrupt users (distinct from parties, which represent a unit of stake). This does *not* increase the amount of adversarially owned stake in the system.

Secure Bootstrapping Assumption. As noted by Bentov, Pass, and Shi [5,23], in this model it is impossible to achieve a secure blockchain protocol using only common knowledge of the initial committee. Therefore we assume a trusted bootstrapping procedure, as Sleepy Consensus [23] and Snow White [5] do. Future work may be able to sidestep the impossibility result using a similar modification to the execution model as Ouroboros Genesis [3].

4.2 Tools

Verifiable Random Functions. A Verifiable Random Function (VRF) [19] takes in a secret key sk_i and a seed s, and returns a random number in the range along with a proof. Anyone who knows the public key pk_i associated with sk_i can verify that $VRF(sk_i, s)$ was computed correctly, but cannot compute $VRF(sk_i, s')$ themselves without knowing sk_i. Due to the complexity of instantiating VRFs when players may choose their own seeds, we model them as random oracles, and direct readers to [7] for a more in-depth treatment of the subject.

Byzantine Agreement. The standard definition of Byzantine Agreement [25] is given below. We say a party is honest if they behave according to the protocol specification throughout its entire execution.

Definition 1. *A protocol $\mathcal{P}$ achieves* **Byzantine Agreement** *with soundness s if, in an execution of $\mathcal{P}$, every honest player j halts with probability 1 and the following two properties both hold with probability $\geq s$:*

1. Agreement: *All honest parties output the same value.*
2. Consistency: *If all honest players input the same value v, then all honest players output v.*

If parties input values in $\{0, 1\}$, we say it achieves binary Byzantine Agreement.

Player Replaceability. The idea of player replaceability was introduced by Chen and Micali [6] as a means of preventing targeted attacks on committee members from disrupting Algorand's binary Byzantine Agreement protocol. Consider a protocol executing over a very large set of players where a small subset of players (the committee) is chosen to carry out the r'th round of a Byzantine Agreement protocol. Informally, a Byzantine Agreement protocol is player replaceable if the protocol still achieves agreement and consistency, despite the following conditions: after each round the old committee may be immediately corrupted and a new committee is selected to carry out round $r + 1$.

Graded Broadcast. Graded broadcast was introduced in [12], and informally allows parties to receive a message from a dealer and express how confident they are that all other parties received the same message.

Definition 2. *A protocol achieves* **Graded Broadcast** *if, in an execution where the dealer D holds value v_D, every player i outputs (g_i, v_i) where $g_i \in \{0, 1, 2\}$ such that:*

1. *If D is honest, then every honest player outputs $(2, v_D)$.*
2. *For any honest parties i and j, $|g_i - g_j| \le 1$.*
3. *For any honest parties i and j, if $g_i > 0$ and $g_j > 0$, then $v_i = v_j$.*

We say a protocol achieves $\{0, 1\}$-graded broadcast [20] if g_i takes values in $\{0, 1\}$, property 3 holds (2 holds trivially), and if players output $(1, v_D)$ when D is honest. For simplicity, in a $\{0, 1\}$-graded broadcast, we say a party *accepts* a value if it has grade 1, and *rejects* a value if it has grade 0.

Graded Consensus. For the reduction of multivalued Byzantine Agreement to binary Byzantine Agreement, we will additionally need the notion of Graded Consensus [6,7], which is a relaxation of consensus, and extends the concept of graded broadcast [12].

Definition 3. *A protocol $\mathcal{P}$ achieves* **Graded Consensus** *if, in an execution of $\mathcal{P}$ where every player i inputs v_i', every player i outputs a grade g_i and a value v_i such that:*

1. *For any honest players i and j, $|g_i - g_j| \le 1$*
2. *For any honest players i and j, if $g_i > 0$ and $g_j > 0$, then $g_i = g_j$*
3. *If there exists a value v such that $v_i' = v$ for all honest players i, then $v_i = v$ and $g_i = 2$ for all honest players i.*

4.3 Other Notation

Additionally, we will use the following pieces of notation which have not been covered so far:

- H represents the set of all honest parties.
- V_i represents participant i's current view of the committee
- N denotes the total amount of online stake at any time in a blockchain.

Proof of Stake Abstraction. In a proof of stake blockchain, users are granted voting power proportional to how much currency they own in the blockchain. Hence, we consider each unit of currency to be a party. Users owning multiple units of currency act as multiple parties.

5   The Blockchain Protocol

We will make use of Algorand's leader election (Algorithm 1) in several of our protocols. The following claim is modified from [6,7] to reflect our treatment of VRFs as random oracles and its usage in the sleepy model.

Proposition 1 [6,7,14]. *At the end of Algorithm 1, if the adversary owns less than $\frac{1}{2}$ the online stake, then with probability $> \frac{1}{2}$, all honest parties output the same message m, which was input by an honest party.*

Proof. If an online honest party has the highest VRF for round r and inputs m, all honest parties output m. Since we model VRFs as random oracles and the adversary owns less than $\frac{1}{2}$ of the online stake, this occurs with probability $> \frac{1}{2}$.

5.1   Committee Selection

The committee view formation algorithm needs to fulfill two different goals. First, views must be majority honest, motivating a uniformly random selection process with proportion to the amount of money (or stake) each user owns. As in Algorand, users may be selected multiple times for the same committee view, so long as they own enough stake. Second, the resulting committee views must be similar enough that our binary Byzantine Agreement protocol will work. Informally, for Byzantine Agreement to work, we need to ensure than any two V_i, V_j overlap on more than half their respective views. The concrete properties we achieve are actually stronger than this, and are described in Lemma 1.

Strawman: Committee Discovery. Starting with the base idea of forming a temporary committee consisting of the n highest VRFs seen, a natural first approach is to attempt to discover the temporary committee members which other honest players have selected and take the most commonly selected parties as your final committee, similar to the participant discovery idea from [1,2]. Intuitively, since each honest temporary view is likely to be majority honest, parties selected by many parties in your temporary view are likely to both be honest and appear in many other honest views. Similarly, parties which are selected by only a few parties in your temporary view are liable to either appear in very few honest views globally, or to have been nominated by dishonest parties. Concretely:

1. All parties send their VRF for the round. Each party i takes the owners of the highest n VRFs received to be its temporary committee V_i^*.

Algorithm 1: Leader Election [6,7,14]

Input: message m_i'
1) Propagate $VRF(i,r), sig_i(m_i')$
2) Set $m_i \leftarrow m_j'$ such that $sig_j(m_j')$ was received and $VRF(j,r)$ was the highest VRF seen
Output: m_i

Algorithm 2: Committee Selection

Input: m_i, committee size n, round r
1) Propagate $VRF(i,r), sig_i(m_i,r)$
2) Set $V_i^* = \{j : VRF(j,r)$ was one of the highest n valid VRFs received during step 1}.
   Propagate $VRF(j,r), sig_j(m_j,r)$ for each $j \in V_i^*$
3) Let $V_{U,i} = \{j : VRF(j,r)$ was one of the highest n valid VRFs received during step 2.}
   Set $V_i = V_i^* \cap V_{U,i}$.
   Set messages $= \{(j, m_j, sig_j(m_j)) : j \in V_i$ and $sig_j(m_j,r)$ was received}
Output: V_i, messages

---

2. All parties propagate their temporary committees. Each party i takes its final committee to be $V_i = \{j : j \in V_k^*$ for more than $\frac{n}{2}$ parties $k \in V_i^*\}$.

At the surface level, this seems quite promising - since temporary committees were selected randomly, each temporary committee is highly likely to be over half honest. Any party seen by the honest portion of your temporary committee will end up in your final committee, and the adversary can't add parties your final view which were not seen by at least one honest party, since that would require $> \frac{n}{2}$ corrupt parties to appear in your temporary committee.

Preventing Majority-Corrupt Committees. Unfortunately, this strategy is not quite as successful at keeping corrupt parties out of your final committee as it might seem. The core issue is that while no single honest party sees many corrupted parties in its temporary committee, different honest parties may see different corrupted parties, and the adversary may use corrupted votes to reach the threshold for acceptance. See the full version for a concrete example of the issue.

The key insight to ensuring honest parties end up with committees which are very similar, but don't include too many corrupted parties, is to *only remove* parties from your temporary committee, rather than allowing them to be added (in the example, adding parties resulted in a majority corrupt committee!).

Generally, we will assume that the committee size n is much smaller than the amount of online stake N at any time.

Lemma 1. *At the end of protocol 2, if the adversary controls $\leq \frac{1}{2} - \epsilon$ fraction of the online stake, then with probability $\approx 1 - \left(1 - 4\epsilon^2\right)^{n/2}$ the following holds:*

1. $\left|\bigcup_{i \in H} V_i\right| \leq n$
2. *$\exists$ set of honest parties H_C such that $|H_C| \geq \frac{n}{2}$ and $H_C \subseteq V_i \; \forall i \in H$.*

Proof (Sketch). Property 1 relies on the fact that every honest player sees every honest temporary committee V_i^*. This means that every honest player will remove at least every VRF in $\bigcup_{i \in H} V_i^*$ beyond the first n. However, they never add additional parties to their view.

For the second property, consider the list of all VRFs of online parties for the round, regardless of what messages they send. Define H_C to be the set of honest parties whose VRF is among the highest n in this list. These will appear in all honest temporary views, and cannot be removed, since there are simply not enough higher VRFs among the online parties.

The size of this set then follows by upper bounding the number of corrupt parties among the highest n VRFs in the complete list. Since there are many more than n online parties, we can approximate this with $Bin(n, \frac{1}{2} - \epsilon)$. A bound by Hoeffding [15] upper bounds the probability that this number is $\geq \frac{n}{2}$.

It is worth noting that the honest core H_C is unknown, though it is guaranteed to exist. We do not know how to find it, but as we will show, it is not necessary to know H_C in order to use it; it is sufficient that it simply exists.

See the full version for a discussion of the committee size requirements using our committee election process.

5.2   Binary Byzantine Agreement

In this section, we discuss the importance of completing the Byzantine agreement protocol in the same step, as well as why that is difficult to achieve adaptively in the sleepy model. Then, we show that both the binary Byzantine Agreement protocol of Micali and Vaikuntanathan [20] and the $\{0, 1\}$ Graded Broadcast protocol used in it still work with our committee selection procedure, despite being designed for the scenario where all honest parties agree on the committee.

Observe that if players were to complete the Byzantine agreement protocol in different steps, then they would begin to do different steps of the overlying blockchain protocol, with some parties operating "in the future". Though we can easily prevent messages sent for different steps of the protocol interfering with each other, it is not so simple for a party lagging behind to "catch up", nor is it easy to convince a party speeding ahead to let the others catch up. Furthermore, splitting the parties like this opens opportunities for the adversary, who may be able to achieve majority online stake in the "future", where only some honest parties are currently operating, despite having minority online stake overall.

Algorand avoids this issue by relying on the fact that if one party accepts a message from a committee member, all other players will also accept that message (as being from a committee member) if they receive it. Thus, a player who sees messages causing them to halt early can ensure that all other players halt early as well by simply propagating those messages.

This strategy does not work under our committee selection, since it is *not* the case that if i accepts k as a committee member, j will too after learning about k. For instance, if k were corrupt, then during a Committee Selection execution (Algorithm 2) it is easy for k to appear in V_i^* but not V_j^* by simply not sending a message to j by the deadline, resulting in k never appearing in V_j. Furthermore, it is extremely important to not expand V_j based on other party's views, since corrupt parties may claim an arbitrarily corrupt view. Thus, we will use the strategy presented in [20], which ensures all parties exit the Byzantine Agreement execution at the same time

To achieve resilience against slightly less than half of any committee view being corrupted, we will need a protocol similar to Graded Broadcast. The only difference in our requirements is in property 1: instead of each $i \in H$ being required to output $(1, m_D)$ when D is honest, i is only required to do so when $D \in H_C$. Algorithm 3 describes a parallel version of this, modified from [20].

Proposition 2. *If at all times, $|V_i| \leq n$ for honest i and there exists a set of honest players H_C of size $> \frac{n}{2}$ common to all honest views, then Algorithm 3 achieves the following properties:*

1. *If $D \in H_{C,1}$ and sends m_D, then i accepts m_D from D.*
2. *If honest parties i, j accept m_D, m'_D, respectively, from D, then $m_D = m'_D$.*

Proof (Sketch). If $D \in H_{C,1}$, then all members of $H_{C,2}$ receive and forward $sig_D(m_D)$. Each honest player therefore receives this from $> \frac{n}{2}$ sources, and do not ever receive $sig_D(m'_D)$ for $m_D \neq m'_D$.

If $i \in H$ accepts a message, then one of the sources they received it from in step 2 was a member of $H_{C,2}$, so all other parties also receive the message i accepts. This means that no $j \in H$ will accept a different message.

Proposition 3. *If $|V_i \bigcup V_j| \leq n$ for all honest parties i, j during an execution of Algorithm 4, then an honest party cannot follow substep (a) in the same step an honest party follows substep (b).*

Proof (Sketch). This would require i and j to see more unique votes combined than exist in the union of their views.

Proposition 4. *If V_i contains at least $\frac{n}{2} + 1$ honest parties and no more than n parties total during an execution of Algorithm 4, then if at some step all honest parties agree on a bit b, all honest parties continue to agree on the same bit b.*

Proof. By Proposition 2 every honest party i accepts at least $\frac{n}{2} + 1$ votes for b from the honest parties in their view and no more than $n - (\frac{n}{2} + 1)$ votes for $1 - b$. Therefore i sets $v_i = b$ at the end of the step.

Algorithm 3: $\{0, 1\}$ Graded Broadcast [20]

Input: v'_i, n, round r
1) $V_{i,1}, ms_1 \leftarrow$ Committee Selection(v'_i, n, r)
2) $V_{i,2}, ms_2 \leftarrow$ Committee Selection(ms_1, n, r)
3) For each $k \in V_{i,1}$, accept m_k if $sig_k(m_k)$ was received from $> \frac{n}{2}$ members of $V_{i,2}$ and no other $sig_k(m'_k)$ was received.

Output: Accepted Messages, $V_{i,1}$

Algorithm 4: Byzantine Agreement [20]

> **Input:** v_i, n
> **for** $i \leftarrow 0$ **to** k **do**
> 1) | Set mc = Leader Election($b \leftarrow$ Uniform($\{0, 1\}$))
> 2) | $\{0,1\}$-Graded Broadcast(v_i)
> | a) **if** *If #(0) accepted* $> \frac{n}{2}$ **then** set $v_i = 0$ b) **else if** *If #(1)*
> | *accepted* $> \frac{n}{2}$ **then** set $v_i = 1$ c) **else** set $v_i = mc$
> **Output:** v_i

Proposition 5. *If $|V_i \bigcup V_j| \leq n$ for all honest parties i, j and V_i contains at least $\frac{n}{2}+1$ honest parties during an execution of Algorithm 4, then with probability at least $\frac{1}{4}$, at the end of step 2 all honest parties are in agreement.*

Proof (Sketch). If an honest party sets $v_i = b$, then all others either set b or set mc, which matches b with probability $\frac{1}{2}$ and is agreed upon with probability $\frac{1}{2}$.

Lemma 2 *If the following properties hold, then Algorithm 4 achieves binary Byzantine Agreement with soundness $> 1 - \frac{3}{4}^k$.*

1. $|V_i \bigcup V_j| \leq n$ for all honest parties i, j.
2. $\exists$ a set of honest players H_C of size $> \frac{n}{2}$ such that $H_C \subseteq V_i \ \forall i \in H$.

Proof. Consistency follows immediately from Proposition 4.

By Proposition 4, agreement will hold at the end of an execution of Algorithm 4 if it holds at the start of any step. By Proposition 5, the probability that this does not occur during any of the k steps is $< \frac{3}{4}^k$.

5.3 Block Proposal

In the binary Byzantine Agreement protocol, parties decide whether or not to add a particular block to the chain. To extend this to deciding *which* block to add to the chain, if any, parties will first attempt to decide a block to vote on during the binary Byzantine Agreement execution. Intuitively, if one honest party i believes the vote is about whether or not to add a block B to the chain, and another honest party j believes the vote is about whether or not to add a different block B' to the chain, then the outcome of the vote should be that no block is added - otherwise, i will add B and j will add B'!

To ensure a nonempty block is only added when all honest parties agree on it, Algorand uses a Graded Consensus protocol before running the binary Byzantine Agreement protocol. Roughly, this ensures that honest parties will decide to add a nonempty block B as a result of the binary Byzantine Agreement execution only if some honest party *knows* that all honest parties think the vote is about whether or not to add B.

We will show that the graded consensus algorithm from [20] surprisingly still works with the notion of "close enough" committees achieved by Algorithm 2 (laid out in Lemma 1). The only modification necessary is the threshold required for a set of signatures to be consistent, since local views of the committee may be different sizes. Algorithm 5 describes the modified graded consensus algorithm.

Algorithm 5: Graded Consensus

Input: v_i', n
1) messages$_1$, $V_{i,1} \leftarrow \{0,1\}$-Graded Broadcast
2) $m_{i,2} \leftarrow \perp$
   if *accepted* $> \frac{n}{2}$ *signatures for* v' *in step 1* **then**
   $\quad | \quad m_{i,2} \leftarrow sig_i(v', 2)$
   messages$_2$, $V_{i,2} \leftarrow \{0,1\}$-Graded Broadcast$(m_{i,2})$
3) $m_{i,3} \leftarrow \perp$
   if $> \frac{n}{2} + 1$ *signatures* $sig_j(v'', 2)$, *for* $j \in V_{i_2}$ **then**
   $\quad | \quad m_{i,3} \leftarrow sig_i(\{sig_j(v'', 2) : sig_j(v'', 2)$ was accepted from $j \in V_{i,2}\})$
   messages$_2$, $V_{i,3} \leftarrow \{0,1\}$-Graded Broadcast$(m_{i,3})$
4) A signature set is *consistent* if it contains $> |V_{i,2}| - \frac{n}{2}$ signatures from members of $V_{i,2}$.
   if $> \frac{n}{2}$ *consistent signatures sets for* $(v''', 2)$ *were accepted in step 3* **then**
   $\quad | \quad$ **Output** $(2, v''')$
   else if ≥ 1 *consistent signature sets for* $(v''', 2)$ *was accepted in step 3* **then**
   $\quad | \quad$ **Output** $(1, v''')$
   else
   $\quad | \quad$ **Output** $(0, \perp)$
   Output: (g_i, v_i)

Proposition 6. *If each view change satisfies* $|V_i \bigcup V_j| \leq n$ *and there exists a set of honest parties* H_C *such that* $|H_C| > \frac{n}{2}$ *and* $H_C \subseteq V_i$ *for any honest players* i, j *then Algorithm 5 achieves graded consensus.*

Proof (Sketch). For the first property, if $g_i = 2$ for an honest player i, then i receives more consistent sets of signatures in step 3 than half its view. One of these must have been from a member of $H_{C,3}$, so all honest parties also receive a set. Since two honest views cannot contain more than n unique parties in their union, all honest parties consider this set consistent.

The second property starts with the observation that if no honest party signs $(v, 2)$ in step 2, then no honest party receives a consistent signature set for $(v, 2)$ in step 4, preventing them from outputting v with a non-zero grade. This follows from honest views containing only $|V_{2,i}| - |H_C|$ corrupted parties. Then, we show that two different values will not be signed by honest parties in step 2, since this would require two honest parties to accept more unique messages in step 1 than exist in the union of their views.

The third property uses the fact that all honest parties accept all messages from members of H_{C_1} during the $\{0,1\}$ graded broadcast, so each these messages are signed by members of $H_{C,2}$ in step 2. This causes every honest party to send its own set, and honest signature sets are consistent for every honest party, leading to an output grade of 2 for v.

To propose a block, every player will begin by creating a candidate block and broadcasting it alongside a VRF and a short description of the block, such as its hash. The block and its description will be propagated separately, so as to allow fast propagation of the description, which is much shorter than the block itself.

After waiting for the network delay to complete, all players will begin Graded Consensus (Algorithm 5) using the block description with the highest associated VRF seen as their input. Finally, the block voted on during Byzantine Agreement will be the value output from Algorithm 5. This is summarized in Algorithm 6.

5.4 Putting It All Together

In this section, we describe how our modifications fit into Algorand as a whole and present our final result.

Our final protocol takes the following parameters, which must be common to all honest players.

- n: the committee size
- k: the number of iterations for the binary Byzantine Agreement
- Δ_N: the network delay

Note that a good parameter choice for n can be determined given a desired safety parameter and an assumed maximum fraction of online stake controlled by the adversary ($\frac{1}{2} - \epsilon$). For this reason, the safety parameter and ϵ may be consider to be parameters in place of the committee size n.

It is also worth noting that the parameter n provides explicit bounds on the committee size, independent of the amount of online stake[2] and in contrast to Algorand, where it is only an expected committee size. By Lemma 1, every honest committee view will have size at least $\frac{n}{2} + 1$, but no more than n, regardless of the amount of online stake. In contrast, committee sizes in Algorand may vary drastically if the amount of online stake is over or underestimated.

Theorem 2. *If less than half of all online stake is adversarially owned and all honest parties input the same parameters to an execution of Algorithm 6, the following properties hold:*

1. *With overwhelming probability, all honest players output the same block B.*
2. *With probability $> \frac{1}{2}$, B is not empty (i.e. contains transactions).*

Proof (Sketch). The first property holds when all honest players output 0 in the Byzantine Agreement protocol, or if all honest players output 1 in the Byzantine Agreement protocol and the same block in the Graded Consensus protocol. With

---

[2] Ignoring the possibility of less than n units of stake being online at all, which we consider to be an extreme corner case.

Algorithm 6: Next Block

Input: committee size n, Byzantine Agreement iterations k, network delay Δ_N, current log L

`// During every subroutine, wait for` Δ_N `time between steps`

1) Wait for Δ_N time to receive transactions. Construct a block $B_i^{(3)}$ from the transactions received.
2) $B_i'' \leftarrow$ Leader Election($B_i^{(3)}$)
3) $(g_i, B_i') \leftarrow$ Graded Consensus(B_i'') During the Graded Consensus execution, ignore invalid blocks. **if** $g_i = 2$ **then** $v_i' \leftarrow 1$ **else** $v_i' \leftarrow 0$
4) $v_i \leftarrow$ Byzantine Agreement(v_i') **if** $v_i = 1$ **then** $B_i \leftarrow B_i'$ **else** $B_i \leftarrow$ empty block

Output: B_i

---

probability $\left(\frac{3}{4}^k + 2k\left(1 - 4\epsilon^2\right)^{n/2}\right)$ and $6\left(1 - 4\epsilon^2\right)^{n/2}$ respectively, these cases do *not* occur, and we can apply a union bound.

Wheneveran honest leader is elected, they propose a non-empty block and that block is unanimously chosen by honest parties. An honest leader is elected with probability $\frac{1}{2}$.

References

1. Alchieri, E.A.P., Bessani, A., Greve, F., da Silva Fraga, J.: Knowledge connectivity requirements for solving byzantine consensus with unknown participants. IEEE Trans. Dependable Secure Comput. **15**(2), 246–259 (2018)
2. Alchieri, E.A.P., Bessani, A.N., da Silva Fraga, J., Greve, F.: Byzantine consensus with unknown participants. In: Baker, T.P., Bui, A., Tixeuil, S. (eds.) OPODIS 2008. LNCS, vol. 5401, pp. 22–40. Springer, Heidelberg (2008). https://doi.org/10.1007/978-3-540-92221-6_4
3. Badertscher, C., Gazi, P., Kiayias, A., Russell, A., Zikas, V.: Ouroboros genesis: composable proof-of-stake blockchains with dynamic availability. In: Lie, D., Mannan, M., Backes, M., Wang, X. (eds.) Proceedings of the 2018 ACM SIGSAC Conference on Computer and Communications Security, CCS 2018, Toronto, ON, Canada, 15–19 October 2018, pp. 913–930. ACM (2018). https://doi.org/10.1145/3243734.3243848
4. Bagaria, V.K., Kannan, S., Tse, D., Fanti, G.C., Viswanath, P.: Prism: Deconstructing the blockchain to approach physical limits. In: Cavallaro, L., Kinder, J., Wang, X., Katz, J. (eds.) Proceedings of the 2019 ACM SIGSAC Conference on Computer and Communications Security, CCS 2019, London, UK, 11–15 November 2019, pp. 585–602. ACM (2019). https://doi.org/10.1145/3319535.3363213
5. Bentov, I., Pass, R., Shi, E.: Snow white: provably secure proofs of stake. IACR Cryptol. ePrint Arch. **2016**, 919 (2016). http://eprint.iacr.org/2016/919
6. Chen, J., Micali, S.: Algorand (2016)
7. Chen, J., Micali, S.: Algorand: a secure and efficient distributed ledger. Theor. Comput. Sci. **777**, 155–183 (2019). https://doi.org/10.1016/j.tcs.2019.02.001

8. David, B., Gaži, P., Kiayias, A., Russell, A.: Ouroboros praos: an adaptively-secure, semi-synchronous proof-of-stake blockchain. In: Nielsen, J.B., Rijmen, V. (eds.) EUROCRYPT 2018. LNCS, vol. 10821, pp. 66–98. Springer, Cham (2018). https://doi.org/10.1007/978-3-319-78375-8_3
9. Dolev, D., et al.: The byzantine generals strike again. J. Algorithms **3**(1), 14–30 (1982)
10. Douceur, J.R.: The sybil attack. In: Druschel, P., Kaashoek, F., Rowstron, A. (eds.) IPTPS 2002. LNCS, vol. 2429, pp. 251–260. Springer, Heidelberg (2002). https://doi.org/10.1007/3-540-45748-8_24
11. Dwork, C., Peleg, D., Pippenger, N., Upfal, E.: Fault tolerance in networks of bounded degree. SIAM J. Comput. **17**(5), 975–988 (1988)
12. Feldman, P., Micali, S.: An optimal probabilistic algorithm for synchronous Byzantine agreement. In: Ausiello, G., Dezani-Ciancaglini, M., Della Rocca, S.R. (eds.) ICALP 1989. LNCS, vol. 372, pp. 341–378. Springer, Heidelberg (1989). https://doi.org/10.1007/BFb0035770
13. Fitzi, M., Gazi, P., Kiayias, A., Russell, A.: Parallel chains: improving throughput and latency of blockchain protocols via parallel composition. IACR Cryptol. ePrint Arch. **2018**, 1119 (2018). https://eprint.iacr.org/2018/1119
14. Gilad, Y., Hemo, R., Micali, S., Vlachos, G., Zeldovich, N.: Algorand: scaling byzantine agreements for cryptocurrencies. In: Proceedings of the 26th Symposium on Operating Systems Principles, pp. 51–68 (2017)
15. Hoeffding, W.: Probability inequalities for sums of bounded random variables. J. Am. Stat. Assoc. **58**(301), 13–30 (1963)
16. Katz, J., Koo, C.-Y.: On expected constant-round protocols for Byzantine agreement. In: Dwork, C. (ed.) CRYPTO 2006. LNCS, vol. 4117, pp. 445–462. Springer, Heidelberg (2006). https://doi.org/10.1007/11818175_27
17. Kiayias, A., Russell, A., David, B., Oliynykov, R.: Ouroboros: a provably secure proof-of-stake blockchain protocol. In: Katz, J., Shacham, H. (eds.) CRYPTO 2017. LNCS, vol. 10401, pp. 357–388. Springer, Cham (2017). https://doi.org/10.1007/978-3-319-63688-7_12
18. Micali, S.: Very simple and efficient byzantine agreement. In: Papadimitriou, C.H. (ed.) 8th Innovations in Theoretical Computer Science Conference, ITCS 2017, LIPIcs, Berkeley, CA, USA, 9–11 January 2017, vol. 67, pp. 6:1–6:1. Schloss Dagstuhl - Leibniz-Zentrum für Informatik (2017). https://doi.org/10.4230/LIPIcs.ITCS.2017.6
19. Micali, S., Rabin, M., Vadhan, S.: Verifiable random functions. In: 40th Annual Symposium on Foundations of Computer Science (cat. No. 99CB37039), pp. 120–130. IEEE (1999)
20. Micali, S., Vaikuntanathan, V.: Optimal and player-replaceable consensus with an honest majority. Technical Reportt MIT-CSAIL-TR-2017-004 (2017). http://hdl.handle.net/1721.1/107927
21. Nakamoto, S., et al.: Bitcoin: a peer-to-peer electronic cash system (2008)
22. Pass, R., Shi, E.: Hybrid consensus: efficient consensus in the permissionless model. In: Richa, A.W. (ed.) 31st International Symposium on Distributed Computing (DISC 2017). Leibniz International Proceedings in Informatics (LIPIcs), vol. 91, pp. 39:1–39:16. Schloss Dagstuhl-Leibniz-Zentrum fuer Informatik, Dagstuhl, Germany (2017). https://doi.org/10.4230/LIPIcs.DISC.2017.39, http://drops.dagstuhl.de/opus/volltexte/2017/8004
23. Pass, R., Shi, E.: The sleepy model of consensus. In: Takagi, T., Peyrin, T. (eds.) ASIACRYPT 2017. LNCS, vol. 10625, pp. 380–409. Springer, Cham (2017). https://doi.org/10.1007/978-3-319-70697-9_14

24. Pass, R., Shi, E.: **Thunderella:** blockchains with optimistic instant confirmation. In: Nielsen, J.B., Rijmen, V. (eds.) EUROCRYPT 2018. LNCS, vol. 10821, pp. 3–33. Springer, Cham (2018). https://doi.org/10.1007/978-3-319-78375-8_1

25. Pease, M., Shostak, R., Lamport, L.: Reaching agreement in the presence of faults. J. ACM (JACM) **27**(2), 228–234 (1980)

26. Turpin, R., Coan, B.A.: Extending binary byzantine agreement to multivalued byzantine agreement. Inf. Process. Lett. **18**(2), 73–76 (1984)

Blockchain CAP Theorem Allows User-Dependent Adaptivity and Finality

Suryanarayana Sankagiri[1]([✉]), Xuechao Wang[1], Sreeram Kannan[2], and Pramod Viswanath[1]

[1] University of Illinois, Urbana-Champaign, IL 61801, USA
ss19@illinois.edu
[2] University of Washington at Seattle, Seattle, WA, USA

Abstract. Longest-chain blockchain protocols, such as Bitcoin, guarantee liveness even when the number of actively participating users is variable, i.e., they are adaptive. However, they are not safe under network partitions, i.e., they do not guarantee finality. On the other hand, classical blockchain protocols, like PBFT, achieve finality but not adaptivity. Indeed, the CAP theorem in the context of blockchains asserts that no protocol can simultaneously offer both adaptivity and finality. We propose a new blockchain protocol, called the checkpointed longest chain, that offers individual users the choice between finality and adaptivity instead of imposing it at a system-wide level. This protocol's salient feature is that it supports two distinct confirmation rules: one that guarantees adaptivity and the other finality. The more optimistic adaptive rule always confirms blocks that are marked as finalized by the more conservative rule, and may possibly confirm more blocks during variable participation levels. Clients (users) make a local choice between the confirmation rules as per their personal preference, while miners follow a fixed block proposal rule that is consistent with both confirmation rules. The proposed protocol has the additional benefit of intrinsic validity: the finalized blocks always lie on a single blockchain, and therefore miners can attest to the validity of transactions while proposing blocks. Our protocol builds on the notion of a finality gadget, a popular technique for adding finality to longest-chain protocols.

1 Introduction

The longest-chain protocol, introduced by Nakamoto in Bitcoin [18], is the prototypical example of a blockchain protocol that operates in a permissionless setting. Put differently, the longest-chain protocol is *adaptive*: it remain safe and live irrespective of the number of active participants (nodes) in the system, as long as the fraction of adversarial nodes among the active ones is less than a half. Adaptivity (also known as dynamic availability) is a desirable property in a highly decentralized system such as a cryptocurrency. The downside of this protocol is that they are insecure during prolonged periods of network partition

---

S. Sankagiri and X. Wang—Equal contribution.

© International Financial Cryptography Association 2021
N. Borisov and C. Diaz (Eds.): FC 2021, LNCS 12675, pp. 84–103, 2021.
https://doi.org/10.1007/978-3-662-64331-0_5

(asynchrony). This is unavoidable; miners in disconnected portions of the network keep extending their blockchains separately, unaware of the other chains. When synchrony resumes, one of the chains wins, which implies that blocks on the other chains get unconfirmed. These features are present not just in the longest-chain protocol, but also in other protocols that are derived from it, e.g., Prism [1].

In stark contrast, committee-based consensus protocols like PBFT [4] and Hotstuff [25] offer strong *finality* guarantees. These protocols remain safe even during periods of asynchrony, and regain liveness when synchrony resumes. Finality is also a desirable property for blockchains, as they may operate under conditions where synchrony cannot be guaranteed at all times. However, all finality-guaranteeing protocols come with a caveat: they are built for the permissioned setting. These protocols make progress only when enough number of votes have been accrued for each block. If a significant fraction of nodes become inactive (go offline), the protocol stalls completely. This prevents them from being adaptive.

We posit that the two disparate class of protocols is a consequence of the CAP theorem, a famous impossibility result in distributed systems. The theorem states that in the presence of a *network partition*, a distributed system cannot guarantee both *consistency* (safety) and *availability* (liveness) [13,14]. The theorem has led to a classification of system designs, on the basis of whether they favor liveness or safety during network partitions. Blockchains, being distributed systems, inherit the trade-offs implicated by the CAP theorem. In particular, we see that the longest-chain class of protocols favor liveness while the committee-based protocols favor safety.

Recently, Lewis-Pye and Roughgarden [16] prove a CAP theorem for blockchains that highlights the adaptivity-finality trade-off explicitly. They show that "a fundamental dichotomy holds between protocols (such as Bitcoin) that are adaptive, in the sense that they can function given unpredictable levels of participation, and protocols (such as Algorand) that have certain finality properties". The essence of this impossibility result is the following: it is difficult to distinguish network asynchrony from a reduced number of participants in the blockchain system. Therefore, a protocol is bound to behave similarly under both these conditions. In particular, adaptive protocols must continue to extend blockchains during asynchrony (thereby compromising finality), while finality-guaranteeing protocols must stall under reduced participation (which means they cannot have adaptivity).

In this paper, we investigate whether the aforementioned trade-off between adaptivity and finality can be resolved at a user level, rather than at a system-wide level. In particular, we seek to build a blockchain system wherein all (honest) nodes follow a *common* block proposing mechanism, but different nodes can choose between two *different confirmation rules*. Under appropriate bounds on adversarial participation, one rule must guarantee adaptivity, while the other must guarantee finality. When the system is operating under desirable conditions, i.e., a large enough fraction of nodes are active and the network is synchronous, the blocks confirmed by both rules must coincide. Protocols with such a dual-confirmation rule (aka dual-ledger) design are termed as "Ebb-and-flow" protocols in [19]. Such a design would be of interest in blockchains for many reasons. For example, for low-value transactions such as buying a coffee, a node may prefer liveness over safety, whereas for high-value transactions, it is natural to choose safety over liveness. Moreover, such a trade-off allows each node to make their own assumptions about the state of the network and choose a confirmation rule appropriately.

At a high level, we are inspired in our formulation from analogous designs to adapt the CAP theorem in practical distributed system settings (Sect. 4 of [14]). More concretely, dual-ledger designs do not fall under the purview of the CAP theorem of [16]; the formulation assumes a single confirmation rule. A second motivation is that a variety of *finality gadgets* (in combination with a blockchain protocol) may also be viewed as providing a user-dependent dual ledger option. We elaborate on some recent proposals in [10,15,24] in Sect. 2.

1.1 Our Contributions

Our main contribution is to propose a new protocol, called the *checkpointed longest chain* protocol, which offers each node in the same blockchain system a choice between two different confirmation rules that have different adaptivity-finality trade-offs.

– **Block Proposal.** Just as in the longest chain protocol, honest miners build new blocks by extending the chain that they currently hold. In addition, some honest users participate in a separate *checkpointing protocol*, that marks certain blocks as checkpoints at regular intervals. An honest user adopts the *longest chain that contains the latest checkpoint*.
– **Confirmation rules.** The protocol's *adaptivity-guaranteeing* confirmation rule is simply the k-deep rule. An honest user confirms a block if it sees k blocks below it, for an appropriate choice of k. The protocol's *finality-guaranteeing* rule is for honest users to treat all blocks in its chain up to the last checkpointed block as confirmed.

The protocol is designed such that new blocks continue to be mined at increasing heights even if the participation level is low, but new checkpoints appear only if there is sufficient participation. This illustrates the adaptivity-guaranteeing property of the k-deep rule. On the other hand, checkpoints are guaranteed to be on a single chain irrespective of network conditions, while the longest chain containing the latest checkpoint may keep alternating between divergent chains. This implies the finality property of the checkpointing rule.

Below, we highlight the key design principles of our protocol, followed by the security guarantees.

Validity of Blockchains. Our protocol keeps intact the intrinsic *validity* of blockchains. Roughly, validity means that the set of blocks that are confirmed all lie on a single, monotonically increasing chain. Thus, the validity of a transaction can be inferred from just the blockchain leading up to the particular block. More precisely, an honest user that is constructing the block has the assurance that if the block is confirmed, all transactions in the block are confirmed, which means it accrues all the transaction rewards. Moreover, a user can infer that a certain transaction is confirmed simply by knowing that the transaction was included in a particular block and that the block was confirmed (as per either rule), without knowledge of the contents of other blocks. These properties are recognized to be important for the blockchain to be incentive-compatible and to enable light clients respectively. Further, validity of blockchains offers spam-resistance and is compatible with existing sharding designs. Although validity of blockchains is a common feature of a majority of protocols, recent high performance designs crucially decouple validation from consensus [1,11]. The Snap-and-Chat design of [19] for the same problem also does not have this feature.

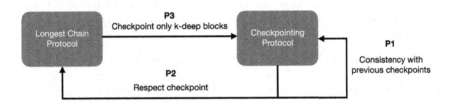

Fig. 1. The checkpointed longest chain

Interaction Between Checkpointing and Longest Chain Protocol. In our design, the longest chain rule (i.e., the block proposal rule) and the checkpointing rule satisfy some constraints with respect to each other. The interlocking structure of constraints between the checkpointing protocol and the longest chain protocol is illustrated in Fig. 1 and detailed below.

- **P1: Consistency with previous checkpoints.** The sequence of checkpoints must be on a chain. This places a self-consistency condition on the checkpointing protocol.
- **P2: Checkpointed longest chain rule.** The longest chain protocol respect the previous checkpoints. Honest users build adopt the longest chain that contains the latest checkpoint and mine new blocks at the tip of this chain.
- **P3: Checkpoints are deep enough.** The checkpointing protocol should only checkpoint blocks that are sufficiently deep in some honestly held chain. Furthermore, such a chain should be made available along with the checkpoint message.

All these three conditions are required to achieve our goals. Condition **P1** is a requisite for a validity preserving protocol (in particular, a validity preserving, finality-guaranteeing confirmation rule). The condition **P2** says that honest nodes should adopt the longest checkpointed chain, rather than the longest chain. Given **P1**, the condition **P2** is required to ensure new checkpoints are produced after a period of asynchrony. Without this condition **P2**, the block proposal rule is simply the longest chain rule. During asynchrony, the longest chain may be one that does not include some of the checkpoints, and there is no correction mechanism to ever bring the longest chain downstream of the last checkpoint. Condition **P3** ensures that during synchrony, any block that is eventually checkpointed would be a part of all honestly held chains. Thus, the dynamics of the protocol would be as if nodes are simply following the longest chain rule, and the known security guarantees would apply. If no such condition is placed, the checkpointing protocol could checkpoint an arbitrary block that possibly forks from the main chain by a large margin. The rule **P2** would force honest nodes to switch to this fork, thereby violating safety of the k-deep rule.

The Checkpointing Protocol. The checkpointing protocol in our design is a BFT consensus protocol. It is a slight modification of Algorand BA, that is presented in [6]. The protocol is extended from a single-iteration byzantine agreement protocol to a multi-iteration checkpointing protocol. In each iteration, nodes run the checkpointing protocol to checkpoint a new block, and **P1** guarantees that the sequence of checkpoints lie on a single chain. Coupled with the chain adoption rule (longest checkpointed chain), these checkpoints offer deterministic finality and safety against network partitions.

We state the safety guarantee of the checkpointing protocol as a basic checkpointing property (CP) as below:

- **CP0: Safety.** All honest users checkpoint the same block in one iteration of the checkpointing protocol, even during network partition. This checkpoint lies on the same chain as all previous checkpoints.

While one might consider different protocols for the checkpointing mechanism, the protocol must further satisfy some key properties during periods of synchrony.

- **CP1: Recency condition.** If a new block is checkpointed at some time, it must have been in a chain held by an honest user at some point in the *recent past*.
- **CP2: Gap in checkpoints.** The interval between successive checkpoints must be large enough to allow **CP1** to hold.
- **CP3: Conditional liveness.** If all honest nodes hold chains that have a common prefix (all but the last few blocks are common), then a new checkpoint will appear within a certain bounded time (i.e., there is an upper bound on the interval between two successive checkpoints).

CP1 helps in bounding the extent to which an honest user may have to drop honest blocks in its chain when it adopts a new checkpoint. Without this condition, (i.e., if arbitrarily old checkpoints can be issued), honest users may have to let go of many honestly mined blocks. This causes a loss in mining power, which we refer to as *bleeding*. Our choice of Algorand BA was made because it has this property. Other natural candidates such as PBFT [4] and HotStuff [25], do not have this property. We discuss this in detail in Appendix D of the full paper [23]. **CP2** ensures that the loss in honest mining power due to the above mechanism is limited. This condition can be incorporated by design. **CP3** is a liveness property of the checkpointing protocol. It ensures new checkpoints appear at frequent intervals, leading to liveness of the finality-guaranteeing confirmation rule.

Security Guarantees (Informal). We show the following guarantees for proof-of-work longest chain along with Algorand BA (augmented with the appropriate validity condition).

1. The k-deep rule is safe and live if the network is synchronous from the beginning and the fraction of adversaries among online users is less than a half.
2. The checkpointing protocol, which is safe by design, is also live soon after the network partition is healed under the partially synchronous model.
3. The ledger from the checkpoint rule is a prefix of the ledger from the k-deep rule from the point of view of any user.

Proof Technique. We prove these security guarantees using the following strategy. First, we show that if all honest users hold chains that obey the k-common prefix condition for an extended period of time, then new blocks get checkpointed at regular intervals, and these blocks are part of the common prefix of the honestly held chains. This tells us that under conditions in which the vanilla longest chain rule is secure, the checkpointed longest chain rule has exactly the same dynamics. It therefore inherits the same security properties of the longest chain rule. Secondly, we show that once sufficient time has passed after a network partition is healed, the chains held by the honest user under the checkpointed longest chain rule are guaranteed to have the common prefix property. Coupled with the first result, we infer that new checkpoints will eventually be confirmed thereby proving liveness of the checkpoint-based confirmation rule under partial synchrony.

Outline. We review related works in Sect. 2 and place our results in the context of several recent works on the same topic as this paper. The similarities and differences in the techniques in our work with closely related works is pictorially illustrated in Fig. 2. We state our network and security models formally in Sect. 3. In Sect. 4, we describe the checkpointed longest chain protocol, highlighting the roles of the miners and precisely stating the two confirmation rules. For clarity, we describe the checkpointing protocol as a black box with certain properties here; we give the full protocol in Appendix A. We state our main theorem, concerning the security guarantees of our protocol, in Sect. 5. In the rest of the section, we give a proof sketch of the theorem. The formal proofs are given in the full version of our paper [23] in Appendices B and C. We conclude the paper with a discussion and pointers for future work in Sect. 6.

2   Related Work

CAP Theorem. The formal connection between the CAP theorem to blockchains is recently made in [16], by providing an abstract framework in which a wide class of blockchain protocols can be placed, including longest chain protocols (both Proof-of-Work based [12] and PoS based, e.g., [8]) as well as BFT-style protocols (e.g., [7]). The main result of [16] says that a protocol (containing a block "encoding" procedure and a block confirmation rule) which is adaptive (i.e., which remains live in an unsized setting) cannot offer finality (i.e., deterministic safety, even under arbitrary network conditions) and viceversa. However, the same paper is mute on the topic of whether different block confirmation rules could offer different guarantees, which is the entire focus of this work. We are inspired in our formulation from analogous designs to adapt the CAP theorem in practical distributed system settings (Section 4 of [14]).

User-Dependent Confirmation Rules. The idea of giving users the option of choosing their own confirmation rule, based on their beliefs about the network conditions and desired security level was pioneered by Nakamoto themself, via choosing the value of k in the k-deep confirmation rule. A recent work [17] allows users the option of choosing between partially synchronous confirmation rule and a synchronous one. However, *neither* of the confirmation rules are adaptive, as the block proposal rule itself is a committee-based one and cannot make progress once the participation is below a required level. Therefore, they do not "break" the CAP theorem as proposed in [16]. In contrast, our protocol offers users the choice of an adaptive system.

Hybrid Consensus. Hybrid consensus [21] is a different technique of incorporating a BFT protocol into the longest-chain protocol. In a nutshell, the idea in this design is to use the longest-chain protocol to randomly select a committee, which then executes a BFT protocol to confirm blocks. The committee consists of the miners of the blocks on the longest chain over a shifting interval of constant size, and is thus re-elected periodically. Hybrid consensus addresses the problem of building a responsive protocol (i.e., latency proportional to network delay) in a PoW setting. It does not, however, address the adaptivity-finality dilemma. In fact, as we illustrate here, the protocol offers neither adaptivity nor finality. Once a miner is elected as a committee member, it is obliged to stay active until the period of its committee is over, which compromises on the adaptivity property. As for finality, although the blocks are confirmed by a finality-based protocol, the committee election mechanism compromises the finality guarantee. During

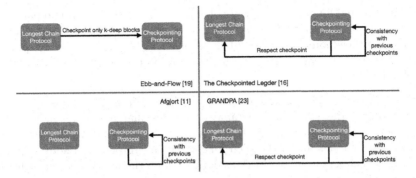

Fig. 2. Four related works in our framework (counterclockwise): In Ebb-and-Flow [19], previous checkpoints are not respected by either the longest chain protocol or the checkpointing protocol. Hence checkpoints may not form a single chain and the final ledger is constructed by sanitization, which makes it impossible to have validation before block proposal. Afgjort [10] takes an off-the-shelf longest chain protocol and keeps checkpointing blocks on it. Due to lack of interaction between the longest chain protocol and the checkpointing protocol, the protocol may fail in a partially synchronous setting when the security of the blockchain is broken. The Checkpointed Ledger [15] and GRANDPA [24] are very similar to our design; the difference is that the checkpoints don't need to be buried deep enough in the longest chain. This minor change makes their protocols become insecure under the variable participation setting.

asynchrony, nodes cannot achieve consensus on who belongs to the committee, and thus the whole protocol loses safety.

Checkpointing is a protocol run on top of the longest chain protocol (run by largely honest parties) that deterministically marks certain blocks as finalized; a simple form of checkpointing was pioneered, and maintained until 2014, by Satoshi Nakamoto (presumably honest). In the context of our work, checkpointing provides finality (essentially by fiat) while the longest chain rule ensures adaptivity. We can interpret our paper as an attempt to provide appropriate conditions on the interaction between the checkpointing and the longest chain protocol, and also to show how to realize such checkpointing in a distributed manner. We note that [15] is a recent work that studies the checkpointed ledger when the longest-chain protocol has super-majority adversaries; this regime is different from that studied in the present paper, where we assume that the longest-chain protocol has majority honest and the checkpointing protocol has 2/3 honest users. For completeness, we have included the architecture of checkpointed ledger in the comparison in Fig. 2.

Casper FFG and Gasper. Casper FFG (*Casper: the Friendly Finality Gadget*), presented in [2], pioneered the study of finality gadgets. Casper FFG also introduced the notion of "economic security". The finality gadget allows cryptographic proofs of malicious behavior which can be used to disincentivize such behavior. We do not explore this aspect of finality gadgets in our paper. Casper FFG, as presented in [2], is not a completely specified protocol. A recent follow-up paper called Gasper [3] provides a complete protocol. Gasper can be viewed as a checkpointed longest chain protocol, with the longest chain rule replaced by the *Latest Message Driven Greediest Heaviest Observed Subtree* (LMD GHOST) rule and the checkpointing protocol being Casper FFG. Gasper does not provide formal security guarantees; in fact, the work by Neu et al. [19] shows a liveness attack on Gasper.

Afgjort. Afgjort [10] is a recent finality gadget proposed by Dinsdale et al., which formally describes the desirable properties that a finality gadget must have, some of them are similar to the ones we require as well. Afgjort has a two-layer design: it takes an off-the-shelf longest chain protocol and adds a finality layer to it. Such a system can work as desired when the network is synchronous, including when the participation levels are variable. However, it is destined to fail in one of two ways in a partially synchronous setting: either the finality gadget stops finalizing new blocks (i.e., violates liveness), or it finalizes "conflicting" blocks, i.e., blocks in two different chains (i.e., violates validity). Thus Afgjort does not provide the guarantees we seek in this work. More generally, any layer-two finality gadget on top of an adaptive protocol would not meet the desired objectives for the same reason; they would be missing rule **P2** (see Fig. 2).

GRANDPA. GRANDPA [24] is another recent finality gadget, proposed by Stewart et al. Just as in our protocol (and unlike Afgjort), GRANDPA alters the underlying block production mechanism to respect blocks that has been finalized by the finality gadget. GRANDPA's security relies on the assumption that the block-production mechanism (longest-chain rule/GHOST) provides a type of "conditional eventual consensus". I.e., If nodes keep building on the last finalized block and don't finalize any new blocks, then eventually they have consensus on a longer chain. This argument, though presumably true, is not a rigorous security analysis; in our work, we prove security for a completely specified model and protocol.

More importantly, comparing Figs. 1 and 2, we see that GRANDPA does not have property **P3**. This leads to a security vulnerability in the variable participation setting. The issue arises due to the following subtlety: in the variable participation setting, a particular block could be 'locked' onto by the checkpointing protocol, but could be checkpointed much later (this does not happen under full participation). A block at the tip of the longest chain could soon be displaced from it by the adversary. If this block is locked while it is on the chain, but checkpointed only when it is out of the chain, the safety of the k-deep rule will be violated. A more detailed description of this attack is given in Appendix D of the full version of our paper [23].

Snap-and-Chat Protocols. A concurrent work by Neu et al. [19] also solves the adaptivity vs finality dilemma posed by the CAP theorem. (Their work appeared online a few weeks prior to ours). They introduce a technique, called Snap-and-Chat, to combine a longest chain protocol with any BFT-style one to obtain a protocol that has the properties we desire. More specifically, their protocol produces two different ledgers (ordered list of transactions), one that offers adaptivity and the other that offers finality. A user can choose to pick either one, depending on its belief about the network condition. These ledgers are proven to be consistent with each other (the finality guaranteeing ledger is a prefix of the adaptive one). While the outcomes of the design of [19] are analogous to ours, the approach adopted and the resulting blockchain protocol are quite different. A major advantage of the approach of [19] is its generality: unlike other existing approaches, it offers a blackbox construction and proof which can be used to combine a variety of adaptive and finality preserving protocols. However, the design of [19] has an important caveat: the sequence of blocks that are confirmed in their protocol do not necessarily form a single chain. Indeed, in the partially synchronous setting, the finality-guaranteeing confirmation rule can finalize blocks on two different forks one after the other. The design of [19] overcomes this apparent issue by constructing a ledger after the blocks have been finalized, and "sanitizing" it at a later step.

The sanitization step implies that not all transactions in a confirmed block may be part of the ledger: for example, if it is a double spend relative to a transaction occurring earlier in the ledger, such transaction will be removed. Put differently, the validity of a particular transaction in a particular block is decided only once the block is confirmed, and not when the block is proposed. Most practical blockchain systems are designed with coupled validation, i.e., an honest block proposer can ensure that blocks contain only valid transactions. Our approach maintains coupled validity of blockchains and does not have this shortcoming, as highlighted in Sect. 1.

3   Security Model

Environment. A blockchain protocol Π is directed by an *environment* $\mathcal{Z}(1^\kappa)$, where κ is the security parameter, i.e., the length of the hash function output. This environment (i) initiates a set of participating nodes $\mathcal{N}$; (ii) manages a public-key infrastructure (PKI) and assigns each node with a unique crypto-graphic identity; (iii) manages nodes through an adversary $\mathcal{A}$ which *corrupts* a subset of nodes before the protocol execution starts; (iv) manages all accesses of each node from/to the environment including broadcasting and receiving messages.

Network Model. The nodes' individual timers do not need to be synchronized or almost synchronized. We only require they have the same speed. In our network, we have a variety of messages, including blocks, votes, etc. The following message delay bounds apply to all messages. Secondly, all messages sent by honest nodes are broadcast messages. Thirdly, all honest nodes re-broadcast any message they have heard. The adversary does not suffer any message delay. In general, we assume that the adversary controls the order of delivery of messages, but the end-to-end network delay between any two honest nodes is subject to some further constraints that are specified below. We operate under either one of the two settings specified below:

- **M1 (Partial synchrony model):** A global stabilization time, GST, is chosen by the adversary, unknown to the honest nodes and also to the protocol designer. Before GST, the adversary can delay messages arbitrarily. After GST, all messages sent between honest nodes are delivered within Δ time. Moreover, messages sent by honest nodes before GST are also delivered by GST $+ \Delta$.
- **M2 (Synchrony model):** All messages sent from one honest node to another are delivered within Δ time.

Participation Model. We introduce the notion of *sized/unsized* number of nodes to capture the notion that node network activity (online or offline) varies over time. It is important to note that we allow for adversarial nodes to go offline as well. A node can come online and go offline at any time during the protocol. An online honest node always executes the protocol faithfully. An offline node, be it honest or adversarial, does not send any messages. Messages that are scheduled to be delivered during the time when the node is offline are delivered immediately after the node comes online again. We consider two different scenarios:

- **U1 (Sized setting):** All nodes stay online at all times.
- **U2 (Unsized setting):** Nodes can come online and offline at arbitrary times, at the discretion of the adversary, provided a certain minimal number of nodes stay online.

Abstract Protocol Model. We describe here our protocol in the abstract framework that was developed in [16]. In this framework, a blockchain protocol is specified as a tuple $\Pi = (I, O, C)$, where I denotes the *instruction set*, O is an *oracle* that abstracts out the leader election process, and C is a confirmation rule (e.g., the k-deep confirmation rule). The bounds on adversarial ratios are also specified through O. The rationale for adopting this framework is to point out precisely how we circumvent the CAP theorem for blockchains, which is the main result of [16].

The theorem states that no protocol $\Pi = (I, O, C)$ can simultaneously offer both finality (safety in the partially synchronous setting) and adaptivity (liveness in the unsized setting). Our checkpointed longest chain protocol is a 4-tuple $\Pi_{\text{CLC}} = (I, O, C_1, C_2)$, with two confirmation rules C_1 and C_2. This entire protocol can be split at a node level into two protocols: $\Pi_{\text{fin}} = (I, O, C_1)$ and $\Pi_{\text{ada}} = (I, O, C_2)$. The protocol Π_{fin} guarantees (deterministic) safety and (probabilistic) liveness under network assumption M1 and participation level U1, just as many BFT-type consensus protocols do. It therefore guarantees finality. Π_{ada} guarantees safety and liveness under network assumption $M2$ and participation level $U2$, just as longest chain protocols do. It thereby guarantees adaptivity. Finally, both Π_{fin} and Π_{ada} are safe and live under conditions $M2$ and $U1$; moreover, the set of blocks confirmed by Π_{fin} at any time is a subset of those confirmed by Π_{ada}. A similar property is proven in [19].

Each node can choose one of the two confirmation rules according to their demands and assumptions. We specify the exact specifications of I, O, C_1 and C_2 and the associated security properties in the next section.

4   Protocol Description

Nodes in the Protocol. In our protocol, let $\mathcal{N}$ denote the set of all participating nodes. Among these, there are two subsets of participating nodes $\mathcal{N}_1$ and $\mathcal{N}_2$. We call nodes in $\mathcal{N}_1$ *miners*, whose role is to propose new blocks. We call nodes in $\mathcal{N}_2$ *checkpointers*, whose role is to vote for blocks on the blockchains they currently hold and mark them as *checkpoints*. Note that we allow for any relation among these sets, including the possibility that all nodes play both roles ($\mathcal{N}_1 = \mathcal{N}_2 = \mathcal{N}$), or the two kinds of nodes are disjoint ($\mathcal{N}_1 \cap \mathcal{N}_2 = \phi$). The instruction set I and the oracle O is different for miners and checkpointers, and is specified below. Note that in the sized/unsized setting, both $\mathcal{N}_1$ and $\mathcal{N}_2$ are sized/unsized.

Before we specify the protocol, we introduce some terminology pertaining to checkpoints. A *checkpoint certificate* is a set of votes from at least 2/3 of the checkpointers for a certain block, that certifies that the block is a checkpoint. When an honest node receives both a checkpoint certificate and a chain that contains the block being checkpointed, we say that the honest node has heard of a checkpoint. We say that a checkpoint *appears at time t* if the t is the first time that an honest node hears of it.

I **for All Nodes.** Every honest node holds a single blockchain at all times, which may be updated upon receiving new messages. They all follow the *checkpointed longest chain rule*, which states that a node selects the longest chain *that extends the last checkpointed block* it has heard of so far. Ties are broken by the adversary. To elaborate, a node keeps track of the last checkpoint it has heard of so far. If a node receives a longer chain that includes the last checkpoint, it adopts the received new chain. A node ignores all chains which do not contain the last checkpoint block as per their knowledge.

I, O **for Miners.** An honest miner adopts the tip of its checkpointed longest chain as the parent block. The miner forms a new block with a *digest* of the parent block and all transactions in its buffer, and broadcasts it when it is chosen as a leader by the oracle. The oracle O chooses miners as leaders at random intervals, that can be modeled as a Poisson process with rate λ. This joint leader election process can be further split into two independent Poisson processes. Let the fraction of online adversarial miners be $\beta < 1/2$. The honest blocks arrive as a Poisson process of rate $(1 - \beta)\lambda$, while the adversarial blocks arrive as an independent Poisson process of rate $\beta\lambda$.

I, O **for Checkpointers.** The checkpointers run a multi-iteration Byzantine Agreement (BA) protocol Π_{BA} to checkpoint blocks, with each iteration checkpointing one block. Our protocol is a slight variant of the Algorand BA protocol from [6]. The complete protocol is described in Appendix A with a minor modification from Algorand, which is highlighted in red. This modification is made so as to enable a consistency check across iterations without losing liveness (i.e., to get a multi-iteration BA from a single iteration one).

Briefly, the protocol works as follows. Each iteration is split into *periods*. Each period has a unique leader chosen by the oracle. Nominally, the values on which consensus is to be achieved amongst all checkpointers are the blockchains held by the checkpointers. In practice, the values may be the hashes of the last block of the blockchain. A key difference from the Algorand protocol is that we allow the checkpointers to change their values at the beginning of each period. The checkpointers aim to achieve consensus amongst these values. The final chain that has been agreed upon is broadcast to all honest nodes (not just checkpointers) together with a certificate. The block that is exactly k-deep in this chain is chosen as the checkpoint block in current iteration. Here, k is a parameter of the protocol Π_{CLC}, and is chosen to be $\Theta(\kappa)$. We call it the *checkpoint depth parameter*.

Confirmation Rules. We propose the following two confirmation rules for Π_{CLC}, which have different security guarantees under different assumptions. Either rule can be adopted by any node in the protocol

- C_1: Confirm the chain up to the last known checkpoint.
- C_2: Confirm all but the last k' blocks in the checkpointed longest chain, i.e., in the chain that is currently held, where $k' = \Theta(\kappa)$

Note that every honest node may choose any value of k' that they wish.

Intuition Behind the Checkpointing Protocol. The checkpointing protocol is designed such that under optimistic conditions, a checkpoint is achieved within one period. These optimistic conditions are that the leader of a period is honest, the network is synchronous, and all chains held by honest checkpointers satisfy the common prefix property. The sequence of leaders for this protocol is guaranteed to be chosen in an i.i.d. fashion amongst online checkpointers by the oracle O. We assume that the fraction of adversarial checkpointers is $\beta' < 1/3$. Thus, the probability of selecting an adversarial leader at any round is $< 1/3$.

We now state some key properties of the checkpointing protocol. These properties, **CP0, CP1, CP2, CP3** were introduced in Sect. 1 and are elaborated upon below.

- **CP0: Safety.** All honest nodes checkpoint the same block in one iteration of the checkpointing protocol, even during network partition. This checkpoint lies on the same chain as all previous checkpoints. This is a safety property of the checkpointing protocol, which will be essential in guaranteeing the safety of Π_{fin}.
- **CP1: Recency condition.** If a new block is checkpointed at some time t by an honest node for the first time, it must have been in a chain held by an honest node at some time $t' \geq t - d$. Here, d is the *recency* parameter of the protocol, and is of the order $O(\sqrt{\kappa}\Delta)$.
- **CP2: Gap in checkpoints.** If a new block is checkpointed at some time t by an honest node for the first time, then the next iteration of the checkpointing

protocol (to decide the next checkpoint) will begin at time $t + e$. Here, e is the *inter-checkpoint interval* and is chosen such that $e \gg d$.

- **CP3: Conditional liveness.** If all honest nodes hold chains that are self-consistent (they satisfy k-common prefix property), during an iteration of the checkpointing protocol, then the checkpointing protocol finishes within $O(\Delta)$ time. Thus, in a period where all honest nodes hold chains that are self-consistent, checkpoints appear within $e + O(\Delta)$ time of each other.

In Appendix B of the full version [23], we prove that the checkpointing protocol we use (modified Algorand BA) satisfies these properties. As such, any protocol that satisfies **CP0–CP3** can be used in our design.

5   Main Result

To state the main security result of our protocol, recall the notations set in Sect. 3. The complete protocol is denoted by $\Pi_{\text{CLC}} = (I, O, C_1, C_2)$ and its two user-dependent variations are $\Pi_{\text{fin}} = (I, O, C_1)$ and $\Pi_{\text{ada}} = (I, O, C_2)$. We also recall the notation M1, M2 for the partially synchronous and synchronous network model, and U1, U2 for the sized and unsized participation models. Clearly, M1 is a more general setting than M2 and U2 is a more general setting than U1. In Theorem 1, a result stated for a general setting also applies to the more restricted setting, but not vice-versa. We first define the notion of safety and liveness that we use for our protocols.

Definition 1 (Safety). *A blockchain protocol Π is safe if the set of blocks confirmed during the execution is a non-decreasing set. Put differently, Π is safe if a block once confirmed by the confirmation rule remains confirmed for all time thereafter.*

Definition 2 (Liveness). *A blockchain protocol Π is live if there exists constants $c, c' > 0$ s.t. the number of new honest blocks confirmed in any interval $[r, s]$ is at least $\lfloor c(s - r) - c' \rfloor$.*

We now state our main theorem, concerning the safety and liveness of Π_{fin} and Π_{ada}.

Theorem 1. *Assume the fraction of adversarial mining power among total honest mining power is bounded by $\beta < 1/2$. Further, assume the fraction of adversarial checkpointers is always less than $1/3$. Then, the protocol Π_{CLC} has the following security guarantees for an execution that runs for a duration of $T_{\max} = O(\text{poly}(\kappa))$ time, where κ is the security parameter, :*

- ***Security of Π_{fin}:*** *The protocol Π_{fin} is safe, and is live after $O(GST + \kappa)$ time in the setting (M1, U1), except with probability negligible in κ.*
- ***Security of Π_{ada}:*** *The protocol Π_{ada} is safe and live in the setting (M2, U2), except with probability negligible in κ.*
- ***Nested Protocols:*** *At any time t, the set of blocks confirmed by Π_{ada} is a superset of the set of blocks confirmed by Π_{fin} in all settings.*

We provide a proof sketch for Theorem 1 below. A detailed proof is relegated to Appendices B and C of the full version of our paper [23].

Proof Sketch. Our proof for Theorem 1 can be split into two parts. First, Appendix B of the full version [23], we show that our checkpointing protocol Π_{BA} satisfies the four checkpointing properties given in Sect. 4, namely **CP0, CP1, CP2, CP3**. Then, in Appendix C of the full version [23], we show that our complete protocol Π_{CLC} satisfies the desired security properties if it uses *any* sub-protocol for checkpointing that satisfies the above properties.

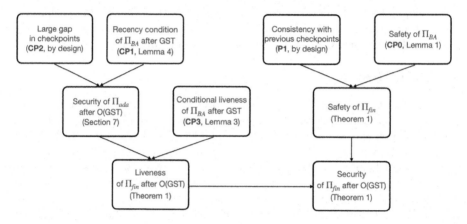

Fig. 3. Flowchart for proving the security property of Π_{fin} under setting $(M1, U1)$

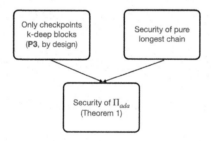

Fig. 4. Flowchart for proving the security property of Π_{ada} under setting $(M2, U2)$

We first highlight some aspects of Theorem 1 that are straightforward to deduce, assuming that Π_{BA} does satisfy the aforementioned properties.

Firstly, the safety of Π_{fin} under setting $(M1, U1)$ can be deduced from two facts: 1) (**CP0**) safety of Π_{BA} holds under setting $(M1, U1)$, and 2) (**P1**) the checkpointed longest chain rule respects all previous checkpoints (see Fig. 3). Specially, **CP0** of Π_{BA} ensure that all checkpoints are uniquely decided by all honest nodes and they lie on a single chain by **P1**, while the checkpointed longest chain protocol instructs honest nodes to always adopt the longest chain with the last checkpoint block. Therefore, an honest node will always keep every checkpoint block it has seen forever.

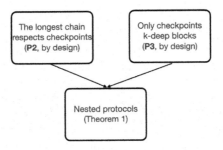

Fig. 5. Flowchart for proving the nesting property of Π_{fin} and Π_{ada}

Secondly, the security of Π_{ada} under setting (M2, U2) are deduced by two facts: 1) security of pure longest chain rule; 2) (**P3**) the checkpointing protocol respects the k-deep rule (see Fig. 4). **P3** ensures that every checkpoint must be at least k-deep in the chain of some honest node when it is decided by Π_{BA}, while a block that is k-deep should remain in the longest chain of all honest nodes forever with high probability under synchrony [9,20,22]. Therefore, every checkpoint will already be present in all honest nodes' chains when it appears. Thus, the chains held by the nodes of the protocol are indistinguishable from the case where they are following the pure longest chain protocol. Given that the confirmation rule is also the same for both protocols (k-deep rule), Π_{ada} inherits the safety and liveness properties of the pure longest chain protocol.

Thirdly, the nesting property of the confirmed blocks also follow immediately by design, given that any checkpointed block must have been already k-deep in a node's chain (**P3**) and the checkpointed longest chain is defined as the longest chain that contains the latest checkpoint (**P2**), (see Fig. 5).

It remains to prove the liveness guarantee of Π_{fin} under setting (M1, U1). In Appendix B (see full version [23]), we evaluate the safety and liveness of our checkpointing protocol Π_{BA} – a modified version of Algorand BA. We show that it satisfies the desired checkpointing properties listed in Sect. 1. A distinguishing property of Π_{BA} is the recency condition (**CP1**). This property states that Π_{BA} only outputs checkpoints that are recently contained in some honest node's chain. Without this property, the adversary could make all honest nodes waste a long time mining on a chain that will never be checkpointed.

In Appendix C (see full version [23]), we prove an important result of Π_{ada} under partial synchronous model: the safety and liveness property will hold after $O(\text{GST})$ time. This is essential to guarantee the liveness of Π_{fin} as a block can be only checkpointed when it lies in the k-common prefix of the checkpointed longest chains of all honest nodes. Finally, combining all these results (see Fig. 3), we show that Π_{fin} is live after $O(\text{GST})$ time with high probability, Thereby completing the proof of the main theorem.

6   Conclusion

In this paper, we presented the design of a new finality gadget, to be used with Proof-of-Work blockchains. The proposed gadget provides each user a choice between an adaptivity guaranteeing confirmation rule and a finality guaranteeing one. This paper underscores the fact that it is possible to circumvent the impossibility result suggested by the CAP theorem by appropriately combining the longest-chain protocol with a committee-based BFT protocol. However, this paper is only a first step towards designing a viable protocol. Several interesting directions of research remain open, which we highlight below.

In our protocol, we used Algorand BA as our checkpointing protocol since it satisfies properties **CP0–CP3**. Other natural candidates, such as PBFT [4], Hotstuff [25] and Streamlet [5] do not satisfy these properties. In particular, they do not satisfy the recency condition **CP1** (we elaborate on this in Appendix D of the full version [23]). It would be interesting to see whether these conditions are necessary, or merely required for the proof. In the latter case, many more BFT protocols could be used for checkpointing.

We have shown that our protocol is essentially a finality gadget, just as Afgjort [10], GRANDPA [24] and Gasper [3]. Through Fig. 2, it we have shown how some of these protocols could be tweaked to enhance their functionality to the level of the protocol we have designed. Formally analyzing the security of GRANDPA, and tweaking Gasper to make it secure (with a formal proof) are interesting open problems that could be tackled using the tools of this paper.

Finality gadgets/checkpointing could potentially offer many more properties. For example, they could protect against a dishonest mining majority, as shown in [15]. They could potentially also be used to have lower latency, and even responsive confirmation of blocks. Designing a protocol that achieves these properties in addition to the ones we show is an exciting design problem. Designing an incentive-compatible finality gadget also remains an open problem. Finally, a system implementation of such protocols could lead to newer considerations, such as communication complexity, latency, which would pave the way for future research.

Acknowledgements. This research is supported in part by a gift from IOHK Inc., an Army Research Office grant W911NF1810332 and by the National Science Foundation under grants CCF 17-05007 and CCF 19-00636.

Appendix

A   Algorand BA is a Checkpointing Protocol

We outline the full Algorand Byzantine Agreement (BA) protocol below for completeness. A minor modification (marked in red), adding validation, is the only addition to the original protocol. Honest checkpointers run a multi-iteration BA to commit checkpoints. The goal of the i-th iteration is to achieve consensus on the i-th checkpoint. Each iteration is divided into multiple periods and view changes will happen across periods.

All checkpointers start period 1 of iteration 1 at the same time (time 0). Checkpointer i starts period 1 of iteration n after it receives $2t + 1$ cert-votes for some value v for the same period p of iteration $n - 1$ and waits for another fixed time e, and only if it has not yet started an iteration $n' > n$. Checkpointer i starts period $p \geq 2$ of iteration n after it receives $2t + 1$ next-votes for some value v for period $p - 1$ of iteration n, and only if it has not yet started a period $p' > p$ for the same iteration n, or some iteration $n' > n$. For any iteration n, checkpointer i sets its starting value for period $p \geq 2$, st_i^p, to v (the value for which $2t + 1$ next-votes were received and based on which the new period was started). For $p = 1$, $st_i^1 = \perp$. The moment checkpointer i starts period p of iteration n, he finishes all previous periods and iterations and resets a local timer $clock_i$ to 0. At the beginning of every period, every honest checkpointer i sets v_i to be the checkpointed longest chain in its view at that time.

Each period has a unique leader known to all checkpointers. The leader is assigned in an i.i.d. fashion by the permitter oracle O. Each checkpointer i keeps a timer $clock_i$ which it resets to 0 every time it starts a new period. As long as i remains in the same period, $clock_i$ keeps counting. Recall that we assume the checkpointers' individual timers have the same speed. In each period, an honest checkpointer executes the following instructions step by step.

Step 1: [Value Proposal by leader]. The leader of the period does the following when $clock_i = 0$; the rest do nothing. If $(p = 1)$ OR $((p \geq 2)$ AND (the leader has received $2t + 1$ next-votes for $\perp$ for period $p - 1$ of iteration $n))$, then it proposes its value v_i. Else if $((p \geq 2)$ AND (the leader has received $2t + 1$ next-votes for some value $v \neq \perp$ for period $p - 1$ of iteration $n))$, then the leader proposes v.

Step 2: [The Filtering Step]. Checkpointer i does the following when $clock_i = 2\Delta$. If $(p = 1)$ OR $((p \geq 2)$ AND (i has received $2t + 1$ next-votes for $\perp$ for period $p - 1$ of iteration $n))$, then i soft-votes the value v proposed by the leader of current period if (it hears of it) AND (the value is VALID OR i has received $2t + 1$ next-votes for v for period $p - 1$). Else if $((p \geq 2)$ AND (i has received $2t + 1$ next-votes for some value $v \neq \perp$ for period $p - 1$ of iteration $n))$, then i soft-votes v.

Step 3: [The Certifying Step]. Checkpointer i does the following when $clock_i \in (2\Delta, 4\Delta)$. If i sees $2t + 1$ soft-votes for some value $v \neq \perp$, then i cert-votes v.

Step 4: [The Period's First Finishing Step]. Checkpointer i does the following when $clock_i = 4\Delta$. If i has certified some value v for period p, he next-votes v. Else if ($(p \geq 2)$ AND (i has seen $2t + 1$ next-votes for $\perp$ for period $p - 1$ of iteration $n))$, he next-votes $\perp$. Else he next-votes his starting value st_i^p.

Step 5: [The Period's Second Finishing Step]. Checkpointer i does the following when $clock_i \in (4\Delta, \infty)$ until he is able to finish period p. If i sees $2t + 1$

soft-votes for some value $v \neq \bot$ for period p, then i next-votes v. If $((p \geq 2)$ AND (i sees $2t + 1$ next-votes for $\bot$ for period $p - 1$) AND (i has not certified in period p)), then i next-votes $\bot$.

Halting condition: Checkpointer i HALTS current iteration if he sees $2t + 1$ cert-votes for some value v for the same period p, and sets v to be his output. Those cert-votes form a certificate for v. The block that is exactly k-deep in v is chosen as the checkpoint in current iteration.

A proposed value v (with block B being exactly k-deep in it) from period p of iteration n is VALID for checkpointer i (in the same period and iteration) if:

- Value v is proposed by the leader of that period;
- Block B is a descendant of all previously checkpointed blocks with smaller iteration number;
- Block B is contained in the checkpointed longest chain that the checkpointer i holds when entering period p.

The only modification to the protocol is in Step 2, in the first condition, where the notion of validity is introduced. This is the only place where new proposals are considered. The validity notion helps transform the Algorand BA protocol into the multi-iteration checkpointing protocol that we desire. In Appendix B (see full version [23]), we show that this protocol indeed satisfies properties **CP0–CP3**, as mentioned in Sect. 4.

References

1. Bagaria, V., Kannan, S., Tse, D., Fanti, G., Viswanath, P.: Prism: deconstructing the blockchain to approach physical limits. In: Proceedings of the 2019 ACM SIGSAC Conference on Computer and Communications Security, pp. 585–602 (2019)
2. Buterin, V., Griffith, V.: Casper the friendly finality gadget. arXiv preprint arXiv:1710.09437 (2017)
3. Buterin, V., et al.: Combining GHOST and Casper. arXiv preprint arXiv:2003.03052 (2020)
4. Castro, M., Liskov, B.: Practical byzantine fault tolerance. In: Proceedings of the Third Symposium on Operating Systems Design and Implementation, OSDI 1999, USA, pp. 173–186. USENIX Association (1999)
5. Chan, B.Y., Shi, E.: Streamlet: textbook streamlined blockchains. IACR Cryptol. ePrint Arch. **2020**, 88 (2020)
6. Chen, J., Gorbunov, S., Micali, S., Vlachos, G.: Algorand agreement: super fast and partition resilient byzantine agreement. IACR Cryptol. ePrint Arch. **2018**, 377 (2018)
7. Chen, J., Micali, S.: Algorand. arXiv preprint arXiv:1607.01341 (2016)
8. Daian, P., Pass, R., Shi, E.: Snow White: robustly reconfigurable consensus and applications to provably secure proof of stake. In: Goldberg, I., Moore, T. (eds.) FC 2019. LNCS, vol. 11598, pp. 23–41. Springer, Cham (2019). https://doi.org/10.1007/978-3-030-32101-7_2
9. Dembo, A., et al.: Everything is a race and Nakamoto always wins. arXiv preprint arXiv:2005.10484 (2020). To appear in CCS 2020

10. Dinsdale-Young, T., Magri, B., Matt, C., Nielsen, J.B., Tschudi, D.: Afgjort: a partially synchronous finality layer for blockchains. In: Security and Cryptography for Networks (SCN) (2020)
11. Fitzi, M., Gazi, P., Kiayias, A., Russell, A.: Parallel chains: improving throughput and latency of blockchain protocols via parallel composition. IACR Cryptol. ePrint Arch. **2018**, 1119 (2018)
12. Garay, J., Kiayias, A., Leonardos, N.: The bitcoin backbone protocol: analysis and applications. In: Oswald, E., Fischlin, M. (eds.) EUROCRYPT 2015. LNCS, vol. 9057, pp. 281–310. Springer, Heidelberg (2015). https://doi.org/10.1007/978-3-662-46803-6_10
13. Gilbert, S., Lynch, N.: Brewer's conjecture and the feasibility of consistent, available, partition-tolerant web services. ACM SIGACT News **33**(2), 51–59 (2002)
14. Gilbert, S., Lynch, N.: Perspectives on the cap theorem. Computer **45**(2), 30–36 (2012)
15. Karakostas, D., Kiayias, A.: Securing proof-of-work ledgers via checkpointing. Cryptology ePrint Archive, Report 2020/173 (2020). https://eprint.iacr.org/2020/173
16. Lewis-Pye, A., Roughgarden, T.: Resource pools and the cap theorem. arXiv preprint arXiv:2006.10698 (2020)
17. Malkhi, D., Nayak, K., Ren, L.: Flexible byzantine fault tolerance. In: Proceedings of the 2019 ACM SIGSAC Conference on Computer and Communications Security, pp. 1041–1053 (2019)
18. Nakamoto, S.: Bitcoin: a peer-to-peer electronic cash system. Technical Report
19. Neu, J., Tas, E.N., Tse, D.: Ebb-and-flow protocols: a resolution of the availability-finality dilemma. arXiv preprint arXiv:2009.04987 (2020)
20. Pass, R., Seeman, L., Shelat, A.: Analysis of the blockchain protocol in asynchronous networks. In: Coron, J.-S., Nielsen, J.B. (eds.) EUROCRYPT 2017. LNCS, vol. 10211, pp. 643–673. Springer, Cham (2017). https://doi.org/10.1007/978-3-319-56614-6_22
21. Pass, R., Shi, E.: Hybrid consensus: efficient consensus in the permissionless model. In: 31st International Symposium on Distributed Computing (DISC) (2017)
22. Ren, L.: Analysis of Nakamoto consensus. IACR Cryptol. ePrint Arch. (2019)
23. Sankagiri, S., Wang, X., Kannan, S., Viswanath, P.: Blockchain cap theorem allows user-dependent adaptivity and finality. arXiv preprint arXiv:2010.13711 (2020)
24. Stewart, A., Kokoris-Kogias, E.: GRANDPA: a byzantine finality gadget. arXiv preprint arXiv:2007.01560 (2020)
25. Yin, M., Malkhi, D., Reiter, M.K., Gueta, G.G., Abraham, I.: HotStuff: BFT consensus with linearity and responsiveness. In: Proceedings of the 2019 ACM Symposium on Principles of Distributed Computing, pp. 347–356 (2019)

PoSAT: Proof-of-Work Availability and Unpredictability, Without the Work

Soubhik Deb[1(✉)], Sreeram Kannan[1], and David Tse[2]

[1] University of Washington, Seattle, USA
{soubhik,ksreeram}@uw.edu
[2] Stanford University, Stanford, USA
dntse@stanford.edu

Abstract. An important feature of Proof-of-Work (PoW) blockchains is full dynamic availability, allowing miners to go online and offline while requiring only 50% of the online miners to be honest. Existing Proof-of-stake (PoS), Proof-of-Space and related protocols are able to achieve this property only partially, either requiring the additional assumption that adversary nodes are online from the beginning and no new adversary nodes come online afterwards, or use additional trust assumptions for newly joining nodes. We propose a new PoS protocol PoSAT which can provably achieve dynamic availability fully without any additional assumptions. The protocol is based on the longest chain and uses a Verifiable Delay Function for the block proposal lottery to provide an arrow of time. The security analysis of the protocol draws on the recently proposed technique of Nakamoto blocks as well as the theory of branching random walks. An additional feature of PoSAT is the complete unpredictability of who will get to propose a block next, even by the winner itself. This unpredictability is at the same level of PoW protocols, and is stronger than that of existing PoS protocols using Verifiable Random Functions.

1 Introduction

1.1 Dynamic Availability

Nakamoto's invention of Bitcoin [26] in 2008 brought in the novel concept of a permissionless Proof-of-Work (PoW) consensus protocol. Following the longest chain protocol, a block can be proposed and appended to the tip of the blockchain if the miner is successful in solving the hash puzzle. The Bitcoin protocol has several interesting features as a consensus protocol. An important one is *dynamic availability*. Bitcoin can handle an uncertain and dynamic varying level of consensus participation in terms of mining power. Miners can join and leave as desired without any registration requirement. This is in contrast to most classical Byzantine Fault Tolerant (BFT) consensus protocols, which assumes a fixed and known number of consensus nodes. Indeed, Bitcoin has been continuously available since the beginning, a period over which the hashrate has varied over a range of 14 orders of magnitude. Bitcoin has been proven to be secure as long

© International Financial Cryptography Association 2021
N. Borisov and C. Diaz (Eds.): FC 2021, LNCS 12675, pp. 104–128, 2021.
https://doi.org/10.1007/978-3-662-64331-0_6

as the attacker has less than 50% of the online hash power (the static power case is considered in [18, 26, 27] and variable hashing power case is considered in [19, 20]).

Recently proof-of-stake (PoS) protocols have emerged as an energy-efficient alternative to PoW. Instead of solving a difficult hash puzzle, nodes participate in a lottery to win the right to append a block to the blockchain, with the probability of winning proportional to a node's stake in the total pool. This replaces the resource intense mining process of PoW, while ensuring fair chances to contribute and claim rewards.

There are broadly two classes of PoS protocols: those derived from classical BFT protocols and those inspired by Nakamoto's longest chain protocol. Attempts at blockchain design via the BFT approach include Algorand [9, 21], Tendermint [7] and Hotstuff [36]. Motivated and inspired by Nakamoto longest chain protocol are the PoS designs of Snow White [4] and the Ouroboros family of protocols [2, 11, 22]. One feature that distinguish the PoS longest chain protocols from the BFT protocols is that they inherit the dynamic availability of Bitcoin: the chain always grows regardless of the number of nodes online. But do these PoS longest chain protocols provide the same level of security guarantee as PoW Bitcoin in the dynamic setting?

1.2 Static vs Dynamic Adversary

Two particular papers focus on the problem of dynamic availability in PoS protocols: the sleepy model of consensus [29] and Ouroboros Genesis [2]. In both papers, it was proved that their protocols are secure if less than 50% of the online nodes are adversary. This condition is the same as the security guarantee in PoW Bitcoin, but there is an additional assumption: *all adversary nodes are always online starting from genesis and no new adversary nodes can join.* While this static adversary assumption seems reasonable (why would an adversary go to sleep?), in reality this can be a very restrictive condition. In the context of Bitcoin, this assumption would be analogous to the statement that the hash power of the adversary is fixed in the past decade (while the total hashing power increased 14 orders of magnitude!) More generally, in public blockchains, PoW or PoS, no node is likely to be adversarial during the launch of a new blockchain token - adversaries only begin to emerge later during the lifecycle.

The static adversary assumption underlying these PoS protocols is not superfluous but is in fact *necessary* for their security. Suppose for the 1st year of the existence of the PoS-based blockchain, only 10% of the total stake is online. Out of this, consider that all nodes are honest. Now, at the beginning of the 2nd year, all 100% of the stake is online out of which 20% is held by adversary. At any point of time, the fraction of online stake held by honest nodes is greater than 0.8. However, both Sleepy and Genesis are not secure since the adversary can use its 20% stake to immediately participate in all past lotteries to win blocks all the way back to the genesis and then grow a chain *instantaneously* from the genesis to surpass the current longest chain (Fig. 1(a)). Thus, due to this "costless simulation", newly joined adversary nodes not only increase the current online adversary stake, but effectively increase past online adversary stake as well. See Appendix A.3 in the full version [12] for further details on how costless simulation renders both sleepy model of consensus and Ouroboros Genesis vulnerable to attacks. In contrast, PoW does not suffer from the same issue because it would take a long time to grow such a chain from the past and that chain will always be behind the current longest chain. Thus, PoW provides an *arrow of time*, meaning nodes cannot "go back in time" to mine blocks for the times at which they were not online. This property is key in endowing PoW protocols with the ability to tolerate fully dynamic adversaries wherein both honest nodes and adversary can have varying participation (Fig. 1(b)).

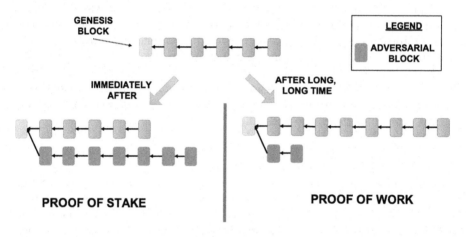

Fig. 1. (a) Newly joined nodes in existing PoS protocols can grow a chain from genesis instantaneously. (b) Newly joined miners in PoW protocol takes a long time to grow such a chain and is always behind.

We point out that some protocols including Ouroboros Praos [11] and Snowhite [4] require that nodes discard chains that fork off too much from the present chain. This feature was introduced to handle nodes with expired stake (or nodes that can perform key grinding) taking over the longest chain. While they did not specifically consider the dynamic adversary issue we highlighted, relying on previous checkpoints can potentially solve the aforementioned security threat. However, as was eloquently argued in Ouroboros Genesis [2], these checkpoints are unavailable to offline clients and newly joining nodes require advice from a trusted party (or a group inside which a majority is trusted). This trust assumption is too onerous to satisfy in practice and is not required in PoW. Ouroboros Genesis was designed to require no trusted joining assumption while being secure to long-range and key-grinding attacks. However, they are not secure against dynamic participation by the adversary: they are vulnerable to the aforementioned attack. This opens the following question:

Is there a fully dynamically available PoS protocol which has full PoW secu-rity guarantee, without additional trust assumptions?

1.3 PoSAT **Achieves PoW Dynamic Availability**

We answer the aforementioned question in the affirmative. Given that arrow-of-time is a central property of PoW protocols, we design a new PoS protocol, PoS with Arrow-of-Time (PoSAT), also having this property using randomness generated from Verifiable Delay Functions (VDF). VDFs are built on top of iteratively sequential functions, i.e., functions that are only computable sequen-tially: $f^\ell(x) = f \circ f \circ ... \circ f(x)$, along with the ability to provide a short and easily verifiable proof that the computed output is correct. Examples of such functions include (repeated) squaring in a finite group of unknown order [8,32], i.e., $f(x) = 2^x$ and (repeated) application of secure hash function (SHA-256) [24], i.e., $f(x) = \text{HASH}(x)$. While VDFs have been designed as a way for prov-ing the passage of a certain amount of time (assuming a bounded CPU speed), it has been recently shown that these functions can also be used to generate an unpredictable randomness beacon [15]. Thus, running the iteration till the random time L when $\text{RANDVDF}(x) = f^L(x) < \tau$ is within a certain threshold will result in L being a geometric random variable. We will incorporate this randomized VDF functionality to create an arrow-of-time in our protocol.

The basic idea of our protocol is to mimic the PoW lottery closely: instead of using the solution of a Hash puzzle based on the parent block's hash as proof of work, we instead use the randomized VDF computed based on the parent block randomness and the coin's public key as the proof of stake lot-tery. In a PoW system, we are required to find a string called "nonce" such that $\text{HASH}(\text{block}, \text{nonce}) < \tau$, a hash-threshold. Instead in our PoS system, we require $\text{RANDVDF}(\text{randSource}, pk, \text{slot}) < \tau$, where randSource is the ran-domness from the parent block, pk is the public key associated with the mining coin and slot represents the number of iterations of the RANDVDF since gene-sis. There are four differences, the first three are common in existing PoS systems: (1) we use "randSource" instead of "block" in order to prevent grinding attacks on the content in the PoS system, (2) we use the public-key "pk" of staking coin instead of PoW "nonce" to simulate a PoS lottery, (3) we use "slot" for ensur-ing time-ordering, (4) instead of using a HASH, we use the RANDVDF, which requires sequential function evaluation thus creating an "arrow of time".

The first two aspects are common to many PoS protocols and is most similar to an earlier PoS protocol [16], however, crucially we use the RANDVDF function instead of a Verifiable random function (VRF) and a time parameter inside the argument used in that protocol. This change allows for full dynamic availability: if adversaries join late, they cannot produce a costless simulation of the time that they were not online and build a chain from genesis instantaneously. It will take the adversary time to grow this chain (due to the sequential nature of the RANDVDF), by which time, the honest chain would have grown and the adversary will be unable to catch up. Thus, PoSAT behaves more like PoW (Fig. 1(b)) rather than existing PoS based on VRF's (Fig. 1(a)). We show that this protocol achieves full dynamic availability: if $\lambda_h(t)$ denotes the honest stake online at t, $\lambda_a(t)$ denotes the online adversarial stake at time t, it is secure as long as

$$\lambda_h(t) > e\lambda_a(t) \qquad \text{for all } t, \tag{1}$$

where e is Euler's number $2.7182\ldots$.

We observe that the security of this protocol requires a stronger condition than PoW protocols. The reason for this is that an adversary can potentially do parallel evaluation of VDF on *all* possible blocks. Since the randomness in each of the blocks is independent from each other, the adversary has many random chances to increase the chain growth rate to out-compete the honest tree. This is a consequence of the nothing-at-stake phenomenon: the same stake can be used to grind on the many blocks. The factor e is the resulting amplification factor for the adversary growth rate. This is avoided in PoW protocols due to the conservation of work inherent in PoW which requires the adversary to split its total computational power among such blocks.

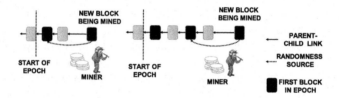

Fig. 2. Left: A node uses randomness from the first block of the epoch. Right: Since a node already won a block in the period, it uses that block's randomness.

We solve this problem in PoSAT by reducing the rate at which the block randomness is updated and hence reducing the block randomness grinding opportunities of the adversary. Instead of updating the block randomness at every level of the blocktree, we only update it once every c levels (called an epoch). The larger the value of the parameter c, the slower the block randomness is updated. The common source of randomness used to run the VDF lottery remains the same for c blocks starting from the genesis and is updated only when (a) the current block to be generated is at a depth that is a multiple of c, or (b) the coin used for the lottery is successful within the epoch of size c. The latter condition is necessary to create further independent winning opportunities for the node within the period c once a slot is obtained with that coin. This is illustrated in Fig. 2. For $c = 1$, this corresponds to the protocol discussed earlier.

The following security theorem is proved about PoSAT for general c, giving a condition for security (liveness and persistence) under *all* possible attacks.

Theorem 1 (Informal). PoSAT with parameter c is secure as long as

$$\frac{\lambda_h^c(t)}{1 + \lambda_{\max}\Delta} > \phi_c\lambda_a(t) \qquad \text{for all } t, \tag{2}$$

where $\lambda_h^c(t)$ is the honest stake this is online at time t and has been online since at least $t - \Theta(c)$, Δ is the network delay between honest nodes, $\lambda_{\max}$ is a constant such that $\lambda_h^c(t) \leq \lambda_{\max}$ for all $t > 0$, ϕ_c is a constant, dependent on c. $\phi_1 = e$ and $\phi_c \to 1$ as $c \to \infty$.

Table 1. Numerically computed values of the adversary amplification factor ϕ_c. The ratio $1/(1 + \phi_c)$ is the adversarial fraction of stake that can be tolerated by PoSAT when $\Delta = 0$.

c	1	2	3	4	5	6	7	8	9	10
ϕ_c	e	2.22547	2.01030	1.88255	1.79545	1.73110	1.68103	1.64060	1.60705	1.57860
$\frac{1}{1+\phi_c}$	$\frac{1}{1+e}$	0.31003	0.33219	0.34691	0.35772	0.36615	0.37299	0.37870	0.38358	0.38780

We remark that in our PoS protocol, we have a known upper bound on the rate of mining blocks (by assuming that the entire stake is online). We can use this information to set $1 + \lambda_{\max}\Delta$ as close to 1 as desired by simply setting the mining threshold appropriately. Furthermore, by setting c large, $\phi_c \approx 1$ and thus PoSAT can achieve the same security threshold as PoW under full dynamic availability. The constant ϕ_c is the amplification of the adversarial chain growth rate due to nothing-at-stake, which we calculate using the theory of branching random walks [33]. The right hand side of (2) can therefore be interpreted as the growth rate of a private adversary tree with the adversary mining on every block. Hence, condition (2) can be interpreted as the condition that the private Nakamoto attack [26] does not succeed. However, Theorem 1 is a *security theorem*, i.e. it gives a condition under which the protocol is secure under *all* possible attacks. Hence what Theorem 1 says is therefore that among all possible attacks on PoSAT, the private attack is the *worst* attack. We prove this by using the technique of blocktree partitioning and Nakamoto blocks, introduced in [13], which reduce all attacks to a union of private attacks.

We note that large c is beneficial from the point of view of getting a tight security threshold. However, we do require c to be finite (unlike other protocols like Ouroboros that continue to work under c being infinite). This is because the latency to confirm a transaction increases linearly in c (see Sect. 4). Furthermore, an honest node on coming online has to wait until encountering the next epoch beginning before it can participate in proposing blocks and the worst-case waiting time increases linearly with c. We note that the adversary cannot use the stored blocks in the next epoch, thus having a bounded reserve of blocks. The total number of blocks stored up by an adversary potentially increases linearly in the epoch size, thus requiring the confirmation depth and thus latency to be larger than $\Theta(c)$. By carefully bounding this enhanced power of the adversary, for any finite c, we show that PoSAT is secure.

Assuming $\lambda_{\max}\Delta$ to be small, the comparison of PoSAT with other protocols is shown in following Table. Here we use Λ_a to be the largest adversary fraction of the total stake online at any time during the execution ($\Lambda_a = \sup_t \lambda_a(t)$). Protocols whose security guarantee assumes all adversary nodes are online all the time effectively assumes that $\lambda_h(t) > \Lambda_a$. Thus existing protocols have limited dynamic availability.

	Ourboros	Snow White/Praos	Genesis/Sleepy	Algorand	PoSAT
Dynamic availability	$\lambda_h(t) > \Lambda_a$	$\lambda_h(t) > \Lambda_a$	$\lambda_h(t) > \Lambda_a$	No	$\lambda_h^c(t) > \phi_c \lambda_a(t)$
Predictability	Global	Local	Local	Local	None

1.4   PoSAT Has PoW Unpredictability

Another key property of PoW protocols is their ability to be unpredictable: no node (including itself) can know when a given node will be allowed to propose a block ahead of the proposal slot. We point out that PoSAT with any parameter c remains unpredictable due to the unpredictability of the RandVDF till the threshold is actually reached. We refer the reader to Fig. 2(a) where if the randomness source is at the beginning of the epoch it is clear that the unpredictability of the randomized VDF implies unpredictability in our protocol. However, in case the miner has already created a block within the epoch (Fig. 2(b)), the randomness source is now her previous block. This can be thought of as a continuation of the iterative sequential function from the beginning of the epoch and hence it is also unpredictable as to when the function value will fall below a threshold. Thus PoSAT achieves true unpredictability, matching the PoW gold standard, where even an all-knowing adversary has no additional predictive power.

The first wave of PoS protocols such as Ouroboros [22] are fully predictable as they rely on mechanisms for proposer election that provide global knowledge of all proposers in an epoch ahead of time. The concept of Verifiable Random Functions (VRF), developed in [14,25], was pioneered in the blockchain context in Algorand [9,21], as well as applied in Ouroboros Praos [11] and Snow White [4]. The use of a private leader election using VRF enables no one else other than the proposer to know of the slots when it is allowed to propose blocks. However, unlike Bitcoin, the proposer itself can predict. Thus, these protocols still allow *local* predictability. The following vulnerability is caused by local predictability: a rational node may then willingly sell out his slot to an adversary. In Ouroboros Praos, such an all-knowing adversary needs to corrupt only 1 user at a time (the proposer) adaptively in order to do a double-spend attack. He will first let the chain build for some time to confirm a transaction, and then get the bribed proposers one at a time to build a competing chain. Algorand is more resilient, but even there, in each step of the BFT algorithm, a different committee of nodes is selected using a VRF based sortition algorithm. These nodes are locally predictable as soon as the previous block is confirmed by the BFT - and thus an all-knowing adversary only needs to corrupt a third of a committee. Assuming each committee is comprised of K nodes (K being a constant), the adversary only needs to corrupt $\frac{K}{3N}$ fraction of the nodes. Refer to Appendix A.4 in [12] for further details.

We summarize the predictability of various protocols in Table 1.

1.5   Related Work

Our design is based on frequent updates of randomness to run the VDF lottery. PoS protocols that update randomness at each iteration have been utilized in practice as well as theoretically proposed [16] - they do not use VDF and have **neither** dynamic availability nor unpredictability. Furthermore, they still face nothing-at-stake attacks. In fact, the amplification factor of e we discussed earlier has been first observed in a Nakamoto private attack analysis in [16]. This analysis was subsequently extended to a full security analysis against *all* attacks in [13,34], where it was shown that the private attack is actually the worst attack. In [34], the idea of c-correlation was introduced to reduce the rate of randomness update and to reduce the severity of the nothing-at-stake attack; we borrowed this idea from them in the design of our VDF-based protocol, PoSAT.

There have been attempts to integrate VDF into the proof-of-space paradigm [10] as well as into the proof-of-stake paradigm [1,23], all using a VRF concatenated with a VDF. But, in [10], the VDF runs for a fixed duration depending on the input and hence is predictable, and furthermore do not have security proofs for dynamic availability. In [1], the randomness beacon is not secure till the threshold of $1/2$ as claimed by the authors since it has a randomness grinding attack which can potentially expand the adverarial power by at least factor e. There are three shortcomings in [23] as compared to our paper: (1) even under static participation, they only focus on an attack where an adversary grows a private chain, (2) there is no modeling of dynamic availability and a proof of security and (3) since the protocol focuses only on $c = 1$, they can only achieve security till threshold $1/1 + e$, not till $1/2$. We note that recent work [6] formalized that a broad class of PoS protocols suffer from either of the two vulnerabilities: (a) use recent randomness, thus being subject to nothing-at-stake attacks or (b) use old randomness, thus being subject to prediction based attacks (even when only locally predictable). We note that PoSAT with large c completely circumvents both vulnerabilities using the additional VDF primitive since it is able to use old randomness while still being fully unpredictable.

We want to point out that dynamic availability is distinct and complementary to *dynamic stake*, which implies that the set of participants and their identities in the mining is changing based on the state of the blockchain. We note that there has been much existing work addressing issues on the dynamic stake setting - for example, the s-longest chain rule in [2], whose adaptation to our setting we leave for future work. We emphasize that the dynamic availability problem is well posed even in the static stake setting (the total set of stakeholders is fixed at genesis).

1.6 Outline

The rest of the paper is structured as follows. Section 2 presents the VDF primitive we are using and the overall protocol. Section 3 presents the model. Section 4 presents the details of the security analysis.

2 Protocol

2.1 Primitives

In this section, we give an overview of VDFs and refer the reader to detailed definitions in Appendix B in the full version [12].

Definition 1 (from [5]). *A VDF $V = (\text{SETUP}, \text{EVAL}, \text{VERIFY})$ is a triple of algorithms as follows:*

- $\text{SETUP}(\lambda, \tau) \rightarrow \mathbf{pp} = (ek, vk)$ *is a randomized algorithm that produces an evaluation key ek and a verification key vk.*
- $\text{EVAL}(ek, input, \tau) \rightarrow (O, proof)$ *takes an input $\in \mathcal{X}$, an evaluation key ek, number of steps τ and produces an output $O \in \mathcal{Y}$ and a (possibly empty) proof.*
- $\text{VERIFY}(vk, input, O, proof, \tau) \rightarrow Yes, No$ *is a deterministic algorithm takes an input, output, proof, τ and outputs Yes or No.*

VDF.EVAL is usually comprised of sequential evaluation: $f^{\ell}(x) = f \circ f \circ \dots \circ f(x)$ along with the ability to provide a short and easily verifiable proof. In particular, there are three separate functions VDF.START, VDF.ITERATE and VDF.PROVE (the first function is used to initialize, the second one operates for the number of steps and the third one furnishes a proof). This is illustrated in Fig. 3a on the left. While VDFs have been designed as a way for proving the passage of a certain amount of time, it has been recently shown that these functions can also be used to generate an unpredictable randomness beacon [15]. Thus, running the iteration till the random time L when $\text{RANDVDF}(x) = f^{L}(x) < \tau$ generates the randomness beacon. This is our core transformation to get a randomized VDF. This is shown in Fig. 3b on the right. Instead of running for a fixed number of iterations, we run the VDF iterations till it reaches a certain threshold. Our transformation is relatively general purpose and most VDFs can be used with our construction. For example, a VDF (which is based on squaring in a group of unknown order) is an ideal example for our construction [30,35]. In the recent paper [15], for that sequential function, a new method for obtaining a short proof whose complexity does not depend (significantly) on the number of rounds is introduced - our protocol can utilize that VDF as well. They show furthermore that they obtain a continuous VDF property which implies that partial VDF computation can be continued by a different party - we do not require this additional power in our protocol.

For the RANDVDF in PoSAT, as illustrated in Fig. 3b, `slot` plays a similar role as the timestamps in other PoS protocols like [29]. The `slot` basically mentions the number of times the RANDVDF has iterated since the genesis and when the speed of the iteration of RANDVDF is constant, slot is an approximation to the time elapsed since the beginning of the operation of the PoS system.

Normally, a VDF will satisfy *correctness* and *soundness*. And we require RANDVDF to also satisfy correctness and soundness as defined in Appendix B in [12].

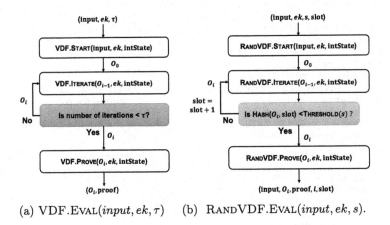

(a) VDF.EVAL($input, ek, \tau$).   (b) RANDVDF.EVAL($input, ek, s$).

Fig. 3. VDF.EVAL($input, ek, \tau$) requires the number of iterations that VDF.ITERATE should run. On the other hand, RANDVDF.EVAL($input, ek, s, slot$) requires the expected number of number of iterations RANDVDF.ITERATE (denoted by s) must run.

A key feature of VDF is that if the VDF takes T steps, then the prover should be able to complete the proof in time (nearly) proportional to T and the verifier should be able to verify the proof in (poly)-logarithmic time. This makes it feasible for any node that receives a block to quickly verify that the VDF in the header is indeed correctly computed, without expending the same effort that was expended by the prover. We refer the reader interested in a detailed analysis of these complexities to Sect. 6.2 in [30] for the efficiency calculation or Sect. 2.3 in [15].

2.2 Protocol Description

The pseudocode for the PoSAT is given in Algorithm 1.

Algorithm 1. PoSAT

1: **procedure** INITIALIZE( )   ▷ all variables are global
2:     blkTree ← SYNC()   ▷ syncing with peers
3:     unCnfTx← ϕ ▷ pool of unconfirmed txs
4:     parentBlk ← blkTree.TIP()   ▷ tip of the longest chain in blkTree
5:     randSource ← None   ▷ will be updated at next epoch beginning
6:     slot ← None   ▷ will be updated at next epoch beginning
7:     **return** False

8: **procedure** POSLEADERELECTION(coin)
9:     (RANDVDF.ek, RANDVDF.vk),(SIGN.vk, SIGN.sk) ← coin.KEYS()
10:     stake ← coin.STAKE(SEARCHCHAINUP(parentBlk))   ▷ update the stake
11:     s ← UPDATETHRESHOLD(stake)   ▷ update the threshold
12:     input ← randSource
13:     // Calling RANDVDF.EVAL
14:     (input, output, proof, randIter, slot) ← RANDVDF.EVAL(input, ek, s, slot)
15:     randSource ← output   ▷ update source of randomness
16:     state ← HASH(parentBlk)
17:     content ← ⟨unCnfTx, coin, input, randSource, proof, randIter, state, slot⟩
18:     **return** ⟨header, content, SIGN(content, SIGN.sk)⟩

19: **procedure** RECEIVEMESSAGE(X)   ▷ receives messages from network
20:     **if** X is a valid tx **then**
21:         unCnfTx ← unCnfTx ∪ {X}
22:     **else if** ISVALIDBLOCK(X) **then**
23:         **if** parentBlk.LEVEL() < X.LEVEL() **then**
24:             CHANGEMAINCHAIN(X)   ▷ if the new chain is longer
25:             parentBlk ← X ▷ update the parent block to tip of the longest chain
26:         **if** X.LEVEL() % c == 0 **then**
27:             randSource ← X.content.randSource
28:         **else**
29:             randSource ← randSource
30:         **if** participate == True **then**
31:             RANDVDF.RESET()   ▷ reset the RANDVDF
32:         // Epoch beginning
33:         **if** (X.LEVEL() % c == 0) & (participate == False) **then**
34:             slot ← X.content.slot
35:             participate = True

36: **procedure** ISVALIDBLOCK(X)   ▷ returns true if a block is valid
37:     **if not** ISUNSPENT(X.content.coin) **then return** False
38:     **if** PARENTBLK(X).content.slot ≥ X.content.slot **then**
39:         **return** False   ▷ ensuring time ordering
40:     s ← UPDATETHRESHOLD(PARENTBLK(X))
41:     **if** HASH(X.content.{randSource, slot}) > THRESHOLD(s) **then return** False
42:     // verifying the work
43:     **return**
44: RANDVDF.VERIFY(X.coin.vk, X.content.{input, randSource, proof, randIter})

45: **procedure** MAIN( )   ▷ main function
46:     participate = INITIALIZE()
47:     STARTTHREAD(RECEIVEMESSAGE)   ▷ parallel thread for receiving messages
48:     **while** True **do**
49:         **if** participate == True **then**
50:             block = POSLEADERELECTION(coin)
51:             SENDMESSAGE(block)   ▷ broadcast to the whole network

---

Initialization. An honest coin n on coming online, calls INITIALIZE() where it obtains the current state of the blockchain, blkTree, by synchronizing with the peers via SYNC() and initializes global variables. However, the coin n can start participating in the leader election only after encountering the next epoch beginning, that is, when the depth of the blkTree is a multiple of c. This is indicated by setting participate$_n$ to False. Observe that if the coin n is immediately allowed to participate in leader election, then, the coin n would have to initiate RANDVDF.EVAL from the randSource contained in the block at the beginning of the current epoch. Due to the sequential computation in RANDVDF, the coin n would never be able to participate in the leader elections for proposing blocks at the tip of the blockchain. In parallel, the coin keeps receiving messages and processes them in RECEIVEMESSAGE(). On receiving a valid block that indicates epoch beginning, randSource$_n$, slot$_n$ and participate$_n$ are updated accordingly (lines 27, 33, 34) for active participation in leader election.

Leader Election. The coin n records the tip of the longest chain of blkTree in parentBlk$_n$ (line 25) and contests leader election for appending block to it. RANDVDF.EVAL(input$_n$, RANDVDF.ek_n, s_n) is used to compute an unpredictable randomness beacon that imparts unpredictability to leader election. The difficulty parameter s_n is set proportional to the current stake$_n$ of the coin n using UPDATETHRESHOLD(stake$_n$) and randSource$_n$ is taken as input$_n$. RANDVDF.EVAL(input$_n$, ek_n, s_n, slot$_n$) is an iterative function composed of:

- RANDVDF.START(input$_n$, RANDVDF.ek_n, IntState$_n$) initializes the iteration by setting initial value of output$_n$ to be input$_n$. Note that IntState$_n$ is the internal state of the RANDVDF.
- RANDVDF.ITERATE(output$_n$, RANDVDF.ek_n, IntState$_n$) is the iterator function that updates output$_n$ in each iteration. At the end of each iteration, it is checked whether HASH(output$_n$, slot$_n$) is less than THRESHOLD(s_n), which is set proportional to s_n. If No, slot$_n$ is incremented by 1 and current output$_n$ is taken as input to the next iteration. If Yes, then it means coin n has won the leader election and output$_n$ is passed as input to RANDVDF.PROVE(.). Observe that the number of iterations, randIter$_n$, that would be required to pass this threshold is unpredictable which lends to randomness beacon. Recall that slot$_n$ is a counter for number of iterations since genesis. In a PoS protocol, it is normally ensured that the timestamps contained in each block of a chain are ordered in ascending order. Here, in PoSAT, instead we ensure that the slot in the blocks of a chain are ordered, irrespective of who proposed it. This is referred to as *time-ordering*. The reader can refer to Appendix A.5 and A.6 in [12] for further details on what attacks can transpire if time-ordering is not ensured. The rationale behind setting THRESHOLD(s_n) proportional to s_n is that even if the stake s_n is sybil over multiple coins, the probability of winning leader election in at least one coin remains the same. See Appendix A.2 in [12] for detailed discussion.

- RANDVDF.PROVE(output$_n$, RANDVDF.ek_n, IntState$_n$)   operates   on output$_n$ using RANDVDF.ek_n and IntState$_n$ to generate proof$_n$ that certifies the iterative computation done in the previous step.

The source of randomness randSource$_n$ can be updated in two ways:

- a block, proposed by another coin, at epoch beginning is received (line 27)
- if coin n wins a leader election and proposes its own block (line 15).

While computing RANDVDF.EVAL(.), if a block is received that updates parentBlk$_n$, then, RANDVDF.RESET() (line 31) pauses the ongoing computation, updates s_n and continues the computation with updated THRESHOLD(s_n). If randSource$_n$ is also updated, then, RANDVDF.RESET() stops the ongoing computation of RANDVDF.EVAL(.) and calls POSLEADERELECTION().

Content of the Block. Once a coin is elected as a leader, all unconfirmed transactions in its buffer are added to the content. The content also includes the identity coin$_n$, input$_n$, randSource$_n$, proof$_n$, randIter$_n$, slot$_n$ from RANDVDF.EVAL(.). The state variable in the content contains the hash of parent block, which ensures that the content of the parent block cannot be altered. Finally, the header and the content is signed with the secure signature SIGN.sk_n and the block is proposed. When the block is received by other coins, they check that the time-ordering is maintained (line 38) and verify the work done by the coin n using RANDVDF.VERIFY(.) (line 44). Note that the leader election is independent of the content of the block and content of previous blocks. This follows a standard practice in existing PoS protocols such as [2] and [29] for ensuring that a grinding attack based on enumerating the transactions won't be possible. The reader is referred to Appendix A.1 in [12] for further details. However, this allows the adversary to create multiple blocks with the same header but different content. Such copies of a block with the same header but different contents are known as a "forkable string" in [22]. We show in the Sect. 4 that the PoSAT is secure against all such variations of attacks.

Confirmation Rule. A block is confirmed if the block is $k-$deep from the tip of the longest chain. The value of k is determined by the security parameter.

3   Model

We will adopt a continuous-time model. Like the Δ-synchronous model in [27], we assume there is a bounded communication delay Δ seconds between the honest nodes (the particular value of latency of any transmission inside this bound is chosen by the adversary).

The blockchain is run on a network of N honest nodes and a set of adversary nodes. Each node holds a certain number of coins (proportional to their stake). We allow nodes to join and leave the network, thus the amount of honest/adversarial stake which is participating in the protocol varies as a function of time. Recall that, as described in Sect. 2, a coin coming online can only participate in the leader election after encountering the next epoch beginning. Let $\lambda_h(t)$ be defined as the stake of the honest coins that are online at time t and has encountered at least one epoch beginning. Thus, $\lambda_h(t)$ is the rate at which honest nodes win leader elections. Let $\lambda_a(t)$ be the stake controlled by the adversary. We will assume there exist constants $\lambda_{\min}, \lambda_{\max} > 0$ such that

$$\lambda_{\min} \leq \lambda_h(t) \leq \lambda_{\max} \quad \forall \quad t \geq 0. \tag{3}$$

The existence of $\lambda_{\max}$ is obvious since we are in a proof-of-stake system, and $\lambda_{\max}$ denotes the rate at which the leader elections are being won if every single stakeholder is online. We need to assume a minimum $\lambda_h(t)$ in order to guarantee that within a bounded time, a new block is created.

An honest node will construct and publicly reveal the block immediately after it has won the corresponding leader election. However, an adversary can choose to not do so. By "private block", we refer to a block whose corresponding computation of RANDVDF.EVAL was completed by the adversary earlier than when the block was made public. Also, by "honest block proposed at time t", we mean that the computation of RANDVDF.EVAL was completed at time t and then the associated honest block was instantaneously constructed and publicly revealed.

The evolution of the blockchain can be modeled as a process $\{(\mathcal{T}(t), \mathcal{C}(t), \mathcal{T}^{(p)}(t), \mathcal{C}^{(p)}(t)) : t \geq 0, 1 \leq p \leq N\}$, N being the number of honest nodes, where:

- $\mathcal{T}(t)$ is a tree, and is interpreted as the *mother tree* consisting of all the blocks that are proposed by both the honest and the adversary nodes up until time t (including private blocks at the adversary).
- $\mathcal{T}^{(p)}(t)$ is an induced (public) sub-tree of the mother tree $\mathcal{T}(t)$ in the view of the p-th honest node at time t.
- $\mathcal{C}^{(p)}(t)$ is the longest chain in the tree $\mathcal{T}^{(p)}(t)$, and is interpreted as the longest chain in the local view of the p-th honest node.
- $\mathcal{C}(t)$ is the common prefix of all the local chains $\mathcal{C}^{(p)}(t)$ for $1 \leq p \leq N$.

The process evolution is as follows.

- **M0**: $\mathcal{T}(0) = \mathcal{T}^{(p)}(0) = \mathcal{C}^{(p)}(0), 1 \leq p \leq N$ is a single root block (genesis).
- **M1**: There is an independent leader election at every epoch beginning, i.e., at every block in the blocktree at level $c, 2c, ..., \ell c, ...$ The leader elections are won by the adversary according to independent Poisson processes of rate $\lambda_a(t)$ at time t, one for every block at the aforementioned levels. The adversary can use the leader election won at a block at level ℓc at time t to propose a block at every block in the next $c - 1$ levels $\ell c, \ell c + 1, ..., \ell c + c - 1$ that are present in the tree $\mathcal{T}(t)$. We refer the reader to Fig. 4 for a visual representation.
- **M2**: Honest blocks are proposed at a total rate of $\lambda_h(t)$ at time t across all the honest nodes at the tip of the chain held by the mining node p, $\mathcal{C}^{(p)}(t)$.

- **M3:** The adversary can replace $T^{(p)}(t^-)$ by another sub-tree $T^{(p)}(t)$ from $T(t)$ as long as the new sub-tree $T^{(p)}(t)$ is an induced sub-tree of the new tree $T^{(p)}(t)$, and can update $C^{(p)}(t^-)$ to a longest chain in $T^{(p)}(t)$.[1]

We highlight the capabilities of the adversary in this model:

- **A1:** Can choose to propose block on multiple blocks of the tree $T(t)$ at any time.
- **A2:** Can delay the communication of blocks between the honest nodes, but no more than Δ time.
- **A3:** Can broadcast private blocks at times of its own choosing: when private blocks are made public at time t to node p, then these blocks are added to $T^{(p)}(t^-)$ to obtain $T^{(p)}(t)$. Note that, under Δ-synchronous model, when private blocks appear in the view of some honest node p, they will also appear in the view of all other honest nodes by time $t + \Delta$.
- **A4:** Can switch the chain where the p-th honest node is proposing block, from one longest chain to another of equal length, even when its view of the tree does not change, i.e., $T^{(p)}(t) = T^{(p)}(t^-)$ but $C^{(p)}(t) \neq C^{(p)}(t^-)$.

It is to be noted that we don't consider the adversary to be *adaptive* in the sense that, although adversarial and honest nodes can join or leave the system as they wish, an adversary can never turn honest nodes adversarial. In order to defend against an adaptive adversary, key evolving signature schemes can be used [11]. However, in order to keep the system simple, we don't consider adaptive adversary.

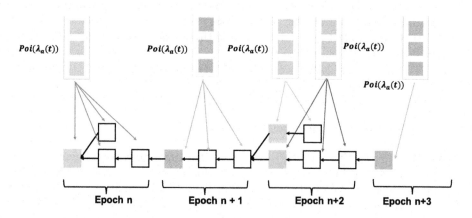

Fig. 4. There is a separate randomness generated for every block in the modulo c position. Blocks generated from that randomness at time t can attach to any block inside the next $c - 1$ blocks that are present in the tree $T(t)$.

---

[1] All jump processes are assumed to be right-continuous with left limits, so that $C(t), T(t)$ etc. include the new arrival if there is a new arrival at time t.

Proving the security (persistence and liveness) of the protocol boils down to providing a guarantee that the chain $\mathcal{C}(t)$ converges fast as $t \to \infty$ and that honest blocks enter regularly into $\mathcal{C}(t)$ regardless of the adversary's strategy.

4   Security Analysis

Our goal is to generate a transaction ledger that satisfies persistence and liveness as defined in [18]. Together, persistence and liveness guarantee robust transaction ledger; honest transactions will be adopted to the ledger and be immutable.

Definition 2 (from [18]). *A protocol* Π *maintains a robust public transaction ledger if it organizes the ledger as a blockchain of transactions and it satisfies the following two properties:*

- *(Persistence) Parameterized by* $\tau \in \mathbb{R}$, *if at a certain time a transaction* tx *appears in a block which is mined more than* τ *time away from the mining time of the tip of the main chain of an honest node (such transaction will be called confirmed), then* tx *will be confirmed by all honest nodes in the same position in the ledger.*
- *(Liveness) Parameterized by* $u \in \mathbb{R}$, *if a transaction* tx *is received by all honest nodes for more than time* u, *then all honest nodes will contain* tx *in the same place in the ledger forever.*

4.1   Main Security Result

To state our main security result, we need to define some basic notations.

Recall that, as described in Sect. 2, a coin coming online can only participate in the leader election after encountering the next epoch beginning. This incurs a random waiting delay for the coin before it can actively participate in the evolution of the blockchain. Hence, the honest mining rate $\lambda_h(t)$, defined in Sect. 3 as the stake of the honest coins that are online at time t and has encountered at least one epoch beginning, is a (random) process that depends on the dynamics of the blockchain. Hence, we cannot state a security result based on conditions on $\lambda_h(t)$. Instead, let us define $\lambda_h^c(t)$ as the stake of the honest coins that are online at time t and has been online since at least time $t - \sigma(c)$, where

$$\sigma(c) = (c - 1) \left(\Delta + \frac{1 + \kappa}{\lambda_{\min}} \right). \tag{4}$$

Here, κ is the security parameter. Intuitively, $\sigma(c)$ is a high-probability worst-case waiting delay, in seconds, of a coin for the next epoch beginning. Note that $\lambda_h^c(t)$ depends only on the stake arrival process and not on the blockchain dynamics.

The theorem below shows that the the private attack threshold yields the true security threshold:

Theorem 1. *If*

$$\frac{\lambda_h^c(t)}{1 + \lambda_{\max}\Delta} > \phi_c\lambda_a(t) \qquad \text{for all } t > 0, \tag{5}$$

then the PoSAT *generate transaction ledgers such that each transaction tx satisfies persistence (parameterized by $\tau = \rho$) and liveness (parameterized by $u = \rho$) in Definition 2 with probability at least $1 - e^{-\Omega(\min\{\rho^{1-\epsilon}, \kappa\})}$, for any $\epsilon > 0$. The constant ϕ_c is dependent on c, with $\phi_1 = e$ and $\phi_c \to 1$ as $c \to \infty$.*

In order to prove Theorem 1, we utilize the concept of blocktree partitioning and Nakamoto blocks that were introduced in [13]. We provide a brief overview of these concepts here.

Let τ_i^h and τ_i^a be the time when the i-th honest and adversary blocks are proposed, respectively; $\tau_0^h = 0$ is the time when the genesis block is proposed, which we consider as the 0-th honest block.

Definition 1. **Blocktree partitioning.** Given the mother tree $\mathcal{T}(t)$, define for the i-th honest block b_i, the *adversary tree* $\mathcal{T}_i(t)$ to be the sub-tree of the mother tree $\mathcal{T}(t)$ rooted at b_i and consists of all the adversary blocks that can be reached from b_i without going through another honest block. The mother tree $\mathcal{T}(t)$ is partitioned into sub-trees $\mathcal{T}_0(t), \mathcal{T}_1(t), \dots \mathcal{T}_j(t)$, where the j-th honest block is the last honest block that was proposed before time t.

The sub-tree $\mathcal{T}_i(t)$ is born at time τ_i^h as a single block b_i and then grows each time an adversary block is appended to a chain of adversary blocks from b_i. Let $D_i(t)$ denote the depth of $\mathcal{T}_i(t)$; $D_i(\tau_i^h) = 0$.

Definition 2 [31]. The j-th honest block proposed at time τ_j^h is called a *loner* if there are no other honest blocks proposed in the time interval $[\tau_j^h - \Delta, \tau_j^h + \Delta]$.

Definition 3. Given honest block proposal times τ_i^h's, define a honest fictitious tree $\mathcal{T}_h(t)$ as a tree which evolves as follows:

1. $\mathcal{T}_h(0)$ is the genesis block.
2. The first honest block to be proposed and all honest blocks within Δ are all appended to the genesis block at their respective proposal times to form the first level.
3. The next honest block to be proposed and all honest blocks proposed within time Δ of that are added to form the second level (which first level blocks are parents to which new blocks is immaterial).
4. The process repeats.

Let $D_h(t)$ be the depth of $\mathcal{T}_h(t)$.

Definition 4 (**Nakamoto block**). Let us define:

$$E_{ij} = \text{event that } D_i(t) < D_h(t - \Delta) - D_h(\tau_i^h + \Delta) \text{ for all } t > \tau_j^h + \Delta. \tag{6}$$

The j-th honest block is called a *Nakamoto block* if it is a loner and

$$F_j = \bigcap_{i=0}^{j-1} E_{ij} \tag{7}$$

occurs.

See Fig. 5 in [13] for illustration of the concepts of blocktree partitioning and Nakamoto blocks.

Lemma 1 *(Theorem 3.2 in [13])* **(Nakamoto blocks stabilize).** *If the j-th honest block is a Nakamoto block, then it will be in the longest chain $\mathcal{C}(t)$ for all $t > \tau_j^h + \Delta$.*

Lemma 1 states that Nakamoto blocks remain in the longest chain forever. The question is whether they exist and appear frequently regardless of the adversary strategy. If they do, then the protocol has liveness and persistence: honest transactions can enter the ledger frequently through the Nakamoto blocks, and once they enter, they remain at a fixed location in the ledger. More formally, we have the following result.

Lemma 2 *(Lemma 4.4 in [13]).* *Define $B_{s,s+t}$ as the event that there is no Nakamoto blocks in the time interval $[s, s+t]$ where $t \sim \Omega\left(\left[\frac{c-1}{\phi_c - 1}\right]^2\right)$. If*

$$P(B_{s,s+t}) < q_t < 1 \tag{8}$$

for some q_t independent of s and the adversary strategy, then the PoSAT *generates transaction ledgers such that each transaction tx satisfies* persistence *(parameterized by $\tau = \rho$) and* liveness *(parameterized by $u = \rho$) in Definition 2 with probability at least $1 - q_\rho$.*

In order to prove Lemma 2, we proceed in six steps as illustrated in Fig. 5.

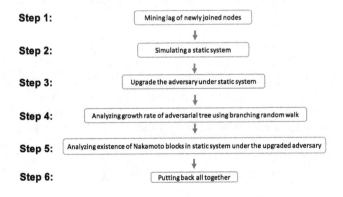

Fig. 5. Flowchart of the proof for Lemma 2.

4.2   Step 1: Mining Lag of Newly Joined Nodes

From Sect. 3, recall that $\lambda_h(t)$ is defined as the stake of the coins that are online at time t but has encountered at least one epoch beginning. That implies, within an epoch, $\lambda_h(t)$ is the effective honest stake that can be used to contribute towards the growth of the longest chain; it remains constant and gets updated only at the epoch beginning. In order to analyze the effect of this lag in a honest node to start mining, we simulate a new dynamic available system, $dyn2$, where, at time t, an honest coin can contribute towards the growth of the longest chain if it has been online in the original dynamic system since at least time $t - \sigma(c)$, where, $\sigma(c) > 0$. Recall that $\lambda_h^c(t)$ be defined as the stake of the coins that are online at time t in the original dynamic system and has been online since at least $t - \sigma(c)$. Clearly, $\lambda_h^c(t)$ is the rate at which the honest nodes win leader election at time t in $dyn2$. We have the following relationship between the original dynamic available system and $dyn2$.

Lemma 3. *For the dynamic available system dyn2 and for all $s, t > 0$, define $B_{s,s+t}^{dyn2}$ as the event that there are no Nakamoto blocks in the time interval $[s, s+t]$. Let κ_0 be the solution for the equation $\ln\left(\frac{\lambda_{\max}}{\lambda_{\min}}(1 + \kappa)\right) = \kappa$. Then, for $\sigma(c) = (c-1)\left(\Delta + \frac{1+\kappa}{\lambda_{\min}}\right)$ and $\kappa \gg \kappa_0$, we have*

$$P(B_{s,s+t}) \leq P(B_{s,s+t}^{dyn2}) + e^{-\Omega(\kappa)}.$$

The proof is given in Appendix C in the full version [12].

4.3   Step 2: Simulating a Static System

Without loss of generality, we assume that the adversarial power is boosted such that $\lambda_a(t)$ satisfies (5) with equality for all t. Let us define η such that $\lambda_a(t) = (1-\eta)\lambda_h(t)$ for all t. Let λ_h be some positive constant. Taking $dyn2$ as the base, we simulate a static system, $ss0$, where both honest nodes and adversary win leader elections with constant rates λ_h and λ_a satisfying $\lambda_a = (1 - \eta)\lambda_h$. This requires, for a local time $t > 0$ in $dyn2$, defining a new local time $\alpha(t)$ for $ss0$ such that

$$\lambda_h^c(u)du = \lambda_h d\alpha \implies \alpha(t) = \int_0^t \frac{\lambda_h^c(u)}{\lambda_h} du. \tag{9}$$

Additionally, for every arrival of an honest or adversarial block in $dyn2$ at a particular level at a tree, there is a corresponding arrival in $ss0$ at the same level in the same tree. For a time t in the local clock of $dyn2$, let $\Delta^{ss0}(t)$ be the network delay of $dyn2$ measured with reference to the local clock of $ss0$. Using (9), we have

$$\frac{\lambda_{\min}}{\lambda_h}\Delta \leq \Delta^{ss0}(t) \leq \frac{\lambda_{\max}}{\lambda_h}\Delta. \tag{10}$$

We have the following relationship between $dyn2$ and $ss0$.

Lemma 4. *Consider the time interval* $[s, s + t]$ *in the local clock of dyn2. For the static system ss0, define* $B^{ss0}_{\alpha(s),\alpha(s+t)}$ *as the event that there are no Nakamoto blocks in the time interval* $[\alpha(s), \alpha(s+t)]$ *in the local clock of ss0. Then,*

$$P(B^{dyn2}_{s,s+t}) = P(B^{ss0}_{\alpha(s),\alpha(s+t)}).$$

The proof for this lemma is given in Appendix D in the full version [12].

4.4   Step 3: Upgrading the Adversary

As the occurrence of Nakamoto blocks is a race between the fictitious honest tree and the adversarial trees from the previous honest blocks, we next turn to an analysis of the growth rate of an adversary tree. However, the growth rate of an adversarial tree would now depend on the location of the root honest block within an epoch which adds to the complexity of the analysis. To get around this complexity, we simulate a new static system, $ss1$ in which the adversary, on winning a leader election after evaluating RANDVDF.EVAL and appending a block to an honest block (that is, growing a new adversarial tree), is given a gift of chain of $c - 1$ extra blocks for which the adversary doesn't have to compute RANDVDF.EVAL. Thus, the adversary has to compute only one RANDVDF.EVAL for the chain of first c blocks in the adversarial tree. At this point, the adversary can assume a new epoch beginning and accordingly update randSource. Hereafter, the evolution of randSource follows the rules in $ss0$. Note that the local clock for both the static systems $ss0$ and $ss1$ are same. Now, we have the following relationship between $ss0$ and $ss1$.

Lemma 5. *Consider the time interval* $[s, s + t]$ *in the local clock of dyn2. For the static system ss1, define* $B^{ss1}_{\alpha(s),\alpha(s+t)}$ *as the event that there are no Nakamoto blocks in the time interval* $[\alpha(s), \alpha(s+t)]$ *in the local clock of ss1. Then,*

$$P(B^{ss0}_{\alpha(s),\alpha(s+t)}) \leq P(B^{ss1}_{\alpha(s),\alpha(s+t)}).$$

The proof for this lemma is given in Appendix E in the full version [12].

For analyzing $P(B^{ss1}_{\alpha(s),\alpha(s+t)})$, we first consider an arbitrary static system $ss2$ where both honest nodes and adversary win leader elections with constant rates λ_h and λ_a, respectively, the honest nodes follows PoSAT, the adversary has similar additional power of gift of chain of $c - 1$ blocks as in $ss1$ but the network delay is a constant, say Δ'. For some $s', t' > 0$ in the local clock of the static system $ss2$, we will determine an upper bound on $P(B^{ss2}_{s',s'+t'})$ in Sects. 4.5 and 4.6 and then use this result to obtain an upper bound on $P(B^{ss1}_{\alpha(s),\alpha(s+t)})$ in Sect. 4.7.

4.5   Step 4: Growth Rate of the Adversarial Tree

For time $t' > 0$, let $\hat{T}_i(t')$ represents the adversarial tree in $ss2$ with i^{th} honest block as its root. The depth $D_i(t')$ at time t' in the local clock of $ss2$ is defined as the maximum depth of the blocks of $\hat{T}_i(t')$ at time t'. In Lemma 6, we evaluate the tail bound on $D_i(t')$.

Lemma 6. *For $x > 0$ so that $\eta_c \lambda_a t' + x$ is an integer,*

$$P(D_i(t') \geq \phi_c \lambda_a t' + cx) \leq e^{-\theta_c^* t'} e^{(\eta_c \lambda_a t' + x - 1)\Lambda_c(\theta_c^*)} g(t'). \qquad (11)$$

where $\phi_c = c\eta_c$, $g(t') = \sum_{i_1 \geq 1} \int_0^{t'} \frac{\lambda_a^{i_1} u^{i_1 - 1} e^{-\lambda_a u}}{\Gamma(i_1)} e^{\theta_c^* u} du$, $\Lambda_{c(\theta_c)} = \log(-\lambda_{a^c}/\theta_c (\lambda_{a-\theta_c})^{c-1})$ and θ_c^* is the solution for the equation $\Lambda_{c(\theta)} = \theta \dot{\Lambda}_{c(\theta)}$

Details on the analysis of $\hat{T}_i(t')$ and the proof of Lemma 6 are in Appendix F in the full version [12].

4.6   Step 5: Existence of Nakamoto Blocks

With Lemma 6, we show below that in the static system $ss2$ in the regime $\phi_c \lambda_a < \frac{\lambda_h}{1 + \lambda_h \Delta'}$, Nakamoto blocks has a non-zero probability of occurrence.

Lemma 7. *If*

$$\phi_c \lambda_a < \frac{\lambda_h}{1 + \lambda_h \Delta'},$$

then, in the static system $ss2$, there is a $p > 0$ such that the probability of the $j-th$ honest block being a Nakamoto block is greater than p for all j.

The proof of this result can be found in Appendix G.2 in the full version [12].

Having established the fact that Nakamoto blocks occurs with non-zero frequency, we can bootstrap on Lemma 7 to get a bound on the probability that in a time interval $[s', s' + t']$, there are no Nakamoto blocks, i.e. a bound on $P(B_{s',s'+t'})$.

Lemma 8. *If*

$$\phi_c \lambda_a < \frac{\lambda_h}{1 + \lambda_h \Delta'},$$

then for any $\epsilon > 0$, there exist constants $\bar{a}_\epsilon, \bar{A}_\epsilon$ so that for all $s' \geq 0$ and $t' > \max \left\{ \left(\frac{2\lambda_h}{1-\eta} \right)^2 \left(\frac{c-1}{\phi_c-1} \right)^2, \left[(c-1) \left(\Delta' + \frac{1}{\lambda_{\min}} \right) \right]^2 \right\}$, we have

$$P(B_{s',s'+t'}^{ss2}) \leq \bar{A}_\epsilon \exp(-\bar{a}_\epsilon t'^{1-\epsilon}) \qquad (12)$$

where $\bar{a}_\epsilon$ is a function of Δ'.

The proof of this result can be found in Appendix G.3 in the full version [12].

4.7   Step 6: Putting Back All Together

In this section, we use the results from Sect. 4.6 to upper bound $P(B_{\alpha(s),\alpha(s+t)}^{ss1})$ and hence, $P(B_{s,s+t})$.

Using Eq. 9, we have $\phi_c \lambda_a(t) < \frac{\lambda_h^c(t)}{1+\lambda_{\max}\Delta} \iff \phi_c \lambda_a < \frac{\lambda_h}{1+\lambda_{\max}\Delta}$. Then, we have the following lemma:

Lemma 9. *If*

$$\phi_c \lambda_a(t) < \frac{\lambda_h^c(t)}{1 + \lambda_{\max} \Delta},$$

then for any $\epsilon > 0$ there exist constants $\bar{a}_\epsilon, \bar{A}_\epsilon$ so that for all $s \geq 0$ and $t >$

$\max \left\{ \left(\frac{2\lambda_h}{1-\eta} \right)^2 \left(\frac{\lambda_h}{\lambda_{\min}} \right) \left(\frac{c-1}{\phi_c-1} \right)^2, \left(\frac{\lambda_h}{\lambda_{\min}} \right) \left[(c-1)\left(\Delta + \frac{1}{\lambda_{\min}} \right) \right]^2 \right\}$, *we have*

$$P(B_{s,s+t}) \leq \bar{A}_\epsilon \exp(-\bar{a}_\epsilon t^{1-\epsilon}) + e^{-\Omega(\kappa)}. \tag{13}$$

The proof for this result is given in Appendix H in the full version [12]. Then, combining Lemma 9 with Lemma 2 implies Theorem 1.

5 Discussion

In this section, we discuss some of the practical considerations in adopting PoSAT.

A key question in PoSAT is what is the right choice of c? If c is low, say 10, then the security threshold is approximately 1.58. At $c = 10$, the protocol is fully unpredictable and the confirmation latency is not too high. Also, any newly joining honest node has to wait for around 10 inter-block arrivals before it can participate in leader election. Thus, if there is a block arrival every second, then, the node has to wait for 10 s. In any standard blockchain, there is always a bootstrap period for the node to ensure that the state is synchronized with the existing peers and 10 s is negligible as compared to the bootstrap period.

In PoSAT, a separate RANDVDF needs to be run for each public-key. In a purely decentralized implementation, all nodes may not have the same rate of computing VDF. This may disadvantage nodes whose rate of doing sequential computation is slower. One approach to solve this problem is to build open-source hardware for VDF - this is already under way through the VDF Alliance. Even under such a circumstance, it is to be expected that nodes that can operate their hardware in idealized circumstances (for example, using specialized cooling equipment) can gain an advantage. A desirable feature of our protocol is that gains obtained by a slight advantage in the VDF computation rate are bounded. For PoSAT, a combination of the VDF computation rate and the stake together yields the net power wielded by a node, and as long as a majority of such power is controlled by honest nodes, we can expect the protocol to be safe.

In our PoSAT specification, the difficulty parameter for the computation of RANDVDF.EVAL was assumed to be fixed. This threshold was chosen based on the entire stake being online - this was to ensure that forking even when all nodes are present remains small, i.e., $\lambda_{\max}\Delta$ remained small. In periods when far fewer nodes are online, this leads to a slowdown in confirmation latency. A natural way to mitigate this problem is to use a variable mining threshold based on past history, similar to the adaptation inherent in Bitcoin. A formal analysis of Bitcoin with variable difficulty was carried out in [19,20], we leave a similar analysis of our protocol for future work.

In our protocol statement, we have used the RANDVDF directly on the randomness prevRand and the public key. The RANDVDF ensures that any other node can only predict a given node's leadership slot at the instant that it actually wins the VDF lottery. However, this still enables an adversary to predict the leadership slots of nodes that are offline and can potentially bribe them to come online to favor the adversary. In order to eliminate this exposure, we can replace the hash in the mining condition by using a verifiable random function [14,25] (which is calculated using the node's secret key but can be checked using the public key). This ensures that an adversary which is aware of all the public state as well as private state of all *online* nodes (including their VRF outputs) still cannot predict the leadership slot of any node ahead of the time at which they can mine the block. This is because, such an adversary does not have access to the VRF output of the offline nodes.

There are two types of PoS protocols: one favoring liveness under dynamic availability and other favoring safety under asynchrony. BFT protocols fall into the latter class and lack dynamic availability. One shortcoming of the longest chain protocol considered in the paper is the reduced throughput and latency compared to the fundamental limits; this problem is inherited from the Nakamoto consensus for PoW [26]. However, a recent set of papers address these problems in PoW (refer Prism [3], OHIE [37] and Ledger Combiners [17]). Adaptations of these ideas to the PoSAT protocol is left for future work. Furthermore, our protocol, like Nakamoto, does not achieve optimal chain quality. Adopting ideas from PoW protocols with optimal chain quality, such as Fruitchains [28], is also left for future work.

Finally, while we specified PoSAT in the context of proof-of-stake, the ideas can apply to other mining modalities - the most natural example is proof-of-space. We note that existing proof-of-space protocols like Chia [10], use a VDF for a fixed time, thus making the proof-of-space challenge predictable. In proof-of-space, if the predictability window is large, it is possible to use slow-storage mechanisms such as magnetic disks (which are asymmetrically available with large corporations) to answer the proof-of-space challenges. Our solution of using a RandVDF can be naturally adapted to this setting, yielding unpredictability as well as full dynamic availability.

Acknowledgements. DT wants to thank Ling Ren for earlier discussions on dynamic availability of Proof-of-Stake protocols.

References

1. Azouvi, S., McCorry, P., Meiklejohn, S.: Betting on blockchain consensus with fantomette. arXiv preprint arXiv:1805.06786 (2018)
2. Badertscher, C., Gaži, P., Kiayias, A., Russell, A., Zikas, V.: Ouroboros genesis: composable proof-of-stake blockchains with dynamic availability. In: Proceedings of the 2018 ACM SIGSAC Conference on Computer and Communications Security, pp. 913–930. ACM (2018)

3. Bagaria, V., et al.: Proof-of-stake longest chain protocols: security vs predictability. arXiv preprint arXiv:1910.02218 (2019)
4. Bentov, I., Pass, R., Shi, E.: Snow white: provably secure proofs of stake. IACR Cryptol. ePrint Arch. **2016**, 919 (2016)
5. Boneh, D., Bonneau, J., Bünz, B., Fisch, B.: Verifiable delay functions. In: Shacham, H., Boldyreva, A. (eds.) CRYPTO 2018. LNCS, vol. 10991, pp. 757–788. Springer, Cham (2018). https://doi.org/10.1007/978-3-319-96884-1_25
6. Brown-Cohen, J., Narayanan, A., Psomas, A., Weinberg, S.M.: Formal barriers to longest-chain proof-of-stake protocols. In: Proceedings of the 2019 ACM Conference on Economics and Computation, pp. 459–473 (2019)
7. Buchman, E., Kwon, J., Milosevic, Z.: The latest gossip on BFT consensus (2018)
8. Cai, J.-Y., Lipton, R.J., Sedgewick, R., Yao, A.-C.: Towards uncheatable benchmarks. In: [1993] Proceedings of the Eigth Annual Structure in Complexity Theory Conference, pp. 2–11. IEEE (1993)
9. Chen, J., Micali, S.: Algorand. arXiv preprint arXiv:1607.01341 (2016)
10. Cohen, B., Pietrzak, K.: The chia network blockchain (2019). https://www.chia.net/assets/ChiaGreenPaper.pdf
11. David, B., Gaži, P., Kiayias, A., Russell, A.: Ouroboros praos: an adaptively-secure, semi-synchronous proof-of-stake blockchain. In: Nielsen, J.B., Rijmen, V. (eds.) EUROCRYPT 2018. LNCS, vol. 10821, pp. 66–98. Springer, Cham (2018). https://doi.org/10.1007/978-3-319-78375-8_3
12. Deb, S., Kannan, S., Tse, D.: PoSAT: proof-of-work availability and unpredictability, without the work. arXiv preprint arXiv:2010.08154 (2020)
13. Dembo, A., et al.: Everything is a race and Nakamoto always wins. In: ACM CCS (2020). See also arXiv preprint arXiv:2005.10484
14. Dodis, Y., Yampolskiy, A.: A verifiable random function with short proofs and keys. In: Vaudenay, S. (ed.) PKC 2005. LNCS, vol. 3386, pp. 416–431. Springer, Heidelberg (2005). https://doi.org/10.1007/978-3-540-30580-4_28
15. Ephraim, N., Freitag, C., Komargodski, I., Pass, R.: Continuous verifiable delay functions. In: Canteaut, A., Ishai, Y. (eds.) EUROCRYPT 2020. LNCS, vol. 12107, pp. 125–154. Springer, Cham (2020). https://doi.org/10.1007/978-3-030-45727-3_5
16. Fan, L., Zhou, H.-S.A.: Scalable proof-of-stake blockchain in the open setting (or, how to mimic Nakamoto's design via proof-of-stake). Cryptology ePrint Archive, Report 2017/656 (2018). Version 20180425:201821
17. Fitzi, M., Gaži, P., Kiayias, A., Russell, A.: Ledger combiners for fast settlement. In: Pass, R., Pietrzak, K. (eds.) TCC 2020. LNCS, vol. 12550, pp. 322–352. Springer, Cham (2020). https://doi.org/10.1007/978-3-030-64375-1_12
18. Garay, J., Kiayias, A., Leonardos, N.: The bitcoin backbone protocol: analysis and applications. In: Oswald, E., Fischlin, M. (eds.) EUROCRYPT 2015. LNCS, vol. 9057, pp. 281–310. Springer, Heidelberg (2015). https://doi.org/10.1007/978-3-662-46803-6_10
19. Garay, J., Kiayias, A., Leonardos, N.: Full analysis of Nakamoto consensus in bounded-delay networks. Cryptology ePrint Archive, Report 2020/277 (2020). https://eprint.iacr.org/2020/277
20. Garay, J.A., Kiayias, A., Leonardos, N.: The bitcoin backbone protocol with chains of variable difficulty. Cryptology ePrint Archive, Report 2016/1048 (2016). https://eprint.iacr.org/2016/1048
21. Gilad, Y., Hemo, R., Micali, S., Vlachos, G., Zeldovich, N.: Algorand: scaling byzantine agreements for cryptocurrencies. In: Proceedings of the 26th Symposium on Operating Systems Principles, pp. 51–68. ACM (2017)

22. Kiayias, A., Russell, A., David, B., Oliynykov, R.: Ouroboros: a provably secure proof-of-stake blockchain protocol. In: Katz, J., Shacham, H. (eds.) CRYPTO 2017. LNCS, vol. 10401, pp. 357–388. Springer, Cham (2017). https://doi.org/10.1007/978-3-319-63688-7_12

23. Long, J., Wei, R.: Nakamoto consensus with verifiable delay puzzle. arXiv preprint arXiv:1908.06394 (2019)

24. Mahmoody, M., Moran, T., Vadhan, S.: Publicly verifiable proofs of sequential work. In: Proceedings of the 4th Conference on Innovations in Theoretical Computer Science, pp. 373–388 (2013)

25. Micali, S., Rabin, M., Vadhan, S.: Verifiable random functions. In: 40th Annual Symposium on Foundations of Computer Science (Cat. No. 99CB37039) (1999), pp. 120–130. IEEE

26. Nakamoto, S.: Bitcoin: a peer-to-peer electronic cash system (2008)

27. Pass, R., Seeman, L., Shelat, A.: Analysis of the blockchain protocol in asynchronous networks. In: Coron, J.-S., Nielsen, J.B. (eds.) EUROCRYPT 2017. LNCS, vol. 10211, pp. 643–673. Springer, Cham (2017). https://doi.org/10.1007/978-3-319-56614-6_22

28. Pass, R., Shi, E.: FruitChains: a fair blockchain. In: Proceedings of the ACM Symposium on Principles of Distributed Computing, pp. 315–324 (2017)

29. Pass, R., Shi, E.: The sleepy model of consensus. In: Takagi, T., Peyrin, T. (eds.) ASIACRYPT 2017. LNCS, vol. 10625, pp. 380–409. Springer, Cham (2017). https://doi.org/10.1007/978-3-319-70697-9_14

30. Pietrzak, K.: Simple verifiable delay functions. In: 10th Innovations in Theoretical Computer Science Conference (ITCS 2019). Schloss Dagstuhl-Leibniz-Zentrum fuer Informatik (2018)

31. Ren, L.: Analysis of Nakamoto consensus. Technical Report. Cryptology ePrint Archive, Report 2019/943. (2019). https://eprint.iacr.org

32. Rivest, R.L., Shamir, A., Wagner, D.A.: Time-lock puzzles and timed-release crypto (1996)

33. Shi, Z.: Branching Random Walks. LNM, vol. 2151. Springer, Cham (2015). https://doi.org/10.1007/978-3-319-25372-5

34. Wang, X., et al.: Proof-of-stake longest chain protocol revisited. arXiv preprint arXiv:1910.02218v2 (2018)

35. Wesolowski, B.: Efficient verifiable delay functions. J. Cryptol. **33**(4), 2113–2147 (2020). https://doi.org/10.1007/s00145-020-09364-x

36. Yin, M., Malkhi, D., Reiter, M.K., Gueta, G.G., Abraham, I.: HotStuff: BFT consensus in the lens of blockchain. arXiv preprint arXiv:1803.05069 (2018)

37. Yu, H., Nikolic, I., Hou, R., Saxena, P.: OHIE: blockchain scaling made simple. arXiv preprint arXiv:1811.12628 (2018)

Payment Channels

Post-Quantum Adaptor Signature for Privacy-Preserving Off-Chain Payments

Erkan Tairi[1]([✉]), Pedro Moreno-Sanchez[2], and Matteo Maffei[1]

[1] TU Wien, Vienna, Austria
{erkan.tairi,matteo.maffei}@tuwien.ac.at
[2] IMDEA Software Institute, Madrid, Spain
pedro.moreno@imdea.org

Abstract. Adaptor signatures (AS) are an extension of digital signatures that enable the encoding of a cryptographic hard problem (e.g., discrete logarithm) within the signature itself. An AS scheme ensures that (i) the signature can be created only by the user knowing the solution to the cryptographic problem; (ii) the signature reveals the solution itself; (iii) the signature can be verified with the standard verification algorithm. These properties have made AS a salient building block for many blockchain applications, in particular, off-chain payment systems such as payment-channel networks, payment-channel hubs, atomic swaps or discrete log contracts. Current AS constructions, however, are not secure against adversaries with access to a quantum computer.

In this work, we present IAS, a construction for adaptor signatures that relies on standard cryptographic assumptions for isogenies, and builds upon the isogeny-based signature scheme CSI-FiSh. We formally prove the security of IAS against a quantum adversary. We have implemented IAS and our evaluation shows that IAS can be incorporated into current blockchains while requiring ∼1500 bytes of storage size on-chain and ∼140 ms for digital signature verification. We also show how IAS can be seamlessly leveraged to build post-quantum off-chain payment applications without harming their security and privacy.

1 Introduction

Bitcoin and many other cryptocurrencies rely on the blockchain, a data structure that logs every single transaction deemed valid by miners through a decentralized consensus protocol. Each transaction is defined in terms of a scripting language that encodes the rules that make a transaction valid. Some cryptocurrencies (e.g., Bitcoin) support just a few operations to encode simple coin transfers authorized by digital signatures, whereas others (e.g., Ethereum) provide a Turing-complete scripting language enabling clients to encode more complex transaction logics.

While logging each single transaction on the blockchain allows for public verifiability, it also introduces evident scalability problems. First, the permissionless nature of the consensus protocol highly limits the transaction rate to few transactions per second – about three orders of magnitude less than traditional credit

---

The full version of this paper is available at https://eprint.iacr.org/2020/1345.

© International Financial Cryptography Association 2021
N. Borisov and C. Diaz (Eds.): FC 2021, LNCS 12675, pp. 131–150, 2021.
https://doi.org/10.1007/978-3-662-64331-0_7

card-based systems [1] – which highly hinders a wider adoption of these cryptocurrencies. Second, miners charge a transaction fee proportional to the size of the scripts included in each transaction and to the computation required by the miners for its validation, which can rapidly become a financial bottleneck.

A promising approach to reduce the transaction size is to manage some of the transaction logic off-chain, that is, encoding the logic as a peer-to-peer protocol between sender and receiver instead of directly in the transaction script. In this setting, A. Polestra introduced the notion of *scriptless scripts* [24], which has been later formalized as *adaptor signatures* [2,17].

Adaptor Signatures (AS). AS can be seen as an extended form of a standard digital signature, where one can create a "pre-signature" that can converted into a (full) signature with respect to an instance of a hard relation (e.g., the discrete logarithm). The resulting signature can then be verified by the miners using the standard verification algorithm from the digital signature scheme. AS provide the following two intuitive properties: (i) only the user knowing the witness of the hard relation can convert the pre-signature into a valid signature; and (ii) anybody with access to the pre-signature and the corresponding signature can extract the witness of the hard relation. This building block has been shown highly useful in practice to build off-chain payment applications such as generalized payment channels [2], payment-channel networks [21], payment-channel hubs [27], and many others, being adopted in real-world blockchain protocols, such as the Lightning Network, the COMIT Network, ZenGo$^\times$ and others.

Related Work and Limitations. Aumayr et al. [2] provides instances of AS based on Schnorr and ECDSA digital signatures. Malavolta et al. [21] show an instance of AS from any one-way homomorphic function and describe how to construct payment-channel networks from AS. Moreno-Sanchez et al. [22] shows an instance of AS based on the linkable ring signature supported in Monero. Tairi et al. [27] leverage AS to build payment-channel hubs.

All these works do not provide security in the post-quantum setting where the discrete logarithm assumption no longer holds against a post-quantum adversary. Therefore, given the relevance in practice of AS, there is a need to design post-quantum instances of them. For instance, there exist several efforts from NIST to standardize quantum resistant algorithms. The blockchain community has also shown interest in migrating towards post-quantum secure alternatives. For example, Ethereum 2.0 Serenity upgrade [5] is planned to have an option for a post-quantum signature and Zcash developers plan to update their protocol with post-quantum alternatives when they are mature enough [16].

Esgin et al. [13] recently came up with a seminal contribution in this field, proposing the first instance of a post-quantum AS, called LAS, which is based on the standard lattice assumptions, such as Module-SIS and Module-LWE. This construction, however, presents a few limitations with regards to correctness, communication overhead, and privacy. From the correctness point of view, LAS requires to use two hard relations, R and R', where R is the base relation and R' is the extended relation that defines the relation for *extracted* witnesses. The reason for this is due to the inherent *knowledge/soundness gap* in lattice-based zero-knowledge proofs [15]. Hence, as mentioned by the authors, LAS only achieves *weak* pre-signature adaptability, which guarantees that only the statement/witness pairs satisfying R are adaptable, and not those satisfying R'. In practice, this implies that the applications that use LAS as a building block require a zero-knowledge proof to guarantee that the extracted witness is of sufficiently small norm and belongs to the relation R, which in turn guarantees that the pre-signature adaptability would work. However, the currently most efficient variant of such a proof has size of 53 KB [14], which would incur significant (off-chain) communication overhead to the applications using LAS.

From the privacy point of view, when LAS is used inside certain applications, such as building payment-channel networks (PCNs), it can leak non-trivial information that hinders the privacy of the overall construction. In a nutshell, the reason for that is that the witness for adapting the pre-signature in LAS is a vector whose infinity norm is 1. Privacy-preserving applications such as PCNs require to encode a randomization factor at each hop, which in LAS is encoded by adding a new vector whose infinity norm is 1 for each hop [13, Section 4.2]. However, this leads to a situation where a node at position k in the payment path receives a vector with infinity norm k with high probability, learning *at least* how many parties are before it on the path. Moreover, if an intermediary observes that the norm is 1, then it knows that (with high probability) the party before it is the sender. Encoding a vector of random but small norm (i.e., padding) for each hop does not help either, as each sender-receiver pair would use a unique norm, breaking thus relationship anonymity (see Sect. 6 for more details).

Finally, given the ongoing standardizations efforts of NIST, we find it interesting to have several candidates of quantum-resistant AS building upon different cryptographic assumptions to aid the related discussion (e.g., if one assumption gets broken, we may still have standing post-quantum constructions). The current state of affairs leads to the following question: *Is it possible to design a quantum resistant AS that preserves the security and privacy guarantees of the off-chain applications built on top of the current non post-quantum alternatives?*

Our Contributions. We affirmatively answer the previous question and propose IAS, the first construction for post-quantum AS that preserves the security and privacy guarantees required by off-chain applications. In particular,

- We design IAS, a construction for AS that builds upon the post-quantum signature scheme CSI-FiSh, and relies on hardness of standard cryptographic assumptions from isogenies. We formally prove the security of IAS.
- We provide a parallelized implementation of IAS and evaluate its performance, showing that it requires ~1500 bytes of storage on-chain (with a parameter set optimized for lower combined public key and signature size) and 140 ms to verify a signature on average (i.e., the computation time for miners). We compare with LAS and observe that the on-chain storage size is 3× smaller than LAS while requiring higher computation time.
- We describe how to build payment-channel networks (PCNs) from IAS, and show that IAS does not diminish the security or privacy guarantees of PCNs.

Thus, IAS seamlessly enables post-quantum off-chain applications as soon as the underlying blockchains support the post-quantum signature scheme CSI-FiSh.

2 Preliminaries

Notation. We denote by 1^λ, for $\lambda \in \mathbb{N}$, the security parameter. We assume this is given as an implicit input to every function, and all our algorithms run in polynomial time in λ. We denote by $x \leftarrow_{\$} \mathcal{X}$ the uniform sampling of the variable x from the set $\mathcal{X}$. We write $x \leftarrow \mathsf{A}(y)$ to denote that a probabilistic polynomial time (PPT) algorithm A on input y, outputs x. We use the same notation also for the assignment of the computational results, for example, $s \leftarrow s_1 + s_2$. If A is a deterministic polynomial time (DPT) algorithm, we use the notation $x := \mathsf{A}(y)$. We use the same notation for the projection of tuples, e.g., we write $\sigma := (\sigma_1, \sigma_2)$ for a tuple σ composed of two elements σ_1 and σ_2. A function $\mathsf{negl} \colon \mathbb{N} \to \mathbb{R}$ is *negligible* in n if for every $k \in \mathbb{N}$, there exists $n_0 \in \mathbb{N}$, such that for every $n \geq n_0$ it holds that $\mathsf{negl}(n) \leq 1/n^k$. Throughout the paper we implicitly assume that negligible functions are negligible in the security parameter (i.e., $\mathsf{negl}(\lambda)$).

2.1 Adaptor Signatures (AS)

We first recall the definition of a hard relation, the notion of AS and informally describe its security goals. We refer the reader to the full version of our paper [28] for more details.

Definition 1 (Hard Relation). *Let R be a relation with statement/witness pairs (Y, y). Let us denote L_R the associated language defined as $L_R := \{Y \mid \exists y \text{ s.t. } (Y, y) \in R\}$. We say that R is a hard relation if the following holds:*

- *There exists a PPT sampling algorithm $\mathsf{GenR}(1^\lambda)$ that on input the security parameter λ outputs a statement/witness pair $(Y, y) \in R$.*
- *The relation is poly-time decidable.*
- *For all PPT adversaries $\mathcal{A}$ there exists a negligible function negl, such that:*

$$\Pr\left[(Y, y^*) \in R \,\middle|\, \begin{array}{c} (Y, y) \leftarrow \mathsf{GenR}(1^\lambda), \\ y^* \leftarrow \mathcal{A}(Y) \end{array}\right] \leq \mathsf{negl}(\lambda),$$

where the probability is taken over the randomness of GenR and $\mathcal{A}$.

Definition 2 (Adaptor Signature Scheme). *An adaptor signature scheme w.r.t. a hard relation R and a signature scheme $\Sigma = (\mathsf{KeyGen}, \mathsf{Sig}, \mathsf{Ver})$ consists of four algorithms $\Xi_{R,\Sigma} = (\mathsf{PreSig}, \mathsf{Adapt}, \mathsf{PreVer}, \mathsf{Ext})$ defined as:*

$\mathsf{PreSig}(\mathsf{sk}, m, Y)$: *is a PPT algorithm that on input a secret key sk, message $m \in \{0,1\}^*$ and statement $Y \in L_R$, outputs a pre-signature $\hat{\sigma}$.*

$\mathsf{PreVer}(\mathsf{pk}, m, Y, \hat{\sigma})$: *is a DPT algorithm that on input a public key pk, message $m \in \{0,1\}^*$, statement $Y \in L_R$ and pre-signature $\hat{\sigma}$, outputs a bit b.*

Adapt$(\hat{\sigma}, y)$: *is a* DPT *algorithm that on input a pre-signature $\hat{\sigma}$ and witness y, outputs a signature σ.*

Ext$(\sigma, \hat{\sigma}, Y)$: *is a* DPT *algorithm that on input a signature σ, pre-signature $\hat{\sigma}$ and statement $Y \in L_R$, outputs a witness y such that $(Y, y) \in R$, or $\bot$.*

Intuitively, an adaptor signature must achieve the following goals:

- *Pre-signature correctness:* An honestly generated pre-signature with respect to a statement $Y \in L_R$ must be a valid pre-signature and can be adapted into a valid signature from which a witness for Y can be extracted.
- *Unforgeability for adaptor signatures:* An adversary must not be able to produce a valid signature on a message m even when given a pre-signature on m w.r.t. a random statement $Y \in L_R$.
- *Pre-signature adaptability:* Any valid pre-signature w.r.t. Y can be adapted into a valid signature using the witness y with $(Y, y) \in R$.
- *Witness extractability:* A valid signature/pre-signature pair $(\sigma, \hat{\sigma})$ for a message/statement pair (m, Y) can be used to extract the witness y of Y.

2.2 Elliptic Curves and Isogenies

Let E be an elliptic curve over a finite field $\mathbb{F}_p$ with p a large prime, and let 0_E be the point at infinity on E. An elliptic curve is called supersingular iff its number of rational points satisfies $\#E(\mathbb{F}_p) = p + 1$. Otherwise, an elliptic curve is called ordinary.We note that in this work we are considering supersingular curves. An isogeny between two elliptic curves E and E' is a rational map $\phi \colon E \to E'$, such that $\phi(0_E) = 0_{E'}$, and which is also a homomorphism with respect to the natural group structure of E and E'. An isomorphism between two ellliptic curves is an injective isogeny. The j-invariant of an elliptic curve, which is a simple algebraic expression in the coefficients of the curve, is an algebraic invariant under isomorphism (i.e., isomorphic curves have the same j-invariant). As isogenies are group homomorphisms, any isogeny comes with a subgroup of E, which is its kernel. Any subgroup $S \subset E(\mathbb{F}_{p^k})$ yields a unique (up to automorphism) separable isogeny $\phi \colon E \to E/S$ with $\ker \phi = S$. The equation for the quotient E and the isogeny ϕ can be computed using Vélu's formulae [29].

The ring of endomorphisms $\mathrm{End}(E)$ consists of all isogenies from E to itself, and $\mathrm{End}_{\mathbb{F}_p}(E)$ denotes the ring of endomorphisms defined over $\mathbb{F}_p$. For an ordinary curve $E/\mathbb{F}_p$ we have that $\mathrm{End}(E) = \mathrm{End}_{\mathbb{F}_p}(E)$, but for a supersingular curve over $\mathbb{F}_p$ we have a strict inclusion $\mathrm{End}_{\mathbb{F}_p}(E) \subsetneq \mathrm{End}(E)$. In particular, for supersingular elliptic curves the ring $\mathrm{End}(E)$ is an order of a quarternion algebra defined over $\mathbb{Q}$, while $\mathrm{End}_{\mathbb{F}_p}(E)$ is isomorphic to an order of the imaginary quadratic field $\mathbb{Q}(\sqrt{-p})$. We will identify $\mathrm{End}_{\mathbb{F}_p}(E)$ with the isomorphic order which we will denote by $\mathcal{O}$.

The ideal class group of $\mathcal{O}$ is the quotient of the group of fractional invertible ideals in $\mathcal{O}$ by the principal fractional invertible ideals, and will be denoted as $\mathrm{Cl}(\mathcal{O})$. There is a natural action of the class group on the class of elliptic curves defined over $\mathbb{F}_p$ with order $\mathcal{O}$. Given an ideal $\mathfrak{a} \subset \mathcal{O}$, we can consider the subgroup defined by the intersection of the kernels of the endomorphisms in

$\mathfrak{a}$, more precisely, $S_{\mathfrak{a}} = \cap_{\alpha \in \mathfrak{a}} \ker \alpha$. As this is a subgroup of E, we can divide out by $S_{\mathfrak{a}}$ and get the isogenous curve $E/S_{\mathfrak{a}}$, which we denote by $\mathfrak{a} \star E$. This isogeny is well-defined and unique up to $\mathbb{F}_p$-isomorphism and the group $\mathrm{Cl}(\mathcal{O})$ acts via the operator $\star$ on the set $\mathcal{E}$ of $\mathbb{F}_p$-isomorphism classes of elliptic curves with $\mathbb{F}_p$-rational endomorphism ring $\mathcal{O}$. One can show that $\mathrm{Cl}(\mathcal{O})$ acts freely and transitively on $\mathcal{E}$ (i.e., $\mathcal{E}$ is a principal homogeneous space for $\mathrm{Cl}(\mathcal{O})$).

Notation. Following [3], we see $\mathrm{Cl}(\mathcal{O})$ as a cyclic group with generator $\mathfrak{g}$, and we write $\mathfrak{a} = \mathfrak{g}^a$ with a random in $\mathbb{Z}_N$ for $N = \#\mathrm{Cl}(\mathcal{O})$ the order of the class group. We write $[a]$ for $\mathfrak{g}^a$ and $[a]E$ for $\mathfrak{g}^a \star E$. We note that under this notation $[a][b]E = [a+b]E$.

2.3   Security Assumptions: GAIP and MT-GAIP

The main hardness assumption underlying group actions based on isogenies is that it is hard to invert the group action.

Definition 3 (Group Action Inverse Problem (GAIP) [9]). Given two elliptic curves E and E' over the same finite field and with $\mathrm{End}(E) = \mathrm{End}(E') = \mathcal{O}$, find an ideal $\mathfrak{a} \subset \mathcal{O}$ such that $E' = \mathfrak{a} \star E$.

The CSI-FiSh signature scheme (see Sect. 3) relies on the hardness of random instance of a multi-target version of GAIP, called MT-GAIP. In [9] it is shown that MT-GAIP reduces tightly to GAIP when the class group structure is known (which is the case for CSI-FiSh).

Definition 4 (Multi-Target GAIP (MT-GAIP) [9]). *Given k elliptic curves $E_1, \ldots, E_k$ over the same field, with $\mathrm{End}(E_1) = \cdots = \mathrm{End}(E_k) = \mathcal{O}$, find an ideal $\mathfrak{a} \subset \mathcal{O}$ s.t. $E_i = \mathfrak{a} \star E_j$ for some $i, j \in \{0 \ldots, k\}$ with $i \neq j$.*

The best known classical algorithm to solve the GAIP (and in this case also the MT-GAIP) has time complexity $O(\sqrt{N})$, where $N = \#\mathrm{Cl}(\mathcal{O})$. On the other hand, the best known quantum algorithm is Kuperberg's algorithm for the hidden shift problem [19,20]. It has a subexponential complexity with the concrete security estimates still being an active area of research [4,23].

3   CSI-FiSh

Isogeny-based cryptography goes back to the works of Couveignes, Rostovtsev and Stolbunov [7,25], with the first isogeny-based signature scheme being proposed by Stolbunov in his thesis [26]. The signature scheme was a Fiat-Shamir transform applied to a standard three-round isogeny-based identification scheme. However, the problem with Stolbunov's scheme is that it required an efficient method to sample in the class group, and that each element of class group should have an efficiently computable unique representation. The roadblock to both of these problems is that the structure of the class group is unknown. Recently, Buellens et al. [3] computed the class group of the quadratic imaginary field

Algorithm 1. CSI-FiSh Signature

1: Public parameters: base curve E_0, class number $N = \#\mathrm{Cl}(\mathcal{O})$, security parameters λ, t_S, S, hash function $\mathcal{H}\colon \{0,1\}^* \to \{-S+1, \ldots, S-1\}^{t_S}$

2: **procedure** KeyGen(1^λ)
3:     **for** $i \in \{1, \ldots, S-1\}$ **do**
4:         $a_i \leftarrow_\$ \mathbb{Z}_N$
5:         $E_i \leftarrow [a_i]E_0$
6:     Set sk $:= [a_i \colon i \in \{1, \ldots, S-1\}]$
7:     Set pk $:= [E_i \colon i \in \{1, \ldots, S-1\}]$
8:     **return** (sk, pk)
9: **procedure** Sig(sk, m)
10:     Parse sk as $(a_1, \ldots, a_{S-1})$
11:     $a_0 \leftarrow 0$
12:     **for** $i \in \{1, \ldots, t_S\}$ **do**
13:         $b_i \leftarrow \mathbb{Z}_N$
14:         $E_i' \leftarrow [b_i]E_0$
15:     $(c_1, \ldots, c_{t_S}) = \mathcal{H}(E_1' \| \cdots \| E_{t_S}' \| m)$
16:     **for** $i \in \{1, \ldots, t_S\}$ **do**
17:         $r_i \leftarrow b_i - \mathrm{sign}(c_i)a_{|c_i|} \bmod N$
18:     **return** $\sigma := (r_1, \ldots, r_{t_S}, c_1, \ldots, c_{t_S})$
19: **procedure** Ver(pk, m, σ)
20:     Parse pk as $(E_1, \ldots, E_{S-1})$
21:     Parse σ as $(r_1, \ldots, r_{t_S}, c_1, \ldots, c_{t_S})$
22:     Define $E_{-i} := E_i^t$ for all $i \in [1, S-1]$
23:     **for** $i \in \{1, \ldots, t_S\}$ **do**
24:         $E_i' \leftarrow [r_i]E_{c_i}$
25:     $(c_1', \ldots, c_t') = \mathcal{H}(E_1' \| \cdots \| E_{t_S}' \| m)$
26:     **if** $(c_1, \ldots, c_{t_S}) == (c_1', \ldots, c_{t_S}')$ **then**
27:         **return** 1
28:     **else**
29:         **return** 0

corresponding to the CSIDH-512 parameter set from [6], which allowed them to construct a more efficient isogeny-based signature scheme, called CSI-FiSh.

Next, we briefly describe the CSI-FiSh signature scheme from [3]. CSI-FiSh is a signature scheme obtained by applying Fiat-Shamir transform to an identification scheme. First, we recall the interactive zero-knowledge identification scheme, where a prover wants to convince a verifier that it knows a secret element $\mathfrak{a} \in \mathrm{Cl}(\mathcal{O})$ of its public key $E_a = \mathfrak{a} \star E_0$, for $\mathfrak{a} = \mathfrak{g}^a$ and $a \in \mathbb{Z}_N$, where E_0 is a publicly known base curve. The scheme is as follows:

- Prover samples a random $\mathfrak{b} = \mathfrak{g}^b$ for $b \in \mathbb{Z}_N$ and commits to $E_b = [b]E_0$ (this corresponds to $E_b = \mathfrak{b} \star E_0$ with our notation).
- Verifier samples a random challenge bit $c \in \{0, 1\}$.
- If $c = 0$, prover replies with $r = b$, otherwise it replies with $r = b - a \bmod N$ (reducing modulo N to avoid any leakage on a).
- If $c = 0$, verifier verifies that $E_b = [r]E_0$, otherwise verifies that $E_b = [r]E_a$.

This scheme is clearly correct, and it has soundness $1/2$. For the zero-knowledge property, it is important that elements in $\mathrm{Cl}(\mathcal{O})$ can be sampled uniformly, and that they have unique representation.

In order to improve soundness, the authors of [3] increased the size of the public key. For a positive integer S, the secret key becomes the vector $(a_1, \ldots, a_{S-1})$ of dimension $S-1$, and public key is set to $(E_0, E_1 = [a_1]E_0, \ldots, E_{S-1} = [a_{S-1}]E_0)$. Then, the prover proves to the verifier that it knows an $s \in \mathbb{Z}_N$, such that $[s]E_i = E_j$ for some pair of curves in the public key (with $i \neq j$). In order to further increase the challenge space, one can exploit the fact that given a curve $E = [a]E_0$, its quadratic twist E^t, which can be computed very

Algorithm 2. Non-interactive zero-knowledge proof for L_j

1: Public parameters: class number $N = \#\mathrm{Cl}(\mathcal{O})$, hash function $\mathcal{F}\colon \{0,1\}^* \to \{0,1\}$

2: **procedure** NIZK.P(x,s) 10: **procedure** NIZK.V(x,π)

3:     Parse x as $(E_1, E_1', \ldots, E_j, E_j')$ 11:   Parse x as $(E_1, E_1', \ldots, E_j, E_j')$

4:     $b \leftarrow_\$ \mathbb{Z}_N$ 12:   Parse π as $((\hat{E}_1, \ldots, \hat{E}_j), r)$

5:     **for** $i \in \{1, \ldots, j\}$ **do**   13: $c = \mathcal{F}(E_1 \| E_1' \| \hat{E}_1 \| \cdots \| E_j \| E_j' \| \hat{E}_j)$

6:        $\hat{E}_i \leftarrow [b]E_i$ 14:   **if** $c = 0$ **then**

7:     $c = \mathcal{F}(E_1 \| E_1' \| \hat{E}_1 \| \cdots \| E_j \| E_j' \| \hat{E}_j)$ 15:   **return** $\bigwedge_{i=1}^{j}([r]E_i = \hat{E}_i)$

8:     $r \leftarrow b - c \cdot s \bmod N$ 16:   **else if** $c = 1$ **then**

9:     **return** $\pi := ((\hat{E}_1, \ldots, \hat{E}_j), r)$ 17:   **return** $\bigwedge_{i=1}^{j}([r]E_i' = \hat{E}_i)$

---

efficiently, is $\mathbb{F}_p$-isomorphic to $[-a]E_0$. Therefore, one can almost double the set of public key curves going from $E_0, E_1, \ldots, E_{S-1}$ to $E_{-S+1}, \ldots, E_0, \ldots, E_{S-1}$, where $E_{-i} = E_i^t$, without any increase in communication cost. Combining all these the soundness error drops to $\frac{1}{2S-1}$. To achieve security level λ (i.e., $2^{-\lambda}$ soundness error), we need to repeat the protocol $t_S = \lambda / \log_2(2S-1)$ times.

The described identification scheme when combined with the Fiat-Shamir heuristic, for a hash function $\mathcal{H}\colon \{0,1\}^* \to \{-S+1, \ldots, S-1\}^{t_S}$, gives the CSI-FiSh signature scheme shown in Algorithm 1, where sign denotes the sign of the integer. In [3] it is shown that CSI-FiSh is SUF-CMA secure under the MT-GAIP assumption, when $\mathcal{H}$ is modeled as a quantum random oracle, hence, it is strongly unforgeable in the quantum random oracle model (QROM) [11].

3.1 Zero-Knowledge Proof for Group Actions

Cozzo and Smart [8] showed how to prove knowledge of a secret isogeny generically. In detail, they showed a zero-knowledge proof for the following relation:

$$L_j := \left\{ \left((E_1, E_1', \ldots, E_j, E_j'), s\right) \colon \bigwedge_{i=1}^{j} \left(E_i' = [s]E_i\right) \right\}.$$

Intuitively, the prover wants to prove in zero-knowledge that it knows a unique witness s for j simultaneous instances of the GAIP. In [8] two variants of such a proof are given, one when $E_1 = \cdots = E_j = E_0$, called Special case with soundness error $1/3$, and another one when that condition does not hold, called General case with soundness error $1/2$. In our paper we only need the General case for $j = 2$. Since the proof has soundness error of $1/2$, we need to repeat it $t_{ZK} = \lambda$ times to achieve a security level of λ. Using a "slow" hash function $\mathcal{F}$, as in CSI-FiSh, which is 2^k times slower than a normal hash function we can reduce the number of repetitions to $t_{ZK} = \lambda - k$. For example, when setting $\lambda = 128$ and $k = 16$, as in the fastest CSI-FiSh parameters, we get $t_{ZK} = 112$. In the random oracle model the proof can be made non-interactive using a hash function $\mathcal{F}$ with codomain $\{0,1\}^{t_{ZK}}$. For brevity, we only present the non-interactive single iteration (i.e., $t_{ZK} = 1$) variant of the proof for L_j in Algorithm 2.

4 IAS: An Adaptor Signature from Isogenies

Despite the fact that CSI-FiSh is simply a signature scheme obtained by applying Fiat-Shamir to multiple repetitions of Schnorr-type identification scheme from isogenies, one cannot trivially construct a Schnorr-type AS as described in [2].

Strawman Approach. Let us consider a single iteration of the identification scheme (i.e., $t_S = 1$), and a hard relation $R_{E_0}^1 \subseteq \mathcal{E} \times \mathrm{Cl}(\mathcal{O})$, for a set of elliptic curves $\mathcal{E}$, to be defined as $R_{E_0}^1 := \{(E_Y, y) \mid E_Y = [y]E_0\}$. A naïve approach to construct an AS from a single-iteration CSI-FiSh, following the Schnorr AS from [2], is to compute the randomness inside the pre-signature algorithm as $E' \leftarrow [b]E_Y$ instead of doing $E' \leftarrow [b]E_0$ as in the original construction, and leave the rest of the algorithm identical to the signing algorithm of CSI-FiSh. However, later during the pre-verification, given the pre-signature $\hat{\sigma} := (\hat{r}, c)$, the statement E_Y and c-th public key E_c, one cannot verify the correctness of the pre-signature $\hat{\sigma}$. More concretely, we have that $\hat{r} = b - \mathrm{sign}(c)a_{|c|} \bmod N$, $E_c = [\mathrm{sign}(c)a_{|c|}]E_0$ and $E_Y = [y]E_0$. Now, using these values we can compute $\hat{E}' = [\hat{r}]E_c = [b]E_0$, but then we cannot combine $\hat{E}'$ with E_Y to obtain $E' = [b]E_Y$, which we need for verification. Analogous problem happens if we first compute the group action $\hat{E}' = [r]E_Y$, and then try to combine it with E_c to obtain the desired E'. The reason behind this problem is that we have a limited algebraic structure. More precisely, the group action is defined as $\star: \mathrm{Cl}(\mathcal{O}) \times \mathcal{E} \to \mathcal{E}$, for class group $\mathrm{Cl}(\mathcal{O})$ and set of elliptic curves $\mathcal{E}$. This implies that we can pair a class group element with an elliptic curve to map it to a new elliptic curve, however, we do not have any meaningful operation over the set $\mathcal{E}$ that would allow us to purely pair two elliptic curves and map to a third one.

4.1 Our Construction

On a high-level, we have to circumvent the limited algebraic structure of CSI-FiSh, which prevents us from extracting the randomness. We solve this problem by means of a zero-knowledge proof showing the validity of the pre-signature construction. This might remind of the ECDSA-based AS construction by Aumayr et al. [2], where a zero-knowledge proof is also used to prove the consistency of the randomness, which would not be otherwise possible due to the lack of linearity of ECDSA. Besides not being post-quantum secure, their cryptographic construction (i.e., the underlying signature scheme and thus the resulting zero-knowledge proof) is, however, fundamentally different because the issue in CSI-FiSh is a limited algebraic structure as opposed to a lack of linearity as in ECDSA.

More concretely, to compute the pre-signature for E_Y, the signer samples a random $b \leftarrow_{\$} \mathbb{Z}_N$, computes $\hat{E}' \leftarrow [b]E_0$ and $E' \leftarrow [b]E_Y$. Then, the signer uses E' as input to the hash function to compute the challenge c, and also includes E' as part of the pre-signature. Lastly, to ensure that the same value b is used in computation of both $\hat{E}'$ and E', a zero-knowledge proof π that $(E_0, \hat{E}', E_Y, E') \in L_2$ is attached to the pre-signature (see Sect. 3.1 for such a proof). So, the pre-signature looks like $\hat{\sigma} := (\hat{r}, c, \pi, E')$. The pre-signature verification of $\hat{\sigma}$ then involves extracting $\hat{E}'$ by computing the group actions $[\hat{r}]E_c$, using it to verify the proof π, and finally, checking that the hash of E' produces the expected challenge c. The pre-signature adaptation is done by adding the corresponding witness y to $\hat{r}$ of the pre-signature to obtain the full valid signature $\sigma := (r, c)$. In an opposite manner, the extraction is done by subtracting r of the valid signature from $\hat{r}$ of the pre-signature.

Since CSI-FiSh involves multiple iterations (more concretely t_S iterations), we extend the hard relation $R_{E_0}^1$ to $R_{E_0}^{t_S} \subseteq \mathcal{E}^{t_S} \times \text{Cl}(\mathcal{O})^{t_S}$, to be defined as $R_{E_0}^{t_S} :=$ $\{(\boldsymbol{E_Y} := (E_Y^1, \dots, E_Y^{t_S}), \boldsymbol{y} := (y_1, \dots, y_{t_S})) \mid E_Y^i = [y_i]E_0 \text{ for all } i \in [1, t_S]\}$, and apply the above described method to every iteration with a different E_Y^i.

Although, the described scheme achieves correctness, one cannot prove its security directly. As we would like to reduce both the unforgeability and witness extractability of the scheme to the strong unforgeability of CSI-FiSh, inside the reduction we need a way to answer the pre-signature queries by only relying on the signing oracle of CSI-FiSh, and without access to the secret key sk or the witness $(y_1, \dots, y_{t_S})$. In order to overcome this issue, we use a modified hard relation. Let $R_{E_0}^*$ consist of pairs $I_Y := (\boldsymbol{E_Y}, \pi_Y)$, where $\boldsymbol{E_Y} \in L_{R_{E_0}^{t_S}}$ is as previously defined, and π_Y is a non-interactive zero-knowledge proof that $\boldsymbol{E_Y} \in L_{R_{E_0}^{t_S}}$. Formally, we have that $R_{E_0}^* := \{((\boldsymbol{E_Y}, \pi_Y), \boldsymbol{y}) \mid \boldsymbol{E_Y} \in L_{R_{E_0}^{t_S}} \wedge \text{NIZK.V}(\boldsymbol{E_Y}, \pi_Y) = 1\}$. Due to the soundness of the proof system, if $R_{E_0}^{t_S}$ is a hard relation, then so is $R_{E_0}^*$. Since we are in the random oracle model, the reduction then can use the random oracle query table to extract a witness from the proof π_Y, and answer the pre-signature oracle queries using this witness.

The resulting AS scheme, which we denote as $\Xi_{R_{E_0}^*, \Sigma_{\text{CSI-FiSh}}}$ and call as IAS, is depicted in Algorithm 3. The security of our construction is captured by the following theorem, which we formally prove in the full version of our paper [28].

Theorem 1. *Assuming that the CSI-FiSh signature scheme $\Sigma_{\text{CSI-FiSh}}$ is SUF-CMA secure and $R_{E_0}^*$ is a hard relation, the adaptor signature scheme $\Xi_{R_{E_0}^*, \Sigma_{\text{CSI-FiSh}}}$, as defined in Algorithm 3, is secure in QROM.*

Optimization. Our construction, as defined in Algorithm 3, makes sure that all t_S parts of the signature are adapted (i.e., each r_i, for $i \in \{1, \dots, t_S\}$, is adapted). This is due to the fact that IAS is based on CSI-FiSh, which in turn is constructed from multiple iterations of a Schnorr-type identification scheme as described in Sect. 3. However, this also points to the fact that CSI-FiSh is just a much less efficient version of Schnorr. Therefore, one can have a more efficient variant of IAS by only adapting one of the iterations (e.g., the first iteration). In this variant, during the pre-signature algorithm we compute π_1 and E_1' using E_Y^1 as defined in Algorithm 3, and attach them to the pre-signature $\hat{\sigma}$ as before. But, for the rest of the iterations (i.e., for $i \in \{2, \dots, t_S\}$), we do not compute any zero-knowledge proof, and compute E_i' using E_0 as done in the signing algorithm of CSI-FiSh (see Sect. 1). This means that the pre-signature $\hat{\sigma}$ is only incomplete in the first component (i.e., only $\hat{r}_1$ needs to be adapted to obtain a valid signature). Hence, the extraction and adaptation only depend

Algorithm 3. Adaptor Signature $\Xi_{R_{E_0}^*,\Sigma_{\text{CSI−FiSh}}}$ (IAS)

1: Public parameters: base curve E_0, class number $N = \#\text{Cl}(\mathcal{O})$, security parameters λ, t_S, S, hash function $\mathcal{H} \colon \{0,1\}^* \to \{-S+1,\ldots,S-1\}^{t_S}$

2: **procedure** PreSig(sk, m, I_Y)
3:     Parse sk as $(a_1, \ldots, a_{S-1})$
4:     Parse I_Y as $(\boldsymbol{E}_Y, \pi_Y)$
5:     Parse $\boldsymbol{E}_Y$ as $(E_Y^1, \ldots, E_Y^{t_S})$
6:     $a_0 \leftarrow 0$
7:     **for** $i \in \{1, \ldots, t_S\}$ **do**
8:         $b_i \leftarrow \mathbb{Z}_N$
9:         $\hat{E}_i' \leftarrow [b_i]E_0$
10:        $E_i' \leftarrow [b_i]E_Y^i$
11:        Set $x_i := (E_0, \hat{E}_i', E_Y^i, E_i')$
12:        $\pi_i \leftarrow \text{NIZK.P}(x_i, b_i)$
13:     $(c_1, \ldots, c_{t_S}) = \mathcal{H}(E_1' \| \cdots \| E_{t_S}' \| m)$
14:     **for** $i \in \{1, \ldots, t_S\}$ **do**
15:        $\hat{r}_i \leftarrow b_i - \text{sign}(c_i)a_{|c_i|} \bmod N$
16:     **return** $\hat{\sigma} := (\hat{r}_1, \ldots, \hat{r}_{t_S}, c_1, \ldots,$
17:            $c_{t_S}, \pi_1, \ldots, \pi_{t_S}, E_1', \ldots, E_{t_S}')$
18: **procedure** PreVer(pk, $m, I_Y, \hat{\sigma}$)
19:     Parse pk as $(E_1, \ldots, E_{S-1})$
20:     Parse I_Y as $(\boldsymbol{E}_Y, \pi_Y)$
21:     Parse $\boldsymbol{E}_Y$ as $(E_Y^1, \ldots, E_Y^{t_S})$
22:     Parse $\hat{\sigma}$ as $(\hat{r}_1, \ldots, \hat{r}_{t_S}, c_1, \ldots, c_{t_S},$
23:           $\pi_1, \ldots, \pi_{t_S}, E_1', \ldots, E_{t_S}')$
24:     Set $E_{-i} = E_i^t$ for all $i \in [1, S-1]$
25:     **for** $i \in \{1, \ldots, t_S\}$ **do**
26:        $\hat{E}_i' \leftarrow [\hat{r}_i]E_{c_i}$

27:        Set $x_i := (E_0, \hat{E}_i', E_Y^i, E_i')$
28:        **if** $\text{NIZK.V}(x_i, \pi_i) \neq 1$ **then**
29:            **return** 0
30:     **if** $(c_1, \ldots, c_{t_S}) == \mathcal{H}(E_1' \| \cdots \| E_{t_S}' \| m)$
    then
31:        **return** 1
32:     **else**
33:        **return** 0
34: **procedure** Ext($\sigma, \hat{\sigma}, I_Y$)
35:     Parse σ as $(r_1, \ldots, r_{t_S}, c_1, \ldots, c_{t_S})$
36:     Parse $\hat{\sigma}$ as $(\hat{r}_1, \ldots, \hat{r}_{t_S}, c_1, \ldots, c_{t_S},$
37:           $\pi_1, \ldots, \pi_{t_S}, E_1', \ldots, E_{t_S}')$
38:     **for** $i \in \{1, \ldots, t_S\}$ **do**
39:        $y_i' \leftarrow r_i - \hat{r}_i$
40:     Set $\boldsymbol{y}' := [y_i' : i \in \{1, \ldots, t_S\}]$
41:     **if** $(I_Y, \boldsymbol{y}') \notin R_{E_0}^*$ **then**
42:        **return** $\perp$
43:     **return** $\boldsymbol{y}'$
44: **procedure** Adapt($\hat{\sigma}, \boldsymbol{y}$)
45:     Parse $\hat{\sigma}$ as $(\hat{r}_1, \ldots, \hat{r}_{t_S}, c_1, \ldots, c_{t_S},$
46:           $\pi_1, \ldots, \pi_{t_S}, E_1', \ldots, E_{t_S}')$
47:     Parse $\boldsymbol{y}$ as $(y_1, \ldots, y_{t_S})$
48:     **for** $i \in \{1, \ldots, t_S\}$ **do**
49:        $r_i \leftarrow \hat{r}_i + y_i \bmod N$
50:     **return** $\sigma := (r_1, \ldots, r_{t_S}, c_1, \ldots, c_{t_S})$

---

on the first component of the pre-signature/signature pair. Using this approach we revert back from the hard relation $R_{E_0}^{t_S}$ to $R_{E_0}^1$, and define a new modified relation $R_{E_0}^\dagger$, which consists of pairs $I_Y := (E_Y, \pi_Y)$, such that $E_Y \in L_{R_{E_0}^1}$ and π_Y is a zero-knowledge proof that $E_Y \in L_{R_{E_0}^1}$. More formally, we have that $R_{E_0}^\dagger := \{((E_Y, \pi_Y), y) \mid E_Y \in L_{R_{E_0}^1} \wedge \text{NIZK.V}(E_Y, \pi_Y) = 1\}$. Due to the soundness of the proof system, if $R_{E_0}^1$ is a hard relation, then so is $R_{E_0}^\dagger$. We call this optimized variant O−IAS, and capture its security with the following theorem, which we formally proof in the full version of our paper [28].

Theorem 2. *Assuming that the CSI-FiSh signature scheme $\Sigma_{\text{CSI−FiSh}}$ is SUF-CMA secure and $R_{E_0}^\dagger$ is a hard relation, the adaptor signature scheme $\Xi_{R_{E_0}^\dagger, \Sigma_{\text{CSI−FiSh}}}$, is secure in QROM.*

Remark 1. Although in this work we specifically focused on CSI-FiSh signature scheme, we note that our techniques to construct an adpaptor signature scheme can also be applied to other isogeny-based signatures that have similar algebraic limitations, such as the recently proposed SQISign [10] signature scheme.

5   Performance Evaluation

In order to evaluate IAS we extended the commit 7a9d30a version of the proof-of-concept implementation of CSI-FiSh (https://github.com/KULeuven-COSIC/CSI-FiSh). The implementation depends on the eXtended Keccak Code Package (https://github.com/XKCP/XKCP) for the implementation of SHAKE256, which is used as the underlying hash function and to expand the randomness. We also use the GMP library [18] for high precision arithmetic. We implemented the optimized variant O−IAS as explained in Sect. 4. Since O−IAS and CSI-FiSh are composed of multiple independent iterations of a non-interactive identification scheme, they are amenable to parallelization. Hence, we provided a parallelized implementation using OpenMP. The source code is available at https://github.com/etairi/Adaptor-CSI-FiSh.

Parameters. CSI-FiSh signature scheme is instantiated with the following parameters: i) S, the number of public keys to use, ii) t_S, the number of repetitions to perform, and iii) k, the rate of the slow hash function (e.g., $k = 16$ means that the used hash function is a factor 2^{16} slower than a standard hash function, such as SHA-3). In order to ensure λ bits of soundness security it suffices to take the parameters such that $S^{-t_S} \leq 2^{-\lambda+k}$. As is described in [3], the parameter S controls the trade-off between on the one hand small public key and fast key generation (when S is small), and on the other hand small signature and fast signing/verification (when S is large).

Testbed. All benchmarks were taken on a KVM-based VM with 2.0 GHz AMD EPYC 7702 processor with 16 cores and 32 GB RAM, running Ubuntu 18.04 LTS, and the code was compiled with gcc 7.5.0.

5.1   Evaluation Results

In this section, we present our evaluation results and discuss the communication size and computation time of O−IAS (i.e., sizes of objects and running times of the algorithms). The results of our evaluation are summarized in Table 1. As shown, playing with the parameters we can obtain different trade-offs, which we explain next. We divide our discussion on: (i) on-chain analysis (i.e., overhead imposed on the blockchain to support O−IAS) and (ii) off-chain analysis (i.e., overhead for peers at the application level).

On-Chain Analysis. In order to support O−IAS, the blockchain only needs to verify that each transaction is accompanied by a signature that correctly verifies under a given public key according to the logic of the verification algorithm of

CSI-FiSh. Thus, the *storage size* imposed by CSI-FiSh is dominated by the signature and public key sizes and the goal is thus to minimize these values. As was already described above, the parameter S can be set to a small value to achieve compact public keys. This, however, yields larger signatures. For instance, we can observe from Table 1 that by setting $S = 2$ one can have public keys of only 128 bytes, but at the cost of signatures of size 1880 bytes.

Similarly, the *computation time* of IAS for the miners is represented by the running time of the verification algorithm of CSI-FiSh. In our evaluation, we observe that increasing the value of S reduces the verification time of CSI-FiSh. However, as was already noted, this increases the public key sizes. Nevertheless, the technique of using Merkle trees to obtain compact and constant size public keys (but large secret keys) as described in [3] can also be applied to our construction. Using that technique one can have public keys of size 32 bytes, signatures of size 1995 bytes and verification algorithm running time of 370 ms with no parallelization, as shown in [3, Table 4], or 60 ms with our parallelized implementation.

Off-Chain Analysis. The operations of O−IAS defined in Algorithm 3 are carried out off-chain, meaning that the creation and verification of pre-signatures is done in a peer-to-peer manner and thus do not need to be stored in the blockchain, nor to be verified by the miners. Yet, we discuss here the computation time and communication size for this part as it illustrates the overhead for applications building upon O−IAS.

In terms of *communication size*, a pre-signature $\hat{\sigma}$ in IAS has size of $\sim$19 KB on average. We can observe from Table 1 that the pre-signature size only varies slightly the change in parameters. The reason for this is that the pre-signature size is dominated by the expensive zero-knowledge proof for L_2 (see Sect. 3.1) that is required during pre-signature computation, which has size $\sim$18 KB and it varies slightly with parameter k (bigger k implies smaller proof size). On the other hand the running times of the pre-signature and pre-verification algorithms decrease with the increased S value, meaning with the decreased number of iterations t_S. The reason for this is that during pre-signature and pre-verification computation our implementation only parallelizes the computation of the

Table 1. Performance of O−IAS. Time is shown in seconds and size in bytes.

S	t_S	k	$|\text{sk}|$	$|\text{pk}|$	$|\hat{\sigma}|$	$|\sigma|$	KeyGen	Sig	Ver	PreSig	PreVer	Ext	Adapt
2^1	56	16	16	128	19944	1880	0.05	0.24	0.23	3.59	3.55	0.005	0.005
2^2	38	14	16	256	19672	1286	0.06	0.16	0.16	2.75	2.68	0.005	0.005
2^3	28	16	16	512	19020	956	0.07	0.13	0.14	2.21	2.15	0.005	0.005
2^4	23	13	16	1024	19338	791	0.07	0.11	0.11	1.99	1.94	0.005	0.005
2^6	16	16	16	4096	18624	560	0.29	0.08	0.09	1.61	1.56	0.005	0.005
2^8	13	11	16	16384	19330	461	1.00	0.08	0.08	1.50	1.44	0.005	0.005
2^{10}	11	7	16	65536	19908	395	3.21	0.06	0.06	1.40	1.36	0.005	0.005
2^{12}	9	11	16	262144	19198	329	12.89	0.06	0.06	1.30	1.25	0.005	0.005
2^{15}	7	16	16	2097152	18327	263	102.02	0.06	0.06	1.16	1.11	0.005	0.005

zero-knowledge proof for L_2, but all the t_S iterations are computed by a single thread. We opted for this approach as the zero-knowledge proof is the dominating cost in IAS, and it requires $\sim$750 ms to compute and verify. On the other hand, extraction and adaptation are generally extremely fast operations for our construction, however, we point out that the time for extraction in Table 1 does not include the verification that the extracted witness $\boldsymbol{y}$, which is a vector of size 1 for O−IAS, satisfies $(I_Y, \boldsymbol{y}) \in R_{E_0}^*$ (line 49 in Algorithm 3). We note that in practice one can just extract the witness, adapt the pre-signature and then check that the signature verifies, which is more efficient than actually checking in $R_{E_0}^*$, which requires verifying an expensive zero-knowledge proof. Lastly, we note that even though the communication size is a bit high these operations are handled off-chain, and the pre-signatures are not stored in the blockchain.

5.2   Comparison with LAS

We compare our evaluation results with those of LAS [13], which is the only other known post-quantum AS, regarding on-chain and off-chain overhead. The authors of [13] did not provide any implementation, but they estimated the size of their signature and pre-signature as 2701 and 3210 bytes, respectively. From this we can observe that our signature sizes are 1.5–10× smaller depending on the parameter choices, however, our pre-signature sizes are $\sim$6× larger. However, due to the *weak* pre-signature adaptability property of LAS (as described in Sect. 1), the applications that use LAS require an expensive zero-knowledge proof to ensure that the extracted witness is of correct norm. In [14] it is shown that such a proof has size of 53 KB, which signifies that our construction is more efficient with respect to both on-chain and off-chain communication size. Moreover, LAS has public key size of 1472 bytes (observed from [12, Table 2]), which implies that using the Merkle tree technique we can have public key sizes that are 42× times smaller. In terms of computation time, LAS is an AS scheme based on Dilithium [12], and thus, it can perform more than hundred sign/verify operations per second, as these operations take less than one millisecond for Dilithium, thereby offering better computational performance than O−IAS.

In summary, our evaluation shows that it is feasible to adopt IAS to extend current blockchains with post-quantum AS at the cost of $\sim$1500 bytes (for combined public key and signature size using parameters $S = 2^3, t_S = 28, k = 16$) of communication size, which will be $\sim$3× smaller than LAS, and requiring only $\sim$100 ms of computation time (for signature verification using the same parameters). Analogous results and reduction in communication size also applies to the off-chain setting, which greatly benefits the off-chain applications using AS as building block, such as payment channels, payment-channel networks, atomic swaps or payment-channel hubs, which are performed over a WAN network, and thus, a reduction in communication is desirable.

6   Building Payment-Channel Networks from IAS

In this section we describe how to use adaptor signatures (AS) and IAS to build post-quantum payment-channel networks (PCNs). In particular, we give the background on PCNs, describe the atomic multi-hop locks (AMHLs) [21], show the current implementation (i.e., one susceptible to post-quantum adversaries), then we explain how to leverage IAS to build post-quantum resistant PCN that achieves both security and privacy, and lastly discuss the privacy challenges of LAS-based PCN from [13].

During our discussion, we assume that the verification algorithm in the underlying cryptocurrency is replaced by the verification algorithm of CSI-FiSh given in Algorithm 1. We further assume that the scripting language supports other application-dependent functionality such as timing conditions, which are available in virtually all cryptocurrencies today.

Background on PCN. Payment channels are a promising and practically relevant approach to mitigate the low throughput provided by permissionless cryptocurrencies such as Bitcoin. In a nuthsell, two users Alice and Bob create a payment channel between them by means of a Bitcoin transaction where they lock coins into a *deposit* Bitcoin address controlled by both of them. Afterwards, Alice and Bob can pay each other by exchanging signed transactions that distribute the coins at the deposit address. These off-chain payments are exchanged in a peer-to-peer manner and stored locally by the users. Only when Alice and Bob decide to close the channel, they include the last transaction that they have agreed on to the Bitcoin blockchain, therefore releasing the coins from the deposit address.

A PCN naturally extends the notion of payment channel to route payments between two users that do not have a payment channel directly between them. Instead, these two users can pay each other by means of multi-hop payments that leverage the payment channels available between intermediaries. A crucial property required in a multi-hop payment is the synchronization of the channels in the path, meaning that either all channels are successfully updated to process the payment or no channel is updated.

The Lightning Network uses the hash-time lock contract (HTLC) for such synchronization task. However, this mechanism presents security (i.e., it is prone to the wormhole attack) and privacy issues (i.e., it leaks who pays to whom). Recently, Malavolta et al. [21][21] have proposed Anonymous Multi-Hop Locks (AMHL) as an alternative synchronization protocol for multi-hop payments that overcomes the aforementioned security and privacy issues. The proposed constructions are, however, based on Schnorr and ECDSA digital signatures, both based on the discrete logarithm problem, and thus, insecure against quantum attackers. Our approach is thus to realize the functionality of AMHL leveraging IAS instead.

Background on AMHL. A multi-hop payment from sender S to receiver R through intermediaries $\{I\}_{1...k}$, which is synchronized with AMHL is divided in three steps: setup, commit and release. During the setup phase, S chooses random strings $l_0, \ldots, l_{k-1}$ and computes $y_j := \sum_{i=0}^{j} l_i$ and $Y_j := f(y_j)$ for $j := 0 \ldots k-1$ where f is an additively homomorphic one-way function. The setup ends when S sends the tuple (Y_{j-1}, Y_j, l_j) to each intermediary I_j and the tuple (Y_{k-1}, y_{k-1}) to the receiver R. At this point, each intermediary can check the correctness of the tuple received from the sender by checking that $f(l_j) \oplus Y_{j-1} = Y_j$, where $\oplus$ denotes the operation in the range of f.

After the setup, the commit phase starts when S makes a conditional payment to I_1 requiring that I_1 provides the pre-image of Y_0. Similarly, each intermediary I_j makes a conditional payment to I_{j+1} with the condition Y_j after they have received the corresponding payment from I_{j-1}. Finally, the release phase is triggered by the receiver R that reveals y_{k-1} to I_{k-1} to claim the coins in the conditional payment previously set during the commit phase. Then, each intermediary claims the coins from the previous neighbor in the path by computing $y_{j-1} := y_j - l_j$. When the release phase is finished, all channels are updated and the payment is finished.

Realizing AMHL with IAS. IAS allows for a smooth realization of AMHL in a post-quantum setting. The random strings l_j in our case are sampled from $\mathbb{Z}_N$ for $N = \#\mathrm{Cl}(\mathcal{O})$ being the order of the class group. The pre-images of the one-way function f in our case are computed as $y_j \leftarrow \sum_{i=0}^{j} l_i$.

The function f becomes the group action computation, and hence, we compute $Y_j \leftarrow [y_j]E$, for the public base curve E. Then, the setup phase continues as described above. We note that analogous to other AMHL realizations [13,21], S also needs to send a zero-knowledge proof π_{j+1} to each intermediary I_{j+1}, for $j \in \{0, \ldots, k-2\}$, which proves that S knows a witness y_j for Y_j. Although, this corresponds to the L_1 variant of the proof described in Sect. 3.1, one can just run an instance of the underlying basic CSI-FiSh identification scheme to prove this statement more efficiently, as it corresponds to a proof of a single secret group action.

Once the setup phase is finalized, the parties proceed to the commit and release phases, which we combine them here under a single phase called payment for brevity. We denote by tx_i the transaction transferring coins from I_j to I_{j+1}. During the payment phase S creates a pre-signature $\hat{\sigma}_0 \leftarrow \mathsf{PreSig}(\mathsf{sk}_0, \mathsf{tx}_0, Y_0)$, and shares it with I_1. Then, for $j \in \{1, \ldots, k-1\}$, each intermediary I_j creates its own pre-signature $\hat{\sigma}_j \leftarrow \mathsf{PreSig}(\mathsf{sk}_j, \mathsf{tx}_j, Y_j)$. Once all pre-signature are generated and shared, R adapts the pre-signature $\hat{\sigma}_{k-1}$ into a valid full signature σ_{k-1} using the witness y_{k-1} that it receives from S. Then, R shares σ_{k-1} with I_{k-1}, which extracts the witness y'_{k-1} using $\hat{\sigma}_{k-1}$ and σ_{k-1}, computes $y''_{k-2} \leftarrow y'_{k-1} - l_{k-1}$, and uses it to adapt its own pre-signature $\hat{\sigma}_{k-2}$. This process continues backwards until S receives σ_0.

This anonymous multi-hop payment construction is shown in Fig. 1.

Security and Privacy Discussion. In terms of security, Malavolta et al. [21] showed that when AMHL is constructed using an AS, the security reduces to the security of the underlying AS scheme. As proved in the full version of our paper

[28], IAS is a secure AS, hence, the security of our AMHL realization follows consequently.

Regarding privacy, we observe that each witness y_j (pre-image of f) is computed as the sum of $j+1$ elements that are uniformly sampled from $\mathbb{Z}_N$. Hence, the resulting value y_j is also uniformly distributed in $\mathbb{Z}_N$. Therefore, when a witness y_j is revealed to an intermediary, it does not leak any information that might be used to harm the privacy. As explained in Sect. 1, this is in contrast with the AMHL construction of LAS [13], where the norm of y_j increases (with high probability) as j increases (i.e., as we move further along the path). This in turn leaks non-trivial information regarding the path, which can be used to break the privacy notions of interest for an AMHL that are described in [21].

Privacy Challenges With LAS in PCNs. Interestingly, Esgin et al. [13] also describe how to realize a post-quantum PCN building on LAS. As the authors of this work point out, LAS is a post-quantum adaptor signature scheme that relies on hardness assumptions from lattices, a design choice that requires to carefully handle challenge inherent to the lattice setting that makes the realization of applications in a secure manner difficult. We refer to [13, Section 4.2] or more details. We observe that the lattice setting (and thus LAS) also presents severe challenges in terms of privacy.

In LAS-based PCN, the sender S during the setup samples k vectors r_j with infinity norm equal 1 [13, Fig. 2]. Then, S sets a vector $s_j := \sum_{i=0}^{j} r_i$ for each intermediary I_j. Thus, each vector s_j has an infinity norm equal j with high probability. This pattern leaks information that allows an honest-but-curious adversarial intermediary to deduce sensitive information. First, if the adversary receives a vector s_j with norm equal 1, then the adversary trivially learns that the sender of the payment is the left neighbor in the path. Second, if an adversary receives a vector with norm k^*, it learns that it is in the k^*-th position within the payment path.

As a possible countermeasure, one could imagine that the sender, during the setup, could set the norm of the vector s_0 (i.e., the first vector in the series s_j) to a value other than 1 chosen at random. This naïve approach has two disadvantages. First, increasing the norm of the vector s_j decreases the efficiency of the signature scheme. In fact, Esgin et al. suggest to keep this value below 50 for practical purposes. Second, this approach also breaks relationship anonymity [21], meaning that an adversarial intermediary can link who pays to whom in a PCN. In particular, as required in the definition of relationship anonymity, assume that two senders S_0 and S_1 simultaneously pay to receiver R_0 and R_1 correspondingly, through a path I_1, I_2, I_3 where I_1 and I_3 are controlled by the adversary. In this setting, when I_1 receives the vector s_0 from sender S_0 with a certain norm x, the adversary can compare it with the norm of the vector s_2 that sends to R_0. If the norm of s_2 is $x+2$, the adversary knows that R_0 is the intended receiver of the payment from S_0. Otherwise, the intended receiver is R_1. We leave the design of a modified version of LAS that preserves the privacy properties of off-chain applications such as PCNs as an interesting future work.

148   E. Tairi et al.

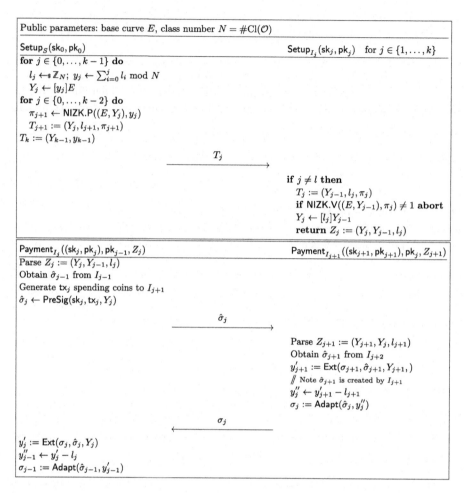

Fig. 1. Anonymous multi-hop payments using IAS. We assume that (i) T_j's are transmitted confidentially, (ii) pre-signature transmission from I_j to I_{j+1} happens only if that from I_{j-1} to I_j already happened, and (iii) signature transmission from I_{j+1} to I_j happens only if that from I_{j+2} to I_{j+1} already happened.

7 Conclusion

Adaptor signatures (AS) are an extension of digital signatures that enable the encoding of a cryptographic hard problem within the signature itself, a functionality that has emerged as a key building block for off-chain applications. However, virtually all current AS constructions are prone to attacks from an adversary with a quantum computer. The recently proposed post-quantum AS construction LAS constitutes a breakthrough in this sense, suffering however from limitations when it comes to performance, communication overhead and, most notably, privacy of the off-chain applications that use it as a building block.

In this work we designed IAS, the first construction for AS that is provably secure in the post-quantum setting that additionally provides the security and privacy notions of interest for off-chain applications built upon it. Our performance evaluation showed that IAS can be incorporated into current blockchains while requiring ~1500 bytes of storage size on-chain and 140 ms for digital signature verification. When compared to LAS, IAS requires 3× small storage while requiring higher computation time, thereby posing a different performance trade-off. Finally, we showed how to build post-quantum PCN from IAS.

Acknowledgements. This work has been partially supported by the European Research Council (ERC) under the European Unions Horizon 2020 research (grant agreement No 771527-BROWSEC); by Netidee through the project EtherTrust (grant agreement 2158) and PROFET (grant agreement P31621); by the Austrian Research Promotion Agency through the Bridge-1 project PR4DLT (grant agreement 13808694); by COMET K1 SBA, ABC; by Chaincode Labs through the project SLN: Scalability for the Lightning Network; by the Austrian Science Fund (FWF) through the Meitner program (project M-2608) and project W1255-N23.

References

1. Stress test prepares visanet for the most wonderful time of the year (2013). https://tinyurl.com/ya35s3uo
2. Aumayr, L., et al.: Generalized bitcoin-compatible channels. Cryptology ePrint Archive, Report 2020/476 (2020). https://eprint.iacr.org/2020/476
3. Beullens, W., Kleinjung, T., Vercauteren, F.: CSI-FiSh: efficient isogeny based signatures through class group computations. In: Galbraith, S.D., Moriai, S. (eds.) ASIACRYPT 2019. LNCS, vol. 11921, pp. 227–247. Springer, Cham (2019). https://doi.org/10.1007/978-3-030-34578-5_9
4. Bonnetain, X., Schrottenloher, A.: Quantum security analysis of CSIDH. In: Canteaut, A., Ishai, Y. (eds.) EUROCRYPT 2020. LNCS, vol. 12106, pp. 493–522. Springer, Cham (2020). https://doi.org/10.1007/978-3-030-45724-2_17
5. Buterin, V.: Understanding serenity, part I: Abstraction (2015). https://blog.ethereum.org/2015/12/24/understanding-serenity-part-i-abstraction/
6. Castryck, W., Lange, T., Martindale, C., Panny, L., Renes, J.: CSIDH: an efficient post-quantum commutative group action. In: Peyrin, T., Galbraith, S. (eds.) ASIACRYPT 2018. LNCS, vol. 11274, pp. 395–427. Springer, Cham (2018). https://doi.org/10.1007/978-3-030-03332-3_15
7. Couveignes, J.M.: Hard homogeneous spaces. Cryptology ePrint Archive, Report 2006/291 (2006). https://eprint.iacr.org/2006/291
8. Cozzo, D., Smart, N.P.: Sashimi: cutting up CSI-FiSh secret keys to produce an actively secure distributed signing protocol. In: PQCrypto (2020)
9. De Feo, L., Galbraith, S.D.: SeaSign: compact isogeny signatures from class group actions. In: Ishai, Y., Rijmen, V. (eds.) EUROCRYPT 2019. LNCS, vol. 11478, pp. 759–789. Springer, Cham (2019). https://doi.org/10.1007/978-3-030-17659-4_26
10. De Feo, L., Kohel, D., Leroux, A., Petit, C., Wesolowski, B.: SQISign: compact post-quantum signatures from quaternions and isogenies. In: Moriai, S., Wang, H. (eds.) ASIACRYPT 2020. LNCS, vol. 12491, pp. 64–93. Springer, Cham (2020). https://doi.org/10.1007/978-3-030-64837-4_3

11. Don, J., Fehr, S., Majenz, C., Schaffner, C.: Security of the Fiat-Shamir transformation in the quantum random-oracle model. In: Boldyreva, A., Micciancio, D. (eds.) CRYPTO 2019. LNCS, vol. 11693, pp. 356–383. Springer, Cham (2019). https://doi.org/10.1007/978-3-030-26951-7_13
12. Ducas, L., Lepoint, T., Lyubashevsky, V., Schwabe, P., Seiler, G., Stehle, D.: CRYSTALS - dilithium: digital signatures from module lattices. Cryptology ePrint Archive, Report 2017/633 (2017). https://eprint.iacr.org/2017/633
13. Esgin, M.F., Ersoy, O., Erkin, Z.: Post-quantum adaptor signatures and payment channel networks. In: Chen, L., Li, N., Liang, K., Schneider, S. (eds.) ESORICS 2020. LNCS, vol. 12309, pp. 378–397. Springer, Cham (2020). https://doi.org/10.1007/978-3-030-59013-0_19
14. Esgin, M.F., Nguyen, N.K., Seiler, G.: Practical exact proofs from lattices: new techniques to exploit fully-splitting rings. Cryptology ePrint Archive, Report 2020/518 (2020). https://eprint.iacr.org/2020/518
15. Esgin, M.F., Steinfeld, R., Sakzad, A., Liu, J.K., Liu, D.: Short lattice-based one-out-of-many proofs and applications to ring signatures. In: Deng, R.H., Gauthier-Umaña, V., Ochoa, M., Yung, M. (eds.) ACNS 2019. LNCS, vol. 11464, pp. 67–88. Springer, Cham (2019). https://doi.org/10.1007/978-3-030-21568-2_4
16. Foundation, Z.: Frequently asked questions. https://z.cash/support/faq/#quantum-computers
17. Fournier, L.: One-time verifiably encrypted signatures a.k.a. adaptor signatures (2019). https://github.com/LLFourn/one-time-VES/blob/master/main.pdf
18. Granlund, T., The GMP Development Team: GNU MP: The GNU Multiple Precision Arithmetic Library, 6.1.2 edn. (2019)
19. Kuperberg, G.: A subexponential-time quantum algorithm for the dihedral hidden subgroup problem. SIAM J. Comput. $35(1)$, 170–188 (2005)
20. Kuperberg, G.: Another subexponential-time quantum algorithm for the dihedral hidden subgroup problem. In: TQC 2013, pp. 20–34 (2013)
21. Malavolta, G., Moreno-Sanchez, P., Schneidewind, C., Kate, A., Maffei, M.: Anonymous multi-hop locks for blockchain scalability and interoperability. In: NDSS (2019)
22. Moreno-Sanchez, P., Blue, A., Le, D.V., Noether, S., Goodell, B., Kate, A.: DLSAG: non-interactive refund transactions for interoperable payment channels in Monero. In: Bonneau, J., Heninger, N. (eds.) FC 2020. LNCS, vol. 12059, pp. 325–345. Springer, Cham (2020). https://doi.org/10.1007/978-3-030-51280-4_18
23. Peikert, C.: He gives C-sieves on the CSIDH. In: Canteaut, A., Ishai, Y. (eds.) EUROCRYPT 2020. LNCS, vol. 12106, pp. 463–492. Springer, Cham (2020). https://doi.org/10.1007/978-3-030-45724-2_16
24. Poelstra, A.: Scriptless scripts. Presentation Slides (2017). https://download.wpsoftware.net/bitcoin/wizardry/mw-slides/2017-05-milan-meetup/slides.pdf
25. Rostovtsev, A., Stolbunov, A.: Public-key cryptosystem based on isogenies. Cryptology ePrint Archive, Report 2006/145 (2006). https://eprint.iacr.org/2006/145
26. Stolbunov, A.: Cryptographic schemes based on isogenies (2012)
27. Tairi, E., Moreno-Sanchez, P., Maffei, M.: A^{2}l: anonymous atomic locks for scalability in payment channel hubs. Cryptology ePrint Archive, Report 2019/589 (2019). https://eprint.iacr.org/2019/589
28. Tairi, E., Moreno-Sanchez, P., Maffei, M.: Post-quantum adaptor signature for privacy-preserving off-chain payments. Cryptology ePrint Archive, Report 2020/1345 (2020). https://eprint.iacr.org/2020/1345
29. Vélu, J.: Isogénies entre courbes elliptiques. CR Acad. Sci. Paris Sér. AB 273(A238–A241), 5 (1971)

FPPW: A Fair and Privacy Preserving Watchtower for Bitcoin

Arash Mirzaei$^{(\boxtimes)}$, Amin Sakzad, Jiangshan Yu, and Ron Steinfeld

Faculty of Information Technology, Monash University, Melbourne, Australia
{arash.mirzaei,amin.sakzad,jiangshan.yu,ron.steinfeld}@monash.edu

Abstract. In this paper, we introduce FPPW, a new payment channel with watchtower scheme for Bitcoin. This new scheme provides fairness w.r.t. all channel participants including both channel parties and the watchtower. It means that the funds of any honest channel participant are safe even assuming that other two channel participants are corrupted and/or collude with each other. Furthermore, the watchtower in FPPW learns no information about the off-chain transactions and hence FPPW provides privacy against the watchtower. As a byproduct, we also define the coverage of a watchtower scheme, that is the total capacity of channels that a watchtower can cover on a scale of 0 to 1, and show that FPPW's coverage is higher than those of PISA and Cerberus. The scheme can be implemented without any update in Bitcoin script.

Keywords: Bitcoin · Security · Privacy · Payment channel · Lightning network · Generalized channel · Watchtower

1 Introduction

Scalability has always been an important limitation of Bitcoin. Payment channel is a promising technique to resolve this issue. It enables two parties to open a channel by locking some funds in a 2-of-2 multi-signature output. Then parties can update the channel state by exchanging off-chain transactions. Finally, they record the last agreed state on-chain and each party receives its deserved amount of funds accordingly. Since off-chain transactions are not recorded on the blockchain, payment channels also provide some privacy guarantees.

Lightning [16] and generalized channels [1] are two important payment channels for Bitcoin. In a Lightning channel, commit transactions represent the channel states and each party has its own version of the transaction. However, in a generalized channel, both parties hold the same version of the state and adaptor signature is effectively used to distinguish the broadcaster of the transaction from its counter-party. Several schemes also exist on Turing complete blockchains (e.g. Ethereum) [6,8,14].

Most payment channels work based on this idea that once a dishonest channel party records an old state on-chain, its counter-party is supposed to provide evidence of invalidity of the published state within a time interval. Otherwise, the channel gets finalized with the recorded old state. Since duration of this time

© International Financial Cryptography Association 2021
N. Borisov and C. Diaz (Eds.): FC 2021, LNCS 12675, pp. 151–169, 2021.
https://doi.org/10.1007/978-3-662-64331-0_8

interval is limited, such payment channels rely on the assumption that channel parties check the blockchain frequently. However, since it is possible that channel parties crash or go offline for a long time, they might delegate the monitoring task to a third-party, called the watchtower. Monitor [5], DCWC [3], Outpust [10], Cerberus [4], and Tee Guard [11] are the existing watchtower schemes for Bitcoin, where Tee Guard follows a different direction as it relies on features of Trusted Execution Environments. There are also some watchtower schemes for Turing complete blockchains [2,12,13].

Monitor [5] is the first watchtower scheme for Lightning network which mainly focuses on the privacy against the watchtower. However, Monitor has two main issues, both of which related to fairness. Firstly, honest watchtowers might be rewarded upon fraud (i.e. broadcast of an old state on-chain), which is unfair with respect to (w.r.t.) the watchtower. Secondly, honest parties cannot penalize the unresponsive watchtower, which is unfair towards an honest hiring party.

DCWC [3] proposes the usage of a network of watchtowers which must cooperate to maximize their interest. This reduces the probability that the channel gets finalized with an old state. However, watchtowers might still crash or get unresponsive without being penalized by the hiring party. Also, the reward mechanism is still unfair w.r.t. the watchtower. Outpost [10] solves the issue of fairness towards the watchtower by paying her per channel update.

Cerberus [4] and PISA [13] elegantly provide fairness w.r.t. the hiring party. However, PISA fails to be deployed in cryptocurrencies with limited script languages such as Bitcoin and Cerberus sacrifices the privacy against the watchtower. In particular, the Cerberus watchtower learns the distribution of funds in the channel. Thus, the main motivation of this paper is designing a watchtower scheme for Bitcoin that achieves both: (1) fairness w.r.t. both the hired watchtower and her hiring party and (2) privacy against the watchtower.

1.1 Our Contribution

The contribution of this paper is as follows:

- We present a new privacy-preserving payment channel with watchtower scheme for Bitcoin called FPPW, which is fair w.r.t. all channel participants and allows the channel parties to go offline for a long period of time (Sect. 4). To be more precise, FPPW is an extension of a new variant of a generalized channel.
- We are the first to define the concepts of fairness, privacy against the watchtower and coverage for a watchtower service (Sect. 3.3), where coverage is a metric that represents the maximum total capacity of channels that the watchtower can cover on a scale of 0 to 1. Furthermore, in Sect. 5, we prove that our design achieves fairness w.r.t. all channel participants and unlike Cerberus, it provides privacy against the watchtower. We also show that the coverage of FPPW is better than that of Cerberus and PISA . Table 1 presents a quick comparison between FPPW and other schemes.

Table 1. Comparison of FPPW with existing watchtower schemes.

Scheme	Bitcoin support	Privacy	β-Coverage[a]	Channel party α-fairness[b]	Watchtower fairness
Monitor [5]	Yes	Yes	$\beta = 1$	$\alpha = 0$	No
DCWC [3]	Yes	Yes	$\beta = 1$	$\alpha = 0$	No
Outpost [10]	Yes	Yes	$\beta = 1$	$\alpha = 0$	Yes
PISA [13]	No	Yes	$\beta = 1/3$	$\alpha = 1$[c]	Yes
Cerberus [4]	Yes	No	$\beta = 1/3$	$\alpha = 1$	Yes
FPPW (this work)	Yes	Yes	$\beta = 1/2$	$\alpha = 1$	Yes

[a]: β is a value between 0 and 1 where the higher β, the higher achievable total capacity for the channels that are monitored by the watchtower.
[b]: α is a value between 0 and 1 and represents that the channel party might lose $(1 - \alpha)$ portion of its balance if the watchtower is unresponsive.
[c]: PISA allows the watchtower to lock an agreed amount of collateral per customer (i.e. $0 < \alpha \leq 1$). PISA also provides β-coverage with $\beta = 1/(1+2\alpha)$. However, in this table, to compare coverage of PISA with those of Cerberus and FPPW, we let PISA's collateral to be equal to the channel capacity (i.e. $\alpha = 1$).

– We propose a fee handling mechanism that allows the channel participants to determine the fee for different transactions at the time when fraud occurs. Furthermore, a proof-of-concept implementation of FPPW channels on Bitcoin is provided.[1]

2   Preliminaries and Notations

2.1   Preliminaries

In this section the underlying cryptographic primitives of FPPW are introduced.

Digital Signature. A digital signature scheme Π includes three algorithms as following:

– **Key Generation.** $(pk, sk) \leftarrow \mathsf{Gen}(1^\kappa)$ on input 1^κ (κ is the security parameter), outputs the public/private key pair (pk, sk).
– **Signing.** $\sigma \leftarrow \mathsf{Sign}_{sk}(m)$ on inputs the private key sk and a message $m \in \{0,1\}^*$ outputs the signature σ.
– **Verification.** $b \leftarrow \mathsf{Vrfy}_{pk}(m; \sigma)$ takes the public key pk, a message m and a signature σ as input and outputs a bit b.

In this work, we assume that the utilized signature schemes are existentially unforgeable under an adaptive chosen-message attack. It guarantees that the probability that an adversary who has access to a signing oracle outputs a valid signature on any new message is negligible. In this paper, we call such signature

---

[1] Due to lack of space, this will be presented in the technical report [15].

schemes secure. ECDSA [9] is a secure signature scheme that is currently being used in Bitcoin. Schnorr [17] is another important secure signature scheme that has been proposed to be introduced in Bitcoin due to its key aggregation and signature aggregation properties.

Hard Relation. A relation $\mathcal{R}$ with statement/witness pairs $(Y; y)$ is called a hard relation if (i) There exists a polynomial time generating algorithm $(Y; y) \leftarrow \mathsf{GenR}(1^\kappa)$ that on input 1^κ outputs a statement/witness pair $(Y; y) \in \mathcal{R}$; (ii) The relation between Y and y can be verified in polynomial time, and (iii) For any polynomial-time adversary $\mathscr{A}$, the probability that $\mathscr{A}$ on input Y outputs y is negligible. We also let $L_\mathcal{R} := \{Y \mid \exists Y \ s.t. \ (Y, y) \in \mathcal{R}\}$. Statement/witness pairs of $\mathcal{R}$ can be public/private key of a signature scheme generated by Gen algorithm.

Adaptor Signature. Adaptor signatures appeared first in [1]. Adaptor signature is used in generalized channels to tie together the authorization of a commit transaction and the leakage of a secret value. In what follows, we recall how an adaptor signature works. Given a hard relation $\mathcal{R}$ and a signature scheme Π, an adaptor signature protocol Ξ includes four algorithms as follows:

- **Pre-Signing.** $\tilde{\sigma} \leftarrow \mathsf{pSign}_{sk}(m, Y)$ is a probabilistic polynomial time (PPT) algorithm that on input a private key sk, message $m \in \{0,1\}^*$ and statement $Y \in L_\mathcal{R}$, outputs a pre-signature $\tilde{\sigma}$.
- **Pre-Verification.** $b \leftarrow \mathsf{pVrfy}_{pk}(m, Y; \tilde{\sigma})$ is a deterministic polynomial time (DPT) algorithm that on input a public key pk, message $m \in \{0,1\}^*$, statement $Y \in L_\mathcal{R}$ and pre-signature $\tilde{\sigma}$, outputs a bit b.
- **Adaptation.** $\sigma \leftarrow \mathsf{Adapt}(\tilde{\sigma}, y)$ is a DPT algorithm that on input a pre-signature $\tilde{\sigma}$ and witness y, outputs a signature σ.
- **Extraction,** $\mathsf{Ext}(\sigma, \tilde{\sigma}, Y)$ is a DPT algorithm that on input a signature σ, pre-signature $\tilde{\sigma}$, and statement $Y \in L_\mathcal{R}$, outputs $\perp$ or a witness y such that $(Y, y) \in \mathcal{R}$.

Correctness of an adaptor signature guarantees that for an honestly generated pre-signature $\tilde{\sigma}$ on the message m w.r.t. a statement $Y \in L_\mathcal{R}$, we have $\mathsf{pVrfy}_{pk}(m, Y; \tilde{\sigma}) = 1$. Furthermore, when $\tilde{\sigma}$ is adapted to the signature σ, we have $\mathsf{Vrfy}_{pk}(m; \sigma) = 1$ and $\mathsf{Ext}(\sigma, \tilde{\sigma}, Y)$ outputs y such that $(Y, y) \in \mathcal{R}$.

An adaptor signature scheme is secure if it is existentially unforgeable under chosen message attack ($\mathsf{aEUF - CMA}$ security), pre-signature adaptable and witness extractable. The $\mathsf{aEUF - CMA}$ security guarantees that it is of negligible probability that any PPT adversary who has access to signing and pre-signing oracles outputs a valid signature for any arbitrary new message m even given a valid pre-signature and its corresponding Y on m. Pre-signature adaptablity guarantees that every pre-signature (possibly generated maliciously) w.r.t. Y can adapt to a valid signature using the witness y with $(Y, y) \in \mathcal{R}$. Witness extractablity guarantees that it is of negligible probability that any PPT adversary who has access to signing and pre-signing oracles outputs a valid signature and a statement Y for any new message m such that the valid signature does not reveal a witness for Y even given a valid pre-signature on m w.r.t. Y. The ECDSA-based and Schnorr-based adaptor signature schemes were constructed and analyzed in [1].

2.2   Notations

In this section, we present the notations for Bitcoin transactions. A Bitcoin transaction Tx_i has some inputs and some outputs and is denoted by:

$$Tx_i = [I_i^1, I_i^2, \ldots] \rightarrow [O_i^1, O_i^2, \ldots],$$

where I_i^j and O_i^j with $j \geq 0$ denote the jth input and the jth output of Tx_i, respectively. If Tx_i has one output, this output is denoted by O_i. Each Bitcoin output O, denoted by $(x \mid \varphi)$, consists of a monetary value x and some conditions φ that must be met when one takes O as an input in another transaction. If an output has several subconditions, they are separated by $\vee$ operation(s); To spend the output, one of the subconditions must be met. Each transaction input I has also two elements where the first one is actually the output of a previously published transaction O and the second element is the witness γ that I uses to meet the condition φ of O. The witness γ has also two elements, first of which is denoted by S and determines the index of the subcondition that I meets. The second element of γ, which is denoted by D, is actually the data that is required to meet the subcondition. To simplify the notations, we denote I by $(O\|S)$. If a transaction Tx_i lacks some required data in witness part of at least one of its inputs, it is denoted by $[Tx_i]$.

The signature and pre-signature of party $\mathcal{P}$ on Tx_i for its jth input is denoted by $\sigma_i^{\mathcal{P},j}$ and $\tilde{\sigma}_i^{\mathcal{P},j}$, respectively, where j can be removed if Tx_i has one input. Since transaction flows might be difficult to follow, we also use charts to illustrate them. For example, $Tx_i = [(O_j^3\|2), (O_k\|1)] \rightarrow [O_i^1, O_i^2, \ldots]$ is illustrated in Fig. 1. Transactions that are already published on-chain are illustrated by doubled edge rectangles (e.g. Tx_j in Fig. 1). Transactions that are ready to be published are illustrated by single edge rectangles (e.g. Tx_i). Dotted edge rectangles show transactions that still lack the required witness for at least one input and hence are unprepared to be propagated in the blockchain network (e.g. $[Tx_k]$ in Fig. 1).

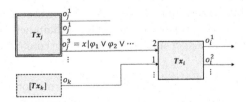

Fig. 1. Transaction flow of $Tx_i = [(O_j^3\|2), (O_k\|1)] \rightarrow [O_i^1, O_i^2, \ldots]$.

For some transactions, the output that is taken as input to the transaction is irrelevant to protocol design. Such inputs are notated by $(x \mid \#_{\mathcal{P}})$ where x and $\mathcal{P}$ denotes the value and owner of that taken output, respectively. For example, the funding transaction of a payment channel between $\mathcal{A}$ and $\mathcal{B}$ is denoted by:

$$Tx_i = [(a \mid \#_{\mathcal{A}}), (b \mid \#_{\mathcal{B}})] \rightarrow [(a+b \mid pk_{\mathcal{A}} \wedge pk_{\mathcal{B}})].$$

Table 2 summarizes the mentioned notations.

Table 2. Notations

Notation	Description
Tx_i	Transaction $Tx_i = [I_i^1, I_i^2, \ldots] \rightarrow [O_i^1, O_i^2, \ldots]$ with inputs I_i^1, I_i^2, etc. and outputs O_i^1, O_i^2, etc.
I_i^j	j^{th} input of transaction Tx_i
O_i^j	j^{th} output of Tx_i. Index j can be removed if Tx_i has a single output
$O = (x \mid \varphi)$	Output with monetary value x and condition φ
γ_i^j	Witness of the input I_i^j
$\sigma_i^{\mathcal{P},j}$ (or $\tilde{\sigma}_i^{\mathcal{P},j}$)	Signature (or pre-signature) of $\mathcal{P}$ on j^{th} input of Tx_i. The index j can be removed if Tx_i has a single input
$I = (O\|S)$	The input that meets S^{th} subcondition of the output O
$[Tx_i]$	Transaction Tx_i with incomplete witness for at least one input
$(x\|\#_{\mathcal{A}})$	Any arbitrary output owned by $\mathcal{A}$ with monetary value of x

3 FPPW Overview

3.1 System Model

Cryptographic primitives that have been used in FPPW are cryptographically secure. There is an authenticated and secure end-to-end communication channel between channel parties. The watchtower and channel parties are rational and might deviate from the protocol if it increases their profit. Also, each pair of participants might collude with each other if it raises the total profit of colluding participants. The watchtower is an always online service provider, but channel parties can go offline for a long period (approximately T rounds). Furthermore, the underlying blockchain contains a distributed ledger that achieves security [7]. When a valid transaction is propagated in the blockchain network, it is definitely included in the blockchain ledger immediately (i.e. the confirmation delay τ is 1).

Remark 1. FPPW channels can work with any confirmation delay. However, we assume that the confirmation delay is 1 to simplify the protocol and its analysis.

3.2 FPPW Overview

A payment channel contains a sequence of state updates between two parties where only its first and last states are recorded on the blockchain. The two channel parties process all the intermediate state updates off-chain. This eliminates the need to confirm every state update, i.e. every transaction, on the blockchain. However, as one may submit an intermediate state (which is already revoked by a later state) to the blockchain, the channel parties will need to get online frequently to monitor and punish such misbehaviours. Such a requirement may be impractical for some users. Thus, watchtower is introduced as a third party to act on behalf of the channel parties.

FPPW is a fair and privacy preserving watchtower service for generalised channels [1]. FPPW provides privacy against the watchtower and hence the watchtower obtains no data on intermediate state updates. To provide fairness towards the watchtower, the FPPW service rewards the watchtower for the channel establishment and per channel update. Furthermore, to achieve fairness w.r.t. channel parties, the watchtower must lock some collateral, which is redeemed if the watchtower is responsive upon fraudulent channel closures. If the watchtower is dishonest and the channel is closed at an old state, protocol guarantees that the cheated party can penalize the watchtower by taking its collateral. Watchtower can reclaim its collateral at any time. Then, the channel parties can update the channel on-chain and hire a new watchtower or continue using the channel. In the latter case, channel parties must get online frequently.

3.3 Watchtower Service Properties

In this section, some properties of a watchtower service are formally defined.

Definition 1 (Channel party α-Fairness). *A payment channel with watchtower is α-party-fair, if the following holds for an honest channel party $\mathcal{P}$:*

- *$\mathcal{P}$ can close the channel at any time and*
- *α is the largest real number such that regardless of the reward that $\mathcal{P}$ pays to the watchtower, $\mathcal{P}$ loses at most $(1 - \alpha) \cdot x_{\mathcal{P}}$ coins in the channel where $x_{\mathcal{P}}$ denotes balance of $\mathcal{P}$ in the latest channel state.*

Note that $0 \leq \alpha \leq 1$, where $\alpha = 1$ implies that the honest party $\mathcal{P}$ will not lose any fund in the channel and $\alpha = 0$ means that $\mathcal{P}$ might lose all of his funds.

Definition 2 (Watchtower Fairness). *A payment channel with watchtower is watchtower-fair, if the following holds for an honest watchtower $\mathcal{W}$:*

- *$\mathcal{W}$ is rewarded with some non-zero amounts of coins and*
- *given that $\mathcal{W}$ has locked some collateral as part of the watching service, it is of negligible probability that the honest watchtower cannot redeem all the collateral once watching terminates according to the watching agreement.*

Monitor [5] and DCWC [3] are called unfair w.r.t the watchtower because for these schemes, it is possible that the watchtower is not rewarded.

Let $x_{\mathcal{P},0}$ with $\mathcal{P} \in \{\mathcal{A}, \mathcal{B}\}$ denote the initial balance of party $\mathcal{P}$ in the channel and the channel capacity be defined as $X := x_{\mathcal{A},0} + x_{\mathcal{B},0}$. The *privacy* is defined by the following *privacy game*.

Challenge. Let there exist two payment channels where the first one is between honest channel parties $\mathcal{A}$ and $\mathcal{B}$ and the second one is between honest channel parties $\mathcal{A}'$ and $\mathcal{B}'$ and both channels have the same number of channel updates n and the same channel setup, i.e. $x_{\mathcal{A},0} = x_{\mathcal{A}',0}$, $x_{\mathcal{B},0} = x_{\mathcal{B}',0}$, $x_{\mathcal{A},n} = x_{\mathcal{A}',n}$ and $x_{\mathcal{B},n} = x_{\mathcal{B}',n}$. Let $\mathbf{x}_{\mathcal{P},[i,j]}$ show the sequence of balance values of party $\mathcal{P}$ between i^{th} to j^{th} states of the payment channel that $\mathcal{P}$ is involved in. Assume that $\mathscr{A}$ is any passive PPT adversarial watchtower excluding $\mathcal{A}$, $\mathcal{B}$, $\mathcal{A}'$ and $\mathcal{B}'$ which watches these two channels. To challenge $\mathscr{A}$, the challenger selects a random bit b and gives the sequence $(\mathbf{x}_{\mathcal{P},[1,n-1]}, \mathbf{x}_{\bar{\mathcal{P}},[1,n-1]})$ to $\mathscr{A}$ where $\mathcal{P} = \mathcal{A}$ and $\bar{\mathcal{P}} = \mathcal{B}$ if $b = 0$ and $\mathcal{P} = \mathcal{A}'$ and $\bar{\mathcal{P}} = \mathcal{B}'$ otherwise.

Output. The adversary $\mathscr{A}$ outputs a bit b' to guess that the received sequence belongs to the first or the second channel. The adversary wins the game if and only if $b = b'$.

Remark 2. For any multihop payment routed via the channel between $\mathcal{A}$ and $\mathcal{B}$ or the channel between $\mathcal{A}'$ and $\mathcal{B}'$, we assume that the passive adversary is not involved as a channel party in routing such payments.

Definition 3 (Weak Privacy Against Watchtower). *A payment channel with watchtower provides weak privacy against the watchtower if according to the privacy game* $| \Pr[b = b'] - 1/2 |$ *is negligible.*[2]

Next, we define β-coverage, which basically measures the capability of a watchtower (on a scale between 0 to 1) in watching all the existing payment channels on a fixed Blockchain.

Definition 4 (Coverage). *For a blockchain $\mathbb{B}$ with N payment channels, a watchtower $\mathcal{W}$ provides β-coverage with $\beta := \frac{X}{C+X}$, where C is the total collateral required by $\mathcal{W}$ to watch all payment channels for both channel parties and X is the total capacity of all channels.*

The parameter β can take any value in the interval $[0, 1]$. For Cerberus and PISA (with $\alpha = 1$), β equals $\frac{1}{3}$ because for these schemes, collateral of the watchtower must be twice the channel capacity if the watchtower is going to be hired by both channel parties. Although, PISA allows lower values of collateral, such values cannot provide channel party α-fairness with $\alpha = 1$ and hence cannot guarantee that the honest party does not lose any funds.

---

[2] If in the defined privacy game, the channel setup for two channels could be different and the sequence $(\mathbf{x}_{\mathcal{P},[0,n]}, \mathbf{x}_{\bar{\mathcal{P}},[0,n]})$ is given to the passive PPT adversarial watchtower, then the privacy guarantee is stronger. While Monitor, DCWC, and Outpost provide such stronger privacy guarantee, PISA provides weak privacy as defined in Definition 3 and Cerberus does not achieve privacy against watchtower.

4   FPPW Channel

The lifetime of an FPPW channel can be divided into 4 phases including establishment, update, closure and abort. We explain these phases through the following sections. The cryptographic primitives, used in these phases, are as following: A digital signature scheme Π = (Gen, Sign, Vrfy); a hard relation $\mathcal{R}$ with generating algorithm GenR = Gen; an adaptor signature scheme $\Xi_{\Pi,\mathcal{R}}$ = (pSign, pVrfy, Adapt, Ext). We assume that the watchtower is hired by both channel parties. However, FPPW can be simply extended to situations where only one party hires the watchtower. FPPW for such scenarios will be provided in the technical report [15].

4.1   FPPW Channel Establishment

FPPW channel establishment phase includes a funding transaction, a commit transaction and a split transaction. The funding transaction locks funds of the channel parties in a 2-of-2 multisig output and can be claimed only if both parties agree and cooperate with each other. The commit transaction is held by both channel parties and sends all the channel funds to a joint account that can be spent by the corresponding split transaction after t rounds. Split transaction actually represents the channel state and distributes the channel funds between the channel parties. The quantity t, which is called the revocation period, exists to ensure that there is enough time for punishing the dishonest channel party in case of fraud (i.e. if the published commit transaction corresponds with a revoked state). Parties finally publish the funding transaction on the blockchain. However, since its output can be spent if both parties cooperate, one party might lock the funds by being unresponsive. To avoid such situations, before signing the funding transaction, both channel parties must sign commit and split transactions.

Additionally, two other transactions are created in this phase including the collateral transaction and the reclaim transaction which are used for watchtower services. Using the collateral transaction, the watchtower locks its collateral in a 3-of-3 multisig output shared between channel parties and the watchtower. Collateral is awarded to the cheated channel party if the watchtower does not appropriately act upon fraud. The value of the collateral equals the channel capacity. Using the reclaim transaction, the watchtower can start the process of reclaiming its collateral. The watchtower can finally redeem its collateral by claiming the output of the reclaim transaction after a large relative timelock of T rounds with $T \gg t$ which is called the penalty period. If channel parties get online at least once every $T-1$ rounds, they will always have enough time to take the dishonest watchtower's collateral as compensation and prevent an unresponsive watchtower from redeeming its collateral. However, if the honest watchtower has published the reclaim transaction to withdraw its service, channel parties will have two options. They can either update the channel on-chain with a new watchtower or remain almost always online to prevent from fraudulent channel closures. Collateral transaction is finally recorded on-chain. However, to avoid any hostage situation, before publishing the collateral transaction, the watch-tower must receive channel parties' signatures on the reclaim transaction.

All the above-mentioned transactions are further explained hereinafter.

- **Funding transaction**: Using this transaction, channel parties $\mathcal{A}$ and $\mathcal{B}$ open an FPPW channel. Funding transaction is defined as follows:

$$Tx_{\mathrm{FU}} := [(a + \epsilon/2 \mid \#_{\mathcal{A}}), (b + \epsilon/2 \mid \#_{\mathcal{B}})] \rightarrow [(a + b + \epsilon \mid (pk_{\mathcal{A}} \wedge pk_{\mathcal{B}}))], \quad (1)$$

where ϵ is the minimum value supported by the Bitcoin blockchain and a and b are the initial balance of $\mathcal{A}$ and $\mathcal{B}$ in the channel (regardless of the negligible value $\epsilon/2$). Output of Tx_{FU} is a 2-of-2 multisig output shared between $\mathcal{A}$ and $\mathcal{B}$. The public keys $pk_{\mathcal{A}}$ and $pk_{\mathcal{B}}$ of $\mathcal{A}$ and $\mathcal{B}$ are generated using the key generation algorithm of the underlying digital signature Gen.

- **Commit transaction**: There exists one commit transaction $Tx_{\mathrm{CM},i}$ per state but only the first one ($Tx_{\mathrm{CM},i}$ with $i = 0$) is created at the channel establishment phase. $Tx_{\mathrm{CM},i}$ is as follows:

$$Tx_{\mathrm{CM},i} := [(O_{\mathrm{FU}}\|1)] \rightarrow [(a + b \mid \varphi_{\mathrm{CM},i}^1), (\epsilon \mid \varphi_{\mathrm{CM},i}^2)], \quad (2)$$

where $\varphi_{\mathrm{CM},i}^1 := \varphi_{\mathrm{CM},i(1)}^1 \vee \varphi_{\mathrm{CM},i(2)}^1$ with $\varphi_{\mathrm{CM},i(1)}^1 := pk_{\mathcal{A}} \wedge pk_{\mathcal{B}} \wedge \Delta_t$, $\varphi_{\mathrm{CM},i(2)}^1 := pk_{\mathcal{A}} \wedge pk_{\mathcal{B}} \wedge pk_{\mathcal{W}}$ and $\varphi_{\mathrm{CM},i}^2 := \varphi_{\mathrm{CM},i(1)}^2 \vee \varphi_{\mathrm{CM},i(2)}^2 \vee \varphi_{\mathrm{CM},i(3)}^2$ with $\varphi_{\mathrm{CM},i(1)}^2 := pk_{\mathcal{B}} \wedge Y_{\mathcal{A},i} \wedge \Delta_t$, $\varphi_{\mathrm{CM},i(2)}^2 := pk_{\mathcal{A}} \wedge pk_{\mathcal{B}} \wedge pk_{\mathcal{W}}$ and $\varphi_{\mathrm{CM},i(3)}^2 := pk_{\mathcal{A}} \wedge Y_{\mathcal{B},i} \wedge \Delta_t$ where $Y_{\mathcal{A},i}$ and $Y_{\mathcal{B},i}$ are statements of a hard relation $\mathcal{R}$ generated by $\mathcal{A}$ and $\mathcal{B}$ for the ith state using the generating algorithm GenR and Δ_t shows relative timelock of t rounds. $O_{\mathrm{CM},i}^1$ is the main output with value of $a+b$. Normally, if parties act honestly and $Tx_{\mathrm{CM},i}$ is published on-chain, the first subcondition of its main output ($pk_{\mathcal{A}} \wedge pk_{\mathcal{B}} \wedge \Delta_t$) is met by $Tx_{\mathrm{SP},i}$ after t rounds. The $O_{\mathrm{CM},i}^2$ with value of ϵ is the auxiliary output, which as will be explained in Sect. 4.2, is only used for watchtower purposes.

The transaction $Tx_{\mathrm{CM},i}$ requires signatures of both parties $\mathcal{A}$ and $\mathcal{B}$ to be published. To generate $\sigma_{\mathrm{CM},i}^{\mathcal{B}}$, party $\mathcal{A}$ generates a statement/witness pair $(Y_{\mathcal{A},i}, y_{\mathcal{A},i})$ and sends the statement $Y_{\mathcal{A},i}$ to $\mathcal{B}$. Then, party $\mathcal{B}$ uses the pre-signing algorithm pSign of the adaptor signature and $\mathcal{A}$'s statement $Y_{\mathcal{A},i}$ to generate a pre-signature $\tilde{\sigma}_{\mathrm{CM},i}^{\mathcal{B}}$ on $[Tx_{\mathrm{CM},i}]$ and sends the result to $\mathcal{A}$. Thus, whenever it is necessary, $\mathcal{A}$ is able to use the adaptation algorithm adapt of the adaptor signature to transform the pre-signature to the signature $\sigma_{\mathrm{CM},i}^{\mathcal{B}}$ and publish $Tx_{\mathrm{CM},i}$ on-chain. This also enables $\mathcal{B}$ to use the extraction algorithm Extract, the published signature and its corresponding pre-signature to extract the witness value $y_{\mathcal{A},i}$. The witness value, as will be seen in Sect. 4.2, might be used to punish a dishonest channel party by claiming all the channel funds or to penalize an unresponsive watchtower.

Remark 3. $\mathcal{A}$ has two public keys in $O_{\mathrm{CM},i}^1$, which for simplicity, we denote them both by $pk_{\mathcal{A}}$. However, in practice such public keys are selected dis-jointly. This is also extended to other participants and other outputs.

– **Split transaction**: $Tx_{\mathrm{SP},i}$ actually represents the ith channel state where only the first one ($Tx_{\mathrm{SP},i}$ with $i = 0$) is created in the channel establishment phase. This transaction is as follows:

$$Tx_{\mathrm{SP},i} := [(O^1_{\mathrm{CM},i}\|1)] \rightarrow [(x^1_{\mathrm{SP},i} \mid \varphi^1_{\mathrm{SP},i}),(x^2_{\mathrm{SP},i} \mid \varphi^2_{\mathrm{SP},i}),\ldots]. \tag{3}$$

The $Tx_{\mathrm{SP},i}$ spends the main output of $Tx_{\mathrm{CM},i}$ by meeting the subcondition $pk_{\mathcal{A}} \wedge pk_{\mathcal{B}} \wedge \Delta_t$.

– **Collateral transaction**: Tx_{CL} locks the collateral of the watchtower on-chain and its output can be spent if $\mathcal{A}$, $\mathcal{B}$ and $\mathcal{W}$ cooperate. Value of collateral c equals $a + b$. The Tx_{CL} is defined as follows:

$$Tx_{\mathrm{CL}} := [(c \mid \#_{\mathcal{W}})] \rightarrow [(c \mid pk_{\mathcal{A}} \wedge pk_{\mathcal{B}} \wedge pk_{\mathcal{W}})]. \tag{4}$$

– **Reclaim transaction**: This transaction spends the output of Tx_{CL} and its output can be spent by $\mathcal{A}$, $\mathcal{B}$ and $\mathcal{W}$ if they cooperate or by $\mathcal{W}$ after a long relative timelock period. The Tx_{RC} is defined as follows:

$$Tx_{\mathrm{RC}} := [(O_{\mathrm{CL}}\|1)] \rightarrow [(c \mid (pk_{\mathcal{A}} \wedge pk_{\mathcal{B}} \wedge pk_{\mathcal{W}}) \vee (pk_{\mathcal{W}} \wedge \Delta_T))]. \tag{5}$$

The second subcondition is used by the watchtower to redeem its collateral after T rounds and withdraw its service. However, as will be mentioned in following sections, the first subcondition is used to penalize the unresponsive watchtower.

Figure 2 summarizes the channel establishment phase. The technical report [15] provides details of the corresponding protocol.

4.2   FPPW Channel Update

Assume that an FPPW channel is in state i with $i \geq 0$ and channel parties decide to update it from state i to $i + 1$. This is performed in two sub-phases. In the first sub-phase, channel parties create a new commit transaction and a new split transaction for the new state. However, to avoid any hostage situation, they sign the split transaction before signing the commit transaction. In the second sub-phase, channel parties revoke the previous state by signing one revocation and two penalty transactions. At most one out of these three transactions might be published on-chain upon fraud (i.e. upon broadcast of the revoked commit transaction). While the revocation transaction might be used to penalize the cheating channel party, penalty transactions might be utilized for punishing the dishonest watchtower.

The revocation transaction is the only transaction that spends both outputs of the revoked commit transaction using their non-timelocked subconditions $pk_{\mathcal{A}} \wedge pk_{\mathcal{B}} \wedge pk_{\mathcal{W}}$. Thus, once a dishonest channel party publishes the revoked commit transaction, the watchtower or the counter-party can immediately publish the revocation transaction. It invalidates both penalty transactions because

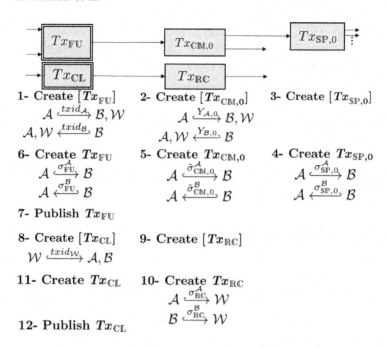

Fig. 2. A summary of FPPW channel establishment.

they also spend the auxiliary output of the revoked commit transaction. The single output of the revocation transaction is spendable by someone who knows witness value y of both channel parties (i.e. party $\mathcal{A}$ can claim it if party $\mathcal{B}$ has published the revoked commit transaction and vice versa).

Now assume that a dishonest channel party publishes the revoked commit transaction but the watchtower does not react in time. Then the dishonest channel party might also publish the corresponding split transaction after t rounds. This spends the main output of the revoked commit transaction and invalidates the revocation transaction. However, since the honest channel party go offline for at most $T - 1$ rounds, it gets online when the watchtower has not completed reclaiming its collateral yet (i.e. the watchtower has not broadcast the reclaim transaction or has not spent its output yet). Thus, the honest party can publish one of two penalty transactions. Both penalty transactions spend the auxiliary output of the revoked commit transaction as well as output of collateral and reclaim transaction, respectively. Similar to the revocation transaction, only the honest cheated party can claim output of the published penalty transaction.

The introduced transactions will be explained further bellow:

– **Revocation transaction**: When parties $\mathcal{A}$ and $\mathcal{B}$ want to revoke $Tx_{\mathrm{CM},i}$, each channel participant ($\mathcal{A}$, $\mathcal{B}$ and $\mathcal{W}$) generates all the required signatures for the revocation transaction $Tx_{\mathrm{RV},i}$ and sends the signatures to other two participants. $Tx_{\mathrm{RV},i}$ is as follows:

$$Tx_{RV,i} := [(O_{CM,i}^1\|2), (O_{CM,i}^2\|2)] \rightarrow [(a + b + \epsilon \mid Y_{A,i} \wedge Y_{B,i})]. \qquad (6)$$

The $Tx_{RV,i}$ spends both outputs of $Tx_{CM,i}$ using the non-timelocked sub-condition $pk_A \wedge pk_B \wedge pk_W$ and sends all the channel funds to an output with condition $Y_{A,i} \wedge Y_{B,i}$. When a dishonest party, let's say A, publishes the revoked $Tx_{CM,i}$, A must wait for t rounds before being able to publish $Tx_{SP,i}$. However, W or B can immediately publish $Tx_{RV,i}$. Since $Tx_{CM,i}$ has been published by A, party B can obtain $y_{A,i}$. Thus, only party B who knows both $y_{A,i}$ and $y_{B,i}$ will own all the channel funds.

- **Penalty transaction 1**: There is one penalty transaction 1 $Tx_{PN_1,i}$ per revoked state which is used to penalize W, given that a dishonest party publishes $Tx_{CM,i}$ and spends its main output using $Tx_{SP,i}$. The $Tx_{PN_1,i}$ is defined as follows:

$$Tx_{PN_1,i} := [(O_{CM,i}^2\|j), (O_{CL}\|1)] \rightarrow [(c + \epsilon \mid Y_{A,i} \wedge Y_{B,i})], \qquad (7)$$

where $j := 1$ given that broadcaster of $Tx_{CM,i}$ is A or $j := 3$ otherwise. When parties want to revoke $Tx_{CM,i}$, A and W (B and W) compute the required signatures for the second input of $Tx_{PN_1,i}$ and send the signatures to B (A). Now assume that one party, let's say A, publishes the revoked $Tx_{CM,i}$ and spends its main output after t rounds. Then, B obtains $y_{A,i}$ and hence can add the required signatures for the first input of $Tx_{PN_1,i}$ and publish it, given that O_{CL} is still unspent. $Tx_{PN_1,i}$ spends the second output of $Tx_{CM,i}$ using the timelocked subcondition $pk_B \wedge Y_{A,i} \wedge \Delta_t$ as well as the output of the collateral transaction. Only B can claim output of $Tx_{PN_1,i}$. A similar scenario can occur if B is the broadcaster of $Tx_{CM,i}$.

- **Penalty transaction 2**: There exists one penalty transaction 2 $Tx_{PN_2,i}$ per state. It is exactly the same as $Tx_{PN_1,i}$, with the only difference that it spends O_{RC} (rather that O_{CL}) using the subcondition $pk_A \wedge pk_B \wedge pk_W$. Thus, it is useful for cases where the watchtower does not react upon fraud but by publishing Tx_{RC} tries to reclaim its collateral. However, since the honest party goes offline for at most $T - 1$ rounds, it gets online when O_{RC} is still unspent. Thus, the honest party can add the required signatures to $[Tx_{PN_2,i}]$ and publish it. The $Tx_{PN_2,i}$ is defined as follows:

$$Tx_{PN_2,i} := [(O_{CM,i}^2\|j), (O_{RC}\|1)] \rightarrow [(c + \epsilon \mid Y_{A,i} \wedge Y_{B,i})], \qquad (8)$$

where $j := 1$ given that broadcaster of $Tx_{CM,i}$ is party A or $j := 3$ otherwise.

Figure 3 summarizes the channel update phase. The technical report [15] provides details of the corresponding protocol.

Remark 4. Watchtower is actively involved in steps 6 and 7 of the channel update phase (See Fig. 3). Therefore, this phase fails to complete if the watchtower is unavailable. The technical report [15] introduces an update protocol for such scenarios.

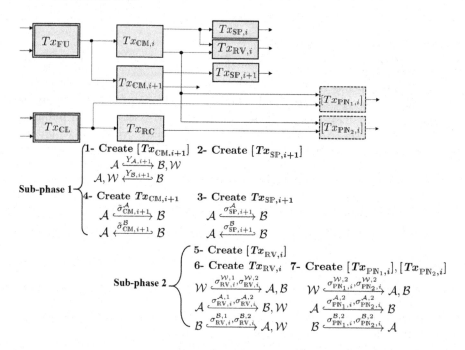

Fig. 3. A summary of FPPW channel update.

4.3   FPPW Channel Closure

Assume that the channel parties $\mathcal{A}$ and $\mathcal{B}$ have updated their channel n times and then $\mathcal{A}$ and/or $\mathcal{B}$ decide to close it. They can close the channel cooperatively. To do so, $\mathcal{A}$ and $\mathcal{B}$ create a new transaction, called modified split transaction $Tx_{\overline{\text{SP}}}$, and publish it on-chain. The $Tx_{\overline{\text{SP}}}$ is defined as follows:

$$Tx_{\overline{\text{SP}}} := [(O_{\text{FU}}\|1)] \rightarrow [(x^1_{\overline{\text{SP}}} \mid \varphi^1_{\overline{\text{SP}}}), (x^2_{\overline{\text{SP}}} \mid \varphi^2_{\overline{\text{SP}}}), \ldots]. \qquad (9)$$

Outputs of this transaction might be similar to those for $Tx_{\text{SP},n}$. Note that the value of auxiliary output of $Tx_{\text{CM},n}$ (ϵ) can also be given to $\mathcal{A}$ and $\mathcal{B}$ ($\epsilon/2$ each) through outputs of $Tx_{\overline{\text{SP}}}$. If one of the channel parties gets unresponsive, its counter-party can still close the channel non-collaboratively by publishing $Tx_{\text{CM},n}$ and then $Tx_{\text{SP},n}$ on-chain.

It is always possible that a channel party publishes a revoked commit transaction $Tx_{\text{CM},i}$ on-chain. Then, the watchtower or the counter-party publishes the corresponding revocation transaction within $t-1$ rounds. Only the honest counter-party can claim output of the revocation transaction. If the watchtower is unresponsive and the honest party is offline, a malicious party can publish a revoked commit transaction $Tx_{\text{CM},i}$ with $i < n$ and its corresponding split transaction $Tx_{\text{SP},i}$ on-chain. Then the honest party, who gets online once every $T-1$ rounds, can penalize the unresponsive watchtower by publishing either $Tx_{\text{PN}_1,i}$ or $Tx_{\text{PN}_2,i}$. Protocols for all the mentioned scenarios can be found in the technical report [15]. Figure 4 depicts transaction flows of FPPW.

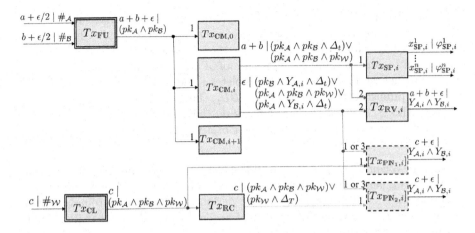

Fig. 4. An FPPW Bitcoin channel.

4.4 FPPW Watchtower Abort

In this phase, $\mathcal{W}$ decides to terminate its employment by $\mathcal{A}$ and $\mathcal{B}$. To do this, $\mathcal{W}$ publishes Tx_{RC} and spends its output after T rounds. Since $\mathcal{A}$ and $\mathcal{B}$ do not go offline for more than $T-1$ rounds, they get online during this T-round interval and observes that Tx_{RC} is on the chain. Then parties can close the channel and open a new one with a new watchtower. Parties can also continue using this channel without any watchtower. To do so, channel parties must check the blockchain at least once every $t-1$ rounds to prevent from fraudulent channel closures. New channel updates can be performed according to generalized channels [1] or its new variant introduced in the technical report [15].

5 Security Analysis

In this section, we analyze fairness, privacy against watchtower and coverage of FPPW protocol through Theorems 1, 2, and 3, respectively. Lemmas 1 and 2 are used to prove Theorem 1. They show how FPPW guarantees that funds of the honest channel party and the honest watchtower are safe in the channel.

Lemma 1. *For an FPPW channel, assume that the honest channel party $\mathcal{P} \in \{\mathcal{A}, \mathcal{B}\}$ checks the blockchain at the end of the channel establishment phase and then gets online periodically with period of at most $T-1$ rounds. The probability that $\mathcal{P}$ loses any funds in the channel is negligible.*

Although, proof of Lemma 1 will be presented in the technical report [15], here we briefly discuss it. Without loss of generality let $\mathcal{P} = \mathcal{A}$. Cheating the honest party $\mathcal{A}$ using any scenario other than broadcast of a revoked commit transaction requires forging the signature of $\mathcal{A}$ and hence is of negligible probability. Channel establishment phase completes when Tx_{CL} is published on-chain. If Tx_{CL} is published through the block BL_j, the next time that $\mathcal{A}$ gets online, BL_{j+k} with $k \leq T-1$ is the latest block on the chain and four possible events might have occurred regarding broadcast of a revoked $Tx_{\mathrm{CM},i}$ or Tx_{RC} during this interval:

- Case 1: When BL_{j+k} is the last block on the blockchain, $\mathcal{A}$ observes that only Tx_{RC} has been published on-chain. Consequently, $\mathcal{A}$ goes offline and checks the blockchain frequently with period of at most $t-1$ rounds. Now if a revoked $Tx_{\mathrm{CM},i}$ is published, it is of negligible probability that its outputs can be spent within $t-1$ rounds without $\mathcal{A}$'s authorization and $\mathcal{A}$ grants such an authorization only on $Tx_{\mathrm{RV},i}$. Also since $\mathcal{A}$ does not go offline for more than $t-1$ rounds, $\mathcal{A}$ will always have at least 1 round time to publish $Tx_{\mathrm{RV},i}$, which is enough according to our assumption regarding the value of the confirmation delay.
- Case 2: When BL_{j+k} is the last block on chain, $\mathcal{A}$ observes that both the revoked $Tx_{\mathrm{CM},i}$ and Tx_{RC} are on the chain. If fewer than $t-1$ blocks have published since broadcast of $Tx_{\mathrm{CM},i}$, $\mathcal{A}$ publishes $Tx_{\mathrm{RV},i}$. Otherwise, $\mathcal{A}$ will have at least 1 round time to publish $Tx_{\mathrm{PN}_2,i}$ which is enough according to our assumption regarding the value of the confirmation delay. The probability of other scenarios is negligible.
- Case 3: When BL_{j+k} is the last block on chain, $\mathcal{A}$ observes that $Tx_{\mathrm{CM},i}$ is on-chain but Tx_{RC} is unpublished. If fewer than $t-1$ blocks have published since broadcast of $Tx_{\mathrm{CM},i}$, party $\mathcal{A}$ can publish $Tx_{\mathrm{RV},i}$. Otherwise, $\mathcal{A}$ publishes $Tx_{\mathrm{PN}_1,i}$. If before publishing $Tx_{\mathrm{PN}_1,i}$, the transaction Tx_{RC} is recorded on-chain, $\mathcal{A}$ publishes $Tx_{\mathrm{PN}_2,i}$. Other scenarios happen with negligible probability.
- Case 4: When BL_{j+k} is the last block on chain, $\mathcal{A}$ observes that neither a revoked $Tx_{\mathrm{CM},i}$ nor Tx_{RC} are on-chain and goes offline for another $T-1$ rounds.

As it is obvious, Cases 1, 2, and 3 result in publishing either of $Tx_{\mathrm{RV},i}$, $Tx_{\mathrm{PN}_1,i}$ or $Tx_{\mathrm{PN}_2,i}$ on the chain. It is of negligible probability that broadcast of $Tx_{\mathrm{RV},i}$, $Tx_{\mathrm{PN}_1,i}$ or $Tx_{\mathrm{PN}_2,i}$ causes the honest party $\mathcal{A}$ to lose any funds in the channel because only $\mathcal{A}$ knows values of both $y_{A,i}$ and $y_{B,i}$. If Case 4 occurs, the process can repeat with all j being replaced with $j+k$.

Lemma 2. *For an FPPW channel, assume that the honest watchtower $\mathcal{W}$ checks the blockchain at the end of the channel establishment phase and then remains online. The probability that $\mathcal{W}$ loses any funds in the channel is negligible.*

As will be seen in the proof of Lemma 2 in the technical report [15], an honest watchtower $\mathcal{W}$ does not lose any funds with non-negligible probability unless first a revoked commit transaction $Tx_{\mathrm{CM},i}$ is recorded on the blockchain and at least t rounds later, either $Tx_{\mathrm{PN}_1,i}$ or $Tx_{\mathrm{PN}_2,i}$ is also published on-chain. However, if a revoked $Tx_{\mathrm{CM},i}$ is published, it is of negligible probability that $O^1_{\mathrm{CM},i}$ or $O^2_{\mathrm{CM},i}$ are spent within $t-1$ rounds using any transaction other than $Tx_{\mathrm{RV},i}$. Thus, once $Tx_{\mathrm{CM},i}$ is published, $\mathcal{W}$ will have at least $t-1$ rounds time to publish $Tx_{\mathrm{RV},i}$ and invalidate both $Tx_{\mathrm{PN}_1,i}$ and $Tx_{\mathrm{PN}_2,i}$.

Theorem 1. *FPPW provides channel party α-fairness with $\alpha = 1$ and watchtower fairness as defined in Definition 1 and 2, respectively.*

Proof. The honest channel party always have at least one non-revoked commit transaction and its corresponding split transaction by broadcasting which she can close the channel. This proves that FPPW meets the first requirement of Definition 1. Furthermore, We know that based on FPPW protocol, the honest channel party checks the chain at least once every $T-1$ rounds and according to the above discussion (see Lemma 1), the probability that the honest channel party loses any funds in the channel is negligible. This proves that FPPW provides channel party α-fairness with $\alpha = 1$.

The watchtower in FPPW is paid for channel establishment and each channel update and hence her reward amount is non-zero. Also, we know that based on FPPW protocol, the honest watchtower always remains online and according to Lemma 2, the probability that such an honest watchtower loses any funds in the channel is negligible. Additionally, the watchtower can publish Tx_{RC} at any time and redeem her collateral after T rounds. Thus, FPPW meets both requirement of Definition 2.

Theorem 2. *FPPW provides weak privacy against watchtower based on Definition 3.*

Proof. Assume that the conditions mentioned in the two-stage privacy game (see Sect. 3.3) are satisfied. By observing different steps and transactions of the protocol, one can see that only split transactions contain information on $x_{\mathcal{A},i}$ and $x_{\mathcal{B},i}$ with $i \in [1, n-1]$. However, these transactions are never published on-chain or sent to the watchtower or any external entity. Other transactions in the protocol contain no information regarding $x_{\mathcal{A},i}$ or $x_{\mathcal{B},i}$ with $i \in [1, n-1]$. Note that monetary value of $O^1_{\mathrm{CM},i}$, $O^2_{\mathrm{CM},i}$, $O^1_{\mathrm{RV},i}$, $O^1_{\mathrm{PN}_1,i}$, $O^1_{\mathrm{PN}_2,i}$, O^1_{CL}, and O^1_{RC} of the first payment channels are the same as those for the second one. Furthermore, Tx_{FU}, $Tx_{\mathrm{SP},n}$ or $Tx_{\overline{\mathrm{SP}}}$ contain no information regarding the ith channel state with $i \in [1, n-1]$. Thus, the view of any passive PPT adversarial watchtower $\mathscr{A}$ on $(\mathbf{x}_{\mathcal{A},[1,n-1]}, \mathbf{x}_{\mathcal{B},[1,n-1]})$ is indistinguishable from its view on $(\mathbf{x}_{\mathcal{A}',[1,n-1]}, \mathbf{x}_{\mathcal{B}',[1,n-1]})$.

Theorem 3. *FPPW provides β-coverage with $\beta = 1/2$ based on Definition 4.*

Proof. Assume that we have N payment channels, with channel capacities $X_i = a_i + b_i$, $i \in [1, N]$. Thus, the total capacity of the channels is $\mathcal{X} = \sum_{i=1}^{N} X_i$. Since the ith channel collateral c_i equals $a_i + b_i$, the total watchtower collateral is $\mathcal{C} = \sum_{i=1}^{N} c_i = \sum_{i=1}^{N} X_i = \mathcal{X}$. Thus, we have $\beta = \frac{\mathcal{X}}{\mathcal{X}+\mathcal{C}} = 1/2$.

6   Fee Handling

Once a revoked commit transaction is recorded on the blockchain, watchtower must record its corresponding revocation transaction within $t-1$ rounds. Otherwise the watchtower might be penalized. However, the time it takes for a transaction to be recorded on the blockchain depends on its fee value and the network congestion. Body of a revocation transaction is created during the channel update phase but it might be broadcast in the blockchain network later upon fraud. Thus, the fee amount must be large enough to ensure the watchtower that the revocation transaction will be accepted by miners within the revocation period. In other words, when channel participants are creating a revocation transaction, they must assume that the blockchain network will be highly congested at the time when fraud will occur.

An alternative approach is usage of SIGHASH of type 0x81 (SIGHASH_ALL | SIGHASH_ANYONECANPAY) for channel parties' signatures for both inputs of revocation transactions. Thus, signature for each input applies to that input and the output. Therefore, when due to network congestion the considered fee for the revocation transaction is low, the watchtower can add some inputs to the revocation transaction to increase the fee amount, sign all inputs using SIGHASH of type 0x01 (SIGHASH_ALL) and submit it to the network. If there exists enough time, the watchtower might even repeat this process several times and raise this extra fee each time until one of the revocation transactions is accepted by the miners. This method can be used if revocation transactions are only held by the watchtower (i.e. if channel parties do not receive signatures of the watchtower on revocation transactions during the channel update phase).

A similar approach can also be used for penalty transactions. Channel parties and the watchtower can use SIGHASH of type 0x02 (SIGHASH_NONE) for the second input of penalty transactions. Then, signatures apply only on all inputs of penalty transactions. In this way, the watchtower can be certain that a penalty transaction cannot be published unless its corresponding commit transaction is on-chain. However, if a revoked $Tx_{\mathrm{CM},i}$ is published by a channel party, let's say $\mathcal{A}$, and its main output is spent by $Tx_{\mathrm{SP},i}$, party $\mathcal{B}$ has the opportunity to set the output value of the penalty transaction according to the network congestion and sign the corresponding penalty transaction (to meet the subcondition $pk_{\mathcal{B}} \wedge Y_{\mathcal{A},i} \wedge \Delta_T$) using SIGHASH of type 0x01 (SIGHASH_ALL). In this way, $\mathcal{B}$ can reduce the output value if the current fee is low and this difference value is used as the extra fee amount. If there exists enough time, $\mathcal{B}$ can even repeat this process multiple times, each time with a higher fee until one penalty transaction is recorded on-chain.

Acknowledgements. This research was partially supported by the Australian Government through the Australian Research Council's Discovery Projects funding scheme (project DP180102199) and Discovery Early Career Award (project DE210100019).

References

1. Aumayr, L., et al.: Generalized Bitcoin-compatible channels. IACR Cryptol. ePrint Arch. **2020**, p. 476 (2020)
2. Avarikioti, G., Kogias, E.K., Wattenhofer, R.: Brick: Asynchronous state channels. arXiv preprint arXiv:1905.11360 (2019)
3. Avarikioti, G., Laufenberg, F., Sliwinski, J., Wang, Y., Wattenhofer, R.: Towards secure and efficient payment channels. arXiv preprint arXiv:1811.12740 (2018)
4. Avarikioti, Z., Thyfronitis Litos, O.S., Wattenhofer, R.: CERBERUS channels: incentivizing watchtowers for Bitcoin. In: Bonneau, J., Heninger, N. (eds.) FC 2020. LNCS, vol. 12059, pp. 346–366. Springer, Cham (2020). https://doi.org/10.1007/978-3-030-51280-4_19
5. Dryja, T., Milano, S.B.: Unlinkable outsourced channel monitoring. Talk transcript) https://diyhpl.us/wiki/transcripts/scalingbitcoin/milan/unlinkable-outsourced-channel-monitoring (2016)
6. Dziembowski, S., Eckey, L., Faust, S., Malinowski, D.: Perun: virtual payment hubs over cryptocurrencies. In: 2019 IEEE Symposium on Security and Privacy (SP), pp. 106–123. IEEE (2019)
7. Garay, J., Kiayias, A., Leonardos, N.: The Bitcoin backbone protocol with chains of variable difficulty. In: Katz, J., Shacham, H. (eds.) CRYPTO 2017, Part I. LNCS, vol. 10401, pp. 291–323. Springer, Cham (2017). https://doi.org/10.1007/978-3-319-63688-7_10
8. Green, M., Miers, I.: Bolt: Anonymous payment channels for decentralized currencies. In: Proceedings of the 2017 ACM SIGSAC Conference on Computer and Communications Security, pp. 473–489 (2017)
9. Johnson, D., Menezes, A., Vanstone, S.: The elliptic curve digital signature algorithm (ECDSA). Int. J. Inf. Secur. **1**(1), 36–63 (2001)
10. Khabbazian, M., Nadahalli, T., Wattenhofer, R.: Outpost: a responsive lightweight watchtower. In: Proceedings of the 1st ACM Conference on Advances in Financial Technologies, pp. 31–40 (2019)
11. Leinweber, M., Grundmann, M., Schönborn, L., Hartenstein, H.: TEE-based distributed watchtowers for fraud protection in the lightning network. In: Pérez-Solà, C., Navarro-Arribas, G., Biryukov, A., Garcia-Alfaro, J. (eds.) DPM/CBT -2019. LNCS, vol. 11737, pp. 177–194. Springer, Cham (2019). https://doi.org/10.1007/978-3-030-31500-9_11
12. Liu, B., Szalachowski, P., Sun, S.: Fail-safe watchtowers and short-lived assertions for payment channels. arXiv preprint arXiv:2003.06127 (2020)
13. McCorry, P., Bakshi, S., Bentov, I., Meiklejohn, S., Miller, A.: Pisa: arbitration outsourcing for state channels. In: Proceedings of the 1st ACM Conference on Advances in Financial Technologies, pp. 16–30 (2019)
14. Miller, A., Bentov, I., Kumaresan, R., McCorry, P.: Sprites: Payment channels that go faster than lightning. CoRR abs/1702.05812 306 (2017)
15. Mirzaei, A., Sakzad, A., Yu, J., Steinfeld, R.: FPPW: A fair and privacy preserving watchtower for Bitcoin. Cryptology ePrint Archive, Report 2021/117 (2021), https://eprint.iacr.org/2021/117
16. Poon, J., Dryja, T.: The Bitcoin lightning network: Scalable off-chain instant payments (2016)
17. Schnorr, C.P.: Efficient signature generation by smart cards. J. Cryptol. **4**(3), 161–174 (1991). https://doi.org/10.1007/BF00196725

Congestion Attacks in Payment Channel Networks

Ayelet Mizrahi$^{(\boxtimes)}$ ⓘ and Aviv Zohar ⓘ

The Hebrew University of Jerusalem, Jerusalem, Israel
{ayelem02,avivz}@cs.huji.ac.il

Abstract. Payment channel networks provide a fast and scalable solution to relay funds, acting as a second layer to slower and less scalable blockchain protocols. In this paper, we present an accessible, low-cost attack in which the attacker paralyzes multiple payment network channels for several days. The attack is based on overloading channels with requests that are kept unresolved until their expiration time. Reaching the maximum allowed unresolved requests (HTLCs) locks the channel for new payments. The attack is in fact inherent to the way off-chain networks are constructed, since limits on the number of unresolved payments are derived from limits on the blockchain. We consider three versions of the attack: one in which the attacker attempts to block as many high liquidity channels as possible, one in which it disconnects as many pairs of nodes as it can, and one in which it tries to isolate individual nodes from the network. We evaluate the costs of these attacks on Bitcoin's Lightning Network and compare how changes in the network have affected the cost of attack. Specifically, we consider how recent changes to default parameters in each of the main Lightning implementations contribute to the attacks. Finally, we suggest mitigation techniques that make these attacks much harder to carry out.

Keywords: Lightning Network · Payment channel networks · Network security · HTLC

1 Introduction

Payment channel networks such as the Lightning Network [27] are a second layer off-chain solution to the scalability problems of blockchains. They require participants to lock funds into channels, which then allows them to send payments to others over several hops. Altogether, they allow both a higher number of transactions as well as faster transaction resolution compared to the underlying blockchain.

In this paper we describe and evaluate a novel attack that locks funds in channels between honest participants that are potentially far away from the attacker, giving the attacker the ability to disrupt the transfer of payments throughout the network. In contrast to previously known attacks that locked liquidity in channels [30], the method we present here requires *lower* costs as it

ⓒ International Financial Cryptography Association 2021
N. Borisov and C. Diaz (Eds.): FC 2021, LNCS 12675, pp. 170–188, 2021.
https://doi.org/10.1007/978-3-662-64331-0_9

requires the attacker to lock a smaller amount of liquidity. We evaluate these costs in the Lightning Network, where we show that spending less than half a bitcoin, the attacker can indefinitely lock up channels holding the majority of the funds currently assigned to the network. To summarize, our contributions are as follows:

- We leverage a known limitation of payment channels (their max HTLC limit) to form two different attacks on the Lightning Network (a network wide DoS attack and a more localized node isolation attack).
- We provide statistics on several aspects of the Lightning Network that are relevant to the attack which may be of independent interest.
- We provide a thorough evaluation of the amount of resources needed to conduct each attack and of the level of harm an attacker can cause.
- We report on small proof of concept experiments using actual lightning nodes (on a local test network) that confirm the feasibility of the attack.
- We propose and discuss several short-term mitigation approaches that make the attack more difficult to carry out and reduce its efficiency.

Our attack is based on the inner workings of the main mechanism that makes payment channel networks possible: Hashed Time-Locked Contracts (HTLC). Essentially, as payments are set up to move along some path in the network, all channels along the path reserve some funds for the transfer that is about to take place. The number of simultaneously reserved and unresolved payments per path is limited. Our attack thus simply opens many small payment requests along extremely long paths and keeps them unresolved for as long as possible. In this way, all channels along the path are unable to relay other transfers.

The vulnerability can be attributed to three fundamental properties of off-chain payment networks.

1. Payments are executed in a trustless manner. Payments are executed using conditional payment contracts (in the form of transactions with HTLCs) that are exchanged between parties and are only sent to the blockchain if disputes arise. These contracts grow in size as more conditional payments are pending, and so the total number of pending payments is limited by transactions sizes that can be placed on the blockchain. Bitcoin's Lightning Network is limited to at most 483 concurrent HTLCs [33], while Raiden [25], Ethereum's network, is limited to at most 160 due to gas costs [24].

2. Expiration times are long. To allow nodes to recover their funds if a malicious partner closes a channel that is part of a pending payment, HTLC expiration times have been set to allow nodes sufficient time to appeal such closures. In Bitcoin's Lightning Network things are even more severe: due to lower expressiveness of its scripting language, HTLC expiration times accumulate over the length of the path, reaching up to 2016 blocks – which typically take the Bitcoin network two weeks to produce.

3. The Privacy of Payments. Payment Channel Networks utilize onion routing that does not allow intermediate nodes on the path to recognize where payments originate and where they are going, allowing the attacker to act with impunity. Payment privacy essentially prevents us from attributing blame to potential attackers and add mechanisms that effectively detect the attack.

A Description of the Attack. In order to paralyze channels, the attacker first adds a new node to the payment network. It then identifies a route suitable to attack, considering some restrictions on the path (maximum route length, lock-time of intermediate nodes, remaining HTLC capacity) and maximizing the attack benefit (to lock channels with a large amount of funds or high betweenness value). It opens channels with the source and target of the route, and requests many tiny payments through this path, exhausting the number of simultaneously open HTLCs. Since the attacker is both the source and destination of this payment, it can choose to delay the final execution of the payment which would remove all pending HTLCs from the path. The path is then locked for long periods of time (up to several days). Just before expiration, the attacker sends an *update_failure* message to the previous node, which cancels the payment and reverts the state, avoiding a forced closure of the attacker's channel. This allows the attacker to re-run the attack once again and lock the same path for an additional period of time.

To successfully carry out the attack, the attacker needs liquidity on its out-going channel as well as liquidity on its incoming channel. While it is easy to open a channel and invest liquidity, this liquidity is on the attacker's side of the channel initially which is suitable for the outgoing channel. The incoming chan-nel's liquidity needs to allow for payments toward the attacker. Liquidity can be shifted in that direction by sending an outgoing payment from the attacker, e.g., to deposit funds in some exchange or purchase goods.

We stress that simple mitigation attempts such as increasing the number of HTLCs allowed per channel are not very effective. First, more allowed HTLCs will imply larger settlement transactions in Lightning (larger than the current block size). Second, the attacker can easily create enough payment requests to lock many more HTLCs (each message locks an HTLC for days and requires little effort).

In this paper we evaluate the attack specifically on the Lightning Network, which is the most prominently used payment channel network. We evaluate three main attack scenarios: First, we consider an attack on the entire network, which attempts to lock as many channels as possible and focuses on channels holding most of the funds in the network. This sort of disruption would severely hinder the volume of payments that can be sent on the Lightning Network. The second attack scenario we consider is one that disconnects as many pairs of nodes as possible and breaks the network into separate components. The main complexity in carrying out these attacks is picking routes in a way that respects limits on the maximal delay incurred along the path, and still targets the channels with the highest connectivity and liquidity. Finally, the third attack variant that we evaluate targets single nodes and paralyzes all channels that connect them to the network.

As far as we are aware, while exhaustion of the HTLCs of a channel is known to paralyze the channel, the attack that we describe has never been evaluated for its effects on the network, or on individual nodes. In particular, there are no available estimates of the cost to attackers from executing either version of the attacks we propose.[1]

Due to ethical concerns, we did not attack the live network. Instead, we worked with two main complementary approaches. In the first, we use the code of actual lightning node implementations to set small local networks to test the basic mechanics underlying the attacks. We validate the behavior of nodes in a series of experiments reported in the full version of the paper [23]. In the second, we perform the attacks on a simulation of the actual network based on topology data we extracted from a live node. We provide the full description and evaluation of the attacks in its different modes in Sects. 4 and 5. In Sect. 7 we discuss prior work, including other DoS attacks on the Lightning Network. Our attack differs in that it requires fewer resources, repeating it indefinitely does not waste fees, and it does not require a direct connection to the victim node.

2   Background on the Lightning Network

The Lightning Network is the most widely used payment channel network to date. As of October 2020, it has more than 14k nodes and 37k channels and holds a total capacity of around 1100 BTC. We introduce some of the basic properties of the Lightning Network.

*Hashed Time Locked Contracts (*HTLCs*)* - conditional payments which promise an intermediate node on the channel that it can receive funds if it submits a cryptographic proof (pre-image of a hash) within a given timeframe (specified as a specific chain height). Each transaction that occurs in the Lightning Network is first set up by adding an additional HTLC output to every channel on its path. Once these are set up, the payment is executed by propagating the pre-image from the payment's recipient back along the path towards the sender. Once the pre-image arrives at some intermediate node, it can essentially guarantee that it can receive the funds (if it posts the transaction with the pre-image to the blockchain). The conditional payment is then removed from the channel and is replaced by a non-conditional reallocation of the funds.

The main problem with the approach above is that if several payments are being set up, the number of HTLCs on a channel grows. This implies that the transaction that will eventually be posted to the blockchain will be large – setting a natural limit on the number of HTLCs that can be simultaneously open on a channel.

HTLC Timeouts - Usually, channels are set up quickly and do not wait long for the pre-image to propagate. An *update_failure* message may sometime be returned instead of the pre-image if one of the intermediate nodes cannot or will

---

[1] We were able to find public record describing the basic idea of the attack, on a single channel [8,31]. We note that no full translation of this vulnerability to the entire network was previously considered. Due to the public nature of these posts, we did not perform a disclosure of the vulnerability to the devs.

not relay the payment. However, malicious nodes may withhold the pre-image and not propagate it back (or alternatively not complete the channel set up with HTLCs). In such cases, HTLCs are designed to expire. This is done using a CheckLockTimeVerify (CLTV) instruction, which essentially does not allow the HTLC to be redeemed after a certain block height. In order to ensure that intermediate nodes do not lose funds, outgoing HTLCs must expire before incoming HTLCs do. Each node specifies a parameter cltv_expiry_delta, which specifies the difference in timeouts it is willing to tolerate. The timeout of payments is therefore the accumulation of the cltv_expiry_deltas from the end of the route towards its beginning (the last node's timeout is limited by a parameter named min_final_cltv_expiry instead of cltv_expiry_delta). As cltv_expiry_deltas are typically either 40 blocks or 144 blocks, the timeouts of HTLCs can accumulate and often take days. Nodes impose a limit on the maximal timeout locktime_max, which is set to 2016 blocks (equivalent to 2 weeks). This high timeout makes the attack extremely potent.

Privacy - One of the goals of the Lightning protocol is to preserve the privacy of users – a fact that eventually aids our attack. For example, routing payments is done via Onion Routing which helps disguise the attacker. Additionally, the expiration of HTLCs is also conveyed along payment paths and to preserve privacy, senders are allowed to add arbitrary values to the initial delay. We exploit this fact to add to the expiration delay of HTLCs (up to the allowed maximum of two weeks).

3   Lightning Network Analysis

We begin our exploration of the current state of the Lightning Network by listing the default values for various parameters in the main implementations of the Lightning protocol. These are of interest since, as we show later below, most nodes use the defaults, and thus these heavily influence the state of the Lightning Network and its vulnerability to our attack.

3.1   Default Parameter Values

The BOLT (Basis of Lightning Technology) [33] specifications detail the protocol of Lightning Networks. In our work, we focus on the main three implementations: LND [18], C-Lightning [5], and Eclair [7]

Each of the implementations uses slightly different default values for parameters of interest. These are depicted in the table below, along with ranges or values specified in the BOLT.[2]

---

[2] We give the defaults used in mainnet. Testnet behavior differs slightly.

	LND	C-lightning	Eclair	BOLT
cltv_expiry_delta	40	14	144	-
min_final_cltv_expiry	40	10	9	9
locktime_max	2016	2016	2016	$<5 \cdot 10^8$
max_concurrent_htlcs	483	30	30	≤ 483
dust_limit_satoshis	573	546	546	-
htlc_minimum_msat	1000	1000	1	-
fee_base_msat	1000	1000	1000	-
fee_proportional_millionths	1	10	100	-

Recent changes to the defaults have in fact made our attack easier to carry out: LND changed their cltv_expiry_delta default from 144 to 40 blocks (on Mar 12th, 2019) [28], which allows chaining more nodes in each path without reaching the locktime_max limit. Nodes running an old version may still hold the 144 default that was used prior to that.

Additionally, a locktime_max of 2016 was agreed upon by Lightning developers, in the 2018 Adelaide meeting to set the BOLT 1.1 specs [6]. This is an increase of previous values used in some implementations. Again, this allows for longer routes and longer expiration delays that make the attack more damaging and easier to carry out.

3.2 Network Statistics

We introduce some statistics on the parameters announced by nodes in channels on the Lightning Network.[3] In order to perform the calculations, we took snapshots of the Lightning Network mainnet. The information was obtained from a continuously running LND node. Our results correspond to a network snapshot taken on September 21st, 2020. We include additional analysis with snapshots taken over a period of 18 months for comparison.

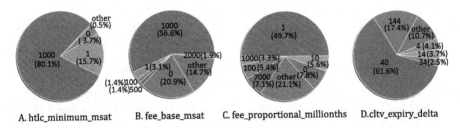

A. htlc_minimum_msat   B. fee_base_msat   C. fee_proportional_millionths   D. cltv_expiry_delta

Fig. 1. Statistics on parameters announced by nodes in channels on the Lightning Network

---

[3] We ignore disabled channels and channels with nodes that do not reveal their policies.

In Fig. 1, we present the most common values of four of the parameters announced by nodes. It is clear that very few values are used. The remaining values appeared less than 3% each (which we grouped together as "other").

Figures 1A, B, C show the distribution of `htlc_minimum_msat`, `fee_base_msat` and `fee_proportional_millionths`. These represent the minimal amounts nodes are willing to transfer, the flat fee for each transfer, and the fee that grows with the transferred amount. These values are small relative to the default configured dust limit, which sets a threshold below which HTLCs would not be added by nodes. Therefore, these parameters have a lower impact on the cost of the attack. We elaborate more on costs in Sect. 4.

Finally, we examine the distribution of `cltv_expiry_delta` - the minimum difference in HTLC timeouts the forwarding node will accept. We recall from the table in Sect. 3.1 that 144, 40, and 14 are the defaults that correspond to the different implementations mentioned previously. In Fig. 1D, we see that the defaults constitute 82.7% of the total.

How do values change over time? In our attack, the route length we can compose is often limited by the values of `cltv_expiry_delta`. Figure 2 shows the changes in `cltv_expiry_delta` over an 18 month period[4]. We show only the most common values. The choice of presented dates was according to available information from our node and was slightly affected by downtime. Since channels are open for a long period of time, the exact day chosen does not impact the topology.

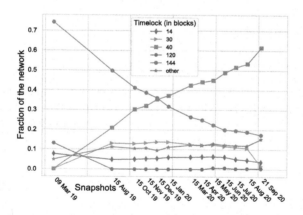

Fig. 2. `cltv_expiry_deltas` in different snapshots

The main change over this period is the decreased use of the value 144 for expiry time and the increase in the use of the value 40. We attribute this to the fact that LND changed their default `cltv_expiry_delta` from 144 to 40 in Mar 2019 [28]. In the full version of the paper [23], we show that LND nodes are both the most common nodes (we estimate that they constitute 91.3% of the network), and also the ones that hold most of the liquidity in the network.

---

[4] The snapshot from Mar 9th, 2019 was taken from [29,30].

4   Attacking the Entire Network

In this section, we consider a malicious node that wishes to disrupt the entire network's operation. Initially, it connects to other nodes in the network by opening channels with them, allowing it to learn the topology of the network and launch the attack. Then, the attacker uses a greedy algorithm in order to pick routes and paralyze as much liquidity or to disconnect as many pairs of nodes as possible. For each route, the attacker will initiate max_concurrent_htlcs payments, and withhold the response, turning all channels along the path unavailable for new requests. Just before expiration, the attacker will announce a failure to complete the payment. This step is repeated for multiple disjoint routes making the network less and less connected.

Examining several heuristics and path selection choices we found that a greedy choice of routes which we fully paralyze one by one makes the most out of every attacker's outgoing channel and achieves approximately optimal results for the attacker as we will present in the following evaluation. The main challenge faced by the attacker in this heuristic is to use routes composed of channels with similar max_concurrent_htlcs so that we do not leave parts of the path unlocked, and to fit as many high-liquidity channels within the limits of 20 hops and locktime_max total delay. Hence, we divide the network to subgraphs with similar max_concurrent_htlcs, and use a greedy algorithm to select routes. The algorithm that we utilized is parametrized by G (a subgraph of the network) and a parameter τ_{min} that denotes the minimal time (measured in blocks) that we would like paths to be locked for. We assign two types of weights to the edges (used in selecting the routes to attack) to support two different modes of attack. The greedy algorithm selects routes one by one, constructing each by consecutively picking high weighted edges. In the first mode we seek to freeze as much liquidity as possible and use the channel capacity as the weight. In the second mode, we seek to disconnect as many pairs of nodes and use the unweighted betweenness centrality measurement of edges as the weight (taking inspiration from the Girvan-Newman Algorithm [10]). A concise description of the algorithm follows (a detailed description is available in the full version of the paper [23]):

1. Pick a channel of maximal weight (capacity/betweenness).
2. Extend it to a route by repeatedly choosing an adjacent channel of maximal weight which meet the constraints of having similar max_concurrent_htlcs value and maintaining route validity (maximum route length and desired route locktime τ_{min}).
3. Remove the route channels from the graph.
4. Repeat until all channels are exhausted.

The result is a partition of G's channels into disjoint routes that can be paralyzed for at least τ_{min} blocks. Note that routes produced by the algorithm are circular (from the attacker to itself) and require two attacker channels: to begin and end each route.

For many channels in the network, the value set for cltv_expiry_delta is different depending on the direction we traverse the channel (this is because nodes may have set different values for this parameter). Our greedy approach excelled at picking directions with lower `cltv_expiry_delta` values naturally, which allows it to form longer routes that paralyze more channels simultaneously. Other approaches that we explored, such as iterating over a single channel back and forth to form a long path, resulted in slightly worse performance.

The greedy algorithm does not optimize over the `htlc_minimum_msat` values when picking routes (the detailed algorithm is available in the full version of the paper [23]). The values set for this parameter are extremely low and their impact on the total cost is minor.

4.1   Evaluation

We run the attack locking channels for at least 3 days ($\tau_{min} = 432$). We begin by attempting to freeze up a large amount of liquidity (setting the weight in the algorithm (available in the full version of the paper [23]) to the channel's capacity).

We infer for each node, which implementation of the protocol it runs (available in the full version of the paper [23]), and then partition the network into two sub-graphs:

1. The network graph reduced to LND nodes. Which has `max_concurrent_htlcs` defaults that are 483.
2. The complementary graph consisting of all channels with at least one Eclair or C-Lightning node. These use a default `max_concurrent_htlcs` of 30.

In the implementation inference process we assume most users use the default values for the `max_concurrent_htlcs` parameter. This assumption is reinforced by Sect. 3.2, which presents distributions of other parameter values displaying high correspondence to their default values.

We visualize the results in Fig. 3a, presenting the fraction of the network's capacity that the attacker succeeds in locking as a function of the resources it invests (the number of channels it opened). We find for example that the attacker can lock 20% of the network's capacity using only 68 channels, and can lock 90% using 1030 channels. We notice that the greedy algorithm is almost optimal on our graph. To do so we compare to an unachievable upper bound which is calculated as follows: The maximum allowed route length is 20. The attacker uses 2 channels to attack any route, hence it can attack at most 18 channels per route. We sort the channels by their capacities and use the highest capacity edges first, disregarding the constraint that paths are connected correctly.

We estimate the attack's costs, by considering two types of costs:

1. The cost of opening channels. The attacker pays the fee required to place channel funding transactions on the blockchain. We estimated the cost of opening a channel to be 2.2 USD (the average transaction fees observed on the date of the snapshot which the evaluation was performed on) [4].
2. The cost of provisioning channels with liquidity. Attackers must lock enough liquidity for payments they will later request. Locked funds are not spent and will return to the attacker once it completes the attack.

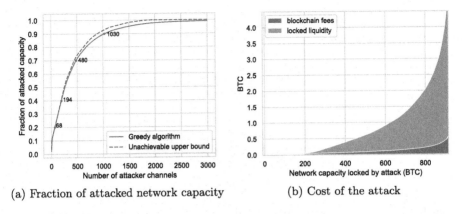

(a) Fraction of attacked network capacity   (b) Cost of the attack

Fig. 3. Evaluation and cost of the attack

Figure 3b displays our evaluation of the costs. It clearly separates the two types of costs mentioned above (non-refundable blockchain fees and locked liquidity). Our results show that the attacker can paralyze most of the liquidity in the Lightning Network for 3 days spending less than half a Bitcoin. We take into account the dust limit configured in the main Lightning implementations which sets a threshold on the payment size below which HTLCs would not be added by nodes. The locked liquidity cost is mainly affected by the dust limit, the rest of the parameters (min HTLC, base fee, minimal channel capacity) have less of an impact because of their small values. The costs we estimate above can be further lowered by opening multiple channels with a single on-chain transaction. Once channels are established, the attack may be repeated again and again with no additional cost to the attacker.

To be able to block a route there needs to be sufficient balance in each channel to allow for a minimum payment (otherwise nodes along the path will reject the payment request). The required balance relies mainly on the dust limit and the max_concurrent_htlcs values configured along the route.

We show more details on the attack results in Fig. 4. The figure shows that the attacker succeeds in attacking long routes (exploiting maximum route length), and that most of the routes are locked for more than the 3 days that were set as the minimal lock time.

In Fig. 5a, we run the attack changing the number of days that channels remain locked for. The results indicate that the number of attacker channels required to lock paths for different periods (from 1 to 6 days) differs only slightly. This can be explained by the relation between the large locktime_max (2016 blocks) value, the small cltv_expiry_deltas, and the 20-hop route length constraint. In other words, most of the liquidity of the network can be attacked using routes that consist of small cltv_expiry_deltas, allowing the attacker to high timeouts and withhold the payments for a long period.

Figure 5b explores how the attack would work on the Lightning Network at different times. We use snapshots taken over several months. The results

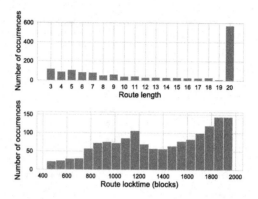

Fig. 4. Histogram of route lengths (including attacker's edges) and route lock times

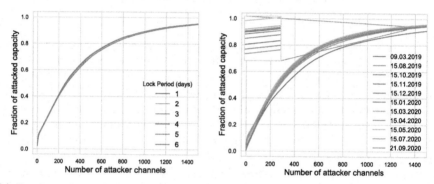

(a) Fraction of attacked network capacity for different lock periods

(b) Fraction of attacked network capacity in different snapshots

Fig. 5. Evaluation of the attack

generally show that the attack gets *easier* as time passes (there is a slight improvement from May 2020). This can be explained by the changes made to default parameters – increasing `locktime_max` to 2016 in all implementations and decreasing `cltv_expiry_delta` from 144 to 40 in LND. Both changes make it easier to construct long routes with high timeouts.

In Fig. 6, we show how the attack affects connectivity between nodes in the network. We explored several algorithms to select the attacked routes and present them in Fig. 6. The algorithms we explored are: Using a greedy algorithm (available in the full version of the paper [23]) which picks channels with high betweenness centrality. The second approach utilizes spectral clustering to repeatedly cut the large connected component using an eigenvector corresponding to the second smallest eigenvalue (Fiedler vector) of the Laplacian matrix of the largest connected component. The sign of the coordinates partitions the vertices of the graph into 2, defining a cut [9]. Finally, we used a simplified version of Kernighan-Lin algorithm [15] that starts with an arbitrary partition that

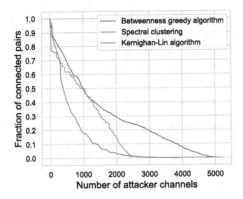

Fig. 6. Fraction of connected pairs of nodes in the network

separates 1/4 of the nodes and greedily swaps nodes across the cut to minimize the cut. This yielded the best results.

While before the attack almost all pairs of nodes (>97%) are connected, using only 32 attacker channels we disconnect 23% of the pairs in the network, while with 385 channels we disconnect 50% of the pairs. We stress that right now different Lightning implementations try only a small handful of paths [36], so even a large fraction of nodes that we noted as connected will not be able to route payments between them.

5 Attacking Hubs - Attack on a Single Node

In this section we consider an attack aimed at disconnecting a single node from the network for an extended period of time. Here, the adversary connects to the victim and paralyzes its adjacent channels one by one using the following steps:

1. The adversary connects to the victim with a new channel.
2. It then initiates a payment to itself via a route that begins with its connection to the victim, and then traverses a single target channel back and forth multiple times, before returning to the attacker. Surprisingly, such paths that traverse channels back and forth are indeed possible (see the full version of the paper [23]).
3. The attacker makes multiple payment requests over this path until the target channel reaches `max_concurrent_htlcs`. In this case, the attacker's own channel is usually not maxed out, and can be used to attack again.

We note that the attack is still possible to carry out if the victim does not accept direct connections (but at a somewhat lower efficiency). In this case, we would connect to neighbors of the victim.

Once the target channel is paralyzed, we move to the next one and apply the same method. We will need to open a new channel between the adversary and the target node every time that the former reaches its `max_concurrent_htlcs`.

Yet, at each payment we withhold only two HTLCs on the adversary's channel while it is possible to reach up to 18 HTLCs in the target channel at the same time. In other words, in order to attack all of the victim's channels, the adversary needs to open a small number of channels relative to the victim's degree.

5.1   Evaluation

We evaluate the attack on prominent nodes in the network. The following table summarizes our results:

Alias	% of Network liquidity	Node's degree	Attacker channels
ACINQ	10.8%	774	151
Bitfinex [lnd1]	6.4%	169	19
OpenNode	4.2%	648	88
Bitrefill	3.8%	229	39
CoinGate	3.1%	609	68
LNBIG (25 nodes)	22.2%	3835	405

The names of nodes were taken from our snapshot data directly. The last entry in the table relates to an attack on LNBIG [17], a single entity that controls 25 nodes which are extremely central to the network, holding a significant share of the network's capacity in multiple channels. We isolate all 25 nodes, without paralyzing links between the nodes themselves. Paths were set so that all links are paralyzed for at least 3 days in each iteration.

We evaluated the cost of attack on *all* nodes in the network using a snapshot from September 21st, 2020, isolating each node for 3 days. Figure 7 presents a histogram of the degree of nodes and shows the relation between the degree and the number of channels attackers needed to perform the attack on each node. Each node is represented by a point in the graph. The number of channels is not directly determined by the degree, because different nodes have set up different values of cltv_expiry_delta. We see that most nodes have a very low degree and are extremely easy to isolate. Even nodes with high degree, require far fewer channels than the degree to attack.

In an additional evaluation (available in the full version of the paper [23]), we show that of the 3 main implementations of the Lightning Network, LND (the most common implementation) nodes are the easiest to attack.

6   Mitigation Techniques

The attack and vulnerabilities described in our work continue to be relevant and have been discussed by the Lightning community [1,3]. In this section we discuss several proposed adjustments to payment channel network protocols that may help mitigate the attack. Specifically, we discuss some ideas that were raised in the Lightning-dev mailing list [8,31], as well as our own suggestions. We discuss weaknesses and strengths of each such suggestion.

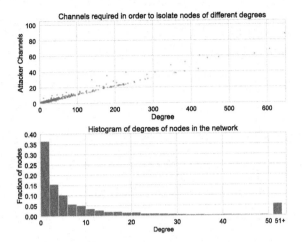

Fig. 7. Degree analysis

Enforcing fast HTLC resolution - This is our most drastic suggestion: While HTLC expiration times allow nodes to remain secure and provide sufficient time to publish transactions to the network, we propose the addition of another timeout mechanism. Specifically, if HTLC secrets are not propagated fast enough from one's neighbor the channel with this neighbor should be closed.

Each node should announce to its successor in the path its own deadline for resolving the HTLC. The node would then be able to communicate an earlier deadline for HTLC resolution to its next hop. If the timeout arrives, and the HTLC was not fulfilled or canceled, the node will wait for the HTLC to naturally expire but will close the channel with its neighbor.

To avoid having all channels along the path closed due to a failure to complete the HTLC in time, and specifically to avoid closing channels between compliant nodes, the last node in the path will provide proof of the channel closure to its predecessors (this can be done using a zero-knowledge proof for example).

We stress that this proposed mechanism does not replace the HTLC timeouts that still ensure the safety with regards to the *current* payment. Our mechanism is a way to disconnect misbehaving peers from the network in order to prevent them from repeating the attack many times at no cost. We note that it is risky to add behavior that automatically closes channels, and so this proposal warrants further evaluation. We leave this to future work.

Reducing route length - We suggest lowering the maximum allowed route length (currently 20 hops), as suggested in previous work [26]. The network graph is a small world network [30] - it is highly connected, and a smaller number of hops should still suffice. We point out that shortest paths between nodes in the network have an average of less than 3 hops and that the network diameter is ~ 6 [30,32], which are significantly lower than the 20 allowed hops. In Fig. 8, we show the fraction of successfully attacked capacity (with respect to the attack described in Sect. 4), assuming that different max route lengths are allowed. The figure shows that attackers need many more channels to attack if they are forced to use shorter route lengths.

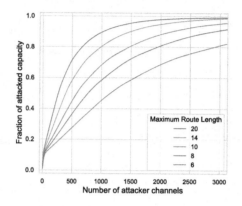

Fig. 8. Fraction of capacity attacked for different max route lengths

Setting number of max concurrent payments based on trust level - Currently, each node configures `max_concurrent_htlcs` to bound the maximum transfers it is willing to hold concurrently. Most nodes use the default value configured by the implementation they run. In all cases this value should not exceed the number 483 which is derived from the blockchain's limitations. We suggest changing the way nodes configure this parameter, adjusting the value according to the level of trust they have in particular peers. Setting a high `max_concurrent_htlcs` for some peer effectively allows it to route many concurrent payments through your node and to do more damage if it is malicious. Therefore, newly created channels with unknown and untrusted nodes should default to a low `max_concurrent_htlcs`. A new pull request has been opened recently (Aug 2020) promoting the basis of our proposal, allowing nodes to limit their exposure to the maximum number of concurrent HTLCs [1].

Loop Avoidance - As our experiments show (available in the full version of the paper [23]), it is possible to construct paths that visit the same node several times, including traversals of the same channel back and forth. It is relatively simple for nodes to disallow such paths. Since HTLCs that belong to the same path use the same hash, they can be easily recognized and rejected. This will make our specific technique to isolate individual nodes harder to carry out, but may not solve the issue entirely.

7   Related Work

A DDoS attack on the Lightning Network occurred in March of 2018. Many nodes were flooded with traffic and around 200 Lightning nodes were taken offline [37]. Several studies explore sophisticated attacks on the Lightning Network. Some focus on privacy issues [14, 34], and others on isolating nodes [26, 30] or disrupting the network in other ways. Rohrer et al. [30] explored an attack that disrupts the liquidity balance of channels. The attacker initiates payments that move all the liquidity to one side, effectively blocking payments in that direction (payments in the other direction are still possible). Our attack differs from this attack [30], as they require direct connections to the victim node, as well as locked liquidity in high amounts (up to the liquidity the victim has), in addition to the payment of fees for large transactions.

A similar attack uses payment griefing but avoids paying the fees [26]. In this variant of the attack, the attacker still sends a payment in one direction that unbalances the channel in order to isolate a node. This time it withholds the HTLC pre-image in order to lock the amount, and never really executes the payment. Unlike our attack, this still requires amounts of locked funds that match the amounts being locked in the victim channel, but does indeed avoid paying most of the fees (channel establishment is still needed).

Tochner et al. [36] presents a denial-of-service attack based on route hijacking within the Lightning Network. They show how connecting with few channels to the network offering low fees draws most of the routes which yields a potent attack. Our work does not rely on the routing strategy of nodes to attack the network.

In a work parallel to ours, Tikhomirov et al. [35] quantify the effect of several attacks on the Lightning Network. They additionally discuss the limitation on the number of concurrent HTLCs and describe the attack vector and its effect on the network's scalability. We describe how to leverage the attack and provide deeper analysis.

The privacy of payments in the Lightning Network is known to be relatively weak. Discovering the current liquidity balance of a channel can be accomplished using techniques from Herrera-Joancomarti et al. research [14]. Tang et al. [34] explore the tradeoff between privacy and utility in PCNs, considering adding noise to channels as well (which adds privacy, but lowers efficiency).

The structural properties of the Lightning Network and its topology in the context of the network's robustness have been studied in several studies [16, 32].

A technique to lower the delay of HTLC expiration is described by Miller et al. [22] and would make our attack less severe in this context. This sort of technique is not applicable to the Bitcoin blockchain, due to its more limited scripting language.

Several protocols improving upon privacy issues in off-chain payment channels are suggested in previous studies [11, 13, 19], as well as advances in payment channel networks like the addition of watchtowers [2, 20].

McCorry et al. [21] presents a technical overview of Bitcoin's payment channel networks. Additional work on off-chain protocols can be found in SoK survey [12].

8   Conclusions and Future Work

In this paper we discussed a fundamental vulnerability that arises in payment channel networks as part of the construction of trust-less multi-hop payments. We presented three types of attacks: the first aims to lock as many high liquidity channels as possible for an extended period, the second disconnects as many pairs of nodes as possible in the network, and the third isolates hubs from the rest of the network. We evaluated these attacks over the Lightning Network. We examined the network's properties and different parameters set by the three main implementations of the Lightning Network. We showed how recent changes in default parameters agreed upon by Lightning Devs have made the attack easier to carry out. Our results show that it is possible to disrupt the Lightning Network at a relatively low cost.

Further work must be conducted in order to mitigate this type of attack. We suggested several solutions to reduce the success rate of these attacks, but such mitigation is generally harder due to the nature of the attack: it relies on several fundamental properties of payment channel networks, and the blockchain.

Acknowledgments. We thank Itay Cohen, Nir Lavee and Zvi Yishai for providing improvements in our network partitioning algorithms and analysis.

This research was supported by the Israel Science Foundation (grant 1504/17) and by a grant from the HUJI Cyber Security Research Center in conjunction with the Israel National Cyber Bureau.

References

1. Fundingmanager: configurable remote max HTLCs [lnd pull request #4527], August 2020. https://github.com/lightningnetwork/lnd/pull/4527
2. Avarikioti, G., Laufenberg, F., Sliwinski, J., Wang, Y., Wattenhofer, R.: Towards secure and efficient payment channels. arXiv preprint arXiv:1811.12740 (2018)
3. Bastien Teinturier, A.R., Jager, J.: Spamming the lightning network, October 2020. https://github.com/t-bast/lightning-docs/blob/master/spam-prevention.md
4. BitInfoCharts: Bitcoin avg. transaction fee historical chart (2020). https://bitinfocharts.com/comparison/bitcoin-transactionfees.html#3m
5. C-Lightning: A lightning network implementation in c (2020). https://github.com/ElementsProject/lightning
6. Dziemian, C.: Summary of the second lightning development summit (2018). https://lists.linuxfoundation.org/pipermail/lightning-dev/2018-November/001595.html. [Lightning-dev]
7. Eclair: A scala implementation of the lightning network (2020). https://github.com/ACINQ/eclair
8. EmelyanenkoK: lightning-rfc issue #182: Payment channel congestion via spam-attack, May 2017. https://github.com/lightningnetwork/lightning-rfc/issues/182
9. Fiedler, M.: Laplacian of graphs and algebraic connectivity. Banach Center Publ. **25**(1), 57–70 (1989)
10. Girvan, M., Newman, M.E.: Community structure in social and biological networks. Proc. Natl. Acad. Sci. **99**(12), 7821–7826 (2002)

11. Green, M., Miers, I.: Bolt: Anonymous payment channels for decentralized currencies. In: Proceedings of the 2017 ACM SIGSAC Conference on Computer and Communications Security, pp. 473–489. ACM, Dallas (2017)
12. Gudgeon, L., Moreno-Sanchez, P., Roos, S., McCorry, P., Gervais, A.: Sok: Off the chain transactions. IACR Cryptology ePrint Archive **2019**, p. 360 (2019)
13. Heilman, E., Alshenibr, L., Baldimtsi, F., Scafuro, A., Goldberg, S.: Tumblebit: an untrusted bitcoin-compatible anonymous payment hub. In: Network and Distributed System Security Symposium, NDSS (2017)
14. Herrera-Joancomarti, J., Navarro-Arribas, G., Pedrosa, A.R., Cristina, P.S., Garcia-Alfaro, J.: On the difficulty of hiding the balance of lightning network channels. Ph.D. thesis, Dépt. Réseaux et Service de Télécom (Institut Mines-Télécom-Télécom SudParis ... (2019)
15. Kernighan, B.W., Lin, S.: An efficient heuristic procedure for partitioning graphs. Bell Syst. Tech. J. **49**(2), 291–307 (1970)
16. Lee, S., Kim, H.: On the robustness of lightning network in bitcoin. Pervasive Mob. Comput. **61**, 101108 (2020)
17. LNBIG: Lnbig lightning nodes (2018–2019). https://lnbig.com/#/our-nodes
18. LND: The lightning network daemon (2020). https://github.com/lightningnetwork/lnd
19. Malavolta, G., Moreno-Sanchez, P., Kate, A., Maffei, M., Ravi, S.: Concurrency and privacy with payment-channel networks. In: Proceedings of the 2017 ACM SIGSAC Conference on Computer and Communications Security, pp. 455–471. ACM, New York (2017)
20. McCorry, P., Bakshi, S., Bentov, I., Meiklejohn, S., Miller, A.: Pisa: arbitration outsourcing for state channels. In: Proceedings of the 1st ACM Conference on Advances in Financial Technologies, pp. 16–30. AFT, Zurich (2019)
21. McCorry, P., Möser, M., Shahandasti, S.F., Hao, F.: Towards Bitcoin payment networks. In: Liu, J.K., Steinfeld, R. (eds.) ACISP 2016, Part I. LNCS, vol. 9722, pp. 57–76. Springer, Cham (2016). https://doi.org/10.1007/978-3-319-40253-6_4
22. Miller, A., Bentov, I., Bakshi, S., Kumaresan, R., McCorry, P.: Sprites and state channels: payment networks that go faster than lightning. In: Goldberg, I., Moore, T. (eds.) FC 2019. LNCS, vol. 11598, pp. 508–526. Springer, Cham (2019). https://doi.org/10.1007/978-3-030-32101-7_30
23. Mizrahi, A., Zohar, A.: Congestion attacks in payment channel networks. arXiv preprint arXiv:2002.06564 (2020)
24. Network, R.: Setting the number of pending transfers keeping the gas limit, July 2018. https://github.com/raiden-network/raiden/commit/107b3c3700a7d6cac3ea e8634f945c1b6095f91c
25. Network, T.R.: An off-chain scaling solution (2020), https://github.com/raiden-network/raiden
26. Pérez-Solà, C., Ranchal-Pedrosa, A., Herrera-Joancomartí, J., Navarro-Arribas, G., Garcia-Alfaro, J.: LockDown: balance availability attack against lightning network channels. In: Bonneau, J., Heninger, N. (eds.) FC 2020. LNCS, vol. 12059, pp. 245–263. Springer, Cham (2020). https://doi.org/10.1007/978-3-030-51280-4_14
27. Poon, J., Dryja, T.: The Bitcoin lightning network: Scalable off-chain instant payments (2016)
28. (Roasbeef), O.O.: Git Commit: "lnd: lower default CLTV delta from 144 to 40". https://github.com/lightningnetwork/lnd/commit/c302f1ea3a91ccfa382d5 6851d23f4c73656208c#diff-356ddb2e7efca712327c3b2d94d3afd3 (Mar 2019)
29. Rohrer, E.: Lightning network snapshots (2018–2019). https://gitlab.tu-berlin.de/rohrer/discharged-pc-data/tree/master/snapshots

30. Rohrer, E., Malliaris, J., Tschorsch, F.: Discharged payment channels: Quantifying the lightning network's resilience to topology-based attacks. arXiv preprint arXiv:1904.10253 (2019)
31. Russell, R.: Loop attack with onion routing, August 2015. https://lists.linuxfoundation.org/pipermail/lightning-dev/2015-August/000135.html [Lightning-dev]
32. Seres, I.A., Gulyás, L., Nagy, D.A., Burcsi, P.: Topological analysis of bitcoin's lightning network. arXiv preprint arXiv:1901.04972 (2019)
33. Specifications, L.N.: Basis of lightning technology (BOLTs) (2020). https://github.com/lightningnetwork/lightning-rfc
34. Tang, W., Wang, W., Fanti, G., Oh, S.: Privacy-utility tradeoffs in routing cryptocurrency over payment channel networks. arXiv preprint arXiv:1909.02717 (2019)
35. Tikhomirov, S., Moreno-Sanchez, P., Maffei, M.: A quantitative analysis of security, anonymity and scalability for the lightning network. IACR Cryptol. ePrint Arch. **2020**, p. 303 (2020)
36. Tochner, S., Schmid, S., Zohar, A.: Hijacking routes in payment channel networks: A predictability tradeoff. arXiv preprint arXiv:1909.06890 (2019)
37. Trustnodes: Lightning network ddos sends 20% of nodes down (2018). https://www.trustnodes.com/2018/03/21/lightning-network-ddos-sends-20-nodes

Payment Trees: Low Collateral Payments for Payment Channel Networks

Maxim Jourenko[1][(✉)], Mario Larangeira[1,2], and Keisuke Tanaka[1]

[1] Department of Mathematical and Computing Sciences, School of Computing,
Tokyo Institute of Technology, Tokyo 152-8550, Japan
`jourenko.m.ab@m.titech.ac.jp`, `mario@c.titech.ac.jp`,
`keisuke@is.titech.ac.jp`
[2] Input Output Hong Kong, Hong Kong, China
`mario.larangeira@iohk.io`
`http://iohk.io`

Abstract. The security of blockchain based decentralized ledgers relies on consensus protocols executed between mutually distrustful parties. Such protocols incur delays which severely limit the throughput of such ledgers. Payment and state channels enable execution of offchain protocols that allow interaction between parties without involving the consensus protocol. Protocols such as Hashed Timelock Contracts (HTLC) and Sprites (FC'19) connect channels into Payment Channel Networks (PCN) allowing payments across a path of payment channels. Such a payment requires each party to lock away funds for an amount of time. The product of funds and locktime is the collateral of the party, i.e., their cost of opportunity to forward a payment. In the case of HTLC, the locktime is linear to the length of the path, making the total collateral invested across the path quadratic in size of its length. Sprites improved on this by reducing the locktime to a constant by utilizing smart contracts. Atomic Multi-Channel Updates (AMCU), published at CCS'19, introduced constant collateral payments without smart contracts. In this work we present the Channel Closure attack on AMCU that allows a malicious adversary to make honest parties lose funds. Furthermore, we propose the Payment Trees protocol that allows payments across a PCN with linear total collateral without the aid of smart contracts; a competitive performance similar to Sprites, and yet compatible to Bitcoin.

Keywords: Blockchain · Payment channel · HTLC · Collateral

1 Introduction

Blockchain based decentralized ledgers as introduced by Nakamoto [12] have enjoyed popularity and received interest from the research community and practitioners. Consensus protocols allow these ledgers to be operated by mutually

This work was supported by the Input Output Cryptocurrency Collaborative Research Chair funded by IOHK, JST CREST JPMJCR14D6, JST OPERA.

N. Borisov and C. Diaz (Eds.): FC 2021, LNCS 12675, pp. 189–208, 2021.
https://doi.org/10.1007/978-3-662-64331-0_10

distrustful parties at the cost of limited throughput. For example, Visa as a centralized system can process orders of magnitude more transactions within a given time frame than the most prominent blockchains as Bitcoin and Ethereum.

The main motivation for the development of offchain protocols is to close the gap in transaction throughput. The idea is to allow parties to interact with each other without interacting with the ledger, while still being able to use it to resolve disputes. Offchain protocols operate on *channels* that are created between two parties. Channels hold a state which can be enforced on the ledger. Payment channels [4,13,15] store the number of coins the two parties have locked inside that channel. Offchain protocols provide a means to alter this state arbitrarily often and thus improving the transaction throughput in the overall system.

Individual channels can be extended to channel networks, e.g. PCNs Lightning [15] and Raiden [1]. This is done using techniques, such as HTLC [2,15], that allow for payments of $b \in \mathbb{N}$ coins across a path of payment channels of length $n \in \mathbb{N}$. This is performed by executing the same payment on each channel within the payment path atomically. All parties on the payment path have to lock the payment amount for a duration of up to *locktime*. The opportunity cost a party has to invest is the *collateral* [10] which equals the payment amount b multiplied by the locktime. In turn, parties can impose fees to invest collateral. In the case of HTLC, a party's collateral equals $\mathcal{O}(nb\Delta)$ in the worst-case where Δ is a parameter of the underlying ledger and is the upper limit of the time it takes for a transaction to be included in the ledger.

High collateral investments can be exploited by malicious adversaries to perform *grieving* and *denial-of-service* attacks [11,14]. For example, an attacker might operate a channel to collect fees by forwarding payments. However, payments might be routed through competing channels instead. To sabotage the competitor, the attacker can route a payment through these channels without the intent of executing it, locking the competing channel's coins for the entirety of the locktime. These channels experience a denial-of-service scenario by being unable to forward any other payments, losing fees that the attacker can collect through their own channel. Performing this attack on a large scale can result in denial-of-service for the whole PCN. On a lower scale, a griever might force parties to lock away their funds for as long as possible by delaying their cooperation until the last moment. An alternative form of this attack involves routing multiple low value payments through a competing channel, up until a point where the channel cannot add any further HTLCs even though it contains enough coins. In the case of the Lightning network, these types of denial-of-service attacks can lock all of a channel's coins for up to around 2 weeks [11].[1]

For HTLC the total collateral locked over a whole payment path is $\mathcal{O}(n^2 b\Delta)$ and therefore quadratic in the payment paths length. Sprites [10] reduce the collateral of each party to $\mathcal{O}(b(n + \Delta))$ and the total collateral to $\mathcal{O}(bn(n + \Delta))$ by utilizing a smart contract. This is considered to be constant and linear respectively, since $n << \Delta$ such that $n + \Delta < 2\Delta$. Sprites mitigate the damage done by a possible attacker but its implementation is limited to ledgers with smart

---

[1] https://cointelegraph.com/news/developer-reveals-biggest-unsolvable-lightning-attack-vector.

contract capability. The Atomic Multi-Channel Updates (AMCU) protocol [7] is an attempt to close this gap and enable payments with constant collateral on ledgers without smart contract capabilities. However, even though AMCU is formalized as a functionality within Canetti's UC Framework [3], the very last, but crucial step, of the updateState function *does not seem to be presented* in the description of the AMCU protocol, and neither addressed by the simulator [7]. This gap results in a vulnerability that can be exploited by a malicious adversary to steal funds from honest parties.

Related Work. Payment channels [4,13,15] themselves allow only for offchain payments between two parties. Offchain protocols such as HTLCs [2,15] and Sprites [10] allow to perform payments across paths of channels allowing for the implementation of PCNs. Prominent examples are the Lightning Network [15] and Raiden [1]. Although offchain protocols exist that create new *virtual* channels out of two existing channels as Perun [5,6] and Lightweight Virtual Payment Channels [8], this work focuses on performing individual payments across a PCN. In the following we consider a payment of $b \in \mathbb{N}$ coins across a path of $n \in \mathbb{N}$ channels involving parties $\mathcal{P}_0, \ldots, \mathcal{P}_n$.

The most prominent technique is based on HTLCs [2,15], which are scripts that perform conditional payments within a channel: The payer locks funds into the contract that are paid out if the payee can present a secret x such that $y = \mathcal{H}(x)$ where $\mathcal{H}$ is a cryptographic hash function. Otherwise, after time *locktime* the payment times-out and the payer can reclaim their funds. This contract is replicated along all channels within a payment path. The payment is performed as soon as $\mathcal{P}_n$ reveals x to their predecessor who then learns the value of x allowing them to claim the payment from their predecessor in turn. An attacker $\mathcal{P}_i, 0 < i \leq n$ might attempt to delay revelation of x to their predecessor until briefly before expiration of the *locktime*. To allow $\mathcal{P}_{i-1}$ to forward x in time, their locktime needs to be increased by at least Δ. This results in a locktime in $\mathcal{O}(n\Delta)$ and a total locktime in $\Theta(n^2\Delta)$.

Sprites [10] aim to reduce the locktime of a party up to a constant $\mathcal{O}(n + \Delta)$ where $n << \Delta$. This is done by setting up a smart contract entity called *PreimageManager*, s.t. submitting x to the PreimageManager allows to broadcast it to all nodes within a payment path in at most n communication rounds. The protocol requires creation of a smart contract, making it unavailable to script based ledgers as Bitcoin. AMCU [7] attempts to close this gap, i.e. compatibility with Bitcoin, by introducing an approach for constant locktime payments without the need of smart contracts. AMCU sets up payments on each channel within a payment path that are performed on the condition that an *Enable* transaction is created, upon which all payments are performed atomically. However, this Enable transactions results in several issues. For one, its size grows linearly in the payment path's length, making its implementation prohibitive for ledgers which have an upper limit for block size and transaction size. Moreover, no party has control over all of the Enable transaction's inputs. A malicious adversary can make two parties collaborate to double spend one of the Enable transaction's inputs, such that no party is able to enforce the payment on the ledger. If the double-spending is timed appropriately, this can lead to an attacker stealing funds from honest parties.

Jourenko et al. [8] proposed an offchain protocol that takes two channels γ_A and γ_B as input, one between $\mathcal{P}_A$ and $\mathcal{P}_I$ and one between $\mathcal{P}_I$ and $\mathcal{P}_B$ and creates a new channel γ^v between $\mathcal{P}_A$ and $\mathcal{P}_B$. As this approach is not optimized for individual payments, using it for this purpose would result in excessive collateral as parties would need to lock away more coins for a longer duration as in existing approaches. However, we re-use techniques from the lightweight virtual payment channel construction for the Payment Tree protocol.

Our Contributions. Our contributions are threefold. 1) We present an attack on AMCU performed by a malicious adversary. 2) We present *Payment Trees* that allow for payments across paths within a PCN without the need of smart contracts, requiring *only* logarithmic individual collateral $\mathcal{O}(b\Delta \log n)$ while requiring only linear total collateral $\mathcal{O}(nb\Delta)$ such that its performance is comparable to Sprites. 3) We provide efficiency and security analysis of Payment Trees, proving the properties *Balance Security* and *Liveness*.

Structure. In the remainder of this work, first, we provide background to this work in Sect. 2. We give an outline of the Channel Closure attack in Sect. 3. Next, we give an informal overview of the Payment Tree protocol in Sect. 4. Afterwards, we introduce the types of transactions used for our construction in Sect. 5 before introducing Payment Trees in Sect. 6 followed by efficiency and security analysis in Sect. 7. We conclude in Sect. 8.

2   Background

Notation. Throughout this work we make use of tuples and use short-hand notations as follows. Let $(a_1, a_2, \ldots, a_n)$ be a definition of a tuple of type A and let α be an instantiation of A. Then $\alpha.a_i$ equals the i-th entry of α.

The UTXO Paradigm. A UTXO is a tuple of the form (b, π) where $b \in \mathbb{N}$ is an amount of coins and $\pi \in \{0,1\}^*$ is a script. The b coins of the UTXO are claimed by providing a witness $w \in \{0,1\}^*$ s.t. $\pi(w) = \text{True}$. The state of the ledger is represented by a set of UTXO S_{utxo}, which can be changed by a transaction of the form (U_{in}, U_{out}, t) where $t \in \mathbb{N}$ is the (absolute) timelock represented as a point in time, U_{out} is the list of unique UTXO for the *outputs* of the transaction, and U_{in} is the set of transaction *inputs* of the form $(\text{ref}(u), w_u)$ where $\text{ref}(u)$ is the pointer to the UTXO u, and w_u is the witness.

A transaction (U_{in}, U_{out}, t) needs to fulfill the following conditions. (1) The locktime has passed, i.e. $t \leq \tau$ where τ is the current time, (2) all witnesses are valid, i.e. $\forall (\text{ref}(u), w) \in U_{in} : u.\pi(w) = \text{True}$ (3) the coins within the newly created UTXO are less or equal to those in the transaction's inputs, i.e. $\Sigma_{(\text{ref}(u),w) \in U_{in}} u.b \geq \Sigma_{u \in U_{out}} u.b$, (4) all UTXOs in the transaction's inputs exist and have not yet been spent, i.e. $\forall (\text{ref}(u), w) \in U_{in} : u \in S_{utxo}$. The transaction has the following effect on the ledger. All UTXOs referenced within U_{in}

are removed from S_{utxo} and all UTXOs defined in U_{out} are added to S_{utxo}. A transaction T is included in the ledger within a duration $\Delta \in \mathbb{N}$. Condition (4) implies that no UTXO can be claimed by two different transactions. After sending T to the ledger, if within time Δ another transaction T' claiming a subset of the same UTXOs as T is sent to the ledger, it would result in a race condition, in which it is non-deterministic whether T or T' will change the ledger's state. We note that while we use Δ as a ledger parameter in practice this value has to be estimated for real-world implementations. Special care has to be taken when selecting a value. A value that is too low breaks our assumptions and the protocol's security. A value too high increases the collateral and therefore the impact of attacks such as congestion and lockdown [11,14].

Transaction Graph. All transactions included in the ledger form a directed and acyclic graph. The set of all transactions form its vertices. An edge (T_0, T_1) from transaction T_0 to transaction T_1 exists, if T_1's inputs contain a pointer to one of T_0's outputs, i.e. $\exists u : u \in T_0.U_{out} \wedge (\text{ref}(u), w) \in T_1.U_{in}$. Note that a transaction can only be included in a ledger if all of its ancestors have been included in the ledger before. In the remainder of this work we reference sets of transactions that are connected to form a sub-tree as *transaction trees*.

Scripting. Scripts in this work specify a UTXOs owner by requiring a signature of the transaction that spends the UTXO with the recipient's verification key. This is extended to 2-out-of-2 multisignatures that require verification keys of two parties $\mathcal{P}$ and $\mathcal{P}'$ effectively creating a shared wallet between both parties that can only be spent with consent of both parties. In the remainder of this work UTXOs requiring 2-out-of-2 multisignatures are termed Funding UTXO. Throughout this work we simplify scripts by only stating the set of parties which need to provide their signatures to spend the respective UTXO.

Channels. A channel γ between two parties consists of sub-protocols setup, closure and dispute. In setup both parties create a transaction Tr_f containing a Funding UTXO between each other which locks their funds into the channel. They create a transaction tree with the Funding UTXO as its ancestor that represents the channel which we reference in the remainder of this work as *channel-tree*. Only after the channel-tree is created and either party holds signatures of its transactions, both parties sign and commit Tr_f to the ledger while holding off commitment of transactions within the channel-tree. Both parties can perform closure of the channel by committing a transaction to the ledger that spends the Funding UTXO unlocking the channel's funds according to its most recent state. In case of a dispute, the dispute sub-protocol enforces the channel's state by committing the channel-tree's transactions onto the ledger.

Offchain Protocols perform a state transition of a channel by transforming its channel-tree. Any honest party must be able to enforce the new channel's state which might require an explicit invalidation step that disables commitment of an older version of the channel-tree or allows for punishment of a party that does so. An efficiency requirement of offchain protocols is that performing them $n \in \mathbb{N}$ times grows the channel-tree by at most $\mathcal{O}(1)$ transactions.

Invalidation by Timelock. Timelocks can be used to define at which point a transaction can be committed to the ledger. Assume there are two transactions that spend the same UTXO, but which have timelocks that are 1) in the future and 2) have a difference of at least Δ. In this case parties can enforce commitment of the transaction with the lower timelock to the ledger. The transaction with the lower timelock *invalidates* the transaction with the higher timelock.

Hashed Timelock Contracts. Let $\mathcal{P}_0, \mathcal{P}_1, \ldots, \mathcal{P}_n, n \in \mathbb{N}$ be parties where parties $\mathcal{P}_{i-1}$ and $\mathcal{P}_i, i \in \{1, \ldots, n\}$ control channel γ_i. HTLCs are used to perform payments of $b \in \mathbb{N}$ coins from $\mathcal{P}_0$ to $\mathcal{P}_n$ by replicating the payment on each channel γ_i within a payment path $\gamma_1, \ldots, \gamma_n$ from $\mathcal{P}_0$ to $\mathcal{P}_n$. (1) On a channel $\gamma_j, j \in \{1, \ldots, n\}$ the payment is performed by extending the channel-tree with a conditional payment: If the payee $\mathcal{P}_j$ can show the pre-image $x \in \mathbb{N}$ of a hashed value $y = H(x)$, where H is a cryptographic hash function, they will receive b coins from the payer $\mathcal{P}_{j-1}$. However, after expiration of a locktime t_j the payment expires and the payer $\mathcal{P}_{j-1}$ will have their coins refunded instead. (2) Only after the conditional payments are set up on all channels, the payment is executed atomically by having $\mathcal{P}_n$ show the pre-image x to $\mathcal{P}_{n-1}$, proving that they have the *capability* to claim the coins on the ledger through the conditional payment. In turn, $\mathcal{P}_{n-1}$ learns the pre-image x s.t. they can show it to party $\mathcal{P}_{n-2}$ reclaiming the coins they forwarded to $\mathcal{P}_n$. The information on x propagates through the whole payment path in this manner. (3) Lastly, to keep the payment offchain, the parties need to consolidate the payment on each channel respectively. This is done by updating the channel-tree. The conditional-payment is removed and the b coins that were locked into the channel are credited to the payee. At this point the channel-tree has the same form as before the payment, but with updated balance distribution to account for the payment. This ensures that the channel-tree does not grow in size with each payment, thus fulfilling the efficiency requirements of an offchain protocol. Note that, if the payer $\mathcal{P}_{j-1}$ does not cooperate with consolidation, payee $\mathcal{P}_i$ can reclaim their coins by resolving the conditional payment on the ledger instead. Due to this the timelock t_j has to be chosen s.t. $\mathcal{P}_i$ has enough time to do so before the conditional payment expires, even if they learn the pre-image from $\mathcal{P}_{i+1}$ at the last moment just shortly before expiration of timelock t_{j+1}. Thus the relation $t_i \geq t_{i+1} + \Delta$ has to hold, making the locktime grow linearly with the payment path's length. This results in a collateral cost of $bt_i \in \mathcal{O}(bn^2\Delta)$ which is quadratic in the path's length.

The Wormhole Attack. The HTLC protocol is vulnerable to the wormhole attack [9]. An adversary controlling two parties $\mathcal{P}_i$, $\mathcal{P}_j$, $1 \leq i \leq j + 2 \leq n - 1$ within a payment path can prevent intermediaries $k, i < k < j$ to participate at the payment and receive their fees by having $\mathcal{P}_i$ forward pre-image x to $\mathcal{P}_{i-1}$ after $\mathcal{P}_j$ learns it from $\mathcal{P}_{j+1}$ and without forwarding it to party $\mathcal{P}_{j-1}$.

Brief Description of AMCU. A payment within the AMCU protocol is performed by replicating the payment on each channel using *Consume* transactions. All Consume transactions share a common ancestor within the protocol's transaction tree which is the *Enable* transaction. The Enable transaction has UTXOs from each individual channel as input and thus requires signatures of all parties within the payment path. As soon as the parties exchange signatures for the Enable transaction, all Consume transaction could be committed on the ledger, thus performing the payment. If any party refuses to collaborate in the creation of the Enable transaction, all parties have their coins refunded using *Lock* transactions after the expiration of the specified locktime period. As we show in the next section, in contrast to HTLCs, AMCU cannot ensure that all parties have the capability to claim their coins on the ledger after the payment. In fact it takes only one pair of parties controlling a channel to spend one of the Enable transaction's inputs with a different transaction s.t. the Enable transaction and transitively the Consume transactions cannot be committed to the ledger. This could be remedied by performing a consolidation step on all channels atomically. Although the functionality PCN$^+$, that models AMCU, correctly performs this consolidation step, the AMCU protocol itself does not.

3   The Channel Closure Attack on AMCU

In the following we present the Channel Closure attack informally. A more detailed description of AMCU and a formal treatment of the attack are supplemented in the full version of the paper.

The Vulnerability. While the Enable transaction is the core of the AMCU construction, it also seems to be its vulnerability. While the Enable transaction receives inputs from each channel, no party has control over all channels within the payment path. At any time, two parties sharing a channel can maliciously spend a UTXO that is provided as input of the transaction, or as input to any of its ancestors within the transaction tree. When this happens, the Enable transaction cannot be committed to the ledger and all parties have their coins refunded through Lock transactions. Effectively, no party can enforce payment after execution of the AMCU protocol. On top of that, an adversary can take this further, performing a Channel Closure attack to steal funds from honest parties. We remark that PCN payments require a consolidation step in which a payment is included within the parties' individual channels. While the functionality PCN$^+$ modeling AMCU performs a consolidation step atomically on all channels, this step is omitted by the AMCU protocol. Second, performing the consolidation step atomically on all channels is highly non-trivial as atomic operations on multiple channels is exactly the problem statement that protocols such as HTLCs, Sprites and AMCU themselves attempt to solve.

The Channel Closure Attack is performed by abusing exactly these two observations. First, the adversary corrupts two parties within a payment path $\mathcal{P}_i$ and $\mathcal{P}_{i+1}$. These parties cooperate in execution of the AMCU protocol right up until the consolidation step. Then, $\mathcal{P}_i$ performs the consolidation step with $\mathcal{P}_{i-1}$ on channel γ_{i-1} while $\mathcal{P}_{i+1}$ does not cooperate with $\mathcal{P}_{i+2}$ to consolidate the payment on channel γ_{i+1}. Next, $\mathcal{P}_i$ and $\mathcal{P}_{i+1}$ close their channel γ_i such that the Enable transaction cannot be committed to the ledger. This allows $\mathcal{P}_{i+1}$ to reclaim coins from $\mathcal{P}_{i+2}$ using their shared Lock transaction. Effectively, $\mathcal{P}_i$ received the payment amount from $\mathcal{P}_{i-1}$ on γ_i through consolidation, while $\mathcal{P}_{i+1}$ did not forward the payment.

4   Protocol Overview

In the following, we define communication and adversarial models, before giving an overview of the protocol. Lastly we define the properties of our construction.

Communication Model. Communication between parties occurs in rounds. Any message sent within one round is available to the recipient at the beginning of the next round. The duration of any round has an upper limit.

Adversarial Model. We define an Adversary $\mathcal{A}$ consistent with related work [7,8,10]: At the beginning of protocol execution, the adversary can statically corrupt up to n of $n + 1$ parties, receiving their internal state and having all communication to and from these parties be routed through the adversary. The adversary is malicious and can make any corrupted party deviate from the protocol. Moreover, within each communication round, the adversary can delay and re-order all messages sent.

We illustrate the life-cycle of the Payment Tree protocol for a payment of 2 coins from Alice to Charlie across two channels using Figs. 1 and 2. The protocol's approach is to take two channels, one between parties Alice and Bob, one between parties Bob and Charlie and construct a transaction tree that effectively creates a virtual channel [8] optimized for a one-time payment between Alice and Charlie. Our construction utilizes two approaches to perform updates to transaction trees atomically. On the one hand, we use these techniques to empower the intermediary Bob to ensure correctness of the protocol, while on the other hand, we incentivise Bob to actually do so by means of punishment. Our construction consists of multiple transaction tree updates. Updates are done using the *invalidation by timelock* technique, but for simplicity we leave the details to Sect. 6.

Constructing Transaction Trees Atomically. We observe that committing a transaction to the ledger requires that all of its ancestors are committed to the ledger beforehand. For a transaction to be able to be committed to the ledger it needs to contain all required witnesses, i.e. signatures. Therefore, (1) we can atomically create a transaction tree rooted in a transaction tr_{root} that is

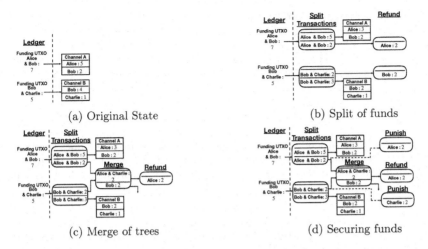

(a) Original State

(b) Split of funds

(c) Merge of trees

(d) Securing funds

Fig. 1. Stepwise construction of a Payment Tree across two channels. Boxes with straight corners represent channel trees displaying their state. Boxes with round corners represent transactions displaying output UTXOs. Edges indicate which transactions spend the UTXO at their origin.

common ancestor to all other transactions. First, we add signatures to all transactions except tr_{root}. Afterwards, adding signatures to tr_{root} makes the whole transaction tree committable to the ledger at the same moment. (2) We assume two transactions, tr_0 and tr_1, that require signatures of Alice and Bob, as well as Bob and Charlie respectively. Bob can enforce that both transactions are created atomically by only providing his signature *after* he received signatures from Alice and Charlie. We note that techniques (1) and (2) can be used in tandem.

Payment Tree Construction. Figure 1 depicts construction of a Payment Tree between Alice, Bob and Charlie. Construction consists of three atomic transaction tree updates. We note that the balance distribution between the parties remains unchanged between the updates and no payment is executed. Alice and Bob as well as Bob and Charlie share a channel as depicted in Fig. 1a. (1) Then, as shown in Fig. 1b we update both trees by introducing a *Split* transaction that spends the channels' Funding UTXOs and creates two new Funding UTXOs each. One UTXO contains the payment amount and is funded by coins from Alice, who is payer, and Bob, who is intermediary, respectively. The other UTXO contains the remaining coins and is used as Funding UTXO to reopen both channels which can be used for further payments within the channels or further Payment Tree constructions. (2) Next as shown in Fig. 1c both separate transaction trees are combined using a Merge transaction. This transaction creates two UTXOs. One UTXO requires Bob's signature to be spent and contains his collateral. The other UTXO is a Funding UTXO requiring the signatures of Alice and Charlie and it contains Alice's payment to Charlie. At this point, the coins are given to Alice. (3) Lastly, as shown in Fig. 1d, before we can proceed with a payment,

(a) Payment   (b) Consolidation

Fig. 2. Payment and Consolidation using Payment Trees. Figure 2a modifies the Payment Tree to forward the funds in the Merge transaction's Funding UTXO to the payee. Figure 2b splits up the Payment Tree and distributes funds according to the Payment Tree's state in Fig. 2a.

the funds within the Merge transaction's Funding UTXOs need to be secured in case two parties, for example Bob and Charlie, collude to spend their Merge transaction's or Split transaction's input with a different transaction. This attack is similar to the Channel Closure attack described in Sect. 3 and would disable commitment of the Merge transaction. However, we observe that all UTXOs that can be spent for this attack require Bob's signature. Respectively, in this scenario we can uniquely identify Bob as malicious. In order to punish Bob and secure the funds of Alice and Charlie respectively we create *Punish* transactions. These transactions spend the same Funding UTXOs as the Merge transaction but have a timelock that is higher than that of the Merge transaction by at least Δ. Due to this, Bob can always avoid commitment of a Punish transaction by committing the Merge transaction to the ledger. However, in case Bob acted maliciously such that the Merge transaction cannot be committed to the ledger, Alice and Charlie can reclaim their coins from Bob through the Punish transactions.

Payment and Consolidation. Figure 2 depicts payment and consolidation using a Payment Tree. Assuming a fully constructed Payment Tree as shown in Fig. 1d a payment is executed by giving the coins within the Merge transaction's Funding UTXO to Charlie instead of Alice. As shown in Fig. 2a this changes the balance distribution represented by the transaction tree, reducing Alice's coins by 2 and adding those to Charlie's balance. A consolidation requires one atomic transaction tree update as shown in Fig. 2b. This update spends the UTXOs within the Merge transaction's inputs and gives the coins to Bob and Charlie respectively. Note that this step does not change the balance distribution between the parties. Bob needs to make sure that this update is done atomically s.t. he avoids commitment of a Punish transaction. At this point the transaction trees are separate and in control of each channels' members respectively. Both pair of parties can now perform a last transaction tree update that replaces the respective transaction tree with a channel as shown in Fig. 1a but that now represents the new balance distribution instead.

System Goals. In the following we define the desired properties of our protocol.

Theorem 1 (Balance Security). *Outside of performing the intended payment, the sum of a honest party's coins is not reduced by participation in the Payment Tree protocol.*

Theorem 2 (Liveness). *Eventually any honest party receives access to their coins through UTXOs spendable with a witness consisting of a signature corresponding to their verification key.*

5   Transactions

We use three types of transactions. Split transactions are used to split off coins from one channel, making them available to our construction in form of a Funding UTXO. Payout transactions take a Funding UTXO as input and pay the money to one of the two parties involved in it. Lastly, the Merge transaction is used to combine the Funding UTXOs that were split off two channels by taking them as input, paying out the intermediary's coins out as collateral and creating a Funding UTXO between the two remaining non-intermediary parties.

Split Transactions are of form $Tr_{\mathsf{split}} = (U_{\mathsf{in}}, U_{\mathsf{out}}, t)$ where $U_{\mathsf{in}} = \{\mathsf{ref}(f_\gamma)\}$ consist of one Funding UTXO provided by the channel-tree of γ, $U_{\mathsf{out}} = \{f_{\mathsf{change}}, f_{\mathsf{pay}}\}$ consists of two Funding UTXOs. It holds that $f_{\mathsf{change}}.b + f_{\mathsf{pay}}.b = f_\gamma$ and $f_{\mathsf{pay}}.b = b$. Moreover, $f_\gamma.\pi = f_{\mathsf{change}}.\pi = f_{\mathsf{pay}}.\pi$, i.e. all Funding UTXOs are shared between the same parties. The function call $\mathsf{SPLIT}(\gamma, b, t)$ creates a Split transaction as described above and returns f_{pay}. A function call to $\mathsf{UNSPLIT}(\gamma)$ consolidates the transaction into the channel by updating the channel's balance distribution with the split off balance. Additionally it sets up a channel between both parties by constructing a channel-tree with Funding UTXO f_{change} as root. *Split* transactions are used to take off b coins from each channel to be used for our construction. They are used to avoid that the existing channels are affected in case a corrupted intermediary misbehaves. Although we represent this by using a Split transactions as done with Virtual Channels and AMCU, it could be included similarly as conditional payments from HTLCs by placing a Funding UTXO instead of a HTLC contract.

Merge Transactions are of form $Tr_{\mathsf{merge}} = (U_{\mathsf{in}}, U_{\mathsf{out}}, t)$ where $U_{\mathsf{in}} = \{f_{\mathsf{pay},0}, f_{\mathsf{pay},1}\}$ and $U_{\mathsf{out}} = \{f_{\mathsf{pay}}, u_{collateral}\}$. The two Funding UTXOs that are provided as input $f_{\mathsf{pay},0}$ and $f_{\mathsf{pay},1}$ are shared between parties $\mathcal{P}_A$ and $\mathcal{P}_B$ as well as between parties $\mathcal{P}_B$ and $\mathcal{P}_C$ respectively. The newly created Funding UTXOs f_{pay} in the output is shared between parties $\mathcal{P}_A$ and $\mathcal{P}_C$. The other UTXO within the outputs is $u_{collateral}$ which pays out funds to $\mathcal{P}_B$. Lastly it holds that the coins in all UTXOs are equal, i.e. $f_{\mathsf{pay},0}.b = f_{\mathsf{pay},1}.b = f_{\mathsf{pay}}.b = u_{collateral}.b = b$. The function call $\mathsf{MERGE}(f_{\mathsf{pay},0}, f_{\mathsf{pay},1}, t)$ is a short-hand notation to construct a Merge transaction. We extend helper function $\mathsf{OUT\_UTXO}$ to accept a Merge transaction as input as well. In this case it returns UTXO f_{pay}. The helper function IN_UTXO takes a Merge transaction as input and outputs the UTXOs that are used within its inputs, i.e. $f_{\mathsf{pay},0}, f_{\mathsf{pay},1}$. *Merge* transactions are used to combine transaction trees into one, essentially opening up a virtual channel between Alice and Charlie that can be used for a one-time payment.

Payout Transactions are of form $Tr_{\mathsf{payout}} = (U_{\mathsf{in}}, U_{\mathsf{out}}, t)$ where $U_{\mathsf{in}} = \{f\}$ is a Funding UTXO and $U_{\mathsf{out}} = \{u_{\mathsf{payout}}\}$. It holds that u_{payout} pays out funds to a party $\mathcal{P}$ and $f.b = u_{\mathsf{payout}}.b$. The function call PAYOUT$(f, \mathcal{P}, t)$ constructs a Payout transaction as described above. We extend helper function IN_UTXO to take a Payout transaction as input in which case it outputs the UTXO f. Payout transactions are used at several points within our construction to serve different roles as shown in Fig. 3. *Refund* transactions are used whenever Funding UTXOs are created. They are used to ensure that no funds are locked away within Funding UTXOs indefinitely even when any other party stops collaboration, which is essential to ensure the liveness property. *Punish* transactions are used to incentivise an intermediary to collaborate and ensure Merge transactions can be committed to the ledger. Without those, in case a Merge transaction is not committed to the ledger it could result in the loss of coins for Charlie in case the Refund transaction between Bob and Charlie is committed to the ledger instead and after the payment between Alice and Charlie has been performed. The *Payment* transaction is used to perform a change of the state, i.e. balance distribution, represented by the transaction tree, effectively performing a payment. Lastly, *Consolidation* transactions are used to deconstruct the transaction tree by applying the payment on both original transaction trees atomically. Without these, we cannot enforce the payment outside of committing the transaction tree to the ledger itself because of which the protocol would not fulfill the efficiency requirements for offchain protocols and thus not being classified as such. We note that the Refund and Punish transactions between Alice and Bob represent the same state s.t. the Punish transaction is redundant. However, for simplicity we opted to include both transactions making the construction symmetric. Whereas similarly the Consolidation and Punish transactions between Bob and Charlie do represent the same state in Fig. 3, it is not possible to remove any of the transactions in the case where fees are paid to Bob which would be included within the Consolidation but not the Punish transactions.

6   Our Payment Tree Construction

We describe the construction of a payment tree in respect to our running example. Let $\mathcal{P}_0, \mathcal{P}_1, \ldots, \mathcal{P}_n, n \in \mathbb{N}$, be parties where parties $\mathcal{P}_{i-1}$ and $\mathcal{P}_i, i \in \{1, \ldots, n\}$ control channel γ_i. The protocol performs a payment of $b \in \mathbb{N}$ coins from $\mathcal{P}_0$ to $\mathcal{P}_n$. The value $\tau \in \mathbb{N}$ represents the current time, whereas $\Delta \in \mathbb{N}$ is the maximum time it takes for a transactions to be included in the ledger after committing it. We illustrate our approach in Fig. 3 for a two-hop payment, i.e. for the case of $n = 2$. It is designed such that it can be extended to payment

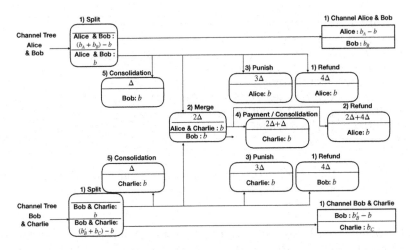

Fig. 3. Transaction tree of a payment of b coins across 2 hops. Beforehand, the respective balances are b_A and b_B for Alice and Bob, b'_B and b_C for Bob in Charlie within their channels. Transactions are boxes with round corners containing the UTXOs they create, whereas referenced UTXOs in inputs are indicated implicitly by arrows originating from the UTXO that is spent. Red numbers indicate timelocks. Numbers atop the transaction indicate order of construction whereas transactions with same numbers are constructed atomically. Channel trees are boxes with straight edges forming a black box. (Color figure online)

paths of arbitrary lengths. The construction is based on the overview given in Sect. 4. Numbers indicate the order in which transactions are created, whereas transactions with the same numbers are created atomically (Fig. 4).

The Payment Tree Protocol. The protocol for constructing a Payment Tree across a path of n channels is depicted in Algorithm 4. It makes use of Algorithm 1 that allows an intermediary to atomically create two transactions, Algorithm 2 that performs a construction step of the Payment Tree, and Algorithm 3 that performs a consolidation step of the Payment Tree.

Helper Functions. Function SIGN(Tr, P_S, P_R) is used to sign and exchange signatures of transactions. It takes a transaction Tr and two sets of parties P_S and P_R as input. Each party in P_S signs Tr and sends the signature to each party in P_R. This includes verification of signatures by the recipients. Function PARTIES takes a Funding UTXO as input and outputs a set containing the two parties of which a signature is required to spend the UTXO. Function INTERMEDIARY(f_0, f_1) takes two Funding UTXOs f_0, f_1 as input, if an intermediary exists, i.e. $|\text{PARTIES}(f_0) \cap \text{PARTIES}(f_1)| = 1$, then it returns the intermediary $\mathcal{P} \in \text{PARTIES}(f_0) \cap \text{PARTIES}(f_1)$. Otherwise it returns $\bot$. Function COUNTERPARY($f, \mathcal{P}$) takes a Funding UTXO and a party as input, if $\mathcal{P} \in \text{PARTIES}(f)$, then it returns its counterparty $\mathcal{P}_C \in (\text{PARTIES}(f)) \setminus \{\mathcal{P}\}$.

Algorithm 1 Atomically signing two Payout transaction

1: **function** ATOMIC_SIGN(Tr_0, Tr_1)
Require: Tr_0, Tr_1 are Payout transactions between three parties.
2:     $f_0, f_1 \leftarrow$ FUTXO(Tr_0), FUTXO(Tr_1)
3:     $\mathcal{P}_I \leftarrow$ INTERMEDIARY(f_0, f_1)
4:     $\mathcal{P}_A, \mathcal{P}_B \leftarrow$ COUNTERPARY($f_0, \mathcal{P}_I$), COUNTERPARY($f_1, \mathcal{P}_I$)
5:     SIGN($Tr_0, \{\mathcal{P}_A\}, \{\mathcal{P}_I\}$), SIGN($Tr_1, \{\mathcal{P}_B\}, \{\mathcal{P}_I\}$)
6:     SIGN($Tr_0, \{\mathcal{P}_I\}, \{\mathcal{P}_A\}$), SIGN($Tr_1, \{\mathcal{P}_I\}, \{\mathcal{P}_B\}$)
7: **end function**

Fig. 4. Algorithm that takes two Payout transactions as input and allows the intermediary party to enforce that either both or no transactions are fully signed.

Atomic Signatures. We assume a setting with two channels between three parties. Protocol *ATOMIC_SIGN* is shown in Algorithm 1. It enables the intermediary party to enforce that two transactions – one on each channel – are created atomically. This is done by having the intermediary party provide signatures to both transactions only after they received all signatures from its counterparties (Fig. 5).

Merging Channels. Protocol *MERGE* as shown in Algorithm 2 takes two Funding UTXOs f_0, f_1, an amount of coins b and a time t as input where f_0 is shared between parties $\mathcal{P}_A$ and $\mathcal{P}_I$, f_1 is shared between parties $\mathcal{P}_I$ and $\mathcal{P}_B$ and it holds that $f_0.b = f_1.b = b$. It creates a Merge transactions with timelock $t_m = t + 2\Delta$ spending both Funding UTXOs, paying out b coins to $\mathcal{P}_I$ and containing a Funding UTXO holding b coins, which are paid out to $\mathcal{P}_A$ after time $t_m + 4\Delta$ by means of a Payout transaction. This transaction tree is created atomically as its root, which is the Merge transaction, is signed last. Only after each party holds a fully signed instance of the Merge transaction, two Punish transactions spending f_0 and f_1 and paying out b coins to $\mathcal{P}_A$ and $\mathcal{P}_B$ respectively are created atomically using *ATOMIC_SIGN*. These have timelocks equal to $t + 3\Delta$. Note that the creation of the Merge transaction must not re-distribute funds, i.e. the funds in f_0 are paid by $\mathcal{P}_A$ and the funds in f_1 are paid by $\mathcal{P}_I$. The Punish transactions are used to secure the funds within the Merge transaction by paying out funds to $\mathcal{P}_A$ and $\mathcal{P}_B$, if the Merge transaction cannot be committed to the ledger. Timelocks are selected to perform transformations on the existing transaction through the invalidation by timelock technique and also to allow the construction to be performed iteratively. Timelock t_m is selected s.t. a Consolidation transaction can be placed with timelock $t + \Delta$ during the protocol's consolidation phase. Timelocks of the Punish transactions are selected s.t. they are invalidated by the Merge transaction *conditionally*, i.e. only if the Merge transaction can be committed to the ledger, the Punish transactions are invalid. The Payout transaction acts as a Refund transaction for the new Merge transaction. Respectively we assign it

---

Algorithm 2 Construction Step of a Payment Tree

1: **function** MERGE(f_0, f_1, b, t)
2:     $\mathcal{P}_I \leftarrow$ INTERMEDIARY(f_0, f_1)
3:     $\mathcal{P}_A, \mathcal{P}_B \leftarrow$ COUNTERPARY($f_0, \mathcal{P}_I$), COUNTERPARY($f_1, \mathcal{P}_I$)
4:     $Tr_{mrg} \leftarrow$ MERGE($f_0, f_1, t + 2\Delta$)
5:     $Tr_{refund} \leftarrow$ PAYOUT(OUT_UTXO(Tr_{mrg}), $\mathcal{P}_A, t + 6\Delta$)
6:     $Tr_{punish,A} \leftarrow$ PAYOUT($f_0, \mathcal{P}_A, t + 3\Delta$)
7:     $Tr_{punish,B} \leftarrow$ PAYOUT($f_1, \mathcal{P}_C, t + 3\Delta$)
8:     SIGN($Tr_{refund}, \{\mathcal{P}_A, \mathcal{P}_B\}, \{\mathcal{P}_A, \mathcal{P}_B\}$)
9:     SIGN($Tr_{mrg}, \{\mathcal{P}_A, \mathcal{P}_B, \mathcal{P}_I\}, \{\mathcal{P}_A, \mathcal{P}_B, \mathcal{P}_I\}$)
10:     ATOMIC_SIGN($Tr_{punish,A}, Tr_{punish,B}$) **return** Tr_{mrg}
11: **end function**

Fig. 5. Creation of a Funding UTXO between two counterparties. The intermediary can enforce atomic construction while Punish transactions provide incentive.

a timelock of $t_m + 4\Delta$ such that Consolidation, Merge and Punish transactions can be placed with timelocks $t_m + \Delta$, $t_m + 2\Delta$ and $t_m + 3\Delta$ respectively. Note that if the Merge transaction is on top of the Payment Tree s.t. it is not used for further channel merges, the Refund transaction's timelock can be reduced to $t_m + 2\Delta$. Lastly, if a transaction spends another transaction, its timelock needs to be larger by at least Δ to ensure that all transactions can be committed to the ledger as soon as their timelocks expire (Fig. 6).

Consolidation. Algorithm 3 takes a Merge transaction as input, invalidates it by creating two Payout transactions atomically using the ATOMIC_SIGN protocol that spend the Merge transaction's inputs. Both consolidation transactions perform a payment by giving the funds to the payee. Note that the protocol can be adjusted to cancel a payment by refunding the funds to the payer instead (Fig. 7).

Payment Trees. Algorithm 4 performs a payment from $\mathcal{P}_0$ to $\mathcal{P}_n$ by iteratively merging Funding UTXOs, s.t. the Merge transactions form the nodes of a balanced binary tree as illustrated in Fig. 8. The algorithm takes the following inputs: (1) The payment path $\gamma_1, \ldots, \gamma_n$, (2) the payment amount b, and (3) time t_{min}. The value t_{min} is negotiated by the parties and represents the maximum amount of time the parties have to execute the protocol. The dispute protocol starts if the protocol is not concluded until t_{min}. Note that even existing methods as HTLCs have to account for t_{min}.

In the following we refer to a certain depth within this binary tree as *level*, beginning with Split transactions on level 0. The algorithm maintains lists of Funding UTXOs F_UTXO_i for each level $i \geq 0$ of the binary tree, as well as lists of Merge transactions MRG_j for each level $j \geq 1$ of the binary tree. The

---

Algorithm 3 Deconstructing Step of a Payment Tree

1: **function** CONSOLIDATE(Tr_{mrg})
2:    $f_0, f_1 \leftarrow$ IN_UTXO(Tr_{mrg})
3:    $\mathcal{P}_I \leftarrow$ INTERMEDIARY(f_0, f_1)
4:    $\mathcal{P}_A, \mathcal{P}_B \leftarrow$ COUNTERPARY($f_0, \mathcal{P}_I$), COUNTERPARY($f_1, \mathcal{P}_I$)
5:    $Tr_A \leftarrow$ PAYOUT($f_0, \mathcal{P}_B, t + \Delta$)
6:    $Tr_B \leftarrow$ PAYOUT($f_1, \mathcal{P}_C, t + \Delta$)
7:    ATOMIC_SIGN(Tr_A, Tr_B)
8: **end function**

Fig. 6. Invalidating a Merge transactions and atomically updating the state on the two original Funding UTXOs.

algorithm proceeds as follows. Add a Funding UTXO from each Split transaction to F_UTXO_0 in order (4–7) and create the Payment Tree by iterative use of the *MERGE* protocol level-by-level (8–18). The Merge transactions and Funding UTXOs created on level j are added to lists MRG_j and F_UTXO_j respectively and in order (12–13). Note that if there is an uneven amount of Funding UTXOs within a level, we leave the odd one to be used in the level above instead (15–17). The payment is executed after construction is concluded (19). Afterwards the payment tree is deconstructed in reverse order by executing the *CONSOLIDATE* protocol on each Merge transaction (20–24). Lastly the Split transactions are removed and consolidation within all original channels concludes (25–27).

Dispute. This protocol is executed at time t_{min} if the payment tree protocol has not come to conclusion in an orderly manner. Every honest party submits their transactions to the ledger as soon as their respective timelocks expire. This will result in commitment of the payment tree onto the ledger where transactions are committed in order of their priority. If a Merge transaction cannot be committed to the ledger, refunds and payments are done via Punish transactions.

Fees. Fees can be paid by the payer $\mathcal{P}_0$ and payee $\mathcal{P}_n$ or either of them alone to the intermediaries to compensate for their invested collateral. Our approach to handling fees is similar to the approach used for HTLCs, however, adapted to the binary tree structure of Payment Trees. Any party acting as intermediary when creating a Merge transaction receives cumulative fees from the other two parties participating in the Merge transaction's construction. The cumulative fee paid to the intermediary is composed of two parts. For one, it contains the fees paid to the intermediary themselves, and for another, it contains coins the party has to forward to the parties who act as intermediaries of Merge transactions on the lower levels of the Payment Tree. For simplicity, in the following we assume that the path's length is a power of 2, i.e. $n = 2^i, i \in \mathbb{N}$, the paid fees f are equal for

---

Algorithm 4 Payment Tree Construction

1: **function** PAYMENTTREE($\gamma_1, \gamma_2, \ldots, \gamma_n, b, t_{min}$)
2:     $F\_UTXO_i \leftarrow [], 0 \leq i \leq \lceil (\log n) - 1 \rceil$
3:     $MRG_i \leftarrow [], 1 \leq i \leq \lceil \log n \rceil$
4:     **for** $1 \leq i \leq n$ **do**
5:         $f_i \leftarrow$ SPLIT(γ_i, b, t_{min})
6:         Append f_i to F_UTXO_0
7:     **end for**
8:     **for** $i = 0$ until $i = \lceil (\log n - 1) \rceil$ **do**
9:         **for** $0 \leq j \leq \lfloor |F\_UTXO_i|/2 \rfloor$ **do**
10:             Retrieve f_{2j}, f_{2j+1} from F_UTXO_i
11:             $Tr_{mrg,j} \leftarrow$ MERGE($f_{2j}, f_{2j+1}, b, t_{min} + 2i\Delta$)
12:             Append OUT_UTXO($Tr_{mrg,j}$) to F_UTXO_{i+1}
13:             Append $Tr_{mrg,j}$ to MRG_{i+1}
14:         **end for**
15:         **if** $|F\_UTXO_i|$ mod $2 = 1$ **then**
16:             Remove last entry of F_UTXO_i and append to F_UTXO_{i+1}
17:         **end if**
18:     **end for**
19:     $Tr_{Payment} \leftarrow$ PAYOUT(OUT_UTXO($MRG_{\lceil \log n \rceil}[0]$), $\mathcal{P}_n, t_{min} + 2\Delta \log n + \Delta$)
20:     **for** $i = \lceil \log n \rceil$ until $i = 1$ **do**
21:         **for** Tr_{mrg} in MRG_i **do**
22:             CONSOLIDATE(Tr_{mrg})
23:         **end for**
24:     **end for**
25:     **for** $1 \leq i \leq n$ **do**
26:         UNSPLIT(γ_i)
27:     **end for**
28: **end function**

Fig. 7. The full Payment Tree protocol from construction to consolidation.

each intermediary and all fees are shared between payer $\mathcal{P}_0$ and payee $\mathcal{P}_n$ equally. Then, a party that acts as intermediary of level i of the Payment Tree receives $f_i = f + 2\frac{f_{i-1}}{2} = f + f_{i-1}$ coins, where $f_1 = f$. The fee f_i is paid equally by the other two parties involved in the Merge transaction's construction. Payment of fees happens within Merge transactions by adding a fee to the collateral the intermediary receives. However, this raises the challenge that we have to ensure that all transactions receive sufficient funding: The coins within a transaction's inputs have to cover all coins within their outputs. Moreover, to ensure that the consolidation step can be performed, the collateral of the intermediary within a Merge transaction has to be at least as high as the coins within the Merge transaction's Funding UTXO [8]. Therefore, when performing the merge step on level i every party has to have an additional balance of $f_{i,cum} = \sum_{j=i}^{h} f_j$, whereas the collateral of a Merge transaction's intermediary equals $b + f_{i,cum} + f_i$ where f_i is paid equally from balances brought by the other two parties.

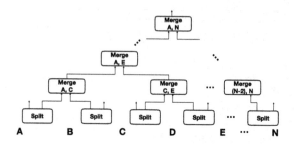

Fig. 8. Payment tree in the shape of a balanced binary tree.

7   Collateral Efficiency and Security Analysis

In this section we discuss properties of the Payment Tree construction.

Efficiency. Figure 9 depicts the efficiency properties of Payment Trees, comparing it to existing approaches. We compare two metrics: (1) The collateral, and (2) the number of transactions that have to be committed to the ledger in case of dispute. We do this for individual parties, as well as for the whole payment.

Commitment of each Merge transaction unlocks the collateral of one party. To commit a Merge transaction located on level i of the payment tree it needs to commit i transactions beforehand, i.e. $i-1$ Merge transaction as well as a Split transaction. This will happen at time $2\Delta i$. As the height of the Payment tree is limited by $\lceil \log n \rceil$ it follows that any party invests $b2\Delta i \in \mathcal{O}(b\Delta \log n)$ collateral and has to commit $i+1 \in \mathcal{O}(\log n)$ transactions. Regarding the total payment, we observe that there are $\frac{n}{2^i}$ Merge transactions on level i of the payment tree. It follows that the total collateral equals the sum $\sum_{i=1}^{\lceil \log n \rceil} b2\Delta i \frac{n}{2^i} = b2\Delta n \sum_{i=1}^{\lceil \log n \rceil} \frac{i}{2^i}$. As $\sum_{i=1}^{\infty} \frac{i}{2^i} = 2$ and each part of the sum is positive, it follows that the total collateral $b2\Delta n \sum_{i=1}^{\lceil \log n \rceil} \frac{i}{2^i} < 4b\Delta n \in \mathcal{O}(b\Delta n)$ is linear in the length of the payment path n. The number of transactions can be computed in a similar fashion, however, an intuitive approach is to recall that the transactions form a balanced binary tree of height $1 + \lceil \log n \rceil$ which has at most $2^{1+\lceil \log n \rceil} \leq 2n \in \mathcal{O}(n)$ nodes. Although the collateral any individual party has to invest is logarithmic, therefore higher than Sprites but lower than HTLCs, the total collateral incurred over the whole payment is linear in the path's length. This is comparable to the performance of Sprites and is by a factor of n lower than the total collateral of HTLCs. A trade-off of Payment Trees is that an individual party might have to commit up to $\mathcal{O}(\log n)$ many transactions. Nevertheless the total number of transactions over the whole payment is comparable to both, HTLCs and Sprites. Payment Trees provide a performance comparable to Sprites without requiring a ledger with smart contract capability.

Method	pp Collateral	pp Tr.	Total Collateral	Total Tr.	Smart Contracts
HTLC [15,2]	$\mathcal{O}(b\Delta n)$	$\mathcal{O}(1)$	$\mathcal{O}(b\Delta n^2)$	$\mathcal{O}(n)$	No
Sprites [10]	$\mathcal{O}(b(n+\Delta))$	$\mathcal{O}(1)$	$\mathcal{O}(b(n+\Delta)n)$	$\mathcal{O}(n)$	Yes
Payment Tree	$\mathcal{O}(b\Delta \log n)$	$\mathcal{O}(\log n)$	$\mathcal{O}(b\Delta n)$	$\mathcal{O}(n)$	No

Fig. 9. Comparison of the performance of Payment Trees across the whole payment (Total) and individually per party (pp).

Denial of Service Attacks. The Payment Tree protocol mitigates existing attacks such as the congestion and lockdown attacks [11,14] on HTLCs that aim to lock a channel's coins within unfulfilled HTLCs. This is done by reducing the total and individual collateral of payments. While a large scale DoS attack on multiple channels is difficult as the total collateral of Payment Trees is linear in the payment path's length, a specific intermediary can be targeted to act a intermediary on the highest level of the Payment Tree to pay a logarithmic collateral. Another aspect of the Lockdown attack is that a channel is blocked by saturating the number of HTLCs applicable to a channel which is limited by the maximum size of a transaction. The Payment Trees protocol mitigates this by using Split transactions. Each pending payment requires the construction of a Split transaction. This prevents that there is any transaction that increases in size depending on the number of pending transactions. However, a tradeoff to using Payment Trees is the increased number of transactions that would need to be committed to the ledger in case of a dispute.

Wormhole Attacks. The Payment Tree protocol pays coins to intermediaries of a Merge transaction and they include fees for all intermediaries on lower levels of respective sub-trees. An attack similar to the wormhole attack can be performed by a corrupted intermediary when creating a Merge transaction by replacing the Merge transaction's inputs with UTXOs they control. Doing this they could take all fees that were intended to be forwarded to other parties while preventing them to participate in the protocol. In contrast to the wormhole attack on HTLCs a wormhole-like attack on the Payment Trees protocol requires making changes to the transaction tree which in-turn can be detected and prevented. We assume that either $\mathcal{P}_0$ and $\mathcal{P}_n$ are honest. Otherwise, if both are corrupted the attack would only redistribute coins between corrupted parties resulting in no net gain to the adversary. During creation of the Payment Tree all intermediaries send their view of the protocol to $\mathcal{P}_0$ and $\mathcal{P}_n$, i.e. the Merge transactions they are involved in. Having this information $\mathcal{P}_0$ and $\mathcal{P}_n$ can verify correctness of the construction and abort the payment in the negative case.

Security Proofs. We provide proof of Theorems 1 and 2 in the full version of the paper.

8 Conclusion

Payment Trees provide competitive performance to state-of-the-art approaches as Sprites, while having fewer restrictions to its employability by not requiring smart contract capability. Thus providing the first secure alternative to HTLCs for the Lightning Network.

References

1. Raiden network. Accessed 03 Sept 2018
2. Bowe, S., Hopwood, D.: Hashed time-locked contract transactions (2017). https://github.com/bitcoin/bips/blob/master/bip-0199.mediawiki. Accessed 29 Aug 2020
3. Canetti, R., Dodis, Y., Pass, R., Walfish, S.: Universally composable security with global setup. In: Vadhan, S.P. (ed.) TCC 2007. LNCS, vol. 4392, pp. 61–85. Springer, Heidelberg (2007). https://doi.org/10.1007/978-3-540-70936-7_4
4. Decker, C., Wattenhofer, R.: A fast and scalable payment network with bitcoin duplex micropayment channels. In: Pelc, A., Schwarzmann, A.A. (eds.) SSS 2015. LNCS, vol. 9212, pp. 3–18. Springer, Cham (2015). https://doi.org/10.1007/978-3-319-21741-3_1
5. Dziembowski, S., Eckey, L., Faust, S., Malinowski, D.: Perun: Virtual payment hubs over cryptocurrencies. In: 2019 IEEE Symposium on Security and Privacy (SP), pp. 106–123. IEEE (2019)
6. Dziembowski, S., Faust, S., Hostáková, K.: General state channel networks. In: Proceedings of the 2018 ACM SIGSAC Conference on Computer and Communications Security, pp. 949–966. ACM (2018)
7. Egger, C., Moreno-Sanchez, P., Maffei, M.: Atomic multi-channel updates with constant collateral in bitcoin-compatible payment-channel networks. In: Cavallaro, L., Kinder, J., Wang, X., Katz, J. (eds.) ACM CCS 2019, pp. 801–815. ACM Press, November 2019. https://doi.org/10.1145/3319535.3345666
8. Jourenko, M., Larangeira, M., Tanaka, K.: Lightweight virtual payment channels. Cryptology ePrint Archive, Report 2020/998 (2020). https://eprint.iacr.org/2020/998
9. Malavolta, G., Moreno-Sanchez, P., Schneidewind, C., Kate, A., Maffei, M.: Anonymous multi-hop locks for blockchain scalability and interoperability. In: Network and Distributed Systems Security Symposium (2019)
10. Miller, A., Bentov, I., Bakshi, S., Kumaresan, R., McCorry, P.: Sprites and state channels: payment networks that go faster than lightning. In: Goldberg, I., Moore, T. (eds.) FC 2019. LNCS, vol. 11598, pp. 508–526. Springer, Cham (2019). https://doi.org/10.1007/978-3-030-32101-7_30
11. Mizrahi, A., Zohar, A.: Congestion attacks in payment channel networks. arXiv preprint arXiv:2002.06564 (2020)
12. Nakamoto, S.: Bitcoin: a peer-to-peer electronic cash system (2008)
13. PDecker, C., Russel, R., Osuntokun, O.: Eltoo: a simple layer2 protocol for bitcoin (2017). https://blockstream.com/eltoo.pdf
14. Pérez-Solà, C., Ranchal-Pedrosa, A., Herrera-Joancomartí, J., Navarro-Arribas, G., Garcia-Alfaro, J.: LockDown: balance availability attack against lightning network channels. In: Bonneau, J., Heninger, N. (eds.) FC 2020. LNCS, vol. 12059, pp. 245–263. Springer, Cham (2020). https://doi.org/10.1007/978-3-030-51280-4_14
15. Poon, J., Dryja, T.: The bitcoin lightning network: scalable off-chain instant payments (2016). https://lightning.network/lightning-network-paper.pdf

BRICK: Asynchronous Incentive-Compatible Payment Channels

Zeta Avarikioti[1]([✉]), Eleftherios Kokoris-Kogias[2], Roger Wattenhofer[1], and Dionysis Zindros[3,4]

[1] ETH Zürich, Zürich, Switzerland
[2] IST Austria, Novi Research, Klosterneuburg, Austria
[3] NKUA, Athens, Greece
[4] IOHK, AthensAthensAthens, Singapore

Abstract. Off-chain protocols (channels) are a promising solution to the scalability and privacy challenges of blockchain payments. Current proposals, however, require synchrony assumptions to preserve the safety of a channel, leaking to an adversary the exact amount of time needed to control the network for a successful attack. In this paper, we introduce BRICK, the first payment channel that remains secure under network asynchrony and concurrently provides correct incentives. The core idea is to incorporate the conflict resolution process within the channel by introducing a rational committee of external parties, called wardens. Hence, if a party wants to close a channel unilaterally, it can only get the committee's approval for the last valid state.

Additionally, BRICK provides sub-second latency because it does not employ heavy-weight consensus. Instead, BRICK uses consistent broadcast to announce updates and close the channel, a light-weight abstraction that is powerful enough to preserve safety and liveness to any rational parties. We formally define and prove for BRICK the properties a payment channel construction should fulfill. We also design incentives for BRICK such that honest and rational behavior aligns. Finally, we provide a reference implementation of the smart contracts in Solidity.

1 Introduction

The prime solution to the scalability challenge [12] of large-scale blockchains, are the so-called *channels* [13,33,36]. The idea is that any two parties that interact (often) with each other can set up a joint account on the blockchain, i.e., a channel. Using this channel, the two parties can transact off-chain, sending money back and forth by just sending each other signed messages. The two parties are relying on the blockchain as a fail-safe mechanism in case of disputes.

The security guarantees of a channel are ensured by a dispute handling mechanism. If one party tries to cheat the other party, in particular by trying to close a channel on the underlying blockchain in an invalid (outdated) state, then the attacked party has a window of time (t) to challenge the fraud attempt. Hence, a channel is secure as long as all parties of the channel are frequently – at least

© International Financial Cryptography Association 2021
N. Borisov and C. Diaz (Eds.): FC 2021, LNCS 12675, pp. 209–230, 2021.
https://doi.org/10.1007/978-3-662-64331-0_11

once in t time – online and monitoring the blockchain. This is problematic in real networks [30], as one party may simply execute a denial-of-service (DoS) attack on the other party. To add insult to injury, the dispute period t is public; the attacking party hence knows the exact duration of the denial-of-service attack.

The issue is well-known in the community, and there were solution attempts using semi-trusted third parties called *watchtowers* [2,6,7,16,29]. The idea is that worrisome channel parties can hire watchtowers that watch the blockchain on their behalf in case they were being attacked. So instead of DoSing a single machine of the channel partner, the attacker might need to DoS the channel partner as well as its watchtower(s). This certainly needs more effort as the adversary must detect a watchtower reacting and then block the dispute from appearing on-chain. However, if large amounts of money are in a channel, it will easily be worth the investment.

While DoS attacks are also possible in blockchains such as the Bitcoin blockchain, DoS attacks on channels have a substantially different threat level. A DoS attack on a blockchain is merely a liveness attack: One may prevent a transaction from entering the blockchain at the time of the attack. However, the parties involved with the transaction will notice this, and can simply re-issue their transaction later. A DoS attack on a channel, on the other hand, will steal all the funds that were in the channel. Once the fraudulent transaction is in the blockchain, uncontested for t time, the attack succeeds, and nobody but the cheated party (and its watchtowers) will know any better.

Channels need a more fundamental solution. Not unlike blockchains, introducing timing parameters is acceptable for liveness. Security on the other hand should be guaranteed even if the network behaves completely asynchronously. To that end we introduce BRICK, a novel incentive-compatible payment channel construction that does not rely on timing assumptions for the delivery of messages to be secure. BRICK provides *proactive security*, detecting and preventing fraud before it appears on-chain. As a result, BRICK can guarantee the channels' security even under censorship[1] [30] or any liveness attack.

To achieve these properties, BRICK needs to address three key challenges. The first challenge is how to achieve this proactive check without using a single trusted third party that approves every transaction [39]. The core idea of BRICK is to provide proactive security to the channel instead of reactive dispute resolution. To this end, BRICK employs a *group of wardens*. If there is a dispute, the wardens make sure the correct state is the only one available for submission on-chain, regardless of the amount of time it takes to make this final state visible. The second challenge for BRICK is cost. To simulate this trusted third party, it would need the wardens to run costly asynchronous consensus [25] for every update. Instead, in BRICK we show that a light-weight *consistent broadcast* protocol is enough to preserve both safety and liveness.

A final challenge of BRICK that we address is *incentives*. While the wardens may be partially byzantine, we additionally want honest behavior to be their

---

[1] This censoring ability is encompassed by the chain-quality property [18] of blockchain systems which is rightly bound to the synchrony of the network.

dominant strategy. Unfortunately, existing watchtower solutions do not align the expected and rational behavior of the watchtower, hence a watchtower is reduced to a trusted third party. Specifically, Monitors [16], Watchtowers [2], and DCWC [6] pay the watchtower upon fraud. Given that the use of a watchtower is public knowledge, any rational channel party will not commit fraud and hence the watchtower will never be paid. Therefore, there is no actual incentive for a third party to offer a watchtower service. On the other hand, Pisa [29] pays the watchtower regularly every time a transaction is executed on the channel. The watchtower also locks collateral on the blockchain in case it misbehaves. However, Pisa's collateral is not linked to the channel or the party that employed the watchtower. Hence, a watchtower that is contracted by more than one channel can double-assign the collateral, making Pisa vulnerable to bribing attacks. Even if the incentives of Pisa get fixed, punishing a misbehaving watchtower in Pisa is still a synchronous protocol (though for a longer period). In BRICK, we employ both rewards and punishment to design the appropriate incentives such that honest and rational behavior of wardens align, while no synchrony assumptions are required, i.e., the punishment of misbehaving wardens is not conditional on timing assumptions.

To evaluate our channel construction we deploy our protocol on a large-scale testbed and show that the overhead of an update is around the round-trip latency of the network (in our case 0.1 s). Unlike existing channels, the parties in BRICK need not wait for the dispute transaction to appear on-chain. Hence, our dispute resolution mechanism is three orders of magnitude faster than existing blockchain systems that need to wait until the transaction is finalized on-chain. We additionally implement the on-chain operations of BRICK in a Solidity smart contract that can be deployed on the Ethereum blockchain. We provide gas measurements for typical operations on the smart contract illustrating that it is practical. Our smart contract implementation is well tested and can be adopted towards a real deployment of BRICK.

In summary, this paper makes the following contributions:

- We introduce BRICK, the first incentive-compatible off-chain construction that operates securely with offline channel participants under full asynchrony with sub-second latency.
- We define the desired channel properties and show they hold for BRICK under a hybrid model of rational and byzantine participants (channel parties and wardens). Specifically, we present elaborate incentive mechanisms (rewards and punishments) for the wardens to maintain the channel properties under collusion or bribing.
- We evaluate the practicality of BRICK by fully implementing its on-chain functionality in Solidity for the Ethereum blockchain. We measure its operational costs in terms of gas and illustrate that its deployment is practical.

2   Protocol Overview

2.1   System Model

Cryptographic Assumptions. We make the usual cryptographic assumptions: the participants are computationally bounded and cryptographically-secure communication channels, hash functions, signatures, and encryption schemes exist.

Blockchain Assumptions and Network Model. We assume that any message sent by an honest party will be delivered to any other honest party within a polynomial number of rounds. We do not make any additional assumptions about the network (e.g., known bounds for message delivery). Furthermore, we do not require a "perfect" blockchain system since BRICK can tolerate temporary liveness attacks. Specifically, if an adversary temporarily violates the liveness property of the underlying blockchain, this may result in violating the liveness property of channels but will not affect the safety. Nevertheless, we assume the underlying blockchain satisfies persistence [18]. In Sect. 7, we discuss a modification of BRICK that is safe *even when persistence is temporarily violated*.

Threat Model. We initially assume that at least one party in the channel is honest to simplify the security analysis. However, later, we show that the security analysis holds as long as the "richest" party of the channel is rational and intentionally deviates from the protocol only if it can increase its profit (utility function). Regarding the committee, we assume that there are at most f out of $n = 3f + 1$ byzantine wardens, and we define a threshold $t = 2f + 1$ to achieve the liveness and safety properties. The non-byzantine part of the committee is assumed rational; we first prove the protocol goals for t honest wardens, and subsequently align the rational behavior to this through incentives.

2.2   Brick Overview

Both parties of a channel agree on a committee of wardens before opening the channel. The wardens commit their identities on the blockchain during the funding transaction of the channel (opening of the channel). After opening the channel on the blockchain, the channel can only be closed either by a transaction published on the blockchain and signed by both parties or by a transaction signed by one of the parties and a threshold (t) of honest wardens. Thus, the committee acts as power of attorney for the parties of the channel. Furthermore, BRICK employs correct incentives for the t rational wardens to follow the protocol, hence it can withstand $t = 2f + 1$ rational and f byzantine wardens, while the richest channel party is assumed rational and the other byzantine.

A naive solution would then instruct the committee to run asynchronous consensus on every new update, which would cost $O(n^4)$ [25] per transaction, a rather big overhead for the critical path of our protocol. Instead in Brick, consensus is not necessary for update transactions, as we only provide guarantees to rational parties (if both parties misbehave one of them might lose its funds).

As a result, every time a new update state occurs in the channel (i.e., a transaction), the parties run a consistent broadcast protocol (cost of $O(n)$) with the committee. Specifically, a party announces to each warden that a state update has occurred. This announcement is a monotonically increasing sequence number to guarantee that the new state is the freshest state, signed by both parties of the channel to signal that they are in agreement. If the consistent broadcast protocol succeeds (t wardens acknowledge reception) then this can serve as proof for both parties that the state update is safe. After this procedure terminates correctly, both parties proceed to the execution of the off-chain state.

At the end of the life-cycle of a channel, a dispute might occur, leading to the unilateral closing of the channel. Even in this case, we can still guarantee the security and liveness of the closing with consistent broadcast. The crux of the idea is that if $2f + 1$ wardens accepted the last sequence number before receiving the closing request (hence the counterparty has committed), then at least one honest warden will not accept the closing at the old sequence number. Instead, the warden will reply to the party that it can only close at the state represented by the last sequence number. As a result we define a successful closing to be at the maximum of all proposed states, which guarantees safety. *Although counterintuitive, this closing process is safe because the transactions are already totally ordered and agreed to by the parties of the channel;* thus, the committee simply acts as shared memory of the last sequence number.

2.3   Reward Allocation and Collateral

To avoid bribing attacks, we enforce the wardens to lock collateral in the channel. The total amount of collateral is proportional to the value of the channel meaning that if the committee size is large, then the collateral per warden is small. More details on the necessary amount of collateral are thoroughly discussed in Sects. 3.2 and 7. Additionally, the committee is incentivized to actively participate in the channel with a small reward that each warden gets when they acknowledge a state update of the channel. This reward is given with a unidirectional channel [21], which does not suffer from the problems BRICK solves. Moreover, the wardens that participate in the closing state of the channel get an additional reward, hence the wardens are incentivized to assist a party when closing in collaboration with the committee is necessary.

2.4   Protocol Goals

To define the goals of BRICK, we first need to define the necessary properties of a channel construction. Intuitively, a channel should ensure similar properties with a blockchain system, i.e., a party cannot cheat another party out of its funds, and any party has the prerogative to eventually spend its funds at any point in time. The first property, when applied to channels, means that no party can cheat the channel funds of the counterparty, and is encapsulated by *Safety*. The second property for a channel solution is captured by *Liveness*; it translates to any party having the right to eventually close the channel at any point in time.

We say that a channel is *closed* when the locked funds of the channel are spent on-chain, while a channel *update* refers to the off-chain change of the channel's state. In addition, we define *Privacy* which is not guaranteed in many popular blockchains, such as Bitcoin [32] or Ethereum [38], but constitutes an important practical concern for any functional monetary (cryptocurrency) system.

First, we define some characterizations on the state of the channel, namely, validity and commitment. Then, we define the properties for the channel construction. Each state of the channel has a discrete sequence number that reflects the order of the state. We assume the initial state of the channel has sequence number 1 and every new state has a sequence number one higher than the previous state agreed by both parties. We denote by s_i the state with sequence number i.

Definition 1. *A state of the channel, s_i, is **valid** if the following hold:*

- *Both parties of the channel have signed the state s_i.*
- *The state s_i is the **freshest** state, i.e., no subsequent state s_{i+1} is valid.*
- *The committee has not invalidated the state. The committee can invalidate the state s_i if the channel closes in the state s_{i-1}.*

Definition 2. *A state of the channel is **committed** if it was signed by at least $2f + 1$ wardens or is valid and part of a block in the persistent[2] part of the blockchain.*

Definition 3 (Safety). *A BRICK channel will only close in the freshest committed state.*

Definition 4 (Liveness). *Any valid operation (update, close) on the state of the channel will eventually[3] be committed (or invalidated).*

Definition 5 (Privacy). *No external (to the channel) party learns about the state of the channel (e.g., the current distribution of funds between the parties of a payment channel) unless at least one of the parties initiate the closing of the channel.*

3   Brick Design

In this section, we first present the BRICK architecture assuming t honest wardens, and then introduce the incentive mechanisms aligning honest and rational behavior.

---

[2] The part of the chain where the probability of fork is negligible hence there is transaction finality, e.g., 6 blocks in Bitcoin.

[3] Depending on the message delivery.

3.1   Architecture

BRICK consists of three phases: *Open*, *Update*, and *Close*. We assume the existence of a smart contract that has two functions, Open and Close, which receive the inputs of the protocols and verify that they adhere to the abstractly defined protocols specified below.

Protocol 1 describes the first phase, *Open*, which is the opening of a channel between two parties. In this phase, the parties create the initial funding transaction, similarly to other known payment channels such as [13,33]. However, in BRICK we also define two additional parameters in the funding transaction: the hashes of the public keys of the wardens of the channel, denoted by $W_1, W_2, \ldots, W_n$, and the threshold t.

Protocol 1: BRICK Open

Data: Parties A, B, wardens $W_1, \ldots, W_n$, initial state s_1.
Result: Open a BRICK payment channel.

```
/* The parties agree on the first update before opening the channel
   */
```
1. Register to $\{M, \sigma(M)\}$ the announcement of Protocol 2 on input (A, B, s_1).

```
/* The parties broadcast the first sequence number to the wardens
   */
```
2. Execute Protocol 3 on input $(M, \sigma(M), A, B, W_1, W_2, \ldots, W_n)$.
                                                   // without an update fee

```
/* The parties open the BRICK channel                              */
```
3. Both parties A, B sign and publish on-chain
   $open(H(W_1), H(W_2), \ldots, H(W_n), t, s_1)$.
```
/* Closing fee F is included in the funding transaction, as well as
      collateral C of each warden along with their signature.        */
```

The second phase, *Update*, consists of two protocols, Protocol 2 (Update), and Protocol 3 (Consistent Broadcast). Both algorithms are executed consecutively every time an update occurs, i.e., when the state of the channel changes. In Protocol 2, the parties of the channel agree on a new state and create an announcement, which they subsequently broadcast to the committee with Protocol 3. To agree on a new state, both parties sign the hash of the new state[4]. This way both parties commit to the new state of the channel, while none of the parties can unilaterally close the channel without the collaboration of either the

---

[4] Blinding the commitment to the state is not necessary for BRICK, but we do it for compatibility with an auditable extension of BRICK [5] where the hash of the state is given to the wardens along with the sequence number. Because the states of a channel may be limited, the salt r_i is used to prevent wardens from retrieving the state by simply hashing all possible states, effectively compromising privacy.

counterparty or the committee. The announcement, on the other hand, is the new sequence number signed by both parties of the channel[5]. The signed sequence number allows the wardens to verify agreement has been reached between the channel parties on the new state, while the state of the channel remains private. Upon receiving a valid announcement from a party, wardens reply with their signature on the announcement. A party executes the new state update when it receives t signatures from the wardens.

Protocol 2: BRICK Update

Data: Parties A, B, current state s.
Result: Create announcement $M, \sigma(M)$ (sequence number of new state signed by both parties).

1. Both parties A, B sign, exchange, and store: $\{H(s_i, r_i), i\}$, where r_i is a random number and s_i the current state.   // The parties store only the current and previous hash

2. Upon receiving the signature of the counterparty on $\{H(s_i, r_i), i\}$, a party replies with its signature on the sequence number $\sigma(i)$.   // creating the announcement $\{M, \sigma(M)\}(M = i)$

Protocol 3: BRICK Consistent Broadcast

Data: Parties A, B, wardens $W_1, \ldots, W_n$, announcement $\{M, \sigma(M)\}$.
Result: Inform the committee of the new update state and verify the validity of the new state.

1. Each party broadcasts to all the wardens $W_1, W_2, \ldots, W_n$ the announcement $\{M, \sigma(M)\}$.   // alongside a fee r

2. Each warden W_j, upon receiving $\{M, \sigma(M)\}$, verifies that both parties' signatures are present, and the sequence number is exactly one higher than the previously stored sequence number. If the warden has published a closing state, it ignores the state update. Otherwise, W_j stores the announcement $\{M, \sigma(M)\}$ (replacing the previous announcement), signs M, and sends the signature $\sigma_{W_j}(M)$ to the parties.   // only to the parties that payed the fee

3. Each party, upon receiving at least t signatures on the announcement M, considers the state committed and proceeds to the state transition.

---

[5] We abuse the notation of signature σ to refer to the multisig of both A and B.

The last phase of the protocol, *Close*, can be implemented in two different ways: the first is similar to the traditional approach for closing a channel (Protocol 4: Optimistic Close) where both parties collectively sign the freshest state (closing transaction) and publish it on-chain. However, in case a channel party is not responding to new state updates or closing requests, the counterparty can unilaterally close the channel in collaboration with the committee of the channel (Protocol 5: Pessimistic Close).

In Protocol 5, a party requests from each warden its signature on the last committed sequence number. A warden, upon receiving the closing request, publishes on-chain a closing announcement, i.e., the stored sequence number signed along with a flag close. When t closing announcements are on the persistent part of the chain, the party recovers the state that corresponds to the maximum sequence number from the closing announcements s_i. Then, the party publishes state s_i and the random number r_i along with the signatures of both parties on the corresponding hash and sequence number $\sigma(H(s_i, r_i), i)$ on-chain. As soon as these data are included in a (permanent) block, the BRICK smart contract performs the following operations: (a) recovers from the submitted state s_i and salt r_i the hash $H(s_i, r_i)$ and the maximum sequence number i, (b) verifies that the signatures of both parties are on the message $\{H(s_i, r_i), i\}$, and (c) there are t submitted announcements that correspond to warden identities committed on-chain in Protocol 1. If all verifications check the smart contract closes the channel in the submitted state s_i.

3.2   Incentivizing Honest Behavior

BRICK actually works without the fees, if we assume one honest party and t honest wardens. However, our goal is to have no honest assumptions and instead align rational behavior to honest through incentives. There are three incentive mechanisms in BRICK:

Protocol 4: BRICK Optimistic Close

Data: Parties A, B, state s.

Result: Close a channel on state s, assuming both parties are responsive and in agreement.

1. A party $p \in \{A, B\}$ broadcasts the request $close(s)$.

2. Both parties A, B sign the state s (if they agree) and exchange their signatures.

3. The party p (or any other channel party) publishes the signed by both parties state, $\sigma_{A,B}(s)$ on-chain.
```
/* The collateral C is returned to each warden          */
/* The closing fee F is returned to the parties          */
```

Protocol 5: BRICK Pessimistic Close

Data: Party $p \in \{A, B\}$, wardens $W_1, \ldots, W_n$, state s_i, random nonce r_i.
Result: Close a channel on state s_i with the assist of the committee.

1. Party p broadcasts to the wardens $W_1, W_2, \ldots, W_n$ the request $close()$.

2. Each warden W_j publishes on-chain a signature on the (last) stored announcement $\sigma_{W_j}(M, close)$ and stops signing new state updates.

3. Party p, upon verifying t on-chain signed announcements by the wardens, recovers the $max(i)$ that is included in the announcements. Then, party p publishes on-chain the state s_i, the random number r_i, and the signature of both parties on $\{H(s_i, r_i), i\}$.

4. After the state is included in a (permanent) block, the smart contract recovers $\{H(s_i, r_i), i\}$, verifies both parties' signatures and the wardens identities, and then closes the channel in state s_i.

Update Fee (r). The parties establish a unidirectional channel [21] with each warden and send a fee when they want a signature for a state update. Note that the update fee is awarded to the wardens at step 1 of Protocol 3.

Closing Fee (F). During phase *Open* (Protocol 1), the parties lock a closing fee F in the channel. If a party closes in a collaboration with the wardens, the closing fee is split only among the first t wardens that publish an announcement on-chain (see Protocol 6). If the channel closes optimistically (Protocol 4), the closing fee returns to the parties.

Collateral (C). During phase *Open*, each warden locks collateral C at least equal to the amount locked in the channel v divided by f. If a warden misbehaves, the closing party can claim the warden's collateral by submitting a proof-of-fraud in the BRICK smart contract during phase *Close*; otherwise, the collateral is returned to the warden when the channel closes (Protocol 6). A proof-of-fraud consists of two conflicting messages signed by the same warden: (a) a signature on an announcement on a state update of the channel, and (b) a signature on an announcement for closing on a previous state of the channel.

In case, a party submits $x \le f$ proofs-of-fraud, the closing process is extended until $x + t$ wardens have published an announcement on-chain. Then, the channel closes in the state with the maximum sequence number from the announcements submitted by the t non-cheating wardens. On the other hand, if a party submits at least $f + 1$ proofs-of-fraud, the party that submitted the proofs-of-fraud claims only the collateral from the cheating wardens, while the entire channel balance is awarded to the counterparty. If no proofs-of-fraud are submitted the channel closes as described in Protocol 5, as it is a subcase of Protocol 6 for $x = 0$.

We further demand that the size of the committee is at least $n > 7$, hence $f > 2$. As a result, we guarantee there is at least one channel party with locked funds

---

Protocol 6: BRICK Pessimistic Close with Incentives

Data: Party $p \in \{A, B\}$, wardens $W_1, \ldots, W_n$, state s_i, random nonce r_i.
Result: Close a channel on state s_i with the assist of the committee.

```
/* Similarly to Protocol 5                                        */
```
1. Party p broadcasts to the wardens $W_1, W_2, \ldots, W_n$ the request $close()$.

2. Each warden W_j publishes on-chain a signature on the (last) stored announcement $\sigma_{W_j}(M, close)$ and stops signing new state updates.

```
/* Closing party submits also proofs-of-fraud                     */
```
3. Party p, upon verifying t on-chain signed announcements by the wardens, recovers the $max(i)$ that is included in the announcements. Then, party p publishes on-chain the state s_i, the random number r_i, the signature of both parties on $\{H(s_i, r_i), i\}$, and any proofs-of-fraud.

```
/* Closing the channel with punishments                           */
```
4. After the state is included in a (permanent) block, the smart contract recovers $\{H(s_i, r_i), i\}$, and verifies both parties' signatures, the wardens identities, and the proofs-of-fraud.
   (a) If the valid proofs-of-fraud $x \leq f$, the smart contract closes the channel as soon as $t + x$ wardens have published an announcement on-chain. The channel closes in the state with the maximum sequence number included in the announcements, s_i.   `// Protocol 5 with $t + x$ wardens`
   (b) If the valid proofs-of-fraud $x \geq f + 1$, the smart contract closes the channel, and awards the entire channel balance to the counterparty.
   The smart contract awards the collateral of cheating wardens to party p, and returns the collateral of all non-cheating wardens. The first t non-cheating wardens whose signature are published on-chain get an equal fraction of the closing fee F/t.

---

greater than each individual warden's collateral, $\frac{v}{2} > \frac{v}{f}$. This restriction along with the aforementioned incentive mechanisms ensure resistance to collusion and bribing of the committee, meaning that following the protocol is the dominant strategy for the rational wardens.

We note that in a network with multiple channels, each channel needs to maintain a unique id which will be included in the announcement to avoid replay attacks. Otherwise, if there exist two channels with the same parties and watchtowers, the parties can unjustly claim the watchtowers' collateral by using signed sequence numbers from the other channel, effectively violating safety.

4   Brick Analysis

We first prove BRICK satisfies *safety* and *liveness* assuming at least one honest channel party and at least t honest wardens. Furthermore, we note that

BRICK achieves *privacy* even if all wardens are byzantine while the channel parties are rational. Then, we show that rational players (parties and wardens) that want to maximize their profit will follow the protocol specification, for the incentive mechanisms presented in Sect. 3.2. Essentially, we show that BRICK enriched with the proposed incentive mechanisms is dominant-strategy incentive-compatible.

Security Under One Honest Participant and t Honest wardens. The core idea for safety is that the channel will close in the state that corresponds to the maximum sequence number submitted by t wardens. In particular, every transaction is broadcast to the wardens and confirmed by at least t wardens before the transaction is executed by the parties. Given that at most f wardens are byzantine and at most another $n - t = 3f + 1 - (2f + 1) = f$ can be slow, then at most $2f$ can publish an outdated sequence number when closing the channel. Since BRICK waits for $t = 2f + 1$ sequence numbers, at least one will be submitted by an honest and up-to-date warden which will bear the maximum sequence number and correspond to the freshest state.

Theorem 1. BRICK *achieves safety in asynchrony assuming one byzantine party and f byzantine wardens.*

Note that a channel can close in two possible states: either the last agreed state by both parties, or the previous one. We still preserve safety in both cases. If the last agreed state is considered valid then it is guaranteed to be the closing state, whereas if the closing state is the previous then the last agreed state never gets validated by t wardens.

Theorem 2. BRICK *achieves liveness in asynchrony assuming one byzantine party and f byzantine wardens.*

Lastly, BRICK achieves *privacy even against byzantine wardens*. They only receive the sequence number of each update. Therefore, as long as parties do not intentionally reveal information, privacy is maintained.

Incentivizing Rational Players. In this section, we show that rational players, parties and wardens, that want to maximize their profit follow the protocols, i.e., deviating from the honest protocol executions can only result in decreasing a player's expected payoff. Therefore, security and liveness hold from Theorems 1 and 2. Note that in our system model $2f + 1$ wardens and the richest party are rational, while the rest can be byzantine. We consider each protocol separately, and evaluate the players' payoff for each possible action.

Intuitively, we provide correct incentives *without utilizing timelocks* because the closing party is the one penalizing the cheating wardens when closing the channel. Although counter-intuitive, the main idea is that the cheating party that convinced the wardens to cheat will profit more from collecting the collateral of the cheating wardens than closing the channel in any old state. Or in other words, the cheating party is actually rationally baiting the possible byzantine wardens to get their collateral. As we show, this leads to rational wardens following the protocol faithfully. We omit the analysis due to space limitation, but can be found in the full version [5].

5   Evaluation of BRICK

We evaluate the cost of consistent broadcast and of on-chain operations. The questions asked are: (a) how deployment costs change as we increase wardens, and (b) how off-chain costs scale.

Solidity Smart Contract. To evaluate the Ethereum deployment cost, we implement on-chain operations as a Solidity 0.5.16 contract[6]. Our gas measurements illustrated in Fig. 1 are based on May 2020 prices (1 ETH = 195.37 EUR and gas = 20 Gwei). We compiled with solc 0.6.8 with optimizations enabled and deployed on a local ganache-cli using truffle and web3. The measurements concern contract deployment, opening, as well as optimistic and pessimistic closing. The contract allows specification of the number n of wardens and their identities. We used the `secp256k1` elliptic curve [11,22] and the `ecrecover` precompiled contract [38] for verification. We performed measurements for $n = 3$ to 30. We recommend $n = 13$ since it is safe, gas-efficient and incentive-compatible.

After deployment, the contract is funded first by Alice and then by Bob. Next, the collateral is calculated and wardens fund it in any order. Thereafter, Alice or Bob can open the channel. Any participant can withdraw prior to opening, at which point the channel is cancelled and everyone else can withdraw as well. Once open, parties continue exchanging states off-chain. If multiple channels are used, the cost of contract deployment is amortized by abstracting common functionality into a library. However, opening and closing costs are recurrent. Our deployment cost (≈ 9 EUR) is comparable to other state channel contracts (e.g., the deployment of Pisa [29] contracts amounts to ≈ 17 EUR).

When the parties agree to close, Alice submits a transaction requesting closure. It contains her claimed closing state. If Bob agrees, he submits a transaction to signal so. The contract then returns the parties' values and the collaterals. If Bob disagrees, the channel becomes unusable and must be closed pessimistically. The optimistic close operation measures the cumulative gas cost of these 2 transactions. The cost is minimal and this is the normal execution path.

Finally, the channel can be closed pessimistically by any party via a request to the wardens. Each warden submits a transaction with the sequence number they last saw signed by both Alice and Bob. The signatures are verified on-chain, along with warden signatures; this operation spends the most gas. The closing party monitors the chain for fraudulent warden claims. As soon as t honest claims appear, the party sends a transaction to close the channel. The transaction includes the fraud proofs, namely the latest announcement for each

---

[6] The source code is available at https://github.com/dionyziz/brick.

warden who made a bad claim. These contain the warden signature on the plaintext which consists of the contract address and sequence number. Closing the channel releases the parties' funds and slashes malicious wardens. After closure, honest wardens redeem their collateral and fee by issuing further transactions. Pessimistic closing was measured when no fraud proofs are provided and includes the transaction of each of the t wardens and the final transaction by one of the parties. We assumed that, while the counterparty is unresponsive, the wardens were responsive and all submitted the same sequence number (limiting the need for multiple signature validations).

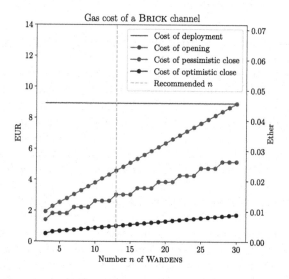

Fig. 1. On-chain gas costs of deployment and operation in Ethereum.

Consistent Broadcast. We implement consistent broadcast in Golang using Kyber [26] and cothority [14]. In Table 1 we evaluate our protocol on Deterlab [15] using 36 physical machines, each having 4 Intel E5-2420 v2 CPUs and 24 GB RAM. To model a WAN, we impose a 100ms rtt latency and a 35Mbps bandwidth limit. The overhead of using a committee is almost equal to the latency. The small overhead is due to the sequential message sending, hence the last message is sent with a small delay. The total latency is close to 100 ms. This is the time parties must wait to execute a transaction safely, meaning we provide fast finality. Our numbers are three orders of magnitude faster than current blockchains. Furthermore, channels are independent and embarrassingly parallel; we can deploy multiple without increased overhead. Contrary to synchronous solutions where finality is guaranteed after closure, BRICK provides instant finality.

Table 1. Microbenchmark of BRICK

Number of wardens	7	34	151
Consistent Broadcast	0.1138 s	0.118 s	0.1338 s

6   Related Work

Payment channels were originally introduced by Spilman [36]. Several payment channels solutions have been proposed [1,13,33], the most notable being the Bitcoin Lightning Network [33]. All these solutions, however, require timelocks to guarantee safety and therefore make strong synchrony assumptions that sometimes fail in practice.

To guarantee safety, traditional payment channels require participants to be frequently online, actively watching the blockchain. To alleviate this necessity, recent proposals introduced third-parties in the channel to act as proxies for the participants of the channel in case of fraud. This idea was initially discussed by Dryja [16], who introduced the Monitors or Watchtowers [2] operating on the Bitcoin Lightning network [33]. Later, Avarikioti et al. proposed DCWC [6], a less centralized distributed protocol for the watchtower service, where every full node can act as a watchtower for multiple channels depending on the network topology. In both these works, the watchtowers are paid upon fraud. Hence, the solutions are not incentive-compatible since in case a watchtower is employed no rational party will commit fraud on the channel and thus the watchtowers will never be paid. This means there will be no third parties offering such a service unless we assume they are altruistic.

In parallel, McCorry et al. [29] proposed Pisa, a protocol that enables the delegation of Sprites [31] channels' safety to third-parties called Custodians. Although Pisa proposes both rewards and penalties similarly to BRICK, it fails to secure the channels against bribing attacks. Particularly, the watchtower's collateral can be double-spent since it is not tied to the channel/party that employed the watchtower. More importantly, similarly to Watchtowers and DCWC, Pisa demands a synchronous network and a perfect blockchain, meaning that transactions must not be censored, to guarantee the safety of channels.

Concurrently to this work, Avarikioti et al. introduced Cerberus channels [7], a modification of Lightning that incorporates rational watchtowers to Bitcoin channels. Although Cerberus channels are incentive-compatible, they still require timelocks, hence their security depends on synchrony assumptions and a perfect blockchain that cannot be censored. Furthermore, Cerberus channels do not guarantee privacy from the watchtowers, as opposed to BRICK.

In a similar work, Lind et al. proposed Teechain [27], a layer 2 payment network that operates securely under asynchrony using hardware trusted execution environments (TEEs) to prevent parties from misbehaving. In contrast, BRICK eliminates the need for TEEs with the appropriate incentive mechanisms.

To summarize, we exhibit the differences of BRICK to the other channel constructions and watchtower solutions in Table 2. We observe that BRICK is the only solution that maintains security under an asynchronous network and offline channel parties while assuming rational watchtowers. Further, BRICK is secure (i.e., no loss of funds) even when the blockchain substrate is censored, and also when the network is congested. Finally, an extension to BRICK that we describe in Sect. 7 enables protection against small scale persistence attacks making it more secure than the underlying blockchain.

Table 2. Comparison with previous work

Protocol safe under	Monitors [16]	DCWC [6]	Pisa [29]	Cerberus [7]	Brick [5]
Rational players	✗	✗	$\sim^a$	✓	✓
Offline parties	✓	✓	$T \gg t_d{}^b$	$T \gg t_d{}^b$	✓
Asynchrony	✗	✗	✗	✗	✓
Censorship	✗	✗	✗	✗	✓
Congestion	✗	✗	✗	✗	✓
Forks	✗	✗	✗	✗	✓^{c}
Privacy	✓	✓	✓	✗	✓
Bitcoin Compat.	✓	✓	✗	✓	✗

[a]The watchtower needs to lock collateral per-channel, equal to the channel's value. Current implementation of Pisa does not provide this.
[b]The party needs to be able to deliver messages and punish the watchtower within a large synchrony bound T.
[c]Possible if consensus is run for closing the channel as described in Sect. 7.

State Channels, Payment Networks, and Sidechains. Payment channels can only support payments between users. To extend this solution to handle smart contracts [37] that allow arbitrary operations and computations, *state channels* were introduced [31]. Recently, multiple state channel constructions have emerged [10,17,31]. However, all these constructions use the same foundations, i.e., the same concept on the operation of two-party channels. And as the fundamental channel solutions are flawed the whole construction inherits the same problems (synchrony and availability assumptions). BRICK's design could potentially extend to an asynchronous state channel solution if there existed a valuation function for the states of the contract (i.e., a mapping of each state to a monetary value for the parties) to correctly align incentives. In this case, the channel can evolve as long as the parties update the state, while in case of an uncooperative counterparty the honest party can always pessimistically close the channel at the last agreed state and continue execution on-chain.

Another solution for scaling blockchains is sidechains [8,19,24]. In this solution, the workload of the main chain is transferred in other chains, the sidechains, which are "pegged" to the main chain. Although the solution is kindred to channels, it differs significantly in one aspect: in channels, the states updates are totally ordered and unanimously agreed by the parties thus a consensus process is not necessary. On the contrary, sidechains must operate a consensus process to agree on the validity of a state update. BRICK lies in the intersection of the two concepts; the states are totally ordered and agreed by the parties, whereas wardens merely remember that agreement was reached at the last state announced.

Finally, an extension to payment channels is payment channel networks (PCN) [9,28,34,35]. The core idea of PCN is that users that do not have a direct channel can route payments using the channels of other users. While BRICK presents a novel channel construction that is safe under asynchrony, enabling asynchronous multi-hop payments remains an open question.

7   Conclusion, Limitations and Extensions

Below, we discuss the rationale of BRICK design, its limitations, and extensions.

Byzantine Players. If both channel parties are byzantine then the wardens' collateral can be locked arbitrarily long since the parties can simply crash forever. This is why in the threat model, we assume that at least the richest channel party is rational to correctly align the incentives. We further demand byzantine fault-tolerance to guarantee a truly robust protocol against arbitrary faults. We assume at most f out of the $3f + 1$ wardens are byzantine, which is necessary to maintain safety, as dictated by well known lower bounds for asynchronous consistent broadcast. Nevertheless, users of BRICK can always assume $f = 0$ and configure the smart contract parameters accordingly.

Warden Unilateral Exit. If both parties are malicious, they might hold the wardens' collateral hostage. A similar situation is indistinguishable from the parties not transacting often. As a result the wardens might want to exit the channel. A potential extension can support this in two ways. First, we can enable committee replacement, meaning that a warden can withdraw its service as long as there is another warden willing to take its place. In such a case, we simply replace the collateral and warden identities with an update of the funding transaction on-chain, paid by the warden that requests to withdraw its service. Second, if a significant number (e.g., $2f + 1$) of wardens declare they want to exit, the smart-contract can release them and convert the channel to a synchronous channel [29]. The parties will now be able to close the channel unilaterally by directly publishing the last valid state. If the counterparty tries to cheat and publishes an old state, the party (or any remaining warden) can catch the dispute on-time and additionally claim the (substantial) closing fee.

Committee Selection. Each channel has its own group of wardens, i.e., the committee is independently selected for each channel by the channel parties. The scalability of the system is not affected by the use of a committee since each channel has its own independent committee of wardens. The size of the committee for each channel can vary but is constrained by the threat model. If we assume at least one honest party in the channel, a single rational warden is enough to guarantee the correct operation of BRICK. Otherwise, we require more than 7 wardens to avoid hostage situations from colluding channel parties (Sect. 3.2). Note that the cost for security for the parties is not dependent on the committee size, but on the value of the channel. If the parties chose a small committee size, the collateral per warden is high, thus the update fees are few but high. On the other hand, if the parties employ many wardens, the collateral per warden is low, thus the update fees are many but low.

Consensus vs Consistent Broadcast. Employing consistent broadcast in a blockchain system typically implies no conflict resolution as there is no liveness guarantee if the sender equivocates. This is not an issue in channels since a valid update needs to be signed by both parties and we provide safety guarantees only to honest and rational parties[7]. The state updates in channels are totally ordered by the parties and each sequence number should have a unique corresponding state. Thereby, it in not the role of the warden committee to enforce agreement, but merely to verify that agreement was reached, and act as a shared memory for the parties. As a result, consistent broadcast is tailored for BRICK as it offers the only necessary property, equivocation protection.

Brick Security Under Execution Fork Attacks. We can extend BRICK to run asynchronous consensus [25] during the closing phase in order to defend against execution fork attacks [23]. This would add an one-off overhead during close but would make BRICK resilient against extreme conditions [4]. For example, in case of temporary dishonest majority the adversary can attack the persistence[8] of the underlying blockchain, meaning that the adversary can double-spend funds. Similarly in channels, if the adversary can violate persistence, the dispute resolution can be reversed, hence funds can be cheated out of a party. However, in BRICK the adversary can only close on the last committed state or the freshest valid (not committed) state. With consensus during close, BRICK maintains safety (i.e., no party loses channel funds) even when persistence is violated. A malicious party can only close the channel in the state that the consensus decides to be last, thus a temporary take-over can only affect the channel's liveness. Therefore, BRICK can protect both against *liveness and persistence attacks*[9] on the underlying blockchain adding an extra layer of protection, and making it safer to transact on BRICK than on the blockchain.

Update Fees. Similarly to investing in stocks for a long period of time, many invest in cryptocurrencies; resulting in large amounts of unused capital. Acting as a warden can simply provide more profit (update fees) to the entities that own this capital complementary to owning such cryptocurrencies. Currently, the update fees are awarded to wardens on every state update via a unidirectional channel. Ideally, these rewards would be included in the state update of the channel. But even if we include an increased fee on every state update, the parties can always invoke Optimistic Close, and update the channel state to their favor when closing. Thus, the incentives mechanism is not robust if the update rewards of the wardens are included in the state updates.

---

[7] Of course if a party crashes we cannot provide liveness, but safety holds.

[8] Persistence states that once a transaction is included in the permanent part of one honest party's chain, then it will be included in every honest party's blockchain.

[9] We assume the channel to be created long before these attacks take place, so the adversary cannot fork the transaction that creates the channel.

Collateral. The collateral for each warden in BRICK is v/f, where v is the total value of the channel and f the number of byzantine wardens. This is slightly higher than the lowest amount $v/(f+1)$ for which security against bribing attacks is guaranteed in asynchrony when both channel parties and wardens are rational. Towards contradiction, we consider a channel where each warden locks collateral $C < v/(f+1)$. Suppose now a rational party p owns 0 coins in the freshest state and v coins in a previous state. Due to asynchrony, p controls the message delivery, hence f wardens may consider this previous state as the freshest one. Consequently, if p bribes $f+1$ wardens, which costs less than $(f+1)v/(f+1) = v$, the party profits from closing the channel in the previous state in collaboration with the bribed and "slow" wardens, violating safety.

In a synchronous network, this attack would not work since the other parties would have enough time to dispute. However, under asynchrony (or offline parties [29]) there is no such guarantee. Further, note that in a naive asynchronous protocol with f byzantine wardens, the previous attack is always possible for any collateral because a rational party can direct the profit from the collateral of the byzantine wardens to bribe the rational wardens. We circumvent this problem in BRICK by changing the closing conditions: we force the closing party to choose between closing the channel in an old state, or claiming the collateral of at least $f+1$ wardens and awarding the channel balance to the counterparty.

Finally, a trade-off for replacing trust is highlighted: online participation with synchrony requirements or appropriate incentive mechanisms to compel the honest behavior of rational players.

Decentralization. In previous payment channel solutions a party only hires a watchtower if it can count on it in case of an attack. Essentially, watchtowers are the equivalent of insurance companies. If the attack succeeds, the watchtower should reimburse the cheated channel party [29]. After all, it is the watchtower's fault for not checking the blockchain when needed. However, in light of network attacks (which are prevalent in blockchains [3,20]), only a few, centrally connected miners will be willing to take this risk. BRICK provides an alternative, that proactively protects from such attacks and we expect to provide better decentralization properties with minimal overhead and fast finality.

Bitcoin Compatibility. We believe BRICK can be implemented in Bitcoin assuming t honest wardens (Protocol 5) using chained transactions. In contrast, we conjecture that the incentive-compatible version of BRICK (Protocol 6) cannot be deployed without timelocks in platforms with limited contracts like Bitcoin.

Acknowledgments. We would like to thank Kaoutar Elkhiyaoui for her valuable feedback as well as Jakub Sliwinski for his impactful contribution to this work.

References

1. Raiden network (2017). https://raiden.network/. Accessed 22 Nov 2020
2. Hertig, A.: Bitcoin Lightning Fraud? Laolu Is Building a 'Watchtower' to Fight It (2018). https://www.coindesk.com/laolu-building-watchtower-fight-bitcoin-lightning-fraud
3. Apostolaki, M., Zohar, A., Vanbever, L.: Hijacking bitcoin: Routing attacks on cryptocurrencies. In: 2017 IEEE Symposium on Security and Privacy (SP), pp. 375–392. IEEE (2017)
4. Avarikioti, G., Käppeli, L., Wang, Y., Wattenhofer, R.: Bitcoin security under temporary dishonest majority. In: Goldberg, I., Moore, T. (eds.) FC 2019. LNCS, vol. 11598, pp. 466–483. Springer, Cham (2019). https://doi.org/10.1007/978-3-030-32101-7_28
5. Avarikioti, G., Kokoris-Kogias, E., Wattenhofer, R., Zindros, D.: Brick: Asynchronous payment channels. arXiv preprint: 1905.11360 (2020)
6. Avarikioti, G., Laufenberg, F., Sliwinski, J., Wang, Y., Wattenhofer, R.: Towards secure and efficient payment channels. arXiv preprint: 1811.12740 (2018)
7. Avarikioti, Z., Thyfronitis Litos, O.S., Wattenhofer, R.: CERBERUS channels: incentivizing watchtowers for bitcoin. In: Bonneau, J., Heninger, N. (eds.) FC 2020. LNCS, vol. 12059, pp. 346–366. Springer, Cham (2020). https://doi.org/10.1007/978-3-030-51280-4_19
8. Back, A., et al.: Enabling blockchain innovations with pegged sidechains (2014). https://www.blockstream.com/sidechains.pdf
9. Bagaria, V., Neu, J., Tse, D.: Boomerang: redundancy improves latency and throughput in payment networks. In: International Conference on Financial Cryptography and Data Security (2020)
10. Coleman, J., Horne, L., Xuanji, L.: Counterfactual: Generalized state channels (2018). https://l4.ventures/papers/statechannels.pdf
11. Courtois, N.T., Grajek, M., Naik, R.: Optimizing SHA256 in bitcoin mining. In: Kotulski, Z., Księżopolski, B., Mazur, K. (eds.) CSS 2014. CCIS, vol. 448, pp. 131–144. Springer, Heidelberg (2014). https://doi.org/10.1007/978-3-662-44893-9_12
12. Croman, K., et al.: On scaling decentralized blockchains. In: Clark, J., Meiklejohn, S., Ryan, P.Y.A., Wallach, D., Brenner, M., Rohloff, K. (eds.) FC 2016. LNCS, vol. 9604, pp. 106–125. Springer, Heidelberg (2016). https://doi.org/10.1007/978-3-662-53357-4_8
13. Decker, C., Wattenhofer, R.: A fast and scalable payment network with bitcoin duplex micropayment channels. In: Pelc, A., Schwarzmann, A.A. (eds.) SSS 2015. LNCS, vol. 9212, pp. 3–18. Springer, Cham (2015). https://doi.org/10.1007/978-3-319-21741-3_1
14. DeDiS cothority (2016). https://www.github.com/dedis/cothority
15. DeterLab network security testbed (2012). http://isi.deterlab.net/
16. Dryja, T.: Unlinkable outsourced channel monitoring (2016). https://youtu.be/Gzg_u9gHc5Q
17. Dziembowski, S., Eckey, L., Faust, S., Malinowski, D.: Perun: virtual payment hubs over cryptocurrencies. In: IEEE Symposium on Security and Privacy, pp. 327–344 (2017)
18. Garay, J., Kiayias, A., Leonardos, N.: The bitcoin backbone protocol: analysis and applications. In: Oswald, E., Fischlin, M. (eds.) EUROCRYPT 2015. LNCS, vol. 9057, pp. 281–310. Springer, Heidelberg (2015). https://doi.org/10.1007/978-3-662-46803-6_10

19. Gaži, P., Kiayias, A., Zindros, D.: Proof-of-Stake Sidechains. In: IEEE Symposium on Security and Privacy, pp. 139–156. IEEE (2019)
20. Gervais, A., Ritzdorf, H., Karame, G.O., Capkun, S.: Tampering with the delivery of blocks and transactions in Bitcoin. In: Proceedings of the 22nd ACM SIGSAC Conference on Computer and Communications Security, pp. 692–705. ACM (2015)
21. Gudgeon, L., Moreno-Sanchez, P., Roos, S., McCorry, P., Gervais, A.: SoK: layer-two blockchain protocols. In: Bonneau, J., Heninger, N. (eds.) FC 2020. LNCS, vol. 12059, pp. 201–226. Springer, Cham (2020). https://doi.org/10.1007/978-3-030-51280-4_12
22. Gura, N., Patel, A., Wander, A., Eberle, H., Shantz, S.C.: Comparing elliptic curve cryptography and RSA on 8-bit CPUs. In: Joye, M., Quisquater, J.-J. (eds.) CHES 2004. LNCS, vol. 3156, pp. 119–132. Springer, Heidelberg (2004). https://doi.org/10.1007/978-3-540-28632-5_9
23. Karame, G.O., Androulaki, E., Capkun, S.: Double-spending fast payments in Bitcoin. In: 19th ACM Conference on Computer and Communications Security, pp. 906–917. ACM (2012)
24. Kiayias, A., Zindros, D.: Proof-of-work sidechains. In: Bracciali, A., Clark, J., Pintore, F., Rønne, P.B., Sala, M. (eds.) FC 2019. LNCS, vol. 11599, pp. 21–34. Springer, Cham (2020). https://doi.org/10.1007/978-3-030-43725-1_3
25. Kokoris-Kogias, E., Malkhi, D., Spiegelman, A.: Asynchronous distributed key generation for computationally-secure randomness, consensus, and threshold signatures. In: 27th ACM SIGSAC Conference on Computer and Communications Security, pp. 1751–1767. ACM (2020)
26. The Kyber Cryptography Library (2010–2018)
27. Lind, J., Naor, O., Eyal, I., Kelbert, F., Sirer, E.G., Pietzuch, P.R.: Teechain: a secure payment network with asynchronous blockchain access. In: Proceedings of the 27th ACM Symposium on Operating Systems Principles, pp. 63–79 (2019)
28. Malavolta, G., Moreno-Sanchez, P., Kate, A., Maffei, M.: SilentWhispers: enforcing security and privacy in decentralized credit networks. In: 24th Annual Network and Distributed System Security Symposium (2017)
29. McCorry, P., Bakshi, S., Bentov, I., Meiklejohn, S., Miller, A.: Pisa: Arbitration outsourcing for state channels. In: Proceedings of the 1st ACM Conference on Advances in Financial Technologies, pp. 16–30. ACM (2019)
30. Miller, A.: Feather-forks: enforcing a blacklist with sub-50% hash power. https://bitcointalk.org/index.php?topic=312668.0. Accessed 22 Nov 2020
31. Miller, A., Bentov, I., Bakshi, S., Kumaresan, R., McCorry, P.: Sprites and state channels: payment networks that go faster than lightning. In: Goldberg, I., Moore, T. (eds.) FC 2019. LNCS, vol. 11598, pp. 508–526. Springer, Cham (2019). https://doi.org/10.1007/978-3-030-32101-7_30
32. Nakamoto, S.: Bitcoin: A Peer-to-Peer Electronic Cash System (2008)
33. Poon, J., Dryja, T.: The bitcoin lightning network: Scalable off-chain instant payments (2015)
34. Prihodko, P., Zhigulin, S., Sahno, M., Ostrovskiy, A., Osuntokun, O.: Flare: an approach to routing in lightning network (2016)
35. Roos, S., Moreno-Sanchez, P., Kate, A., Goldberg, I.: Settling payments fast and private: Efficient decentralized routing for path-based transactions. In: 25th Annual Network and Distributed Systems Security Symposium (2018)
36. Spilman, J.: Anti DoS for tx replacement. https://lists.linuxfoundation.org/pipermail/bitcoin-dev/2013-April/002433.html. Accessed 22 Nov 2020
37. Szabo, N.: Formalizing and securing relationships on public networks. First Monday **2**(9) (1997)

38. Wood, G.: Ethereum: A secure decentralised generalised transaction ledger. Ethereum Project Yellow Paper (2014)
39. Zamyatin, A., et al.: SoK: communication across distributed ledgers. IACR Cryptology ePrint Archive, Report 2019/1128 (2019)

Mining

Ignore the Extra Zeroes: Variance-Optimal Mining Pools

Tim Roughgarden[1] and Clara Shikhelman[2]([⊠])

[1] Columbia University, New York, NY 10027, USA
[2] Chaincode Labs, New York, NY 10017, USA

Abstract. Mining pools decrease the variance in the income of cryptocurrency miners (compared to solo mining) by distributing rewards to participating miners according to the shares submitted over a period of time. The most common definition of a "share" is a proof-of-work for a difficulty level lower than that required for block authorization—for example, a hash with at least 65 leading zeroes (in binary) rather than at least 75.

The first contribution of this paper is to investigate more sophisticated approaches to pool reward distribution that use multiple classes of shares—for example, corresponding to differing numbers of leading zeroes—and assign different rewards to shares from different classes. What's the best way to use such finer-grained information, and how much can it help? We prove that the answer is *not at all*: using the additional information can only increase the variance in rewards experienced by every miner.

Our second contribution is to identify variance-optimal reward-sharing schemes. Here, we first prove that pay-per-share rewards simultaneously minimize the variance of all miners over all reward-sharing schemes with long-run rewards proportional to miners' hash rates. We then show that, if we impose natural restrictions including a no-deficit condition on reward-sharing schemes, then the pay-per-last-N-shares method is optimal.

Keywords: Blockchains · Cryptocurrencies · Mining pools · Variance-minimization

1 Introduction

In Bitcoin [13] and many other cryptocurrencies (Ethereum [3], for example), *miners* produce proofs-of-work to authorize blocks of transactions in exchange for rewards. A solo miner controlling a small fraction of the overall hashrate will receive no reward for long stretches of time (e.g., for a Bitcoin miner with 0.1% of the overall hashrate, for roughly a week on average). To spread payouts more evenly over time, many miners join *mining pools* in which multiple miners join forces and work to authorize a block in tandem.

© International Financial Cryptography Association 2021
N. Borisov and C. Diaz (Eds.): FC 2021, LNCS 12675, pp. 233–249, 2021.
https://doi.org/10.1007/978-3-662-64331-0_12

When a mining pool successfully authorizes a block (e.g., finding a nonce so that the block hashes to a number with at least 75 leading zeroes in binary[1]), the reward collected by the pool owner must be distributed to the participating miners (perhaps less a commission) so that they continue to contribute. There are many ways to distribute rewards (as evident already from the early survey of Rosenfeld [16]); here, we isolate two of the design decisions involved.

Design decision #1: What information from miners should be the basis for their rewards?

Typically, rewards are based on the *shares* submitted by each miner over a period of time, where a "share" is a proof-of-work for a difficulty level lower than that required for block authorization (e.g., 65 leading zeroes instead of 75). This difficulty level is chosen to be low enough that a typical miner can produce shares reasonably frequently (thereby receiving a somewhat steady payout) but high enough that neither miners nor the pool are overwhelmed by the number of shares that must be communicated. There is no obvious reason to restrict designs to a simple uniform notion of shares, however. An example of a more sophisticated approach would be to use multiple classes of shares—for example, differing numbers of leading zeroes—and assign different rewards to shares from different classes.

Design decision #2: How should the information submitted by miners determine their rewards?

For example, with a single class of shares, two of the approaches common in practice are *pay-per-share (PPS)*, in which there is a fixed reward for each share (independent of any block authorization events); and *pay-per-last-N-shares (PPLNS)*, in which the reward associated with each successful block authorization is distributed equally among the most recently submitted N shares. Is there a good reason to prefer one of these approaches over the other? Is some other way of distributing rewards "better" than both of them?

The goal of this paper is to identify mining pool reward-sharing schemes that are "optimal" in a precise sense.

1.1   Our Contributions

Model for Identifying Variance-Optimal Reward-Sharing Schemes. Given that the primary raison d'être of mining pools is to reduce the variance in miners' rewards [16], we focus on the objective of minimizing variance.[2] Our first contribution is the definition of a formal model that allows us to identify every

---

[1] Technically, in Bitcoin this is defined by finding a hash that is smaller than a number that gets adjusted over time. For ease of discussion we will continue to refer to the number of leading zeros.

[2] Rosenfeld [16] computed the variance of some specific reward-sharing schemes and briefly considered multi-class shares (in [16, §7.5]) but did not pursue optimality results. A discussion on variance minimization can also be found in [17].

reward-sharing scheme with a statistical estimator (of the miner hashrate distribution) and formally compare the variance properties of different schemes. We then use this model to investigate the two design decisions above. We focus on schemes that are *unbiased* in the sense that the long-run rewards to a miner are proportional to the fraction of the overall hashrate controlled by that miner (as is the case for all of the most popular reward-sharing schemes).

Single-Class Shares are Optimal. It is intuitively clear that, at least in some scenarios, multi-class shares can lead to higher payoff variance than single-class shares. For example, consider a sequence of t consecutive messages, generated by the miners, that qualify for some type of reward (say, because each starts with at least 65 zeroes). In the extreme case in which there is only a single miner, with 100% of the hashrate, the variance of that miner's reward under standard (single-class) PPS in such a sequence is zero (as all t messages must have been generated by that miner, and each pays the same reward). With multi-class shares, by contrast, there would be positive variance in the miner's payoff across such sequences because of (say) the varying number of zeroes across different messages.

Our second contribution shows that variance degradation from multiple classes of shares is a fundamental phenomenon and not just an edge case: for every possible miner hashrate vector, every deviation from the dominant-in-practice single-class model can only increase the variance in rewards of *every* miner. For example, a version of PPLNS or PPS that conditions rewards on the number of leading zeroes in a hash (e.g., with a smaller reward for 65 zeroes and a larger reward for 75) would be worse for all miners than PPLNS or PPS (respectively) with all shares treated equally. As shown in Fig. 1, the difference in variance between single-class and multi-class shares can be significant.

Pay-per-Share is Optimal. Our third contribution identifies a sense in which the pay-per-share method is variance-optimal: for every possible miner hashrate vector, it simultaneously minimizes the variance of all miners over all unbiased reward-sharing schemes. We stress that there is no a priori guarantee that a scheme with such a guarantee exists—conceivably, small miners would be better off under one scheme and larger miners under a different one. Our result shows that no trade-offs between different miners are necessary—from the perspective of variance-minimization, all miners prefer pay-per-share. We also provide a second statistical justification of the pay-per-share method by showing that it corresponds to the maximum likelihood estimator for the miner hashrate distribution.

Pay-per-Last-N-Shares is Optimal Within a Restricted Class. One drawback of the PPS scheme is that, in the short run, it might be obligated to pay out rewards to miners that exceed the rewards that the pool has actually earned to date. (Whereas, in the long run, the reward per share is set so that the pool can almost surely cover its obligations with its earned rewards.) This issue motivates our fourth contribution, in which we study practically motivated subclasses of

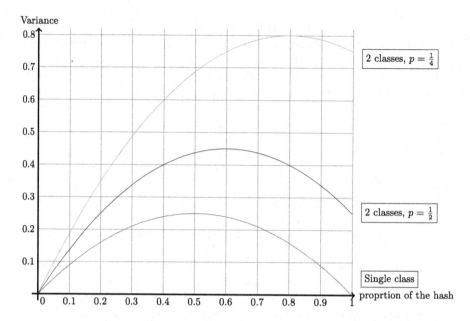

Fig. 1. Example variances in miner reward (over sequences of messages of a fixed length t) under the PSS RSS, as a function of the miner's fraction of the overall hashrate. For the single-class case, we use a reward of 1 per share. For the 2-class cases, we assume every share belonging to the second class (e.g., with at least 66 or at least 67 zeroes) belongs also to the first class (e.g., with at least 65 zeroes). Let p denote the probability that a share that belongs to the first class also belongs to the second (e.g., $\frac{1}{2}$ or $\frac{1}{4}$). We use a reward of $\frac{1}{2}$ per share in the first class and an additional bonus for each share in the second class. The bonus is set so that the expected value of a share from the first class (which may or may not also belong to the second) is 1 (e.g., a bonus of 1 for $p = \frac{1}{2}$ and a bonus of 2 for $p = \frac{1}{4}$).

reward sharing schemes (RSSes), such as those that never run a deficit and must distribute any block reward immediately. We prove that the pay-per-last-N-shares method is variance-optimal among RSSes in a natural subclass (and not variance-optimal if the subclass restrictions are relaxed).

1.2 Related Work

The goals of this paper are closely related to those of Fisch et al. [7], although the model and conclusions differ. In [7], miner risk aversion is modeled via a concave utility function of the form $u(x) = x^\alpha$ (where x is the reward and $\alpha \in (0, 1)$); here, we assume that each miner's preference is to minimize reward variance (subject to the expected reward being proportional to their hashrate).[3] Fisch et al. [7] then define "optimality" in terms of a global objective function, namely

---

[3] Variance-minimization has been regarded as a key objective function for mining pool design since Rosenfeld's seminal analysis of Bitcoin mining pools [16].

maximizing the total discounted utility of all miners. Because our optimality results apply to all miners simultaneously (and not just e.g. for the total variance of all miners), we are not forced to choose any method of aggregating benefits across miners. Finally, Fisch et al. [7] consider only what they call "pure" pooling strategies which do not allocate any rewards prior to a block authorization event (which have the advantage of never running a deficit) and thus the PPS scheme is outside of their model. (PPS does not run a deficit in the long run, but it can in the short run.) Because of these differences, the main result in [7] advocates for a geometric reward scheme (with the reward-per-share decaying with the share's distance from the next block authorization) to maximize total discounted utility; our theory singles out the pay-per-share scheme as variance-optimal. (Though our Theorem 5 does incorporate a no-deficit constraint to prove a restricted variance-optimality result for the pay-per-last-N-shares method.)

Much of the previous theoretical work on mining pools has focused on incentive aspects. For example, there are incentive issues both between different pools (e.g., pool-hopping [16]) and within a single pool (e.g., the miner's dilemma [5] or the delayed reporting of shares [18]). Another game-theoretic analysis of mining pools can be found in Lewenberg et al. [12], where the authors study the dynamics of a network with several mining pools. They show that there exists an instability in the choice of pools by miners, and that the miners will often switch pools, given some natural topological assumptions on the network. Along related lines, Laszka et al. [10] and Johnson et al. [8] examine the incentive of mining pools to attack each other. They show that in certain cases pools can benefit from such attacks.

We stress that while the present work does not focus on incentive issues per se (excepting the discussion in Sect. 4.4), our main results nevertheless advocate (on the basis of variance-minimization) for rules that happen to possess good incentive properties (such as PPS, see e.g. [18]). That is, our results optimize over all (not necessarily incentive-compatible) schemes and yet they champion schemes with strong incentive-compatibility properties.

Another line of works considers the forces behind and consequences of centralization (either outside of a mining pool or within a mining pool). An empirical study of this issue can be found in a recent paper by Romiti et al. [15]. The results of this study point to centralization tendencies inside pools, with a small number of miners reaping a large portion of the rewards. This raises incentive and security concerns motivated by the power that a small group may hold. In [6] Eyal and Sirer show that the Bitcoin protocol is not incentive compatible, in the sense that colluding miners could gain profits larger than their proportional hash power. As a counterpoint, in [9] the authors analyze mining as a stochastic game and show that as long as all of the miners are small, honest mining is a Nash equilibrium.

Others have studied the setting where there are a few miners with large mining power (one can think of them as mining pools, but this does not have to be the case) and many small miners. For Bitcoin this was studied in [11]. For Ethereum, which has a slightly different reward allocation rule in which a miner can be rewarded for finding a block that does not end up in the main chain (known as "uncle" rewards), it was shown in [21] that powerful miners can attack weak miners.

A different approach taken in [1] takes into account the cost of mining equipment purchased by miners. There it is shown that with time one can expect that there will only be a small set of strong miners. These strong miners again can be interpreted as mining pools.

An axiomatic approach to reward allocation for miners was taken by Chen et al. in [4]. They start by stating the desired properties of reward allocation rule, such as symmetry, sybil-proofness, collusion-proofness, and others. They proceed to study which allocation rules satisfy these properties, showing that Bitcoin's allocation rule is the unique solution that satisfies a strong set of properties and that this is no longer the case for slightly weaker properties or if the miners are risk-averse.

Finally, we point the reader to two surveys that may be of interest. The first is a Systematization of Knowledge paper [2], where the authors examine results in the fields of game theory, cryptography, and distributed systems. The second [20] offers a systematic study of blockchain networks, focusing on the incentive aspects in the design of such systems.

2   Preliminaries

2.1   Model of Miners

We assume there is a finite set of miners, and use $[k] := \{1, 2, \ldots, k\}$ to denote their possible identities (public keys). (Any number of miner identities may belong to the same actor.) We assume that there is a finite message space M, such as $\{0, 1\}^{256}$ (e.g., all possible hash function outputs). By a *signed message* (s, m) we mean a miner $s \in [k]$ and a message $m \in M$. The sets $[k]$ and M are known to all in advance. We assume that, due to capacity and communication considerations, a mining pool is willing to accept only a subset $A \subseteq M$ of the possible messages (e.g., those with at least 65 leading zeroes).[4]

Each miner s has a nonnegative hashrate h_s, not known a priori to the designer, which controls the rate at which s can generate signed messages. We model miner s as a Poisson process with rate h_s, with each generated message of the form (s, m) with m drawn uniformly at random from the message space M (e.g., the output of SHA-256 on a block with a specific nonce, under the random oracle assumption).[5] We assume that a miner s sends one of its generated messages (s, m) to the mining pool if and only if $m \in A$ (e.g., a miner doesn't bother to send hashes with less than 65 zeroes). We can assume without loss of

---

[4] Our results remain the same if each miner has its own subset A_i of acceptable messages, provided the A_i's all have the same size.

[5] The Poisson assumption is for convenience. The important property is that the identity of the sender of a new signed message is distributed proportionally to the hashrate distribution, independent of the past.

generality that the total hashrate is 1 ($\sum_{s=1}^{k} h_s = 1$) and hence the vector $\mathbf{h}$ of hashrates can be interpreted as a probability distribution, called the *hashrate distribution*.

The *message distribution* $\mathcal{M}(\mathbf{h})$ induced by a hashrate distribution $\mathbf{h}$ is the distribution over signed messages arriving at the mining pool. A sample (s, m) from $\mathcal{M}(\mathbf{h})$ can be generated by independently choosing a miner identity s according to the hashrate distribution and an acceptable message m uniformly at random from A. Each signed message received by the mining pool is an i.i.d. sample from the message distribution.

2.2 Reward Sharing Schemes

A *reward sharing scheme (RSS)* ascribes a (possibly random) reward to the sender of each signed message, given the messages received thus far. Formally, an RSS is a random function φ from finite sequences $(s_1, m_1), \ldots, (s_t, m_t)$ of signed messages to real-valued rewards (for the miner s_t). An RSS is *memoryless* if its output is independent of all but the most recent signed message. We write $\varphi(s, m)$ for the (random) output of a given memoryless RSS φ on a given signed message (s, m).

For example, the *pay-per-share (PPS)* RSS deterministically pays a fixed reward for each message received. That is,

$$\text{PPS}(s, m) = c$$

for some $c > 0$.[6]

For a more involved example, consider the *pay-per-last-N-shares (PPLNS)* RSS, which distributes a fixed reward to the most recent N messages leading up to the pool's successful authorization of a block. Here, a miner's reward for a message depends on the future—on the number of blocks mined by the pool over the course of the next N messages. (Note, however, the miner's reward is independent of the past.) We can model this uncertainty in our RSS framework using random rewards:

$$\text{PPLNS}(s, m) = c \cdot X,$$

where $c > 0$ is a constant and $X \sim Bin(N, p)$ is a binomial random variable, where the number of trials is N and the success probability p is the probability that a sample from the message distribution leads to a block authorization (e.g., if the acceptable messages A have 65 leading zeroes and 75 are necessary to authorize a block, then $p = 2^{-10}$).[7]

---

[6] The constant $c > 0$ would typically be chosen so that the rate at which rewards are granted to miners equals the rate at which the pool accrues block rewards (and possibly transaction fees), less a commission.

[7] Other schemes with future-dependent rewards can be similarly modeled. The key requirement is that the probability distribution over the reward associated with a share (with respect to future samples from the message distribution) is independent of the hashrate distribution $\mathbf{h}$. This is the case for most of the well-studied RSSes (including e.g. the geometric reward schemes studied in [7]).

An example of a natural RSS that is not memoryless is the *proportional* RSS, which upon a block authorization distributes the corresponding reward to miners proportionally to the number of signed messages each miner sent since the most recent successful block authorization. Here, the reward to a miner for a signed message depends on the past, and specifically on how many signed messages the pool has received since the most recent successful block authorization.

2.3 Message-Independence and Symmetrization

An RSS φ is *message-independent* if $\varphi((s_1, m_1), \ldots, (s_t, m_t))$ is independent of $m_1, m_2, \ldots, m_t$, that is, the RSS does not take into account the content of the message $m_1, \ldots, m_t$.[8] Message-independence corresponds to the notion of "single-class shares" from the introduction—the RSS does not consider the contents of a message beyond its acceptability (i.e., membership in A). Thus our results about the optimality of single-class shares will be formalized as optimality results for message-independent RSSes.

The PPS, PPLNS, and proportional RSSes are all message-independent. (To avoid confusion, remember that every message reaching the RSS belongs to A; non-acceptable messages are filtered out beforehand.) Conditioning a reward on, for example, the number of leading zeroes in an acceptable message would lead to a non-message-independent RSS.

For a (not necessarily message-independent) RSS φ, define its *symmetrization* φ^{sym} by

$$\varphi^{sym}((s_1, m_1), \ldots, (s_t, m_t)) = \mathbb{E}_{u_1, \ldots, u_t \sim A}[\varphi(s_i, m_i)],$$

where the u_i's are i.i.d. uniformly random messages from A. For the special case of a memoryless RSS φ, we can write

$$\varphi^{sym}(s, m) = \mathbb{E}_{u \sim A}[\varphi(s, m)].$$

We immediately have:

Proposition 1. *For every RSS φ, its symmetrization φ^{sym} is message-independent.*

2.4 A Reward-Sharing Scheme as a Hashrate Estimator

To compare the statistical properties (such as variance-minimization) of different RSSes, it is useful to view an RSS as a statistical estimator of the hashrate distribution. By an *estimator*, we mean a function that associates each sequence $(s_1, m_1), \ldots, (s_t, m_t)$ with a probability distribution over the miners $[k]$.

---

[8] All of the common RSSes that motivate this work are also *anonymous*, meaning that $\varphi((s_1, m_1), \ldots, (s_t, m_t))$ is independent of $s_1, s_2, \ldots, s_t$. While anonymity is natural (and arguably unavoidable) in a permissionless blockchain setting, our positive results do not require that assumption. In any case, the RSSes advocated by our results are anonymous.

Specifically, given an RSS φ, the corresponding estimator f_φ associates each sequence $(s_1, m_1), \ldots, (s_t, m_t)$ of signed messages with the k-vector $\mathbf{p}$ in which the jth component p_j is the fraction of the rewards awarded to miner j:

$$p_j = \frac{1}{Z} \cdot \sum_{i \in [t] \,:\, s_i = j} \varphi((s_1, m_1), \ldots, (s_i, m_i)), \tag{1}$$

where $Z = \sum_{i=1}^{t} \varphi((s_1, m_1), \ldots, (s_i, m_i))$ is a normalizing factor. For a memoryless rule φ one can write $\varphi(s_i, m_i)$ instead of $\varphi((s_1, m_1), \ldots, (s_i, m_i))$ in (1). If the RSS φ is randomized, so is the corresponding estimator f_φ (even for a fixed sample).

The *likelihood* of a sequence $(s_1, m_1), \ldots, (s_t, m_t)$ of signed messages with a hashrate distribution $\mathbf{h}$ is the probability that t i.i.d. draws from the message distribution $\mathcal{M}(\mathbf{h})$ induced by $\mathbf{h}$ is $(s_1, m_1), \ldots, (s_t, m_t)$. A *maximum likelihood estimator (MLE)* maps each sequence $(s_1, m_1), \ldots, (s_t, m_t)$ to a hashrate distribution maximizing the likelihood of that sequence. There is no a priori requirement that an MLE is induced by an RSS, though we'll see in Theorem 2 that the PPS RSS induces an MLE.

Some kind of unbiasedness assumption is required for meaningful variance-minimization results (otherwise, a constant function can achieve zero variance). Formally, we call an estimator f *unbiased* if, for every positive integer t and hashrate distribution $\mathbf{h}$,

$$\mathbb{E}[f((s_1, m_1), \ldots, (s_t, m_t))] = \mathbf{h}, \tag{2}$$

where the expectation is over t i.i.d. samples from $\mathcal{M}(\mathbf{h})$ and any randomization internal to the estimator. For example, the PPS, PPLNS, and proportional RSSes all induce unbiased estimators. Also, because the message m_i in a sample (s_i, m_i) from $\mathcal{M}(\mathbf{h})$ is chosen uniformly at random from A:

Proposition 2. *For every unbiased RSS φ, its symmetrization φ^{sym} is also unbiased.*

An estimator is *unbiased for miner s* if the identity in (2) holds in the sth coordinate. (An estimator is thus unbiased if and only if it is unbiased for every miner.)

For a given estimator f, positive integer t, and hashrate distribution $\mathbf{h}$, we can define its *miner-s t-sample variance* as

$$\mathbb{E}[(f((s_1, m_1), \ldots, (s_t, m_t)))_s - h_s)^2],$$

where the expectation is again over t i.i.d. samples from $\mathcal{M}(\mathbf{h})$ and any randomization internal to the estimator. The *t-sample variance* of an estimator f for a hashrate distribution $\mathbf{h}$ is the vector of all such variances (ranging over the miner s).

2.5   When t is Random

The t-sample variance refers to a fixed number t of samples, corresponding to a fixed number of miner shares. If one instead fixes an amount of *time*, then t itself is a random variable (the number of shares found during that time window, which is distributed according to a Poisson distribution). All of our t-sample variance-optimality results (such as Theorems 4 and 5) hold simultaneously for all positive integers t. Thus, by the law of total variance (see Eq. (3)), these variance-optimality results carry over to the case in which t is a random variable (e.g., the case of a fixed time window).

3   Warm-Up: Maximizing Likelihood

We begin with an observation that champions PPS from a statistical prediction perspective—the corresponding estimator is in fact a maximum likelihood estimator for the hashrate distribution $\mathbf{h}$ (given t i.i.d. samples from the message distribution $\mathcal{M}(\mathbf{h})$).[9,10] The next section describes the main results of this paper, on variance-optimality.

Theorem 1 (PPS Is an MLE). *The estimator f_{PPS} induced by the PPS reward-sharing scheme is an MLE.*

Before we prove Theorem 1, we need to state the following result that can be found, for example, in [19]. Let $X_1, ..., X_n$ be i.i.d random variables with a discrete support $[k]$. For $s \in [k]$ let $n_s = |\{X_i = s\}|$. We say that $\mathbf{p} = (p_1, ..., p_k)$ is the *maximum likelihood estimate* if

$$\mathbf{p} = argmax_{\mathbf{q} \in Q} \prod_{s=1}^{n} q_s^{n_s}$$

where $Q = \{\mathbf{q} \in \mathbb{R}^k : \sum_{s=0}^{k} q_s = 1, \forall s \ q_s \geq 0\}$ denotes the simplex.

Theorem 2. *The maximum likelihood estimate is given by the empirical distribution defined by*

$$p_s = \frac{n_s}{n}$$

for all $s \in [k]$.

We are now ready to prove Theorem 1.

Proof (Proof of Theorem 1). First note that the values of the s_i's are i.i.d. For every i, s_i is chosen by the hash distribution, and for any $i \neq j$, s_i is independent of s_j as the Poisson process is memoryless. Furthermore, the estimator induced

---

[9] MLEs are deterministic (up to tie-breaking). Thus no randomized RSS (such as PPLNS or the estimator induced by the proportional rule) can be a MLE.

[10] A similar result can be found in [14] under the reasonable assumption that the shares follow the Poisson distribution.

by PPS is the empirical distribution. Indeed, when focusing on PPS (with a fixed reward of c per share), the identity in (1) specializes to

$$p_s = \frac{1}{c \cdot t} \cdot \sum_{i \in [t] \, : \, s_i = s} c$$

$$= \frac{|\{i \, : \, s_i = s\}|}{t}.$$

Theorem 1 now follows from Theorem 2.

While we believe Theorem 1 is a novel way to single out one RSS among many, the primary purpose of mining pools is variance-minimization, not prediction per se. We therefore proceed to our main results on variance-optimality, in which the PPS RSS will continue to play a central role.

4   Main Results: Variance-Optimality

4.1   Single-Class Shares Are Optimal

Our first result proves that single-class shares are optimal, in the sense that symmetrization can only reduce the variance of every miner.

Theorem 3 (Message-Independence Minimizes Variance). *For every unbiased RSS φ, hashrate distribution $\mathbf{h}$, positive integer t, and miner $j \in [k]$, the miner-j t-sample variance under the estimator f_φ is at least as large as under its symmetrization $f_{\varphi^{sym}}$.*

Proof. The law of total variance states that for X and Y, random variables over the same probability space,

$$\text{Var}[X] = \mathbb{E}[\text{Var}[X \mid Y]] + \text{Var}[\mathbb{E}[X \mid Y]]. \tag{3}$$

For an unbiased RSS, we have that $\mathbb{E}[(f((s_1, m_1), \dots, (s_t, m_t)))_j - h_j)^2] = \text{Var}[(f_\varphi((s_1, m_1), \dots, (s_t, m_t)))_j]$, and so we can apply the above. Here we take $X = f_\varphi(\mathbf{s}, \mathbf{m})_j$, where $\mathbf{s} = (s_1, \dots, s_t)$ and $\mathbf{m} = (m_1, \dots m_t)$. Note that $\mathbb{E}_\mathbf{m}[f_\varphi(\mathbf{s}, \mathbf{m})_j \mid \mathbf{s}] = f_{\varphi^{sym}}(\mathbf{s}, \mathbf{m})_j$.

Plugging this into (3) we find that

$$\text{Var}[f_\varphi(\mathbf{s}, \mathbf{m})_j] = \mathbb{E}_\mathbf{s}[\text{Var}[f_\varphi(\mathbf{s}, \mathbf{m})_j \mid \mathbf{s}]] + \text{Var}[f_{\varphi^{sym}}(\mathbf{s}, \mathbf{m})_j].$$

The first term on the right-hand side is always nonnegative, and it equals 0 if $f_\varphi = f_{\varphi^{sym}}$. This completes the proof.

For example, consider a version of the PPLNS scheme that uses two classes of shares (e.g., corresponding to at least 65 and at least 75 leading zeroes), with different rewards (e.g., more for 75 zeroes). Theorem 3 implies that all miners would enjoy lower variance (and the same expectation) if instead every share of either type was rewarded according to the expected reward of a share in one of the two classes (where the expectation is over a uniformly random message from A).

4.2   PPS is Variance-Optimal

Theorem 3 is agnostic to all aspects of an RSS other than message-independence—for example, it offers no opinion on which of PPS or PPLNS is "better." Our next result singles out PPS as variance-optimal among all unbiased RSSes. We discuss this point further and revisit PPLNS after the proof of Theorem 5.

Theorem 4 (PPS is Variance-Optimal). *For every hashrate distribution* **h**, *positive integer* t, *and miner* $j \in [k]$, *the PPS RSS minimizes the miner-j t-sample variance over all estimators that are unbiased for miner j.*

To prove this, we show the following general statement:

Lemma 1. *Let* $x = (m, \mathbf{b})$ *be such that* m *is chosen uniformly from some set* $\mathcal{F}$ *and* **b** *are the results of* l *coin flips for some constant* l. *Let* $\{F_i\}$ *be pairwise disjoint subsets of* $\mathcal{F} \times \{0, 1\}^l$. *Let*

$$X = \sum_i a_i \mathbf{1}_{x \in F_i}$$

and assume that $\mathbb{E}[X] = R$ *for some constant* R. *Then the choice of* a_i *that minimizes the variance of* X *is* $a_i = \frac{R}{\Pr[x \in \cup F_i]}$.

Intuitively we can think about the elements of Lemma 1 as follows. Assume that a bitcoin mining pool runs a version of PPS where the reward for a miner is a function of the number of leading zeroes in the hash. Then each F_i will be the set of messages with a given number of leading zeroes, and for such a message the pool will give a reward of a_i.

If there is some extra randomness beyond the sampling of the miner, say as in PPLNS, then this randomness will appear in the coin flips **b**. In this case, a family F_i could be, for example, all the messages with the number of leading zeros between 65 and 70, for which the coin flips sum up to exactly 5.

The reward given for the family F_i can be a function also of the history $(s_1, m_1), ..., (s_{t-1}, m_{t-1})$.

Lemma 1 essentially shows that the minimum variance is obtained by giving the same reward for every family F_i, that is, discarding any information given by the message or the randomness of the RSS.

Proof (of Lemma 1). Let $X = \sum_i a_i \mathbf{1}_{x \in F_i}$. Remembering that $\mathrm{Var}[X] = \mathbb{E}[[X - \mathbb{E}[X]]^2]$ we have that the smallest possible variance $\mathrm{Var}[X] = 0$ is obtained if and only if $X = \mathbb{E}[X]$.

In our notation, this means that for every i and i' we must have that $a_i = a_{i'}$, and as $\mathbb{E}[X] = R$ this gives us that for every i, $a_i = \frac{R}{\Pr[x \in \cup F_i]}$ as needed.

It is left to deduce Theorem 4 from Lemma 1.

Proof (of Theorem 4). To show this, we first choose $\mathcal{F} = A$, the family of all messages that can be sent to the pool. Second, for a given RSS we define as F_i

the set of all the messages and result of the extra randomness that get the reward a_i. The expectation R is given by the assumption that the RSS is unbiased.

Note that in an unbiased RSS a miner j cannot get paid for the a message sent by another miner (e.g., if $h_j = 0$ then any payment to j would make the RSS biased). To minimize the variance of miner j it is left to decide on the reward of messages sent by them. By Lemma 1 we have that the smallest variance will be obtained by giving the same reward for every message and flipping no extra coins. This is exactly the definition of PPS.

Finally, we note that Theorem 4 considers minimizing the variance of some fixed miner $s \in [k]$. As the optimal RSS is PPS (independent of s), it is actually variance-optimal for all of the miners simultaneously. More precisely, we have the following:

Corollary 1 (Miner-Optimality). *For every hashrate distribution $\mathbf{h}$ and positive integer t, the PPS RSS simultaneously minimizes the variance of the miner-s t-sample for all s over all unbiased estimators.*

It is interesting to note that Corollary 1 holds even if each miner chooses their own difficulty of shares (as is common in some mining pools). A miner that is free to choose its difficulty in the PPS RSS can lower the variance further by choosing the smallest possible difficulty.

We emphasize that there is no a priori guarantee that a statement like Corollary 1 should hold for any RSS—for example, it is conceivable that small miners would fare better under one scheme and large miners under a different one. Corollary 1 shows that no trade-offs between different miners are necessary. This is particularly interesting if we add other restrictions on the RSS.

4.3   Variance-Optimality of PPLNS

A shortcoming of PPS is that for any fixed reward per share, there is a constant probability that at some point the pool will not have the funds to pay the miners. The PPLNS method is common in practice and does not suffer from this drawback. Does PPLNS become variance-optimal if we impose additional constraints on an RSS?

We consider four constraints on an RSS.

(P1) *No-deficit.* An RSS can only distribute block rewards that have been earned to date.

(P2) *Liquidating.* An RSS must distribute each block reward as soon as the block is found.

(P3) *N-bounded.* The reward given for a share depends on at most the next N shares found.

(P4) *Past-agnostic.* The distribution of the reward for a share should not depend on the realizations of past rewards or on past blocks found.

The PPLNS method is variance-optimal for all miners, subject to (P1)–(P4).

Theorem 5. *For every hashrate distribution* **h** *and positive integer* t, *the PPLNS RSS simultaneously minimizes the variance of the miner-s t-sample for all s over all unbiased RSSes that satisfy properties (P1)–(P4).*

Before proceeding to the proof, we note that PPLNS is *not* variance-optimal if any of the properties (P1)–(P4) are relaxed. Most of the RSSes that demonstrate this are not particularly attractive, however, as they suffer from serious incentive problems (see Sect. 4.4 for further discussion). The point of Theorem 5 is not so much to argue that PPLNS is the only reasonable RSS for variance-minimization, but rather to clarify the types of transgressions required by any RSS that does better.

Proof (of Theorem 5). Let f be an unbiased RSS that follows constraints (P1)–(P4) and has minimum variance. By (P1) we know that it can distribute only block rewards that were already obtained, and by (P2) we know that it has to distribute the reward immediately when a block is found. Thus, it is enough to determine its behavior at the appearance of a block. Furthermore, by (P3) we know that the reward can only be distributed among the last N shares, and so f takes as an input only the last N messages before the block, even if $t > N$. Thus, we can focus on a function that given the fact that share j is a block, distributes the reward found among the shares $j - N - 1, j - N - 2, ..., j$. Call this function f_j and note that $f = \sum_{j \text{ is block}} f_j$.

By (P4), f_j cannot depend on whether any of the other N shares is a block or if the share already received a reward from a different block. The information available for f_j is the message sent with the shares, the arrival time of the share with respect to the block, and the identity of the sender. This makes f_j independent of any $f_{j'}$, for $j \neq j'$, and so it is enough to minimize the variance of each f_j separately.

After considering (P1)–(P4) we see that f_j is an unbiased RSS over an N-sample. By Corollary 1, PPS minimizes the variance for all of the miners simultaneously, and so in the context of f_j this means that each of the N shares receives the same reward. By (P2) all of the block reward needs to be distributed, so each shares gets $1/N$ of the block reward, which is exactly the definition of PPLNS.

4.4   Relaxing the Constraints

All the properties (P1)–(P4) are required for the variance-optimality result in Theorem 5. For starters, if the no-deficit condition, (P1), is dropped, the PPS method has smaller variance.

Suppose the liquidating constraint (P2) is dropped. That is, an RSS need not allocate the full block reward. With partial reward distributions, we can again find an RSS with a smaller variance: For each share, reward a fixed amount if in the next N shares at least one block is found. (The reward is the same, whether 1 or 17 blocks are found over the next N shares.) This RSS has smaller variance than PPLNS as the reward does not depend on the number of blocks found. The variance of this RSS becomes smaller as a function of N, but a direct consequence of this is that a large portion of funds will not be distributed. Furthermore, it might incentivize miners to delay the publication of blocks until they have published enough shares.

If N-boundedness (P3) is dropped, consider the following RSS. For a fixed N let M be the expected number of blocks within N shares. For each share, reward a sum proportional to M/N. If there are not enough funds in the pool, wait for the next block to be found and start paying shares, ordered from the oldest to the newest. This results in an RSS very similar to PPS, but with the risk of funds delaying significantly. This RSS suffers from incentive issues, however: As the delays inevitably grow, miners are incentivized to leave the pool for greener pastures.

Finally, an RSS which is not past agnostic (P4) and has a smaller variance is the following. Assume, again, that we expect to find M blocks for every N shares. Then, for every block found, look back at the last N shares and reward each one with a sum that will make their reward as close to M/N as possible. If not all of the reward was distributes or if the reward is not enough to bring the shares to M/N, distribute the reward in a way that will make the reward of all of the N shares as even as possible. Although this RSS has a smaller variance, it creates a negative incentive to mine if no block was found for a while.

Although the examples above have obvious incentive problems, it is not clear that any such relaxation will create these issues. Studying this further may be of interest.

5   Conclusions and Discussion

In this work, we have proposed a model for investigating the variance-minimization properties of different mining pool reward-sharing schemes. We focused on two design decisions: (i) What information from miners should be the basis for their rewards?; and (ii) How should the information submitted by miners determine their rewards? Our results strongly support the common practice of using a single class of shares, as the use of finer-grained information can only increase the variance experienced by every miner. This holds true across different ways of translating single-class shares into miner rewards (PPS, PPLNS, etc.). Our results also strongly support the pay-per-share scheme, which can be justified both as a maximum likelihood estimator for the miner hashrate distribution and as the scheme that minimizes the variance of all miners simultaneously, over all unbiased estimators.

This work focused single-mindedly on variance-minimization. This tunnel vision is deliberate, both because it enables a tractable theory with particularly crisp and interpretable results, and because in many cases it only makes our results stronger. For example, our main results do not restrict consideration to reward-sharing schemes with desirable incentive properties, but nevertheless advocate (as variance-optimal) schemes that do have such properties.

Needless to say, there are many other scientifically interesting and practically relevant dimensions along which one can compare reward-sharing schemes, all of which should be taken into account in a real design. For example, in some settings the variance-minimization benefits of the pay-per-share scheme may be outweighed by the risk that would be taken on by the pool owner.

References

1. Arnosti, N., Weinberg, S.M: Bitcoin: a natural oligopoly. arXiv preprint arXiv:1811.08572 (2018)
2. Azouvi, S., Hicks, A.: Sok: tools for game theoretic models of security for cryptocurrencies. arXiv preprint arXiv:1905.08595 (2019)
3. Buterin, V., et al.: Ethereum: a next-generation smart contract and decentralized application platform (2014). https://github.com/ethereum/wiki/wiki/%5BEnglish%5D-White-Paper
4. Chen, X., Papadimitriou, C., Roughgarden, T.: An axiomatic approach to block rewards. In: Proceedings of the 1st ACM Conference on Advances in Financial Technologies, pp. 124–131 (2019)
5. Eyal, I.: The miner's dilemma. In: 2015 IEEE Symposium on Security and Privacy, pp. 89–103. IEEE (2015)
6. Eyal, I., Sirer, E.G.: Majority is not enough: bitcoin mining is vulnerable. In: Christin, N., Safavi-Naini, R. (eds.) FC 2014. LNCS, vol. 8437, pp. 436–454. Springer, Heidelberg (2014). https://doi.org/10.1007/978-3-662-45472-5_28
7. Fisch, B., Pass, R., Shelat, A.: Socially optimal mining pools. In: Devanur, N.R., Lu, P. (eds.) WINE 2017. LNCS, vol. 10660, pp. 205–218. Springer, Cham (2017). https://doi.org/10.1007/978-3-319-71924-5_15
8. Johnson, B., Laszka, A., Grossklags, J., Vasek, M., Moore, T.: Game-theoretic analysis of DDoS attacks against bitcoin mining pools. In: Böhme, R., Brenner, M., Moore, T., Smith, M. (eds.) FC 2014. LNCS, vol. 8438, pp. 72–86. Springer, Heidelberg (2014). https://doi.org/10.1007/978-3-662-44774-1_6
9. Kiayias, A., Koutsoupias, E., Kyropoulou, M., Tselekounis, Y.: Blockchain mining games. In: Proceedings of the 2016 ACM Conference on Economics and Computation, pp. 365–382 (2016)
10. Laszka, A., Johnson, B., Grossklags, J.: When bitcoin mining pools run dry. In: Brenner, M., Christin, N., Johnson, B., Rohloff, K. (eds.) FC 2015. LNCS, vol. 8976, pp. 63–77. Springer, Heidelberg (2015). https://doi.org/10.1007/978-3-662-48051-9_5
11. Leonardos, N., Leonardos, S., Piliouras, G.: Oceanic games: centralization risks and incentives in blockchain mining. In: Pardalos, P., Kotsireas, I., Guo, Y., Knottenbelt, W. (eds.) Mathematical Research for Blockchain Economy. SPBE, pp. 183–199. Springer, Cham (2020). https://doi.org/10.1007/978-3-030-37110-4_13
12. Lewenberg, Y., Bachrach, Y., Sompolinsky, Y., Zohar, A., Rosenschein, J.S.: Bitcoin mining pools: a cooperative game theoretic analysis. In: Proceedings of the 2015 International Conference on Autonomous Agents and Multiagent Systems, pp. 919–927. Citeseer (2015)
13. Nakamoto, S.: Bitcoin: a peer-to-peer electronic cash system. Technical report, Manubot (2019)
14. Paszek, E.: Introduction to statistics (2007)
15. Romiti, M., Judmayer, A., Zamyatin, A., Haslhofer, B.: A deep dive into bitcoin mining pools: an empirical analysis of mining shares. arXiv preprint arXiv:1905.05999 (2019)

16. Rosenfeld, M.: Analysis of bitcoin pooled mining reward systems. arXiv preprint arXiv:1112.4980 (2011)
17. Rosenfeld, M., et al.: A short note about variance and pool payouts (2011). https://bitcointalk.org/index.php?topic=5264.0
18. Schrijvers, O., Bonneau, J., Boneh, D., Roughgarden, T.: Incentive compatibility of bitcoin mining pool reward functions. In: Grossklags, J., Preneel, B. (eds.) FC 2016. LNCS, vol. 9603, pp. 477–498. Springer, Heidelberg (2017). https://doi.org/10.1007/978-3-662-54970-4_28
19. Shashua, A.: Introduction to machine learning: class notes 67577 (2009)
20. Wang, W., et al.: A survey on consensus mechanisms and mining strategy management in blockchain networks. IEEE Access **7**, 22328–22370 (2019)
21. Zamyatin, A., Wolter, K., Werner, S., Harrison, P.G., Mulligan, C.E.A., Knottenbelt, W.J.: Swimming with fishes and sharks: beneath the surface of queue-based Ethereum mining pools. In: 2017 IEEE 25th International Symposium on Modeling, Analysis, and Simulation of Computer and Telecommunication Systems (MASCOTS), pp. 99–109. IEEE (2017)

HaPPY-Mine: Designing a Mining Reward Function

Lucianna Kiffer[✉] and Rajmohan Rajaraman

Northeastern University, Boston, MA, USA
{lkiffer,rraj}@ccs.neu.edu

Abstract. In cryptocurrencies, the block reward is meant to serve as the incentive mechanism for miners to commit resources to create blocks and in effect secure the system. Existing systems primarily divide the reward in proportion to expended resources and follow one of two static models for total block reward: (i) a fixed reward for each block (e.g., Ethereum), or (ii) one where the block reward halves every set number of blocks (e.g., the Bitcoin model of halving roughly every 4 years) but otherwise remains fixed between halvings. In recent work, a game-theoretic analysis of the static model under asymmetric miner costs showed that an equilibrium always exists and is unique [4]. Their analysis also reveals how asymmetric costs can lead to large-scale centralization in blockchain mining, a phenomenon that has been observed in Bitcoin and Ethereum and highlighted by other studies including [11,16].

In this work we introduce a novel family of mining reward functions, HaPPY-Mine (HAsh-Pegged Proportional Yield), which peg the value of the reward to the hashrate of the system, decreasing the reward as the hashrate increases. HaPPY-Mine distributes rewards in proportion to expended hashrate and inherits the safety properties of the generalized proportional reward function established in [9]. We study HaPPY-Mine under a heterogeneous miner cost model and show that an equilibrium always exists with a unique set of miner participants and a unique total hashrate. Significantly, we prove that a HaPPY-Mine equilibrium is more decentralized than the static model equilibrium under a set of metrics including number of mining participants and hashrate distribution. Finally, we show that any HaPPY-Mine *equilibrium* is also safe against collusion and sybil attacks, and explore how the market value of the currency affects the equilibrium.

1 Introduction

Existing cryptocurrencies rely on block rewards for two reasons: to subsidize the cost miners incur securing the blockchain and to mint new coins. Miners in major cryptocurrencies like Bitcoin and Ethereum participate in the protocol by packaging user transactions into blocks and incorporating those blocks into

We thank the anonymous reviewers and Yonatan Sompolinsky for their helpful comments. The first author was supported by a Facebook Fellowship and Dfinity Scholarship. This work was also partially supported by NSF grant CCF-1909363. This work was initiated when the first author was at an internship at DAGlabs.

N. Borisov and C. Diaz (Eds.): FC 2021, LNCS 12675, pp. 250–268, 2021.
https://doi.org/10.1007/978-3-662-64331-0_13

the blockchain (the global record of all transactions that have taken place in the system). Creating a block involves significant computational power where the miner preforms iterations of some kind of computation, the *proof of work*, generally iterating over a hash function. This *work*, whether on a CPU, GPU or other specialized hardware, comes at a cost to the miner. To compensate miners for incurring this cost and to incentivize more miners to join, miners collect a *block reward* of newly minted coins for each block that gets added to the blockchain. In expectation, miners are rewarded in proportion to the resources they contribute. This computational work is also what cryptographically ties each block in the blockchain together and makes it so that anyone wanting to *fork* the blockchain, i.e. erase transactions by creating their own version of a subset of the chain, would have to redo an equivalent amount of work. The more resources miners invest in the system, the greater the system hashrate, the more expensive this attack becomes. In effect, the computational work of miners secures the blockchain system by making the blockchain immutable.

There are two common frameworks for the block reward function in terms of distribution of supply. Bitcoin's protocol has a set maximum number of coins that will ever be minted, therefore the mining reward diminishes over time. The mining reward halves every 210,000 blocks (approximately every 4 years). For now, miners continue to profit since the value of each Bitcoin has increased over time making up for the decrease in reward with increases system hashrate. Eventually though, the mining reward will reach zero and miners will be repaid solely in transaction fees for the transactions they include in the blocks they mine. Another cryptocurrency, Ethereum, currently has in its protocol a fixed mining reward of 5 Ethers for all blocks ever. This means that the supply of Ether is uncapped and the mining hashrate can grow linearly in the market value of Ether.

In general miner costs are asymmetric [1] with miners with access to low-cost electricity or mining hardware being at an advantage. This has led to large centralization in both Bitcoin and Ethereum mining, with a significant portion of the hashrate being controlled by a few mining pools [2,3,11]. This prevents other players from having a share of the market. We ask the question, can we design a mining reward function that alleviates these problems?

1.1 Main Contributions

In this paper, we develop a novel hashrate-based mining reward function, HaPPY-Mine, which sets the block reward based on the system hashrate. HaPPY-Mine is defined so that as the system hashrate increases, the block reward smoothly decreases. We now outline the main contributions of this paper.

1. We introduce the notion of a *hashrate-pegged mining reward function*, and formally argue that it can help in decentralizing the blockchain by reducing the hashrate that a new miner is incentivized to buy.
2. We present HaPPY-Mine, a family of hashrate-pegged mining reward functions that dispense rewards in proportion to the expended hashrate. We conduct a rigorous equilibrium analysis of the HaPPY-Mine family under general

miner costs. We establish that equilibria always exist, and are more decentralized than an equlibrium under the static reward function: in particular, HaPPY-Mine equilibria have at least as many participating miners as and lower total hashrate than an equilibrium for the static reward function.

3. We show that HaPPY-Mine equilibria (as well as that of a static reward function) are resistant to any collusion attack involving fewer than half the miners, and that a Sybil attack does not increase the utility of the attacker.

4. We finally consider the scenario where rewards are issued in the currency of the blockchain and study the effect of the change in the currency's value on the equilibrium. We show that in HaPPY-Mine, an increase in the value of the cryptocurrency allows more higher cost miners to participate, again resulting in greater decentralization as compared to an equilibrium under the static reward function.

Outline of the Paper. We begin in Sect. 2 with a description of the equilibrium analysis of [4], which provides a basic game-theoretic framework that we build on. We also describe the properties satisfied by the *generalized proportional allocation rule* of [9], of which our function is a special case. In Sect. 3 we introduce our hash-pegged mining reward function and in Sect. 4 we analyze its equilibria. We analyze other factors that impact the equilibria in Sect. 5. We conclude with a discussion on the practicality of implementing the hash-pegged mining reward function in a system and with future and related work in Sects. 6 and 7.

2   Background

In this paper, we follow a miner model of asymmetric costs with rewards being awarded in proportion to expended resources(hashrate). Our study builds on an analysis framework developed in [4]. In this section, we first summarize the model of [4] and their equilibrium analysis of a static reward function for mining. We next review proportional allocation, used in both the static reward function and HaPPY-Mine, and state salient properties established in [9].

Equilibrium Analysis of Static Reward Function. The *simple proportional model* introduced in [4] has n miners with costs $c_1, c_2, \ldots, c_n$ where $c_1 \leq c_2 \leq \cdots \leq c_n \leq \infty$. A miner i who invests q_i hashrate at a cost of $c_i q_i$ has mining reward and utility given by

$$x_i(q) = \frac{q_i}{\sum_j q_j} \text{ and } U_i(q) = x_i(q) - c_i q_i,$$

respectively. The main result of [4] is that there is a *unique pure strategy equilibrium* where each miner invests

$$q_i = \frac{1}{c^*} \max(1 - c_i/c^*, 0)$$

for the unique value c^* s.t. $X(c^*) = 1$ where

$$X(c) = \sum_i \max(1 - c_i/c, 0).$$

The value c^* thus serves as a bound for which miners participate, with a miner i participating if $c_i < c^*$. They also show that the number of miners must be finite for there to be an equilibrium strategy and that even countably infinite miners would not have an equilibrium strategy.

Properties of Proportional Allocation. In [9], the authors define a set of properties that allocation rules can satisfy: non-negativity, budget-balance (*strong-* means all the reward is allocated, *weak-* means less or all of the reward is allocated), symmetry (two miners with equal hashrate get equal reward), sybil-proofness (can't split hashrate and get more reward) and collusion-proofness (can't join hashrates and get more). They prove that the proportional allocation rule is the only rule that satisfies all of the above properties. They also define a *generalized proportional allocation rule* as

$$x_i(q) = f(\sum_j q_j) \frac{q_i}{\sum_j q_j}$$

for some function f which takes in the sum of hashrate and returns the amount of reward that will be allocated. The static reward function is an example of the generalized proportional allocation rule with $f(\sum_j q_j) = 1$. In HaPPY-Mine, we provide a family of functions for f. These functions follow the generalized proportional allocation rule and, hence, satisfy all of the above properties with a *weak* budget-balance as, by definition, the full reward value is not always rewarded (i.e. $f(\sum_j q_j) \leq 1$).

3   Hashrate-Pegged Block Reward

We now introduce the notion of a *hash-pegged mining reward function*. We consider a miner's decision of how much hashrate to purchase when they are joining the system. In this section, we consider a simplified model where the network currently has hashrate 1 with network operational cost c and mining reward of 1 per block such that mining is profitable, i.e. $c < 1$ and the *system's* utility is $U = 1 - c$. Given the network hashrate $H = \sum_j q_j$, we consider block reward

$$r(H) = \left(\frac{1}{H}\right)^\delta$$

for a given parameter $\delta \geq 0$ such that any additional hashrate added to the system decreases the block reward[1].

The focus of this section is on answering the following question: Given a new miner with cost c_i, how much hashrate is this new miner incentivized to buy? That is, what q_i maximizes their utility

$$U_i(q) = \frac{q_i}{1 + q_i} r(1 + q_i) - c_i q_i?$$

---

[1] Note that our $r(H)$ function is replacing [9]'s c function. We change notation so as not to confuse the reward with the cost of hashrate.

Case: $\delta = 0$, Static Reward. First consider the fixed reward system where the reward is always 1. A new miner joining the system with hashrate q_i will have utility $U_i(q) = \frac{q_i}{q_i+1} - c_i q_i$ which they want to maximize. By solving for $U_i'(q) = 0$ with $q_i > 0$ and $c_i < 1$, we find that the miner maximizes their utility by buying hashrate $q_i = \sqrt{\frac{1}{c_i}} - 1$.

Case: $\delta = 1$, Linear Decrease in Reward. With $r(H) = \frac{1}{H}$, a miner now wants to maximize $U_i(q) = \frac{q_i}{(q_i+1)^2} - c_i q_i$. We can't easily solve for $U_i'(q) = \frac{1}{(q_i+1)^2} - \frac{2q_i}{(q_i+1)^3} - c_i = 0$. What we can observe is that $U_i''(q) = \frac{6q_i}{(q_i+1)^4} - \frac{4}{(q_i+1)^3}$ and that $U_i''(q) < 0$ for $q_i < 2$, i.e. $U_i(q)$ is concave down when a miner buys less than double the current hashrate of the system. Since $U_i'(q_i = \sqrt{\frac{1}{c_i}} - 1) = 2c_i(\sqrt{c_i} - 1) < 0$ for $c_i < 1$, we obtain that for a miner that's acquiring less than twice the current system hashrate, *the hashrate bought by the miner under a linearly diminishing reward ($\delta = 1$) is less than that bought under a static reward ($\delta = 0$).* (For a miner buying more than twice the hashrate ($q_i \geq 2$), c_i would have to be sufficiently small for this to be profitable i.e. $c_i < \frac{1}{(1+q_i)^2} < \frac{1}{9}$.)

General δ. We now analyze the impact of a more drastic decay function (larger δ) on the optimal hashrate bought by a new miner joining the system. When a new miner joins with additional hashrate q_i, the mining reward becomes $(\frac{1}{q_i+1})^{\delta}$, where $0 \leq \delta < \infty$. The utility function is now $U_i(q) = \frac{q_i}{q_i+1}(\frac{1}{q_i+1})^{\delta} - c_i q_i = \frac{q_i}{(q_i+1)^{\delta+1}} - c_i q_i$.

Proposition 1. *The optimal hashrate for a new miner decreases with increasing δ.*

Our proof proceeds in two steps. We show that (1) the utility is a concave function at the maxima and (2) the derivative of the utility w.r.t. q_i is decreasing in δ. We then obtain that the utility maximum (i.e. the q_i s.t. $U_i'(q) = 0$) is decreasing with an increase in δ. Due to space constraints, we defer the proof to the full version of this paper [14].

Thus, if we increase the δ exponent in the total block reward, we decrease the hashrate that a new miner is incentivized to buy. While this may not have an effect for smaller miners who do not have the resources to purchase their maximal utility hashrate, Proposition 1 demonstrates that a hash-pegged reward function can be a useful decentralization tool that disincentivizes rational big miners from joining the system with a large fraction of the hashrate.

Note that Proposition 1 does not take into account the dynamic game between different miner's choices. We now formally define the above family of hash-pegged mining reward functions for arbitrary system hashrate as HaPPY-Mine and analyze the equilibria given a set of miners with asymmetric costs.

4   HaPPY-Mine Equilibrium Analysis

Building on the model of [4] we define a non-cooperative game between m miners with cost $c_1 \leq c_2 \leq \cdots \leq c_m$ where each miner i with hashrate q_i has utility

$$U_i(q) = x_i(q) - c_i q_i.$$

In HaPPY-Mine we set the maximal block reward to be 1 and have the reward start to decrease after the system's hashrate surpasses Q, for a parameter $Q > 0$. We define the reward for miner i as

$$x_i(q) = \frac{q_i}{\sum_j q_j} r(q) \quad \text{where} \quad r(q) = \min\left(1, \left(\frac{Q}{\sum_j q_j}\right)^\delta\right)$$

for system parameter $\delta \in [0, \infty)$.

The main results of this section concern the existence and properties of pure Nash equilibria for the above HaPPY-Mine game. We begin our analysis by differentiating $r(q)$ and $x_i(q)$ with respect to q_i, and finding the derivative of $U_i(q)$ w.r.t. q_i.

$$U_i'(q) = \begin{cases} \frac{\sum_j q_j - q_i}{(\sum_j q_j)^2} - c_i & \text{if } \sum_j q_j < Q \\ \frac{Q^\delta}{(\sum_j q_j)^{\delta+2}}[\sum_j q_j - (\delta+1)q_i] - c_i & \text{if } \sum_j q_j > Q \end{cases}$$

Recall that for equilibria we need that $U_i'(q) \leq 0$ with equality for $q_i > 0$. (For the case $\sum_j q_j = Q$, we need the left and right derivatives to be nonnegative and nonpositive, respectively.)

4.1   Examples with Diverse Cost Scenarios

We work through some cost examples to gain intuition for the equilibrium analysis of the above reward function.

Example 1. First we consider a general 2-miner case with δ and Q set to 1. In this model we have 2 miners with costs c_1, c_2 s.t. $c_1 \leq c_2$. See the full version of this paper [14] for the full analysis. If $c_1 + c_2 > 1$ we use the analysis of [4] with reward 1 and obtain that the equilibrium hashrate is $q_1 + q_2 < Q = 1$ with $q_i = \frac{1}{c_1+c_2}(1 - \frac{c_i}{c_1+c_2})$. If $c_1 + c_2 \leq 1$, then there are multiple equilibria where $\alpha + \beta = 1$ with $\frac{1-c_1}{2} \leq \alpha \leq 1 - c_1$ and $\frac{1-c_2}{2} \leq \beta \leq 1 - c_2$. Note the equilibria system hashrate with two miners is always $\leq Q = 1$.

Taking $c_1 + c_2 \leq 1$, let us consider the total utility of an equilibrium.

$$\max_{\alpha,\beta}(U_1 + U_2) = \max_{\alpha,\beta}(1 - c_1\alpha - c_2\beta) = \max_\alpha(1 - c_2 + (c_2 - c_1)\alpha)$$

Thus, a utilitarian equilibrium is one where α is maximized, i.e. $\alpha = 1 - c_1$. The utilitarian equilibrium is thus the one with maximal utility for the miner with least cost and lowest utility for the miner with most cost.

Example 2. $c_i = \frac{i}{i+1}$ We now consider an example from [4] where the cost function $c_i = \frac{i}{i+1}$, still considering $\delta = Q = 1$. This case is interesting because in the static reward case (i.e. $U_i(q) = \frac{q_i}{\sum_i q_i} - q_i c_i$) the equilibrium strategy has that $\sum_i q_i > 1$ and that only the first 7 miners participate. This equilibrium point would have less reward in HaPPY-Mine and thus may no longer be the equilibrium point. We solve this in the full version of this paper [14] and find that

$$q_i = \frac{1}{2}\sqrt{\frac{n-2}{\sum_{j=1}^n \frac{j}{j+1}}}\left(1 - \frac{(n-2)i}{\sum_{j=1}^n \frac{j}{j+1}(i+1)}\right)$$

for all miners that participate in equilibrium. We can iterate over n to find that with this strategy, equilibrium exists at $n = 25$, i.e. for $n > 25$ only the first 25 miners participate otherwise all miners participate. Thus HaPPY-Mine with $\delta = 1$ results in an equilibrium with *more miners participating* than in the equilibrium under a static reward function.

Example 3. $c_i = c$ **for All** i. The next example we consider is the case of homogeneous cost with m miners, $Q = 1$ and any δ. See the full version of this paper [14] for the full analysis. For $c > \frac{m-1}{m}$, we can use the analysis of [4] and obtain $q_i = \frac{m-1}{m^2 c}$ with $\sum_i q_i = \frac{m-1}{mc} < 1$. For $\frac{m-\delta-1}{m} \leq c \leq \frac{m-1}{m}$, an equilibrium exists at $\sum_i q_i = 1$ where $q_i = \frac{1}{m}$. Finally for $c < \frac{m-\delta-1}{m}$ we get an equilibrium strategy with $\sum_i q_i > 1$ where $q_i = \frac{1}{m}\sqrt[\delta+1]{\frac{m-\delta-1}{cm}}$. In each case the equilibrium hashrate for HaPPY-Mine for any δ is less than or equal to that of the static reward equilibria. In Corollary 2 below, we show this in fact holds for any set of costs.

4.2   General Analysis of HaPPY-Mine

We now analyze the equilibria for the general case of HaPPY-Mine with $m > \delta + 1$ miners with costs $c_1 \leq c_2 \leq \ldots \leq c_m < c_{m+1} = \infty$. Recall the utility function

$$U_i(q) = \begin{cases} \frac{q_i}{\sum_j q_j} - q_i c_i & \text{if } \sum_j q_j \leq Q \\ \frac{q_i}{\sum_j q_j}\left(\frac{Q}{\sum_j q_j}\right)^\delta - q_i c_i & \text{o/w} \end{cases}$$

In the propositions below we first derive necessary conditions for an equilibrium to exist in different cases depending on how the system hashrate $\sum_i q_i$ compares with Q. Taking these propositions we derive lemmas proving the existence of equilibria given any set of miner costs. The lemmas also prove the impossibility of equilibria to exist simultaneously for different values of $\sum_i q_i$, i.e. the uniqueness of the equilibria. We finish this section with our final theorem statement defining the equilibria values given a set of costs, as well as corollaries on the properties of the equilibria.

Proposition 2 (Necessary condition for equilibrium with total hashrate less than Q, [4]). *If $\sum_i q_i < Q$ at equilibrium then there exists a $c^* > 1/Q$ such that $X(c^*) = 1$ and all miners i with $c_i < c^*$ participate with $q_i = \frac{1}{c^*}(1 - c_i/c^*)$.*

Proof. If $\sum_i q_i < Q$ then miners have utility function $U_i(q) = \frac{q_i}{\sum_j q_j} - q_i c_i$ which is the same as the simple proportional model of [4] where there is an equilibrium strategy with $q_i = \frac{1}{c^*} \max(1 - c_i/c^*, 0)$ for c^* such that $X(c^*) = 1$. In this analysis $\sum_j q_j = \frac{1}{c^*}$, and so for $\sum_j q_j < Q$ we have $c^* > 1/Q$. $\quad\square$

Proposition 3 (Necessary condition for equilibrium with total hashrate equal to Q). *If $\sum_i q_i = Q$ at equilibrium then all miners with cost $c_i < 1/Q$ participate and satisfy*

$$\frac{1}{\delta + 1}(Q - c_i Q^2) \le q_i \le Q - c_i Q^2$$

Proof. Assume there is an equilibrium strategy such that $\sum_i q_i = Q$. The utility of a miner i is given by

$$U_i(q) = q_i(\frac{1}{Q} - c_i) \le 0$$

so miners with cost $c_i > 1/Q$ will not participate; those with $c_i < 1/Q$ will.

We take the n miners for which $c_i \le 1/Q$. $\sum_i q_i = Q$ is an equilibrium *iff*,

$$U_i'(q) = \begin{cases} \frac{1}{Q^2}[Q - q_i] - c_i \ge 0 & \text{for } \sum_j q_j < Q \\ \frac{Q^\delta}{Q^{\delta+2}}[Q - (\delta + 1)q_i] - c_i \le 0 & \text{for } \sum_j q_j > Q \end{cases}$$

and thus, any equilibrium strategy satisfies

$$\frac{1}{\delta + 1}(Q - c_i Q^2) \le q_i \le Q - c_i Q^2$$

Note that $c_i = 1/Q$ implies $q_i = 0$, so a miner with cost $1/Q$ does not participate. Thus, exactly those miners with $c_i < 1/Q$ participate in an equilibrium. $\quad\square$

Proposition 4 (Necessary condition for equilibrium with total hashrate more than Q). *If $\sum_i q_i > Q$ at equilibrium then there exists a $c^\dagger < 1/Q$ such that $X(c^\dagger) = \delta + 1$ and all miners with cost $c_i < c^\dagger$ participate with*

$$q_i = \frac{\sqrt[\delta+1]{Q^\delta}}{(\delta + 1)\sqrt[\delta+1]{c^\dagger}}(1 - c_i/c^\dagger)$$

Proof. Assume first there exists an equilibrium where miner $i + 1$ participates and miner i does not with sum of hashrate H. This means

$$U_{i+1}'(q) = \frac{Q^\delta}{H^{\delta+2}}[H - (\delta + 1)q_{i+1}] - c_{i+1} = 0,$$

and thus $c_{i+1} = \frac{Q^\delta}{H^{\delta+2}}[H - (\delta + 1)q_{i+1}]$. For $q_i = 0$ we get $U_i'(q) = \frac{Q^\delta}{H^{\delta+1}} - c_i \le 0$ which means $\frac{Q^\delta}{H^{\delta+1}} \le c_i$, putting both together we get

$$\frac{Q^\delta}{H^{\delta+1}} \le c_i \le c_{i+1} = \frac{Q^\delta}{H^{\delta+2}}[H - (\delta + 1)q_{i+1}],$$

which implies $q_{i+1} \leq 0$, a contradiction to miner $i+1$ participating. Thus in any equilibrium, if miner $i+1$ participates, then miner i must also participate.

Letting $H = \sum_i q_i > Q$, for a miner i that participates in equilibrium

$$U_i'(q) = \frac{Q^\delta}{H^{\delta+2}}[H - (\delta+1)q_i] - c_i = 0 \implies q_i = \frac{H}{\delta+1}\left(1 - \frac{H^{\delta+1}}{Q^\delta}c_i\right).$$

Assuming that only the first n miners participate in equilibrium, we solve for H

$$H = \sum_{i=1}^n q_i = \sum_{i=1}^n \frac{H}{\delta+1}\left(1 - \frac{H^{\delta+1}}{Q^\delta}c_i\right) = \sqrt[\delta+1]{\frac{Q^\delta(n-\delta-1)}{\sum_{i=1}^n c_i}}.$$

This also means player $n+1$ must have $U_{n+1}'(q) \leq 0$ at $q_{n+1} = 0$, so we get

$$U_{n+1}'(q) = \frac{Q^\delta}{H^{\delta+1}}[H - (\delta+1)q_{n+1}] - c_{n+1} = \frac{Q^\delta}{H^{\delta+1}} - c_{n+1} \leq 0,$$

$$\implies \frac{Q^\delta}{H^{\delta+1}} = \frac{\sum_{i=1}^n c_i}{n-\delta-1} \leq c_{n+1}.$$

Let $c^\dagger$ be the bound for which miners participate, i.e. miner i participates iff $c_i < c^\dagger$. Then from the above we get that $c^\dagger = \frac{\sum_{i=1}^n c_i}{n-\delta-1}$. Rewriting this and using the fact that $c_i/c^* \geq 1$ for $c_i \geq c^\dagger$, we obtain

$$\sum_i \max(1 - c_i/c^\dagger, 0) = \delta+1,$$

co-opting the $X(c)$ equation for $c^\dagger$ s.t. $X(c^\dagger) = \delta+1$. Since $c^\dagger = \frac{Q^\delta}{H^{\delta+1}}$ it must be that $c^\dagger < 1/Q$. Lastly we plug $c^\dagger$ into the equation for q_i and get

$$q_i = \frac{\sqrt[\delta+1]{Q^\delta}}{(\delta+1)\sqrt[\delta+1]{c^\dagger}}(1 - c_i/c^\dagger). \qquad \square$$

We now use Propositions 2, 3, and 4 to establish the following lemmas, which will help prove our main theorem. We first define c^* as the value for which $X(c^*) = 1$ and, for $m > \delta+1$, $c^\dagger$ as the value for which $X(c^\dagger) = \delta+1$. Note that $X(c)$ is a continuous increasing function in c and thus $c^* < c^\dagger$.

Lemma 1 (Equilibrium when $c^* > 1/Q$). *If $c^* > 1/Q$, then there exists a unique equilibrium strategy with $\sum_i q_i < Q$*

Proof. We know from Proposition 2 that there is an equilibrium strategy with $\sum_i q_i = \frac{1}{c^*} < Q$. Since $c^* > 1/Q$ that implies $c^\dagger > 1/Q$ so by Proposition 4 there is not an equilibrium strategy with $\sum_i q_i > Q$. Finally, lets assume there is an equilibrium strategy with $\sum_i q_i = Q$. Recall from Proposition 3 that all miners with cost $< 1/Q$ participate, so let n be those miners s.t. $c_i < 1/Q$ for $i \leq n$. From the definition of $X(c)$ we have that $\sum_{i=1}^n 1 - c_i/c^* \leq 1$ which we can solve to be $c^*(n-1) \leq \sum_{i=1}^n c_i$ and we get $\frac{n-1}{Q} < \sum_{i=1}^n c_i$. From Proposition 3 we have that $q_i \leq Q - c_i Q^2$ for all $i \leq n$. Thus $\sum_{i=1}^n q_i \leq \sum_{i=1}^n Q - c_i Q^2$ which solves to $\sum_{i=1}^n c_i \leq \frac{n-1}{Q}$, and thus there is no equilibrium at $\sum_i q_i = Q$. $\square$

Lemma 2 (Equilibrium when $c^* \leq 1/Q \leq c^{\dagger}$). *If $c^* \leq 1/Q \leq c^{\dagger}$ then there exists at least one equilibrium at $\sum_i q_i = Q$ and any equilibrium strategy has $\sum_i q_i = Q$ with a miner i participating iff $c_i < 1/Q$.*

Proof. First, since $c^* \leq 1/Q$ we know from Proposition 2 there is no equilibrium at $\sum_i q_i < Q$, and since $c^{\dagger} \geq 1/Q$ we know from Proposition 4 there is no equilibrium at $\sum_i q_i > Q$. Finally from Proposition 3, for there to be an equilibrium at $\sum_i q_i = Q$ we need for each miner i with $c_i < 1/Q$, q_i must satisfy

$$\frac{1}{\delta+1}(Q - c_i Q^2) \leq q_i \leq Q - c_i Q^2.$$

Summing over all n s.t. $c_i < 1/Q$ for $i \leq n$, and simplifying, we derive

$$\frac{n-\delta-1}{Q} \leq \sum_{i=1}^{n} c_i \leq \frac{n-1}{Q}$$

Taking the fact that $c^* \leq 1/Q$ we get $\sum_{i=1}^{n} 1 - c_i/c^* \geq 1$ which simplifies to $c^*(n-1) \geq \sum_{i=1}^{n} c_i$. Taking the fact that $c^{\dagger} \geq 1/Q$ we get $\sum_{i=1}^{n} 1 - c_i/c^{\dagger} \leq \delta+1$ which simplifies to $c^{\dagger}(n - \delta - 1) \leq \sum_{i=1}^{n} c_i$. Putting these together, we obtain

$$\frac{n-1}{Q} \geq \sum_{i=1}^{n} c_i \geq \frac{n-\delta-1}{Q} \qquad \qquad \square$$

Lemma 3 (Equilibrium when $c^{\dagger} < 1/Q$). *If $c^{\dagger} < 1/Q$ then there exists a unique equilibrium strategy with $\sum_i q_i > Q$.*

Proof. We know from Proposition 4 that there is a unique equilibrium strategy with $\sum_i q_i = \sqrt[\delta+1]{\frac{Q^{\delta}}{c^{\dagger}}} > Q$. Since $c^* < c^{\dagger}$ we know from Proposition 2 there is not an equilibrium strategy with $\sum_i q_i < Q$. Take the n miners s.t $c_i < c^{\dagger}$ for $i \leq n$. From the definition of $X(c)$ we have

$$\sum_{i=1}^{n} 1 - c_i/c^{\dagger} = \delta + 1 \implies \sum_{i=1}^{n} c_i = c^{\dagger}(n - \delta - 1) < \frac{n-\delta-1}{Q}.$$

Assume there is an equilibrium with $\sum_i q_i = Q$. By Proposition 3, miner i s.t. $c_i < 1/Q$ participates with $\frac{1}{\delta+1}(Q - c_i Q^2) \leq q_i$. If there are n miners s.t. $c_i < c^{\dagger}$,

$$\sum_{i=1}^{n} \frac{1}{\delta+1}(Q - c_i Q^2) \leq \sum_{i=1}^{n} q_i \leq Q \implies \frac{n-\delta-1}{Q} \leq \sum_{i=1}^{n} c_i$$

which is a contradiction. Thus, there is no equilibrium with $\sum_i q_i = Q$. $\qquad \square$

We can now put together the above lemmas to get our main result:

Theorem 1. *For any $\delta \in [0, \infty)$ and $m \geq 2$ miners with costs $c_1 \leq c_2 \leq ... \leq c_m < c_{m+1} = \infty$, let*

$$X(c) = \sum_i \max(1 - c_i/c, 0)$$

and c^* s.t $X(c^*) = 1$ and (if $m > \delta + 1$) let $c^\dagger$ s.t. $X(c^\dagger) = \delta + 1$. HaPPY-Mine with $Q > 0$ has equilibria as follows with system hashrate $\sum_i q_i = H$:

(a) *if $c^* > 1/Q$, there is a unique equilibrium with $H = \frac{1}{c^*} < Q$ with*

$$q_i = \max(\frac{1}{c^*}(1 - c_i/c^*), 0)$$

(b) *if $c^* \leq 1/Q \leq c^\dagger$ or $c^* \leq 1/Q$ and $m \leq \delta + 1$, there exists an equilibrium and every equilibrium satisfies $H = Q$, with $q_i = 0$ for $c_i \geq 1/Q$, and otherwise*

$$\frac{1}{\delta + 1}(Q - c_i Q^2) \leq q_i \leq Q - c_i Q^2$$

(c) *if $c^\dagger < 1/Q$, $m > \delta + 1$, there is a unique equilibrium with $H = \sqrt[\delta+1]{\frac{Q^\delta}{c^\dagger}} > Q$,*

$$q_i = \max(\frac{\sqrt[\delta+1]{Q^\delta}}{(\delta + 1)\sqrt[\delta+1]{c^\dagger}}(1 - c_i/c^\dagger), 0)$$

Proof. The case $c^* > 1/Q$ follows directly from Lemma 1. Next we consider $c^* \leq 1/Q$ and $m \leq \delta + 1$. Since $c^* \leq 1/Q$ we know from Proposition 2 there is no equilibrium at $\sum_i q_i < Q$. For equilibria with $\sum_i q_i = H > Q$ we need that $U_i'(q) = 0$ for all miners who participate which gives us that $q_i = \frac{H}{\delta+1}[1 - c_i \frac{H^{\delta+1}}{Q^\delta}]$. Assuming only the first n miners participate, we get $H = \sum_i^n q_i = \sum_i^n \frac{H}{\delta+1}[1 - c_i \frac{H^{\delta+1}}{Q^\delta}]$. We can simplify this to be $\frac{H^{\delta+1}}{Q^\delta} \sum_i^n c_i = n - \delta - 1 < 0$ which is not satisfiable. The only option for equilibria is then for $\sum_i q_i = Q$ which we get from Proposition 3 iff $\frac{1}{\delta+1}[Q - Q^2 c_i] \leq q_i \leq Q - Q^2 c_i$ for all miners with $c_i < 1/Q$. Summing over all miners $i \leq n$ s.t $c_i < 1/Q$ we get $\frac{n-\delta-1}{Q} \leq \sum_i^n c_i \leq \frac{n-1}{Q}$ must be satisfied. Notice that the left-most expression is negative so the left expression is satisfied. We know $c^* \leq 1/Q$ thus $X(1/Q) = \sum_i^n 1 - c_i Q \geq 1$ which simplifies to $\sum_i^n c_i \leq \frac{n-1}{Q}$. Finally for $m > \delta + 1$, the case for $c^* \leq 1/Q \leq c^\dagger$ follows from Lemma 2 and the case for $c^\dagger < 1/Q$ follows from Lemma 3. □

In the following two corollaries we examine how the equilibria of HaPPY-Mine changes with the parameter δ in terms of miner participation and the system hashrate. In particular we show that any HaPPY-Mine equilibria has at least as many miners participating (with at most the same system hashrate) as in the static reward function equilibria.

Corollary 1. *For any m miners with costs $c_1 \leq c_2 \leq ... \leq c_m$, HaPPY-Mine with any Q, δ has equilibria with at least as many miners participating as the static reward function. Furthermore, the number of miners participating in equilibria for HaPPY-Mine monotonically increases in δ.*

Proof. By the analysis of [4] under the simple proportional model, the static reward function has a unique equilibrium with all miners whose cost $c_i < c^*$ participating s.t $X(c^*) = 1$. HaPPY-Mine has at least all the same miners participating in 3 scenarios: $c_i < c^*$ for $c^* > 1/Q$, $c_i < 1/Q$ for $c^* \leq 1/Q$ and $m \leq \delta + 1$ or $1/Q \leq c^\dagger$ and $c_i < c^\dagger$ for $c^\dagger < 1/Q$ where $c^* < c^\dagger$, i.e. in all four cases, all miners with $c_i < c^*$ are participating and possibly additional miners.

For the general statement, take any δ-HaPPY-Mine equilibrium. If $c^* > 1/Q$, regardless of how you change δ, c^* remains fixed so by Lemma 1, the equilibrium remain the same with the same miners. Suppose instead $c^* \leq 1/Q \leq c^\dagger$, as δ increases $c^\dagger$ increases. Thus for a larger δ, the equilibrium remains at $\sum_i q_i = Q$ with the same miners of cost $c_i < 1/Q$ participating. If $c^\dagger < 1/Q$, then since $c^\dagger$ acts as an upper-bound for which miners participate, as δ increases, this upper bound increases. This upper bound caps at $1/Q$; then we switch to the second equilibrium case where all miners with $c_i < 1/Q$ participate. □

Corollary 2. *HaPPY-Mine has equilibria with hashrate at most that of the static reward function. Furthermore, HaPPY-Mine equilibria hashrate is monotonically non-increasing with an increase in δ.*

Proof. We prove the second part of the statement and note that the static reward function is HaPPY-Mine with $\delta = 0$, so the first statement follows. Given a set of costs, we consider the possible values of c^* and $c^\dagger$. (a) If $c^* > 1/Q$, then for any δ, H is always $1/c^*$. (b) If $c^* \leq 1/Q \leq c^\dagger$ for some δ, then the equilibria hashrate for that δ is $H = Q$. As δ increases, the value of $c^\dagger$ increases so the equilibrium hashrate will continue to be Q for any $\delta' > \delta$. (c) If $c^\dagger < 1/Q$ for some δ, we that $H > Q$ and we have two cases to consider for $\delta' > \delta$. Since $c^\dagger$ increases as δ increases, either it increases s.t. $c^\dagger_{new}$ becomes $\geq 1/Q$ or $m < \delta' + 1$, in either case the new equilibrium hashrate would be $H' = Q < H$. The last case is that $c^\dagger < c^\dagger_{new} < 1/Q$ and $m \geq \delta' + 1$. In this case we first assume $H < H'$, i.e.

$$
\begin{aligned}
H &= \frac{Q^{\delta/(\delta+1)}}{(c^\dagger)^{1/(\delta+1)}} \\
&= \frac{Q^{\delta'/(\delta'+1)}Q^{\delta/(\delta+1)-\delta'/(\delta'+1)}}{(c^\dagger)^{1/(\delta+1)}} \\
&\geq \frac{Q^{\delta'/(\delta'+1)}Q^{\delta/(\delta+1)-\delta'/(\delta'+1)}}{(c^\dagger_{new})^{1/(\delta+1)}} && (c^\dagger < c^\dagger_{new}) \\
&= \frac{Q^{\delta'/(\delta'+1)}}{(c^\dagger_{new})^{1/(\delta'+1)}} \frac{Q^{\delta/(\delta+1)-\delta'/(\delta'+1)}}{(c^\dagger_{new})^{1/(\delta+1)-1/(\delta'+1)}} \\
&= H' \frac{Q^{(\delta-\delta')/(\delta+1)(\delta'+1)}}{(c^\dagger_{new})^{(\delta'-\delta)/(\delta+1)(\delta'+1)}} \\
&= H' \left(\frac{1}{c^\dagger_{new}Q}\right)^{(\delta'-\delta)/(\delta+1)(\delta'+1)} \\
&\geq H' && (c^\dagger_{new}Q < 1 \text{ and } \delta' > \delta)
\end{aligned}
$$

□

The previous corollaries together say that as δ increases, the number of miners who participate in equilibrium increases with the total hashrate of the system at equilibrium decreasing. We now explore what the impact of this is on the market share of miners. In particular we want to check that the new equilibrium does not disproportionately advantage lower cost miners. Unfortunately we can't make such a strong statement, owing to the presence of multiple equilibria when the sum of hashrates equals Q. Instead, we get the following corollary which states that for *most cases*, a miner's relative market share to any higher-cost miner does not go up. Formally, given two miners i, j with costs $c_i < c_j$ and δ s.t. $q_i, q_j > 0$ at equilibrium (i.e. both miners participate at equilibrium), we define the *relative market share* $r_{ij}(\delta)$ as follows. If $\sum_i q_i \neq Q$, then there is a unique equilibrium, so we define $r_{ij}(\delta)$ to be q_i/q_j. Otherwise, there may be multiple equilibria and we define $r_{ij}(\delta)$ to be the ratio of the maximum value of q_i to the maximum value of q_j in equilibrium (defining it to be the ratio of the minimum values yields the same ratio).

Corollary 3. *For any two miners i, j with costs $c_i < c_j$, parameters δ, δ' such that both miners participate in equilibrium at parameter δ, and $\delta' > \delta$, $r_{ij}(\delta')$ is at least $r_{ij}(\delta)$.*

Proof. Consider a miner who participates at equilibrium with a certain δ. Given a set of costs, we consider the possible values of c^* and $c^\dagger$. (a) If $c^* > 1/Q$, then for any δ, the equilibrium stays the same. (b) for $c^* \leq 1/Q \leq c^\dagger$, any increase in δ does not change this inequality and thus the equilibrium conditions do not change and thus maintain the same equilibria maximum and minimum ratios (i.e. $r_{ij}(\delta) = r_{ij}(\delta')$ for all δ').

The only interesting case is thus (c) $c^\dagger < 1/Q$, as δ increases $c^\dagger$ increases. Given a $\delta' > \delta$, we compare the relative market share of two miners i, j where $c_i < c_j$ as $r_{ij}(\delta') = \frac{c^\dagger_{new} - c_i}{c^\dagger_{new} - c_j}$ which is decreasing with an increase in $c^\dagger_{new}$ (i.e. increasing δ'). Thus, while $c^\dagger_{new} < 1/Q$, a miner's relative market share to any higher cost miner is decreasing.

The only case left to consider is a $\delta' > \delta$ s.t. $c^\dagger_{new} \geq 1/Q$. The new equilibrium hashrate q'_i for miners participating is bounded by $\frac{1}{\delta+1}(Q - c_i Q^2) \leq q'_i \leq Q - c_i Q^2$. If we compare q'_i, q'_j at the bounds we get $r_{ij}(\delta') = \frac{1 - c_i Q}{1 - c_j Q}$ which is less than the old relative market share of $\frac{1 - c_i/c^\dagger}{1 - c_j/c^\dagger}$ since $c^\dagger < 1/Q$. □

5   Impact of Attacks and Currency on Equilibria

Our equilibrium analysis in Sect. 4 assumes that the number of miners and their costs are known, and that the miner costs and rewards are in the same currency unit. In this section, we analyze certain attacks and events that may impact equilibria. We begin with the question: if miners are able to collude (two miners pretend to be a single miner) or duplicate themselves (a single miner pretends to be multiple miners), can they increase their own utility? In other words, are HaPPY-Mine equilibria resistant to miner collusion and sybil strategies? We show that HaPPY-Mine equilibria are resistant to collusion and Sybil attacks. We also study the effect of variable coin market value when reward is given in the coin of the blockchain. Due to space constraints, we state the main results for collusion resistance and the effect of variable coin market value, and refer the reader to the full version of this paper [14] for Sybil resistance and the missing proofs in this section.

Collusion Resistance. We consider the case of m homogeneous miners.

Lemma 4. *Suppose m miners with uniform costs participate in HaPPY-Mine with parameters δ, Q. If $k \leq m/2$ of the miners collude and act as one miner (so the game now has $m - k + 1$ miners), with each colluding miner receiving $1/k$ of the colluding utility, the utility achieved in an equilibrium with collusion is at most that achieved without collusion, assuming m is sufficiently large.*

In the heterogeneous cost model, it is unclear what collusion would mean for two miners with different costs, but one could imagine models where there are some miners with the same cost and they choose to collude. We leave this further analysis for future work. The general intuition we get from Lemma 4 is that with fewer miners, the equilibrium hashrate decreases thus the reward may increase as the cost decreases. So for the miners who don't collude, the equilibrium utility increases. But for miners who collude, they must then share the increased utility with all colluders, and it is unclear if the increase is enough to make up for splitting the utility into k parts.

Variable Coin Market Value. In Sect. 4, we view the miner cost and reward in terms of the same currency unit. In reality, the reward is given in the coin of the blockchain being mined while cost is a real-world expense generally paid in the currency of the country where the mining is taking place. To bridge this gap we must understand how to convert real-world change in the price of the cryptocurrency to the relationship between the reward and the cost to miners.

Consider the equilibrium analysis to be saying that a hashrate of 1 for miner i costs c_i unit of cost (say dollars) and that one coin of the reward has 1 unit of worth (i.e. \$1). Now, say the value of the currency changes by R, so one unit of currency is now worth \$$R$. We are now interested in understanding what happens to the equilibrium of the system, i.e. which miners would now participate at equilibrium and with what hashrate?

Lemma 5. *In the static-reward model, an increase in the value of the cryptocurrency by a factor of R results in a new equilibrium strategy where the same miners participate with Rq_i hashrate where q_i is the previous equilibrium hashrate. The new system hashrate thus increases by a factor of R.*

Lemma 6. *In HaPPY-Mine, an increase in the value of the cryptocurrency by a factor of R results in the participation cost threshold to increase (allowing higher cost miners to participate), and the system hashrate to increase by a factor of R until it reaches Q, then increase by a factor of $\sqrt[\delta+1]{R}$.*

6 Discussion

In this paper we've presented a novel family of mining reward functions which adjust to the hashrate of the system. Our functions fall in the class of *generalized proportional allocation rules* of [9] and thus inherit the properties of non-negativity, weak budget-balance, symmetry, sybil-proofness and collusion-proofness. These properties are defined based solely on the expectation of the reward of a miner and not under any equilibrium. In this work we've shown that for all $Q > 0$ and $\delta \geq 0$ HaPPY-Mine has an equilibrium at a unique hashrate and set of miners, and if that hashrate is equal to Q there may be multiple equilibria at Q. We further show that the equilibrium includes at least as many miners as the static-reward function and is at a hashrate at most that for the static-reward function. We also discuss collusion and sybil-proofness in equilibrium and that as the market value of the coin increases, the equilibrium shifts to include more miners at an increased hashrate that is sub-linear in the value of the coin after the system hashrate surpasses Q (unlike the static-reward function whose equilibrium hashrate increases linearly indefinitely).

We show that by relaxing the budget-balance property from [9], we are able to improve upon fairness properties of a mining reward function. A question for future work is whether we can generalize this into an axiomatic framework for mining reward *fairness* and if there exists other functions in the generalized proportional allocation family that can improve upon our fairness results.

Long-Term Dynamics. As our analysis focuses on equilibria, a natural question to ask is whether we introduce any unfavorable long-term dynamics by pegging our reward to the system hashrate. One such concern is on the control of supply of the system. Two current versions of coin issuance are the Bitcoin and Ethereum models. In Bitcoin the reward per block halves every 210K blocks (approximately every 4 years until it is 0), so that half the total supply ever was mined in the first 4 years. In Ethereum the block reward is set at 5 Ethers so that the total supply will never be capped. Our proposed model is novel in that assuming a steady increase in hashrate, the issuance will decrease smoothly over time. The rate of decrease, δ, is a parameter set by the system designer.

In the start of any new cryptocurrency the coins have no value, thus the miners that initially mine are speculating that the coins will have value in the future making up for the cost. During this time the hashrate is generally low so the existing miners do not incur much cost. When the currency does have more value, it appears older coins were mined for "cheap". One could argue that those early miners mine speculatively, and for systems whose coin reward goes down over time, early miners may also control a large portion of the supply. The steeper the decline in the reward, the larger fraction of supply early miners control. As an example, it is estimated that the creator of Bitcoin, Satoshi Nakamoto, and assumed first miner, holds approximately 1 million Bitcoins[2], about 5% of the total supply ever, probably mined at a cost of only a few dollars [13,18].

---

[2] Currently valued at 10 billion Dollars but which have never been spent and are assumed to stay out of circulation.

As a currency grows in value, new miners are incentivized to start mining in the system until the cost to mine a block becomes close to the value of the reward for that block. Since the total supply of the currency is tied to the hashrate we get the interesting phenomena that as the system gains users (miners) the projected total supply decreases, but inversely, if the system decreases in value and starts to lose miners, HaPPY-Mine works a bit like a fail safe where the reward will increase and hopefully aid in incentivizing the remaining miners to stay, stabilizing the value of the system as opposed to a death spiral of miners leaving and the reward just losing value. In this paper, we model the utility of the miner as the per-block profit. To understand the long-term dynamics at play, a future analysis of the evolving game should incorporate market share into the utility of the miner and its impact on market centralization.

Setting Q and δ. We show that an increase in δ comes with an increase in good decentralization properties we want, like more miners mining at equilibrium and big miners joining with less hashrate. The more you increase δ however, the more constrained the issuance of the currency becomes, which could lead to centralization in the market control to early adopters. Setting Q and δ is thus a balancing game and involves practical considerations.

The δ exponent in HaPPY-Mine controls how quickly the block reward declines. A low δ would correspond to a gradual decrease in the block reward as the hashrate increases. Q is the threshold from which point the reward starts to decrease. One way to think of Q is as a security lower-bound for the system. When the hashrate reaches Q, any additional hashrate would lower the reward. A system designer should then choose a Q based on the mining hardware of the system (e.g. ASICs,GPUs, etc.) and some understanding of likely advancements in its performance and choose Q to be a conservative bound on the cost to amass enough hardware to attack the system (e.g. a 51% attack). Based on this and the issuance rate the system designer is targeting a δ can be set.

Since any change to parameters in blockchain systems generally require a *hardfork* in the code, i.e. a change that breaks consensus between adopters and non-adopters, the Bitcoin model of blockchain software development is to avoid such changes unless absolutely critical. Other, more expressive systems (e.g. Ethereum and Zcash), have relied on hardforks to implement changes and increase functionality on a more regular basis. Though setting Q and δ could be thoughtfully done only once in the inception of a new system, another approach would be to periodically update their values if the system's growth (both miner hashrate and value of the currency) is not within the predicted bounds. One such concern would be if the target hashrate Q underestimated the growth of the system hashrate and thus stagnating the cost to attack the system. It would then be incentive compatible to increase Q as it would incentivize higher hashrates (increase security) while also increasing the reward for the miners. One idea is to set Q based on a long-term expected growth and have periodic updates (on the scale of years) to adjust Q based on miner increase and mining hardware trends.

7 Related Work

In this paper we've provided an equilibrium analysis of HaPPY-Mine, a new family of mining reward functions pegged to the network hashrate. As stated above, HaPPY-Mine is an example of the generalized proportional model of [9]. We compare HaPPY-Mine with the equilibrium of the static reward function of [4] associated with most cryptocurrencies. Other papers have looked at different games involved in mining including the game between participants in mining pools and different reward functions for how the pool rewards are allocated [20]. In [17], the authors present a continuous mean-field game for bitcoin mining which captures how miner wealth and strategies evolve over time. They are able to capture the "rich get richer" effect of initial wealth disparities leading to greater reward imbalances. [12] models the blockchain protocol as a game between users generating transactions with fees and miners collecting those fees and the block reward. They show if there is no block reward, then there is an equilibria of transaction fee and miner hashrate. Higher fees incentivize higher miner hashrate which leads to smaller block times (in between difficulty adjustments). When you introduce a high static block reward, the users may no longer be incentivized to introduce mining fees and there may no longer be an equilibrium.

In contrast, [8] also studies the case where there is no block reward, and analyzes new games in which miners may use transactions left in the mempool (pending transactions) to incentivize other miners to join their fork. Another work exploring the mining game when there is no block reward is that of [21] who introduce *the gap game* to study how miners choose periods of times when not to mine (gaps) as they await more transactions (and their fees). They show that gap strategies are not homogeneous for same cost miners and that the game incentivizes miner coalitions reducing the decentralization of the system.

Previous work on rational attacks in cryptocurrency mining includes [5] who study the security of Bitcoin mining under rational adversaries using the Rational Protocol Design framework of [10] as a rational-cryptographic game. Also, [6] who analyze the Bitcoin mining game as a sequential game with imperfect information, and [19] analyze selfish mining by looking at the minimal fraction of resources required for a profitable attack, tightening the previous lower-bounds and further extending the analysis to show how network delays further lower the computational threshold to attack. In [15], the authors explore the game of Bitcoin mining cost and reward focusing on incentives to participate honestly. They outline the choices different players can make in a blockchain system and their possible consequences, but their analysis does not take into account block withholding attacks. Another work related to the incentives at play in cryptocurrency mining is [7] which looks at the coordination game of Bitcoin miners in choosing which fork to build on when mining. They find the longest chain rule is a Markov Perfect equilibrium strategy in a synchronous network and explore other miner strategies, some that result in persistent forks.

References

1. Here's how much it costs to mine a single bitcoin in your country. https://www.marketwatch.com/story/heres-how-much-it-costs-to-mine-a-single-bitcoin-in-your-country-2018-03-06
2. Pool distribution. https://btc.com/stats/pool?pool_mode=month3
3. Top 25 miners by blocks. https://etherscan.io/stat/miner?blocktype=blocks
4. Arnosti, N., Matthew Weinberg, S.: Bitcoin: a natural oligopoly. In 10th Innovations in Theoretical Computer Science Conference (ITCS 2019). Schloss Dagstuhl-Leibniz-Zentrum fuer Informatik (2018)
5. Badertscher, C., Garay, J., Maurer, U., Tschudi, D., Zikas, V.: But why does it work? A rational protocol design treatment of bitcoin. In: Nielsen, J.B., Rijmen, V. (eds.) EUROCRYPT 2018. LNCS, vol. 10821, pp. 34–65. Springer, Cham (2018). https://doi.org/10.1007/978-3-319-78375-8_2
6. Beccuti, J., Jaag, C., et al.: The bitcoin mining game: on the optimality of honesty in proof-of-work consensus mechanism. Swiss Economics Working Paper 0060 (2017)
7. Biais, B., Bisiere, C., Bouvard, M., Casamatta, C.: The blockchain folk theorem. Rev. Fin. Stud. 32(5), 1662–1715 (2019)
8. Carlsten, M., Kalodner, H., Matthew Weinberg, S., Narayanan, A.: On the instability of bitcoin without the block reward. In: Proceedings of the 2016 ACM SIGSAC Conference on Computer and Communications Security, pp. 154–167 (2016)
9. Chen, X., Papadimitriou, C., Roughgarden, T.: An axiomatic approach to block rewards. In: Proceedings of the 1st ACM Conference on Advances in Financial Technologies, pp. 124–131 (2019)
10. Garay, J., Katz, J., Maurer, U., Tackmann, B., Zikas, V.: Rational protocol design: cryptography against incentive-driven adversaries. In 2013 IEEE 54th Annual Symposium on Foundations of Computer Science, pp. 648–657. IEEE (2013)
11. Gervais, A., Karame, G.O., Capkun, V., Capkun, S.: Is bitcoin a decentralized currency?. IEEE Secur. Privacy 12(3), 54–60 (2014)
12. Iyidogan, E.: An equilibrium model of blockchain-based cryptocurrencies. Available at SSRN 3152803 (2019)
13. Kenton, W.: Satoshi Nakamoto. https://www.investopedia.com/terms/s/satoshi-nakamoto.asp
14. Kiffer, L., Rajaraman, R.: Happy-mine: designing a mining reward function. arXiv e-prints, pages arXiv-2103 (2021)
15. Kroll, J.A., Davey, I.C., Felten, E.W.: The economics of bitcoin mining, or bitcoin in the presence of adversaries. In: Proceedings of WEIS, vol. 2013, p. 11 (2013)
16. Leonardos, N., Leonardos, S., Piliouras, G.: Oceanic games: centralization risks and incentives in blockchain mining. In: Pardalos, P., Kotsireas, I., Guo, Y., Knottenbelt, W. (eds.) Mathematical Research for Blockchain Economy. SPBE, pp. 183–199. Springer, Cham (2020). https://doi.org/10.1007/978-3-030-37110-4_13
17. Li, Z.: A Max Reppèn, and Ronnie Sircar. A mean field games model for cryptocurrency mining. arXiv preprint arXiv:1912.01952 (2019)
18. Redman, J.: Bitcoin's early days: how crypto's past is much different than the present. https://news.bitcoin.com/bitcoins-early-days-how-cryptos-past-is-much-different-than-the-present/
19. Sapirshtein, A., Sompolinsky, Y., Zohar, A.: Optimal selfish mining strategies in bitcoin. In: Grossklags, J., Preneel, B. (eds.) FC 2016. LNCS, vol. 9603, pp. 515–532. Springer, Heidelberg (2017). https://doi.org/10.1007/978-3-662-54970-4_30

20. Schrijvers, O., Bonneau, J., Boneh, D., Roughgarden, T.: Incentive compatibility of bitcoin mining pool reward functions. In: Grossklags, J., Preneel, B. (eds.) FC 2016. LNCS, vol. 9603, pp. 477–498. Springer, Heidelberg (2017). https://doi.org/10.1007/978-3-662-54970-4_28
21. Tsabary, I., Eyal, I.: The gap game. In: Proceedings of the 2018 ACM SIGSAC Conference on Computer and Communications Security, pp. 713–728 (2018)

Selfish Mining Attacks Exacerbated by Elastic Hash Supply

Yoko Shibuya[1(✉)], Go Yamamoto[1], Fuhito Kojima[1], Elaine Shi[2],
Shin'ichiro Matsuo[1,3], and Aron Laszka[4]

[1] NTT Research, San Francisco, USA
yshibuya@stanford.edu
[2] Cornell University, Ithaca, USA
[3] Georgetown University, Washington, D.C., USA
[4] University of Houston, Houston, USA

Abstract. Several attacks have been proposed against Proof-of-Work blockchains, which may increase the attacker's share of mining rewards (e.g., selfish mining, block withholding). A further impact of such attacks, which has not been considered in prior work, is that decreasing the profitability of mining for honest nodes incentivizes them to stop mining or to leave the attacked chain for a more profitable one. The departure of honest nodes exacerbates the attack and may further decrease profitability and incentivize more honest nodes to leave. In this paper, we first present an empirical analysis showing that there is a statistically significant correlation between the profitability of mining and the total hash rate, confirming that miners indeed respond to changing profitability. Second, we present a theoretical analysis showing that selfish mining under such elastic hash supply leads either to the collapse of a chain, i.e., all honest nodes leaving, or to a stable equilibrium depending on the attacker's initial share.

Keywords: Blockchain · Selfish mining · Hash supply · Proof of Work

1 Introduction

When blockchains were first introduced, it was believed that profitable attacks require at least 50% of the total mining power. However, several attacks have been found to go against proof-of-work blockchains, such as selfish mining [2] and block withholding against mining pools [1]. A common goal of many such attacks is, at a high level, to increase the attacker's share of the mining rewards by reducing other miners' effective mining power. Prior work found that such attacks may be profitable even if the attacker's original share of the total mining power is less than 50%. An important limitation of prior work is that they do not

---

The complete version of this paper [6] is available on arXiv: https://arxiv.org/abs/2103.08007.

E. Shi—This work was performed while the author was consulting for NTT Research during summer 2020.

N. Borisov and C. Diaz (Eds.): FC 2021, LNCS 12675, pp. 269–276, 2021.
https://doi.org/10.1007/978-3-662-64331-0_14

consider how honest miners react to changes in profitability when attacks occur. Most models assume that the total hash supply in a chain is *fixed* and does not respond to changes in the profitability of the chain. In practice, however, most miners are profit-oriented and choose which currency to mine (or to not mine at all) based on their profitability.

In this paper, we first document real-world evidence of miner's profit-oriented behavior, using data from three different cryptocurrencies. We found a positive and statistically significant correlation between total hash supply and per-hash mining revenue, i.e., the evidence of *elastic* hash supply with respect to miners' revenue. We then provide a new analysis of selfish mining that takes into account the elasticity of hash supply. In an elegant work by Huberman et al. [4], the authors point out that Bitcoin mining is a free-entry, two-sided market. If there is a profit to be made, more miners will enter, which will then trigger the difficulty adjustment algorithm, making mining more difficult, and thus everyone's expected mining revenue decreases. In the equilibrium state, miners break even, i.e., the revenue that they earn from mining is equal to their cost. Inspired by this principle, we incorporate a free-entry condition in a model of selfish mining, and thus our analysis essentially characterizes the long-term effects of selfish mining on the eco-system in the equilibrium state.

During a selfish mining attack, because a fraction of the honest mining power is being erased, the erased fraction is essentially not gaining rewards. The immediate effect is that the cost of mining to earn each unit of reward becomes proportionally higher for honest miners; and if the honest miners' profitability plunges below zero, they start to leave the system. As honest miners leave, the impact of the attack on the remaining miners is magnified as a higher fraction of their mining power is now erased, which in turn drives more miners away. At the same time, as honest miners leave, the total mining power decreases. Therefore, the mining difficulty drops, and thus mining becomes cheaper—this second effect somewhat counteract the decreased profitability for honest miners that stems from being the victim of selfish mining. When hash power is elastic, what happens in the equilibrium state is driven simultaneously by the above two opposite effects. We show that for a wide range of parameter regimes, the first effect dominates and leads to a "collapse scenario"—specifically, selfish mining drives costs up for honest miners, and *all* honest miners end up leaving the system as a result. In some other parameter regimes, however, because the two effects somewhat counteract each other, the system reaches a new equilibrium after some but not all honest nodes have left. In either scenario, the unfairness of selfish mining is significantly exacerbated by the elasticity of hash power.

The rest of the paper is organized as follows. Section 2 shows our empirical evidence on the elasticity of hash supply, which motivates our model setting. Section 3 describes our theoretical model of selfish mining under elastic hash supply.

2   Empirical Findings

Only few pieces of literature have worked on measuring elasticity of hash supply [5], but our paper distinguishes itself from the prior literature in terms of length and coverage of time-series data. We study the elasticity of hash supply with respect to miners' revenue using data from 3 different currencies (Bitcoin, Ethereum, and Ethereum Classic) from 2015–2020.

Data and Empirical Strategy. We downloaded cryptocurrency data from three sources: Bitcoin data from Quandl, Ethereum data from Etherscan, and Ethereum Classic data from crypto-ethereum-classic public library on BigQuery. We use three variables in our regression analysis: daily price, network difficulty, and total hash rate of each cryptocurrency. Different currencies have different lengths of history, and thus we use data from 2017/1/1 to 2020/7/31 for Ethereum and Ethereum Classic, and from 2015/1/1 to 2020/7/31 for Bitcoin. We computed daily per-hash revenue from coinbase using daily price and network difficulty (and data on cryptocurrency halving). We focus on miner's revenue from coinbase and not from transaction fees because transaction fees have been randomly fluctuating over the recent years in these cryptocurrencies.

Technological advancements in cryptocurrency mining over the past 10 years pose a challenge for regression analysis since they add significant time trends to time-series variables. In order to deal with the trend issue, we apply time-detrending filters that are commonly used in macroeconomics. Time-detrending filters allow us to separate the slow-moving trend component from the shorter-horizon cyclical fluctuations ([3]). We apply three types of time-detrending filters: Hodrick-Prescott (HP), Baxter-King (BK), and Christiano-Fitzgerald (CF) filters.[1] Figure 1 shows the decomposition of the logarithm of the total hash rate in the Bitcoin network over the past three years, using HP filter. The total hash rate of the Bitcoin network has an increasing trend over this time period, and the filter removes out the trend. In the later regression analysis, we use the cycle components of the variables after applying filters. To estimate the elasticity of total hash rate with respect to per-hash revenue, we consider the following regression equation:

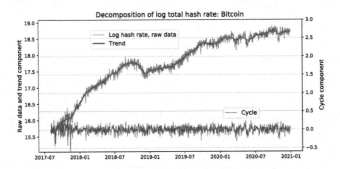

Fig. 1. Application of HP filter to raw hash-rate data from Bitcoin.

---

[1] For HP filter, we use $\lambda = 10,000$. For BK filter we use (7, 90, 12) for high, low frequencies, and lead-lag length, respectively. For CF filter, we use (7, 90) for high and low-frequency length.

$$\Delta \log \text{THR}_{i,t} = \alpha_i \Delta \log \text{MRC}_{i,t} + \epsilon_{i,t}, \qquad (1)$$

where THR stands for total hash rate, MRC stands for miners' per-hash revenue from coinbase. Parameter i is an index representing the cryptocurrency (Bitcoin, Ethereum, or Ethereum Classic), and t is an index for time (day). Variables with Δ are cycle components of the logged variables.[2] We include year-month fixed effect in the regression to take out some year/month fixed events such as regulation changes, which might not be taken out by time-detrending filters.

Results. Table 1 summarizes the results of running the above regression for the three cryptocurrencies. The main result of the regression analysis is that with any type of time-detrending filter, in any time period, and for any currency, the coefficients on $\Delta \log \text{MRC}$ are *positive and statistically significant*. In other words, the total hash rate is elastic with respect to the miners' per-hash revenue from coinbase. The magnitude of the coefficient varies across different time-detrending methods and different currencies, but the elasticity ranges from 0.028 to 0.183. One percentage change in the miners' per-hash revenue from coinbase causes 0.027 to 0.183% change in the total hash rate. Regression with a longer sample period for Bitcoin data gives us a more interesting result. Table 2 summarizes the regression results for Bitcoin data with different sample periods. Interestingly, elasticity is higher and more statistically significantly positive in the recent period (2018–2020) compared to the beginning of the sample period (2015–2017). This shows the possibility that the hash rate becomes more responsive to the miners' revenue as a currency grows.

Table 1. Regression results for three currencies in sample period 2017/1/1–2020/7/31

	Bitcoin			Ethereum			Ethereum classic		
	HP	BK	CF	HP	BK	CF	HP	BK	CF
$\Delta \log \text{MRC}$	0.175***	0.183***	0.181***	0.028***	0.033***	0.079***	0.041***	0.048***	0.027***
	(5.53)	(8.83)	(1.30)	(3.69)	(5.08)	(12.54)	(3.20)	(3.12)	(2.57)
No. of obs	1308	1296	1308	1308	1296	1308	1308	1296	1308

Table 2. Regression results for Bitcoin data with three different sample periods

	2015/1–2017/12			2018/1–2020/7			2015/1–2020/7		
	HP	BK	CF	HP	BK	CF	HP	BK	CF
$\Delta \log \text{MRC}$	0.082*	0.108***	0.078***	0.163***	0.152***	0.194***	0.126***	0.132***	0.143***
	(2.02)	(3.83)	(3.62)	(4.85)	(6.88)	(11.76)	(4.80)	(7.38)	(10.65)
No. of obs.	1096	1084	1096	943	931	943	2039	2015	2039

*** $p < 0.01$, ** $p < 0.05$, * $p < 0.1$, t-values in parentheses.

---

[2] For regressions with Ethereum Classic data, we use daily difference in total hash rate as an independent variable. The reasons for this is that total hash rate of Ethereum Classic is volatile at high frequency, and does not exhibit any time trend.

3   Model with Elastic Hash Supply

We first explain our baseline model without selfish mining and illustrate how total hash rate is determined endogenously in an equilibrium by free-entry condition. We then analyze the model with selfish mining, building on the seminal work by Eyal and Sirer [2]. Lastly, we discuss the stability of equilibria.

In our model of selfish mining with elastic hash supply, the equilibrium state is determined by the two opposing effects. An attack increases the cost of mining for honest miners and thus makes honest miners leave. At the same time, when some honest miners leave, the total mining power decreases and so does the cost of mining for honest miners. [3] Which effect dominates depends on the attacker's initial share of mining power. We derive a threshold for the attacker's initial share such that (a) if the attacker's share is below the threshold, the system has a stable equilibrium with a positive hash supply by honest miners; and (b) if the attacker's share is above the threshold, all honest miners leave and the system collapses. In either case, some or all honest miners leave the system, and thus the effect of selfish mining is significantly exacerbated under elastic hash supply.

Notations. The following notations and basic assumptions are employed:

- B = expected reward for a new block, including both the coinbase and the transaction fee. For example, as of December 2020, B is 6.25 BTC $\approx$ 169,441 USD coinbase plus transaction fees for Bitcoin.
- C = expected cost of mining per unit of hash-rate until some miner finds a new block. This includes electricity costs, depreciation, and other operational costs. We assume that a miner's cost is proportional to its hash rate, and the cost per unit of hash-rate is the same for all miners. For example, C is the cost per unit of hash-rate for 10 min for Bitcoin. On the online marketplace NiceHash (nicehash.com), as of December 2020, the lowest-price offer for 1 PH/s of mining power[4] for 24 h is 0.0069 BTC. From this, we can estimate C as 0.0069 BTC / (PH/s) / 24 h · 10 min $\approx$ 1.31 USD / (PH/s).
- H = honest miners' hash rate in total.
- M = attacking pool's hash rate.

Baseline Model Without Selfish Mining. We consider a system with a group of honest miners (with mining power H) and an attacking pool (with mining power M). We assume *elastic hash supply* in the system: the equilibrium mining power of honest miners (H^*) is determined such that honest miners make

---

[3] In practice, as miners leave and the total mining power decreases, the price of the cryptoccurrency may drop, thereby decreasing the revenue of the remaining honest miners. Similar to the attacker's increasing share due to miners leaving, this effect exacerbates the impact of the attack, and in this sense, magnifies the phenomenon that we identified in this paper. We leave the modeling and formal analysis of this effect to future work.

[4] We use PH/s and EH/s to denote peta-hash per second and exa-hash per second.

zero profit with mining power H^*. The attacking pool's mining power (M), block rewards (B) and cost (C) are assumed to be fixed and to satisfy $M < B/C$.

Without selfish mining attack, the honest miners' profit per unit hash rate is

$$\mathcal{U}^N(H) = B\frac{1}{H+M} - C. \tag{2}$$

In an equilibrium, the elastic hash supply assumption implies $\mathcal{U}^N(H^*) = 0$. We can solve for H^*:

$$H^* = \frac{B}{C} - M > 0 \tag{3}$$

Model with Selfish Mining. Now, we assume that the attacking pool performs selfish mining as defined by [2].[5] We can calculate the expected mining reward per block discovery, including the hidden block discoveries, as

$$B_{\text{attacker}} = B\frac{\left(-2\alpha^4 + 5\alpha^3 - 4\alpha^2 + \alpha\right)\gamma + 4\alpha^4 - 9\alpha^3 + 4\alpha^2}{2\alpha^3 - 4\alpha^2 + 1}.$$

for the attacking pool, and

$$B_{\text{honest}} = B\frac{\left(2\alpha^4 - 5\alpha^3 + 4\alpha^2 - \alpha\right)\gamma - 4\alpha^4 + 10\alpha^3 - 6\alpha^2 - \alpha + 1}{2\alpha^3 - 4\alpha^2 + 1}$$

for the honest miners, where we denote by $\alpha = \frac{M}{H+M}$ the fraction of the attacking pool's mining power out of the total mining power, and by γ the ratio of honest miners that choose to mine on the attacking pool's block. The total effective mining power in the system under attack is $(B_{\text{honest}} + B_{\text{attacker}})(H+M)/B$.[6] The honest miners' effective mining power is given by $B_{\text{honest}}(H+M)/B = \frac{B_{\text{honest}}}{(1-\alpha)B}H$ and the attacking pool's effective mining power is $B_{\text{attacker}}(H+M)/B = \frac{B_{\text{attacker}}}{\alpha B}M$.

Then, the honest miners' per hash-rate profit under selfish mining attack is

$$\mathcal{U}^S(H) = B\frac{B_{\text{honest}}}{(1-\alpha)B}\frac{B}{(B_{\text{attacker}} + B_{\text{honest}})(H+M)} - C. \tag{4}$$

In an equilibrium, honest miners' hash supply is again derived from $\mathcal{U}^S(H^*) = 0$:

$$\mathcal{U}^S(H^*) = B\frac{1}{M}\left\{\frac{\alpha^* \cdot B_{\text{honest}}(\alpha^*)}{(1-\alpha^*)(B_{\text{attacker}}(\alpha^*) + B_{\text{honest}}(\alpha^*))} - \kappa\right\} = 0 \tag{5}$$

for $\alpha^* = \frac{M}{H^*+M}$ and $\kappa = M \cdot \frac{C}{B}$.

A natural question is whether the above equilibrium condition has a solution $H^* > M$. If not, then the system cannot find an equilibrium where honest miners stay in the system under selfish mining attack. This simple theorem answers that the attacker's hash rate must be bounded to avoid collapsing the system.

---

[5] It is well-known that selfish mining attack proposed by [2] is not the optimal attacker strategy, and thus please note that the actual equilibrium may be different.

[6] These calculations should coincide $B_{\text{attacker}} = B \cdot r_{\text{pool}}$ and $B_{\text{honest}} = B \cdot r_{\text{others}}$, where r_{pool} and r_{others} are from Eq. (6) and (7) in [2].

Theorem 1. *For any given γ, there exists M_{max} such that a solution H^* of $\mathcal{U}^S(H^*) = 0$ with $H^* > M(> 0)$ exists if and only if $M \leq M_{max}$.*

Proof. $B_{\text{attacker}}(\alpha)$ and $B_{\text{honest}}(\alpha)$ have the following properties: (A) $B_{\text{honest}}(\alpha)$ and $B_{\text{attacker}}(\alpha)$ are continuous for $0 \leq \alpha \leq 1/2$, (B) $B_{\text{honest}}(1/2) = 0$, and (C) $B_{\text{honest}}(\alpha) + B_{\text{attacker}}(\alpha) > 0$ for all $0 \leq \alpha \leq 1/2$. Let us define a function $f(\alpha) = \frac{\alpha \cdot B_{\text{honest}}(\alpha)}{(1-\alpha)(B_{\text{attacker}}(\alpha) + B_{\text{honest}}(\alpha))}$. First, $f(\alpha)$ is continuous for $0 \leq \alpha \leq 1/2$ because of property (A) and property (C). Since f is continuous, there exists $\alpha_{\max} \in [0, 1/2]$ that achieves the maximum of $f(\alpha)$ for $0 \leq \alpha \leq 1/2$. Let $M_{\max} = \frac{B}{C} f(\alpha_{\max})$. If $M_{\max} < M$, then $\mathcal{U}^S(H) < 0$ for all H such that $H > M$, so solution H^* does not exist. To complete the proof it suffices to find a solution $H^* > M$ of $\mathcal{U}^S(H) = 0$ for constant M that satisfies $0 < M \leq M_{\max}$. There exists some $\alpha^* \in (0, 1/2)$ such that $f(\alpha^*) = \frac{C}{B}M$ because f is continuous, $f(0) = f(1/2) = 0$ by property (B), and $0 < \frac{C}{B}M \leq \frac{C}{B}M_{\max} = f(\alpha_{\max})$. We find H^* by solving $\alpha^* = \frac{M}{H^*+M}$, and $H^* > M$ because $\alpha^* < 1/2$. $\square$

We can find $\alpha_{\max}$ by solving $f'(\alpha) = 0$:

$$\gamma = \frac{4\alpha^6 - 16\alpha^5 + 26\alpha^3 - 16\alpha^2 + 1}{2\alpha^6 - 8\alpha^5 - \alpha^4 + 14\alpha^3 - 10\alpha^2 + 2\alpha}. \tag{6}$$

With elastic hash supply, selfish mining attacks reduce the profitability of honest miners, making honest miners leave the system, which in turn increases the attacker's share, further decreasing profitability for honest miners. If the attacking pool's share is large enough, the negative propagation effect forces all honest miners to leave the system. For example, when $\gamma = 1$, we find that $f(\alpha_{\max})$ is approximately 0.292. Since $H^* + M = \frac{B}{C}$ in the equilibrium without selfish mining attacks, this implies that if the attacking pool's share is larger than 29.2%, then the attack makes all the honest miners eventually leave the system. When $0 \leq \gamma \leq 1$, $f(\alpha_{max})$ is decreasing in γ, ranging from 0.3475 at $\gamma = 0$ to 0.2919 at $\gamma = 1$.

When the system does not collapse, we can find a stable equilibrium from the honest miners' response. It is straightforward to check that (Eq. 6) has only one solution in $0 \leq \alpha \leq 1/2$.[7] This implies that we have only two equilibria H_1^* and H_2^* when $M < M_{\max}$. We assume $H_1^* < H_2^*$ without loss of generality. Since $f'(\frac{M}{H_1^*+M}) < 0$ and $f'(\frac{M}{H_2^*+M}) > 0$, we obtain the following proposition.

Proposition 1. *For any given γ and $M < M_{max}$, there are two equilibria, H_1^* and H_2^* ($H_2^* > H_1^*$), where H_2^* is stable and H_1^* is unstable.*

Figure 2 illustrates the honest miners' per-hash revenue and cost, given parameters B, C, γ, and M.[8] Under the free entry condition, the equilibria correspond to points H_1^* and H_2^* where the revenue curve intersects the cost,

---

[7] We omit the details due to the restriction of space.

[8] We set $B = 169,441$ USD, $C = 1.31$ USD/(PH/s), $\gamma = 1$, and $M = 0.25\frac{B}{C}$ for Fig. 2. We computed values of B based on Bitcoin price and block-reward and C based on the most competitive offer from nicehash.com on December 29th, 2020.

i.e., points with zero profit. In this case, equilibrium H_2^* is stable, while H_1^* is not. When honest miners' mining power increases (decreases) by any small amount $\epsilon > 0$ from point H_1^*, positive (negative) profit will be generated and more honest miners will enter (leave) the system, ending up reaching equilibrium H_2^* (or an equilibrium $H = 0$).[9] On the other hand, when mining power increases (decreases) from point H_2^*, negative (positive) profit will be generated and honest miners leave (enter) the system. Therefore, equilibrium H_2^* is the only stable equilibrium.

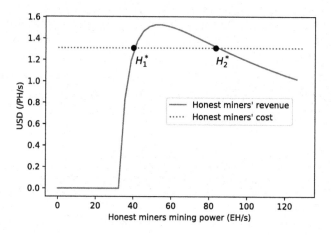

Fig. 2. Honest miners' per hash-rate revenue and cost (PH/s: peta-hash per second, EH/s: exa-hash per second)

References

1. Eyal, I.: The miner's dilemma. In: 36th IEEE Symposium on Security and Privacy (S&P), pp. 89–103. IEEE (2015)
2. Eyal, I., Sirer, E.G.: Majority is not enough: bitcoin mining is vulnerable. In: Christin, N., Safavi-Naini, R. (eds.) FC 2014. LNCS, vol. 8437, pp. 436–454. Springer, Heidelberg (2014). https://doi.org/10.1007/978-3-662-45472-5_28
3. Hamilton, J.D.: Time Series Analysis. Princeton University Press, Princeton (2020)
4. Huberman, G., Leshno, J., Moallemi, C.C.: An economic analysis of the Bitcoin payment system. Technical report, pp. 17–92, Columbia Business School (2019)
5. Noda, S., Okumura, K., Hashimoto, Y.: An economic analysis of difficulty adjustment algorithms in proof-of-work blockchain systems. In: 21st ACM Conference on Economics and Computation (EC), p. 611 (2020)
6. Shibuya, Y., Yamamoto, G., Kojima, F., Shi, E., Matsuo, S., Laszka, A.: Selfish mining attacks exacerbated by elastic hash supply. In: Borisov, N., Diaz, C. (eds.) FC 2021. LNCS, vol. 12675, pp. xx–yy (2021)

---

[9] While $H = 0$ is an equilibrium, we do not consider cases where $H < M$ in our analysis since it is well known that such cases are unsustainable.

Scaling Blockchains

Fraud and Data Availability Proofs: Detecting Invalid Blocks in Light Clients

Mustafa Al-Bassam[1(✉)], Alberto Sonnino[1], Vitalik Buterin[2], and Ismail Khoffi[3]

[1] University College London, London, UK
{m.albassam,a.sonnino}@cs.ucl.ac.uk
[2] Ethereum Research, Zug, Switzerland
vitalik@ethereum.org
[3] LazyLedger Labs, Vaduz, Liechtenstein
ismail@lazyledger.io

Abstract. Light clients, also known as Simple Payment Verification (SPV) clients, are nodes which only download a small portion of the data in a blockchain, and use indirect means to verify that a given chain is valid. Instead of validating blocks, they assume that the chain favoured by the blockchain's consensus algorithm only contains valid blocks, and that the majority of block producers are honest. By allowing such clients to receive fraud proofs generated by fully validating nodes that show that a block violates the protocol rules, and combining this with probabilistic sampling techniques to verify that all of the data in a block actually is available to be downloaded so that fraud can be detected, we can eliminate the honest-majority assumption for block validity, and instead make much weaker assumptions about a minimum number of honest nodes that rebroadcast data. Fraud and data availability proofs are key to enabling on-chain scaling of blockchains while maintaining a strong assurance that on-chain data is available and valid. We present, implement, and evaluate a fraud and data availability proof system.

1 Introduction and Motivation

Due to the scalability limitations of existing blockchains, popular services have stopped accepting Bitcoin [24] payments due to transactions fees rising as high as $20 [16,25], and a popular Ethereum [7] contract caused the pending transactions backlog to increase six-fold [36]. Users pay higher fees as they compete to get their transactions included on the chain, due to space being limited, *e.g.*, by Bitcoin's block size limit [2] or Ethereum's block gas limit [37].

While increasing on-chain capacity limits would yield higher transaction throughput, there are concerns that this creates a trade-off that would decrease decentralisation and security. This is because increasing on-chain capacity would increase the computational resources required for ordinary users to fully download and verify the blockchain, to check that all transactions are correct and valid. Consequently fewer users would afford to run fully validating nodes (full nodes) that independently verify the blockchain, requiring users to instead run

© International Financial Cryptography Association 2021
N. Borisov and C. Diaz (Eds.): FC 2021, LNCS 12675, pp. 279–298, 2021.
https://doi.org/10.1007/978-3-662-64331-0_15

light clients that assume that the chain favoured by the blockchain's consensus algorithm only contains valid transactions [22].

Light clients operate well under normal circumstances, but have weaker assurances compared to full nodes when the majority of the consensus (*e.g.*, miners or block producers) is dishonest (also known as a '51% attack'). When running a full node, a 51% attack on the Bitcoin or Ethereum network can only censor, reverse or double spend transactions, *i.e.*, by forking the chain. However if users run light clients, a 51% attack can generate blocks that contain invalid transactions that, for example, steal funds or create new money out of thin air, and light clients would not be able to detect this as they do not verify the chain. This increases the incentive for conducting a 51% attack. On the other hand, full nodes would reject those invalid blocks immediately as they verify the chain.

In this paper, we decrease the on-chain capacity vs. security trade-off by making it possible for light clients to receive and verify fraud proofs of invalid blocks from any full node that generates such proofs, so that they too can reject them. This gives light clients a level of security similar to full nodes. We also design a data availability proof system, a necessary complement to fraud proofs, so that light clients have assurance that the block data required for full nodes to generate fraud proofs from is available, given that there is a minimum number of honest light clients to reconstruct missing data from blocks. This solves the 'data availability problem', which asks: how can light clients efficiently check that all the data for a block has been made available by the block producer?

We also implement and evaluate the security and efficiency of our overall design, and show in Sect. 5.4 that less than 1% of block data needs to be downloaded in order to check that the entire data of the block is available with 99% probability. Fraud proofs for invalid blocks are in the order of kilobytes; with practical parameters we show in Sect. 6 that for a 1 MB block, fraud proofs are under 27 KB.

Our work also plays a key role in efforts to scale blockchains with sharding [1,8,18], as in a sharded system no single node in the network is expected to download and validate the state of all shards, and thus fraud proofs are necessary to detect invalid blocks from malicious shards. By running light clients that download block headers for shards, nodes can receive fraud proofs for invalid shard block using the techniques described in this paper.

2   Background

Blockchains. The data structure of a blockchain consists of a chain of blocks. Each block contains two components: a header and a list of transactions. In addition to other metadata, the header stores at minimum the hash of the previous block, and the root of the Merkle tree of all transactions in the block.

Validity Rule. Blockchain networks have a consensus algorithm [3] to determine which chain should be favoured in the event of a fork, *e.g.*, if proof-of-work [24] is used, then the chain with the most accumulated work is favoured. They also have a set of transaction validity rules that dictate which transactions are valid, and thus blocks that contain invalid transactions will never be favoured by the consensus algorithm and should in fact always be rejected.

Full Nodes and Light Clients. Full nodes (also known as fully-validating nodes) are nodes which download block headers as well as the list of transactions, verifying that the transactions are valid according to the transaction validity rules. Light clients only download block headers, and assume that the list of transactions are valid according to the transaction validity rules. Light clients verify blocks against the consensus rules, but not the transaction validity rules, and thus assume that the consensus is honest in that they only included valid transactions (unlike full nodes). Light clients may also receive Merkle proofs from full nodes that a specific transaction or state is included in a block header.

Sparse Merkle Trees. A Sparse Merkle tree [11,19] is a Merkle tree that allows for commitments to key-value maps, where values can be updated, inserted or deleted trivially on average in $O(\log(k))$ time in a tree with k keys. The tree is initialised with n leaves where n is extremely large (*e.g.*, $n = 2^{256}$), but where almost all of the leaves have the same default empty value (*e.g.*, 0). The index of each leaf in the tree is its key. Sub-trees with only empty descendant leaves can be replaced by a placeholder value, and sub-trees with only one non-empty descendant leaf can be replaced by a single node. Therefore despite the extremely large number of leaves, each operation takes $O(\log(k))$ time.

Erasure Codes and Reed-Solomon Codes. Erasure codes are error-correcting codes [13,28] working under the assumption of bit erasures rather than bit errors; in particular, the users knows which bits have to be reconstructed. Error-correcting codes transform a message of length k into a longer message of length $n > k$ such that the original message can be recovered from a subset of the n symbols. Reed-Solomon (RS) codes [35] have various applications and are among the most studied error-correcting codes. They can correct up to any combination of k of $2k$ known erasures, and operate over a finite field of order q (where q is a prime power) such that $k < n \leq q$. RS codes have been generalised to multidimensional codes [12,32] in various ways [31,33,38]. In a p multidimensional code, the message is encoded p times along p orthogonal axis, and can be represented as coding in different dimensions of a multidimensional array.

3   Assumptions and Threat Model

We present the network and threat model under which our fraud proofs (Sect. 4) and data availability proofs (Sect. 5) apply. First, we present some primitives that we use in the rest of the paper.

- hash(x) is a cryptographically secure hash function that returns the digest of x (*e.g.*, SHA-256).
- root(L) returns the Merkle root for a list of items L.
- $\{e \to r\}$ denotes a Merkle proof that an element e is a member of the Merkle tree committed by root r.
- VerifyMerkleProof($e, \{e \to r\}, r, n, i$) returns true if the Merkle proof is valid, otherwise false, where n additionally denotes the total number of elements in the underlying tree and i is the index of e in the tree. This verifies that e is at index i, as well as its membership.
- $\{k, v \to r\}$ denotes a Merkle proof that a key-value pair k, v is a member of the Sparse Merkle tree committed by root r.

3.1 Blockchain Model

We assume a generalised blockchain architecture, where the blockchain consists of a hash-based chain of block headers $H = (h_0, h_1, ...)$. Each block header h_i contains a Merkle root txRoot$_i$ of a list of transactions T_i, such that root(T_i) = txRoot$_i$. Given a node that downloads the list of unauthenticated transactions N_i from the network, a block header h_i is considered to be valid if (i) root(N_i) = txRoot$_i$ and (ii) given some validity function

$$\mathsf{valid}(T, S) \in \{\mathsf{true}, \mathsf{false}\}$$

where T is a list of transactions and S is the state of the blockchain, then valid(T_i, S_{i-1}) must return true, where S_i is the state of the blockchain after applying all of the transactions in T_i on the state from the previous block S_{i-1}. We assume that valid(T, S) takes $O(n)$ time to execute, where n is the number of transactions in T.

In terms of transactions, we assume that given a list of transactions $T_i = (t_i^0, t_i^1, ..., t_i^n)$, where t_i^j denotes a transaction j at block i, there exists a state transition function transition that returns the post-state S' of executing a transaction on a particular pre-state S, or an error if the transition is illegal:

$$\mathsf{transition}(S, t) \in \{S', \mathsf{err}\}$$

$$\mathsf{transition}(\mathsf{err}, t) = \mathsf{err}$$

We introduce the concept of intermediate state, which is the state of the chain after processing only some of the transactions in a given block. Thus given the intermediate state $I_i^j = \mathsf{transition}(I_i^{j-1}, t_i^j)$ after executing the first j transactions $(t_i^0, t_i^1, ..., t_i^j)$ in block i where $j \leq n$, and the base case $I_i^{-1} = S_{i-1}$, then $S_i = I_i^n$. In other words, the final intermediate state of a block is the post-state.

Therefore, valid(T_i, S_{i-1}) = true if and only if $I_i^n \neq \mathsf{err}$.

Aim. The aim of this paper is to prove to clients that for a given block header h_i, valid(T_i, S_{i-i}) returns false in less than $O(n)$ time and less than $O(n)$ space, relying on as few security assumptions as possible.

3.2   Participants and Threat Model

Our protocol assumes a network that consists of full nodes and light clients.

Full Nodes. These nodes download and verify the entire blockchain, generating and distributing fraud proofs if a block is invalid. Full nodes store and rebroadcast valid blocks that they download to other full nodes, and broadcast block headers associated with valid blocks to light clients. Some of these nodes may participate in consensus by producing blocks, which we call block producers.

Full nodes may be dishonest, *e.g.*, they may not relay information (*e.g.*, fraud proofs), or they may relay invalid blocks. However we assume that the graph of honest full nodes is well connected, a standard assumption made in previous work [17,18,21,24]. This results in a broadcast network, due to the synchrony assumption we will make below.

Light Clients. These nodes have computational capacity and network bandwidth that is too low to download and verify the entire blockchain. They receive block headers from full nodes, and on request, Merkle proofs that some transaction or state is a part of the block header. These nodes receive fraud proofs from full nodes in the event that a block is invalid.

As is the status quo in prior work [7,24], we assume that each light client is connected to at least one honest full node (*i.e.*, is not under an eclipse attack [15]), as this is necessary to achieve a synchronous gossiping network (discussed below). However when a light client is connected to multiple full nodes, they do not know which nodes are honest or dishonest, just that at least one of them is. Consequently, light clients may be connected to dishonest full nodes that send block headers that have consensus (state agreement) but correspond to invalid or unavailable blocks (violating state validity), and thus need fraud and data availability proofs to detect this.

For data availability proofs, we assume a minimum number of honest light clients in the network to allow for a block to be reconstructed, as each light client downloads a small chunk of every block. The specific number depends on the parameters of the system, and is analysed in Sect. 5.4.

Network Assumptions. We assume a synchronous peer-to-peer gossiping network [5], a standard assumption in the consensus protocols of most blockchains [18,21,24,26,40] due to FLP impossibility [14]. Specifically, we assume a maximum network delay δ; such that if one honest node can connect to the network and download some data (*e.g.*, a block) at time T, then it is guaranteed that any other honest node will be able to do the same at time $T' \leq T + \delta$. In order to guarantee that light clients do not accept block headers that do not have state validity, they must receive fraud proofs in time, hence a synchrony assumption is required. Block headers may be created by adversarial actors, and thus may be invalid, and we cannot rely on an honest majority of consensus-participating nodes for state validity.

4   Fraud Proofs

In order to support efficient fraud proofs, it is necessary to design a blockchain data structure that supports fraud proof generation by design. Extending the model described in Sect. 3.1, a block header h_i at height i contains at least the following elements (not including any extra data required *e.g.*, for consensus):

prevHash$_i$. The hash of the previous block header.
dataRoot$_i$. The root of the Merkle tree of the data (*e.g.*, transactions) included in the block.
dataLength$_i$. The number of leaves represented by dataRoot$_i$.
stateRoot$_i$. The root of a Sparse Merkle tree of the state of the blockchain (to be described in Sect. 4.1).

Additionally, the hash of each block header blockHash$_i$ = hash(h_i) is also stored by clients and nodes. Note that typically blockchains have the Merkle root of transactions included in headers. We have abstracted this to a 'Merkle root of data' called dataRoot$_i$, because as we shall see, as well as including transactions in the block data, we also need to include intermediate state roots.

4.1   State Root and Execution Trace Construction

To instantiate a blockchain based on the state-based model described in Sect. 3.1, we make use of Sparse Merkle trees, and represent the state as a key-value map. In a UTXO-based blockchain *e.g.*, Bitcoin [24], keys would be UTXO identifiers, and values would be booleans representing if the UTXOs are unspent or not. The state keeps track of all data relevant to block processing.

We now define a variation of the function transition defined in Sect. 3.1, called rootTransition, that performs transitions without requiring the whole state tree, but only the state root and Merkle proofs of parts of the state tree that the transaction reads or modifies (which we call "state witness", or w for short). These Merkle proofs are effectively a deep sub-tree of the same state tree.

$$\text{rootTransition}(\text{stateRoot}, t, w) \in \{\text{stateRoot}', \text{err}\}$$

A state witness w consists of a set of (k, v) key-value pairs and their associated Sparse Merkle proofs in the state tree, $w = \{(k_0, v_0, \{k_0, v_0 \rightarrow \text{stateRoot}\}), (k_1, v_1, \{k_1, v_1 \rightarrow \text{stateRoot}\}), ...\}$.

After executing t on the parts of the state shown by w, if t modifies any of the state, then the new resulting stateRoot$'$ can be generated by computing the root of the new sub-tree with the modified leafs. If w is invalid and does not contain all of the state required by t during execution, then err is returned.

Let us denote, for the list of transactions $T_i = (t_i^0, t_i^1, ..., t_i^n)$, where t_i^j denotes a transaction j at block i, then w_i^j is the state witness for transaction t_i^j for stateRoot$_i$.

Given the intermediate state root interRoot$_i^j$ = rootTransition(interRoot$_i^{j-1}$, t_i^j, w_i^j) after executing the first j transactions $(t_i^0, t_i^1, ..., t_i^j)$ in block i where $j \leq n$, and the base case $\mathsf{interRoot}_i^{-1} = \mathsf{stateRoot}_{i-1}$, then $\mathsf{stateRoot}_i = \mathsf{interRoot}_i^n$. Hence, $\mathsf{interRoot}_i^j$ denotes the intermediate state root at block i after applying the first j transactions $t_i^0, t_i^1, ..., t_i^j$ in block i.

4.2 Data Root and Periods

The data represented by the $\mathsf{dataRoot}_i$ of a block contains transactions arranged into fixed-size chunks of data called 'shares', interspersed with intermediate state roots called 'traces' between transactions. We denote trace_i^j as the jth intermediate state root in block i. It is necessary to arrange data into fixed-size shares to allow for data availability proofs as we shall see in Sect. 5. Each leaf in the data tree represents a share.

Given a list of shares $(sh_0, sh_1, ...)$ we define a function $\mathsf{parseShares}$ which parses these shares and outputs an ordered list of messages $(m_0, m_1, ...)$, which are either transactions or intermediate state roots. For example, $\mathsf{parseShares}$ on some shares in the middle of some block i may return $(\mathsf{trace}_i^1, t_i^4, t_i^5, t_i^6, \mathsf{trace}_i^2)$.

$$\mathsf{parseShares}((sh_0, sh_1, ...)) = (m_0, m_1, ...)$$

Note that as the block data does not necessarily contain an intermediate state root after every transaction, we assume a 'period criterion', a protocol rule that defines how often an intermediate state root should be included in the block's data. For example, the rule could be at least once every p transactions, or b bytes or g gas (i.e., in Ethereum [37]).

We thus define a function $\mathsf{parsePeriod}$ which parses a list of messages, and returns a pre-state intermediate root trace_i^x, a post-state intermediate root trace_i^{x+1}, and a list of transaction $(t_i^g, t_i^{g+1}, ..., t_i^{g+h})$ such that applying these transactions on trace_i^x is expected to return trace_i^{x+1}. If the list of messages violate the period criterion, then the function may return err, for example if there too many transactions in the messages to constitute a period.

$$\mathsf{parsePeriod}((m_0, m_1, ...)) \in \{(\mathsf{trace}_i^x, \mathsf{trace}_i^{x+1}, (t_i^g, t_i^{g+1}, ..., t_i^{g+h})), \mathsf{err}\}$$

Note that trace_i^x may be nil if no pre-state root was parsed, as this may be the case if the first messages in the block are being parsed, and thus the pre-state root is the state root of the previous block $\mathsf{stateRoot}_{i-i}$. Likewise, trace_i^{x+1} may be nil if no post-state root was parsed i.e., if the last messages in the block are being parsed, as the post-state root would be $\mathsf{stateRoot}_i$.

4.3 Proof of Invalid State Transition

A malicious block producer may provide a bad $\mathsf{stateRoot}_i$ in the block header that modifies the state an invalid way, i.e., it does not match the new state root that should be returned according to $\mathsf{rootTransition}$. We can use the execution trace provided in $\mathsf{dataRoot}_i$ to prove that some part of the execution trace resulting in stateRoot$_i$ was invalid, by pin-pointing the first intermediate state root that is invalid. We define a function VerifyTransitionFraudProof and its parameters which verifies fraud proofs of invalid state transitions received from full nodes. We denote d_i^j as share number j in block i.

Summary of VerifyTransitionFraudProof. A state transition fraud proof consists of (i) the relevant shares in the block that contain the bad state transition, (ii) Merkle proofs that those shares are in dataRoot$_i$, and (iii) the state witnesses for the transactions contained in those shares. The function takes as input this fraud proof, then (i) verifies the Merkle proofs of the shares, (ii) parses the transactions from the shares, and (iii) checks if applying the transactions on the intermediate pre-state root results in the intermediate post-state root specified in the shares. If it does not, then the fraud proof is valid, and the block that the fraud proof is for should be permanently rejected by the client.

VerifyTransitionFraudProof(blockHash$_i$,

$$(d_i^y, d_i^{y+1}, ..., d_i^{y+m}), y, \qquad \qquad \text{(shares)}$$

$$(\{d_i^y \to \text{dataRoot}_i\}, \{d_i^{y+1} \to \text{dataRoot}_i\}\}, ..., \{d_i^{y+m} \to \text{dataRoot}_i\}\}),$$

$$(w_i^y, w_i^{y+1}, ..., w_i^{y+m}), \qquad \qquad \text{(tx witnesses)}$$

) $\in \{true, false\}$

VerifyTransitionFraudProof returns true if all of the following conditions are met, otherwise false is returned:

1. blockHash$_i$ corresponds to a block header h_i that the client has downloaded and stored.
2. For each share d_i^{y+a} in the proof, VerifyMerkleProof($d_i^{y+a}, \{d_i^{y+a} \to$ dataRoot$_i\}$, dataRoot$_i$, dataLength$_i$, $y + a$) returns true.
3. Given parsePeriod(parseShares(($d_i^y, d_i^{y+1}, ..., d_i^{y+m}$))) $\in \{(\text{trace}_i^x, \text{trace}_i^{x+1}, (t_i^g, t_i^{g+1}, ..., t_i^{g+h})), \text{err}\}$, the result must not be err. If trace$_i^x$ is nil, then $y = 0$ is true, and if trace$_i^{x+1}$ is nil, then $y + m = $ dataLength$_i$ is true.
4. Check that applying $(t_i^g, t_i^{g+1}, ..., t_i^{g+h})$ on trace$_i^x$ results in trace$_i^{x+1}$. Formally, let the intermediate state roots after applying every transaction in the proof one at a time be interRoot$_i^j = $ rootTransition(interRoot$_i^{j-1}, t_i^j, w_i^j$). If trace$_x$ is not nil, then the base case is interRoot$_i^y = $ trace$_x$, otherwise interRoot$_i^y = $ stateRoot$_{i-1}$. If trace$_{x+1}$ is not nil, trace$_{x+1} = $ interRoot$_i^{g+h}$ is true, otherwise stateRoot$_i = $ interRoot$_i^{y+m}$ is true.

5 Data Availability Proofs

A malicious block producer could prevent full nodes from generating fraud proofs by withholding the data needed to recompute dataRoot$_i$ and only releasing the block header to the network. The block producer could then only release the data—which may contain invalid transactions or state transitions—long after the block has been published, and make the block invalid. This would cause a rollback of transactions on the ledger of future blocks. It is therefore necessary for light clients to have a high level of assurance that the data matching dataRoot$_i$ is indeed available to the network.

We propose a data availability scheme based on Reed-Solomon erasure coding, where light clients request random shares of data to get high probability guarantees that all the data associated with the root of a Merkle tree is available. The scheme assumes there is a sufficient number of honest light clients making the same requests such that the network can recover the data, as light clients upload these shares to full nodes, if a full node who does not have the complete data requests it. It is fundamental for light clients to have assurance that all the transaction data is available, because it is only necessary to withhold a few bytes to hide an invalid transaction in a block.

A naive data availability proof scheme may simply apply a standard one dimenisonal Reed-Solomon encoding to extend the block data. However a malicious block producer could incorrectly generate the extended data. In that case, proving that the extended data is incorrectly generated would be equivalent to sending the entire block itself, as clients would have to re-encode all data themselves to verify the mismatch with the given extended data. It is therefore necessary to use multi-dimensional encoding, so that proofs of incorrectly generated codes are limited to a specific axis, rather than the entire data—limiting the size of the proof to $\mathcal{O}(\sqrt[d]{t})$ for d dimensions instead of $\mathcal{O}(t)$. For simplicity, we will only consider bi-dimensional Reed-Solomon encodings in this paper, but our scheme can be easily generalised to higher dimensions.

We first describe how dataRoot$_i$ should be constructed under the scheme in Sect. 5.1, and how light clients can use this to have assurance that the full data is available in Sect. 5.2.

5.1   2D Reed-Solomon Encoded Merkle Tree Construction

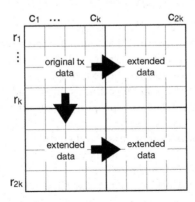

Fig. 1. Diagram showing a 2D Reed-Solomon encoding process.

Let extend be a function that takes in a list of k shares, and returns a list of $2k$ shares that represent the extended shares encoded using a standard one dimensional Reed-Solomon code.

$$\text{extend}(\text{sh}_1, \text{sh}_2, ..., \text{sh}_k) = (\text{sh}_1, \text{sh}_2, ..., \text{sh}_{2k})$$

The first k shares that are returned are the input shares, and the latter k are the coded shares. Recall that all $2k$ shares can be recovered with knowledge of any k of the $2k$ shares. A 2D Reed-Solomon Encoded Merkle tree can then be constructed as follows from a block of data:

1. Split the original data into shares of size shareSize each, and arrange them into a $k \times k$ matrix O_i; apply padding if the last share is not exactly of size shareSize, or if there are not enough shares to complete the matrix. In the next step, we extend this $k \times k$ matrix to a $2k \times 2k$ matrix M_i with Reed-Solomon encoding.
2. For each row in the original $k \times k$ matrix O_i, pass the k shares in that row to extend($\text{sh}_1, \text{sh}_2, ..., \text{sh}_k$) and append the extra shares outputted ($\text{sh}_{k+1}, ...,$ sh_{2k}) to the row to create an extended row of length $2k$, thus extending the matrix horizontally. Repeat this process for the columns in O_i to extend the matrix vertically, so that each original column now has length $2k$. This creates an extended $2k \times 2k$ matrix with the upper-right and lower-left quadrants filled, as shown in Fig. 1. Then finally apply Reed-Solomon encoding horizontally on each row of the vertically extended portion of the matrix to complete the bottom-right quadrant of the $2k \times 2k$ matrix. This results in the extended matrix M_i for block i.
3. Compute the root of the Merkle tree for each row and column in the $2k \times 2k$ matrix, where each leaf is a share. We have $\text{rowRoot}_i^j = \text{root}((M_i^{j,1}, M_i^{j,2}, ..., M_i^{j,2k}))$ and $\text{columnRoot}_i^j = \text{root}((M_i^{1,j}, M_i^{2,j}, ..., M_i^{2k,j}))$, where $M_i^{x,y}$ represents the share in row x, column y in the matrix.
4. Compute the root of the Merkle tree of the roots computed in step 3 and use this as dataRoot_i. We have $\text{dataRoot}_i = \text{root}((\text{rowRoot}_i^1, \text{rowRoot}_i^2, ..., \text{rowRoot}_i^{2k}, \text{columnRoot}_i^1, \text{columnRoot}_i^2, ..., \text{columnRoot}_i^{2k}))$.

We note that in step 2, we have chosen to extend the vertically extended portion of the matrix horizontally to complete the extended matrix, however it would be equally acceptable to extend the horizontally extended portion of the matrix vertically to complete the extended matrix; this will result in the same matrix because Reed-Solomon coding is linear and commutative with itself [32]. The resulting matrix has the property that all rows and columns have reconstruction capabilities.

The resulting tree of dataRoot_i has $\text{dataLength}_i = 2 \times (2k)^2$ elements, where the first $\frac{1}{2}\text{dataLength}_i$ elements are in leaves via the row roots, and the latter half are in leaves via the column roots.

In order to allow for Merkle proofs from dataRoot_i to individual shares, we assume a wrapper function around VerifyMerkleProof called VerifyShareMerkle Proof with the same parameters which takes into account how the underlying

Merkle trees deal with an unbalanced number of leaves, as $\mathsf{dataRoot}_i$ is composed from multiple trees constructed independently from each other.

The width of the matrix can be derived as $\mathsf{matrixWidth}_i = \sqrt{\frac{1}{2}\mathsf{dataLength}_i}$. If we are only interested in the row and column roots of $\mathsf{dataRoot}_i$, rather than the actual shares, then we can assume that $\mathsf{dataRoot}_i$ has $2 \times \mathsf{matrixWidth}_i$ leaves when verifying a Merkle proof of a row or column root.

A light client or full node is able to reconstruct $\mathsf{dataRoot}_i$ from all the row and column roots by recomputing step 4. In order to gain data availability assurances, all light clients should at minimum download all the row and column roots needed to reconstruct $\mathsf{dataRoot}_i$ and check that step 4 was computed correctly, because as we shall see in Sect. 5.3, they are necessary to generate fraud proofs of incorrectly generated extended data.

We nevertheless represent all of the row and column roots as a a single $\mathsf{dataRoot}_i$ to allow 'super-light' clients which do not download the row and column roots, but these clients cannot be assured of data availability and thus do not fully benefit from the increased security of allowing fraud proofs.

5.2   Random Sampling and Network Block Recovery

In order for any share in the 2D Reed-Solomon matrix to be unrecoverable, then at least $(k+1)^2$ out of $(2k)^2$ shares must be unavailable (see Theorem 1), as opposed to $k+1$ out of $2k$ with a 1D code. When light clients receive a new block header from the network, they should randomly sample $0 < s \le (2k)^2$ distinct shares from the extended matrix, and only accept the block if they receive all shares. The higher the s, the greater the confidence a light client can have that the data is available (this will be analysed in Sect. 5.4). Additionally, light clients gossip shares that they have received to the network, so that the full block can be recovered by honest full nodes.

The protocol between a light client and the full nodes that it is connected to works as follows:

1. The light client receives a new block header h_i from one of the full nodes it is connected to, and a set of row and column roots $R = (\mathsf{rowRoot}_i^1, \mathsf{rowRoot}_i^2, ...,$ $\mathsf{rowRoot}_i^{2k}, \mathsf{columnRoot}_i^1, \mathsf{columnRoot}_i^2, ..., \mathsf{columnRoot}_i^{2k})$. If the check $\mathsf{root}(R)$ $= \mathsf{dataRoot}_i$ is false, then the light client rejects the header.

2. The light client randomly chooses a set of unique (x,y) coordinates $S = \{(x_0,y_0)(x_1,y_1), ..., (x_n,y_n)\}$ where $0 < x \le \mathsf{matrixWidth}_i$ and $0 < y \le \mathsf{matrixWidth}_i$, corresponding to points on the extended matrix, and sends them to one or more of the full nodes it is connected to.

3. If a full node has all of the shares corresponding to the coordinates in S and their associated Merkle proofs, then for each coordinate (x_a, y_b) the full node responds with $M_i^{x_a,y_b}, \{M_i^{x_a,y_b} \to \mathsf{rowRoot}_i^a\}$ or $M_i^{x_a,y_b}, \{M_i^{x_a,y_b} \to \mathsf{columnRoot}_i^b\}$. Note that there are two possible Merkle proofs for each share; one from the row roots, and one from the column roots, and thus the full node must also specify for each Merkle proof if it is associated with a row or column root.

4. For each share $M_i^{x_a,y_b}$ that the light client has received, the light client checks VerifyMerkleProof$(M_i^{x_a,y_b}, \{M_i^{x_a,y_b} \rightarrow \mathsf{rowRoot}_i^a\}, \mathsf{rowRoot}_i^a, \mathsf{matrixWidth}_i, b)$ is true if the proof is from a row root, otherwise if the proof is from a column root then VerifyMerkleProof$(M_i^{x_a,y_b}, \{M_i^{x_a,y_b} \rightarrow \mathsf{columnRoot}_i^b\}, \mathsf{columnRoot}_i^b, \mathsf{matrixWidth}_i, a)$ is true.

5. Each share and valid Merkle proof that is received by the light client is gossiped to all the full nodes that the light client is connected to if the full nodes do not have them, and those full nodes gossip it to all of the full nodes that they are connected to.

6. If all the proofs in step 4 succeeded, and no shares are missing from the sample made in step 2, then the block is accepted as available if within $2 \times \delta$ no fraud proofs for the block's erasure code is received (Sect. 5.3).

Recovery and Selective Share Disclosure. There must be a sufficient number of light clients to sample at least $(2k)^2 - (k+1)^2$ different shares in total for the block to be recoverable; recall if $(k+1)^2$ shares are unavailable, the Reed-Solomon matrix may be unrecoverable. Additionally, the block producer can selectively releases shares as light clients ask for them, and always pass the sampling challenge of the clients that ask for the first $(2k)^2 - (k+1)^2$ shares, as they will accept the blocks as available despite them being unrecoverable. The number of light clients will be discussed in Sect. 5.4.

Table 1 in Sect. 5.4 will show that the number of light clients that this may apply to is in the hundreds to low thousands if s is set to a reasonable size, which is extremely low (less than $\sim 0.2\%$ of users) compared to for example 1M+ users who have installed a popular Bitcoin Android SPV client [4]. Alternatively, block producers can be prevented from selectively releasing shares to the first clients if one assumes an enhanced network model where each sample request for each share is anonymous (*i.e.*, sample requests cannot be linked to the same client) and the distribution in which every sample request is received is uniformly random, for example by using a mix net [10]. As the network would not be able to link different per-share sample requests to the same clients, shares cannot be selectively released on a per-client basis. This also prevents adversarial block producers from targeting a specific light client via its known IP address, by only releasing shares to that light client. See Appendix A.2 for proofs.

5.3   Fraud Proofs of Incorrectly Generated Extended Data

If a full node has enough shares to recover any row or column, and after doing so detects that recovered data does not match its respective row or column root, then it should distribute a fraud proof consisting of enough shares in that row or column to be able to recover it, and a Merkle proof for each share.

We define a function VerifyCodecFraudProof and its parameters that verifies these fraud proofs, where $\mathsf{axisRoot}_i^j \in \{\mathsf{rowRoot}_i^j, \mathsf{columnRoot}_i^j\}$. We denote axis and ax_j as row or column boolean indicators; 0 for rows and 1 for columns.

Summary of VerifyCodecFraudProof. The fraud proof consists of (i) the Merkle root of the incorrectly generated row or column, (ii) a Merkle proof that the row or column root is in the data tree, (iii) enough shares to be able to reconstruct that row or column, and (iv) Merkle proofs that each share is in the data tree. The function takes as input this fraud proof, and checks that (i) all of the supplied Merkle proofs are valid, (ii) all of the shares given by the prover are in the same row or column and (iii) that the recovered row or column indeed does not match the row or column root in the block. If all these conditions are true, then the fraud proof is valid, and the block that the fraud proof is for should be permanently rejected by the client.

$$\text{VerifyCodecFraudProof}(\text{blockHash}_i,$$

$$\text{axisRoot}_i^j, \{\text{axisRoot}_i^j \rightarrow \text{dataRoot}_i\}, j, \qquad\qquad \text{(row or column root)}$$

$$\text{axis}, \qquad\qquad\qquad\qquad\qquad\qquad\qquad\qquad \text{(row or column indicator)}$$

$$((\text{sh}_0, \text{pos}_0, \text{ax}_0), (\text{sh}_1, \text{pos}_1, \text{ax}_1), ..., (\text{sh}_k, \text{pos}_k, \text{ax}_k)), \qquad\qquad \text{(shares)}$$

$$(\{\text{sh}_0 \rightarrow \text{dataRoot}_i\}, \{\text{sh}_1 \rightarrow \text{dataRoot}_i\}\}, ..., \{\text{sh}_k \rightarrow \text{dataRoot}_i\}\})$$

$$) \in \{\text{true}, \text{false}\}$$

Let recover be a function that takes a list of shares and their positions in the row or column $((\text{sh}_0, \text{pos}_0), (\text{sh}_1, \text{pos}_1), ..., (\text{sh}_k, \text{pos}_k))$, and the length of the extended row or column $2k$. The function outputs the full recovered shares $(\text{sh}_0, \text{sh}_1, ..., \text{sh}_{2k})$ or err if the shares are unrecoverable.

$$\text{recover}(((\text{sh}_0, \text{pos}_0), (\text{sh}_1, \text{pos}_1), ..., (\text{sh}_k, \text{pos}_k)), 2k) \in \{(\text{sh}_0, \text{sh}_1, ..., \text{sh}_{2k}), \text{err}\}$$

VerifyCodecFraudProof returns true if all of the following conditions are met:

1. blockHash_i corresponds to a block header h_i that the client has downloaded and stored.
2. If axis = 0 (row root), VerifyMerkleProof($\text{axisRoot}_i^j, \{\text{axisRoot}_i^j \rightarrow \text{dataRoot}_i\}$, $\text{dataRoot}_i, 2 \times \text{matrixWidth}_i, j$) returns true.
3. If axis = 1 (col. root), VerifyMerkleProof($\text{axisRoot}_i^j, \{\text{axisRoot}_i^j \rightarrow \text{dataRoot}_i\}$, $\text{dataRoot}_i, 2 \times \text{matrixWidth}_i, \frac{1}{2}\text{dataLength}_i + j$) returns true.
4. For each $(\text{sh}_x, \text{pos}_x, \text{ax}_x)$, VerifyShareMerkleProof($\text{sh}_x, \{\text{sh}_x \rightarrow \text{dataRoot}_i\}$, $\text{dataRoot}_i, \text{dataLength}, \text{index}$) returns true, where index is the expected index of the sh_x in the data tree based on pos_x assuming it is in the same row or column as axisRoot_i^j. See Appendix A.2 for how *index* can be computed. Note that full nodes can specify Merkle proofs of shares in rows or columns from either the row or column roots *e.g.*, if a row is invalid but the full nodes only has Merkle proofs for the row's share from column roots. This also allows for full nodes to generate fraud proofs if there are inconsistencies in the data between rows and columns *e.g.*, if the same cell in the matrix has a different share in its row and column trees.
5. $root(\text{recover}(((\text{sh}_0, \text{pos}_0), (\text{sh}_1, \text{pos}_1), ..., (\text{sh}_k, \text{pos}_k))))) = \text{axisRoot}_i^j$ is false.

If VerifyCodecFraudProof for blockHash$_i$ returns true, then the block header h_i is permanently rejected by the light client.

5.4   Security Probability Analysis

We present how the data availability scheme presented in Sect. 5 can provide lights clients with a high level of assurance that block data is available to the network.

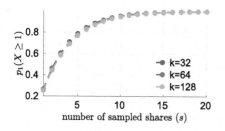

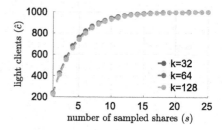

Fig. 2. $p_1(X \geq 1)$ versus the number of samples.

Fig. 3. Light clients $\hat{c}$ for which $p_c(Y > \hat{c}) \geq 0.99$.

Unrecoverable Block Detection. Figure 2 shows the probability $p_1(X \geq 1)$ that a single light client samples at least one unavailable share in a matrix with $(k + 1)^2$ unavailable shares, thus detecting that a block may be unrecoverable (see Theorem 2 in Appendix A.1). Figure 2 shows how this probability varies with the number of samples s for $k = 32, 64, 128$; each light client samples at least one unavailable share with about 60% probability after 3 samplings (*i.e.,* after querying respectively 0.073% of the block shares for $k = 32$ and 0.005% of the block shares for $k = 128$), and with more than 99% probability after 15 samplings (*i.e.,* after querying respectively 0.4% of the block shares for $k = 32$ and 0.02% of the block shares for $k = 128$). Furthermore, this probability is almost independent of k for large values of k (see Corollary 2 in Appendix A.1).

Table 1. Minimum number of light clients (c) required to achieve $p_e(Z \geq \gamma) > 0.99$ for various values of k and s. The approximate values have been approached numerically as evaluating Theorem 4 can be extremely resource-intensive for large values of k.

$p_e(Z \geq \gamma)$	$s = 2$	$s = 5$	$s = 10$	$s = 20$	$s = 50$
$k = 16$	692	277	138	69	28
$k = 32$	2805	1,122	561	280	112
$k = 64$	11,289	4,516	2,258	1,129	451
$k = 128$	>40,000	~18,000	~9,000	~4,500	1,811

Multi-client Unrecoverable Block Detection. $p_c(Y > \hat{c})$ is the probability that more than $\hat{c}$ out of c light clients sample at least one unavailable share in a matrix with $(k+1)^2$ unavailable shares (see Theorem 3 in Appendix A.1). Figure 3 shows the variation of the number of light clients $\hat{c}$ for which $p_c(Y > \hat{c}) \geq 0.99$ with the sampling size s, fixing $c = 1000$, and the matrix sizes are $k = 64, 128, 256$. $p_c(Y > \hat{c})$ is almost independent of k, and can be used to determine the number of light clients that will detect incomplete matrices with high probability $(p_c(Y > \hat{c}) \geq 0.99)$; there is little gain in increasing s over 15.

Recovery and Selective Share Disclosure. Table 1 presents the probability $p_e(Z \geq \gamma) > 0.99$ that light clients collectively samples enough shares to recover every share of the $2k \times 2k$ matrix (see Corollary 3 in Appendix A.1). We are interested in the probability that light clients—each sampling s distinct shares—collectively samples at least γ distinct shares, where γ is the minimum number of distinct shares (randomly chosen) needed to have the certainty to be able to recover the $2k \times 2k$ matrix (see Corollary 1 in Appendix A.1).

6 Performance and Implementation.

We implemented the data availability proof scheme described in Sect. 5 and a prototype of the state transition fraud proof scheme described in Sect. 4 in 2,683 lines of Go code and released the code as a series of free and open-source libraries.[1] We perform the measurements on a laptop with an Intel Core i5 1.3GHz processor and 16GB of RAM, and use SHA-256 for hashing.

Table 2 shows the space complexity and sizes for different objects. We observe that the size of the state transition fraud proofs only grows logarithmically with the size of the block and state; this is because the number of transactions in a period remains static, but the size of the Merkle proof for each transaction

Table 2. Worst case space complexity and illustrative sizes for various objects for 250 KB and 1MB blocks. p represents the number of transactions in a period, w represents the number of witnesses for those transactions, d is short for dataLength, and s is the number of key-value pairs in the state tree. For the illustrative sizes, we assume that a period consists of 10 transactions, the average transaction size is 225 bytes, and that conservatively there are 2^{30} non-default nodes in the state tree.

Object	Space complexity	250 KB block	1MB block
State fraud proof	$O(p + p\log(d) + w\log(s) + w)$	14,090b	14,410b
Availability fraud proof	$O(d^{0.5} + d^{0.5}\log(d^{0.5}))$	12,320b	26,688b
Single sample response	$O(\text{shareSize} + \log(d))$	320b	368b
Header	$O(1)$	128b	128b
Header + axis roots	$O(d^{0.5})$	2,176b	4,224b

---

[1] "https://github.com/musalbas/rsmt2d".

Table 3. Worst case time complexity and benchmarks for various actions for 250 KB and 1MB blocks (mean over 10 repeats), where [G] means generate and [V] means verify. p represents the number of transactions in a period, b represents the number of transactions in the block, w represents the number of witnesses for those transactions, d is short for dataLength, and s is the number of key-value pairs in the state tree. For the benchmarks, we assume that a period consists of 10 transactions, the average transaction size is 225 bytes, and each transaction writes to one key in the state tree.

Action	Time complexity	250 KB block	1 MB block
[G] State fraud proof	$O(b + p\log(d) + w\log(s))$	41.22 ms	182.80 ms
[V] State fraud proof	$O(p + p\log(d) + w)$	0.03 ms	0.03 ms
[G] Availability fraud proof	$O(d\log(d^{0.5}) + d^{0.5}\log(d^{0.5}))$	4.91 ms	19.18 ms
[V] Availability fraud proof	$O(d^{0.5}\log(d^{0.5}))$	0.05 ms	0.08 ms
[G] Single sample response	$O(log(d^{0.5}))$	< 0.00001 ms	< 0.00001 ms
[V] Single sample response	$O(log(d^{0.5}))$	< 0.00001 ms	< 0.00001 ms

increases logarithmically. On the other hand, the availability fraud proofs (as well as block headers with the axis roots) grow at least in proportion to the square root of the size of the block, as the size of a single row or column is proportional to the square root of the size of the block.

Table 3 shows the time complexity and benchmarks for various actions. To generate and verify availability fraud proofs, we use an algorithm based on Fast Fourier Transforms (FFT) to perform the encoding and decoding, which has a $O(k\log(k))$ complexity for a message of k shares [20, 30]. As expected, verifying an availability fraud proof is significantly quicker than generating one. This is because generation requires checking the entire data matrix, whereas verification only requires checking one row or column.

7   Related Work

The Bitcoin paper [24] briefly mentions the possibility of 'alerts', which are messages sent by full nodes to alert light clients that a block is invalid, prompting them to download the full block to verify the inconsistency. Little further exploration has been done on this, partly due to the data availability problem.

There have been online discussions about how one may go about designing a fraud proof system [29,34], but no complete design that deals with all block invalidity cases and data availability has been proposed. These earlier systems have taken the approach of attempting to design a fraud proof for each possible way to create a block that violates the protocol rules (*e.g.*, double spending inputs, mining a block with a reward too high, etc.), whereas this paper generalises the blockchain into a state transition system with only one fraud proof.

On the data availability side, Perard *et al.* [27] have proposed using erasure coding to allow light clients to voluntarily contribute to help storing the blockchain without having to download all of it, however they do not propose a scheme to allow light clients to verify that the data is available via random sampling and fraud proofs of incorrectly generated erasure codes.

Error coding as a potential solution has been briefly discussed on IRC chatrooms with no analysis, however these early ideas [23] require semi-trusted third parties to inform clients of missing samples, and do not make use of 2D coding and proofs of incorrectly generated codes and are thus vulnerable to block producers that generate invalid codes.

Cachin and Stefano [9] introduce verifiable information dispersal, which stores files by distributing them amongst a set of servers in a storage-efficient way, where up to one third of the servers and an arbitrary number of clients may be malicious. Data availability proofs on the other hand do not make any honest majority assumptions about nodes, however require a minimum number of honest light clients.

7.1 SParse FrAud pRotection (SPAR)

Since the release of this paper's pre-print, new work by Yu *et al.* [39] on data availability proofs was presented in FC'20 that builds on this work, which adopts our security definitions and framework. An alternative data availability proof scheme called SPAR is proposed where only an $O(1)$ hash commitment is required in each header with respect to the size of the block, compared to an $O(\sqrt{n})$ commitment in our scheme. The scheme uses a Merkle tree where each layer of the tree is coded with an LDPC code [6]. The scheme considers sampling with two types of adversarial block producers: a strong adversary and a weak adversary. A strong adversary can find, with NP-hardness, the specific shares that must be hidden (the stopping set) in order to make the data unavailable. A weak adversary cannot find the stopping set, and thus randomly selects shares to withhold. Under a threat model that assumes a strong adversary, clients must therefore sample more shares to achieve the same data availability guarantees.

According to the evaluation of the scheme in the paper [39], light clients are required to download 2.5–4x more samples than our 2D-RS scheme from each block to achieve the same level of data availability guarantee under a weak adversary, and 10–16x more under a strong adversary. Furthermore, the size of each sample is increased as shares must be downloaded from multiple layers of the tree, as opposed to only the bottom layer in our 2D-RS scheme. However, the overall amount of data that needs to be downloaded only increases logarithmically with the block size as the size of the Merkle proofs only increase logarithmically, while the header size is $O(1)$ instead of $O(\sqrt{n})$.

Figure 4 in Appendix C compares the overall header and sampling bandwidth cost for different block sizes for both the 2D-RS scheme and the SPAR scheme, with a target data availability guarantee of 99% and 256 byte shares (used in the evaluation in both this paper and SPAR). We observe that due to the high sampling cost of SPAR, it outperforms 2D-RS in bandwidth costs only when the block size is greater than 50 MB under the weak adversary model. After 50 MB, the fact that the bandwidth cost only increases logarithmically in SPAR becomes advantageous.

On the other hand, the size of each SPAR sample is smaller when the size of the shares are smaller. To compare the best case scenario, Fig. 5 in Appendix C shows the comparison between SPAR and 2D-RS assuming 32 byte shares (*i.e.*, the size of shares are equivalent to the size of the SHA-256 hash). This shows that SPAR outperforms 2D-RS for blocks greater than 6 MB under the weak adversary model. However, decreasing the share size increases the fraud proof size and decoding complexity—we refer readers to the SPAR paper [39] for metrics.

8   Conclusion

We presented, implemented and evaluated a complete fraud and data availability proof scheme, which enables light clients to have security guarantees almost at the level of a full node, with the added assumptions that there is at least one honest full node in the network that distributes fraud proofs within a maximum network delay, and that there is a minimum number of light clients in the network to collectively recover blocks.

Acknowledgements. Mustafa Al-Bassam is supported by a scholarship from The Alan Turing Institute and Alberto Sonnino is supported by the European Commission Horizon 2020 DECODE project under grant agreement number 732546.

Thanks to George Danezis, Alexander Hicks and Sarah Meiklejohn for helpful discussions about the mathematical proofs.

Thanks to our shephard Sreeram Kannan for providing helpful feedback.

Appendix

See the full version of the paper at https://fc21.ifca.ai/papers/83.pdf.

References

1. Al-Bassam, M., Sonnino, A., Bano, S., Hrycyszyn, D., Danezis, G.: Chainspace: A sharded smart contracts platform. In: Proceedings of the Network and Distributed System Security Symposium (NDSS) (2018)
2. Antonopoulos, A.M.: Mastering bitcoin: unlocking digital crypto-currencies. O'Reilly Media Inc. 1st edn. (2014)
3. Bano, S., Sonnino, A., Al-Bassam, M., Azouvi, S., McCorry, P., Meiklejohn, S., Danezis, G.: Consensus in the age of blockchains. CoRR abs/1711.03936 (2017). https://arxiv.org/abs/1711.03936
4. Bitcoin Wallet Developers: Bitcoin wallet - apps on Google Play (2018). https://play.google.com/store/apps/details?id=de.schildbach.wallet
5. Boyd, S., Ghosh, A., Prabhakar, B., Shah, D.: Randomized gossip algorithms. IEEE Trans. Inf. Theory **52**(6), 2508–2530 (2006)
6. Burshtein, D., Miller, G.: Asymptotic enumeration methods for analyzing ldpc codes. IEEE Trans. Inf. Theory **50**(6), 1115–1131 (2004). https://doi.org/10.1109/TIT.2004.828064

7. Buterin, V.: Ethereum: the ultimate smart contract and decentralized application platform (white paper) (2013). http://web.archive.org/web/20131228111141/vbuterin.com/ethereum.html
8. Buterin, V.: Ethereum sharding FAQs (2018). https://github.com/ethereum/wiki/wiki/Sharding-FAQs/c54cf1b520b0bd07468bee6950cda9a2c4ab4982
9. Cachin, C., Tessaro, S.: Asynchronous verifiable information dispersal. In: 24th IEEE Symposium on Reliable Distributed Systems (SRDS'05), pp. 191–201. IEEE (2005)
10. Chaum, D.L.: Untraceable electronic mail, return addresses, and digital pseudonyms. Commun. ACM 24(2), 84–90 (1981)
11. Dahlberg, R., Pulls, T., Peeters, R.: Efficient sparse merkle trees. In: Brumley, B., Röning, J. (eds.) NordSec 2016. LNCS, vol. 10014, pp. 199–215. Springer, Cham (2016). https://doi.org/10.1007/978-3-319-47560-8_13
12. Dudáček, L., Veřtát, I.: Multidimensional parity check codes with short block lengths. In: Telecommunications Forum (TELFOR), 2016 24th, pp. 1–4. IEEE (2016)
13. Elias, P.: Error-free coding. Trans. IRE Prof. Group Inf. Theory 4(4), 29–37 (1954)
14. Fischer, M.J., Lynch, N.A., Paterson, M.S.: Impossibility of distributed consensus with one faulty process. J. ACM (JACM) 32(2), 374–382 (1985)
15. Heilman, E., Kendler, A., Zohar, A., Goldberg, S.: Eclipse attacks on Bitcoin's peer-to-peer network. In: 24th USENIX Security Symposium (USENIX Security 15), pp. 129–144. USENIX Association, Washington, D.C. (2015). https://www.usenix.org/conference/usenixsecurity15/technical-sessions/presentation/heilman
16. Karlo, T.: Ending Bitcoin support (2018). https://stripe.com/blog/ending-Bitcoin-support
17. Kiayias, A., Russell, A., David, B., Oliynykov, R.: Ouroboros: a provably secure proof-of-stake blockchain protocol. In: Katz, J., Shacham, H. (eds.) CRYPTO 2017. LNCS, vol. 10401, pp. 357–388. Springer, Cham (2017). https://doi.org/10.1007/978-3-319-63688-7_12
18. Kokoris-Kogias, E., Jovanovic, P., Gasser, L., Gailly, N., Syta, E., Ford, B.: OmniLedger: a secure, scale-out, decentralized ledger via sharding. In: Proceedings of IEEE Symposium on Security and Privacy. IEEE (2018)
19. Laurie, B., Kasper, E.: Revocation transparency (2012). https://www.links.org/files/RevocationTransparency.pdf
20. Lin, S.J., Chung, W.H., Han, Y.S.: Novel polynomial basis and its application to Reed-Solomon erasure codes. In: Proceedings of the 2014 IEEE 55th Annual Symposium on Foundations of Computer Science, pp. 316–325. FOCS '14, IEEE Computer Society, Washington, DC, USA (2014). https://doi.org/10.1109/FOCS.2014.41, http://dx.doi.org/10.1109/FOCS.2014.41
21. Luu, L., Narayanan, V., Zheng, C., Baweja, K., Gilbert, S., Saxena, P.: A secure sharding protocol for open blockchains. In: Proceedings of the 2016 ACM SIGSAC Conference on Computer and Communications Security, pp. 17–30. CCS '16, ACM, New York, NY, USA (2016). https://doi.org/10.1145/2976749.2978389
22. Marshall, A.: Bitcoin scaling problem, explained (2017). https://cointelegraph.com/explained/Bitcoin-scaling-problem-explained
23. Maxwell, G.: (2017). https://botbot.me/freenode/bitcoin-wizards/2017-02-01/?msg=80297226&page=2
24. Nakamoto, S.: Bitcoin: a peer-to-peer electronic cash system (2008). http://bitcoin.org/bitcoin.pdf

25. Orland, K.: Your Bitcoin is no good here–Steam stops accepting cryptocurrency (2017). https://arstechnica.com/gaming/2017/12/steam-drops-Bitcoin-payment-option-citing-fees-and-volatility/
26. Pass, R., Seeman, L., Shelat, A.: Analysis of the blockchain protocol in asynchronous networks. In: Coron, J.S.ébastien., Nielsen, J. (eds.) EUROCRYPT 2017. LNCS, vol. 10211, pp. 643–673. Springer, Cham (2017). https://doi.org/10.1007/978-3-319-56614-6_22
27. Perard, D., Lacan, J., Bachy, Y., Detchart, J.: Erasure code-based low storage blockchain node. In: IEEE International Conference on Blockchain (2018)
28. Peterson, W.W., Wesley, W., Weldon Jr Peterson, E., Weldon, E., Weldon, E.: Error-correcting codes. MIT Press (1972)
29. Ranvier, J.: Improving the ability of SPV clients to detect invalid chains (2017). https://gist.github.com/justusranvier/451616fa4697b5f25f60
30. Reed, I., Scholtz, R., Truong, T.K., Welch, L.: The fast decoding of Reed-Solomon codes using Fermat theoretic transforms and continued fractions. IEEE Trans. Inf. Theory **24**(1), 100–106 (1978). https://doi.org/10.1109/TIT.1978.1055816
31. Saints, K., Heegard, C.: Algebraic-geometric codes and multidimensional cyclic codes: a unified theory and algorithms for decoding using Grobner bases. IEEE Trans. Inf. Theory **41**(6), 1733–1751 (1995)
32. Shea, J.M., Wong, T.F.: Multidimensional codes. Encyclopedia of Telecommunications (2003)
33. Shen, B.Z., Tzeng, K.: Multidimensional extension of reed-solomon codes. In: Information Theory 1998 Proceedings 1998 IEEE International Symposium on, p. 54. IEEE (1998)
34. Todd, P.: Fraud proofs (2016). https://diyhpl.us/wiki/transcripts/mit-bitcoin-expo-2016/fraud-proofs-petertodd/
35. Wicker, S.B.: Reed-solomon codes and their applications. IEEE Press, Piscataway, NJ, USA (1994)
36. Wong, J.I.: CryptoKitties is causing Ethereum network congestion (2017). https://qz.com/1145833/cryptokitties-is-causing-ethereum-network-congestion/
37. Wood, G.: Ethereum: a secure decentralised generalised transaction ledger - Byzantium version, p. e94ebda (yellow paper) (2018). https://ethereum.github.io/yellowpaper/paper.pdf
38. Wu, J., Costello, D.: New multilevel codes over GF(q). IEEE Trans. Inf. Theory **38**(3), 933–939 (1992)
39. Yu, M., Sahraei, S., Li, S., Avestimehr, S., Kannan, S., Viswanath, P.: Coded merkle tree: solving data availability attacks in blockchains. In: Financial Cryptography and Data Security (2020)
40. Zamani, M., Movahedi, M., Raykova, M.: Rapidchain: Scaling blockchain via full sharding. In: Proceedings of the 2018 ACM SIGSAC Conference on Computer and Communications Security, pp. 931–948 (2018)

ACeD: Scalable Data Availability Oracle

Peiyao Sheng[1(✉)], Bowen Xue[2], Sreeram Kannan[2], and Pramod Viswanath[1]

[1] University of Illinois, Urbana-Champaign, IL 61801, USA
psheng2@illinois.edu
[2] University of Washington, Seattle, WA, USA

Abstract. A popular method in practice offloads computation and storage in blockchains by relying on committing only hashes of off-chain data into the blockchain. This mechanism is acknowledged to be vulnerable to a stalling attack: the blocks corresponding to the committed hashes may be unavailable at any honest node. The straightforward solution of broadcasting all blocks to the entire network sidesteps this data availability attack, but it is not scalable. In this paper, we propose ACeD, a scalable solution to this data availability problem with $O(1)$ communication efficiency, the first to the best of our knowledge. The key innovation is a new protocol that requires each of the N nodes to receive only $O(1/N)$ of the block, such that the data is guaranteed to be available in a distributed manner in the network. Our solution creatively integrates coding-theoretic designs inside of Merkle tree commitments to guarantee efficient and tamper-proof reconstruction; this solution is distinct from Asynchronous Verifiable Information Dispersal [7] (in guaranteeing efficient proofs of malformed coding) and Coded Merkle Tree [25] (which only provides guarantees for random corruption as opposed to our guarantees for worst-case corruption). We implement ACeD with full functionality in 6000 lines of Rust code, integrate the functionality as a smart contract into Ethereum via a high-performance implementation demonstrating up to 10,000 transactions per second in throughput and 6000x reduction in gas cost on the Ethereum testnet Kovan. Our code is available in [1].

1 Introduction

Public blockchains such as Bitcoin and Ethereum have demonstrated themselves to be secure in practice (more than a decade of safe and live operation in the case of Bitcoin), but at the expense of poor performance (throughput of a few transactions per second and hours of latency). Design of high performance (high throughput and low latency) blockchains without sacrificing security has been a major research area in recent years, resulting in new proof of work [4,13,23, 24], proof of stake [3,9,10,15,18], and hybrid [6,20] consensus protocols. These solutions entail a wholesale change to the core blockchain stack and existing blockchains can only potentially upgrade with very significant practical hurdles

---

The full version of paper is available in https://arxiv.org/abs/2011.00102
P. Sheng and B. Xue—Contributed equally to this work.

© International Financial Cryptography Association 2021
N. Borisov and C. Diaz (Eds.): FC 2021, LNCS 12675, pp. 299–318, 2021.
https://doi.org/10.1007/978-3-662-64331-0_16

(e.g.: hard fork of existing ledger). To address this concern, high throughput scaling solutions are explored via "layer 2" methods, including payment channels [11,19] and state channels [17,21,22]. These solutions involve "locking" a part of the ledger on the blockchain and operating on this trusted, locked state on an application layer outside the blockchain; however the computations are required to be semantically closely tied to the blockchain (e.g.: using the same native currency for transactions) and the locked nature of the ledger state leads to limited applications (especially, in a smart contract platform such as Ethereum).

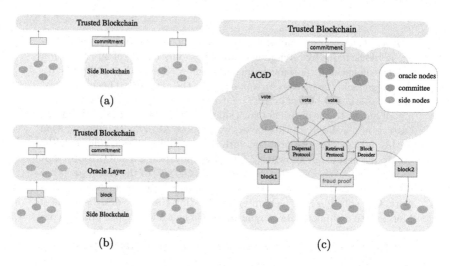

Fig. 1. (a) Side blockchains commit the hashes of blocks to a larger trusted blockchain. (b) An oracle layer is introduced to ensure data availability. (c) ACeD is a data availability oracle.

In practice, a popular form of scaling blockchain performance is via the following: a smaller blockchain (henceforth termed "side blockchain") derives trust from a larger blockchain (henceforth termed "trusted blockchain") by committing the hashes of its blocks periodically to the trusted blockchain (Fig. 1a). The ordering of blocks in the side blockchain is now determined by the order of the hashes in the trusted blockchain; this way the security of the side blockchain is directly derived from that of the trusted blockchain. This mechanism is simple, practical and efficient – a single trusted blockchain can cheaply support a large number of side blockchains, because it does not need to store, process or validate the semantics of the blocks of the side blockchains, only storing the hashes of them. It is also very popular in practice, with several side blockchains running on both Bitcoin and Ethereum; examples include donation trace (Binance charity [14]) and diplomas and credentials verification (BlockCert used by MIT among others [16]).

For decentralized operations of this simple scaling mechanism, any node in the side blockchain should be able to commit hashes to the trusted blockchain. This simple operation, however, opens up a serious vulnerability: an adversarial side blockchain node can commit the hash of a block without transmitting the block to any other side blockchain node. Thus, while the hash is part of the ordering according to the trusted blockchain, the block corresponding to the hash is itself unavailable at any side blockchain node; this *data availability attack* is a serious threat to the liveness of the side blockchain. The straightforward solution to this data availability attack is to store all blocks on the trusted blockchain, but the communication and storage overhead for the trusted blockchain is directly proportional to the size of the side blockchains and the mechanism is no longer scalable.

We propose an intermediate "data availability oracle" layer that interfaces between the side blockchains and the trusted blockchain (Fig. 1b). The oracle layer accepts blocks from side blockchains, pushes verifiable commitments to the trusted blockchain and ensures data availability to the side blockchains. The N oracle layer nodes work together to reach a consensus about whether the proposed block is retrievable (i.e., data is available) and only then commit it to the trusted blockchain. The key challenge is how to securely and efficiently share the data amongst the oracle nodes to verify data availability; if all oracle nodes maintain a copy of the entire side blockchain data locally (i.e., repetition), then that obviously leads to simple majority vote-based retrievability but is not scalable. If the data is dispersed among the nodes to reduce redundancy (we call this "dispersal"), even one malicious oracle node can violate the retrievability. Thus it appears there is an inherent trade-off between security and efficiency.

The main point of this paper is to demonstrate that the trade-off between security and efficiency is not inherent; the starting point of our solution is the utilization of an erasure code such that different oracle nodes receive different coded chunks. A key issue is how to ensure the integrity and correctness of the coded chunks. Intuitively we can use a Merkle tree to provide the proof of inclusion for any chunk, but a malicious block producer can construct a Merkle tree of a bunch of nonsense symbols so that no one can successfully reconstruct the block. To detect such attacks, nodes can broadcast what they received and meanwhile download chunks forwarded by others to decode the data and check the correctness. Such a method is used in an asynchronous verifiable information dispersal (AVID) protocol proposed by [7]. AVID makes progress on storage savings with the help of erasure code but sacrifices communication efficiency. Nodes still need to download all data chunks; hence, the communication complexity is $O(Nb)$. An alternative approach to detect incorrect coding attacks is via an *incorrect-coding proof* (also called fraud proof), which contains symbols that fail the parity check and can be provided by any node who tries to reconstruct the data; consider using an (n, k) Reed-Solomon code (which is referred as 1D-RS), with k coded symbols in the fraud proof, essentially not much better than downloading the original block (n symbols). For reducing the size of fraud proof, 2D-RS [2] places a block into a $(\sqrt{k}, \sqrt{k})$ matrix and apply $(\sqrt{n}, \sqrt{k})$ Reed-Solomon code on all columns and rows to generate n^2 coded symbols; 2D-RS reduces the fraud proof size to $O(\sqrt{b} \log b)$ if we assume symbol size is constant.

In summary (Table 1), to find a scalable solution for the data availability oracle problem, erasure code based methods must defend against the incorrect coding attack while minimizing the storage and communication cost. 1D-RS has low communication complexity but when the storing node is adversarial, the storage and download overhead are factor b worse than optimal. The storage and download overhead of AVID remains optimal even under adversarial storing node but the communication complexity is factor N worse than optimal. A full analysis on each performance entry in the table is provided in full paper.

Our main technical contribution is a new protocol, called Authenticated Coded Dispersal (ACeD), that provides a scalable solution to the data availability oracle problem. ACeD achieves near-optimal performance on all parameters (defined in Table 2): optimal storage, download and communication overhead under the normal path, and near-optimal (worse by a logarithmic factor) storage and download overhead when the storing node is adversarial, cf. Table 1. We state and prove the security of the data availability guarantee and efficiency properties of ACeD in a formal security model (Sect. 2).

Table 1. Performance metrics for different data availability oracles (N: number of oracle nodes, b: block size).

	Maximal adversary fraction	Normal case		Worst case		Communication complexity
		Storage overhead	Download overhead	Storage overhead	Download overhead	
Uncoded (repetition)	1/2	$O(N)$	$O(1)$	$O(N)$	$O(1)$	$O(Nb)$
Uncoded (dispersal)	1/N	$O(1)$	$O(1)$	$O(1)$	$O(1)$	$O(b)$
AVID [7]	1/3	$O(1)$	$O(1)$	$O(1)$	$O(1)$	$O(Nb)$
1D-RS	1/2	$O(1)$	$O(1)$	$O(b)$	$O(b)$	$O(b)$
2D-RS [2]	1/2	$O(1)$	$O(1)$	$O(\sqrt{b}\log b)$	$O(\sqrt{b}\log b)$	$O(b)$
ACeD	1/2	$O(1)$	$O(1)$	$O(\log b)$	$O(\log b)$	$O(b)$

Table 2. System performance metrics

Metric	Formula	Explanation
Maximal adversary fraction	β	The maximum number of adversaries is βN
Storage overhead	D_{store}/D_{info}	The ratio of total storage used and total information stored
Download overhead	$D_{download}/D_{data}$	The ratio of the size of downloaded data and the size of reconstructed data
Communication complexity	D_{msg}	Total number of bits communicated

Technical Summary of ACeD. There are four core components in ACeD, as is shown in Fig. 1c with the following highlights.

- ACeD develops a novel coded commitment generator called *Coded Interleaving Tree* (CIT), which is constructed layer by layer in an interleaved manner embedded with erasure codes. The interleaving property avoids downloading extra proof and thus minimizes the number of symbols needed to store.
- A dispersal protocol is designed to disperse tree chunks among the network with the least redundancy and we show how feasible dispersal algorithms ensure the reconstruction of all data.

- A hash-aware peeling decoder is used to achieve linear decoding complexity. The fraud proof is minimized to a *single parity equation*.

Performance Guarantees of ACeD. Our main mathematical claim is that safety of ACeD holds as long as the trusted blockchain is secure, and ACeD is live as long as the trusted blockchain is live and a majority of oracle nodes are honest (i.e., follow protocol) (Sect. 4.1). ACeD is the first scalable data availability oracle that promises storage and communication efficiency while providing a guarantee for security with a provable bound and linear retrieval complexity; see Table 1 with details deferred to Sect. 4.2. The block hash commitment on the trusted blockchain and the size of fraud proof are both in constant size.

Incentives. From a rational action point of view, oracle nodes are naturally incentivized to mimic others' decisions without storing/operating on their own data. This "information cascade" phenomenon is recognized as a basic challenge of actors abandoning their own information in favor of inferences based on actions of earlier people when making sequential decisions [12]. In the context of ACeD, we carefully use the semantics of the data dispersal mechanisms to design a probabilistic auditing mechanism that ties the vote of data availability to an appropriate action by any oracle node. This allows us to create a formal rational actor model where the incentive mechanism can be mathematically modeled: we show that the honest strategy is a strong Nash equilibrium; the details are deferred to full paper.

Algorithm to System Design and Implementation. We design an efficient system architecture implementing the ACeD components. Multithreaded erasure code encoding and block pipelining designs significantly parallelize the operations leading to a high performing architecture. We implement this design in roughly 6000 lines of code in Rust and integrate ACeD with Ethereum (as the trusted blockchain). We discuss the design highlights and implementation optimizations in Sect. 5.

Evaluation. ACeD is very efficient theoretically, but also in practice. Our implementation of ACeD is run by lightweight oracle nodes (e.g.: up to 6 CPU cores) communicating over a wide area network (geographically situated in three continents) and is integrated with the Ethereum testnet Kovan with full functionality for the side blockchains to run Ethereum smart contracts. Our implementation scales a side blockchain throughput up to 10,000 tx/s while adding a latency of only a few seconds. Decoupling computation from Ethereum (the trusted blockchain) significantly reduces gas costs associated with side blockchain transactions: in our experiments on a popular Ethereum app Cryptokitties, we find that the gas (Ethereum transaction fee) is reduced by a factor of over 6000. This is the focus of Sect. 6.

We conclude the paper with an overview of our contributions in the context of the interoperability of blockchains in Sect. 7.

2   System and Security Model

The system is made up of three components: a trusted blockchain (that stores commitments and decides ordering), clients (nodes in side blockchains who propose data), and an intermediate oracle layer ensuring data availability (see Fig. 1c).

2.1   Network Model and Assumptions

There are two types of nodes in the network: oracle nodes and clients.

Oracle nodes are participants in the oracle layer. They receive block commitment requests from clients, including block headers, and a set of data chunks. After verifying the integrity and correctness of the data, they vote to decide whether the block is available or not and submit the results to the trusted blockchain.

Clients propose blocks and request the oracle layer to store and commit the blocks. They periodically update the local ledger according to the commitment states from the trusted blockchain and ask oracle nodes for the missing blocks on demand.

One of the key assumptions of our system is that the trusted blockchain has a persistent order of data and liveness for its service. Besides, we assume that in the oracle layer, there is a majority of honest nodes. For clients, we only assume that at least one client is honest (for liveness). Oracle nodes are connected to all clients. The network is synchronous, and the communication is authenticated and reliable.

2.2   Oracle Model

The oracle layer is introduced to offload the storage and ensure data availability. The network of oracle layer consists of N oracle nodes, which can interact with clients to provide data availability service. There exists an adversary that is able to corrupt up to βN oracle nodes. Any node if not corrupted is called honest.

The basic data unit for the oracle layer is a *block*. A data availability oracle comprises of the following primitives which are required for committing and retrieving a block B.

1. **Generate chunks:** When a client wants to commit a block B to the trusted blockchain, it runs (generate_commitment(B, M)) to generate a commitment c for the block B and a set of M chunks $c_1, ..c_M$ which the block can be reconstructed from.
2. **Disperse chunks:** There is a dispersal protocol disperse$(B, (c_1, .., c_M), N)$ which can be run by the client and specifies which chunks need to be sent to which of the N oracle nodes.
3. **Oracle finalization:** The oracle nodes run a finalization protocol to finalize and accept certain blocks whose commitments are written into the trusted blockchain.
4. **Retrieve Data:** Clients can initiate a request (retrieve, c) for retrieving a set of chunks for any commitment c that has been accepted by the oracle.
5. **Decode Data:** There is a primitive decode$(c, \{c_i\}_{i \in S})$ that any client can run to decode the block from the set of chunks $\{c_i\}_{i \in S}$ retrieved for the commitment. The decoder also returns a proof that the decoded block B is related to the commitment.

We characterize the security of the oracle model and formally define data availability oracle as follows,

Definition 1. *A data availability oracle for a trusted blockchain accepts blocks from clients and writes commitments into the trusted blockchain with the following properties:*

1. **Termination:** *If an honest client initiates a* **disperse** *request for a block B, then block B will be eventually accepted and the commitment c will be written into the trusted blockchain.*
2. **Availability:** *If a dispersal is accepted, whenever an honest client requests for retrieval of a commitment c, the oracle is able to deliver either a block B or a null block ∅ and prove its relationship to the commitment c.*
3. **Correctness:** *If two honest clients on running (**retrieve**, c) receives B_1 and B_2, then $B_1 = B_2$. If the client that initiated the dispersal was honest, we require furthermore that $B_1 = B$, the original dispersed block.*

A naive oracle satisfying all above expectations is trivial to construct, e.g., sending all oracle nodes a full copy of data. However, what we want is a **scalable** data availability oracle. To better understand this motivation, in the next section, we will introduce some metrics to concretize the oracle properties.

3   Technical Description of ACeD

In this section, we describe the four components of ACeD: CIT, dispersal protocol, retrieval protocol and block peeling decoder.

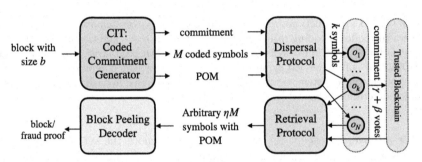

Fig. 2. The pipeline for a block to be committed in trusted blockchain.

3.1   Coded Interleaving Tree

The first building block of ACeD is a coded commitment generator which takes a block proposed by a client as an input and creates three outputs: a commitment, a sequence of *coded symbols*, and their proof of membership POM – see Fig. 2. The commitment is the root of a coded interleaving tree (CIT), the coded symbols are the leaves of CIT in the base layer, and POM for a symbol includes the Merkle proof (all siblings' hashes from each layer) and a set of *parity symbols* from all intermediate layers. A brief overview to erasure coding can be found in full paper.

The construction process of an example CIT is illustrated in Fig. 3. Suppose a block has size b, and its CIT has ℓ layers. The first step to construct the CIT is to divide the block evenly into small chunks, each is called a *systematic symbol*. The size of a systematic symbol is denoted as c, so there are $s_\ell = b/c$ systematic symbols. And we apply erasure codes with coding ratio $r \leq 1$ to generate $m_\ell = s_\ell/r$ coded symbols in base layer. Then by aggregating the hashes of every q coded symbols we get m_ℓ/q systematic symbols for its parent layer (layer $\ell - 1$), which can be further encoded to $m_{\ell-1} = m_\ell/(qr)$ coded symbols. We aggregate and code the symbols iteratively until the number of symbols in a layer decays to t, which is the size of the root.

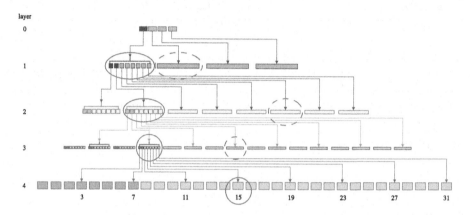

Fig. 3. (1) CIT construction process of a block with $s_\ell = 8$ systematic symbols, applied with erasure codes of coding ratio $r = \frac{1}{4}$. The batch size $q = 8$ and the number of hashes in root is $t = 4$. (2) Circled symbols constitute the 15th base layer coded symbol and its POM. The solidly circled symbols are the base layer coded symbol and its Merkle proof (intermediate systematic symbols), the symbols circled in dash are parity symbols sampled deterministicly.

For all layers j except for root, $1 \leq j \leq \ell$, denote the set of all m_j coded symbols as M_j, which contains two disjoint subsets of symbols: systematic symbols S_j and parity symbols P_j. The number of systematic symbols is $s_j = rm_j$. Specifically, we set $S_j = [0, rm_j)$ and $P_j = [rm_j, m_j)$. Given a block of s_ℓ systematic symbols in the base layer, the aggregation rule for the k-th systematic symbol in layer $j - 1$ is defined as follows:

$$Q_{j-1}[k] = \{H(M_j[x]) \mid x \in [0, M_j), k = x \bmod rm_{j-1}\} \tag{1}$$

$$M_{j-1}[k] = H(\text{concat}(Q_{j-1}[k])) \tag{2}$$

where $1 \leq j \leq \ell$ and H is a hash function. $Q[k]$ is the tuple of hashes that will be used to generate k-th symbol in the parent layer and concat represents the string concatenation function which will concatenate all elements in an input tuple.

Generating a POM for a base layer symbol can be considered as a layer by layer sampling process as captured by the following functions:

$$f_\ell : [m_\ell] \to \binom{m_{\ell-1}}{2}, \cdots, f_2 : [m_\ell] \to \binom{m_1}{2};$$

Each function maps a base layer symbol to two symbols of the specified layer: one is a systematic symbol and the other is a parity symbol. We denote the two symbols with a tuple of functions $f_j(i) = (p_j(i), e_j(i))$, where $p_j(i)$ is the sampled systematic symbol and $e_j(i)$ is the sampled parity symbol, each is defined as follows:

$$p_j(i) = i \bmod rm_{j-1}; \quad e_j(i) = rm_{j-1} + (i \bmod (1-r)m_{j-1}) \qquad (3)$$

where $p_j : [m_\ell] \to [0, rm_{j-1})$ and $e_j : [m_\ell] \to [rm_{j-1}, m_{j-1})$. Note that the sampled non-base layer systematic symbols are automatically the Merkle proof for both systematic and parity symbols in the lower layer.

There are two important properties of the sampling function. (1) It guarantees that if at least $\eta \leq 1$ ratio of distinct base layer symbols along with their POM are sampled, then in every intermediate layer, at least η ratio of distinct symbols are already picked out by the collected POM. It ensures the reconstruction of each layer of CIT (Lemma 2, *reconstruction* property). (2) All sampled symbols at each layer have a common parent (Lemma 3, *sibling* property), which ensures the space efficiency of sampling.

As described above, CIT can be represented by parameters $\mathcal{T} = (c, t, r, \alpha, q, d)$. All parameters have been defined except α, which is the *undecodable ratio* of an erasure code and d, which is the number of symbols in a failed *parity equation*. Both of them will be discussed in the decoder section (Sect. 3.3).

Comparison with CMT. (1) CIT is designed for the Push model (the client sends different chunks to different nodes) whereas CMT is designed for the Pull model (the nodes decide which chunks to sample from the client). (2) The CIT provides an ideal property (Lemma 2) that ensures reconstruction from any set of nodes whose size is greater than a given threshold. Thus as long as enough signatures are collected and we can be assured that the honest subset represented therein is larger than this threshold, we are guaranteed reconstruction in CIT. This is not the case in CMT, whose guarantees are probabilistic since each node samples data in a probabilistic manner. (3) On the technical side, CIT requires a new interleaving layer as well as a dispersal mechanism which decides how to assign the different symbols from intermediate layers to different groups. (4) Furthermore, CMT requires an assumption of an anonymous network whereas CIT does not require an anonymous network.

3.2 Dispersal Protocol

Given the commitment, coded symbols and POM generated by CIT, the dispersal protocol is used to decide the chunks all oracle nodes need to store. Consider a simple model where there are $M = b/(cr)$ chunks to be distributed to N nodes (each node may receive k chunks) such that any γ fraction of nodes together contains η fraction of chunks. The efficiency of the dispersal protocol is given by $\lambda = M/(Nk)$. We define the dispersal algorithm formally as follows,

Definition 2. *The chunk dispersal algorithm is said to achieve parameters set* $(M, N, \gamma, \eta, \lambda)$ *if there is a collection of sets* $\mathcal{C} = \{A_1, ..., A_N\}$ *such that* $A_i \subseteq [M]$, $|A_i| = \frac{M}{N\lambda}$. *Also, for any* $S \subseteq [N]$ *with* $|S| = \gamma N$, *it holds that* $|\bigcup_{i \in S} A_i| \geq \eta M$.

To simplify the 5 dimensional region, we consider the tradeoff on the three quantities: a certain triple (γ, η, λ) is said to be achievable if for any N, there exists M such that the chunk dispersal algorithm can achieve parameters set $(M, N, \gamma, \eta, \lambda)$. In the ACeD model, γ is constrained by security threshold β since the clients can only expect to collect chunks from at most $(1 - \beta)N$ nodes. η is constrained by the undecodable ratio α of the erasure code since the total chunks a client collects should enable the reconstruction. So for a given erasure code, there is a trade-off between dispersal efficiency and security threshold.

Our main result is the demonstration of a dispersal protocol with near optimal parameters (Lemma 1).

Lemma 1. *If* $\frac{\gamma}{\lambda} < \eta$, *then* (γ, η, λ) *is not feasible. If* $\frac{\gamma}{\lambda} > \log(\frac{1}{1-\eta})$ *then* (γ, η, λ) *is feasible and there exists a chunk dispersal protocol with these parameters.*

We provide a sketch of proof. If $\frac{\gamma}{\lambda} < \eta$, the maximum number of distinct symbols is $\frac{M}{N\lambda} \cdot \gamma M = \frac{M\gamma}{\lambda} < \eta M$, so (γ, η, λ) is not feasible.

If $\frac{\gamma}{\lambda} > \log(\frac{1}{1-\eta})$, we prove that the probability of $\mathcal{C}$ is not a valid code can vanish to as small as we want. The problem is transformed to the upper bound of $P(Y < \eta M)$ use a standard inequality from the method of types [8], where Y is the number of distinct chunks sampled. By sampling $\frac{\gamma}{\lambda}M$ chunks from a set of M chunks randomly, we have $P(Y < \eta M) \leq e^{-f(\cdot) \cdot M}$, where $f(\cdot)$ is a positive function. So the probability of $\mathcal{C}$ is a valid code can be positive, which proves the existence of a *deterministic* chunk distribution algorithm. And we can control the probability of $\mathcal{C}$ is not a valid code to be vanishingly small. The detailed proof of the result can be found in full paper.

In the dispersal phase, all oracle nodes wait for a data commitment c, k assigned chunks and the corresponding POM. The dispersal is accepted if $\gamma + \beta$ fraction of nodes vote that they receive the valid data.

3.3   Retrieval Protocol and Block Decoding

When a client wants to retrieve the stored information, the retrieval protocol will ask the oracle layer for data chunks. Actually, given erasure codes with undecodable ratio α, an arbitrary subset of codes with the size of over ratio $1 - \alpha$ is sufficient to reconstruct the whole block. When enough responses are collected, a hash-aware peeling decoder introduced in [25] will be used to reconstruct the block. The decoding starts from the root of CIT to the leaf layer and for each layer, it keeps checking all degree-0 parity equations and then finding a degree-1 parity equation to solve in turn. Eventually, either all symbols are decoded or there exists an invalid parity equation. In the second case, a logarithmic size incorrect-coding proof is prepared, which contains the inconsistent hash, d coded symbols in the parity equation and their Merkle proofs. After an agreement is reached on the oracle layer, the logarithmic size proof is stored in the trusted blockchain to permanently record the invalid block. Oracle nodes then remove all invalid symbols to provide space for new symbols. In the special case when the erasure code used by the CIT requires more than $(1 - \alpha)$ ratio of symbols to decode the original block, oracle nodes need to invoke a bad code handling protocol to reset a better code. We leave details in the full paper.

3.4 Protocol Summary

In summary, an ACeD system with N oracle nodes and block size b using CIT $\mathcal{T}$ and dispersal protocol $\mathcal{D}$ can be represented by parameters $(b, N, \mathcal{T}, \mathcal{D})$, where $\mathcal{T} = (c, t, r, \alpha, q, d)$ and $\mathcal{D} = (\gamma, \eta, \lambda)$. The pipeline to commit a block to the trusted blockchain is as follows (see Fig. 2).

- A client proposes a block of size b, it first generates a CIT with base layer symbol size c, number of hashes in root t, coding ratio r and batch size q. There are $M = b/(cr)$ coded symbols in the base layer. And then it disperses M coded symbols, their POM and the root of CIT to N oracle nodes using the dispersal protocol $\mathcal{D} = (\gamma, \eta, \lambda)$.
- Oracle nodes receive the dispersal request, they accept chunks and commitment, verify the consistency of data, POM and root, vote their results. A block is successfully committed if there are at least $\beta + \gamma$ votes. Upon receiving retrieval requests, oracle nodes send the stored data to the requester. Upon receiving the fraud proof of a block, oracle nodes delete the stored data for that block.
- Other clients send retrieval requests to the oracle nodes on demand. Upon receiving at least $\eta \geq 1 - \alpha$ fraction of chunks from at least γ oracle nodes, they reconstruct the block, if a coding error happens, the fraud proof will be sent to the trusted blockchain.

4   Performance Guarantees of ACeD

Theorem 1. *Given an adversarial fraction $\beta < \frac{1}{2}$ for an oracle layer of N nodes, ACeD is a data availability oracle for a trusted blockchain with $O(b)$ communication complexity, $O(1)$ storage and download overhead in the normal case, and $O(\log b)$ storage and download overhead in the worst case.*

This result follows as a special case of a more general result below (Theorem 2).

Proof. Suppose χ is an ACeD data availability oracle with parameters $(b, N, \mathcal{T}, \mathcal{D})$ where $\mathcal{T} = (c, t, r, \alpha, q, d)$ and $\mathcal{D} = (\gamma, \eta, \lambda)$. There are at most $\beta < \frac{1}{2}$ fraction of adversarial nodes in the oracle layer. Then by setting $r, q, d, t = O(1), c = O(\log b), b \gg N, \chi$ is secure as long as $\beta \leq \frac{1}{2}(1 - \lambda \log(\frac{1}{\alpha}))$; the communication complexity of χ is $O(b)$ because

$$Nyt + \frac{b}{\lambda r} + \frac{(2q - 1)by}{cr\lambda} \log_{qr} \frac{b}{ctr} = O(N) + O(b) + O(b) = O(b)$$

the storage and download overhead in the normal case is $O(1)$, because

$$\frac{Nyt}{b} + \frac{1}{\lambda r} + \frac{(2q-1)y}{cr\lambda} \log_{qr} \frac{b}{ctr} = O(1) + O(1) + O(\frac{1}{\log b} \log(\frac{b}{\log b})) = O(1)$$

the storage and download overhead in the worst case is $O(\log b)$, because

$$\frac{c(d-1)}{y} + d(q-1) \log_{qr} \frac{b}{ctr} = O(\log b) + O(\log_{qr}(\frac{b}{\log b})) = O(\log b)).$$

A complete description of the security and performance guarantees of ACeD is below.

Theorem 2. *ACeD is a data availability oracle for the trusted blockchain tolerating at most $\beta \leq 1/2$ fraction of adversarial oracle nodes in an oracle layer of N nodes. The ACeD is characterized by the system parameters $(b, N, \mathcal{T}, \mathcal{D})$, where $\mathcal{T} = (c, t, r, \alpha, q, d)$ and $\mathcal{D} = (\gamma, \eta, \lambda)$. y is a constant size of a hash digest, then*

1. *ACeD is secure under the conditions that*

$$\beta \leq \frac{1-\gamma}{2}; \ \frac{\gamma}{\lambda} > \log(\frac{1}{1-\eta}); \ \eta \geq 1-\alpha$$

2. *Communication complexity is*

$$Nyt + \frac{b}{\lambda r} + \frac{(2q-1)by}{cr\lambda} \log_{qr} \frac{b}{ctr}$$

3. *In normal case, both the storage and download overhead are*

$$\frac{Nyt}{b} + \frac{1}{\lambda r} + \frac{(2q-1)y}{cr\lambda} \log_{qr} \frac{b}{ctr}$$

4. *In worst case, both storage and download overhead are*

$$\frac{c(d-1)}{y} + d(q-1) \log_{qr} \frac{b}{ctr}$$

Proof. We prove the security and efficiency guarantees separately.

4.1   Security

To prove that ACeD is secure as long as the trusted blockchain is persistent and

$$1 - 2\beta \geq \gamma; \ \frac{\gamma}{\lambda} > \log(\frac{1}{1-\eta}); \ \eta \geq 1-\alpha,$$

we prove the following properties as per Definition 1.

- **Termination.** In ACeD, a dispersal is accepted only if there is a valid commitment submitted to the trusted blockchain. Suppose an honest client requests for dispersal but the commitment is not written into the trusted blockchain, then either the commitment is not submitted or the trusted blockchain is not accepting new transactions. Since $1 - 2\beta \geq \gamma$, thus $\beta + \gamma \leq 1 - \beta$, even if all corrupted nodes remain silent, there are still enough oracle nodes to vote that the data is available and the commitment will be submitted, hence the trusted blockchain is not live, which contradicts our assumption.

- **Availability.** If a dispersal is accepted, the commitment is on the trusted blockchain and $\beta + \gamma$ oracle nodes have voted for the block. Since the trusted blockchain is persistent, whenever a client wants to retrieve the block, it can get the commitment and at least γ nodes will respond with the stored chunks. On receiving chunks from γ fraction of nodes, for a CIT applying an erasure code with undecodable ratio α and a feasible dispersal algorithm (γ, η, λ) (Lemma 1), because $\eta \geq 1 - \alpha$, the base layer is reconstructable. Then we prove the following lemma ensures the reconstruction of all intermediate layers.

Lemma 2 *(Reconstruction). For any subset of base layer symbols W_ℓ, denote $W_j := \bigcup_{i \in W_\ell} f_j(i)$ as the set of symbols contained in POM of all symbols in W_ℓ. If $|W_\ell| \geq \eta m_\ell$, then $\forall j \in [1, \ell]$, $|W_j| \geq \eta m_j$.*

The proof of Lemma 2 utilizes the property when generating POM given base layer symbols. (See details in full paper). Thus the entire tree is eventually reconstructed and the oracle can deliver a block B, and the proof for B's relationship to commitment c is the Merkle proof in CIT. If a client detects a failed parity equation and outputs a null block $\emptyset$, it will generate an incorrect-coding proof.

- **Correctness.** Suppose for a given commitment c, two honest clients reconstruct two different blocks B_1 and B_2, the original dispersed block is B.
  (1) If the client that initiated the dispersal was honest, according to the availability property, $B_1, B_2 \neq \emptyset$, both clients can reconstruct the entire CIT. If $B_1 \neq B_2$, the commitment $c_1 \neq c_2$, which contradicts our assumption that the trusted blockchain is persistent.
  (2) If the client that initiated the dispersal was adversary and one of the reconstructed blocks is empty, w.l.o.g suppose $B_1 = \emptyset$, the client can generate a fraud proof for the block. If $B_2 \neq \emptyset$, the entire CIT is reconstructed whose root is commitment c_2. Since there is no failed equation in the CIT of B_2, $c_1 \neq c_2$, which contradict our assumption that the trusted blockchain is persistent.
  (3) If the client that initiated the dispersal was adversary and $B_1, B_2 \neq \emptyset$, both clients can reconstruct the entire CIT. If $B_1 \neq B_2$, the commitment $c_1 \neq c_2$, which contradict our assumption that the trusted blockchain is persistent.
  Thus we have $B_1 = B_2$, and if the client that initiated the dispersal is honest, $B_1 = B$.

4.2   Efficiency

Prior to computing the storage and communication cost for a single node to participate dispersal, we first claim a crucial lemma:

Lemma 3. *For any functions $p_j(i)$ and $e_j(i)$ defined in Eq. 3, where $1 \leq j \leq \ell$, $0 \leq i < m_\ell$, $p_j(i)$ and $e_j(i)$ are siblings.*

Lemma 3 indicates that in each layer, there are exactly two symbols included in the POM for a base layer symbol and no extra proof is needed since they are siblings (see proof details in the full version of paper). For any block B, oracle nodes need to store two parts of data, the hash commitment, which consists of t hashes in the CIT root, and k dispersal units where each unit contains one base layer symbol and two symbols per intermediate layer. Denote the total storage cost as X, we have

$$X = ty + kc + k[y(q-1) + yq] \log_{qr} \frac{b}{ctr} \qquad (4)$$

where y is the size of hash, b is the size of block, q is batch size, r is coding rate, and c is the size of a base layer symbol. Notice that $k = \frac{b}{Nrc\lambda}$, we have

$$X = ty + \frac{b}{Nr\lambda} + \frac{(2q-1)by}{Nrc\lambda} \log_{qr} \frac{b}{ctr}. \qquad (5)$$

It follows that the communication complexity is NX. In the normal case, each node only stores X bits hence the storage overhead becomes $\frac{NX}{b}$, and similarly when a client downloads data from N nodes, its overhead is $\frac{NX}{b}$. In the worst case, we use incorrect-coding proof to notify all oracle nodes. The proof for a failed parity equation which contains d coded symbols consist of $d-1$ symbols and their Merkle proofs, denote the size as P, we have

$$P = (d-1)c + dy(q-1) \log_{qr} \frac{b}{ctr}. \qquad (6)$$

The storage and download overhead in this case is $\frac{P}{y}$, the ratio of the proof size and the size of reconstructed data, a single hash y.

5   Algorithm to System Design and Implementation

ACeD clients are nodes associated with a number of side blockchains; the honest clients rely on ACeD and the trusted blockchain to provide an ordering service of their ledger (regardless of any adversarial fraction among the peers in the side blockchain). A client proposes a new block to all peers in the side blockchain by running ACeD protocol. An honest client confirms to append the new block to the local side blockchain once the block hash is committed in the trusted blockchain and the full block is downloaded. As long as there is a *single honest* client in the side blockchain, we have the following claim:

Claim. Once a block is confirmed by an honest client, security is guaranteed as long as the trusted blockchain is safe, even if the oracle layer is dishonest majority. Liveness is guaranteed when the trusted blockchain is live and the majority of the oracle layer is honest.

The claim indicates that in side blockchains, the safety of a confirmed block only relies on the trusted blockchain because the commitment on it is irrefutable once the trusted blockchain is safe, and the honest client has already downloaded the full block. So even if the oracle layer is occupied by the dishonest majority, those confirmed blocks are still safe. However, the liveness relies on the liveness of both ACeD and the trusted blockchain. As for the side blockchain network, because data persistence is guaranteed by ACeD, any client inside the network can safely conduct a transaction and reconstruct the ledger without worrying about a dishonest majority; similarly a valid transaction will eventually join the ledger as long as there is a single honest client who can include the transaction into a block.

Next we discuss the practical parameter settings for ACeD. We use these parameter choices to design and implement an ACeD oracle layer that interfaces with Ethereum as the trusted blockchain.

Parameter Specifications. We study an ACeD system with $N = 9000$ oracle nodes with adversarial fraction $\beta = 0.49$; the block size b is 12 MB and therefore $b \gg N$. In each block, the base layer symbol size c is $2000 \log b \approx 48$ kB, which corresponds to $\frac{b}{c} \approx 256$ uncoded symbols in the base layer. Within the setup, we construct a CIT of five layers with parameters: number of root symbols $t = 16$, hash size $y = 32$ bytes, coding ratio $r = 0.25$, aggregation batch size $q = 8$ and 4 erasure codes of size (256,128,64,32) for each non-root layer. For selecting erasure code properties, we use codes with undecodable ratio $\alpha = 0.125$, maximal parity equation size $d = 8$. In the dispersal protocol, we use $\eta = 0.875 = 1 - \alpha$, which translates to a dispersal efficiency $\lambda \leq \frac{1-2\beta}{\log \frac{1}{1-\eta}} = 1/150$, and therefore each oracle node needs to store roughly 17 symbols. With ACeD characterized by those parameters, the total communication cost for a client to commit a 12 MB block is roughly 5.38 GB; this represents a $0.5N$ factor boost over storing just one block. In the normal path, after accepting the 12 MB block, each oracle node only has to store 448 kB of data, a 3.7% factor of the original data; if there is an incorrect-coding attack, oracle layer will together upload data of size 339 kB incorrect-coding proof to the trusted blockchain. To download a block in the normal path, a client can use a naive method of collecting all symbols from all oracle nodes. Despite the conservative approach at block reconstruction, the entire download takes 5.38 GB. A simple optimization involving selectively querying the missing symbols can save significant download bandwidth: a client only needs 896 coded symbols in the base layer to reconstruct the block; thus, in the best case only 42 MB is needed to directly receive those symbols. When there is an incorrect-coding attack, a new user only needs to download the fraud proof which has been generated by other nodes (either client or oracle nodes); the proof is only of the size of 339 kB. Table 3 tabulates the performance metrics of ACeD (and baseline schemes) with these parameter settings. The calculation details of other protocols are described in the full paper.

Table 3. Performance metrics under a specific system parameterization.

	Maximal adversary fraction	Normal case		Worst case		Communication complexity
		Storage cost[a]	Download cost[a,b]	Storage cost[a]	Download cost[a]	
Uncoded (repetition)	0.49	12 MB	12 MB	12 MB	12 MB	108 GB
uncoded (dispersal)	0	1.3 kB	12 MB	1.2 kB	12 MB	12 MB
AVID [7]	0.33	4.37 kB	13.4 MB	32B	32B	354 GB
1D-RS	0.33	4.37 kB	13.4 MB	13.4 MB	13.4 MB	39.4 MB
1D-RS	0.49	67.1 kB	12.1 MB	12.1 MB	12.1 MB	604 MB
2D-RS	0.33	5.4 kB	16.6 MB	232.1 KB	232.1 KB	48.9 MB
2D-RS	0.49	72.1 kB	13 MB	925.6 KB	925.6 KB	648.6 MB
ACeD	0.33	50.3 kB	42 MB	339 kB	339 kB	452 MB
ACeD	0.49	597 kB	42 MB	339 kB	339 kB	5.38 GB

[a] cost is derived by $\frac{b}{N} \cdot$ overhead

[b] best case

The ACeD oracle layer interacts with the side blockchains and the trusted blockchain. For a high performance (high throughput, low gas), the oracle layer and its interaction protocols have to be carefully designed for software implementation. In this section, we discuss our system design decisions that guided the implementation.

Architecture. We use Ethereum as the trusted blockchain. The oracle nodes interact with Ethereum via a special (ACeD) smart contract; the contract is owned by a group of permissioned oracle nodes, who individually cannot update the contract, except that a majority of the oracle nodes together agree and perform a single action on the smart contract. The contract only changes its state after accepting a multisignature of majority votes [5]. We implement both the oracle nodes and side blockchain nodes in RUST; the architecture is depicted in Fig. 4. A detailed discussion of the design and implementation optimizations of these four blocks is provided in full paper, which also discusses the data structures that maintain the state of ACeD.

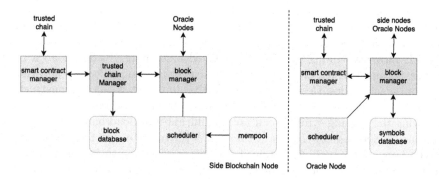

Fig. 4. The left figure depicts a block diagram of a side node; the right figure depicts an oracle node. The sharp rectangle represents an active thread; round rectangles are system states.

6   Evaluation

We aim to answer the following questions through our evaluation. (a) What is the highest throughput (block confirmation rate) that ACeD can offer to the side blockchains in a practical integration with Ethereum? (b) What latency overhead does ACeD pose to block confirmation? (c) How much is the gas cost reduced, given the computation (smart contract execution) is not conducted on the trusted blockchain? (d) What are the bottleneck elements to performance?

Testbed. We deploy our implementation of ACeD on Vultr Cloud hardware of 6 core CPU, 16 GB memory, 320 GB SSD and a 40 Gpbs network interface (for both oracle and side blockchain nodes). To simplify the oracle layer, we consider all of oracle nodes are committee members, which is reflected in the experiment topology: all the oracle nodes are connected as a complete graph, and each side blockchain node has TCP connections to each of the oracle nodes. We deploy a smart contract written in Solidity using the Truffle development tool on a popular Ethereum testnet: Kovan. Oracle nodes write their smart contracts using Ethereum accounts created with MetaMask, each loaded with sufficient Keth to pay the gas fee of each Ethereum transaction. We use an LDPC code of $\frac{b}{c} = 128$ input symbols with a coding rate of $r = 0.25$ to construct CIT with $q = 8, d = 8, \alpha = 0.125, \eta = 0.875, t = 16$. We fix the transaction length to be 316 bytes, which is sufficient for many Ethereum transactions.

Experiment Settings. We consider four separate experiments with varying settings of four key parameters (Table 4): the number of oracle nodes, the number of side blockchain nodes, block generation rate, and block size. The experiment results are in Fig. 5.

Table 4. Four different experiments varying the parameters of ACeD.

	# side blockchain nodes	# oracle nodes	Block size(MB)	Block generation rate(sec/blk)
A	5	5,10,15,25	4	5
B	5,10,20	10	4	5
C	5	10	4,8,16	5
D	3,5,8,10	10	4	8.33,5,3.125,2.5

(1) **Throughput.** We measure the rate of state update in the trusted blockchain as viewed from each oracle blockchain nodes; the throughput is then the rate averaged across time and across oracle blockchain nodes. The throughput performance changes with four parameters: In experiments A and B, the throughput is not noticeably impacted as the number of oracles or side blockchain nodes increases. In experiment C, the block size has roughly a linear effect on throughput, which continues until coding the block is too onerous (either it costs too much memory or takes too long). In experiment D, we fix the product of the block generating rate and the number of side blockchain node to constant, while

increasing the block generation rate, the throughput increases linearly; the performance will hit a bottleneck when the physical hardware cannot encode a block in a time smaller than the round time.

(2) The **latency** of ACeD is composed of three major categories: block encoding time, oracle vote collection time and time to update the trusted blockchain. We find latency stays relatively constant in all experiments (the exception is experiment C where block encoding is onerous).

(3) **Gas saving**. ACeD transactions cost significantly less gas than a regular Ethereum transaction, independent of the computational complexity of the transaction itself. The cost of an ACeD transaction voted by 10 oracles nodes on a 4MB block costs on average 570K gas. Based on a historical analysis of 977 Crytokitties transactions, we estimate a 220 byte transaction costing roughly 180,000 gas: ACeD gas savings are thus over a factor 6000. We emphasize that the saving in gas is independent of block generation rate or the block size, since the smart contract only needs the block header and a list of the oracle signatures.

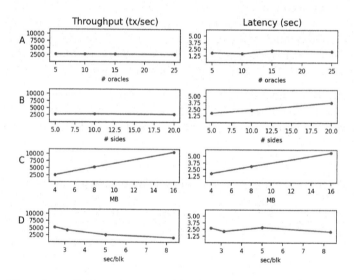

Fig. 5. Throughput (left) and Latency (right) for the 4 experiments A, B, C, D.

7   Conclusion and Discussion

Interoperability across blockchains is a major research area. Our work can be viewed as a mechanism to transfer the trust of an established blockchain (e.g.: Ethereum) to many small (side) blockchains. Our proposal, ACeD, achieves this by building an oracle that guarantees data availability. The oracle layer enabled by ACeD is run by a group of permissioned nodes which are envisioned to provide an *interoperability service* across blockchains; we have provided a detailed specification of ACeD, designed incentives to support our requirement of an honest majority among the oracle nodes, and designed and evaluated a high performance implementation.

ACeD solves the data availability problem with near optimal performance on all metrics. However, when instantiating the system with specific parameters, we observe that some metrics have to be computed with constant factors which give rise to acceptable but non-negligible performance loss. The critical bottleneck for ACeD is the lower undecodable ratio (the fraction of symbols in the minimum stopping set) compared to 1D-RS coding; this undermines dispersal efficiency and increases the communication cost under the existence of strong adversary. Therefore, finding a *deterministic* LDPC code with a higher undecodable ratio will immediately benefit the practical performance of ACeD; the construction of such LDPC codes is an exciting direction of future work and is of independent interest.

Acknowledgements. This research is supported in part by a gift from IOHK Inc., an Army Research Office grant W911NF1810332 and by the National Science Foundation under grant CCF 1705007.

References

1. Aced library. https://github.com/simplespy/ACeD.git
2. Al-Bassam, M., Sonnino, A., Buterin, V.: Fraud and data availability proofs: maximising light client security and scaling blockchains with dishonest majorities (2019)
3. Badertscher, C., Gaži, P., Kiayias, A., Russell, A., Zikas, V.: Ouroboros genesis: Composable proof-of-stake blockchains with dynamic availability. In: Proceedings of the 2018 ACM SIGSAC Conference on Computer and Communications Security, pp. 913–930 (2018)
4. Bagaria, V., Kannan, S., Tse, D., Fanti, G., Viswanath, P.: Prism: deconstructing the blockchain to approach physical limits. In: Proceedings of the 2019 ACM SIGSAC Conference on Computer and Communications Security, pp. 585–602 (2019)
5. Breidenbach, L., Daian, P., Juels, A., Sirer, E.G.: An in-depth look at the parity multisig bug (2017) http://hackingdistributed.com/2017/07/22/deepdive-parity-bug
6. Buterin, V., Griffith, V.: Casper the friendly finality gadget. arXiv preprint arXiv:1710.09437 (2017)
7. Cachin, C., Tessaro, S.: Asynchronous verifiable information dispersal. In: 24th IEEE Symposium on Reliable Distributed Systems (SRDS 2005), pp. 191–201. IEEE (2005)
8. Csiszár, I.: The method of types [information theory]. IEEE Trans. Inf. Theory **44**(6), 2505–2523 (1998)
9. Daian, P., Pass, R., Shi, E.: Snow White: robustly reconfigurable consensus and applications to provably secure proof of stake. In: Goldberg, I., Moore, T. (eds.) FC 2019. LNCS, vol. 11598, pp. 23–41. Springer, Cham (2019). https://doi.org/10.1007/978-3-030-32101-7_2
10. David, B., Gaži, P., Kiayias, A., Russell, A.: Ouroboros Praos: an adaptively-secure, semi-synchronous proof-of-stake blockchain. In: Nielsen, J.B., Rijmen, V.

(eds.) EUROCRYPT 2018. LNCS, vol. 10821, pp. 66–98. Springer, Cham (2018). https://doi.org/10.1007/978-3-319-78375-8_3

11. Decker, C., Wattenhofer, R.: A fast and scalable payment network with bitcoin duplex micropayment channels. In: Pelc, A., Schwarzmann, A.A. (eds.) SSS 2015. LNCS, vol. 9212, pp. 3–18. Springer, Cham (2015). https://doi.org/10.1007/978-3-319-21741-3_1

12. Easley, D., Kleinberg, J., et al.: Networks, Crowds, and Markets, vol. 8. Cambridge University Press, Cambridge (2010)

13. Fitzi, M., Gazi, P., Kiayias, A., Russell, A.: Parallel chains: Improving throughput and latency of blockchain protocols via parallel composition. IACR Cryptol. ePrint Arch. **2018**, 1119 (2018)

14. Foti, A., Marino, D.: Blockchain and charities: a systemic opportunity to create social value. In: Marino, D., Monaca, M.A. (eds.) Economic and Policy Implications of Artificial Intelligence. SSDC, vol. 288, pp. 145–148. Springer, Cham (2020). https://doi.org/10.1007/978-3-030-45340-4_11

15. Gilad, Y., Hemo, R., Micali, S., Vlachos, G., Zeldovich, N.: Algorand: scaling byzantine agreements for cryptocurrencies. In: Proceedings of the 26th Symposium on Operating Systems Principles, pp. 51–68 (2017)

16. Jirgensons, M., Kapenieks, J.: Blockchain and the future of digital learning credential assessment and management. J. Teach. Educ. Sustain. **20**(1), 145–156 (2018)

17. Kalodner, H., Goldfeder, S., Chen, X., Weinberg, S.M., Felten, E.W.: Arbitrum: scalable, private smart contracts. In: 27th {USENIX} Security Symposium ({USENIX} Security 2018), pp. 1353–1370 (2018)

18. Kiayias, A., Russell, A., David, B., Oliynykov, R.: Ouroboros: a provably secure proof-of-stake blockchain protocol. In: Katz, J., Shacham, H. (eds.) CRYPTO 2017. LNCS, vol. 10401, pp. 357–388. Springer, Cham (2017). https://doi.org/10.1007/978-3-319-63688-7_12

19. Miller, A., Bentov, I., Kumaresan, R., McCorry, P.: Sprites: payment channels that go faster than lightning. CoRR abs/1702.05812 306 (2017)

20. Pass, R., Shi, E.: Hybrid consensus: Efficient consensus in the permissionless model. In: 31st International Symposium on Distributed Computing (DISC 2017). Schloss Dagstuhl-Leibniz-Zentrum fuer Informatik (2017)

21. Poon, J., Buterin, V.: Plasma: scalable autonomous smart contracts. White paper, pp. 1–47 (2017)

22. Teutsch, J., Reitwießner, C.: A scalable verification solution for blockchains. arXiv preprint arXiv:1908.04756 (2019)

23. Yang, L., et al.: Prism: Scaling bitcoin by 10,000 x. arXiv preprint arXiv:1909.11261 (2019)

24. Yu, H., Nikolić, I., Hou, R., Saxena, P.: OHIE: blockchain scaling made simple. In: 2020 IEEE Symposium on Security and Privacy (SP), pp. 90–105. IEEE (2020)

25. Yu, M., Sahraei, S., Li, S., Avestimehr, S., Kannan, S., Viswanath, P.: Coded Merkle Tree: solving data availability attacks in blockchains. In: Bonneau, J., Heninger, N. (eds.) FC 2020. LNCS, vol. 12059, pp. 114–134. Springer, Cham (2020). https://doi.org/10.1007/978-3-030-51280-4_8

Efficient State Management
in Distributed Ledgers

Dimitris Karakostas[1,2]($\boxtimes$), Nikos Karayannidis[2], and Aggelos Kiayias[1,2]

[1] University of Edinburgh, Edinburgh, UK
dimitris.karakostas@ed.ac.uk, akiayias@inf.ed.ac.uk
[2] IOHK, Singapore, Singapore
nikos.karagiannidis@iohk.io

Abstract. Distributed ledgers implement a storage layer, on top of which a shared state is maintained in a decentralized manner. In UTxO-based ledgers, like Bitcoin, the shared state is the set of all unspent outputs (UTxOs), which serve as inputs to future transactions. The continuously increasing size of this shared state will gradually render its maintenance unaffordable. Our work investigates techniques that minimize the shared state of the distributed ledger, i.e., the in-memory UTxO set. To this end, we follow two directions: a) we propose novel transaction optimization techniques to be followed by wallets, so as to create transactions that reduce the shared state cost and b) propose a novel fee scheme that incentivizes the creation of "state-friendly" transactions. We devise an abstract ledger model, expressed via a series of algebraic operators, and define the transaction optimization problem of minimizing the shared state; we also propose a multi-layered algorithm that approximates the optimal solution to this problem. Finally, we define the necessary conditions such that a ledger's fee scheme incentivizes proper state management and propose a state efficient fee function for Bitcoin.

1 Introduction

The seminal work of Shostak, Pease, and Lamport, during the early'80s, introduced the consensus problem [19,27] and extended our understanding of distributed systems. 30 Years later, Bitcoin [25] introduced what is frequently referred to as "Nakamoto consensus" and the blockchain data structure, followed by widespread research on distributed ledgers.

In ledger systems, participants maintain a shared state which consists of three objects: i) the public ledger, i.e., the list of transactions which form the system's history; ii) the mempool, i.e., the set of, yet unpublished, transactions; iii) the active state which, in systems like Bitcoin, consists of the UTxO set. To support thousands (or millions) of participants, a decentralized system's state management should be well-designed, primarily focused on minimizing the shared state. Our work focuses on the third type, as poorly designed management often leads to performance issues and even Denial-of-Service (DoS) attacks. In Ethereum, during a 2016 DoS attack, an attacker added 18 million accounts to the state,

© International Financial Cryptography Association 2021
N. Borisov and C. Diaz (Eds.): FC 2021, LNCS 12675, pp. 319–338, 2021.
https://doi.org/10.1007/978-3-662-64331-0_17

increasing its size by 18 times [33]. Bitcoin saw similar spam attacks in 2013 [31] and 2015 [2], when millions of outputs were added to the UTxO set.

Problem Statement. Mining nodes and full nodes incur costs for maintaining the shared state in the Bitcoin network. This cost pertains to the resources (i.e., CPU, disk, network bandwidth, memory) that are consumed with every transaction transmitted, validated, and stored. An expensive part of a transaction is the newly created outputs, which are added to the in-memory UTxO set. As the system's scale increases, the cost of maintaining the UTxO set gradually leads to a shared-state bloat, which makes the cost of running a full node prohibiting.

Moreover, the system's incentives, which are promoted via transaction fees, only deteriorate the problem. For example, assume two transactions τ_A and τ_B: τ_A spends 5 inputs and creates 1 output, while τ_B spends 1 input and creates 2 outputs. Assuming the size of a UTxO is equal to the size of consuming it (200 bytes) and that transaction fees are 30 satoshi per byte, τ_A costs $30 \times 200 \times (5 + 1) = 36000$ satoshi and τ_B costs $30 \times 200 \times (1 + 2) = 18000$ satoshi. Although τ_B burdens the UTxO set by creating a net delta of $(2 - 1 = 1)$ new UTxO, while τ_A reduces the shared state by consuming $(1 - 5 = -4)$ UTxOs, τ_B is cheaper in terms of fees. Clearly, the existing fee scheme penalizes the consumption of multiple inputs, dis-incentivizing minimizing the shared state.

Our Contributions. Our goal is to devise a set of techniques that minimize the shared state of a distributed ledger, i.e., the in-memory UTxO set. Our approach is twofold: a) we propose transaction optimization techniques which, when employed by wallets, help reduce the shared state's cost; b) propose a novel fee scheme that incentivizes "shared state-friendly" transactions.

In particular, we propose a UTxO model, which abstracts UTxO ledgers and enables evaluating the cost of a ledger's shared state. We then propose a transaction optimization framework, based on three levels of optimization: a) b) a declarative (rule-based) level, c) a logical/algebraic (cost-based) level, and d) a physical/algorithmic (cost-based) level. Following, we propose three transaction optimization techniques based on the aforementioned optimization levels: a) a rule-driven optimal total order of transactions (the *last-payer rule*), b) a logical transaction transformation (the *2-for-1 transformation*), and c) a novel *input selection* algorithm that minimizes the UTxO set increase, i.e., favors consumption over creation of UTxOs. We then define the transaction optimization problem and propose a 3-step dynamic programming algorithm to approximate the optimal solution. Finally, we define the state efficiency property that a fee function should have, in order to correctly reflect a transaction's shared-state cost, and propose a state efficient fee function for Bitcoin.

Related Work. The problem of unsustainable growth of the UTxO set has concerned developers for years. It has been discussed in community articles [13,15], some [1] offering estimations on the level of inefficiency in Bitcoin. Additionally, research papers [8,12,26,28] have analyzed Bitcoin's and other cryptocurrencies' UTxO sets to gain further insight. Engineering efforts, e.g., in Bitcoin Core's newer releases [22], have also focused on improving performance by reducing the UTxO memory requirements. Various solutions have been proposed to reduce the state of a UTxO ledger, e.g., consolidation of outputs [32] can help reduce the cost of spending multiple small outputs. Alternatively, Utreexo [11], uses cryptographic accumulators to reduce the size of the UTxO set in memory, while BZIP [17] explores lossless compression of the UTxO set.

An important notion in this line of research is the "stateless blockchain" [30]. Such blockchain enables a node to participate in transaction validation without storing the entire state of the blockchain, but only a short commitment to it. Chepurnoy *et al.* [7] employ accumulators and vector commitments to build such blockchain. Concurrently, Boneh *et al.* [5] introduce batching techniques for accumulators in order to build a stateless blockchain with a trustless setup which requires constant amount of storage. We consider an orthogonal problem, i.e., constructing transactions in an incentive-compatible manner that minimizes the state, so these tools can act as building blocks in our proposed techniques.

The role of fees in blockchain systems has also been a topic of interest in recent years. Luu *et al.* [20] explored incentives in Ethereum, focusing on incentivizing miners to correctly verify the validity of scripts run on this "global consensus computer". Möser and Böhme [24] investigate Bitcoin fees empirically and observe that users' behavior depends primarily on the client software, rather than a rational cost estimation. Finally, in an interesting work, Chepurnoy *et al.* [6] propose a fee structure that considers the storage, computation, and network requirements; their core idea is to classify each transaction on one of the three resource types and set its fees accordingly.

2   A UTxO Model

We abstract a distributed ledger as a state machine on which parties act. Specifically, we consider only *payments*, i.e., value transfers between parties; a more elaborate model could take into account arbitrary computations on the ledger's data. We note that our model considers only *fungible* assets.

Initially, we assume a ledger state $\mathcal{S}_{init}$, on which a *transaction* is applied to move the ledger to a new state. Transactions that may be applied on a state are *valid*, following a validation predicate. Each transaction is unique and moves the system to a unique state; with hindsight, we assume that the ledger never transitions to the same state (cf. Definition 5), i.e., valid transactions do not form cycles.

Our formalism is similar to chimeric ledgers [34], though focused on UTxO-based ledgers. Following, we provide some basic definitions in a "top-down" approach, starting with the ledger $\mathcal{L}$, which is an ordered list of transactions; our notation of functions is the one typically used in functional programming languages, for example a function $f : A \to B \to C$ takes two input parameters of type A and B respectively and returns a value of type C.

Definition 1. *A ledger $\mathcal{L}$ is a list of valid transactions:* $\mathcal{L} \overset{def}{=} List[Transaction]$.

A transaction τ transitions the system from one state to another. UTxO-based transactions are thus a product of *inputs*, which define the ownership of assets, and *outputs*, which define the rules of re-transferring the acquired value.

Definition 2. *A UTxO-based transaction τ is defined as: Transaction $\stackrel{def}{=}$ (inputs : Set[Input], outputs : List[UTxO], forge : Value, fee : Value)*

An *unspent transaction output (UTxO)* represents the ownership of some value from a party, which is represented via an *address* α. Intuitively, in the real world, an output is akin to owning a physical coin of an arbitrary denomination.

Definition 3. *A UTxO is defined as follows: UTxO $\stackrel{def}{=}$ (α : Address, value : Value, created : Timestamp).*

A transaction's input is a reference to a UTxO, i.e., an output that is owned by the party that creates the transaction. An input consists of two objects: i) the *id* of the transaction that created it (typically its hash) and ii) an index, which identifies the specific output among all UTxOs of the referenced transaction.

Definition 4. *An input is defined as: Input $\stackrel{def}{=}$ (id : Hash, index : Int).*

Given an input and a ledger, three functions retrieve: i) the corresponding output, ii) the corresponding transaction, and iii) the input value. All returned values are wrapped in `Option`, denoting that a value may not be returned.

- UTxO : Input $\rightarrow$ $\mathcal{L}$ $\rightarrow$ Option[UTxO]
- τ : Input $\rightarrow$ $\mathcal{L}$ $\rightarrow$ Option[*Transaction*]
- *value* : Input $\rightarrow$ $\mathcal{L}$ $\rightarrow$ Option[*Value*]

A transaction defines some value that is given as a *fee* to the *miner*, i.e., the party who publishes the transaction into the ledger $\mathcal{L}$. We require that all transactions must preserve value as follows: $\tau.forged + \sum_{i \in \tau.inputs} value(i, \mathcal{L}) = \tau.fee + \sum_{o \in \tau.outputs} o.value$. We note that this applies only on standard transactions, not "coinbase" transactions which create new coins.

Finally, we define the ledger's state $\mathcal{S}$. $\mathcal{S}$ comprises the *UTxO set*, i.e., the set of all outputs of transactions whose value has not been re-transferred and can be used as inputs to new transactions.

Definition 5. *The ledger's state is defined as: State $\stackrel{def}{=}$ Set[Input].*

We now return to the state machine model. A transaction is applied on a ledger state $\mathcal{S}_1$ and results in a ledger state $\mathcal{S}_2$ via the function:

$$\text{txRun} : Transaction \rightarrow LedgerState \rightarrow LedgerState$$

An ordered list of transactions $\mathbb{T} = [\tau_1, \tau_2, \ldots, \tau_N]$ can be applied sequentially on state $\mathcal{S}_1$ to transit to state $\mathcal{S}_N$: $\mathcal{S}_N = (\text{txRun}(\tau_N). \ldots .\text{txRun}(\tau_2).\text{txRun}(\tau_1))(\mathcal{S}_1)$, assuming the function composition operator ".".

Finally, every ledger state S corresponds to some cost C. We assume a cost function, which assigns a signed integer of cost units to a ledger state.

$$\mathsf{cost} : LedgerState \rightarrow Cost$$

This function is employed in Definition 6, which defines a transaction's cost; minimizing this cost will be the target of our optimization. Observe that the transaction's cost might be negative, e.g., if the transaction reduces the state.

Definition 6. *The cost of a transaction τ applied to a state S is the difference between the cost of the final state minus the cost of the initial state:*

$$\mathsf{costTx} : Transaction \rightarrow LedgerState \rightarrow Cost$$
$$\mathsf{costTx}(\tau, S) = cost(\mathsf{txRun}(\tau, S)) - cost(S)$$

The cost of an ordered list of transactions $[T]$ applied to a state S is the difference between the cost of the final state minus the cost of the initial state:

$$\mathsf{costTotTx} : [Transaction] \rightarrow LedgerState \rightarrow Cost$$
$$\mathsf{costTotTx}([T], S) = cost((\mathsf{txRun}(\tau_N). \ \ldots \ .\mathsf{txRun}(\tau_2).\mathsf{txRun}(\tau_1))(S_1)) - cost(S)$$

We note that, in the rest of the paper, cost represents the size of the ledger's state. However, our model is generic enough to accommodate alternative cost designs as well. For instance, cost could represent the computational effort of producing or verifying the state, such that a cost unit would be a computational cycle. Therefore, our analysis would also be directly applicable in that case, by accordingly adapting some parts of the subsequent optimization framework like the heuristics.

3   Transaction Optimization

The purpose of a distributed ledger is to execute payments, i.e., transfer value from one party to another via transactions. Multiple transactions can perform the same transfer of value between two parties. Such transactions are *equivalent* in terms of their final result, i.e., transferring some value between parties A and B, but may vary in their cost to the ledger state. *Transaction optimization* is the problem of finding the equivalent transaction with minimum cost; our work is heavily inspired by the seminal research on database query optimization [16].

The cost difference between equivalent transactions may be significant. For example, assume that Alice wants to give Bob 100 coins and owns a UTxO of 100 coins and 100 UTxOs of 1 coin each. Consider the two equivalent plans: 1) Alice spends the single UTxO of value 100 and creates 100 outputs of value 1 for Bob; 2) Alice spends the 100 UTxOs of 1 coin value and defines a single UTxO of value 100 to transfer to Bob. The cost of the two approaches exemplifies the ledger state impact that equivalent transactions may have. The first plan increases the ledger's state by 99 UTxOs, while the second decreases it by the same amount.

Following, we use the terms plan and transaction interchangeably, i.e., an alternative plan that achieves the same goal is expressed as an alternative, equivalent transaction. Definition 7 describes transaction equivalency, while Definition 8 defines equivalency between two ordered lists of transactions.

Definition 7. *Transactions* τ_1, τ_2 *are equivalent (denoted* $\tau_1 \equiv \tau_2$*) if, when applied to the same state* $\mathcal{S}_A$ *of a ledger* $\mathcal{L}$*, they result in states* $\mathcal{S}_1$ *and* $\mathcal{S}_2$ *respectively, with the same total accumulated value per unique address* α*:*

$$\forall \alpha \in A \sum_{\substack{i \in \mathcal{S}_1 \\ o_i = \mathsf{UTxO}(i, \mathcal{L}) \\ o_i.address = \alpha}} o_i.value = \sum_{\substack{j \in \mathcal{S}_2 \\ o_j = \mathsf{UTxO}(j, \mathcal{L}) \\ o_j.address = \alpha}} o_j.value$$

where A *is the set of all addresses of the parties participating in the ledger system.*

Definition 8. *Two different totally ordered sets of the same* N *transactions* $[T_i]$ *and* $[T_j]$ *are equivalent (denoted as* $[T_i] \equiv [T_j]$*) if, when applied to the same ledger state* $\mathcal{S}_A$ *of a ledger* $\mathcal{L}$*, they result in states* $\mathcal{S}_1$ *and* $\mathcal{S}_2$ *respectively, where the total accumulated value per unique address* α *is the same in both states:*

$$\forall \alpha \in A \sum_{\substack{i \in \mathcal{S}_1 \\ o_i = \mathsf{UTxO}(i, \mathcal{L}) \\ o_i.address = \alpha}} o_i.value = \sum_{\substack{j \in \mathcal{S}_2 \\ o_j = \mathsf{UTxO}(j, \mathcal{L}) \\ o_j.address = \alpha}} o_j.value$$

where A *is the set of addresses of all participants in the distributed ledger system.*

Following, we define the basic logical operators for expressing a transaction and explore optimization techniques for compiling the optimal transaction plan.

3.1 Transaction Logical Operators - Ledger State Algebra

First, we introduce some basic *logical* operators, i.e., functions used to form a transaction. The operators are regarded as basic logical steps for executing a transaction, i.e., irrespective of their particular implementation. However, depending on their implementation, each step may correspond to different cost. The operators operate on and produce a state, forming *transactions* which may be equivalent (cf Definition 7). The operators and operands form a *ledger state algebra* and, as the state is a set of UTxOs (cf. Definition 5), all common set operators are applicable. In case of failure, they return the empty state $\varnothing$.

1. **Input Selection** $\sigma_{(P_{id}, V)}$: *LedgerState* $\rightarrow$ *LedgerState*
   $\sigma_{(P_{id}, V)}$ is a unary operator, which is given as input parameter a pair *(Party id, Value)*. *Party id* is an abstraction of a set of UTxOs, e.g., it could abstract a *wallet* that controls a set of addresses, each owning multiple UTxOs. When applied on a state $\mathcal{S}_i$, $\sigma_{(P_{id}, V)}$ produces a new state $\mathcal{S}_f \subset \mathcal{S}_i$, where $\forall o \in \mathcal{S}_f : o \in P_{id}$ and $\sum_{o \in P_{id}} o.value \geq V$. Essentially, σ is a filter over a state, selecting the UTxOs with aggregate value larger than, or equal to the input V.

2. **Output Creation** $\pi_{[(a_1,v_1),...,(a_n,v_n)]}$: *LedgerState* $\rightarrow$ *LedgerState*
   $\pi_{[(a_1,v_1),...,(a_n,v_n)]}$ is a unary operator, which is given a set of *(Address, Value)* pairs and is applied on a state $\mathcal{S}_i$. It produces a new UTxO set $\mathcal{S}_f$ with $\mathcal{S}_f \cap \mathcal{S}_i = \varnothing$, i.e., $\mathcal{S}_f$ includes only new UTxOs. Also $\forall o \in \mathcal{S}_f$: $(o.address, \sum_{o.address} o.value) \in [(a_1,v_1),...a_n,v_n)]$, i.e., the aggregate output value per address is equal to the input parameter. We require that value is preserved, i.e., the total value in $\mathcal{S}_i$ is greater than (or equal to) the total value in $\mathcal{S}_f$; the value difference is is the miners' fee.
3. **Transaction Validation** $\tau_{V_R,\mathcal{S}_i}$: *LedgerState* $\rightarrow$ *LedgerState* $\rightarrow$ *LedgerState*
   $\tau_{V_R,\mathcal{S}_i}$ is a binary operator that validates input and output states $\mathcal{S}_I, \mathcal{S}_O$, against a set of rules V_R, over an initial state $\mathcal{S}_G$. If validation succeeds, it returns an updated state $\mathcal{S}_f = (\mathcal{S}_G - \mathcal{S}_I) \cup \mathcal{S}_O$.

Figure 1 depicts the simplest transaction under our algebra, i.e., a tree with a root and two branches. The root is the transaction validation operator (τ) that receives two inputs: a) the set of selected inputs (σ on the left branch) and b) the set of outputs to be created (π on the right branch). Algebraically we express this transaction as: $T = (\sigma_{Alice,V})'\tau'(\pi_{Bob,V})$, $'\tau'$ being the infix validation operator.

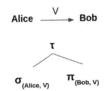

Fig. 1. The simplest expression of a transaction.

Moving one step further, we assume three transactions τ_1, τ_2 and τ_3. The execution of these transactions is *totally ordered*, i.e., $\tau_1 \rightarrow \tau_2 \rightarrow \tau_3$. Figure 2 depicts this expression. Here, τ_1 is nested within τ_2 and both are nested within τ_3. Such tree is executed from bottom to top, therefore τ_2 is given the ledger state generated after τ_1 is executed; similarly, τ_3 is given the ledger state generated after both τ_1 and τ_2 are executed. Given the above, we next define *subtransactions*; interestingly, transactions may spend outputs created from their subtransactions, thus we also define the notion of *correlated transactions*.

Definition 9. *A subtransaction is a transaction nested within a "parent" transaction; it is executed first, so its impact on the ledger state is visible to the parent.*

Definition 10. *Two transactions τ_1, τ_2 are correlated, if τ_1 is a subtransaction of τ_2 and τ_2 spends at least one output created by τ_1.*

3.2   A Transaction Optimization Framework

We now identify different phases in the transaction optimization process; in a hypothetical *transaction optimizer* each phase would be a distinct module. These phases are different approaches to producing equivalent transactions. The phases operate on three levels of optimization: a) a declarative (rule-based) level, b) a logical/algebraic (cost-based) level, and c) a physical/algorithmic (cost-based) level, as depicted in Fig. 3. The input of the process is a transaction set $[\tau_x]$, that we want to optimize, and the output is the optimal transaction $\tau_{x-Optimal}$.

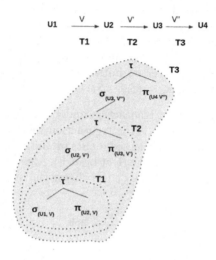

Fig. 2. The expression tree entails a transaction execution total order.

Rules: This phase is declarative, as it does not depend on the cost; instead, when applied, it necessarily produces a better transaction. Essentially it consists of *heuristic rules* that are applied by default to produce an equivalent transaction; example of such rules are "create a single output per address" or "consume as many inputs and create as few outputs as possible".

Algebraic Transformations: These are transformations at the level of logical operators that define a transaction's execution. Generally the efficiency of such transformation is evaluated based on the entailed cost. Examples of such transformations are the 2-for-1 transformation (cf. Definition 11) and different transaction orderings (cf. Definition 9).

Methods and Structures: This phase optimizes the algorithm that implements a logical operator. For instance, given two algorithms A, B result in transaction costs C_A, C_B, if $C_A < C_B$ we would choose A; one such example is the different implementations of the input selection operator σ, as shown in Fig. 4. Optimizations in this phase may also change the data structure used to access the underlying data, which in our case is the ledger state.

Planning and Searching: This phase employs a *searching strategy* to explore the available space of candidate solutions, i.e., equivalent transaction plans. This space consists of the transactions produced from the above phases, each evaluated based on their cost, under the available cost model.

3.3 Transaction Optimization Techniques

In this section, we propose three transaction optimization techniques based on the aforementioned optimization levels: a) heuristic rule-based, b) logical/algebraic transformation cost-based, and c) physical/algorithmic cost-based.

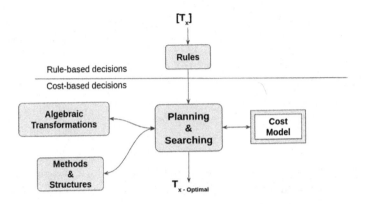

Fig. 3. The transaction optimization process.

Input Selection Optimization. We demonstrate this technique with an example. Assume Alice wants to give Bob 5 coins. Figure 4 depicts three equivalent transactions for implementing this payment. Observe that each plan is represented as a tree, where the intermediate nodes are the previously defined logical operators (that act on a ledger state) and the leaf nodes are ledger states. We also assume that the state cost is the number of elements (UTxOs) in the state. The three transactions have the same structure, i.e., they are the same logical expression, but result to different ledger states with different costs. The transactions differ only in the output of the input selection operator ($\sigma_{(Alice,5)}$), a difference which may be attributed to different implementations of the operator; in the paper's full version [18], we provide a novel input selection algorithm that minimizes the net delta of created UTxOs; it favors UTxO consumption over creation.

The 2-for-1 Transformation. We again consider the example where Alice wants to give Bob 5 coins. Figure 5 depicts a fourth, more complex, equivalent transaction. This transaction consists of two subtransactions (cf. Definition 9), where Alice first gives Bob 17 coins and then receives 12. When the first transaction is completed, an intermediate state (S_i') is created, which is then given as input to the second transaction, that produces the final ledger state S_f of cost 3. Observe that, although more complex, this transaction minimizes the final ledger state (72% cost reduction). Intuitively, this transaction spends all of Alice's outputs with the first sub-transaction and then does the same for Bob with the second sub-transaction. Therefore, the optimal cost does not depend on input selection (like the 3rd plan of Fig. 4), but requires the combination of two transactions that implement a single payment, under a specific amount (12). Definition 11 provides a formal specification of the *2-for-1* logical (algebraic) transformation.

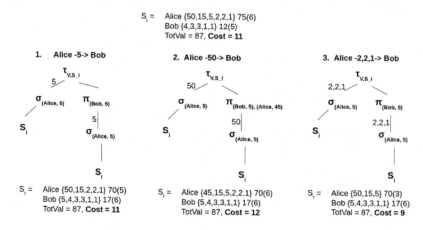

Fig. 4. An example of three equivalent transactions that transfer 5 tokens from Alice to Bob but incur different state costs.

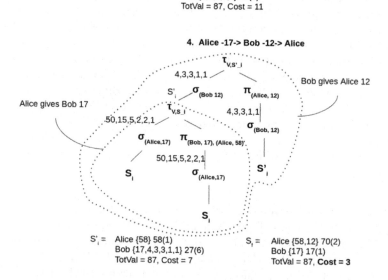

Fig. 5. A 2-for-1 transaction that transfers 5 tokens from Alice to Bob.

Definition 11. *Given a transaction τ_1, which transfers an amount V from party A to B, the algebraic 2-for-1 transformation creates an equivalent transaction τ_2, which consists of (a) (b) a subtransaction, which transfers $V + V_c$ from party A to B and (c) an outer transaction, which transfers V_c from party B to A.*

Figure 6 depicts the 2-for-1 algebraic transformation based on an amount V_c. To implement such a scheme we require an *atomic operation*, where the grouped transactions are executed simultaneously. One method to implement the atomic transfers is CoinJoin [21], which was proposed for increasing the privacy in Bitcoin; in CoinJoin, the transaction is constructed and signed gradually by each party that contributes its inputs. A similar concept is Algorand's atomic transfers [14], that groups transactions under a common id.

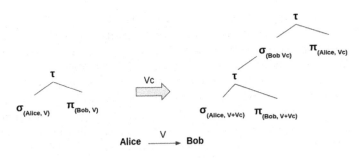

Fig. 6. The 2-for-1 algebraic transformation.

Intuitively, 2-for-1 reduces the transaction's cost by also consuming UTxOs of the receiving party, instead of only consuming outputs of the sending party. Specifically, assume the initial state $\mathcal{S}_i = \{|A|, |B|\}$, where $|A|$ denotes the number of outputs owned by party A. When issuing a payment to B, party A can consume all outputs and consolidate its remaining value to a single UTxO, the "change" output. Such transaction results in state $\mathcal{S}_f = \{1, |B| + 1\}$ with cost $cost(\mathcal{S}_f) = |B| + 2$. If we apply the 2-for-1 transformation, the final state is $\mathcal{S}_f' = \{1 + 1, 1\}$ with a cost of $cost(\mathcal{S}_f') = 3$; if $|B| > 1$, then $cost(\mathcal{S}_f') < cost(\mathcal{S}_f)$. Therefore, if the receiving party has multiple outputs, this transformation creates a transaction with a smaller cost. Consequently, by giving the opportunity to the receiving party of a transaction to spend also its outputs, the 2-for-1 transformation *always* results in a greater shared state cost reduction than the individual un-transformed transaction in the case where there are no fee constraints and thus outputs can be spent freely; otherwise it is a cost-based decision.

Transaction Total Ordering and the Last-Payer Heuristic Rule. Assume the following four transactions: (1) T_1: Alice $\xrightarrow{V_1}$ Charlie, (2) T_2: Bob $\xrightarrow{V_2}$ Charlie, (3) T_3: Eve $\xrightarrow{V_3}$ Alice, and (4) T_4: Eve $\xrightarrow{V_4}$ Bob. which are applied on an initial ledger state $\mathcal{S}_i = \{|Alice| = 5, |Bob| = 5, |Charlie| = 2, |Eve| = 3\}$ with cost

$cost(\mathcal{S}_i) = 15$; as before, $|A|$ denotes the number of outputs owned by party A and the state cost is the number of all UTxOs.

A first execution order is as follows: $T_1 \rightarrow T_2 \rightarrow T_3 \rightarrow T_4$. For simplicity and without loss of the generality, we assume that when a party pays, it always consumes all available outputs, thus having a single output afterwards (the leftover balance). Similarly, when a party gets paid, the number of UTxOs that it owns increases by one. The state changes with each executed transaction:

i) $\mathcal{S}_i = \{|Alice| = 5, |Bob| = 5, |Charlie| = 2, |Eve| = 3\}, cost = 15$

ii) $T_1 : \{|Alice| = 1, |Bob| = 5, |Charlie| = 3, |Eve| = 3\}, cost = 12$

iii) $T_2 : \{|Alice| = 1, |Bob| = 1, |Charlie| = 4, |Eve| = 3\}, cost = 8$

iv) $T_3 : \{|Alice| = 2, |Bob| = 1, |Charlie| = 4, |Eve| = 1\}, cost = 8$

v) $T_4 : \{|Alice| = 2, |Bob| = 2, |Charlie| = 4, |Eve| = 1\}, cost = 9$

Under a different order, $T_3 \rightarrow T_4 \rightarrow T_1 \rightarrow T_2$, the cost of the final state would be 7. Evidently, the different execution order results in different resulting state cost. Therefore, by changing the nesting order of the transactions in an expression tree, different plans may conduct the same payment with different cost.

Intuitively, parties should have the ability to consume outputs that are produced by the other transactions. For instance, regarding T_1 and T_3, the order $T_3 \rightarrow T_1$ is more cost effective ($cost = 10$) than $T_1 \rightarrow T_3$ ($cost = 11$), since Alice can consume the output created by Eve. Specifically, if in the last transaction where $\mathcal{P}$ participates, either as a sender or a receiver, $\mathcal{P}$ is the sender, then it can minimize its state cost; we call this the *last-payer heuristic rule*.

Ensuring that each party participates in their last transaction as a sender is not always feasible. Specifically, conflicts may arise in cyclic situations, where $\mathcal{P}_1$ pays $\mathcal{P}_2$ (T_{12}) and also $\mathcal{P}_2$ pays $\mathcal{P}_1$ (T_{21}). Here, it is impossible for both $\mathcal{P}_1$ and $\mathcal{P}_2$ to be the sender in their last transaction. Algorithm 1 below, achieves a transaction ordering based on the last-payer heuristic that bypasses conflicts. This algorithm has a time complexity of $O(M \log M)$ in the number M of participants.

We provide a short example to demonstrate the inner-workings of Algorithm 1. Assume the four transactions: $T_{12} : \mathcal{P}_1 \rightarrow \mathcal{P}_2$, $T_{21} : \mathcal{P}_2 \rightarrow \mathcal{P}_1$, $T_{13} : \mathcal{P}_1 \rightarrow \mathcal{P}_3$, and $T_{23} : \mathcal{P}_2 \rightarrow \mathcal{P}_3$. First (line 2), the algorithm sorts the list of participants in ascending order of receiving payments, i.e., the more payments a party receives, the more last-payers will conflict, so it should not be considered early-on as a last-payer. In our example, where $\mathcal{P}_3$ receives the most (2) payments, this results in order: $\mathcal{P}_1, \mathcal{P}_2, \mathcal{P}_3$. Next (lines 4 - 11), for each party $\mathcal{P}$ in the ordered list, the algorithm tries to find a transaction where $\mathcal{P}$ pays a party who has not been already considered as a last-payer (thus avoiding conflicts); if such transaction exists, it is placed last in the final transaction ordering. Finally, the list of remaining transactions is inserted to the head of the list (line 12). In our example, the transaction ordering through each iteration is: 1st iteration : $[T_{12}]$, 2nd iteration : $[T_{12}, T_{23}]$, 3rd iteration : $[T_{12}, T_{23}]$, final : $[T_{21}, T_{13}, T_{12}, T_{23}]$. As per the Last-Payer heuristic rule, each party is the sender in their last transaction, except for party $\mathcal{P}_3$ which only receives payments.

Algorithm 1: Transaction ordering algorithm based on the Last-Payer heuristic rule.

Input: A set of M participants $Set[\mathcal{P}_1, \mathcal{P}_2, \ldots, \mathcal{P}_M]$

Input: A set of k transactions $Set[T_{ij}], i, j = 1, 2, \ldots, M$ among these participants to be ordered. Assume that in transaction T_{ij} party $\mathcal{P}_i$ pays party $\mathcal{P}_j$ ($\mathcal{P}_i \xrightarrow{V_{ij}} \mathcal{P}_j$). Also assume that the transactions are not correlated (see definition 10) and thus all orders are equivalent (see definition 8).

Output: A totally ordered set of transactions $[T_{ij}]$.

1   $output \longleftarrow \emptyset$ $[FinalOrderOfTransactions] \longleftarrow \emptyset$
2   $[OrderedParticipants] \longleftarrow$ Order the input set of participants in an ascending order of the number of received payments.
3   $[ParticipantsLastPaymentAdded] \longleftarrow \emptyset$
4   **while** $[OrderedParticipants] \neq \emptyset$ **do**
5      $\mathcal{P}_{current} \longleftarrow$ get and remove first item from $[OrderedParticipants]$
6      $T_X \longleftarrow$ Find and then remove from $Set[T_{ij}]$, a transaction that $\mathcal{P}_{current}$ pays some participant $\mathcal{P}$ where $\mathcal{P} \notin [ParticipantsLastPaymentAdded]$
7   **if** $T_x == \emptyset$ **then**
8   continue;   /* continue to the next participant */
9   **else**
10        $[FinalOrderofTransactions] \longleftarrow T_x$; /* Put it last in the final ordered list */
11        $[ParticipantsLastPaymentAdded] \longleftarrow \mathcal{P}_{current}$

12   $[FinalOrderOfTransactions] \longleftarrow Set[T_{ij}]$;   /* Add the remaining transactions of the initial set at the beginning (head) of the ordered list */
13   $ouput \longleftarrow [FinalOrderOfTransactions]$

Assuming k transactions among M parties, Algorithm 1 is executed locally by each party $\mathcal{P}_i$ after the M participants have coordinated off-chain the k transactions. Specifically, the wallet of each participant exchanges information, in order to gather all k transactions, and then executes the algorithm. The produced total order of transactions will be expressed as a tree of the form depicted in Fig. 2 and will be implemented as an atomic operation in a similar manner to the 2-for-1 transformation discussed above. Such off-chain coordination for transaction posting is not unique to our work, e.g., this is also how CoinJoin [21] works.

Interestingly, the grouping of many transactions into an atomic operation in general, is a method that can be also aimed at increasing privacy. Therefore, it is an interesting direction for future research to see if it is possible to combine both privacy and space efficiency considerations.

3.4 The Transaction Optimization Problem

Using the above ideas, we now formally define the transaction optimization problem as a typical *optimization problem*, assuming a set of available input selection algorithms $\{Sel_1, Sel_2, \ldots, Sel_l\}$.

Definition 12. *Given N payments between M parties $\mathcal{P}_1, \mathcal{P}_2, \ldots, \mathcal{P}_M$ and a search space $\mathcal{S}$ of equivalent (cf. Definition 8), ordered lists of transaction plans that execute the N payments, called* candidate solutions, *find the candidate $\tau \in \mathcal{S}$, such that $eval(\tau) \leq eval(\rho)$, for all $\rho \in \mathcal{S}$. Specifically:*

1. *A candidate $\rho \in S$ is an ordered list of transaction plans*[1] $||T_1|| \to ||T_2|| \to \cdots \to ||T_k||$, *where the transaction plan of a transaction T_x is the pair:* $||T_x|| \overset{def}{=}$ *(Logical Expression, Input Selection Algorithm).*
2. *The search space S is defined by all candidates* $||T_1|| \to ||T_2|| \to \cdots \to ||T_k||$, *where, for each transaction T_i, an input selection algorithm is chosen from* $\{Sel_1, Sel_2, \ldots, Sel_l\}$ *and, possibly, the 2-for-1 logical transformation (cf. Definition 11) is applied.*
3. *eval evaluates the cost of every candidate $\rho \in S$ (cf. Definition 6) as follows:*

$$eval : [Transaction] \to LedgerState \to Cost,$$
$$eval([T_1, T_2, \ldots, T_k], S_{init}) =$$
$$cost((txRun(T_k). \ldots .txRun(T_2).txRun(T_1))(S_{init})) - cost(S_{init})$$

where $cost(S) = |S|$ is the size of a ledger state (cf. Definition 5) and $(txRun(T_k). \ldots .txRun(T_2).txRun(T_1))(S_{init})$ *outputs the final state after the list of transactions is executed on state S_{init} for each plan $||T_i||$.*

Solving the Transaction Optimization Problem. We now present a 3-step, dynamic programming algorithm, which solves the transaction optimization problem via an exhaustive search and dynamically pruning candidate solutions:

Step 1: Create N transactions $T_{ij}, i, j \in [1, M]$, corresponding to the N payments $(\mathcal{P}_i \xrightarrow{V_{ij}} \mathcal{P}_j)$, as follows: $T_{ij} = (\sigma_{\mathcal{P}_i, V_{ij}}(S_{init}))'\tau'(\pi_{\mathcal{P}_j, Vij}(S_{init}))$ where V_{ij} is the amount to be paid from $\mathcal{P}_i$ to $\mathcal{P}_j$. For each transaction T_{ij}, find the input selection algorithm in $\{Sel_1, Sel_2, \ldots, Sel_l\}$ that minimizes $eval(T_{ij}, S_{init})$. Then, enforce the *heuristic rule* to create a *single* output per recipient address for each transaction. At the end of this step, the algorithm outputs N transaction plans, i.e., N pairs of transaction's T_{ij} logical expression and the chosen input selection algorithm:

$$||T_{ij}|| = ((\sigma_{\mathcal{P}_i, V_{ij}}(S_{init}))'\tau'(\pi_{\mathcal{P}_j, Vij}(S_{init})), \ Sel_s)$$

Step 2: On each transaction plan output of Step 1, perform a 2-for-1 transformation (cf. Definition 11). This step produces a transformed transaction as depicted in Fig. 7, based on an amount $p \times V_{ij}$, where p is a configuration parameter of the algorithm, typically in the range $0 < p \leq 1$. Then, for each of the two transactions that comprise the 2-for-1 transformation, choose the input selection algorithm that minimizes the *eval* function and enforce the heuristic rule of a *single* output per recipient address. Finally, accept the 2-for-1 transformed transaction only if its cost (given by *eval*) is smaller than the non-transformed transaction.

---

[1] We assume that transactions are non-correlated (cf. Definition 10) and all orderings are equivalent (cf. Definition 8).

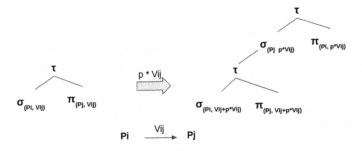

Fig. 7. Applying the 2-for-1 transformation to each separate transaction.

At the end of this step, the algorithm outputs k transaction plans, $k \geq N$, comprising of the 2-for-1 transformed and the non-transformed transactions, along with their input selection algorithms. Importantly, at this point, the algorithm has an optimal plan for each *individual* payment ($\mathcal{P}_i \xrightarrow{V_{ij}} \mathcal{P}_j$), based on an exhaustive search of solutions and cost-driven choices.

Step 3: In this step, the algorithm finds the optimal execution order for the k transactions produced in Step 2. Given the $k!$ permutations, the search space is pruned using the *Last-Payer heuristic rule* (cf. Section 3.3). Finally, the algorithm outputs an ordered list of transaction plans that execute the N payments with a minimum state ledger cost.

As shown, step 2 produces optimal transaction plans, w.r.t. executing the individual transactions, since it performs an exhaustive search for the minimum-cost solution. Step 3 though is based on a heuristic (Last-Payer) to prune the search space, thus only approximating the optimal solution. Future work will evaluate this rule's efficiency and explore techniques to achieve optimality.

4   State Efficiency in Bitcoin

We now define the *state efficiency* property. Our goal is to incentivize users to minimize the global state, without impacting the system's functionality. In that case, if all users are rational, i.e., operate following the incentives, then the state will be minimized as much as possible. Future work will explore the actual impact of deploying such incentives in real-world systems.

To achieve state efficiency, a transaction's fee should be proportional to the incurred state cost. In other words, the more a transaction increases the ledger's state, the higher its fees should be. Specifically, a transaction's fee should reflect: i) the transaction's size, i.e., the cost of storing a transaction permanently on the ledger and ii) the transaction's state cost. A distributed ledger's fee model should aim at incentivizing users to minimizing both storage types, i.e., the distributed ledger and the global state.

First, we define the *fee function F*, i.e., the function that assigns an (integer) fee on a transaction, given a ledger state: $F : Transaction \rightarrow LedgerState \rightarrow Int$. Following, Definition 13 describes *state efficiency*. This property instructs the fee function to (monotonically) increase fees, if a transaction increases the state. Intuitively, between two equivalent transactions, the transaction that incurs greater state cost should also incur a larger fee.

Definition 13. *A fee function F is* state efficient *if*

$$\forall \mathcal{S} \in \mathbb{S} \forall \tau_1, \tau_2 \in \mathbb{T} \mid \tau_1 \equiv \tau_2 \wedge costTx(\tau_1, \mathcal{S}) > costTx(\tau_2, \mathcal{S}) : F(\tau_1, \mathcal{S}) > F(\tau_2, \mathcal{S})$$

for transaction cost function (cf. Definition 6) and equivalence (cf. Definition 7).

Evidently, if the utility of users is to minimize transaction fees, a state efficient fee function ensures that they are also incentivized to minimize the global state. Finally, Definition 14 sets *narrow state efficiency*, a special case of state efficiency which compares equivalent transactions that differ only in their inputs.

Definition 14. *A fee function F is* narrow state efficient *if*

$$\forall \mathcal{S} \in \mathbb{S} \forall \tau_1, \tau_2 \in \mathbb{T} \mid$$
$$\tau_1 \equiv \tau_2 \wedge \tau_1.\mathsf{outputs} = \tau_2.\mathsf{outputs} \wedge costTx(\tau_1, \mathcal{S}) > costTx(\tau_2, \mathcal{S}) :$$
$$F(\tau_1, \mathcal{S}) > F(\tau_2, \mathcal{S})$$

for transaction cost function (cf. Definition 6) and equivalence (cf. Definition 7).

Bitcoin's State Management. Bitcoin's consensus model does not consider fees. Specifically, the user decides a transaction's fees and the miners choose whether to include a transaction in a block. Therefore, it has been stipulated that the level of fees is the balance between the rational choices of miners, who supply the market with block space, and users, who demand part of said space [3].

In practice, most users follow the client software's choice even when not needed [24], e.g., when blocks are not full. Similarly, miners usually follow the hard-coded software rules and may accept even zero-fee transactions. The reference rules of the Bitcoin Wiki [3] define the *fee rate x*, which is the fraction of fees per transaction size, Miners sort transactions based on this metric and solve the Knapsack problem to fill a new block with transactions that maximize it. Some notable alternatives also focus on fee rate [10,29], while reference rules [3] used to also take into account the UTxO age.

As before, a transaction consists of inputs and outputs, i.e., old UTxOs which are spent and newly-created UTxOs. Inputs and UTxOs have a fixed size ι and ω respectively.[2] The size of a transaction is the sum of its inputs and outputs, i.e., is a linear combination of ι and ω, while a transaction's cost is the difference

---

[2] This assumption slightly diverges from the real-world, where UTxOs are typically of varying size depending on the operations in the ScriptPubKey.

between the number of its UTxOs minus its inputs. Bitcoin's fee function is $F = \beta \cdot \mathsf{size}(\tau)$, where $\mathsf{size}(\tau)$ is τ's size in bytes and β is a fixed fee per byte.[3]

We break the fee efficiency of F via a counterexample. Assume two transactions which are applied on the same ledger state $\mathcal{S}$; for ease of notation, in the rest of the section $F(\tau)$ denotes $F(\tau, \mathcal{S})$. First, τ_1 has 1 input and 1 output, so its state cost is $\mathsf{costTx}(\tau_1, \mathcal{S}) = 0$ and its fee is $F(\tau_1) = \beta \cdot (\iota + \omega)$. Second, τ_2 has 2 inputs and 1 output, i.e., its state cost is $\mathsf{costTx}(\tau_2, \mathcal{S}) = -1$, since it decreases the state; however, its fee is $F(\tau_2) = \beta \cdot (2 \cdot \iota + \omega) = F(\tau_1) + \beta \cdot \iota$. Thus, although $\mathsf{costTx}(\tau_1) > \mathsf{costTx}(\tau_2)$, τ_2's fee is higher, since it is larger.

A better alternative fee function is the following: $F' = \beta \cdot \mathsf{size}(\tau) + \psi \cdot \mathsf{costTx}(\tau, \mathcal{S})$. Note that this is state-efficient in our model for a sufficiently small value of β (cf. Sect. 4.1). Observe with this function, when increasing the UTxO set, a user needs to pay an extra fee ψ per UTxO. Given this change, the reference rules are updated so that, instead of only the fee rate, miners use the scoring function: $\mathsf{score}(\tau) = \frac{\mathsf{fees}(\tau) - \psi \cdot \mathsf{costTx}(\tau, \mathcal{S})}{\mathsf{size}(\tau)}$, where $\mathsf{fees}(\tau)$ are τ's total fees. In market prices, 1 byte of RAM costs $\$3.35 \cdot 10^{-9}$ [23]. The average size of a Bitcoin UTxO is 61 Bytes [9], so a single Bitcoin UTxO costs $\psi = 61 \cdot 3.35 \cdot 10^{-9} = \$2 \cdot 10^{-7}$. Given 10000 full nodes[4], which maintain the ledger and keep the UTxO in memory, the cost becomes $\psi = \$0.002$; equivalently, denominated in Bitcoin[5], the cost of creating a UTxO is $\psi = 22$ satoshi.

This solution incorporates the operational costs of miners, thus it is the rational choice for miners who aim at maximizing their profit. Observe that, after subtracting the fees that relate to UTxO costs, the scoring mechanism behaves the same as the one currently used by Bitcoin miners. Therefore, if users wish to prioritize their transactions, they would again simply increase their transaction's fees; in that case, the UTxO portion of the fees (i.e., $\psi \cdot \mathsf{costTx}(\tau, \mathcal{S})$) remains the same, hence higher fees result in a higher score, similar to the existing mechanism. Also we note that this mechanism is directly enforceable on Bitcoin without the need of a fork.

4.1   A State Efficient Bitcoin

Intuitively, to make F state efficient we force the creator of a UTxO to subsidize its consumption, i.e., to pay the user who later consumes it. Our fee function is again: $F' = \beta \cdot \mathsf{size}(\tau) + \psi \cdot \mathsf{costTx}(\tau, \mathcal{S})$. Assume two transactions τ_1, τ_2 with i_1, i_2 inputs and o_1, o_2 outputs respectively:

$$\mathsf{costTx}(\tau_1) > \mathsf{costTx}(\tau_2) \Leftrightarrow o_1 - i_1 > o_2 - i_2 \Leftrightarrow o_2 - o_1 < i_2 - i_1 \tag{1}$$

---

[3] $\beta = 0.0067\$/\text{byte}$ [September 2020] (https://bitinfocharts.com).
[4] https://bitnodes.io [July 2020].
[5] $1 BTC = \$9000$ [July 2020] (https://coinmarketcap.com)

F' is state efficient (cf. Definition 13) if:

$$F'(\tau_1) > F'(\tau_2) \Rightarrow$$
$$\mathsf{size}(\tau_1) \cdot \beta + \mathsf{costTx}(\tau_1) \cdot \psi > \mathsf{size}(\tau_2) \cdot \beta + \mathsf{costTx}(\tau_2) \cdot \psi \Rightarrow$$
$$(i_1 \cdot \iota + o_1 \cdot \omega) \cdot \beta + (o_1 - i_1) \cdot \psi > (i_2 \cdot \iota + o_2 \cdot \omega) \cdot \beta + (o_2 - i_2) \cdot \psi \Rightarrow$$
$$(o_1 - i_1) \cdot \psi - (o_2 - i_2) \cdot \psi > (i_2 \cdot \iota + o_2 \cdot \omega) \cdot \beta - (i_1 \cdot \iota + o_1 \cdot \omega) \cdot \beta \Rightarrow$$
$$(i_2 - i_1 + o_1 - o_2) \cdot \psi > ((i_2 - i_1) \cdot \iota + (o_2 - o_1) \cdot \omega) \cdot \beta \overset{(1)}{\Longrightarrow}$$
$$\psi > \frac{(i_2 - i_1) \cdot \iota + (o_2 - o_1) \cdot \omega}{(i_2 - i_1) - (o_2 - o_1)} \cdot \beta \qquad (2)$$

If F' is narrow state efficient, then $o_1 = o_2$ and the inequality is simplified:

$$\psi > \iota \cdot \beta \qquad (3)$$

We turn again to the previous example. For transaction τ_1, with 1 input and 1 output, $F'(\tau_1) = (\iota + \omega) \cdot \beta$ and for transaction τ_2, with 2 inputs and 1 output, $F'(\tau_2) = (2 \cdot \iota + \omega) \cdot \beta - \psi = F'(\tau_1) + \beta \cdot \iota - \psi$. Since Inequalities 2 and 3 ensure that $\psi > \iota \cdot \beta$, the size fee of the extra input in τ_2 is offset by the extra fee ψ, which is paid by the user who creates it. Again to evaluate these variables we consider market prices. The size of a typical, pay-to-script-hash or pay-to-public-key-hash, UTxO is 34 Bytes [4], while the size of consuming it is 146 bytes. Therefore, to make and make present-day Bitcoin (narrow) state efficient, we can set $\omega = 34$, $\iota = 146$, $\beta = 0.0067\$$, and thus $\psi > 0.0978\$$.

However, this approach presents a number of challenges. To enforce F', the fee policy should be incorporated in the consensus protocol and a transaction's validity will depend on its amount of fees. As long as $F'(\tau) > 0$, i.e., a transaction cannot have negative fees, the fee function can be enforced via a *soft* fork. Specifically, this change is backwards compatible, as miners that do not adopt this change will still accept transactions that follow the new fee scheme. However, if $\mathsf{costTx}(\tau) \ll 0$ and possibly $F'(\tau) < 0$, to implement F' we need to establish a "pot" of fees. When a user creates τ with fee $F' = \beta \cdot \mathsf{size}(\tau) + \psi \cdot \mathsf{costTx}(\tau, \mathcal{S})$, the first part $(\beta \cdot \mathsf{size}(\tau))$ is awarded to the miners as before. The second part $(\psi \cdot \mathsf{costTx}(\tau, \mathcal{S}))$ is deposited to (or, in case of negative cost, withdrawn from) the pot. In case of negative cost, the transaction defines a special UTxO for receiving the reimbursement. At any point in time, the size of the pot is directly proportional to the UTxO set. Observe that the miners receive the same rewards as before, so their business model is not affected by this change. Finally, the cost of flooding the system with UTxOs increases by ψ per UTxO which, depending on ψ, can render attacks ineffective.

5   Conclusion

Our paper explores optimizations that minimize the state which is shared among the participants of a distributed ledger system. We compose a framework for optimizing transactions on multiple levels, including heuristic rules, algebraic transformations, and alternative sub-routines. Next, we formally define the optimization problem of constructing state efficient transactions and present an algorithm that approximates the optimal solution. Finally, we explore how fees can incentivize proper state management and propose an amended, state efficient fee function for Bitcoin. Our work also proposes various questions. For instance, complex cost models could also consider a UTxO's in-memory lifespan. Furthermore, future work could explore the implications of using a memory hierarchy, instead of storing the entire state in memory.

Acknowledgements. This research was partially supported by H2020 project PRIVILEDGE #780477.

References

1. Andresen, G.: Utxo uh-oh... (2015). http://gavinandresen.ninja/utxo-uhoh
2. Bitcoin: July 2015 flood attack (2015). https://en.bitcoin.it/wiki/July_2015_flood_attack
3. Bitcoin: Miner fees (2020). https://en.bitcoin.it/wiki/Miner_fees
4. Bitcoin: Protocol documentation (2020). https://en.bitcoin.it/wiki/Protocol_documentation
5. Boneh, D., Bünz, B., Fisch, B.: Batching techniques for accumulators with applications to IOPs and stateless blockchains. Cryptology ePrint Archive, Report 2018/1188 (2018). https://eprint.iacr.org/2018/1188
6. Chepurnoy, A., Kharin, V., Meshkov, D.: A systematic approach to cryptocurrency fees. In: Zohar, A., et al. (eds.) FC 2018. LNCS, vol. 10958, pp. 19–30. Springer, Heidelberg (2019). https://doi.org/10.1007/978-3-662-58820-8_2
7. Chepurnoy, A., Papamanthou, C., Zhang, Y.: Edrax: a cryptocurrency with stateless transaction validation. Cryptology ePrint Archive, Report 2018/968 (2018). https://eprint.iacr.org/2018/968
8. Delgado-Segura, S., Pérez-Solà, C., Navarro-Arribas, G., Herrera-Joancomartí, J.: Analysis of the bitcoin UTXO set. Cryptology ePrint Archive, Report 2017/1095 (2017). https://eprint.iacr.org/2017/1095
9. Delgado-Segura, S., Pérez-Solà, C., Navarro-Arribas, G., Herrera-Joancomartí, J.: Analysis of the Bitcoin UTXO set. In: Zohar, A., et al. (eds.) FC 2018. LNCS, vol. 10958, pp. 78–91. Springer, Heidelberg (2019). https://doi.org/10.1007/978-3-662-58820-8_6
10. Dos Santos, S., Chukwuocha, C., Kamali, S., Thulasiram, R.K.: An efficient miner strategy for selecting cryptocurrency transactions. In: 2019 IEEE International Conference on Blockchain (Blockchain), pp. 116–123 (2019)
11. Dryja, T.: Utreexo: a dynamic hash-based accumulator optimized for the bitcoin UTXO set. Cryptology ePrint Archive, Report 2019/611 (2019). https://eprint.iacr.org/2019/611
12. Easley, D., O'Hara, M., Basu, S.: From mining to markets: the evolution of bitcoin transaction fees. J. Finan. Econ. **134**(1), 91–109 (2019)
13. Frost, E., van Wirdum, A.: Bitcoin's growing utxo problem and how utreexo can help solve it (2019). https://bitcoinmagazine.com/articles/bitcoins-growing-utxo-problem-and-how-utreexo-can-help-solve-it

14. Fustino, R.: Algorand atomic transfers (2019). https://medium.com/algorand/algorand-atomic-transfers-a405376aad44
15. Ichiba Hotchkiss, G.: The 1.x files: The state of stateless ethereum (2019). https://blog.ethereum.org/2019/12/30/eth1x-files-state-of-stateless-ethereum
16. Ioannidis, Y.E.: Query optimization. ACM Comput. Surv. **28**(1), 121–123 (1996)
17. Jiang, S., et al.: Bzip: a compact data memory system for utxo-based blockchains. In: 2019 IEEE International Conference on Embedded Software and Systems (ICESS), pp. 1–8. IEEE (2019)
18. Karakostas, D., Karayannidis, N., Kiayias, A.: Efficient state management in distributed ledgers. Cryptology ePrint Archive, Report 2021/183 (2021). https://eprint.iacr.org/2021/183
19. Lamport, L., Shostak, R., Pease, M.: The byzantine generals problem. ACM Trans. Program. Lang. Syst. (TOPLAS) **4**(3), 382–401 (1982)
20. Luu, L., Teutsch, J., Kulkarni, R., Saxena, P.: Demystifying incentives in the consensus computer. In: Ray, I., Li, N., Kruegel, C. (eds.) ACM CCS 2015: 22nd Conference on Computer and Communications Security, pp. 706–719. ACM Press, Denver, CO, USA, 12–16 October 2015. https://doi.org/10.1145/2810103.2813659
21. Maxwell, G.: Coinjoin: Bitcoin privacy for the real world (2013). https://bitcointalk.org/index.php?topic=279249.msg2983902#msg2983902
22. Maxwell, G.: A deep dive into bitcoin core v0.15 (2017). http://diyhpl.us/wiki/transcripts/gmaxwell-2017-08-28-deep-dive-bitcoin-core-v0.15/
23. McCallum, J.C.: Historical memory prices 1957+ (2020). https://en.bitcoin.it/wiki/Miner_fee://jcmit.net/memoryprice.htm
24. Möser, M., Böhme, R.: Trends, tips, tolls: a longitudinal study of bitcoin transaction fees. In: Brenner, M., Christin, N., Johnson, B., Rohloff, K. (eds.) FC 2015. LNCS, vol. 8976, pp. 19–33. Springer, Heidelberg (2015). https://doi.org/10.1007/978-3-662-48051-9_2
25. Nakamoto, S.: Bitcoin: a peer-to-peer electronic cash system (2008)
26. Nicolas, H.: The economics of bitcoin transaction fees. SSRN Electron. J. (2014). https://doi.org/10.2139/ssrn.2400519
27. Pease, M., Shostak, R., Lamport, L.: Reaching agreement in the presence of faults. J. ACM (JACM) **27**(2), 228–234 (1980)
28. Pérez-Solà, C., Delgado-Segura, S., Navarro-Arribas, G., Herrera-Joancomart, J.: Another coin bites the dust: an analysis of dust in UTXO based cryptocurrencies. Cryptology ePrint Archive, Report 2018/513 (2018). https://eprint.iacr.org/2018/513
29. Rizun, P.R.: A transaction fee market exists without a block size limit (2015)
30. Todd, P.: Making UTXO set growth irrelevant with low-latency delayed TXO commitments (2016). https://petertodd.org/2016/delayed-txo-commitments
31. Vasek, M., Thornton, M., Moore, T.: Empirical analysis of denial-of-service attacks in the bitcoin ecosystem. In: Böhme, R., Brenner, M., Moore, T., Smith, M. (eds.) FC 2014. LNCS, vol. 8438, pp. 57–71. Springer, Heidelberg (2014). https://doi.org/10.1007/978-3-662-44774-1_5
32. Bitcoin Wiki: How to cheaply consolidate coins to reduce miner fees (2020). https://en.bitcoin.it/wiki/How_to_cheaply_consolidate_coins_to_reduce_miner_fees
33. Wilcke, J.: The ethereum network is currently undergoing a DOS attack (2016). https://blog.ethereum.org/2016/09/22/ethereum-network-currently-undergoing-dos-attack/
34. Zahnentferner, J.: Chimeric ledgers: translating and unifying UTXO-based and account-based cryptocurrencies. Cryptology ePrint Archive, Report 2018/262 (2018). https://eprint.iacr.org/2018/262

Fast Isomorphic State Channels

Manuel M. T. Chakravarty[1], Sandro Coretti[2], Matthias Fitzi[2(✉)], Peter Gaži[3],
Philipp Kant[4], Aggelos Kiayias[5,6], and Alexander Russell[7,8]

[1] IOHK, Utrecht, The Netherlands
manuel.chakravarty@iohk.io
[2] IOHK, Zürich, Switzerland
{sandro.coretti,matthias.fitzi}@iohk.io
[3] IOHK, Bratislava, Slovakia
peter.gazi@iohk.io
[4] IOHK, Berlin, Germany
philipp.kant@iohk.io
[5] IOHK, Edinburgh, UK
[6] University of Edinburgh, Edinburgh, UK
akiayias@inf.ed.ac.uk
[7] IOHK, Storrs, USA
[8] University of Connecticut, Storrs, USA
acr@cse.uconn.edu

Abstract. State channels are an attractive layer-two solution for improving the throughput and latency of blockchains. They offer optimistic off-chain settlement of payments and expedient offchain evolution of smart contracts between multiple parties without any assumptions beyond those of the underlying blockchain. In the case of disputes, or if a party fails to respond, cryptographic evidence collected in the offchain channel is used to settle the last confirmed state onchain, such that in-progress contracts can be continued under mainchain consensus.

In this paper, we introduce *Hydra*, an *isomorphic* multi-party state channel. Hydra simplifies offchain protocol and smart-contract development by directly adopting the layer-one smart contract system, allowing the same code to be used on- and off-chain. Taking advantage of the *extended UTxO model*, we develop a fast off-chain protocol for evolution of Hydra *heads* (our isomorphic state channels) that has smaller round complexity than all previous proposals and enables the state channel processing to advance on-demand, concurrently and asynchronously. We establish strong security properties for the protocol, and we present and evaluate extensive simulation results that demonstrate that Hydra approaches the physical limits of the network in terms of transaction confirmation time and throughput while keeping storage requirements at the lowest possible. Finally, our experimental methodology may be of independent interest in the general context of evaluating consensus protocols.

1 Introduction

Permissionless distributed ledger protocols suffer from serious scalability limitations, including high latency (transaction settlement time), low throughput

© International Financial Cryptography Association 2021
N. Borisov and C. Diaz (Eds.): FC 2021, LNCS 12675, pp. 339–358, 2021.
https://doi.org/10.1007/978-3-662-64331-0_18

(number of settled transactions per unit of time), and excessive storage required to maintain the state of the system and its ever-growing transaction history.

Several approaches to mitigating these issues by improving the underlying ledger protocols have been proposed. Such direct adaptations for scalability are often referred to as *layer-one* solutions. Layer-one solutions face inherent limitations, however, as settlement remains a unwieldy process involving the participation of a large, dynamic set of parties and requiring exchange of significant amounts of data. An alternative approach to improve scalability are *layer-two* (or *offchain*) solutions that overlay a new protocol on top of the (layer-one) blockchain. Layer-two solutions allow parties to securely transfer funds from the blockchain into an offchain protocol instance, settle transactions in this instance (quasi) independently of the underlying chain, and safely transfer funds back to the underlying chain as needed.

Offchain solutions have the advantage that they do not require trust assumptions beyond those of the underlying blockchain, and that they can be very efficient in the optimistic case where all participants of an offchain protocol instance behave as expected.

The most prominent offchain solution are payment channels [7, 15, 28]. A payment channel is established among two parties, allowing them to pay funds back and forth on this channel without notifying the layer-one protocol in the optimistic case. Payment channels gave rise to payment channel networks, such as Lightning [28], virtual payment channels, such as Perun [18], state channels which generalize from payments to smart contracts [4], followed by state channel networks [14, 20, 25], multiparty state channels [26] and virtual state channels [17].

Despite the significant advances, important challenges remain:

- establishing high offchain processing performance that approximates the physical limits of the underlying network; and
- reducing the significant conceptual and engineering overhead: In current solutions, the offchain contract state must be verified in a non-native representation as the state of a contract to be evolved in a state channel needs to be isolated and represented in a form that permits its manipulation both offchain, and by the onchain smart contract scripting system in case of an offchain dispute. Thus, computations performed offchain are no longer in the representation used by the ledger itself; i.e., they are non-native.

Hydra. Hydra tackles both these challenges with the introduction of *isomorphic* multi-party state channels. These are state channels that are capable of reusing the exact state representation of the underlying ledger and, hence, inherit the ledger's scripting system as is. Thus, state channels effectively yield parallel, offchain ledger siblings, which we call *heads*—the ledger becomes multi-headed. The creation of a new head follows a similar commitment scheme as is common in state channels. However, once a state channel is closed, the head state is seamlessly absorbed into the underlying ledger state and the same smart contract code as used offchain is now used onchain. This is possible, even without a priori registration of the contracts used in a head, because one and the same state representation and contract (binary) code is used offchain and onchain.

Not every blockchain scripting system is conducive to isomorphic state channels. Building them requires to efficiently carve out arbitrary chunks of blockchain state, process them independently, and be able at any time to efficiently merge them back in. We observe that the Bitcoin-style UTxO ledger model [5,29] is particularly well suited as a uniform representation of onchain and offchain state, while simultaneously promising increased parallelism in transaction processing. While the main restriction of the plain UTxO model has traditionally been its limited scripting capabilities, the introduction of the *Extended UTxO model (EUTxO)* [11] has lifted this restriction and enabled support for general state machines. Extended UTxO models form the basis for the smart contract platforms of existing blockchains, such as Cardano [13] and Ergo [16]; hence, the work presented in this paper would also be of immediate practical relevance.

Like the UTxO ledger representation, the EUTxO ledger representation makes all data dependencies explicit without introducing *false dependencies*: two transactions only depend on each other if there is an actual data dependency between them. This avoids the over-sequentialization of systems depending on a global state and is optimal as far as parallel transaction processing is concerned [8].

Exploiting the EUTxO ledger representation, we design an offchain protocol with unparalleled performance. In particular, the offchain protocol is capable of processing asynchronously and concurrently between different members of the head, utilizing merely 3 rounds of interaction for updates.

In more detail, in Hydra, a set of parties *commit* a set of UTxOs (owned by the parties) into an offchain protocol, called the *head protocol*. That UTxO set constitutes the initial head state, which the parties can then evolve by handling transactions among themselves without blockchain interaction in the optimistic case.

In case of disputes or in case some party wishes to terminate the offchain protocol, the parties *decommit* the current state of the head back to the blockchain. Ultimately, a decommit will result in an updated blockchain state that is consistent with the offchain protocol evolution on the initially committed UTxO set. To reduce mainchain overhead, the mainchain is oblivious of the detailed transaction history of the head protocol that leads to the updated state. Crucially, the time required to decommit is independent of the number of parties participating in a head or the size of the head state. Finally, Hydra allows incremental commits and decommits, i.e., UTxOs can be added to and removed from a running head without closing it.

Cross-head Networking. In this paper, we focus solely on the analysis of the Hydra head protocol. Nevertheless, the existence of multiple, partially overlapping heads off the mainchain can give rise to cross-head communication (as in the Lightning Network [28]), using similar techniques to [17,20].

Experimental Evaluation. We conducted detailed simulations of head performance under a variety of load and networking scenarios, including both geographically localized heads and heads with participants spread over multiple continents, incurring large network delays.

Instead of focusing on absolute metrics such as transactions per second (TPS), we develop a "baseline" methodology where the protocol is vetted against well-defined ideal baselines revealing its intrinsic design qualities while factoring away experimental environment specificities. We found that our head protocol, in the optimistic case, achieves progress that rivals the speed and throughput of the network in all configurations; this is aided by the concurrency afforded by the partial-only transaction ordering permitted by the graph-structure underlying UTxO ledgers. Moreover, the storage required by the protocol for the participating nodes is maintained at the lowest level possible via a snapshot "garbage collection" mechanism that incurs only a marginal overhead.

Comparison to Previous Work. A number of previous works study state channel protocols. The Sprites protocol by Miller et al. [26] allows a set of parties to initiate a smart contract instance onchain and take it offchain. The offchain protocol runs in phases of 4 asynchronous rounds where a leader coordinates the confirmation of new transactions among the off-chain participants (compared to Hydra's 3 asynchronous rounds). Similarly to Hydra, the Sprites protocol allows to add/remove funds from the offchain contract while it is running.

Dziembowski et al. [17] utilize pairwise state channels and allow the instantiation of a multi-party state channel among any set of parties that are connected by paths of pairwise state channels—the instantiation of the multi-party channel does not require any interaction with the mainchain. The offchain protocol proceeds in phases of at least 3 *synchronous* rounds to confirm new transactions without the need for a coordinating leader.

By resolving disputes in a shared (onchain) contract, both of the above works [17,26]—much like the Hydra protocol—achieve dispute resolution in $O(\Delta)$ time (and independently of the number of state-channel participants), where Δ is the onchain settlement time.

Our experimental evaluation in Sect. 4 includes a comparison to the Sprites protocol [26]. We focused on a comparison to Sprites since it is an asynchronous off-chain protocol as well. In contrast, a fair comparison to the (synchronous) protocol in [17] seems difficult as we would have to choose a respective delay bound, thereby introducing a tradeoff between offchain protocol performance and contestations due to exceeded network delays.

An additional advantage over [26] and [17] is that those fix the set of contracts that can be evolved in a given state channel at channel creation time. In Hydra, new contracts can be introduced in a head after creation in the native EUTxO language of the underlying blockchain. Finally, Hydra is isomorphic and thus reuses the existing smart contract system and code for offchain computations. This is not the case for [26] and [17]. For example, if we consider the sample Solidity contract of [26], it would have to incorporate a whole state machine capable of executing EVM bytecode to achieve contract (system) reuse—and hence, isomorphic state channels.

There exist other smart-contract-enabled ledger models that share some of the structural organization of the (E)UTxO model. In particular, the *records nano-kernel* of ZEXE [10]. We believe that it ought to be possible to transfer the approach that we are describing in the present paper from EUTxO to the records nano-kernel. However, ZEXE's privacy requirements raise a number of additional questions, such as the amount of information that is being leaked by the mainchain contract and the offchain protocol. These additional questions prompted us to base our work on the EUTxO model, which does not have these additional requirements. We leave those questions to future work.

There is also a large number of non-peer reviewed proposals for state-channel-based solutions such as [2,14,24,25]. These proposals come with various degrees of formal specification and provable security guarantees and their systematization is outside of our current scope; it suffices to observe that none of them provides the isomorphism property or comes with a complete formal security analysis and an experimental evaluation.

Two concepts related, but distinct, from state channels are *sidechains* (e.g., [6,21,22]) and *non-custodial chains* (e.g., [3,19,23,27]), including plasma and rollups. Sidechains enable the transfer of assets between a mainchain and a sidechain via a pegging mechanism; contrary to a state channel, funds may be lost in case of a sidechain security collapse. Non-custodial chains delegate mainchain transaction processing to an untrusted aggregator and are capable, like state channels, to protect against a security failure. However, as the aggregator is a single-point-of-failure, in a setting where a large number of users are served by the same non-custodial chain, this gives rise to the "mass-exit" problem (see e.g., [19]); state-channels are similar in the sense that any single user may unilaterally close the channel, however scaling to a large number of users can be also achieved via *state channel networks* [20] (as opposed to a single monolithic state channel) and in such settings multiple pathways may exist for any single subset of users wishing to achieve a particular task; this diffuses the single-point of failure problem—subject to the underlying channel network topology (note that we do not exclude the possibility that "non-custodial chain networks" may be devised to address this problem in a similar manner). Finally, work in progress on optimistic rollups, reported in [3], claims a feature similar to our isomorphic property, but without the latency benefits of our approach as their settlement still advances with the underlying mainchain.

2 Preliminaries

The basis for our fast isomorphic state channels is Bitcoin's UTxO ledger model [5,29]. It arranges transactions in a directed acyclic graph structure, thus making the available parallelism explicit: any two transactions that are not directly or indirectly dependent on each other can be processed independently.

Extended UTxO. The *Extended UTxO Model (EUTxO)* [11] preserves this structure, while enabling more expressive smart contracts, including multi-transaction state machines, which serve as the basis for the mainchain portion of the work presented here.

In addition to the basic EUTxO extension, we generalize the currency *values* recorded on the ledger from integral numbers to *generalized user-defined tokens* [1]. Put simply (sufficient to understand the concepts in this paper), values are sets that keep track of how many units of which tokens of which currency are available. For example, the value $\{\mathsf{Coin} \mapsto \{\mathsf{Coin} \mapsto 3\}, c \mapsto \{t_1 \mapsto 1, t_2 \mapsto 1\}\}$ contains 3 Coin coins (there is only one (fungible) token Coin for a payment currency Coin), as well as (non-fungible) tokens t_1 and t_2, which are both of currency c. Values can be naturally added by component-wise addition for each currency. In the following, $\varnothing$ is the empty value, and $\{t_1, \ldots, t_n\}$::c is used as a shorthand for $\{c \mapsto \{t_1 \mapsto 1, \ldots, t_n \mapsto 1\}\}$.

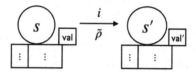

Fig. 1. Transactions representing successive states in a CEM transition relation $s \xrightarrow{i} (s', \mathrm{tx}^{\equiv})$. Fields val and val$'$ are the value fields of the SM outputs and $\tilde{\rho}$ is the additional data.

EUTxO-ledger *transactions* are quintuples $\mathrm{tx} = (I, O, \mathsf{val}_{\mathsf{Forge}}, r, \mathcal{K})$ comprising a set of *inputs* I, a list of *outputs* O, values of *forged/burned tokens* $\mathsf{val}_{\mathsf{Forge}}$, a *slot range* $r = (r_{\min}, r_{\max})$, and public keys $\mathcal{K}$. Each input $i \in I$ is a pair of an *output reference* out-ref (formed by a transaction ID and an index identifying an output of the transaction) and a *redeemer* ρ (used to supply data for validation). Each output $o \in O$ is a triple $(\mathsf{val}, \nu, \delta)$ consisting of a value val, a validator script ν, and a datum δ. The slot range r indicates the slots within which tx may be confirmed and, finally, $\mathcal{K}$ are the public keys under which tx is signed.

To validate a transaction tx with input set I, for each output $o = (\mathsf{val}, \nu, \delta)$ referenced by an $i = (\mathsf{out\text{-}ref}, \rho) \in I$, the corresponding validator ν is run on the following inputs: $\nu(\mathsf{val}, \delta, \rho, \sigma)$, where the *validation context* σ consists of tx and *all* outputs referenced by some $i \in I$ (not just o). Ultimately, tx is valid if and only if all validators return true.

State Machines (SMs). A convenient abstraction for EUTxO contracts spanning a sequence of related transactions are SMs; specifically, *constraint emitting machines (CEMs)* [11]. Based on Mealy machines, they consist of a set of states S_{CEM}, a set of inputs I_{CEM}, a predicate $final_{\mathrm{CEM}} : S_{\mathrm{CEM}} \to Bool$ identifying final states, and a step relation $s \xrightarrow{i} (s', \mathrm{tx}^{\equiv})$, which takes a state s on an input i to a successor state s' if the constraints $\mathrm{tx}^{\equiv}$ are satisfied.

We implement CEMs on an EUTxO ledger (the mainchain) by representing a sequence of CEM states as a sequence of transactions. Each of these transactions has got an *SM input* i_{CEM} and an *SM output* o_{CEM}, where the latter is locked by a validator ν_{CEM}, implementing the step relation. The only exceptions are the initial and final state, which have got no SM input and output, respectively. More specifically, given two transactions tx and tx$'$, they represent successive states under $s \xrightarrow{i} (s', \mathrm{tx}^{\equiv})$ iff

- SM output $o_{\text{CEM}} = (\text{val}, \nu_{\text{CEM}}, s)$ of tx is consumed by SM input $i'_{\text{CEM}} = (\text{out-ref}, \rho)$ of tx′, whose redeemer is $\rho = i$ (i.e., the redeemer provides the SM input) and
- either $final_{\text{CEM}}(s') = \texttt{true}$ and tx' has no SM output, or $o'_{\text{CEM}} = (\text{val}', \nu_{\text{CEM}}, s')$ and tx′ meets all constraints $\text{tx}^{\equiv}$.

Sometimes it is useful to have additional data $\tilde{\rho}$ provided as part of the redeemer, i.e., $\rho = (i, \tilde{\rho})$. A state transition of the described type is represented by two connected transactions as shown in Fig. 1. For simplicity, SM inputs and outputs are not shown, except for the value fields val and val′ of the SM output.

3   The Hydra Protocol

The Hydra protocol locks a set of UTxOs on a blockchain (referred to as the *mainchain*) and evolves it inside an offchain *head*, independently of the mainchain. At any point, the head can be closed with the effect that the locked set of UTxOs on the mainchain is replaced by the latest set of UTxOs inside the head. The protocol guarantees wealth preservation: no funds can be generated offchain, and no responsive honest party involved in the head can lose funds other than by consenting to give them away.

For space reasons, this paper presents a simplified version of Hydra, concentrating on its basic concepts and ideas. More details are given in the online version of the paper [12].

3.1   Protocol Setup

To create a head-protocol instance, any party may take the role of an *initiator* and ask a set of parties, the *head members*, to participate in the head by announcing the identities of the parties. The members then exchange cryptographic key material establishing, amongst others, a public-key infrastructure. Note that this process does not happen on the mainchain but out of band.[1] The setup procedure is detailed in [12], App. C.

3.2   Mainchain (Simplified)

The mainchain part of the Hydra protocol fulfills two principal functions: (1) it locks the mainchain UTxOs committed to the head while the head is active, and (2) it facilitates the settlement of the final head state back to the mainchain after the head is closed. In combination, these two functions effectively result in replacing the initial head UTxO set by the final head UTxO set on the mainchain in a manner that respects the complete set of head transactions (but without posting any other information about these transactions).

The mainchain state machine (SM), depicted in Fig. 2, comprises the four states initial, open, closed, and final, where the first two realize (1) and the second

---

[1] The process also may fail due to member corruption.

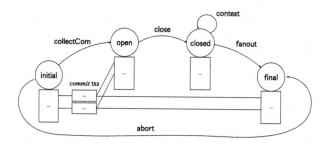

Fig. 2. Mainchain state diagram for a simplified version of Hydra.

two realize (2). Observe that SMs inherently sequentialize all actions involving the machine state; this simplifies both reasoning about and implementing the protocol but might hurt performance as steps that could otherwise be taken in parallel now need to be sequentialized. Where such sequentialization would severely affect protocol performance, we employ a (to our knowledge) novel technique to parallelize the progression of the SM on the mainchain.

We use said technique to parallelize the construction of the initial UTxO set.[2] To create a head instance, the initiator submits a transaction *initial* containing the protocol parameters, and establishing the state initial. Each member can now attach a *commit* transaction (to a dedicated output of *initial*), which locks (on the mainchain) the UTxOs that they want to commit to the head.

The commit transactions are subsequently collected by the *collectCom* transaction causing a transition from initial to open. Once *collectCom* is confirmed, the members are ready to run the offchain head protocol. In case some members fail to post a *commit* transaction, the head can be aborted by an *abort* transaction, directly transitioning the state machine from initial to final.

To ensure exactly one commit transaction per member and that the *collectCom* transaction collects *all* commits, transaction *initial* issues a single non-fungible token, a so-called *participation token*, to each member. Each token must be consumed by the corresponding member's commit transaction, and the *collectCom* transaction, to be valid, must collect the full set of participation tokens.

To close a head, any head member can post a *close* transaction, which takes the SM state from open to closed. Transaction *close* supplies to the SM information about the UTxO set to be restored along with a validity certificate, which is checked by the SM. During a contestation period, *contest* transactions can be posted, leaving the SM in the state closed but providing more up-to-date certified information about the head UTxO state. Once the contestation period is over, the *fanout* transaction can be posted, which takes the SM from closed to final, such that the outputs of the *fanout* transaction correspond exactly to the final head UTxO set.

The detailed workings of the mainchain SM is described in [12], App. D.

---

[2] Without parallelization, all n members would have to post their UTxOs in sequence, requiring a linear-size chain of n transactions, each causing one state transition.

3.3 Head (Simplified)

For ease of overall readability, in this section, we present a simplified version of the head protocol and restrict ourselves to a high-level treatment of the execution model and protocol security. In particular, we omit the graceful handling of (potentially legitimate) transaction conflicts arising from two parties concurrently trying to redeem the same UTxO.[3] A description of the full head protocol together with explicit definitions and a full security proof are given in [12], App. E.

A depiction of the simplified head protocol is given in Fig. 3.

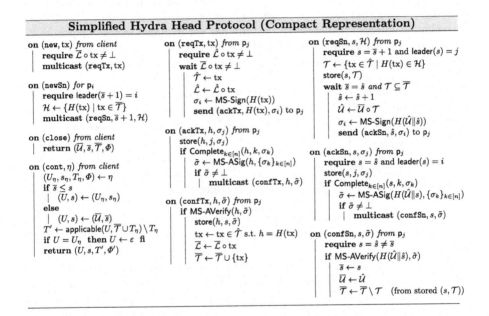

Fig. 3. Head-protocol machine for the *simple protocol* from the perspective of party p_i. All relevant notation is explained in the text.

Quick Summary. The head protocol starts with an initial UTxO set U_0, which is identical to the UTxOs locked onchain.

Transactions. Individual transactions are *confirmed* in full concurrency by collecting and distributing multisignatures (cf. [12], App. B for the definition of multisignatures) on each issued transaction separately. As soon as such a transaction is confirmed, it irreversibly becomes part of the head UTxO state evolution—the transaction's outputs are immediately spendable in the head or can be safely transferred back onchain in case of a head closure.

---

[3] For now, such conflicts are treated like malicious ones, thus resulting in head closure.

Snapshots. To minimize local storage requirements and to allow for closing a head via a transaction whose size is independent of the offchain transaction history, the protocol continuously generates UTxO snapshots $U_1, U_2, \ldots$. Unlike transactions, snapshots are generated sequentially, where the head members take turns acting as *snapshot leaders*.

Once a snapshot gets confirmed via a multisignature, participants can safely delete all included transactions; the multisignature is now evidence that this state once existed during head evolution.

Closing the Head. A party wanting to close the head decommits their local state by posting, onchain, the latest observed confirmed snapshot U_ℓ together with those confirmed transactions that are not yet included in this snapshot, so-called *hanging transactions*. During the subsequent contestation period, other head members may post their own local confirmed states if they are newer.

UTxOs and Transactions. In the UTxO model, independent transactions can be processed concurrently; the exact order of transaction application is irrelevant as long as the partial order imposed by the DAG structure is respected.

Given UTxO set U and transaction tx, by $U' = U \circ \text{tx}$ we express that U' results from U by applying tx, where $U' = \bot$ if the validation fails. For a *set* of transactions T, by $U' = U \circ T$ we express that U' results from U by applying all transactions in T where $U' = \bot$ if the full transaction set cannot be applied.

Tools and Objects. A multisignature scheme from the initial setup is used to certify protocol updates as confirmed, i.e., that every head member has approved the respective update.

Every party maintains local objects to represent transactions, snapshots, and their local state (current view of the head UTxO set). These objects exist in two versions: a *seen* object has been signed by the party (the party has approved the event), and a *confirmed* object has an associated valid multisignature (i.e., all parties have approved the event). A seen object X is denoted by $\hat{X}$, and a confirmed object by $\overline{X}$. Every party locally maintains

- $\hat{s}$ and $\overline{s}$, the index of the latest seen/confirmed snapshot;
- $\hat{\mathcal{U}}$ and $\overline{\mathcal{U}}$, the latest seen/confirmed snapshot;
- $\hat{T}$ and $\overline{T}$, the current set of seen/confirmed transactions that have not yet been considered by a confirmed snapshot;
- $\hat{\mathcal{L}}$ and $\overline{\mathcal{L}}$, the current seen/confirmed UTxO state—thus maintaining $\hat{\mathcal{L}} = \overline{\mathcal{U}} \circ \hat{T}$ and $\overline{\mathcal{L}} = \overline{\mathcal{U}} \circ \overline{T}$.

Code Conventions. The protocol machine is described from the perspective of a generic head party p_i. We assume that the parties communicate over pairwise authenticated channels, and that a party only accepts messages authenticated by its claimed sender. For simplicity, whenever a party p_i sends a message to all head parties, it also sends the message to itself.

By **require**(P) we express that predicate P must be satisfied for the further execution of a routine—if P is not satisfied, the routine is exited immediately.

By **wait**(P) we express a non-blocking wait for predicate P to be satisfied. On $\neg P$, the execution of the routine is stopped, queued, and reactivated as soon as P is satisfied. Finally, for simplicity, we assume the code executions of each routine to be atomic—except for blocks of code that may be put into the wait queue for later execution, in which case we assume the wait block to be atomic.

To facilitate reasoning about protocol security, in the code, we write **output** (seen, tx) (**output** (conf, tx)) to make explicit (to the execution environment) that a given transaction tx has been seen (confirmed) by a particular party.

3-*round object confirmation.* Transactions and snapshots are confirmed in an asynchronous 3-round process:

- req: The issuer of a transaction or snapshot requests to confirm the object by sending the object to every head member.
- ack: The head members acknowledge the object by replying with their signatures on the object to the issuer.
- conf: The issuer collects all signatures, combines the multisignature, and sends the multisignature to all head members.

Initializing the Head. Initially, the parties collect the public-key data from the initial transaction corresponding to the head and verify that it is consistent with the data exchanged during the setup phase. The parties then set $\overline{\mathcal{L}} = \hat{\mathcal{L}} = \overline{\mathcal{U}} = \hat{\mathcal{U}} = U_0$, where U_0 is the initial UTxO set extracted from the *collectCom* transaction. The initial transaction sets are empty, $\overline{\mathcal{T}} = \hat{\mathcal{T}} = \emptyset$, and $\overline{s} = \hat{s} = 0$.

Confirming New Transactions. (new). At any time, by calling (new, tx), a head party can (asynchronously) inject a new transaction tx to the head protocol. For this, the transaction must be applicable to the current confirmed local state: $\overline{\mathcal{L}} \circ \text{tx} \neq \bot$. If the test passes, the issuer initiates a 3-round confirmation process for tx as described above by sending out a (reqTx, tx) request.

(reqTx). Upon receiving a request (reqTx, tx), transaction tx is only signed if tx applies to the local *seen* UTxO state: $\hat{\mathcal{L}} \circ \text{tx} \neq \bot$. Party p_i then waits until his *confirmed* UTxO state $\overline{\mathcal{L}}$ has "caught up": $\overline{\mathcal{L}} \circ \text{tx} \neq \bot$. Finally, in case the preconditions are satisfied, a signature on the hash of tx, $\sigma = \text{MS-Sign}(H(\text{tx}))$, is delivered back to the transaction issuer by replying with (ackTx, $H(\text{tx}), \sigma$).

(ackTx). Upon receiving an acknowledgment (ackTx, h, σ_j) (corresponding to a transaction issued by p_i), p_i stores the received signature. As soon as a signature has been received from every party, p_i creates a multisignature $\tilde{\sigma} \leftarrow \text{MS-ASig}(h, \{\sigma_k\}_{k=[n]})$ and sends it to all parties in a (confTx, $h, \tilde{\sigma}$) message.

(confTx). Upon receiving a confirmation (confTx, $h, \tilde{\sigma}$) (from the transaction issuer) containing a valid multisignature $\tilde{\sigma}$, p_i fetches the transaction tx with $H(\text{tx}) = h$ from storage and updates $\overline{\mathcal{T}} = \overline{\mathcal{T}} \cup \{\text{tx}\}$ and $\overline{\mathcal{L}} = \overline{\mathcal{L}} \circ \text{tx}$.

Creating Snapshots. Snapshots are generated in a sequential round-robin manner. The party responsible for issuing the ith snapshot is called the *leader* of snapshot i. The head protocol in Fig. 3 uses a generic leader schedule defined by the function leader : $\mathbb{N} \rightarrow [n]$, which assigns a head member to every snapshot number. For concreteness, assume that $\text{leader}(s) = (s \mod n) + 1$.

(newSn). On activation via (newSn), if p_i is the snapshot leader, they send message $(\text{reqSn}, \overline{s} + 1, \mathcal{H})$ where $\mathcal{H} = \{H(\text{tx}) \mid \text{tx} \in \overline{\mathcal{T}}\}$, indicating their wish to include in the next snapshot the transaction set $\overline{\mathcal{T}}$—the confirmed transactions from the leader's view that have not yet been processed by a snapshot.

(reqSn). Upon receiving request $(\text{reqSn}, s, \mathcal{H})$, party p_i checks that s is the next snapshot number and that the sending party p_j is its snapshot leader. In $\mathcal{T}$, all (seen) transactions from $\hat{\mathcal{T}}$ are collected whose hashes are contained in $\mathcal{H}$.

The party waits until the previous snapshot is confirmed ($\overline{s} = \hat{s}$) and all transactions in $\mathcal{T}$ are confirmed. Only then, p_i builds the new snapshot, computes a signature $\sigma_i = \text{MS-Sign}(H(\hat{\mathcal{U}}\|\hat{s}))$, and replies $(\text{ackSn}, \overline{s}, \sigma_i)$ to p_j.[4]

(ackSn). Upon receiving acknowledgment $(\text{ackSn}, s, \sigma_j)$, the snapshot leader stores the received signature. Once a signature has been received from every party, the leader creates a multisignature $\tilde{\sigma} \leftarrow \text{MS-ASig}(H(\hat{\mathcal{U}}\|\overline{s}), \{\sigma_k\}_{k=[n]})$ and sends it to all parties in a $(\text{confSn}, h, \tilde{\sigma})$ message.

(confSn). Upon receiving confirmation $(\text{confSn}, s, \tilde{\sigma})$ with a valid multisignature $\tilde{\sigma}$ from the snapshot leader, p_i obtains $\mathcal{T}$ from storage and updates $\overline{s} = s$ and $\overline{\mathcal{U}} = \hat{\mathcal{U}}$. The set of confirmed transactions can now be reduced by excluding the transactions that have been processed by $\overline{\mathcal{U}}$: $\overline{\mathcal{T}} \leftarrow \overline{\mathcal{T}} \setminus \mathcal{T}$.

Closing the Head. (close). To close a head, a party triggers the head-protocol event (close), which returns the latest confirmed snapshot $\overline{\mathcal{U}}$ together with the hanging transactions $\overline{\mathcal{T}}$ and all respective multisignatures. In Fig. 3, the multisignatures on $\overline{\mathcal{U}}$ and the transaction in $\overline{\mathcal{T}}$ are summarized as Φ.

(cont). To contest the current state closed on the mainchain, a party causes the head-protocol event (cont, η), with input η being the latest observed head status that has been aggregated onchain for this head so far (by *close* and *contest* transactions). The algorithm then computes "differential" data between the current onchain head status and the contester's confirmed view: the latest confirmed snapshot (if newer than seen onchain) and the set of hanging transactions (not yet considered by η). From the hanging transactions we only want to publish those not yet contained in T_η and not yet processed by the (possibly newer) snapshot from η. This is achieved by applying function applicable that tests, for each transaction in $\text{tx} \in \overline{\mathcal{T}} \cup T_\eta$ in appropriate order, whether $U \circ \text{tx} \neq \bot$ is still applicable, and by removing T_η from the applicable set.

---

[4] Note that no UTxO sets have to be exchanged in this process as the parties can locally compute a new snapshot using the given transaction hashes.

Security. We now sketch the security definition and a proof of security for the basic protocol without conflict resolution as described above. A comprehensive security analysis of the protocol (with conflict resolution) is given in [12], App. E.

Recall that the head protocol gives different security guarantees depending on the level of adversarial corruption. It provides correctness (safety) independently of both, the number of corrupted parties, and network delays, in the head. However, the guarantee that the protocol makes progress (i.e., that new transactions get confirmed in the head) can only be provided in the case that no head parties are corrupted and that all head-protocol messages are eventually delivered.

We apply a game-based security proof that reflects the above distinction by considering two different adversaries, an active adversary $\mathcal{A}$ with full control over the protocol, and a network adversary $\mathcal{A}_\emptyset$ that does not corrupt any head parties but arbitrarily schedules message delivery in the head protocol under the restriction to eventually deliver all sent network messages.

We capture protocol security by the following events, and prove the protocol secure by showing that, in a random execution of the protocol, no (probabilistic-polynomial-time) adversary can violate any of the following events except for a negligible probability.

- CONSISTENCY (UNDER $\mathcal{A}$): No two uncorrupted parties observe conflicting transactions confirmed.
- CONFLICT-FREE LIVENESS: Under adversary $\mathcal{A}_\emptyset$, if no conflicting transactions are ever issued during the head protocol, then every transaction becomes confirmed at some point.
- SOUNDNESS (UNDER $\mathcal{A}$)): The final UTxO set accepted on the mainchain results from a set of seen transactions.
- COMPLETENESS (UNDER $\mathcal{A}$): All transactions observed as confirmed by an honest party at the end of the protocol are considered on the mainchain.

We now sketch the arguments why the above events are satisfied.

Consistency. Follows from the fact that an honest party never signs a transaction in conflict with his own view of the confirmed UTxO state, and that a confirmed transaction implies that every party signed it.

Conflict-Free Liveness. Assume that all parties are honest and that no conflicting transactions are ever published. A transaction is only issued if it is consistent with the issuing party's *confirmed* UTxO state (see new), implying, by conflict-freeness, that the transaction is (immediately) consistent with the *seen* states of all parties, who will thus eventually confirm the transaction by signing it (see reqTx).

Soundness. Follows from the fact that only confirmed transactions eventually affect the mainchain, and that a confirmed transaction has been seen by all honest parties.

Completeness. Upon head closure, mainchain security guarantees that each honest party gets to have included, in the mainchain ledger, a more recent confirmed snapshot and/or hanging transactions (by a *close* and *contest* mainchain transaction). By consistency and the fact that only confirmed information is included in the aggregated mainchain state η, every transaction ever observed as confirmed by an honest party will finally have been integrated into the final aggregated state on the mainchain.

3.4   Extensions for the Full Protocol

To improve on the basic protocol, we change the mainchain state machine to include (1) incremental commits and decommits (adding UTxOs to or removing them from the head without closing), (2) optimistic one-step head closure without the need for onchain contestation, (3) pessimistic two-step head closure with an $O(\Delta)$ contestation period, independent of n, where Δ is the onchain settlement time of a transaction, and (4) split onchain decommit of the final UTxO set (in case it is too large to fit into a single transaction). These changes are described in [12], App. F, as well as the handling of transaction fees in order to fund onchain state-machine progress.

4   Experimental Evaluation

This section investigates the latency (transaction settlement time) and throughput (rate of transaction processing) of Hydra, using timing-accurate simulations. Instead of simply providing particular numbers (such as transactions-per-second (TPS)), we derive "baselines" that represent the theoretical optimum for *any consensus protocol* and compare the results of our simulations to these baselines. The comparison reveals that Hydra is near-optimal in terms of both throughput and latency. Our methodology features two types of baselines:

The universal baseline considers only the cost of processing transactions and disseminating them across the network of nodes in the state channel; observe that any iterated consensus algorithm that yields full state at each node must necessarily carry out both operations. As this protocol-independent baseline is one against which any iterated consensus algorithm can be compared, near optimality with respect to this baseline reflects ideal throughput.

The *unlimited baseline* focuses on the characteristics of the protocol itself. In particular it asks how the protocol's implementations compare to an idealized execution of the protocol by a set of nodes that experience no local contention for resources. This baseline comparison is meant to be complementary to the universal baseline and helps answer the following question: Whenever there is divergence between the universal baseline and the actual consensus protocol execution in the experiment, how much of this divergence is to be attributed to the inherent cost of running the consensus protocol vs. the costs arising due to contention for resources within each node?

In this section we provide an overview of how we apply this methodology, present graphs of our experimental setup, and discuss the results. Further notes on the experiments are provided in [12], App. A.

4.1 Applying the Methodology

The experimental setup involves a fixed set of nodes, with a specified network bandwidth per node and geographic location of each node that determines the network latency between each pair of nodes. Each node submits transactions with a specified *transaction concurrency* c: it sends c transactions as fast as its resources allow, and then sends another one whenever one of the transactions it sent previously gets confirmed. This controls the number of inflight transactions to be c per node. *Snapshots* are performed regularly: nodes take turns to produce snapshots, and whenever the current leader obtains a new confirmed transaction, it creates a snapshot subsuming all the confirmed transactions it knows about. Testing the system under heavy load like this allows us to determine its maximal throughput. It also gives us a worst-case estimate for the latency; running at capacity will only increase the latency compared to operation below capacity.

In order to properly gauge the simulation results, we compare them to baseline scenarios that are sufficiently simple to facilitate optimistic performance limits exactly. We derive those limits by considering each sequence of events that has to happen in order for a number of transactions to be confirmed, and summing up the time for each event in those sequences. In particular, we have three resources that potentially limit the transaction rate: (1) the *CPU capacity* at each node determines how fast transactions can be validated, and signatures be created or verified; (2) the inbound and outbound *network bandwidth* limits how many message bytes can be received and sent by each node in a given time; (3) each message between two nodes is delayed by the *network latency* between those nodes. Depending on the configuration of the system, the most utilized of these resources will limit the transaction rate. This is an idealization: in a real execution, additional contention effects will cause even the scarcest resource to be blocked and idle occasionally. We thus expect experimental results to be bounded by the baselines, and interpret the difference as the impact of such contention effects. In addition to the universal baseline, where we assume perfect trust between all participants (each transaction is only validated once by the submitting node, no signatures have to be used), and which sets an upper limit for the transaction throughput of *any* protocol that distributes and validates transactions in a distributed system, we consider two protocol specific baselines:

Hydra Unlimited: This scenario resembles the head protocol, but executed under ideal circumstances, ignoring contention effects as described above. In contrast to a real execution of the protocol, where the snapshot size is an emergent property depending on how fast transactions are confirmed, in the baseline, we can directly control how many transactions are contained in a snapshot.

Sprites Unlimited: In order to compare to prior work, we also include a baseline according to an optimal execution of the off-chain protocol from [26]. A deciding difference to the head protocol is that in Sprites, all nodes send their inputs to a leader, which collates them and collects signatures for a whole batch of transactions. Compared to Hydra, this batching reduces the demand on CPU time and number of messages (less signatures) at the expense of additional network roundtrips and higher network bandwidth usage at the current leader node.

4.2 Experimental Results

We now summarize our simulations results (a detailed evaluation is given in [12]).

We performed experiments for three clusters with different geographic distributions of nodes: a *local* deployment of three nodes within the same AWS region, a *continental* deployment across multiple AWS regions on the same continent (Ireland, London, and Frankfurt), and a *global* deployment (Oregon, Frankfurt, and Tokyo)—see the next section for results with larger clusters. For each of those clusters, we measure the dependency of confirmation time and transaction throughput on bandwidth and transaction concurrency, and compare them with the baselines described above. The numerical results depend on a number of parameters that we set, representing the time that elementary operations within the protocol take. We use the settings described below.

Transaction Size. We use two transaction types: (1) *simple* UTxO transactions with two inputs and two outputs, whose size are 265 bytes, and (2) *script* transactions containing larger scripts of 10 kbytes. We use transaction references of 32 bytes. For each message, we allow for a protocol-level overhead of 2 bytes.

Transaction Validation Time. This is the CPU time that a single node will expend in order to check the validity of a transaction. We use conservative values here: 0.4 ms for simple transactions, and 3 ms for script transactions.

Time for Multisignature Operations. We performed benchmarks for the multisignature scheme [9] resulting in the following estimates: 0.15 ms for MS-Sign, 0.01 ms for MS-ASig, and 0.85 ms for MS-AVerify.

Transaction Throughput. Figure 4 displays results for simple UTxO transactions. The different rows correspond to the different geographical setups of the clusters, while the columns differ in transaction concurrency.

As expected, the Universal baseline consistently gives the highest transaction rate. For Hydra Unlimited, three different snapshot sizes (number of contained transactions) are considered (dotted, dashed, and solid lines). Comparing the Universal and Hydra Unlimited baselines, we see that they are identical whenever the transaction rate is limited by the network latency—since the baselines only differ with respect to their demand for CPU time and network bandwidth.

The Sprites Unlimited baseline shows the effect of batching via a leader: as the leader needs to send all transactions to all other nodes, its networking interface is a frequent bottleneck. The additional leader roundtrips reduce throughput whenever the network latency is the limiting resource. In contrast, when roundtrip times are short, and bandwidth is sufficient for the CPU time to become the limiting resource—as in the high-bandwidth region of the upper right panel of Fig. 4—the savings by signing batches instead of single transactions become apparent, and the Sprite baseline nearly reaches the Universal one.

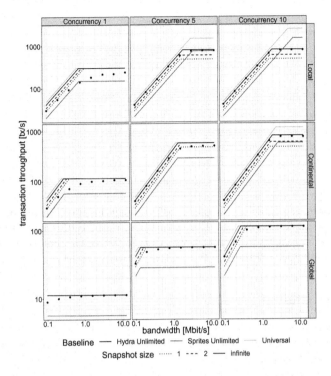

Fig. 4. Transaction rates for the head protocol, compared with the baseline scenarios. Simple UTxO transactions with 2 inputs and 2 outputs. The lines represent the baselines, while the dots are measurements of the transaction rate from our simluations, using a sample of 2000 transactions per measurement.

Comparing our experimental Hydra-protocol performance to the Hydra Unlimited baseline, we see that in most cases, the simulation of the protocol (bold dots) approximates the optimal curve quite well. We only get sizable differences for low concurrency and insufficient bandwidth. Furthermore, the data reveals that performing snapshots has a negligible impact on transaction throughput.

Transaction Confirmation Times. For Hydra Unlimited, we can derive a minimal confirmation time by adding up the times for validating a transaction two times (once at the issuing node, once at every other node), sending the `reqTx` and `ackTx` messages across the longest path in the network, and creating and validating the aggregate signature.

Figure 5 illustrates the conditions under which we achieve minimal confirmation time. With sufficient bandwidth, we get very close to the baseline, indicated by the line. While increasing concurrency improves transaction throughput, individual transactions are more likely to be slowed down by network congestion.

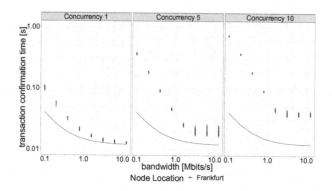

Fig. 5. Confirmation times for simple UTxO transactions, in a cluster located in one AWS region. Each dot represents the measurement of the confirmation time of a single transaction. From panel to panel, we increase the transaction concurrency. The theoretically minimal confirmation time is represented by a line.

4.3 Larger Clusters

In addition to three-node clusters, we have also evaluated how the results depend on cluster size by running simulations with clusters of up to 100 nodes (located in the same AWS region):

- The transaction rates of a larger cluster are close to those for a three-node cluster. This is due to the amount of computation per node per transaction not depending on the number of participants[5].
- The bandwidth needed at each node to reach the maximal transaction rate *does* depend on the cluster size. This is not surprising, since each node needs to communicate with more peers.
- For the same reason, the confirmation time of transactions increases with the cluster size.

Note that these simulations still use a communication pattern where everyone sends messages to everyone, which is suboptimal for large clusters. Instead, we ought to construct a graph to broadcast messages, keeping the number of peers for direct communication small. An advantage of the Hydra approach is that we can easily have different versions of the head protocol, or different implementations of the same head protocol, optimized for different cluster sizes.

---

[5] Note that aggregating signatures and verifying an aggregate signature do depend on the number of participants. However, this does not impact the transaction rates in our simulations, for three reasons: i) we assume that we aggregate the verification keys once at the beginning of the head protocol, and only perform verification against the already computed aggregate verification key during the protocol, ii) even for 100 participants, combining the signatures is quicker than producing a single signature, iii) combining signatures is performed concurrently with the rest of the protocol (see [12], App. A.2).

4.4   Discussion

Hydra consistently achieves subsecond settlement, even for globally distributed heads. When we allocate sufficient networking resources, and choose low concurrency, we do get optimal confirmation times.

Regarding transaction throughput, more important than raw numbers are the comparisons with the theoretical limits from the baselines scenarios:

- We saw that we do not pay a significant cost for creating snapshots, neither in terms of transaction throughput, nor in terms of confirmation time. This is a crucial point: compared to other state channel protocols, Hydra utilizes the UTxO parallelism to avoid having to sequentialize transactions. Snapshots are necessary for that approach, since otherwise, the decommit transactions would become unwieldy. Seeing that snapshots do not slow down the protocol in any significant way thus validates the design of Hydra.
- Comparing the Universal baseline, Hydra Unlimited, and the experimental results, we see that we approach the theoretical limits in regions where we can expect to. When the cost of achieving consensus via multisignatures is dominated by network roundtrip times and transaction validation, we get close to the Universal scenario. We see sizable deviations from Hydra Unlimited only when we have low transaction concurrency and bandwidth.

Acknowledgments. Aggelos Kiayias was supported in part by EU Project No.780477, PRIVILEDGE. We want to thank Duncan Coutts and Neil Davies for advice on technical aspects of the simulations, and Neil Davies for providing the measurements of round trip times between different AWS regions.

References

1. EUTxO with multi-currency. https://github.com/hydra-supplementary-material/eutxo-spec/blob/master/extended-utxo-specification.pdf
2. The Connext Network. https://docs.connext.network/en/latest/background/architecture.html
3. John, A.: The why's of optimistic rollup. https://medium.com/@adlerjohn/the-why-s-of-optimistic-rollup-7c6a22cbb61a, November 2019
4. Ian, A.: Ethereum's Vitalik Buterin explains how state channels address privacy and scalability. International Business Times (2017)
5. Nicola, A., Massimo, B., Stefano, L., Roberto, Z.: A formal model of Bitcoin transactions. In: Financial Cryptography and Data Security, FC 2018, Nieuwpoort, Curaçao, 2018, Revised Selected Papers, pp. 541–560 (2018)
6. Back, A., et al.: Enabling blockchain innovations with pegged sidechains (2014)
7. Bitcoin Wiki. Payment channels. https://web.archive.org/web/20191106110154/https://en.bitcoin.it/wiki/Payment_channelsWiki article. Accessed 11 June 2019
8. Blelloch, G.E.: Programming parallel algorithms. Commun. ACM **39**, 85–97 (1996)
9. Boldyreva, A.: Threshold signatures, multisignatures and blind signatures based on the gap-diffie-hellman-group signature scheme. In: Desmedt, Y.G. (ed.) PKC 2003. LNCS, vol. 2567, pp. 31–46. Springer, Heidelberg (2003). https://doi.org/10.1007/3-540-36288-6_3

10. Bowe, S., Chiesa, A., Green, M., Miers, I., Mishra, P., Wu, H.: Zexe: enabling decentralized private computation. In: 2020 IEEE Symposium on Security and Privacy (SP), pp. 947–964 (2020)
11. Chakravarty, M.M.T., James, C., Kenneth, M., Orestis, Me., Michael, P.J., Philip, W.: The extended UTxO model. In: 4th Workshop on Trusted Smart Contracts (2020). http://fc20.ifca.ai/wtsc/WTSC2020/WTSC20_paper_25.pdf
12. Chakravarty, M.M.T., et al.: Fast isomorphic state channels. Financial Cryptography and Data Security, Web version (2021). https://fc21.ifca.ai/papers/162.pdf
13. Chakravarty, M.M.T., et al.: Functional blockchain contracts, May 2019. https://iohk.io/en/research/library/papers/functional-blockchain-contracts/
14. Coleman, J., Horne, L., Li, X.: Generalized state channels, Counterfactual (2018)
15. Decker, C., Wattenhofer, R.: A fast and scalable payment network with bitcoin duplex micropayment channels. In: Pelc, A., Schwarzmann, A.A. (eds.) SSS 2015. LNCS, vol. 9212, pp. 3–18. Springer, Cham (2015). https://doi.org/10.1007/978-3-319-21741-3_1
16. Ergo Developers. Ergo: A resilient platform for contractual money, May 2019. https://ergoplatform.org/docs/whitepaper.pdf
17. Stefan, D., Lisa, E., Sebastian, F., Julia, H., Kristina, H.: Multi-party virtual state channels. In: Advances in Cryptology - EUROCRYPT 2019, Proceedings, Part (I), pp. 625–656. Springer (2019). https://doi.org/10.1007/978-3-030-17653-2_21
18. Stefan, D., Lisa, E., Sebastian, F., Daniel, M.: Perun: virtual payment hubs over cryptocurrencies. In: 2019 IEEE Symposium on Security and Privacy (SP), pp. 106–123. IEEE (2019)
19. Stefan, D., Grzegorz, F., Sebastian, F., Siavash, R.: Lower bounds for off-chain protocols: Exploring the limits of plasma. Cryptology ePrint Archive, Report 2020/175 (2020). https://eprint.iacr.org/2020/175
20. Stefan, D., Sebastian, F., Kristina, H.: General state channel networks. In: Proceedings of the 2018 ACM SIGSAC Conference on Computer and Communications Security, pp. 949–966. ACM (2018)
21. Gaži, P., Kiayias, A., Zindros, D.: Proof-of-stake sidechains. In: 2019 2019 IEEE Symposium on Security and Privacy (SP), pp. 677–694. IEEE Computer Society, Los Alamitos, CA, USA, May 2019
22. Kiayias, A., Zindros, D.: Proof-of-work sidechains. IACR Cryptology ePrint Archive 2018, vol. 1048 (2018)
23. Georgios, K.: Plasma cash: Towards more efficient plasma constructions (2019)
24. Jeremy, L., Oliver, H.: Funfair technology roadmap and discussion (2017)
25. ScaleSphere Foundation Ltd., Celer network: Bring internet scale to every blockchain (2018)
26. Miller, A., Bentov, I., Bakshi, S., Kumaresan, R., McCorry, P.: Sprites and state channels: payment networks that go faster than lightning. In: Goldberg, I., Moore, T. (eds.) FC 2019. LNCS, vol. 11598, pp. 508–526. Springer, Cham (2019). https://doi.org/10.1007/978-3-030-32101-7_30
27. Poon, J., Buterin, V.: Plasma: Scalable autonomous smart contracts. http://plasma.io/plasma.pdf
28. Joseph, P., Thaddeus, D.: The bitcoin lightning network: scalable off-chain instant payments (2016)
29. Zahnentferner, J.: An abstract model of UTxO-based cryptocurrencies with scripts. IACR Cryptology ePrint Archive 2018, vol. 469 (2018)

Authentication and Usability

What's in Score for Website Users: A Data-Driven Long-Term Study on Risk-Based Authentication Characteristics

Stephan Wiefling[1,2]($\boxtimes$) (iD), Markus Dürmuth[2], and Luigi Lo Iacono[1] (iD)

[1] H-BRS University of Applied Sciences, Sankt Augustin, Germany
{stephan.wiefling,luigi.lo_iacono}@h-brs.de
[2] Ruhr University Bochum, Bochum, Germany
{stephan.wiefling,markus.duermuth}@rub.de

Abstract. Risk-based authentication (RBA) aims to strengthen password-based authentication rather than replacing it. RBA does this by monitoring and recording additional features during the login process. If feature values at login time differ significantly from those observed before, RBA requests an additional proof of identification. Although RBA is recommended in the NIST digital identity guidelines, it has so far been used almost exclusively by major online services. This is partly due to a lack of open knowledge and implementations that would allow any service provider to roll out RBA protection to its users.

To close this gap, we provide a first in-depth analysis of RBA characteristics in a practical deployment. We observed N = 780 users with 247 unique features on a real-world online service for over 1.8 years. Based on our collected data set, we provide (i) a behavior analysis of two RBA implementations that were apparently used by major online services in the wild, (ii) a benchmark of the features to extract a subset that is most suitable for RBA use, (iii) a new feature that has not been used in RBA before, and (iv) factors which have a significant effect on RBA performance. Our results show that RBA needs to be carefully tailored to each online service, as even small configuration adjustments can greatly impact RBA's security and usability properties. We provide insights on the selection of features, their weightings, and the risk classification in order to benefit from RBA after a minimum number of login attempts.

Keywords: Risk-based authentication (RBA) · Authentication features · Big data analysis · Usable security

1 Introduction

Despite their long known weaknesses [5,12,15,19,29,48], passwords are still used for authentication on most online services [35]. However, threats to password-based authentication continue to evolve to attacks involving targeted guessing [32] or stolen credentials sourced from data breaches [43].

© International Financial Cryptography Association 2021
N. Borisov and C. Diaz (Eds.): FC 2021, LNCS 12675, pp. 361–381, 2021.
https://doi.org/10.1007/978-3-662-64331-0_19

Thus, online services need to implement alternative or additional measures to protect their user base. Two-factor authentication (2FA) is such a measure, but tends to be only accepted in online banking use cases [17,36,45]. Also, universal second factor (U2F) or biometric authentication require additional hardware and active user enrollment, which makes them impractical for online services [13,21].

For these reasons, several major online services deployed risk-based authentication (RBA) to protect their users [46]. RBA is an adaptive authentication mechanism which increases password security with minimal impact on the user. It achieves better usability than comparable 2FA methods [45] and is recommended by NIST [22] to mitigate credential stuffing.

During the password entry, RBA monitors and records features that are available in this context. These feature range from network information, or device information, to behavioral information. Based on these features, RBA calculates a risk score related to the login attempt. The score is typically classified by an access threshold into low, medium, and high risk [20,24,28]. Based on the estimated risk, the RBA system can invoke multiple actions. If the score is under the threshold, i.e., a low risk, access is granted. If the score is above this threshold, i.e., medium or high risk, the online service asks for additional information (e.g., confirming an email address) or even blocks access.

RBA schemes, their configuration, and features have not been researched thus far. These are, however, of crucial importance, since they can highly impact security and usability for website users. A feature might reduce the number of re-authentication requests but could also weaken the attack protection. To further investigate this topic, we formulated the following research questions.

Research Questions. With these research questions, we aim to provide answers on how RBA performs in a practical deployment and how RBA can be configured to provide the best balance between security and usability.

RQ1: a) How often does RBA request for re-authentication in a practical deployment?
   b) How many user sessions need to be captured and stored in the login history to achieve a stable and reliable RBA setup?
RQ2: a) Which RBA features have to be chosen to achieve good security?
   b) How do RBA features need to be combined to achieve good security?
   c) How often will different RBA feature combinations request legitimate users for re-authentication?
RQ3: a) How practical are different RBA configurations regarding performance?
   b) How scalable and cost-efficient are different RBA configurations?

Contributions. We provide the first long-term data-driven analysis of RBA characteristics. (i) We monitored and recorded the login behavior and features of 780 users on a real-world online service for over 1.8 years. (ii) We derived two RBA models based on the majority of deployments used in current practice. (iii)

We evaluated the two models on our data set and identified features that, in combination, provide good security and usability. (iv) We proposed and tested a new feature that had not yet been seen in the RBA and browser fingerprinting context before. (v) We derived how specific factors influence RBA's performance.

The results show that even small changes to RBA settings, e.g., the feature set or access threshold, can strongly affect the usability and security properties of RBA. Our work supports service owners regarding RBA design decisions on their website. It helps administrators select suitable RBA properties—including the RBA scheme, feature set, and weightings—for their website's characteristics and needs. Finally, researchers obtain insights on RBA's inner workings in practice. Understanding these factors can provide a comprehensive understanding of RBA and foster a widespread adoption that goes beyond the current use by only major online services.

2   RBA Models

We derived and evaluated two RBA models based on observations on the RBA behavior of major online services [46] and algorithm descriptions in literature.

The **simple model** (SIMPLE) extends the single-feature model used in the open source single sign-on solution OpenAM [31] and is assumed to be used at GOG.com [46]. It also partly reflects models given in literature [16,24,42]. We based our implementation on OpenAM, since it is freely available and probably widely used. The SIMPLE algorithm checks a number of features for an exact match in the user's login history. The risk score is the number of inspected features with at least one match in the login history divided by the total number of considered features. Thus, the risk score granularity increases with the number of observed features. We tested this model in two variations to observe the potential of OpenAM's original implementation. For a fair comparison with an influential RBA algorithm in literature [20], the first variation used the features *IP address* with *IP-based geolocation*, and *user agent string* (SIMPLE-IPUA). In the second variation, we enabled the maximum number of features in the OpenAM solution to test its maximum potential (SIMPLE-ALL). Besides the three features, there were *registered client* (HTML5 canvas and WebGL fingerprint), and *last login* (i.e., logged in within the last 31 days).

The **extended model** (EXTEND) is comparable to the multi-features model that Google, Amazon, and LinkedIn used [46] and presumably still use in some form. We based this model on Freeman et al. [20], since it was the only comparable algorithm described in the literature. The model calculates the risk score S for a user u and a given feature set $(x^1, ..., x^d)$ with d features as [20]:

$$S_u(x) = \left(\prod_{k=1}^{d} \frac{p(x^k)}{p(x^k|u, legitimate)} \right) \frac{p(u|attack)}{p(u|legitimate)} \tag{1}$$

$p(x^k)$ is the probability of a feature value in the global login history and $p(x^k|u, legitimate)$ is the probability that a legitimate user has this feature value in its own login history. Since we did not collect attack data, we assumed that all users are equally likely to be attacked. Thus, we set $p(u|attack) = \frac{1}{|U|}$, where U is the set of users with $u \in U$. The probability of legitimate logins for the user is based on the proportion of logins, i.e., $p(u|legitimate) = \frac{Number\ of\ user\ logins}{Number\ of\ all\ logins}$. Since the risk score depends on the global login history size, the risk score granularity increases with the number of entries in the global login history.

We smoothed the features with linear interpolation to add probabilities for previously unseen but plausible values [20]. We also subdivided some features into subfeatures with individual weightings (IP address → autonomous system number (ASN) and country; user agent string → browser/OS name and version, and device type, i.e., mobile or desktop). Freeman et al. evaluated these features and subfeatures with the help of LinkedIn [20]. Thus, these potentially represent a practical RBA feature set, which is why we chose and tested them as a baseline.

3   Data Set

We evaluated the RBA models with a data set containing real-world user behavior to identify the model characteristics in a practical deployment.

Data Collection. We recorded user data from August 2018 to June 2020 on an e-learning website for medical students. During course enrollment, they were registered at the website by the faculty staff. The students used this online service to exercise for their study courses and exams. After each successful login, we collected 247 different features of the user's online browser, network, and device (see the pre-proceedings paper version [44] for the full list of features). The features were relevant in the field of device fingerprinting [3,34] and could help to identify users in RBA as well.

The data set is very challenging for RBA since the users are mostly located in the same city. Thus, they could get similar feature values, e.g., IP addresses, with higher probability. Testing this data will answer whether practical RBA deployments can protect users in such a challenging scenario.

Survey. The e-learning website collected usernames, hashed passwords, and features only. After the collection phase, we surveyed users between July and August 2020 to improve data quality (see Appendix A for the questionnaire).

We recruited via a mailing list of the University of Cologne, addressing students who potentially used the e-learning website between August 2018 and June 2020. We introduced the study as a survey on the overall website perception. We drew 12 Amazon vouchers worth €10 among all participants after the study.

After verifying their account, the users were redirected to the survey. Besides demographics, we included some questions about the website experience to distract from our actual study purpose. To improve data quality, we asked whether the users knew about someone illegitimately logging into their website account. We based this question on Shay et al. [39].

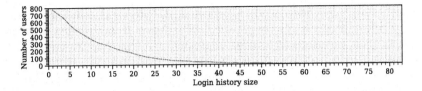

Fig. 1. Login history sizes and number of users in our data set

Demographics. In total, 182 website users (26.6% of login sessions) answered the survey. 168 users passed the attention check. The users were 61.3% female and 38.1% male (0.6% did not state the gender). The majority of users (79.7%) were between 18 and 24 years old. The remaining users were 25–34 years (18.5%), and 35–54 years old (1.8%). The age and gender distribution corresponds to the expected demographics for such a study course.

Login Sessions. The data set consisted of 780 users and 9555 logins. The users mostly logged in daily (44.3%) or several times a week (39.2%). They logged in between one and 83 times (mean: 12.25, median: 9, SD: 11.18; see Fig. 1). They used desktop (81.1%) and mobile devices (18.9%). The desktop devices were Windows (62.5%), macOS (37.2%), and Linux (0.3%) based. Mobile devices were iOS (75.2%) and Android (24.8%) based. The browsers were mainly Safari (40.4%), Chrome (29.0%), Firefox (26.1%), and Edge (3.3%). To improve the quality and validity of our results, we removed users who stated an illegitimate login attempt in the survey. However, there were no such users (93.5% did not notice, 6.5% did not know).

Feature Optimization. To improve the expected performance of some of the features, we optimized them based on procedures found in literature [3,20,24,42] and as described in the following.

We extracted additional subfeatures from the IP address, user agent string, and timestamp features. Besides only extracting the hour [24], we also extracted combinations of weekday and hour to gain more information.

Administrators aiming to deploy the EXTEND model need to adjust the feature weightings to appropriate values. Freeman et al. [20] did not provide subfeature weightings for IP address and user agent string. Thus, we calculated weightings for our data set following the method described in their paper. As a result, we set the weightings for the IP address (IP address: 0.6, ASN: 0.3, country: 0.1) and user agent (full string: 0.53, browser: 0.27, OS: 0.19, device type: 0.01). We chose the weightings based on the value of information when present. They only relate to our specific data set, but can give an impression of their distribution in practice.

New Feature: Round-Trip Time. We propose a new feature that has not been seen in RBA and browser fingerprinting literature at the time of study. In concurrent and independent work, Rivera et al. [37] proposed a similar idea based on the work-in-progress resource timing API. Apart from it being a different approach, their feature is also client originated and thus less trustworthy than our solution.

The web sockets technology [27], which is present in most online browsers today [9], allows measuring the round-trip-time (RTT). The server requests a data packet from the client and measures the time until the response. Popular online browsers Chrome and Firefox did not display this process (ping and pong frames) inside their developer tools at the time of study. RTTs can give information on whether the user's device is really located in the indicated region, or whether the location was potentially spoofed, e.g., by VPNs or proxies [1,8]. This is also true in the presence of Content Delivery Networks (CDNs), where the CDN edge node can be linked to the RTT. This results in an even better measurement, since the edge nodes close to the user's device are also considered.

When users entered the login credentials, we measured the RTT five times. Then, we stored the smallest RTT value to get the best possible value and to mitigate larger RTT variations, e.g., due to mobile connectivity. Besides the RTT in microseconds (RTT-RAW), we stored RTTs in milliseconds (RTT-MS), and rounded to the nearest five (RTT-5MS) and ten milliseconds (RTT-10MS).

Legal and Ethical Considerations. The participants were part of a model medical education program. During enrollment, they signed a consent form agreeing to the data collection for study purposes. They were always able to view their data on request. The collected data was stored on encrypted hard drives. Only the study researchers had access to them. The passwords on the website were hashed with scrypt [33]. All participants gave informed consent on these procedures. All survey questions included a "don't know" option.

We do not have a formal IRB process at our university. But besides our ethical considerations above, we made sure to minimize potential harm by complying with the ethics code of the German Sociological Association (DGS) and the standards of good scientific practice of the German Research Foundation (DFG). We also made sure to comply with the EU General Data Protection Regulation.

4   Attacker Models

We evaluated the RBA systems using three attacker models based on known ones in the RBA context [20,47]. All attackers possess the victim's login credentials (see Fig. 2).

Fig. 2. Overview of the attacker models tested in the study

The **naive attacker** tries to log in via an IP address of a random ISP located somewhere in the world and uses popular user agent strings. We simulate these attackers using a random subset of IP addresses sourced from real-world online attacks [18]. Other feature values not related to the IP address are sourced from our data set. The **VPN attacker** knows the same as the naive attacker plus the correct country of the victim. The attacker spoofs the IP geolocation with VPN services and uses popular user agent strings. We simulate these attackers with known attacker IP addresses [18] located in the victim's country. Feature values not derived from the IP address are sourced from our data set. We also included IP addresses not directly related to VPN services to consider services that tunnel traffic through client devices. The **targeted attacker** extends the knowledge of the VPN attacker by including locations and user agents of the victim. The attacker accesses IP addresses of ISPs in that location, likely including the victim's ones. This attacker is identical to Freeman et al.'s *phishing attacker* [20]. We used a different term, however, as phishing is just one of the ways to obtain this level of knowledge. We simulate this attacker with our data set. The feature values are taken from all users except the victim. Since location dependent feature values in our data set were in close proximity to each other, our simulated attacker is aware of these circumstances and chooses feature values in a similar way.

5   Evaluating RBA Practice (RQ1)

Below, we analyze the RBA behavior in a practical deployment. We describe our methodology to reproduce the RBA behavior and present the results.

Step 1: Calibrating Risk Scores. The risk scores of the RBA models have different granularity (see Sect. 2). For a fair comparison, we calibrated the risk score access thresholds of both RBA models. We adjusted regarding the percentage of blocked attacks in each attacker model, which we call the true positive rate (TPR), as in related work [20]. We approximated the TPRs as close as possible. However, due to their granularity properties, SIMPLE TPRs were more coarse-grained than those of EXTEND.

Step 2: Determine Re-authentication Count. By replaying user sessions, we determined how often the data set's legitimate users were asked for re-authentication based on the number of logins. For each login attempt, we (i) restored the state at the time of the login attempt, (ii) calculated the risk score with the RBA model, and (iii) finally applied the calibrated RBA access threshold to the risk score and stored the access decision.

To provide an average estimation of the RBA behavior, we calculated the median re-authentication counts and rates for each login history size.

5.1   Results

Figure 3 shows the results for the targeted attacker case. We answer our research questions regarding practical RBA deployments in the following.

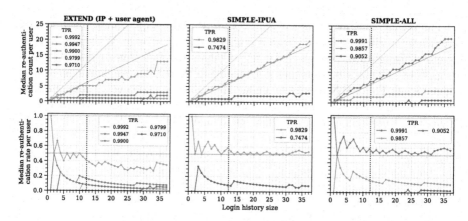

Fig. 3. Median re-authentication counts (top) and rates (bottom) per user based on the login history size. The TPR (percentage of blocked attacks) relates to targeted attackers. We added the baseline for 2FA (light grey line), the stable setup threshold (dark grey line), and the mean login count (dotted black line) for orientation. Below the stable setup threshold, users had to re-authenticate less than every 2nd login attempt.

Table 1. Median login count until re-authentication when blocking targeted attackers

Model	TPR	Median logins until re-authentication	Model	TPR	Median logins until re-authentication	Model	TPR	Median logins until re-authentication
EXTEND	0.9992	2.4	SIMPLE-ALL	0.9991	1.71	SIMPLE-IPUA	0.9829	1.71
	0.9947	6		0.9857	6		0.7474	12
	0.9900	12		<0.9857	∞		<0.7474	∞
	0.9799	12						
	<0.9799	∞						

Login history size: 12

Number of Re-authentication Requests in Practice (RQ1a).

The users logged into the website 12.25 times on mean. Thus, we considered a login history size of 12 to determine the re-authentication count for the average user in our data set. We define the median login count until re-authentication as the login history size divided by the median re-authentication count. In the following, we show the results with TPRs adjusted for each attacker model. Note that due to the risk score characteristics, attackers of lower hierarchy were always blocked as well (e.g., all naive attackers were blocked when blocking all VPN attackers).

Even when blocking all **naive attackers** with the highest possible TPR, legitimate users were never asked for re-authentication at all, except for SIMPLE-IP with TPR 0.999 (every 12th time). When **VPN attackers** were blocked, legitimate users were mostly not asked for re-authentication at all. In the other cases, they were prompted every 2.4th time (TPR 0.9995) and every 12th time (TPR 0.9946, 0.9903) with EXTEND, every 12th time with SIMPLE-IP (TPR 0.9933), and every 6th time with SIMPLE-ALL (TPR 0.9999). When blocking **targeted attackers**, our legitimate users were never asked for re-authentication with TPRs lower than 0.98 in most cases (see Table 1 and Fig. 3).

Overall, the median re-authentication rate became lower with an increase in the login history size. For very high TPRs, however, the numbers did not decrease to a high degree, especially with the SIMPLE model.

Concluding the results, RBA rarely requests re-authentication for most cases in our real-world data set, even when blocking targeted attackers up to a TPR of over 0.9945 with EXTEND. However, the re-authentication rate strongly depends on the RBA model and the assumed attacker model. The influence of the feature set and the feature weightings will be analyzed in Sect. 6.

Required Login History Size (RQ1b). Since RBA is designed to request less re-authentication than 2FA for legitimate users, this difference needs to be noticeable in sensible RBA deployments. As a baseline to request less than every second login attempt, we defined the required login history size as the size above which the median re-authentication rate remains below 0.5. For statistical validity, we considered login history sizes lower than 38 since these had at least 30 users (see Sect. 3).

In our data set, most TPRs required one or even no history entry for blocking targeted attackers in both models (see Fig. 3). However, EXTEND required ten entries for TPR 0.9992. The SIMPLE models partly did not fulfill the requirement (TPRs: 0.9829 SIMPLE-IPUA, 0.9991 SIMPLE-ALL). Based on our results, we conclude that storing one entry is already sufficient for a stable setup that blocks more than 99.45% of targeted attackers with the EXTEND model. To block 99.92% of attack attempts, ten entries are needed in our use case.

5.2   Discussion

Small variations of the access thresholds (see Sect. 1) can greatly affect the TPR. For instance, changing a tiny fraction of the threshold lowered the TPR from a very good 0.9829 to 0.7474 in SIMPLE-IPUA. We assume that this can make it difficult for administrators to adjust the access thresholds correctly. To foster a widespread RBA adoption in the wild, we suggest that RBA properties must be easy for administrators to estimate, apply, and control. A possible solution could be a dashboard showing the aggregated re-authentication rates and risk scores per user. These metrics can help to control and adjust the thresholds continuously and whenever necessary.

Even in settings involving a high TPR, the RBA models hardly ask for re-authentication at all. While this is a very good sign for the security properties of RBA, this influences users. Users will only feel protected by RBA if they get prompted for re-authentication at least once [45]. To support users in feeling protected, we suggest to inform about RBA being active.

6   Analyzing RBA Features (RQ2)

Based on our 247 collected features, we determined a subset that is suitable for RBA use. To be qualified for RBA use, we defined necessary criteria. The features need to: (A) **Have both a good level of stability and at least minimum entropy**: In contrast to fingerprinting properties for tracking purposes [34], we require a certain level of entropy to make it harder for attackers to reproduce the feature values by simply brute forcing them. This might cause RBA to ask for re-authentication at a higher frequency. However, showing RBA presence by very few re-authentication requests can lead to increased (perceived) security [45]. (B) **Be spoofable only with a high amount of effort**: Easy-to-guess features will not bring any attack detection advantage to the RBA feature set baseline. (C) **Increase differentiation between legitimate users and attackers**: When added to the baseline feature set, risk scores differences between legitimate users and attackers should increase.

6.1 Study Setup

Based on the defined criteria, we developed and conducted several big data computing jobs to analyze the performance of all features in our data set.

Test A: Entropy. To identify easy-to-spoof features, we calculated the Shannon entropy of the feature values x_{i_j} of each feature $x_i \in X$ in the login history with $n = |x_i|$:

$$H_{x_i} = -\sum_{j=0}^{n} x_{i_j} \cdot log_2(x_{i_j}) \qquad (2)$$

We calculated two variants of entropy. To observe overall differences, we calculated the entropy $H_{global_{x_i}}$ for the global login history. To observe the feature stability inside the login history of each user, we calculated the mean Shannon entropy $\overline{H_{user_{x_i}}}$ of each feature in the user's login history. As a result, features with $H_{global_{x_i}} = 0$ did not contain any information to distinguish between users. Similarly, features with $\overline{H_{user_{x_i}}} = 0$ did not change inside the users' login histories.

Test B: Number of Feature Values. Some of the collected features can be spoofed by attackers with low effort. This is especially true for client submitted features, e.g., output of a JavaScript function executed in the user's browser.

To make features harder to guess for attackers, they need to have a large range of values with equal distribution. Assuming that accounts will be locked after RBA detected an illegitimate login, it will be difficult for attackers to guess correct feature values with increasing numbers of unique feature values.

Test C: Risk Score Changes. We studied the risk score behavior of the features to evaluate their potential to improve the detection of attackers and legitimate users. We tested the features with the EXTEND model since it provides fine grained risk scores.

For each feature, we calculated the risk scores of all illegitimate login attempts by targeted attackers per user (attacker risk scores). We then calculated the risk scores of all legitimate login attempts (legitimate risk scores). After that, we determined the risk score relation (RSR) as the relation between the mean attacker and mean legitimate risk scores:

$$RSR_{basic} = \frac{mean\ attacker\ risk\ score}{mean\ legitimate\ risk\ score} \tag{3}$$

To ease comparison, we normalized the RSRs for each feature $x_i \in X$ to the baseline:

$$RSR_{x_i} = RSR_{basic_{x_i}} - RSR_{basic_{baseline}} \tag{4}$$

The feature baseline varied depending on the feature being compared to, e.g., the IP address when all compared features were added to the IP address. When testing only one feature, the baseline was a feature without any entropy, to observe risk score differences when entropy was added. If the RSR of a feature $x_i \in X$ is greater than the baseline RSR, i.e., $RSR_{x_i} > 0.0$, this feature increased the differentiation between legitimate users and attackers compared to the baseline.

Subset Extraction. For each test, we defined the following thresholds to extract a subset of suitable features for RBA use: (Test A) To extract features having at least minimum entropy, we only considered features with $H_{global_{x_i}} > 0.1$ and $\overline{H_{user_{x_i}}} > 0.1$. Based on the third quantile and the specific characteristics of the data set, we chose this threshold as a minimum baseline. (Test B) To focus on harder-to-guess features for RBA, we considered those with more than ten unique feature values. More features were considered for both desktop and mobile users in the global login history to adequately address security. We made sure to check both mobile and desktop devices since mobile devices tend to have less unique RBA feature values than desktop devices [40]. (Test C) To ignore features causing only small RSR improvements, we considered features with $RSR_{x_i} > 0.1$.

Feature Reliability. The extracted features were present on all user sessions but were very diverse, ranging from client originated to server side recorded. Thus, we labeled them by the following properties: (i) **Server side**: These features are measured on the server side. Since they do not depend on client originated input, they add a high level of trust. (ii) **Client side JavaScript not required**: There might be users that deactivated JavaScript, e.g., for privacy reasons. To ensure compatibility, we labeled features that can be measured without JavaScript.

Based on the properties, we distinguished three categories of RBA features: **Single features** add a high level of reliability and provide good RBA performance on their own. **Major add-on features** are similar, but they only achieve good RBA performance when added to a single feature. Both feature types can

Table 2. Single and major add-on features that qualified for RBA use. The only single feature is the IP address (bold). The other ones are major features that can be used in addition to a single feature. All features are server originated and hence hard to spoof.

Feature	JavaScript not required	RSR	H_{global}	$\overline{H_{user}}$	Unique values	Median logins until re-authentication
IP address	●	1.20	10.51	1.96	●●●●●	**2.00
RTT-10MS	○	1.75	2.45	1.04	●●○○○	1.50
RTT-5MS	○	1.37	3.27	1.33	●●○○○	1.71
ASN (IP)	●	0.91	3.17	0.76	●●○○○	3.00
RTT-MS	○	0.56	5.43	2.00	●●●●○	2.00
Hour	●	0.23	4.06	2.31	●○○○○	4.00
Region (IP)	●	0.15	1.20	0.31	●○○○○	1.71
Weekday and hour	●	0.15	6.72	2.78	●●●○○	4.00

Significantly higher than the baseline: ** $p < 0.01$
Baselines: Zero entropy feature (single feature), IP address (major add-on feature)
Unique values: Five dot scale (very low, low, medium, high, very high) mapped to the values (10–24, 25–74, 75–149, 150–300, >300).

be used with high weighting and are measured on the server side. **Add-on features** are not as reliable as the features above but can be used in addition to single features. They are client originated. Therefore, it is possible that some of them could be blocked or modified, e.g., by anti-tracking measures [7].

Re-authentication Count Changes. We assume that less requests for re-authentication can increase RBA usability and user acceptance [45]. Thus, we measured whether certain features have the potential to decrease the requests for legitimate users. We calculated the median login count until re-authentication for average legitimate users (i.e., 12 logins) and a TPR of 0.8 (targeted attackers) for each feature. We selected the TPR to allow all features to get a TPR close to the desired TPR for fair comparison. Also, selecting targeted attackers allowed us to test the features against the best possible attacker.

High re-authentication counts can signal administrators to weigh this feature lower, in combination with other features having lower counts, to balance usability.

6.2   Results

In the following, we present our results ordered by the three RBA feature categories. For statistical testing, we used Kruskal-Wallis tests for the omnibus cases and Dunn's multiple comparison test with Bonferroni correction for post-hoc analysis. We considered p-values lower than 0.05 as significant.

We calculated the risk scores on a high-performance computing (HPC) cluster with more than 2400 CPU cores. This was necessary since such calculations were computationally intensive. Using the HPC cluster reduced the calculation time to approximately two days for all features (instead of 123.5 days using 32 cores).

After combining the features that passed all three tests, only the IP address qualified as a **single feature** for RBA use. When being used in addition to the IP address, seven features qualified as **major add-on features**, all of them network or behavior based (see Table 2). Since the IP address was the only appropriate single feature for this case, we extracted the **add-on features** using this feature. 27 features qualified by passing all three tests (see Table 3).

Table 3. Add-on features that qualified for RBA use in addition to single features. In comparison to major add-on features, they are client originated and thus spoofable.

Feature	JavaScript not required	RSR	H_{global}	$\overline{H_{user}}$	Unique values	Median logins until re-authentication
Session Cookie	●	22.39	9.51	0.51	●●●●●	**12.00
User agent string (w/ subfeatures)	●	10.33	7.43	1.21	●●●●●	**12.00
Screen width and height	○	3.28	4.70	0.64	●●●●○	3.00
WebGL fingerprint	○	3.14	4.12	0.55	●●●○○	4.00
Accept language header	●	3.01	2.57	0.33	●●●○○	3.00
App version	○	2.74	6.29	1.01	●●●●●	2.40
Available width and height	○	2.72	6.36	0.95	●●●●●	3.00
OS full version	●	2.64	3.90	0.59	●●●○○	2.40
WebGL Version	○	2.59	2.14	0.36	●●○○○	2.40
WebGL extensions	○	2.52	3.62	0.56	●●○○○	6.00
HTML5 canvas fingerprint	○	2.28	6.45	0.77	●●●●●	3.00
OS name and version	●	2.27	3.91	0.59	●●●○○	2.40
Browser major version	●	2.03	4.28	0.80	●●○○○	**6.00
Device pixel ratio	○	1.94	2.66	0.51	●●○○○	2.40
User agent string (no subfeatures)	●	1.74	7.43	1.21	●●●●●	3.00
Main language	○	1.61	1.35	0.24	●○○○○	3.00
Browser full version	●	1.27	5.49	0.96	●●●○○	**12.00
Browser name and version	●	1.14	5.85	1.02	●●●●○	**6.00
Local IP address	○	1.13	3.27	0.49	●●●●●	1.00
Webkit temporary storage	○	0.92	3.30	0.39	●●●●●	1.00
Battery discharging time	○	0.75	1.95	0.48	●●●●●	1.00

Significantly higher than the baseline: ** p < 0.01
Unique values: Five dot scale (very low, low, medium, high, very high) mapped to the values (10–24, 25–74, 75–149, 150–300, >300).
The session cookie was set by the server. RBA simply compared the stored value.
We omitted similar features for space reasons (see Table 4 in Appendix B for all results).

Conclusion. In summary, a set of features has to be chosen in most cases rather than a single feature to achieve good RBA security. Using only one feature for RBA risk estimation will make it hard to reliably distinguish between attackers and legitimate users. The feature set needs to at least include features that we identified as single or major add-ons (see Table 2) for good RBA security.

6.3   Discussion

The results confirm our previous findings [46] that IP address, user agent, display resolution, language, and login time are useful RBA features and hence, find adoption in the wild. The results also show that most of the 247 analyzed features are not suitable for RBA use. Many of them had few unique values or low RSRs. This is good for privacy, as few features need to be collected. Also, many of the popular features [46] are collected on the server side anyway, e.g., in the logs [25]. Still, some of them may contain sensitive data [6] and must be protected against data breaches. But, as we considered all features as categorical data, these can be hashed, or even truncated to some degree, to produce the same results. Our results suggest a set of relevant RBA features may provide security benefits while preserving usability. This set is rather small compared to the 247 evaluated features. Thus, we discuss how to design a minimal RBA feature set to also balance privacy. We discuss a selection of relevant features and feature combinations based on our results and findings in literature below.

Features. The **IP address** proved to be the only RBA feature that can be used as a single feature. The **region** and **ASN** are also hard to fake and to obtain since they require network access from a specific ASN in a specific location.

The **RTT** turned out as a promising new RBA feature when being rounded to milliseconds at least. Attackers need access to a device physically located inside the victim's location to forge this feature. Thus, using the RTT would add high costs for attackers. However, due to more re-authentication requests, the RTT needs to be weighted lower than other features to balance usability.

Timing features like **weekday and hour** increased security attributes while having few re-authentication requests. Successful attacks need to estimate the victim's usual login times right to the day and hour, which can be greater effort. This is especially the case for services that are not used on a daily basis.

The **user agent string** performed very well when used in combinations with a subfeature hierarchy, confirming findings of Freeman et al. [20].

Since it can be used as a unique session identifier, the **cookie** seems to be an obvious feature choice, and our results would support this view. However, cookies should only be used very carefully or not at all as a RBA feature. They would have to be stored permanently in the login history. Since there is no revocation mechanism in the current RBA models, every cookie inside the login history would always be valid. Thus, a stolen and even outdated cookie might have a negative impact on the risk score, leading to false positives.

Feature Combinations. The **IP address and user agent string** features are often named in literature [20,24,40]. According to our observations related to the data set, they increased the RSR and significantly reduced re-authentications compared to the single features.

RBA models in literature often use **user agent strings** to identify a browser [16,20,24,40,46]. However, **HTML5 canvas and WebGL fingerprints** [14,

30] are newer approaches considered more difficult to fake. Both approaches received lower RSRs and significantly higher re-authentication counts compared to the user agent string in our data set. Following that, if canvas or WebGL fingerprinting should be used to strengthen security, one should consider using them with lower weightings.

7 Analyzing RBA Configuations (RQ3)

For good usability, the latency between submitting the login credentials and getting the risk decision needs to be low. An acceptable delay ranges below 300 ms when considering the page load time [41]. Thus, we analyzed which properties have an impact on the risk score calculation time. This can help to design RBA systems with both good security and a low authentication time.

We replayed all legitimate logins with both models and measured the time it took to calculate the risk score. We measured on a server with Intel Xeon Gold 6130 processor (2.1 GHz, 64 cores), 480 GB SSD storage, and 64 GB RAM. We used Kruskal-Wallis tests to check for significant differences between features. For variables suggesting a relation, we calculated the linear least squares regression between them. We determined the effect sizes based on Cohen [11].

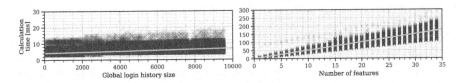

Fig. 4. Relationship between risk score calculation time and the size of the global login history (left) or number of features (right) for EXTEND. The diagonal line represents the fitted linear regression model. Left: We limited the y-axis to 30 ms for readability.

(Test 1) We first measured the calculation times for **every feature**. The median calculation times ranged 4.5–8 ms for EXTEND (median: 5.63; SD: 0.9), and 0.07–2.7 ms for SIMPLE (median: 0.08; SD: 0.17). There were no significant differences between the features. However, there was a large significant effect between the calculation time and the global login history size for EXTEND. The linear regression yielded $y = 4.1912 + 0.0003 \cdot x$, with y being the time in ms and x the global login history size ($R^2 = 0.42$; f = 0.85; p $\ll$ 0.0001).

(Test 2) We then measured the calculation time based on the **number of features** in the feature set. However, testing all $2^{247} - 1$ combinations was not feasible. Since there were no significant differences between all features in Test 1, we chose the feature that ranged in the middle of all median calculation times. We did this to select a feature that matches all features as well as possible. We took this feature, added it to the feature set, measured the times, and did it again until we reached the maximum number of features found in RQ2.

The results showed significant effects between the number of features and the calculation time (see Fig. 4). The fitted linear regression model resulted in $y = 1.5568 + 5.0038 \cdot x$ and a large effect size for EXTEND ($R^2 = 0.93$; f = 3.71; p $\ll$ 0.0001), with y being the time in ms and x the number of features. Linear regression for SIMPLE resulted in $y = -0.0119 + 0.0013 \cdot x$ and a medium effect ($R^2 = 0.12$; f = 0.37; p $\ll$ 0.0001). However, the latter effects were hardly noticeable.

Discussion. Administrators need to keep track of the included global login history and features to ensure an acceptable authentication speed. The results show that including a high amount of features impacts the performance for EXTEND. However, our results for RQ1 already showed that capturing few features was sufficient for good security and usability.

8 Limitations

We implemented the RBA models using Python. High-level programming languages like C++ might have reduced the calculation time. Nevertheless, our results can still give estimates on factors that influence RBA performance.

The results are limited to the data set tested and the users who participated. Our results are not representative of large-scale online services, but represent a typical use case scenario of a daily to weekly use online service in a certain country. We assume that the IP country feature would have qualified with an international user base [20]. To allow a fair comparison of all features, we weighted all features equally. We expect, however, that service owners weigh features individually, possibly improving the RBA performance. Thus, we assume that our study results represent a RBA performance baseline.

As in similar studies, we can never fully exclude that the website was targeted by intelligent attackers. However, we implemented multiple countermeasures. The website URL was only provided to students signing an informed consent. The URL was not accessible via search engines due to geoblocking and other measures to disallow crawling the site. IP scans reaching the website's IP address only received a white page instead of the e-learning website. The TLS certificate also did not reveal the real DNS entry in this case. The fact that users did not notice illegitimate login attempts and no data breaches were known underlines that the website was likely not infiltrated.

9 Related Work

In previous work, we studied RBA's usability characteristics [45,47]. The results helped to estimate the usability of RBA characteristics in this study. To the best of our knowledge, no studies analyzing RBA characteristics with long-term login data exist in literature. Freeman et al. [20] tested their RBA model on a

LinkedIn data set using only IP address and user agent string as features. In contrast to them, we tested their model with a huge set of features.

There is also related work regarding browser fingerprinting features for user authentication purposes. Alaca and van Oorschot [3] classified 29 fingerprinting features which have the potential to be used for user authentication. They selected the features based on literature research but, in contrast to our study, did not test them on real data. Spooren et al. [40] tested OpenAM's RBA mechanism on simulated data with six features, which were screen resolution, browser plugins, fonts, timezone, user agent, and geolocation. They found that mobile devices were less reliable in terms of being uniquely identified. We were able to confirm their findings for these six features. However, our study shows that there are other features that can reliably identify mobile device users. Campobasso and Allodi [8] studied a criminal infrastructure that tries to bypass RBA on malware infected victim devices. Since its geolocation spoofing relied on SOCKS5 proxies, our new RTT feature can detect these attacks. Andriamilanto et al. [4] tested fingerprints of website users regarding their capability to be used for authentication purposes. In contrast to our study, their data set did not relate to login attempts, contained only client originated features, and was not tested on RBA.

10 Conclusion

As long as password-based authentication predominates, constantly evolving data breaches and targeted attacks with breached passwords [2] increase the need of RBA for online services to protect their users. NIST recommends RBA use since 2017 [22]. However, the current body of knowledge does not provide insights on RBA characteristics. Understanding these is important to ensure that practical RBA deployments protect users as much as possible while balancing usability. To close this gap, we studied RBA characteristics with long-term usage data of a real-world online service. Our results show that RBA can achieve low re-authentication rates for legitimate users when blocking more than 99.45% of targeted attacks with the EXTEND model. Moreover, our findings also show that only few of the 247 collected features can be considered useful for practical RBA deployments. The IP address is confirmed to be a must-have feature in general, but it should be enriched by add-on features. Among them, the introduced RTT showed to be a new promising feature. Cookies, however, should only be used with great care or not at all, as stolen credentials together with a stolen cookie might outweigh other features and falsely grant access.

Our contribution indicates that simply acquiring one of the commercially or freely available RBA solutions is not sufficient. They still need to be customized for the targeted online service in order to be optimized in terms of security and usability. We provided insights on how to select proper features, their weightings, and the access threshold. Based on our findings, we recommend to use RBA algorithms comparable to the introduced EXTEND model, since its security and usability properties outweighed the SIMPLE model. Overall, RBA protection should be put in place shortly after the first deployment, as the login history size did not affect it in our study.

Acknowledgments. Thanks to the anonymous reviewers, our shepherd Gunes Acar, and Florian Dehling for their detailed feedback, which greatly helped improve the paper. We would like to thank Rudolf Berrendorf and Javed Razzaq for providing us a huge amount of computational power for our big data analysis. We also thank Gaston Pugliese for providing us his fingerprinting script, Annette Ricke and Jan Herrmann for their support and cooperation, and Tanvi Patil for proofreading the paper. This research was supported by the research training group "Human Centered Systems Security" (NERD.NRW) sponsored by the state of North Rhine-Westphalia. The Platform for Scientific Computing was supported by the German Ministry for Education and Research, and the Ministry for Culture and Science of the state North Rhine-Westphalia (research grant 13FH156IN6).

A   Survey

We balanced all survey questions where applicable to mitigate social desirability bias [38]. The questions were presented in random order to randomly distribute ordering effects [26]. We varied the scale direction of the questions for a random half of survey participants. For questions without an ordinal scale, we randomized the response options for each participant. We did all this to randomly distribute response order bias [10,23]. We also included an attention check similar to previous work [47].

A.1   Online Service

Question (ii) and (iii) were on a five-point Likert scale including a "don't know" option.

(i) Which of these online services did you use at least once in the last three years? *[Multiple choice]* ○ *[website]* ○ Google ○ Facebook ○ Twitch ○ *[made-up online service that did not exist]* ○ Other: _____
   The order of the subquestions varied randomly in this question.

(ii) How much or little did *[website]* support you in learning the lecture material?
   (5 - Did fully support, 1 - Did not support at all)

(iii) Please rate your agreement : I think I would recommend *[website]* to other students.
   (5 - Strongly agree, 1 - Strongly disagree)

(iv) As far as you know, has anyone ever illegitimately logged into your personal *[website]* account? ○ Yes, more than once ○ Yes, only once ○ No ○ I don't know

A.2   Demographics

(i) How old are you? ○ 18–24 ○ 25–34 ○ 35–44 ○ 45–54 ○ 55–64 ○ 65–74 ○ 75 or older ○ Prefer not to say

(ii) What is your gender? ○ Female ○ Male ○ Non-Binary ○ Prefer not to say

B   Features

Table 4. List of single (bold) and (major) add-on features that qualified for RBA use. All features are present in all sessions of the data set.

Feature	Server side	JS not required	RSR	H_{global}	$\overline{H_{user}}$	Unique values	Median logins until re-auth.	p
IP address	●	●	1.20	10.51	1.96	4073	**2.00	<0.0001
Session Cookie	○	●	22.39	9.51	0.51	1534	**12.00	<0.0001
User agent string (w/ subfeatures)	○	●	10.33	7.43	1.21	638	**12.00	<0.0001
Screen width and height	○	○	3.28	4.70	0.64	176	3.00	-
WebGL fingerprint	○	○	3.14	4.12	0.55	90	4.00	0.8057
Screen height	○	○	3.09	4.34	0.64	126	4.00	0.3426
Accept language header	○	●	3.01	2.57	0.33	91	3.00	-
Available screen width	○	○	2.93	4.38	0.69	150	3.00	-
Screen width	○	○	2.93	4.28	0.63	138	4.00	0.8883
App version	○	○	2.74	6.29	1.01	534	2.40	-
Available width and height	○	○	2.72	6.36	0.95	411	3.00	-
OS full version	○	●	2.64	3.90	0.59	93	2.40	-
Available screen height	○	○	2.59	5.91	0.95	289	3.00	-
WebGL Version	○	○	2.59	2.14	0.36	56	2.40	-
Supported languages	○	○	2.53	2.54	0.36	87	3.00	-
WebGL extensions	○	○	2.52	3.62	0.56	69	6.00	0.1601
HTML5 canvas fingerprint	○	○	2.28	6.45	0.77	386	3.00	-
OS name and version	○	●	2.27	3.91	0.59	95	2.40	-
Browser major version	○	●	2.03	4.28	0.80	57	**6.00	0.0046
Device pixel ratio	○	○	1.94	2.66	0.51	70	2.40	-
RTT-10MS	●	○	1.75	2.45	1.04	51	1.50	-
User agent string (no subfeatures)	○	●	1.74	7.43	1.21	635	3.00	-
Main language	○	○	1.61	1.35	0.24	21	3.00	-
RTT-5MS	●	○	1.37	3.27	1.33	67	1.71	-
Browser full version	○	●	1.27	5.49	0.96	118	**12.00	0.0005
Browser name and version	○	●	1.14	5.85	1.02	161	**6.00	0.0064
Local IP address	○	○	1.13	3.27	0.49	716	1.00	-
Webkit temporary storage	○	○	0.92	3.30	0.39	735	1.00	-
ASN (IP)	●	●	0.91	3.17	0.76	43	3.00	-
Battery discharging time	○	○	0.75	1.95	0.48	1007	1.00	0.0860
Battery level	○	○	0.73	2.36	0.75	99	1.00	0.0935
RTT-MS	●	○	0.56	5.43	2.00	170	2.00	-
Hour	●	●	0.23	4.06	2.31	24	4.00	-
Region (IP)	●	●	0.15	1.20	0.31	16	1.71	-
Weekday and hour	●	●	0.15	6.72	2.78	145	4.00	0.2117

Significantly higher than the baseline: * $p < 0.05$
** $p < 0.01$
We omitted p-values of 1.0 for readability reasons.

References

1. Abdou, A., van Oorschot, P.C.: Secure client and server geolocation over the Internet. Login **43**(1), 19–25 (2018)
2. Akamai: Credential Stuffing: Attacks and Economies. [state of the internet]/security 5 (Special Media Edition) (April 2019)
3. Alaca, F., van Oorschot, P.C.: Device fingerprinting for augmenting web authentication: classification and analysis of methods. In: ACSAC 2016 (December 2016)
4. Andriamilanto, N., Allard, T., Guelvouit, G.L.: Guess Who?. In: IMIS 2020 (2021)
5. Bonneau, J.: The science of guessing: analyzing an anonymized corpus of 70 million passwords. In: SP 2012 (May 2012)
6. Bonneau, J., Felten, E.W., Mittal, P., Narayanan, A.: Privacy concerns of implicit secondary factors for web authentication. In: WAY 2014 (2014)
7. Bujlow, T., Carela-Espanol, V., Lee, B.R., Barlet-Ros, P.: A survey on web tracking: mechanisms, implications, and defenses. Proc. IEEE **105**(8), 1476–1510 (2017)
8. Campobasso, M., Allodi, L.: Impersonation-as-a-service: characterizing the emerging criminal infrastructure for user impersonation at scale. In: CCS 2020 (November 2020)
9. caniuse.com: Web sockets (July 2020)
10. Chan, J.C.: Response-order effects in Likert-type scales. Educ. Psychol. Meas. **51**(3), 531–540 (1991)
11. Cohen, J.: Statistical Power Analysis for the Behavioral Sciences, 2nd edn. (1988)
12. Das, A., Bonneau, J., Caesar, M., Borisov, N., Wang, X.: The tangled web of password reuse. In: NDSS 2014 (February 2014)
13. Das, S., Dingman, A., Camp, L.J.: Why Johnny doesn't use two factor a two-phase usability study of the FIDO U2F security key. In: Meiklejohn, S., Sako, K. (eds.) FC 2018. LNCS, vol. 10957, pp. 160–179. Springer, Heidelberg (2018). https://doi.org/10.1007/978-3-662-58387-6_9
14. Daud, N.I., Haron, G.R., Othman, S.S.S.: Adaptive authentication: implementing random canvas fingerprinting as user attributes factor. In: ISCAIE 2017 (April 2017)
15. Dhamija, R., Tygar, J.D., Hearst, M.: Why phishing works. In: CHI 2006 (April 2006)
16. Djosic, N., Nokovic, B., Sharieh, S.: Machine learning in action: securing IAM API by risk authentication decision engine. In: CNS 2020 (June 2020)
17. Dutson, J., Allen, D., Eggett, D., Seamons, K.: "Don't punish all of us": measuring user attitudes about two-factor authentication. In: EuroUSEC 2019 (June 2019)
18. FireHOL: All cybercrime ip feeds (August 2020). http://iplists.firehol.org/?ipset=firehol_level4
19. Florencio, D., Herley, C.: A large-scale study of web password habits. In: WWW 2007 (May 2007)
20. Freeman, D., Jain, S., Dürmuth, M., Biggio, B., Giacinto, G.: Who are you? A statistical approach to measuring user authenticity. In: NDSS 2016 (February 2016)
21. Gaddam, A.: Usage of behavioral biometric technologies to defend against bots. In: Enigma 2019 (January 2019)
22. Grassi, P.A., et al.: Digital identity guidelines: authentication and lifecycle management. Tech. rep. NIST SP 800–63b, NIST, Gaithersburg, MD (June 2017)
23. Hartley, J.: Some thoughts on Likert-type scales. Int. J. Clin. Health Psychol. **14**(1), 83–86 (2014)

24. Hurkała, A., Hurkała, J.: Architecture of context-risk-aware authentication system for web environments. In: ICIEIS 2014 (September 2014)
25. IBM: Log File Formats: NCSA Combined Log Format (2003)
26. Kalton, G., Schuman, H.: The effect of the question on survey responses: a review. J. R. Stat. Soc. Ser. A (Gen.) **145**(1), 42–57 (1982)
27. Melnikov, A., Fette, I.: The WebSocket Protocol. No. 6455 in Request for Comments (December 2011)
28. Molloy, I., Dickens, L., Morisset, C., Cheng, P.C., Lobo, J., Russo, A.: Risk-based security decisions under uncertainty. In: CODASPY 2012 (February 2012)
29. Morris, R., Thompson, K.: Password security. Commun. ACM **22**(11), 594–597 (1979)
30. Mowery, K., Shacham, H.: Pixel perfect. In: W2SP 2012 (May 2012)
31. Open Identity Platform: OpenAM: Adaptive Authentication Module (August 2016). https://git.io/JteWg
32. Pal, B., Daniel, T., Chatterjee, R., Ristenpart, T.: Beyond credential stuffing: password similarity models using neural networks. In: SP 2019 (May 2019)
33. Percival, C., Josefsson, S.: The scrypt password-based key derivation function. Tech. rep. RFC7914 (August 2016)
34. Pugliese, G., Riess, C., Gassmann, F., Benenson, Z.: Long-term observation on browser fingerprinting. Proc. PETS **2020**(2), 558–577 (2020)
35. Quermann, N., Harbach, M., Dürmuth, M.: The state of user authentication in the wild. In: WAY 2018 (August 2018)
36. Reynolds, J., Smith, T., Reese, K., Dickinson, L., Ruoti, S., Seamons, K.: A tale of two studies: the best and worst of yubikey usability. In: SP 2018 (May 2018)
37. Rivera, E., Tengana, L., Solano, J., Castelblanco, A., López, C., Ochoa, M.: Risk-based authentication based on network latency profiling. In: AISec 2020 (2020)
38. Shaeffer, E.M.: Comparing the quality of data obtained by minimally balanced and fully balanced attitude questions. Public Opin. Q. **69**(3), 417–428 (2005)
39. Shay, R., Ion, I., Reeder, R.W., Consolvo, S.: My religious aunt asked why i was trying to sell her viagra. In: CHI 2014 (April 2014)
40. Spooren, J., Preuveneers, D., Joosen, W.: Mobile device fingerprinting considered harmful for risk-based authentication. In: EuroSec 2015 (April 2015)
41. Stadnik, W., Nowak, Z.: The impact of web pages' load time on the conversion rate of an e-commerce platform. In: ISAT 2017 (September 2018)
42. Steinegger, R.H., Deckers, D., Giessler, P., Abeck, S.: Risk-based authenticator for web applications. In: EuroPlop 2016 (June 2016)
43. Thomas, K., et al.: Protecting accounts from credential stuffing with password breach alerting. In: USENIX Security 2019 (August 2019)
44. Wiefling, S., Dürmuth, M., Lo Iacono, L.: What's in score for website users: a data-driven long-term study on risk-based authentication characteristics. In: FC 2021 (Pre-Proceedings) (March 2021). https://nbn-resolving.org/urn:nbn:de:hbz:1044-opus-53053
45. Wiefling, S., Dürmuth, M., Lo Iacono, L.: More than just good passwords? A study on usability and security perceptions of risk-based authentication. In: ACSAC 2020 (December 2020)
46. Wiefling, S., Lo Iacono, L., Dürmuth, M.: Is this really you? An empirical study on risk-based authentication applied in the wild. In: IFIP SEC 2019 (June 2019)
47. Wiefling, S., Patil, T., Dürmuth, M., Lo Iacono, L.: Evaluation of risk-based re-authentication methods. In: IFIP SEC 2020 (September 2020)
48. von Zezschwitz, E., De Luca, A., Hussmann, H.: Honey, I shrunk the keys. In: NordiCHI 2014 (October 2014)

DAHash: Distribution Aware Tuning
of Password Hashing Costs

Wenjie Bai and Jeremiah Blocki$^{(\boxtimes)}$

Department of Compucter Science, Purdue University, West Lafayette, IN, USA
{bai104,jblocki}@purdue.edu

Abstract. An attacker who breaks into an authentication server and steals all of the cryptographic password hashes is able to mount an offline-brute force attack against each user's password. Offline brute-force attacks against passwords are increasingly commonplace and the danger is amplified by the well documented human tendency to select low-entropy password and/or reuse these passwords across multiple accounts. Moderately hard password hashing functions are often deployed to help protect passwords against offline attacks by increasing the attacker's guessing cost. However, there is a limit to how "hard" one can make the password hash function as authentication servers are resource constrained and must avoid introducing substantial authentication delay. Observing that there is a wide gap in the strength of passwords selected by different users we introduce DAHash (Distribution Aware Password Hashing) a novel mechanism which reduces the number of passwords that an attacker will crack. Our key insight is that a resource-constrained authentication server can dynamically tune the hardness parameters of a password hash function based on the (estimated) strength of the user's password. We introduce a Stackelberg game to model the interaction between a defender (authentication server) and an offline attacker. Our model allows the defender to optimize the parameters of DAHash e.g., specify how much effort is spent in hashing weak/moderate/high strength passwords. We use several large scale password frequency datasets to empirically evaluate the effectiveness of our differentiated cost password hashing mechanism. We find that the defender who uses our mechanism can reduce the fraction of passwords that would be cracked by a rational offline attacker by up to 15%.

Keywords: Password hashing · DAHash · Stackelberg game

1 Introduction

Breaches at major organizations have exposed billions of user passwords to the dangerous threat of offline password cracking. An attacker who has stolen the cryptographic hash of a user's password could run an offline attack by comparing the stolen hash value with the cryptographic hashes of every password in a large dictionary of popular password guesses. An offline attacker can check as many

© International Financial Cryptography Association 2021
N. Borisov and C. Diaz (Eds.): FC 2021, LNCS 12675, pp. 382–405, 2021.
https://doi.org/10.1007/978-3-662-64331-0_20

guesses as s/he wants since each guess can be verified without interacting with the authentication server. The attacker is limited only by the cost of checking each password guess i.e., the cost of evaluating the password hash function.

Offline attacks are a grave threat to security of users' information for several reasons. First, the entropy of a typical user chosen password is relatively low e.g., see [9]. Second, users often reuse passwords across multiple accounts to reduce cognitive burden. Finally, the arrival of GPUs, FPGAs and ASICs significantly reduces the cost of evaluating a password hash functions such as PBKDF2 [18] millions or billions of times. Blocki et al. [8] recently argued that PBKDF2 *cannot* adequately protect user passwords without introducing an intolerable authentication delay (e.g., 2 min) because the attacker could use ASICs to reduce guessing costs by many orders of magnitude.

Memory hard functions (MHFs) [5,25] can be used to build ASIC resistant password hashing algorithms. The Area x Time complexity of an ideal MHF will scale with t^2, where t denotes the time to evaluate the function on a standard CPU. Intuitively, to evaluate an MHF the attacker must dedicate t blocks of memory for t time steps, which ensures that the cost of computing the function is equitable across different computer architectures i.e., RAM on an ASIC is still expensive. Because the "full cost" [35] of computing an ideal MHF scales quadratically with t it is also possible to rapidly increase guessing costs without introducing an untenable delay during user authentication—by contrast the full cost of hash iteration based KDFs such as PBKDF2 [18] and BCRYPT [26] scale linearly with t. Almost all of the entrants to the recent Password Hashing Competition (PHC) [34] claimed some form of memory-hardness.

Even if we use MHFs there remains a fundamental trade-off in the design of good password hashing algorithms. On the one hand the password hash function should be sufficiently expensive to compute so that it becomes economically infeasible for the attacker to evaluate the function millions or billions of times per user—even if the attacker develops customized hardware (ASICs) to evaluate the function. On the other hand the password hashing algorithm cannot be so expensive to compute that the authentication server is unable to handle the workload when multiple users login simultaneously. Thus, even if an organization uses memory hard functions it will not be possible to protect all user passwords against an offline attacker e.g., if the password hashing algorithm is not so expensive that the authentication server is overloaded then it will almost certainly be worthwhile for an offline attacker to check the top thousand passwords in a cracking dictionary against each user's password. In this sense all of the effort an authentication server expends protecting the weakest passwords is (almost certainly) wasted.

Contributions. We introduce DAHash (Distribution Aware Hash) a password hashing mechanism that minimizes the damage of an offline attack by tuning key-stretching parameters for each user account based on password strength. In many empirical password distributions there are often several passwords that are so popular that it would be infeasible for a resource constrained authentication server to dissuade an offline attacker from guessing these passwords e.g., in the

Yahoo! password frequency corpus [7,9] the most popular password was selected by approximately 1% of users. Similarly, other users might select passwords that are strong enough to resist offline attacks even with minimal key stretching. The basic idea behind DAHash is to have the resource-constrained authentication server shift more of its key-stretching effort towards saveable password i.e., passwords the offline attacker could be disuaded from checking.

Our DAHash mechanism partitions passwords into τ groups e.g., weak, medium and strong when $\tau = 3$. We then select a different cost parameter k_i for each group G_i, $i \leq \tau$ of passwords. If the input password pw is in group G_i then we will run our moderately hard key-derivation function with cost parameter k_i to obtain the final hash value h. Crucially, the hash value h stored on the server will not reveal any information about the cost parameter k_i or, by extension, the group G_i.

We adapt a Stackelberg Game model of Blocki and Datta [6] to help the defender (authentication server) tune the DAHash cost parameters k_i to minimize the fraction of cracked passwords. The defender (leader) groups passwords into different strength levels and selects the cost parameter k_i for each group of passwords (subject to maximum workload constraints for the authentication server) and then the offline attacker selects the attack strategy which maximizes his/her utility (expected reward minus expected guessing costs). The attacker's expected utility will depend on the DAHash cost paremeters k_i as well, the user password distribution, the value v of a cracked password to the attacker and the attacker's strategy i.e., an ordered list of passwords to check before giving up. We prove that an attacker will maximize its utility by following a simple greedy strategy. We then use an evolutionary algorithm to help the defender compute an optimal strategy i.e., the optimal way to tune DAHash cost parameters for different groups of passwords. The goal of the defender is to minimize the percentage of passwords that an offline attacker cracks when playing the utility optimizing strategy in response to the selected DAHash parameters $k_1, \ldots, k_\tau$.

Finally, we use several large password datasets to evaluate the effectiveness of our differentiated cost password hashing mechanism. We use the empirical password distribution to evaluate the performance of DAHash when the value v of a cracked password is small. We utilize Good-Turing frequency estimation to help identify and highlight uncertain regions of the curve i.e., where the empirical password distribution might diverge from the real password distribution. To evaluate the performance of DAHash when v is large we derive a password distirbution from guessing curves obtained using the Password Guessing Service [29]. The Password Guessing Service uses sophisticated models such as Probabilistic Context Free Grammars [19,31,33], Markov Chain Models [11,12,20,29] and even neural networks [22] to generate password guesses using Monte Carlo strength estimation [13]. We find that DAHash reduces the fraction of passwords cracked by a rational offline attacker by up to 15% (resp. 20%) under the empirical distribution (resp. derived distribution).

2   Related Work

Key-stretching was proposed as early as 1979 by Morris and Thomson as a way to protect passwords against brute force attacks [23]. Traditionally key stretching has been performed using hash iteration e.g., PBKDF2 [18] and BCRYPT [26]. More modern hash functions such as SCRYPT and Argon2 [5], winner of the password hashing competition in 2015 [34], additionally require a significant amount of memory to evaluate. An economic analysis Blocki et al. [8] suggested that hash iteration based key-derivation functions no longer provide adequate protection for lower entropy user passwords due to the existence of ASICs. On a positive note they found that the use of memory hard functions can significantly reduce the fraction of passwords that a rational adversary would crack.

The addition of "salt" is a crucial defense against rainbow table attacks [24] i.e., instead of storing $(u, H(pw_u))$ and authentication server will store $(u, s_u, H(s_u, pw_u))$ where s_u is a random string called the salt value. Salting defends against pre-computation attacks (e.g., [14]) and ensures that each password hash will need to be cracked independently e.g., even if two users u and u' select the same password we will have $H(s_{u'}, pw_{u'}) \neq H(s_u, pw_u)$ with high probability as long as $s_u \neq s_{u'}$.

Manber proposed the additional inclusion of a short random string called "pepper" which would not be stored on the server [21] e.g., instead of storing $(u, s_u, H(s_u, pw_u))$ the authentication server would store $(u, s_u, H(s_u, x_u, pw_u))$ where the pepper x_u is a short random string that, unlike the salt value s_u, is not recorded. When the user authenticates with password guess pw' the server would evaluate $H(s_u, x, pw')$ for each possible value of $x \leq x_{max}$ and accept if and only if $H(s_u, x, pw') = H(s_u, x_u, pw_u)$ for some value of x. The potential advantage of this approach is that the authentication server can usually halt early when the legitimate user authenticates, while the attacker will have to check every different value of $x \in [1, x_{max}]$ before rejecting an incorrect password. Thus, on average the attacker will need to do more work than the honest server.

Blocki and Datta observed that non-uniform distributions over the secret pepper value $x \in [1, x_{max}]$ can sometimes further increase the attacker's workload relative to an honest authentication server [6]. They showed how to optimally tune the pepper distribution by using Stackelberg game theory [6]. However, it is not clear how pepper could be effectively integrated with a modern memory hard function such as Argon2 or SCRYPT. One of the reasons that MHFs are incredibly effective is that the "full cost" [35] of evaluation can scale quadratically with the running time t. Suppose we have a hard limit on the running time t_{max} of the authentication procedure e.g., 1 second. If we select a secret pepper value $x \in [1, x_{max}]$ then we would need to ensure that $H(s_u, x, pw')$ can be evaluated in time at most t_{max}/x_{max}—otherwise the total running time to check all of the different pepper values sequentially would exceed t_{max}. In this case the "full cost" to compute $H(s_u, x, pw')$ for every $x \in [1, x_{max}]$ would be at most $O\left(x_{max} \times (t_{max}/x_{max})^2\right) = O\left(t_{max}^2/x_{max}\right)$. If instead we had not used pepper then it would have been possible to ensure that the full cost could be as large as $\Omega(t_{max}^2)$ simply by allowing the MHF to run for time t_{max} on a single input. Thus, in most scenarios it would be preferable for the authentication server to use a memory-hard password hashing algorithm without incorporating pepper.

Boyen's work on "Halting Puzzles" is also closely related to our own work [10]. In a halting puzzle the (secret) running time parameter $t \leq t_{max}$ is randomly chosen whenever a new account is created. The key idea is that an attacker will need to run in time t_{max} to definitively reject an incorrect password while it only takes time t to accept a correct password. In Boyen's work the distribution over running time parameter t was the same for all passwords. By contrast, in our work we assign a fixed hash cost parameter to each password and this cost parameter may be different for distinct passwords. We remark that it may be possible to combine both ideas i.e., assign a different maximum running time parameter $t_{max,pw}$ to different passwords. We leave it to future work to explore whether or not the composition of both mechanisms might yield further security gains.

3 DAHash

In this section, we first introduce some preliminaries about passwords then present the DAHash and explain how the authentication process works with this mechanism. We also discuss ways in which a (rational) offline attacker might attempt to crack passwords protected with the differentiated cost mechanism.

3.1 Password Notation

We let $\mathcal{P} = \{pw_1, pw_2, \ldots,\}$ be the set of all possible user-chosen passwords. We will assume that passwords are sorted so that pw_i represents the i'th most popular password. Let $\Pr[pw_i]$ denote the probability that a random user selects password pw_i we have a distribution over $\mathcal{P}$ with $\Pr[pw_1] \geq \Pr[pw_2] \geq \ldots$ and $\sum_i \Pr[pw_i] = 1$.

The distributions we consider in our empirical analysis have a compressed representation. In particular, we can partition the set of passwords $\mathcal{P}$ into n' equivalence sets $es_1, \ldots, es_{n'}$ such that for any i, $pw, pw' \in es_i$ we have $\Pr[pw] = \Pr[pw'] = p_i$. In all of the distributions we consider we will have $n' \ll |\mathcal{P}|$ allowing us to efficiently encode the distribution using n' tuple $(|es_1|, p_1), \ldots, (|es_{n'}|, p_{n'})$ where p_i is the probability of any password in equivalence set es_i. We will also want to ensure that we can optimize our DAHash parameters in time proportional to n' instead of $|\mathcal{P}|$.

3.2 DAHash

Account Creation: When a new user first register an account with user name u and password $pw_u \in \mathcal{P}$ DAHash will first assign a hash cost parameter $k_u = $ GetHardness(pw_u) based on the (estimated) strength of the user's password. We will then randomly generate a L bit string $s_u \leftarrow \{0,1\}^L$ (a "salt") then compute hash value $h_u = H(pw_u, s_u; k_u)$, at last store the tuple (u, s_u, h_u) as the record for user u. The salt value s_u is used to thwart rainbow attacks [24] and k_u controls the cost of hash function[1].

Authentication with DAHash: Later, when user u enters her/his password pw'_u, the server first retrieves the corresponding salt value s_u along with the hash value h_u, runs GetHardness(pw'_u) to obtain k'_u and then checks whether the hash $h'_u = H(pw'_u, s_u; k'_u)$ equals the stored record h_u before granting access. If $pw'_u = pw_u$ is the correct password then we will have $k'_u = k_u$ and $h'_u = h_u$ so authentication will be successful. Due to the collision resistance of cryptographic hash functions, a login request from someone claiming to be user u with password $pw'_u \neq pw_u$ will be rejected. The account creation and authentication processes are formally presented in Algorithms 1 and 2 (see Appendix A).

In the traditional (distribution oblivious) key-stretching mechanism GetHardness(pw_u) is a constant function which always returns the same cost parameter k. Our objective will be to optimize GetHardness(pw_u) to minimize the percentage of passwords cracked by an offline attacker. This must be done subject to any workload constraints of the authentication server and (optionally) minimum protection constraint, guiding the minimum acceptable key-stretching parameters for any password.

The function GetHardness(pw_u) maps each password to a hardness parameter k_u which controls the cost of evaluating our password hash function H. For hash iteration based key-derivation functions such as PBKDF2 we would achieve cost k_u by iterating the underling hash function $t = \Omega(k)$ times. By contrast, for an ideal memory hard function the full evaluation cost scales quadratically with the running time t_u so we have $t_u = O\left(\sqrt{k_u}\right)$ i.e., the attacker will need to allocate t_u blocks of memory for t_u time steps. In practice, most memory hard functions will take the parameter t as input directly. For simplicity, we will assume that the cost parameter k is given directly and that the running time t (and memory usage) is derived from k.

Remark. We stress that the hardness parameter k returned by GetHardness(pw_u) should not be stored on the server. Otherwise, an offline attacker can immediately reject an incorrect password guess $pw' \neq pw_u$ as soon as he/she observes that $k \neq$ GetHardness(pw'). Furthermore, it should not possible to directly infer k_u from the hash value $h_u \leftarrow H(pw_u, s_u; k_u)$. Any MHF candidate such as SCRYPT [25], Argon2 [5] or DRSample [3] will satisfy this property. While the hardness parameter k_u is not stored on the server, we do assume that an offline attacker who has breached the authentication server will have access to the function GetHardness(pw_u) (Kerckhoff's Principle) since the code for this function would be stored on the authentication server. Thus, given a password guess pw'

---

[1] We remark that the hardness parameter k is similar to "pepper" [21] in that it is not stored on the server. However, the hardness parameter k is distinct from pepper in that it is derived deterministically from the input password pw_u. Thus, unlike pepper, the authentication server will not need to check the password for every possible value of k.

the attacker can easily generate the hardness parameter $k' = \mathsf{GetHardness}(pw')$ for any particular password guess.

Defending against Side-Channel Attacks. A side-channel attacker might try to infer the hardness parameter k (which may in turn be correlated with the strength of the user's password) by measuring delay during a successful login attempt. We remark that for modern memory hard password hashing algorithms [3, 5, 25] the cost parameter k is modeled as the product of two parameters: memory and running time. Thus, it is often possible to increase (decrease) the cost parameter without affecting the running time simply by tuning the memory parameter[2]. Thus, if such side-channel attacks are a concern the authentication server could fix the response time during authentication to some suitable constant and tune the memory parameter accordingly. Additionally we might delay the authentication response for a fixed amount of time (e.g., 250 milliseconds) to ensure that there is no correlation between response time and the user's password.

3.3   Rational Adversary Model

We consider an untargeted offline adversary whose goal is to break as many passwords as possible. In the traditional authentication setting an offline attacker who has breached the authentication server has access to all the data stored on the server, including each user's record (u, s_u, h) and the code for hash function H and for the function $\mathsf{GetHardness}()$. In our analysis we assume that H can only be used as a black box manner (e.g., random oracle) to return results of queries from the adversary and that attempts to find a collision or directly invert $H(\cdot)$ succeed with negligible probability. However, an offline attacker who obtains (u, s_u, h) may still check whether or not $pw_u = pw'$ by setting $k' = \mathsf{GetHardness}(pw')$ and checking whether or not $h = H(pw', s_u; k')$. The only limitation to adversary's success rate is the resource she/he would like to put in cracking users' password.

We assume that the (untargeted) offline attacker has a value $v = v_u$ for password of user u. For simplicity we will henceforth use v for password value since the attacker is untargetted and has the same value $v_u = v$ for every user u. There are a number of empirical studies of the black market [2, 17, 28] which show that cracked passwords can have substantial value e.g., Symantec reports that passwords generally sell for $4 – $30 [15] and [28] reports that e-mail passwords typically sell for $1 on the Dark Web. Bitcoin "brain wallets" provide another application where cracked passwords can have substantial value to attackers [30].

We also assume that the untargetted attacker has a dictionary list which s/he will use as guesses of pw_u e.g., the attacker knows pw_i and $\Pr[pw_i]$ for each password i. However, the attacker will not know the particular password pw_u selected by each user. Therefore, in cracking a certain user's account the attacker has to enumerate all the candidate passwords and check if the guess is

---

[2] By contrast, the cost parameter for PBKDF2 and BCRYPT is directly proportional to the running time. Thus, if we wanted to set a high cost parameter k for some groups of passwords we might have to set an intolerably long authentication delay [8].

correct until there is a guess hit or the attacker finally gives up. We assume that the attacker is rational and would choose a strategy that would maximize his/her expected utility. The attacker will need to repeat this process independently for each user u. In our analysis we will focus on an individual user's account that the attacker is trying to crack.

4   Stackelberg Game

In this section, we use Stackelberg Game Theory [32] to model the interaction between the authentication server and an untargeted adversary so that we can optimize the DAHash cost parameters. In a Stackelberg Game the leader (defender) moves first and then the follower (attacker) plays his/her best response. In our context, the authentication server's (leader's) move is to specify the function GetHardness(). After a breach the offline attacker (follower) can examine the code for GetHardness() and observe the hardness parameters that will be selected for each different password in $\mathcal{P}$. A rational offline attacker may use this knowledge to optimize his/her offline attack. We first formally define the action space of the defender (leader) and attacker (follower) and then we formally define the utility functions for both players.

4.1   Action Space of Defender

The defender's action is to implement the function GetHardness(). The implementation must be efficiently computable, and the function must be chosen subject to maximum workload constraints on the authentication server. Otherwise, the optimal solution would simply be to set the cost parameter k for each password to be as large as possible. In addition, the server should guarantee that each password is granted with at least some level of protection so that it will not make weak passwords weaker.

In an idealized setting where the defender knows the user password distribution we can implement the function GetHardness(pw_u) as follows: the authentication server first partitions all passwords into τ mutually exclusive groups G_i with $i \in \{1, \cdots, \tau\}$ such that $\mathcal{P} = \bigcup_{i=1}^{\tau} G_i$ and $\Pr[pw] > \Pr[pw']$ for every $pw \in G_i$ and $pw' \in G_{i+1}$. Here, G_1 will correspond to the weakest group of passwords and G_τ corresponds to the group of strongest passwords. For each of the $|G_i|$ passwords $pw \in G_i$ we assign the same hash cost parameter $k_i = $ GetHardness(pw).

The cost of authenticating a password that is from G_i is simply k_i. Therefore, the amortized server cost for verifying a correct password is:

$$C_{SRV} = \sum_{i=1}^{\tau} k_i \cdot \Pr[pw \in G_i], \tag{1}$$

where $\Pr[pw \in G_i] = \sum_{pw \in G_i} Pr[pw]$ is total probability mass of passwords in group G_i. In general, we will assume that the server has a maximum amortized cost C_{max} that it is willing/able to incur for user authentication. Thus, the authentication server must pick the hash cost vector $\mathbf{k} = \{k_1, k_2, \cdots, k_\tau\}$ subject to the cost constraint $C_{SRV} \leq C_{max}$. Additionally, we require that $k(pw_i) \geq k_{min}$ to ensure a minimum acceptable level of protection for all accounts.

4.2   Action Space of Attacker

After breaching the authentication server the attacker may run an offline dictionary attack. The attacker must fix an ordering π over passwords $\mathcal{P}$ and a maximum number of guesses B to check i.e., the attacker will check the first B passwords in the ordering given by π. If $B = 0$ then the attacker gives up immediately without checking any passwords and if $B = \infty$ then the attacker will continue guessing until the password is cracked. The permutation π specifies the order in which the attacker will guess passwords, i.e., the attacker will check password $pw_{\pi(1)}$ first then $pw_{\pi(2)}$ second, etc. Thus, the tuple (π, B) forms a *strategy* of the adversary. Following that strategy the probability that the adversary succeeds in cracking a random user's password is simply sum of probability of all passwords to be checked:

$$P_{ADV} = \lambda(\pi, B) = \sum_{i=1}^{B} p_{\pi(i)} \ . \tag{2}$$

Here, we use short notation $p_{\pi(i)} = \Pr[pw_{\pi(i)}]$ which denotes the probability of the ith password in the ordering π.

4.3   Attacker's Utility

Given the estimated average value for one single password v the expected gain of the attacker is simply $v \times \lambda(\pi, B)$ i.e., the probability that the password is cracked times the value v. Similarly, given a hash cost parameter vector $\mathbf{k}$ the expected cost of the attacker is $\sum_{i=1}^{B} k(pw_{\pi(i)}) \cdot (1 - \lambda(\pi, i - 1))$. We use the shorthand $k(pw) = k_i = \mathsf{GetHardness}(pw)$ for a password $pw \in G_i$. Intuitively, the probability that the first $i - 1$ guesses are incorrect is $(1 - \lambda(\pi, i - 1))$ and we incur cost $k(pw_{\pi(i)})$ for the i'th guess if and only if the first $i - 1$ guesses are incorrect. Note that $\lambda(\pi, 0) = 0$ so the attacker always pays cost $k(pw_{\pi(1)})$ for the first guess. The adversary's expected utility is the difference of expected gain and expected cost:

$$U_{ADV}(v, \mathbf{k}, (\pi, B)) = v \cdot \lambda(\pi, B) - \sum_{i=1}^{B} k(pw_{\pi(i)}) \cdot (1 - \lambda(\pi, i - 1)) \ . \tag{3}$$

4.4   Defender's Utility

After the defender (leader) moves the offline attacker (follower) will respond with his/her utility optimizing strategy. We let P_{ADV}^* denote the probability that the attacker cracks a random user's password when playing his/her optimal strategy.

$$P_{ADV}^* = \lambda(\pi^*, B^*) \ , \quad \text{where} \quad (\pi^*, B^*) = \arg\max_{\pi, B} U_{ADV}(v, \mathbf{k}, (\pi, B)) \ . \tag{4}$$

P^*_{ADV} will depend on the attacker's utility optimizing strategy which will in turn depend on value v for a cracked password, the chosen cost parameters k_i for each group G_i, and the user password distribution. Thus, we can define the authentication server's utility as

$$U_{SRV}(\boldsymbol{k}, v) = -P^*_{ADV} \, . \tag{5}$$

The objective of the authentication is to minimize the success rate $P^*_{ADV}(v, \boldsymbol{k})$ of the attacker by finding the optimal action i.e., a good way of partitioning passwords into groups and selecting the optimal hash cost vector $\boldsymbol{k}$. Since the parameter $\boldsymbol{k}$ controls the cost of the hash function in passwords storage and authentication, we should increase k_i for a specific group G_i of passwords only if this is necessary to help deter the attacker from cracking passwords in this group G_i. The defender may not want to waste too much resource in protecting the weakest group G_1 of passwords when password value is high because they will be cracked easily regardless of the hash cost k_1.

4.5   Stackelberg Game Stages

Since adversary's utility depends on (π, B) and $\boldsymbol{k}$, wherein (π, B) is the responses to server's predetermined hash cost vector $\boldsymbol{k}$. On the other hand, when server selects different hash cost parameter for different groups of password, it has to take the reaction of potential attackers into account. Therefore, the interaction between the authentication server and the adversary can be modeled as a two stage Stackelberg Game. Then the problem of finding the optimal hash cost vector is reduced to the problem of computing the equilibrium of Stackelberg game.

In the Stackelberg game, the authentication server (leader) moves first (stage I); then the adversary follows (stage II). In stage I, the authentication server commits hash cost vector $\boldsymbol{k} = \{k_1, \cdots k_\tau\}$ for all groups of passwords; in stage II, the adversary yields the optimal strategy (π, B) for cracking a random user's password. Through the interaction between the legitimate authentication server and the untargeted adversary who runs an offline attack, there will emerge an equilibrium in which no player in the game has the incentive to unilaterally change its strategy. Thus, an equilibrium strategy profile $\{\boldsymbol{k}^*, (\pi^*, B^*)\}$ must satisfy

$$\begin{cases} U_{SRV}(\boldsymbol{k}^*, v) \geq U_{SRV}(\boldsymbol{k}, v), & \forall \boldsymbol{k} \in \mathcal{F}_{C_{max}}, \\ U_{ADV}(v, \boldsymbol{k}^*, (\pi^*, B^*)) \geq U_{ADV}(v, \boldsymbol{k}^*, (\pi, B)), & \forall (\pi, B) \end{cases} \tag{6}$$

Assuming that the grouping $G_1, \ldots, G_\tau$ of passwords is fixed. The computation of equilibrium strategy profile can be transformed to solve the following optimization problem, where $\Pr(pw_i)$, $G_1, \cdots, G_\tau$, C_{max} are input parameters and (π^*, B^*) and $\boldsymbol{k}^*$ are variables.

$$\min_{k^*, \pi^*, B*} \lambda(\pi^*, B^*)$$

$$\text{s.t.} \quad U_{ADV}\left(v, \boldsymbol{k}, (\pi^*, B^*)\right) \geq U_{ADV}\left(v, \boldsymbol{k}, (\pi, B)\right), \quad \forall(\pi, B),$$

$$\sum_{i=1}^{\tau} k_i \cdot \Pr[pw \in G_i] \leq C_{max}, \tag{7}$$

$$k_i \geq k_{min}, \ \forall i \leq \tau.$$

The solution of the above optimization problem is the equilibrium of our Stackelberg game. The first constraint implies that adversary will play his/her utility optimizing strategy i.e., given that the defender's action $\boldsymbol{k}^*$ is fixed the utility of the strategy (π^*, B^*) is at least as large as any other strategy the attacker might follow. Thus, a rational attacker will check the first B^* passwords in the order indicated by π^* and then stop cracking passwords. The second constraint is due to resource limitations of authentication server. The third constraint sets lower-bound for the protection level. In order to tackle the first constraint, we need to specify the optimal checking sequence and the optimal number of passwords to be checked.

5   Attacker and Defender Strategies

In the first subsection, we give an efficient algorithm to compute the attacker's optimal strategy (π^*, B^*) given the parameters v and $\boldsymbol{k}$. This algorithm in turn is an important subroutine in our algorithm to find the best strategy $\boldsymbol{k}^*$ for the defender.

5.1   Adversary's Best Response (Greedy)

In this section we show that the attacker's optimal ordering π^* can be obtained by sorting passwords by their "bang-for-buck" ratio. In particular, fixing an ordering π we define the ratio $r_{\pi(i)} = \frac{p_{\pi(i)}}{k(pw_{\pi(i)})}$ which can be viewed as the priority of checking password $pw_{\pi(i)}$ i.e., the cost will be $k(pw_{\pi(i)})$ and the probability the password is correct is $p_{\pi(i)}$. Intuitively, the attacker's optimal strategy is to order passwords by their "bang-for-buck" ratio guessing passwords with higher checking priority first. Theorem 1 formalizes this intuition by proving that the optimal checking sequence π^* has no inversions.

We say a checking sequence π has an *inversion* with respect to $\boldsymbol{k}$ if for some pair $a > b$ we have $r_{\pi(a)} > r_{\pi(b)}$ i.e., $pw_{\pi(b)}$ is scheduled to be checked before $pw_{\pi(a)}$ even though password $pw_{\pi(a)}$ has a higher "bang-for-buck" ratio. Recall that $pw_{\pi(b)}$ is the b'th password checked in the ordering π. The proof of Theorem 1 can be found in the Appendix of full version of this paper [4]. Intuitively, we argue that consecutive inversions can always be swapped without decreasing the attacker's utility.

Theorem 1. *Let (π^*, B^*) denote the attacker's optimal strategy with respect to hash cost parameters $\boldsymbol{k}$ and let π be an ordering with no inversions relative to $\boldsymbol{k}$ then*

$$U_{ADV}\left(v, \boldsymbol{k}, (\pi, B^*)\right) \geq U_{ADV}\left(v, \boldsymbol{k}, (\pi^*, B^*)\right) .$$

Theorem 1 gives us *an easy way to compute* the attacker's optimal ordering π^* over passwords i.e., by sorting passwords according to their "bang-for-buck" ratio. It remains to find the attacker's optimal guessing budget B^*. As we previously mentioned the password distributions we consider can be compressed by grouping passwords with equal probability into equivalence sets. Once we have our cost vector $\boldsymbol{k}$ and have implemented GetHardness() we can further partition password equivalence sets such that passwords in each set additionally have the same bang-for-buck ratio.

Theorem 2 tells us that the optimal attacker strategy will either guess *all* of the passwords in such an equivalence set es_j or *none* of them. Thus, when we search for B^* we only need to consider $n' + 1$ possible values of this parameter. We will use this observation to improve the efficiency of our algorithm to compute the optimal attacker strategy.

Theorem 2. *Let (π^*, B^*) denote the attacker's optimal strategy with respect to hash cost parameters $\boldsymbol{k}$. Suppose that passwords can be partitioned into n' equivalence sets $es_1, \ldots, es_{n'}$ such that passwords $pw_a, pw_b \in es_i$ have the same probability and hash cost i.e., $p_a = p_b = p^i$ and $k(pw_a) = k(pw_b) = k^i$. Let $r^i = p^i / k^i$ denote the bang-for-buck ratio of equivalence set es_i and assume that $r^1 \geq r^2 \geq \ldots \geq r^{n'}$ then $B^* \in \left\{0, |es_1|, |es_1| + |es_2|, \cdots, \sum_{i=1}^{n'} |es_i|\right\}$.*

The proof of both theorems can be found in Appendix of the full version of this paper [4]. Theorem 2 implies that when cracking users' accounts the adversary increases number of guesses B by the size of the next equivalence set (if there is net profit by doing so). Therefore, the attacker finds the optimal strategy (π^*, B^*) with Algorithm BestRes$(v, \boldsymbol{k}, D)$ in time $\mathcal{O}(n' \log n')$ — see Algorithm 3 in Appendix A. The running time is dominated by the cost of sorting n' equivalence sets.

5.2   The Optimal Strategy of Selecting Hash Cost Vector

In the previous section we showed that there is an efficient greedy algorithm BestRes$(v, \boldsymbol{k}, D)$ which takes as input a cost vector $\boldsymbol{k}$, a value v and a (compressed) description of the password distribution D computes the attacker's best response (π^*, B^*) and outputs $\lambda(\pi^*, B^*)$—the fraction of cracked passwords. Using this algorithm BestRes$(v, \boldsymbol{k}, D)$ as a blackbox we can apply derivative-free optimization to the optimization problem in Eq. (7) to find a good hash cost vector $\boldsymbol{k}$ which minimizes the objective $\lambda(\pi^*, B^*)$ There are many derivative-free optimization solvers available in the literature [27], generally they fall into two categorizes, deterministic algorithms (such as Nelder-Mead) and evolutionary algorithm (such as BITEOPT [1] and CMA-EA). We refer our solver to as

$\mathsf{OptHashCostVec}(v, C_{max}, k_{min}, D)$. The algorithm takes as input the parameters of the optimization problem (i.e., password value v, C_{max}, k_{min}, and a (compressed) description of the password distribution D) and outputs an optimized hash cost vector $\boldsymbol{k}$.

During each iteration of $\mathsf{OptHashCostVec}(\cdot)$, some candidates $\{\boldsymbol{k}_{c_i}\}$ are proposed, together they are referred as *population*. For each candidate solution $\boldsymbol{k}_{c_i}$ we use our greedy algorithm $\mathsf{BestRes}(v, \boldsymbol{k}_{c_i}, D)$ to compute the attacker's best response (π^*, B^*) i.e., fixing any feasible cost vector $\boldsymbol{k}_{c_i}$ we can compute the corresponding value of the objective function $P_{adv,\boldsymbol{k}_{c_i}} := \sum_{i=1}^{B^*} p_{\pi^*(i)}$. We record the corresponding success rate $P_{adv,\boldsymbol{k}_{c_i}}$ of the attacker as "fitness". At the end of each iteration, the population is updated according to fitness of its' members, the update could be either through deterministic transformation (Nelder-Mead) or randomized evolution (BITEOPT, CMA-EA). When the iteration number reaches a pre-defined value *ite*, the best fit member $\boldsymbol{k}^*$ and its fitness P_{adv}^* are returned.

6   Empirical Analysis

In this section, we design experiments to analyze the effectiveness of DAHash. At a high level we first fix (compressed) password distributions D_{train} and D_{eval} based on empirical password datasets and an implementation of $\mathsf{GetHardness}()$. Fixing the DAHash parameters v, C_{max} and k_{min} we use our algorithm $\mathsf{OptHashCostVec}(v, C_{max}, k_{min}, D_{train})$ to optimize the cost vector $\boldsymbol{k}^*$ and then we compute the attacker's optimal response $\mathsf{BestRes}(v, \boldsymbol{k}^*, D_{eval})$. By setting $D_{train} = D_{eval}$ we can model the idealized scenario where the defender has perfect knowledge of the password distribution. Similarly, by setting $D_{train} \neq D_{eval}$ we can model the performance of DAHash when the defender optimizes $\boldsymbol{k}^*$ without perfect knowledge of the password distribution. In each experiment we fix $k_{min} = C_{max}/10$ and we plot the fraction of cracked passwords as the value to cost ratio v/C_{max} varies. We compare DAHash with traditional password hashing fixing the hash cost to be C_{max} for every password to ensure that the amortized server workload is equivalent. Before presenting our results we first describe how we define the password distributions D_{train} and D_{eval} and how we implement $\mathsf{GetHardness}()$.

6.1   The Password Distribution

One of the challenges in evaluating DAHash is that the exact distribution over user passwords is unknown. However, there are many empirical password datasets available due to password breaches. We describe two methods for deriving password distributions from password datasets.

Empirical Password Datasets. We consider nine empirical password datasets (along with their size N): Bfield (0.54 million), Brazzers (0.93 million), Clixsense

(2.2 million), CSDN (6.4 million), LinkedIn (174 million), Neopets (68.3 million), RockYou (32.6 million), 000webhost (153 million) and Yahoo! (69.3 million). Plaintext passwords are available for all datasets except for the differentially private LinkedIn [16] and Yahoo! [7,9] frequency corpuses which intentionally omit passwords. With the exception of the Yahoo! frequency corpus all of the datasets are derived from password breaches. The differentially LinkedIn dataset is derived from cracked LinkedIn passwords[3]. Formally, given N user accounts $u_1, \ldots, u_N$ a dataset of passwords is a list $D = pw_{u_1}, \ldots, pw_{u_N} \in \mathcal{P}$ of passwords each user selected. We can view each of these passwords pw_{u_i} as being sampled from some unkown distribution D_{real}.

Empirical Distribution. Given a dataset of N user passwords the corresponding password frequency list is simply a list of numbers $f_1 \geq f_2 \geq \ldots$ where f_i is the number of users who selected the ith most popular password in the dataset— note that $\sum_i f_i = N$. In the empirical password distribution we define the probability of the ith most likely password to be $\hat{p}_i = f_i/N$. In our experiments using the empirical password distribution we will set $D_{train} = D_{eval}$ i.e., we assume that the empirical password distribution is the real password distribution and that the defender knows this distribution.

In our experiments we implement GetHardness() by partitioning the password dataset D_{train} into τ groups $G_1, \ldots, G_\tau$ using $\tau - 1$ frequency thresholds $t_1 > \ldots > t_{\tau-1}$ i.e., $G_1 = \{i : f_i \geq t_1\}$, $G_j = \{i : t_{j-1} > f_i \geq t_j\}$ for $1 < j < \tau$ and $G_\tau = \{i : f_i < t_{\tau-1}\}$. Fixing a hash cost vector $\boldsymbol{k} = (k_1, \ldots, k_\tau)$ we will assign passwords in group G_j to have cost k_j i.e., GetHardness(pw)$= k_j$ for $pw \in G_j$. We pick the thresholds to ensure that the probability mass $Pr[G_j] = \sum_{i \in G_j} f_i/N$ of each group is approximately balanced (without separating passwords in an equivalence set). While there are certainly other ways that GetHardness() could be implemented (e.g., balancing number of passwords/equivalence sets in each group) we found that balancing the probability mass was most effective.

Good-Turing Frequency Estimation. One disadvantage of using the empirical distribution is that it can often overestimate the success rate of an adversary. For example, let $\hat{\lambda}_B := \sum_{i=1}^B \hat{p}_i$ and $N' \leq N$ denote the number of distinct passwords in our dataset then we will *always* have $\hat{\lambda}_{N'} := \sum_{i \leq N'} \hat{p}_i = 1$ which is inaccurate whenever $N \leq |\mathcal{P}|$. However, when $B \ll N$ we will have $\hat{\lambda}_B \approx \lambda_B$ i.e., the empirical distribution will closely match the real distribution. Thus, we will use the empirical distribution to evaluate the performance of DAHash when the value to cost ratio v/C_{max} is smaller (e.g., $v/C_{max} \ll 10^8$) and we will highlight uncertain regions of the curve using Good-Turing frequency estimation.

---

[3] The LinkedIn password is derived from 174 million (out of 177.5 million) cracked password hashes which were cracked by KoreLogic [16]. Thus, the dataset omits 2% of uncracked passwords. Another caveat is that the LinkedIn dataset only contains 164.6 million unique e-mail addresses so there are some e-mail addresses with multiple associated password hashes.

Let $N_f = |\{i : f_i = f\}|$ denote number of distinct passwords in our dataset that occur exactly f times and let $B_f = \sum_{i>f} N_i$ denote the number of distinct passwords that occur more than f times. Finally, let $E_f := |\lambda_{B_f} - \hat{\lambda}_{N_{B_f}}|$ denote the error of our estimate for λ_{B_f}, the total probability of the top B_f passwords in the real distribution. If our dataset consists of N independent samples from an unknown distribution then Good-Turing frequency estimation tells us that the total probability mass of all passwords that appear exactly f times is approximately $U_f := (f+1)N_{f+1}/N$ e.g., the total probability mass of unseen passwords is $U_0 = N_1/N$. This would imply that $\lambda_{B_f} \geq 1 - \sum_{j=0}^{f} U_j = 1 - \sum_{j=0}^{i} \frac{(j+1)N_{j+1}}{N}$ and $E_f \leq U_f$.

Table 1 below plots our error upper bound U_f for $0 \leq f \leq 10$ for 9 datasets. Fixing a target error threshold ϵ we define $f_\epsilon = \min\{i : U_i \leq \epsilon\}$ i.e., the minimum index such that the error is smaller than ϵ. In our experiments we focus on error thresholds $\epsilon \in \{0.1, 0.01\}$. For example, for the Yahoo! (resp. Bfield) dataset we have $f_{0.1} = 1$ (resp. $j_{0.1} = 2$) and $j_{0.01} = 6$ (resp. $j_{0.01} = 5$). As soon as we see passwords with frequency *at most* $j_{0.1}$ (resp. $j_{0.01}$) start to get cracked we highlight the points on our plots with a red (resp. yellow) .

Table 1. Error Upper Bounds: U_i for different password datasets

	Bfield	Brazzers	Clixsense	CSDN	Linkedin	Neopets	Rockyou	000webhost	Yahoo!
U_0	0.69	0.531	0.655	0.557	0.123	0.315	0.365	0.59	0.425
U_1	0.101	0.126	0.095	0.092	0.321	0.093	0.081	0.124	0.065
U_2	0.036	0.054	0.038	0.034	0.043	0.051	0.036	0.055	0.031
U_3	0.02	0.03	0.023	0.018	0.055	0.034	0.022	0.034	0.021
U_4	0.014	0.02	0.016	0.012	0.018	0.025	0.017	0.022	0.015
U_5	0.01	0.014	0.011	0.008	0.021	0.02	0.013	0.016	0.012
U_6	0.008	0.011	0.009	0.006	0.011	0.016	0.011	0.012	0.01
U_7	0.007	0.01	0.007	0.005	0.011	0.013	0.01	0.009	0.009
U_8	0.006	0.008	0.006	0.004	0.008	0.011	0.009	0.008	0.008
U_9	0.005	0.007	0.005	0.004	0.007	0.01	0.008	0.006	0.007
U_{10}	0.004	0.007	0.004	0.003	0.006	0.009	0.007	0.005	0.006

Monte Carlo Distribution. As we observed previously the empirical password distribution can be highly inaccurate when v/C_{max} is large. Thus, we use a different approach to evaluate the performance of DAHash when v/C_{max} is large. In particular, we subsample passwords, obtain guessing numbers for each of these passwords and fit our distribution to the corresponding guessing curve. We follow the following procedure to derive a distribution: (1) subsample s passwords D_s from dataset D with replacement; (2) for each subsampled passwords $pw \in D_s$ we use the Password Guessing Service [29] to obtain a guessing number #guessing(pw) which uses Monte Carlo methods [13] to estimate how many guesses an attacker would need to crack pw^4. (3) For each $i \leq 199$ we fix guessing thresholds $t_0 < t_1 < \ldots < t_{199}$ with $t_0 := 0$, $t_1 := 15$, $t_i - t_{i-1} = 1.15^{i+25}$, and $t_{199} = \max_{pw \in D_s}\{\#\mathsf{guessing}(pw)\}$. (4) For each $i \leq 199$ we compute g_i, the number of samples $pw \in D_s$ with $\#\mathsf{guessing}(pw) \in [t_{i-1}, t_i)$. (5) We output a compressed distribution with 200 equivalences sets using histogram density i.e., the ith equivalence set contains $t_i - t_{i-1}$ passwords each with probability $\frac{g_i}{s \times (t_i - t_{i-1})}$.

In our experiments we repeat this process twice with $s = 12,500$ subsamples to obtain two password distributions D_{train} and D_{eval}. One advantage of this approach is that it allows us to evaluate the performance of DAHash against a state of the art password cracker when the ratio v/C_{max} is large. The disadvantage is that the distributions D_{train} and D_{eval} we extract are based on *current* state of the art password cracking models. It is possible that we optimized our DAHash parameters with respect to the wrong distribution if an attacker develops an improved password cracking model in the future.

Implementing $\mathsf{GetHardness}()$**for Monte Carlo Distributions.** For Monte Carlo distribution $\mathsf{GetHardness}(pw)$ depends on the guessing number $\#\mathsf{guessing}(pw)$. In particular, we fix thresholds points $x_1 > \ldots > x_{\tau-1}$ and (implicitly) partition passwords into τ groups $G_1, \ldots, G_\tau$ using these thresholds i.e., $G_i = \{pw : x_{i-1} \geq \#\mathsf{guessing}(pw) > x_i\}$. Thus, $\mathsf{GetHardness}(pw)$ would compute $\#\mathsf{guessing}(pw)$ and assign hash cost k_i if $pw \in G_i$. As before the thresholds $x_1, \ldots, x_{\tau-1}$ are selected to (approximately) balance the probability mass in each group.

6.2   Experiment Results

Figure 1 evalutes the performance of DAHash on the empirical distributions empirical datasets. To generate each point on the plot we first fix $v/C_{max} \in \{i \times 10^{2+j} : 1 \leq i \leq 9, 0 \leq j \leq 5\}$, use $\mathsf{OptHashCostVec}()$ to tune our DAHash parameters $\boldsymbol{k}^*$ and then compute the corresponding success rate for the attacker. The experiment is repeated for the empirical distributions derived from our 9 different datasets. In each experiment we group password equivalence sets into τ groups ($\tau \in \{1, 3, 5\}$) $G_1, \ldots, G_\tau$ of (approximately) equal probability mass. In addition, we set $k_{min} = 0.1 C_{max}$ and iteration of BITEOPT to be 10000. The yellow (resp. red) regions correspond to unconfident zones where we expect that the our results for empirical distribution might differ from reality by 1% (resp. 10%).

Figure 2 evaluates the performance of DAHash for Monte Carlo distributions we extract using the Password Guessing Service. For each dataset we extract two distributions D_{train} and D_{eval}. For each $v/C_{max} \in \{j \times 10^i : 3 \leq i \leq 11, j \in \{2, 4, 6, 8\}\}$ we obtain the corresponding optimal hash cost $\boldsymbol{k}^*$ using

---

[4] The Password Guessing Service [29] gives multiple different guessing numbers for each password based on different sophisticated cracking models e.g., Markov, PCFG, Neural Networks. We follow the suggestion of the authors [29] and use the minimum guessing number (over all autmated approached) as our final estimate.

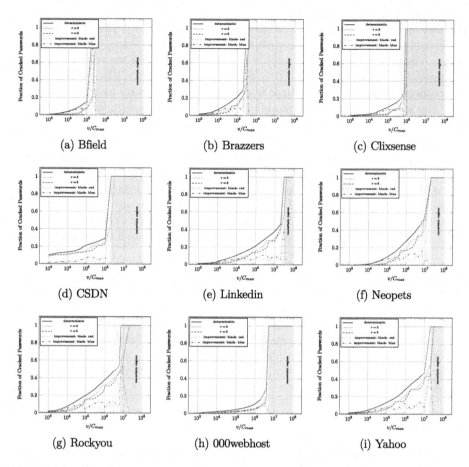

Fig. 1. Adversary Success Rate vs v/C_{max} for Empirical Distributions the red (resp. yellow) shaded areas denote unconfident regions where the empirical distribution might diverges from the real distribution $U_i \geq 0.1$ (resp. $U_i \geq 0.01$). (Color figure online)

OptHashCostVec() with the distribution D_{train} as input. Then we compute success rate of attacker on D_{eval} with the same cost vector $\boldsymbol{k}^*$. We repeated this for 6 plaintext datasets: Bfield, Brazzers, Clixsense, CSDN, Neopets and 000webhost for which we obtained guessing numbers from the Password Guessing Service.

Figures 1 and 2 plot P_{ADV} vs v/C_{max} for each different dataset under empirical distribution and Monte Carlo distribution. Each sub-figure contains three separate lines corresponding to $\tau \in \{1,3,5\}$ respectively. We first remark that $\tau = 1$ corresponds to the status quo when all passwords are assigned the same cost parameter i.e., getHardness(pw_u) = C_{max}. When $\tau = 3$ we can interpret our mechanism as classifying all passwords into three groups (e.g., weak, medium and strong) based on their strength. The fine grained case $\tau = 5$ has more strength levels into which passwords can be placed.

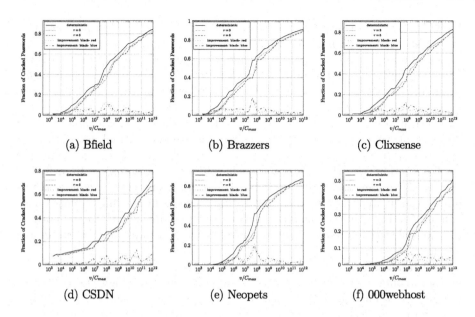

Fig. 2. Adversary success rate vs v/C_{max} for Monte Carlo distributions

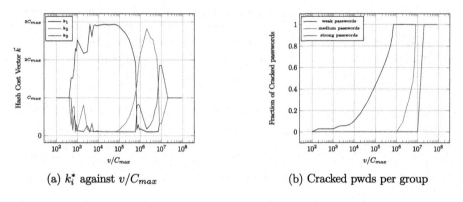

(a) k_i^* against v/C_{max} (b) Cracked pwds per group

Fig. 3. Hash costs and cracked fraction per group for RockYou (Empirical Distribution)

DAHash Advantage: For empirical distributions the improvement peaks in the uncertain region of the plot. Ignoring the uncertain region the improvement is still as large as 15%. For Monte Carlo distributions we find a 20% improvement e.g., 20% of user passwords could be saved with the DAHash mechanism.

Figure 3a explores how the hash cost vector k is allocated between weak/medium/strong passwords as v/C_{max} varies (using the RockYou empirical distribution with $\tau = 3$). Similarly, Fig. 3b plots the fraction of weak/medium/strong passwords being cracked as adversary value increases. We discuss these each of these figures in more detail below.

How Many Groups (τ)? We explore the impact of τ on the percentage of passwords that a rational adversary will crack. Since the untargeted adversary attacks all user accounts in the very same way, the percentage of passwords the adversary will crack is the probability that the adversary succeeds in cracking a random user's account, namely, P^*_{ADV}. Intuitively, a partition resulting in more groups can grant a better protection for passwords, since by doing so the authentication server can deal with passwords with more precision and can better tune the fitness of protection level to password strength. We observe in Figs. 1 and 2 for most of time the success rate reduction when $\tau = 5$ is larger compared to $\tau = 3$. However, the marginal benefit plummets, changing τ from 3 to 5 does not bring much performance improvement. A positive interpretation of this observation is that we can glean most of the benefits of our differentiated hash cost mechanism without making the getHardness() procedure too complicated e.g., we only need to partition passwords into three groups weak, medium and strong.

Our hashing mechanism does not overprotect passwords that are too weak to withstand offline attack when adversary value is sufficiently high, nor passwords that are strong enough so that a rational offline attacker loses interest in cracking. The effort previously spent in protecting passwords that are too weak/strong can be reallocated into protecting "savable" passwords at some v/C_{max}. Thus, our DAHash algorithm beats traditional hashing algorithm without increasing the server's expected workload i.e., the cost parameters $\boldsymbol{k}$ are tuned such that expected workload is always C_{max} whether $\tau = 1$ (no differentiated costs), $\tau = 3$ (differentiated costs) or $\tau = 5$ (finer grained differentiated costs). We find that the defender can reduce the percentage of cracked passwords P^*_{ADV} without increasing the workload C_{max}.

Understanding the Optimal Allocation $\boldsymbol{k}^*$. We next discuss how our mechanism re-allocates the cost parameters across $\tau = 3$ different groups as v/C_{max} increases—see Fig. 3a. At the very beginning v/C_{max} is small enough that a rational password gives up without cracking any password even if the authentication server assigns equal hash costs to different groups of password, e.g., $k_1 = k_2 = k_3 = C_{max}$.

As the adversary value increases the Algorithm OptHashCostVec() starts to reallocate $\boldsymbol{k}$ so that most of the authentication server's effort is used to protect the weakest passwords in group G_1 while minimal key-stretching effort is used to protect the stronger passwords in groups G_2 and G_3 In particular, we have $k_1 \approx 3C_{max}$ for much of the interval $v/C_{max} \in [4*10^3, 10^5]$ while k_2, k_3 are pretty small in this interval e.g., $k_2, k_3 \approx 0.1 \times C_{max}$. However, as the ratio v/C_{max} continues to increase from 10^6 to 10^7 Algorithm OptHashCostVec() once again begins to reallocate $\boldsymbol{k}$ to place most of the weight on k_2 as it is now necessary to protect passwords in group G_2. Over the same interval the value of k_1 decreases sharply as it is no longer possible to protect all of the weakest passwords group G_1.

As v/C_{max} continues to increase Algorithm OptHashCostVec() once again reallocates $\boldsymbol{k}$ to place most of the weight on k_3 as it is now necessary to protect the strongest passwords in group G_3 (and no longer possible to protect all of the medium strength passwords in group G_2). Finally, v/C_{max} gets too large it is no longer possible to protect passwords in any group so Algorithm OptHashCostVec() reverse back to equal hash costs , i.e., $k_1 = k_2 = k_3 = C_{max}$.

Figures 3a and 3b tell a complementary story. Weak passwords are cracked first as v/C_{max} increases, then follows the passwords with medium strength and the strong passwords stand until v/C_{max} finally becomes sufficiently high. For example, in Fig. 3b we see that initially the mechanism is able to protect all passwords, weak, medium and strong. However, as v/C_{max} increases from 10^5 to 10^6 it is no longer possible to protect the weakest passwords in group G_1. Up until $v/C_{max} = 10^6$ the mechanism is able to protect all medium strength passwords in group G_2, but as the v/C_{max} crosses the 10^7 threshold it is not feasible to protect passwords in group G_2. The strongest passwords in group G_3 are completely projected until v/C_{max} reaches 2×10^7 at which point it is no longer possible to protect any passwords because the adversary value is too high.

Viewing together with Fig. 3a, we observe that it is only when weak passwords are about to be cracked completely (when v/C_{max} is around 7×10^5) that the authentication server begin to shift effort to protect medium passwords. The shift of protection effort continues as the adversary value increases until medium strength passwords are about to be massively cracked. The same observation applies to medium passwords and strong password. While we used the plots from the RockYou dataset for discussion, the same trends also hold for other datasets (concrete thresholds may differ).

Robustness. We remark that in Figs. 1 and 2 the actual hash cost vector $\boldsymbol{k}$ we chose is not highly sensitive to small changes of the adversary value v (only in semilog x axis fluctuation of $\boldsymbol{k}$ became obvious). Therefore, DAHash may still be useful even when it is not possible to obtain a precise estimate of v or when the attacker's value v varies slightly over time.

Incentive Compatibility. One potential concern in assigning different hash cost parameters to different passwords is that we might inadvertently provide incentive for a user to select weaker passwords. In particular, the user might prefer a weaker password pw_i to pw_j ($\Pr[pw_i] > \Pr[pw_j]$) if s/he believes that the attacker will guess pw_j before pw_i e.g., the hash cost parameter $k(pw_j)$ is so small that makes $r_j > r_i$. We could directly encode incentive compatibility into our constraints for the feasible range of defender strategies $\mathcal{F}_{C_{max}}$ i.e., we could explicitly add a constraints that $r_j \leq r_i$ whenever $\Pr[pw_i] \leq \Pr[pw_j]$. However, Fig. 3b suggest that this is not necessary. Observe that the attacker does not crack any medium/high strength passwords until *all* weak passwords have been cracked. Similarly, the attacker does not crack any high strength passwords until *all* medium strength passwords have been cracked.

7   Conclusions

We introduce the notion of DAHash. In our mechanism the cost parameter assigned to distinct passwords may not be the same. This allows the defender to focus key-stretching effort primarily on passwords where the effort will influence the decisions of a rational attacker who will quit attacking as soon as expected costs exceed expected rewards. We present Stackelberg game model to capture the essentials of the interaction between the legitimate authentication server (leader) and an untargeted offline attacker (follower). In the game the defender (leader) commits to the hash cost parameters k for different passwords and the attacker responds in a utility optimizing manner. We presented a highly efficient algorithm to provably compute the attacker's best response given a password distribution. Using this algorithm as a subroutine we use an evolutionary algorithm to find a good strategy k for the defender. Finally, we analyzed the performance of our differentiated cost password hashing algorithm using empirical password datasets . Our experiments indicate that DAHash can dramatically reduce the fraction of passwords that would be cracked in an untargeted offline attack in comparison with the traditional approach e.g., by up to 15% under empirical distributions and 20% under Monte Carlo distributions. This gain comes without increasing the expected workload of the authentication server. Our mechanism is fully compatible with modern memory hard password hashing algorithms such as SCRYPT [25], Argon2id [5] and DRSample [3].

Acknowledgment. The work was supported by the National Science Foundation under grants CNS #1704587, CNS #1755708 and CNS #1931443. The authors wish to thank Matteo Dell'Amico (shepherd) and other anonymous reviewers for constructive feedback which helped improve the paper.

A   Algorithms

Algorithm 1. Account creation

Input: u, pw_u, L
1: $s_u \xleftarrow{\$} \{0,1\}^L$;
2: $k \leftarrow$ GetHardness(pw_u);
3: $h \leftarrow H(pw_u, s_u; k)$;
4: StoreRecord (u, s_u, h)

Algorithm 2. Password authentication

Input: u, pw'_u
1: $(u, s_u, h) \leftarrow$ FindRecord(u);
2: $k' \leftarrow$ GetHardness(pw'_u);
3: $h' \leftarrow H(pw_u, s_u; k')$;
4: **Return** $h == h'$

Algorithm 3. The adversary's best response $\mathsf{BestRes}(v, \boldsymbol{k}, D)$,

Input: $\boldsymbol{k}, v, D$
Output: (π^*, B^*)
1: sort $\{\frac{p_i}{k_i}\}$ and reindex such that $\frac{p_1}{k_1} \geq \cdots \geq \frac{p_{n'}}{k_{n'}}$ to get π^*;
2: $B^* = \arg\max U_{ADV}(v, \boldsymbol{k}, (\pi^*, B))$
3: **return** (π^*, B^*);

B   FAQ

Could DAHash Harm User's Who Pick Weak Passwords?

The simple answer is that it depends on whether or not our estimation of the attacker's value v is reasonably accurate. If our estimation of the value v of a cracked password is way too high then it is indeed possible that the DAHash parameters would be misconfigured in a way that harms users with weak passwords. However, even in this case we can ensure that every password receives a minimum level of acceptable protection by tuning the parameter k_{min} which controls minimum acceptable hash cost for any password. If our estimation of v is accurate and it is feasible to deter an attacker from cracking weaker passwords then DAHash will actually tend to provide stronger protection for these passwords. On the other hand if the password is sufficiently weak that we cannot deter an attacker then these weak passwords will always be cracked no matter what actions we take. Thus, DAHash will reallocate key-stretching effort to focus on protecting stronger passwords.

References

1. Biteopt algorithm. https://github.com/avaneev/biteopt
2. Allodi, L.: Economic factors of vulnerability trade and exploitation. In: Thuraisingham, B.M., Evans, D., Malkin, T., Xu, D. (eds.) ACM CCS 2017, Dallas, TX, USA, pp. 1483–1499. ACM Press, 31 October–2 November 2017. https://doi.org/10.1145/3133956.3133960
3. Alwen, J., Blocki, J., Harsha, B.: Practical graphs for optimal side-channel resistant memory-hard functions. In: Thuraisingham, B.M., Evans, D., Malkin, T., Xu, D. (eds.) ACM CCS 2017, Dallas, TX, USA, pp. 1001–1017. ACM Press, 31 October–2 November 2017. https://doi.org/10.1145/3133956.3134031
4. Bai, W., Blocki, J.: Dahash: Distribution aware tuning of password hashing costs (2021). https://arxiv.org/abs/2101.10374
5. Biryukov, A., Dinu, D., Khovratovich, D.: Argon2: new generation of memory-hard functions for password hashing and other applications. In: 2016 IEEE European Symposium on Security and Privacy (EuroS&P), pp. 292–302. IEEE (2016)
6. Blocki, J., Datta, A.: CASH: a cost asymmetric secure hash algorithm for optimal password protection. In: IEEE 29th Computer Security Foundations Symposium, pp. 371–386 (2016)
7. Blocki, J., Datta, A., Bonneau, J.: Differentially private password frequency lists. In: NDSS 2016, San Diego, CA, USA. The Internet Society, 21–24 February 2016

8. Blocki, J., Harsha, B., Zhou, S.: On the economics of offline password cracking. In: 2018 IEEE Symposium on Security and Privacy, San Francisco, CA, USA, pp. 853–871. IEEE Computer Society Press, 21–23 May 2018. https://doi.org/10.1109/SP.2018.00009

9. Bonneau, J.: The science of guessing: analyzing an anonymized corpus of 70 million passwords. In: 2012 IEEE Symposium on Security and Privacy, San Francisco, CA, USA, pp. 538–552. IEEE Computer Society Press, 21–23 May 2012. https://doi.org/10.1109/SP.2012.49

10. Boyen, X.: Halting password puzzles: hard-to-break encryption from human-memorable keys. In: Provos, N. (ed.) USENIX Security 2007, pp. 6–10, Boston, MA, USA. USENIX Association, August 2007

11. Castelluccia, C., Chaabane, A., Dürmuth, M., Perito, D.: When privacy meets security: Leveraging personal information for password cracking. arXiv preprint arXiv:1304.6584 (2013)

12. Castelluccia, C., Dürmuth, M., Perito, D.: Adaptive password-strength meters from Markov models. In: NDSS 2012, San Diego, CA, USA, The Internet Society, 5–8 February 2012

13. Dell'Amico, M., Filippone, M.: Monte Carlo strength evaluation: fast and reliable password checking. In: Ray, I., Li, N., Kruegel, C. (eds.) ACM CCS 2015, Denver, CO, USA, pp. 158–169. ACM Press, 12–16 October 2015. https://doi.org/10.1145/2810103.2813631

14. Dodis, Y., Guo, S., Katz, J.: Fixing cracks in the concrete: random oracles with auxiliary input, revisited. In: Coron, J.-S., Nielsen, J.B. (eds.) EUROCRYPT 2017. LNCS, vol. 10211, pp. 473–495. Springer, Cham (2017). https://doi.org/10.1007/978-3-319-56614-6_16

15. Fossi, M., et al.: Symantec report on the underground economy, November 2008. Accessed 1 August 2013

16. Harsha, B., Morton, R., Blocki, J., Springer, J., Dark, M.: Bicycle attacks considered harmful: Quantifying the damage of widespread password length leakage. Comput. Secur. **100**, 102068 (2021)

17. Herley, C., Florêncio, D.: Nobody sells gold for the price of silver: dishonesty, uncertainty and the underground economy. In: Moore, T., Pym, D., Ioannidis, C. (eds.) Economics of Information Security and Privacy, pp. 33–53. Springer, Boston (2010). https://doi.org/10.1007/978-1-4419-6967-5_3

18. Kaliski, B.: Pkcs# 5: password-based cryptography specification version 2.0 (2000)

19. Kelley, P.G., et al.: Guess again (and again and again): Measuring password strength by simulating password-cracking algorithms. In: 2012 IEEE Symposium on Security and Privacy, pp. 523–537. IEEE Computer Society Press, San Francisco, CA, USA, 21–23 May 2012. https://doi.org/10.1109/SP.2012.38

20. Ma, J., Yang, W., Luo, M., Li, N.: A study of probabilistic password models. In: 2014 IEEE Symposium on Security and Privacy, pp. 689–704. IEEE Computer Society Press, Berkeley, CA, USA, 18–21 May 2014. https://doi.org/10.1109/SP.2014.50

21. Manber, U.: A simple scheme to make passwords based on one-way functions much harder to crack. Comput. Secur. **15**(2), 171–176 (1996)

22. Melicher, W., et al.: Fast, lean, and accurate: Modeling password guessability using neural networks. In: Holz, T., Savage, S. (eds.) USENIX Security 2016, Austin, TX, USA, pp. 175–191. USENIX Association, 10–12 August 2016

23. Morris, R., Thompson, K.: Password security: a case history. Commun. ACM **22**(11), 594–597 (1979). http://dl.acm.org/citation.cfm?id=359172

24. Oechslin, P.: Making a faster cryptanalytic time-memory trade-off. In: Boneh, D. (ed.) CRYPTO 2003. LNCS, vol. 2729, pp. 617–630. Springer, Heidelberg (2003). https://doi.org/10.1007/978-3-540-45146-4_36

25. Percival, C.: Stronger key derivation via sequential memory-hard functions. In: BSDCan 2009 (2009)

26. Provos, N., Mazieres, D.: Bcrypt algorithm. In: USENIX (1999)

27. Rios, L.M., Sahinidis, N.V.: Derivative-free optimization: a review of algorithms and comparison of software implementations. J. Global Optim. **56**(3), 1247–1293 (2013)

28. Stockley, M.: What your hacked account is worth on the dark web, August 2016. https://nakedsecurity.sophos.com/2016/08/09/what-your-hacked-account-is-worth-on-the-dark-web/

29. Ur, B., et al.: Measuring real-world accuracies and biases in modeling password guessability. In: Jung, J., Holz, T. (eds.) USENIX Security 2015. pp. 463–481. USENIX Association, Washington, DC, USA, 12–14 August 2015

30. Vasek, M., Bonneau, J., Castellucci, R., Keith, C., Moore, T.: The bitcoin brain drain: examining the use and abuse of bitcoin brain wallets. In: Grossklags, J., Preneel, B. (eds.) FC 2016. LNCS, vol. 9603, pp. 609–618. Springer, Heidelberg (2017). https://doi.org/10.1007/978-3-662-54970-4_36

31. Veras, R., Collins, C., Thorpe, J.: On semantic patterns of passwords and their security impact. In: NDSS 2014. The Internet Society, San Diego, CA, USA, 23–26 February 2014

32. Von Stackelberg, H.: Market Structure and Equilibrium. Springer, Heidelberg (2010). https://doi.org/10.1007/978-3-642-12586-7

33. Weir, M., Aggarwal, S., de Medeiros, B., Glodek, B.: Password cracking using probabilistic context-free grammars. In: 2009 IEEE Symposium on Security and Privacy, Oakland, CA, USA, pp. 391–405. IEEE Computer Society Press, 17–20 May 2009. https://doi.org/10.1109/SP.2009.8

34. Wetzels, J.: Open sesame: The password hashing competition and Argon2. Cryptology ePrint Archive, Report 2016/104 (2016), http://eprint.iacr.org/2016/104

35. Wiener, M.J.: The Full Cost of Cryptanalytic Attacks. Journal of Cryptology **17**(2), 105–124 (2003). https://doi.org/10.1007/s00145-003-0213-5

Short Paper: Organizational Security: Implementing a Risk-Reduction-Based Incentivization Model for MFA Adoption

Sanchari Das[1,2]($\boxtimes$), Andrew Kim[2], and L. Jean Camp[2]

[1] University of Denver, Denver, US
[2] Indiana University Bloomington, Bloomington, US
anykim@iu.edu

Abstract. Multi-factor authentication (MFA) is a useful measure for strengthening authentication. Despite its security effectiveness, the adoption of MFA tools remains low. To create more human-centric authentication solutions, we designed and evaluated the efficacy of a risk-reduction-based incentivization model and implemented our proposed model in a large-scale organization with more than $92,025$ employees, and collected survey data from 287 participants and interviewed 41 participants. We observed negative perceptions and degraded understandings of MFA technology due to the absence of proper risk and benefit communication in the control group. Meanwhile, the experimental group employees showed positive perceptions of MFA use for their work and personal accounts. Our analysis and implementation strategy are critical for reducing users' risks, creating positive security tool usage experiences, and motivating users to enhance their security practices.

Keywords: Authentication · User studies · Multi-factor authentication · Security awareness · Organizational security · Usable security · Risk communication

1 Introduction

Organizations and companies have often required their employees to use multi-factor authentication (MFA) for protecting their accounts [10]. Although MFA provides substantial added security, it has several user experience hindrances [11]. While making MFA mandatory on some accounts may improve users' online security, it often detrimentally affects users' perceptions and mental models of MFA [4]. Because MFA is usually rolled out without proper supplemental communication, users may come to see it as an unnecessary blocker in their daily workflow rather than as an effective security measure [9]. Regarding risk communication, Albayram et al. explored the use of visual methods for explaining MFA benefits to users, noting that the themes of risk and self-efficacy were compelling for communication [1].

Elaborating on the prior study, to test our understanding of risk communication and MFA with users, we implemented and tested an incentivization

© International Financial Cryptography Association 2021
N. Borisov and C. Diaz (Eds.): FC 2021, LNCS 12675, pp. 406–413, 2021.
https://doi.org/10.1007/978-3-662-64331-0_21

model for MFA risk and benefits communication in an organizational setting. For the study, we conducted a preliminary information gathering interview with $M = 19$ employees of an organization involved with the procurement, development, implementation, and maintenance of MFA. This was done before the pilot study to obtain data for developing the communication model. After that, we conducted a survey with $N1 = 287$ employees and interviewed $N2 = 22$ employees at a large organization that had recently required users to enroll in MFA via the Okta authentication application[1].

Contrary to popular belief, we found that users are receptive to longer text- and video-based communication. Our proposed model for this study, which was tested on the experimental group ($N = 187$ out of a total of $N1 = 287$ survey takers), consisted of an introduction to MFA and a text-based or video-based communication that briefly outlined the security benefits of MFA while explaining the potential risks of not adopting MFA. We wanted to examine how users in a real-world organizational setting responded to such communication, providing further details about improving MFA (or, in general, any security-focused tool) rollout strategies.

2 Related Work

While multi-factor authentication improves online account security, MFA's adoption has been hindered by negative user perception of MFA technologies [3].

Risk Communication and Mental Models: Previous research has explored risk communication for improving the security behavior of individuals [8]. It has been shown that risk perception is often unrealistically low and increasingly vulnerable to online threats [15]. This aligns with Harbach et al.'s work, where they pointed out the need for learning about user mental models and how risk communication can be utilized as a useful tool for improving users' security hygiene [7]. Albayram et al. evaluated visual modes of risk communication, where users were motivated through informative and self-sufficient videos [1]. They identified high-priority tasks (e.g., security content to address) and approaches to avoid (e.g., using computer-generated voices) for improved outcomes for risk communication. We extended these prior works to test the efficacy of different risk communication modes (text and video) in a large-scale organizational setting.

User Experiences with MFA: MFA tools often have usability and accessibility issues due to their lack of user-friendly terminology, risk communication, and misaligned visual cues [4,16]. Braz et al. pointed out that changes in an interface's design impact users' overall experience with MFA [2]. Reynolds et al. identified a lack of usability in U2F applications, specifically during the setup procedures [12]. The focus of our work is to analyze participants' risk perceptions, address the concerns of MFA users, and identify effective ways to communicate the benefits of MFA while being aligned with users' risk mental models.

---

[1] https://www.okta.com.

3   Methodology

We conducted our study in two phases (interview and survey) at a large international organization ($92,025$ full and temporary employees). At the beginning, we conducted a series of semi-structured interviews with: 3 decision-making leaders, 5 core developers, 5 members of the communications and distribution team, 3 technological policy makers, and 3 members of the technical support team.

We then engaged the outreach community and employees of the organization to establish text- and video-based risk communication strategies. Initially, the content focused on the data breaches and employee negligence that had led to broad negative impacts on the organization. However, during our initial pilot testing (which included 23 employees), participants expressed concerns about the pure focus on negative implications and the fear-mongering technique used in the messaging. This led us to question how the negative messaging could impact other participants. Thus, we went through nine more iterations of each of the text- and video-based communications with the same 23 employees before arriving at the finalized messages, which focused on MFA's benefits instead.

In the second phase of the study, we conducted a survey with with employees who worked in the organization's technological field to remove the variability of technical knowledge and expertise. In the first part of the survey, participants ($N1 = 287$) were randomly assigned to one of two groups: the control group ($N11 = 100$) or the experimental group ($N12 = 187$). Those in the experimental group were also divided into two groups: one group presented with the text-based risk communication and incentivization messaging (90) and one group that would be presented with the video-based risk communication incentivization messaging (97). In the second section of the survey, participants were asked specific questions about Okta and their understanding of their MFA usage in general (e.g., For which of the following accounts or services do you use multifactor authentication (MFA)?).

In the third section, participants were presented with the specific risk and benefits communication messaging they had been randomly assigned. They were instructed to read/watch before they answered questions about the benefits of using MFA and the risks of not using it. The control group participants were not given any form of risk and benefits communication messaging but were still asked to answer questions about the benefits and risk trade-offs of MFA to compare and contrast the effectiveness of the proposed model. In the fourth section of the survey, we asked participants questions about their future expectations regarding MFA at their organization. This included questions such as: What other digital identification methods would you like to use to log in to your accounts for password-less access? Finally, a small subset of the participants ($M = 22$) was randomly selected from our participant pool to complete an additional semi-structured interview to gather further information on their MFA usage. The study design and implementation were approved by the organization's digital experiences, strategies, policies, and communications review board.

4   Results

The organization utilized two forms of multi-factor authentication: one for on-premise authentication and the other for off-premise authentication. Due to the company's employee list's dynamic nature, we limited our collection of data from May 2019–September 2019. By the end of this study, we observed that 71, 115 employees were successfully enrolled in some form of MFA through Okta, including push notification, call, etc. Of those 71, 115 users, 63, 964 were enrolled in push and one-time-password (OTP) application-based authentication, and 49, 589 were enrolled in call-based authentication. These users were not mutually exclusive, as 41, 435 users were enrolled in both. A small number of employees (462 employees) were given Yubico security tokens[2] as the second factor of authentication.

User Risk Perception and Mental Models: Though the participants seemed to be aware of online identity theft, their overall lack of knowledge of MFA's works was alarming and was made worse due to their blind trust in security experts. This is critical, as developers, designers, and users often make false assumptions about everyday systems' underlying security [14]. Table 1 outlines participants' responses to various statements about MFA. Only 58% of participants responded that they understood how MFA works, and only 61% indicated that they understood MFA benefits. 60% of participants reported that they believed MFA would make their online data more secure, confirming the need to make MFA enrollment and day-to-day usage easier for users.

Understudied Organizational Population: Prior studies conclude that users often perceive MFA as challenging to set up and a hassle to use. Our study show the impact of a common solution for increased adoption: making security tools mandatory [5,13]. Our results show that requiring the use of tools without properly justifying said requirement is often futile, leading users to adopt negative behaviors, such as authentication tool sharing. Another significant contribution of this paper is the inclusion of the proof-of-concept in a large-scale organizational setting.

Users' Preferred Authentication Methods: We asked users about their likelihood of using any of the popular variations of multi-factor authentication. Users were asked to rate the forms of MFA on a scale from "extremely likely" to use to "unlikely" to use, including codes sent by email/text messages, hardware tokens, biometrics, etc. Users noted that they would be open to using all of the various forms of MFA. Push notifications seemed to be immensely popular among the organization's employees, with nearly 86% of participants rating that they would be "extremely likely" to use MFA via this method. This is most likely due to their previous experience with Okta, which uses a mobile-application-based MFA implementation.

---

[2] https://www.yubico.com/product/security-key-by-yubico/.

Table 1. Participants' understanding of and perception of MFA

Statement	Strongly agree	Agree	Neither agree nor disagree	Disagree	Strongly disagree
I Understand How MFA Works	83	83	13	55	53
I Understand the Benefits of MFA	101	73	6	53	53
I Think MFA Will Make My Online Data More Secure	94	78	11	52	52
I Trust MFA	64	101	17	54	51
I Think MFA Will Be Risky	5	67	77	105	33
I Think MFA Will Be Easy to Use	41	99	39	57	51

Evaluation of Incentivization Model Through Risk and Benefits Communication: In addition to filling out Likert scales, participants were also given the option to submit open-ended responses regarding any questions/concerns they may have had regarding MFA after viewing the videos and reading the text. We asked similar questions to the control group. Users in the experimental group understood clear benefits of MFA usage based on text- (90/90 said yes when asked about MFA benefits) and video- (81/97) information provided to them in comparison to the control group (20/100 said they understood the benefits of MFA). One participant noted:

"I think the video did a good job explaining it [what MFA is and its benefits]."

A small fraction of users stressed that MFA might be useful in reducing risks, but only marginally.

"I'm always concerned about my online data. Although MFA reduces the concern, there will always be the risk of exposing my online data. Nothing is safe, and when one process is shut-down, a new one pops-up to replace it."

Finally, another user said that both the videos and text made them wonder why MFA is not more popular:

"I am concerned that not everything is already MFA-ed... I do not understand why are we not MFA-ing all the things?"

Implementation and Adoption Issues. To further understand the effectiveness of the risk and benefits communications, we also conducted semi-structured interviews with a subset of the participants who completed the survey. From the developers' perspective, the primary problem was that users were unaware of what MFA did and was often forced to use MFA due to mandatory policies.

> *"every day, we get multiple emails; usually, they are easy to address. However, it is mostly when application developers do not have a clear understanding of the Okta (MFA) usage and often ask why Okta (MFA) integration is required for access."* (P1, Developer)

Another problem occurred when users used both security questions and their phones as a second authentication factor but did not carry their devices.

> *"Often, they (users) need to reset the passwords for which they need to go through Okta for the added layer of verification. They forget to bring their devices since they did not know how to use MFA for a password reset, and we need to do the reset for them."* (P3, Developer)

5   Discussions and Implications

Our results prove the overall notion that our incentivization model for risk reduction can be effective when used as part of a MFA rollout strategy in a real-world, large-scale organization. It is important to note that the goal of our research was not to criticize mandatory MFA policies as a security strategy, nor was it to prove the effectiveness of text over video (or vice versa) as a communication medium. Rather, we suggest that mandatory MFA policies in organizations should be complemented with additional risk and benefit communications that align with users' mental models and backgrounds. Both the text- and video-based communications received positive responses; thus, the emphasis should not be on the medium of communication as much as it should be on the content and the timeliness of delivery to users.

Given prior academic research [6], we found that communicated risks and benefits are treated as incentives that help with users' decision-making in adopting security tools and techniques. In order to encourage tool adoption, we must provide users with the reasoning behind why such tools are necessary without overwhelming them with too many technical details. Similarly, for multi-factor authentication, we address the complications of the added steps to login by explaining why such additional steps benefit the users and aligning our communications with the organization for which they work.

6   Limitations and Future Work

We found that our risk-reduction-based incentivization model most positively influenced the security decision-making when added during rollout. However, our studied organization was MFA-compliant when the study started, with some of the participants already using MFA. Thus, further research can explore the model's effectiveness in an organization that has yet to require MFA usage among its users. Additional experiments would help test our model across multiple organizations to see its effectiveness with varying MFA policies and cultural backgrounds of employees.

7   Conclusion

With the rise of users' online presence, authentication has become more challenging and critical, especially for organizations where employees' identities are tightly coupled with the organization's essential information. Our research focused on mitigating risks by exploring how to encourage improved authentication technologies—namely, MFA. Despite the security benefits, usability remains challenging for MFA. To resolve this issue, we proposed implementing risk and benefits communication through text- and video-based messaging to improve user adoption of new security tools and technologies. The user study implemented a preliminary interview, a survey, and a semi-structured interview with the ultimate goal of learning how effective a communication model could be during real-world MFA implementations. Participants responded mostly positively to both text- and video-based forms of risk communication, indicating the importance of mandating technologies and explaining them without security jargon to the end-users. We propose that our risk-reduction-based incentivization model be part of all MFA implementation strategies and policies to encourage positive decision-making regarding security tool usage.

Acknowledgments. We would like to thank the organization and its employees where the study was conducted, the University of Denver, Indiana University Bloomington. Any opinions, findings, and conclusions or recommendations expressed in this material are solely those of the author(s).

References

1. Albayram, Y., Khan, M.M.H., Fagan, M.: A study on designing video tutorials for promoting security features: a case study in the context of two-factor authentication (2fa). Int. J. Human Comput. Interact **33**(11), 927–942 (2017). https://doi.org/10.1080/10447318.2017.1306765
2. Braz, C., Robert, J.M.: Security and usability: the case of the user authentication methods. In: Proceedings of the 18th Conference on L'Interaction Homme-Machine. pp. 199–203. IHM '06, ACM, New York, NY, USA (2006). https://doi.org/10.1145/1132736.1132768, http://doi.acm.org.proxyiub.uits.iu.edu/10.1145/1132736.1132768
3. Das, S., Dingman, A., Camp, L.J.: Why johnny doesn't use two factor a two-phase usability study of the FIDO U2F security key. In: Meiklejohn, S., Sako, K. (eds.) FC 2018. LNCS, vol. 10957, pp. 160–179. Springer, Heidelberg (2018). https://doi.org/10.1007/978-3-662-58387-6_9
4. Das, S., Wang, B., Tingle, Z., Camp, L.J.: Evaluating user perception of multi-factor authentication: a systematic review. In: Proceedings of the 13th International Symposium on Human Aspects of Information Security and Assurance (HAISA 2019). HAISA (2019)
5. Furnell, S.M., Bryant, P., Phippen, A.D.: Assessing the security perceptions of personal internet users. Comput. Secur. **26**(5), 410–417 (2007)

6. Garg, V., Camp, L.J., Connelly, K., Lorenzen-Huber, L.: Risk communication design: video vs. text. In: Fischer-Hübner, S., Wright, M. (eds.) PETS 2012. LNCS, vol. 7384, pp. 279–298. Springer, Heidelberg (2012). https://doi.org/10.1007/978-3-642-31680-7_15
7. Harbach, M., Fahl, S., Smith, M.: Who's afraid of which bad wolf? a survey of it security risk awareness. In: 2014 IEEE 27th Computer Security Foundations Symposium. pp. 97–110. IEEE (2014)
8. Harbach, M., Hettig, M., Weber, S., Smith, M.: Using personal examples to improve risk communication for security and privacy decisions. In: Proceedings of the 32nd Annual ACM Conference on Human Factors in Computing Systems. pp. 2647–2656. ACM (2014)
9. Krol, K., Philippou, E., De Cristofaro, E., Sasse, M.A.: They brought in the horrible key ring thing! analysing the usability of two-factor authentication in uk online banking. arXiv preprint arXiv:1501.04434 (2015)
10. Lang, J., Czeskis, A., Balfanz, D., Schilder, M., Srinivas, S.: Security keys: practical cryptographic second factors for the modern web. In: Grossklags, J., Preneel, B. (eds.) FC 2016. LNCS, vol. 9603, pp. 422–440. Springer, Heidelberg (2017). https://doi.org/10.1007/978-3-662-54970-4_25
11. Petsas, T., Tsirantonakis, G., Athanasopoulos, E., Ioannidis, S.: Two-factor authentication: is the world ready? quantifying 2fa adoption. In: Proceedings of the 8th European Workshop on System Security, p. 4. ACM (April 2015). https://doi.org/10.1145/2751323.2751327
12. Reynolds, J., Smith, T., Reese, K., Dickinson, L., Ruoti, S., Seamons, K.: A tale of two studies: the best and worst of yubikey usability. In: 2018 IEEE Symposium on Security and Privacy (SP). pp. 872–888. IEEE (2018). DOI: https://doi.org/10.1109/SP.2018.00067
13. Sedera, D., Dey, S.: User expertise in contemporary information systems: conceptualization, measurement and application. Inf. Manage 50(8), 621–637 (2013)
14. Viega, J., Kohno, T., Potter, B.: Trust and mistrust in secure applications. Commun. ACM 44(2), 31–36 (2001)
15. Weinstein, N.D.: Unrealistic optimism about future life events. J. Pers. Soc. Psychol. 39(5), 806 (1980)
16. Weir, C.S., Douglas, G., Richardson, T., Jack, M.: Usable security: user preferences for authentication methods in ebanking and the effects of experience. Interact. Comput. 22(3), 153–164 (2010). https://doi.org/10.1016/j.intcom.2009.10.001

Measurement

Lost in Transmission: Investigating Filtering of COVID-19 Websites

Anjali Vyas[1], Ram Sundara Raman[1], Nick Ceccio[1], Philipp M. Lutscher[2], and Roya Ensafi[1(✉)]

[1] University of Michigan, Ann Arbor, USA
{anjvyas,ramaks,ceccion,ensafi}@umich.edu
[2] University of Oslo, Oslo, Norway
philipp.lutscher@stv.uio.no

Abstract. After the unprecedented arrival of the COVID-19 pandemic, the Internet has become a crucial source of essential information on the virus. To prevent the spread of misinformation and panic, many authorities have resorted to exercising higher control over Internet resources. Although there is anecdotal evidence that websites containing information about the pandemic are blocked in specific countries, the global extent of these censorship efforts is unknown. In this work, we perform the first global censorship measurement study of websites obtained from search engine queries on COVID-19 information in more than 180 countries. Using two remote censorship measurement techniques, Satellite and Quack, we collect more than 67 million measurements on the DNS and Application layer blocking of 1,291 domains containing COVID-19 information from 49,245 vantage points in 5,081 ASes. Analyzing global patterns, we find that blocking of these COVID-19 websites is relatively low—on average, 0.20%–0.34% of websites containing information about the pandemic experience interference. As expected, we see higher blocking in countries known for censorship such as Iran, China, and Kazakhstan. Surprisingly, however, we also find significant blocking of websites containing information about the pandemic in countries generally considered as "free" in the Internet space, such as Switzerland (DNS), Croatia (DNS), and Canada (Application layer). We discover that network filters in these countries flag many websites related to COVID-19 as phishing or malicious and hence restrict access to them. However, our investigation suggests that this categorization may be incorrect—most websites do not contain serious security threats—causing unnecessary blocking. We advocate for stricter auditing of filtering policies worldwide to help prevent the loss of access to relevant information.

Keywords: Censorship · COVID-19 · Filtering · Phishing

1 Introduction

The COVID-19 pandemic has necessitated heavy reliance on the Internet by people all over the world. Essential information about the pandemic, including details about the virus and the disease, state- and country-level spread,

© International Financial Cryptography Association 2021
N. Borisov and C. Diaz (Eds.): FC 2021, LNCS 12675, pp. 417–436, 2021.
https://doi.org/10.1007/978-3-662-64331-0_22

guidelines, and tracing are primarily accessed through the Internet [21]. However, at the same time, there has also been a surge of misinformation which has prompted authorities to exercise greater control over Internet resources [34]. Although restricting access to malicious resources may be necessary in order to protect users, several studies have shown that access to legitimate information also may be restricted [12, 24, 38, 55].

Recent work by the censorship measurement community has pointed to the blocking of specific websites related to the COVID-19 pandemic in certain countries. OONI [45], a censorship measurement platform, investigated Myanmar's government directive that all Internet service providers must block websites supposedly containing "fake news" regarding the pandemic [24]. In addition, the Citizen Lab [46] found that sources of COVID-19 information that criticize the government are being actively censored on Chinese social media [12, 38]. These investigations reveal that governments are engaging in possibly detrimental censorship of COVID-19 information. However, efforts to measure censorship of COVID-19 information have so far been restricted to certain countries and a small number of websites. The global extent of blocking of legitimate COVID-19 information is as yet unknown.

In this paper, we present the first global censorship study of websites that provide potentially factual information about the pandemic. We use two recently introduced remote censorship measurement techniques, Satellite/Iris (we use just "Satellite" for briefness) [32, 39] and Quack [48] and study the DNS and Application layer blocking (respectively) of 1,291 domains related to COVID-19 in more than 180 countries. Specifically, we aim to answer the following research questions:

1. What is the share of COVID-related websites blocked?
2. Where are COVID-related websites blocked?
3. What categories of COVID-related websites are blocked?
4. Why are COVID-related websites blocked?

To answer these research questions, we first gather a list of 81 neutral search terms that yield potentially factual information about the pandemic from Google Trends [21]. We then perform geo-distributed search engine crawls using three popular search engines in nine different countries. We collect the top ten websites from each crawl, resulting in a set of 1,291 domains most related to the pandemic (which we refer to as "COVID-related test list"). We then perform remote censorship measurements to 29,113 Satellite vantage points and 20,989 Quack vantage points, resulting in a pool of 67 million measurement points. We make our list of domains and measurement data public for other researchers to use [49]. We additionally add over 86 million measurements for domains that are popular [2] and politically sensitive [10], but not strictly related to the pandemic. This set of domains (which we term "Censorship Measurement test list") has been used extensively by censorship studies in the past [43, 45] and provides a point of comparison.

Analyzing patterns in the data, we find that the global blocking of websites in the COVID-related test list is relatively low—On average, 0.20%–0.34% of the websites on our COVID-related test list experienced interference compared to 0.70%–1.04% of websites in the Censorship measurement test list. As expected, we see more blocking in both test lists in countries known for censorship such as Iran, China, and Kazakhstan. However, more surprisingly, our measurements show significant blocking of COVID-related websites in many countries with high Internet freedom scores [11] such as Switzerland (DNS), Croatia (DNS), and Canada (Application layer). Upon investigation, we find that networks in these countries employ web filters such as Fortiguard [19], which categorize many COVID-related websites as containing phishing or other malicious content, resulting in their unavailability from vantage points in these networks.

We utilize different URL classifying services [7,29,50] and manual investigation to determine whether 46 COVID-related websites blocked by web filters have harmful phishing or other malicious content. Interestingly, while Fortiguard classifies 91.30% of the websites as phishing or malicious, our results show that only 0–36.96% of websites are marked as containing security risks by other services, illustrating the wide variance in categorization and, transitively, blocking policies of web filters. Our manual investigation further suggests that only 2.17% of websites actually contain harmful and evident security threats.

Our findings show that such 'benevolent blocking' may restrict the amount of factual and, in some cases, essential information available on the Internet. With that in mind, we advocate for stricter auditing of censorship policies and for more transparency regarding what is being blocked by groups making use of these filtering services. Only with such transparency can we ensure that valuable information is kept open and available to Internet users.

2 Background and Related Work

The COVID-19 Pandemic and the Internet. On March 12, 2020, the World Health Organization (WHO) officially declared the Coronavirus outbreak as a pandemic. At the time of writing, more than two million deaths were confirmed caused by COVID-19 worldwide [53]. Whereas there has been, and there still is, a lot of variation in how governments respond to the pandemic, most governments imposed regional or country-wide shutdowns, banned mass gatherings, encouraged social distancing, made the wearing of face masks mandatory, and invested in their health care systems to slow down the spread of the virus [8].

Apart from direct disease control, many authorities also increased their efforts in controlling (mis)information during this global pandemic [3]. Reports emphasize that conspiracy theories and disinformation attempts related to COVID-19 have drastically increased [28]. Several studies show that bots and ordinary users promote misinformation on social media [6,9,18,41]. As a response, many authorities enacted policies to counter this so-called "infodemic." Governments passed laws to criminalize falsehood related to public health, created special units to remove disinformation, and delegated this task to social media or private Internet companies [34,55]. However, there is tentative evidence that legitimate information on the pandemic is also blocked. For instance, reports by the Citizen Lab and the New York Times show that regime-criticizing information on the pandemic is actively censored in Chinese social media [12,38,55]. A report by OONI shows that the Myanmar government has been ordering long Internet shutdowns and blocking COVID-19 related content in a non-transparent manner [24]. The pandemic offers an opportunity to intensify online censorship efforts and undemocratic policies [22,25]. However, these case studies only highlight specific cases of censorship in a few countries. To our knowledge, our study is the first that systematically investigates the share of online blocking of COVID-19 related websites worldwide.

Censorship Studies. Censorship mechanisms vary across countries and networks, and therefore many censorship measurement techniques have been proposed to measure and quantify what is being blocked and how the blocking is occurring. On a technical level, network censorship is defined as the deliberate disruption or blocking of certain types of Internet communication by a network adversary. At the coarsest level, an adversary may prevent access to Internet connectivity completely for a user population, a phenomenon termed as *Internet shutdowns* [13,14]. These are out of the scope of our study. Rather, we investigate *Internet censorship* where access to specific websites is blocked. There are commonly three stages of a network connection that could be blocked. First, a censor may restrict access during the TCP handshake stage of an Internet connection between a client and server, based on the server's IP address. This method is not widely used because of the emergence of Content Delivery Networks (CDNs), but is still used to block access to circumvention proxies [1]. Second, a censor may inject a DNS query response with a non-routable IP, an IP that leads to a blockpage, or may not return an IP at all [4,32]. Finally, a censor may also inspect specific HTTP and TLS packets and on observing a particular keyword, reset the connection, inject blockpages or drop packets [44,48]. In this paper, we focus on DNS poisoning and application-layer blocking as they are two common methods of censorship implementation.

Censorship measurements can be conducted from within countries of Interest ("Direct Measurement") or remotely from outside the country ("Remote Measurement"). *Direct Measurement* uses volunteer devices or accessible vantage points inside countries to send network packets to possibly blocked hosts. There has been a plethora of studies that have directly measured censorship within a specific country [5,17,26,45,51,54,56]. This kind of measurement is highly useful for in-depth analysis of censorship, but due to scale, coverage, continuity, and safety limitations is not ideal for widespread global measurement [43].

More recently, *Remote Measurement* techniques that can measure censorship without accessible vantage points or volunteers have enabled global measurements of high scale and coverage [31,32,39,42–44,48]. These techniques use side channels in existing Internet protocols for interacting with remote systems, and infer whether the connection is disrupted from their responses. In this paper, we use two types of remote measurement techniques, Quack and Satellite.

- **Satellite** Satellite sends DNS requests from a single measurement machine towards many infrastructural Open DNS resolvers and control resolvers in

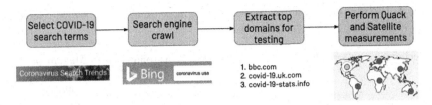

Fig. 1. Flowchart of methodology steps

different countries [32,39]. Satellite then compares the responses from the Open DNS resolvers and control resolvers using a set of 5 heuristics to determine the presence of network interference [32].

– **Quack** Quack uses infrastructural servers that have the TCP Echo functionality enabled on Port 7 as vantage points to measure censorship of specific keywords [48]. Quack uses a retry-based mechanism to send HTTP-lookalike requests containing both sensitive and benign payloads to the Echo server vantage point. In the absence of any censorship, both types of requests would be reflected back to the sender as is. However, in case the sensitive keyword is censored (through injecting a blockpage, reset, or forcing the connection to timeout), the expected response would not be received. Quack also uses Echo's sibling protocol, Discard, to determine directionality of blocking. In the case of Discard, the remote vantage point is expected to drop all of the packets, but a censor acting on incoming packets may choose to inject a reset or a blockpage.

3 Methodology

To collect data on the blocking of potentially important information related to the COVID-19 pandemic, we assemble a list of search keywords that yield factual information related to COVID-19 and perform search engine crawls to gather popular domains. We then test reachability to these domains using remote censorship measurement techniques. Figure 1 provides a flowchart summarizing the data collection methodology.

Selection of Search Engine Crawl Keywords. We first use Google Trends to assemble a list of 81 different search terms meant to yield factual information on COVID-19 in search engine results [21]. Google Trends provides data about the most common Internet searches related to the pandemic performed by Google Search users. We note that most search terms provided by Google consisted of the word 'coronavirus' followed by another word or the name of a country, such as 'coronavirus cases' or 'coronavirus usa.' We add 26 such keywords to our list, followed by the same keywords with the word 'coronavirus' replaced with 'covid' or 'covid-19.' Finally, four general terms ('coronavirus',

Table 1. Distribution of vantage points used for measurement (CR: Covid-related test list, CM: Censorship Measurement test list)

Technique	# VPs		# Countries		# Autonomous Systems (ASes)		Median # of ASes Per Country	
	CR	CM	CR	CM	CR	CM	CR	CM
Satellite	29,113	28,415	165	166	4,073	3,920	5	5
Quack Echo	20,799	10,607	151	125	2,089	1,350	3.5	3
Quack Discard	7,730	7,993	112	112	1,165	1,184	3	3

'corona virus', 'covid', and 'covid-19') complete the list. We utilize this list of frequently-searched keywords as they are more likely to yield factual and important information on COVID-19 that should be available to anyone around the world.

Forming the Test List. Using the list of 81 search terms (shown in Appendix 1), we perform search engine crawls to gather the URLs of websites containing information on COVID-19. To ensure that our list of URLs accurately reflect genuine websites people across the globe would access for COVID-19 information, we execute this crawl on nine different geo-distributed vantage points located in England, France, Germany, Ireland, Canada, Japan, South Korea, Singapore, and Australia. Using Selenium [40], we query Google, Bing, and DuckDuckGo with each of our search terms, recording the URLs of the top ten websites.

We take the union of the list of URLs recorded, which results in a list of 4,155 unique URLs hosted on 1,291 live domains. We use these 1,291 domains, termed as the *COVID-related test list* as input to our measurements testing for blocking. Since these websites form top search results for the different countries, a censor aiming to block factual information on COVID-19 would likely block these websites. These websites fall into 43 categories according to categorization by Fortiguard's URL filter service [19]. The most common categories are News and Media, Government, and Health.

In addition to these 1,291 COVID-related domains, we also create an additional *Censorship Measurement test list* composed of 2,128 sensitive and popular domains from Citizen Lab [10] and Alexa [2] that are regularly tested by other censorship measurement platforms [43,45]. The overlap between the COVID-related test list and the Censorship Measurement test list is very small, consisting of only 70 domains, and as such, the two test lists provide a point of comparison.

Censorship Measurement. We use Quack and Satellite to determine whether the domains in the test input lists are being filtered. Measurements using these techniques were performed for the COVID-related test list and the Censorship

Measurement test list over a period of two weeks, from June 12, 2020, to June 26, 2020, from different machines in North America. For Quack, we performed both Echo and Discard measurements. The number and distribution of vantage points used by each technique for measurements (of the COVID-related and Censorship Measurement test lists) is shown in Table 1.

Ethics. We follow all the recommendations made in previous studies that have performed remote censorship measurements [31,32,35,43,44,48] and have only used "infrastructural" vantage points. Specifically, we only use nameservers for DNS measurements [32] and servers and routers for Quack measurements in countries with strict Internet control [48]. We also follow all the Internet measurement recommendations made in the line of work using Internet-wide scans such as ZMap [16]. We rate limit our measurements, close all connections, and host a web server on our measurement machines which provides details of our research and offers administrators the option to opt-out.

Data Analysis. Overall, we collect around 153 million censorship measurements using our list of vantage points and the two test lists. We perform around 67 million measurements for our COVID-related test list. We augment our measurements with country information from Maxmind [27] and AS information combined from Maxmind [27], Routeviews [37], and Censys [15]. We perform measurements in 186 countries and 5,081 Autonomous Systems (ASes).

Our measurement techniques perform multiple probes during each test, and the test is marked as interfered only if all the probes fail. This helps to prevent false positives from momentary glitches in the network. In addition, we manually remove false positives originating from rogue vantage point responses and use blockpage and false positive fingerprints recorded in previous studies [43,44] to label our data and avoid false inferences.

We next calculate the average blocking rate across each of the countries covered by our measurements. More precisely, we calculated the average blocking rate in a country cc with n vantage points as:

$$\text{Avg. Blocking Rate}_{\text{cc}} = \frac{\sum_{i=1}^{n} \% \text{ domains blocked}_{\text{vp}_i}}{n} \qquad (1)$$

We use this quantitative value in our results. For our country-level aggregates to be more accurate, we only report aggregate results for countries with 10 or more vantage points in our results.

4   Results

The worldwide measurement of COVID-19-related websites allows us to answer our research questions outlined in the introduction.

4.1   What Is the Share of COVID-related Websites Blocked?

On a positive note, the global average blocking rate of COVID-19 related websites seems to be relatively low. On average, only 0.20%–0.34% (depending on the

Table 2. Top five countries having the highest average blocking rate across the three sets of domains (CC: Covid-containing, CR: Covid-related, CM: Censorship measurement) in Satellite, Quack Echo, and Quack Discard

Satellite			Quack Echo			Quack Discard		
CC	CR	CM	CC	CR	CM	CC	CR	CM
CH (4.32%)	CN (10.74%)	CN (15.71%)	EC (2.50%)	IR (8.98%)	IR (29.50%)	CN (1.52%)	IR (7.77%)	IR (33.27%)
HR (2.39%)	IR (1.76%)	IR (14.95%)	CN (1.17%)	CN (4.30%)	CN (11.81%)	CA (1.42%)	CN (4.45%)	CN (11.44%)
KZ (2.23%)	KZ (0.57%)	IQ (2.96%)	IR (1.09%)	EC (2.29%)	BD (2.94%)	TW (0.78%)	VN (0.37%)	KZ (1.82%)
AU (1.55%)	SG (0.56%)	ID (2.46%)	CA (0.82%)	SI (1.25%)	PK (2.48%)	IR (0.48%)	EG (0.28%)	TR (1.57%)
DK (1.26%)	CH (0.52%)	AF (2.10%)	BD (0.79%)	TN (0.71%)	TN (1.74%)	RO (0.31%)	RU (0.19%)	EG (0.93%)

protocol tested) of websites experience some sort of interference. This is lower compared to an average blocking rate of 0.70%–1.04% per country from the Censorship Measurement test list of politically sensitive and popular domains. Nevertheless, our measurements still find many COVID-related websites filtered in networks in a considerable number of countries. Perhaps the most surprising finding is that several countries previously not known for Internet censorship observe the highest blocking rates for these websites.

To showcase this, we create an additional set of domains from the COVID-related test set that consists exclusively of the domains that have the phrases "covid", "corona" or "korona" in them. These domains likely became live after the pandemic started with the purpose to provide users with information related to COVID-19. We call this list *COVID-containing* and use it as an indicator of blocking specifically related to the pandemic. There are 1,291 distinct domains in our COVID-related set, out of which 152 are in our COVID-containing set. These websites appear in the top search engine results for common COVID-19 queries, and as such may provide useful information to Internet users on the pandemic.

Table 2 shows the top 5 countries in which we observe the highest average blocking rates for these three sets of domains in Satellite and Quack. Whereas we observe the highest average blocking rate in China and Iran in most test lists, countries previously not known for Internet censorship (Switzerland, Croatia, and Canada) appear in the top 5 in the COVID-containing and COVID-related test lists.

To investigate this finding more systematically, we correlate our measurements to a qualitative Internet censorship measure quantified by "Varieties of Democracies" [11]. This measure is judged for 202 countries by several country experts. Figure 2 illustrates the results. The labeled countries exhibit blocking that is higher than 90% of blocking observed in all countries. A simple linear regression shows a positive correlation between the level of Internet censorship and the average blocking rate in most test sets. Nevertheless, in particular for the COVID-containing list, we find many countries with low censorship scores from "Varieties of Democracies" that experience relatively high website blocking rates in our tests.

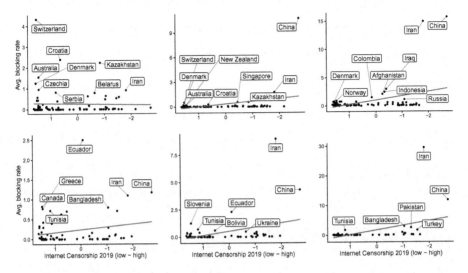

Fig. 2. Correlation between qualitatively measured Internet censorship level (2019) and blocking with Satellite (top) and Quack Echo (bottom) for the *Covid-containing* (left), *Covid-related* (middle) and *Censorship Measurement* (right) test sets—Note: X-axes are reversed. The blue lines display the linear regression for each measurement and test list. Correlation coefficients are $\beta = .02$ (p=.76) [Satellite, CC], $\beta = -.33/-.04$ (p = .0/.04) [Satellite, CR], $\beta = -.76/-.04$ (p = .00/.44) [Satellite, CM], $\beta = -.07$ (p=.09) [Echo, CC], $\beta = -.38/-.17$ (p = .00/.01) [Echo, CR], $\beta = -1.55/-1.25$ (p = .00/.01) [Echo, CM]. Negative coefficients reflect a higher average blocking rate when a country is qualitatively rated as more restrictive. The second values, if applicable, show the coefficients after removing influential observations with a Cook's distance above 1. Discard measurements are comparable to the Echo measurements.

4.2   Where Are COVID-related Websites Blocked?

Based on the results in Table 2 and Fig. 2, we analyze the blocking of COVID-related domains for certain countries in detail. We first explore two countries, Switzerland and Croatia. Both countries are not typically known for online censorship but many DNS probes containing websites from our COVID-containing and COVID-related domains appear to be filtered in networks that are in these countries. Second, we look at Canada as another unexpected country for which we found high average blocking rates for the COVID-containing test list using Quack measurements. Finally, we summarize results for some of the other countries in which we found high censorship: China, Iran, and Kazakhstan.

Switzerland. According to "Varieties of Democracies" [11], Switzerland can be considered one of the freest countries when it comes to Internet freedom. However, our DNS measurements in Switzerland detect a high average blocking rate (4.32%) in particular for keywords in our COVID-containing test list.

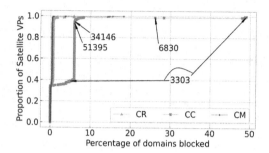

Fig. 3. CDF showing blocking of COVID-related, COVID-containing, and Censorship Measurement domains in Switzerland—The AS numbers of the vantage points experiencing filtering of COVID-containing domains are annotated.

Fig. 4. Switzerland blockpages—The blockpages in the top left and right are ISP blockpages, while the blockpage in the bottom left is a known blockpage of the web filter Fortinet [44].

How is the Blocking Spread Out? We performed measurements to 922 Satellite vantage points spanning 34 ASes in Switzerland. As shown in Fig. 3, the number of domains blocked differs by vantage point, even within the same AS. Six out of 34 ASes have at least one vantage point observing blocking of keywords from our COVID-related and COVID-containing test lists. The AS with the largest amount of vantage points, AS3303 (846 vantage points), observes high blocking of content related to the pandemic. 82 out of the 152 domains in the COVID-containing test list are filtered in our probes to at least one vantage point in this AS. 599 vantage points in AS3303 observe blocking of at least one keyword from the COVID-related list. This AS is the second largest in Switzerland according to Censys [15].

What is the Censored Response? We find that 601 out of the 607 (99%) vantage points experiencing blocking in Switzerland observed five distinct IP addresses for DNS resolutions of filtered domains, all of which hosted a visible blockpage. Ten vantage points in AS3303 responded with two IP addresses hosting the

Table 3. Top 10 filtered domains in Switzerland (DNS)

Domain	Category	% of VPs	Domain	Category	% of VPs
www.covid-19.uk.com	Phishing	66.44	covid-19-stats.info	Phishing	65.74
coronavirus-realtime.com	Malicious	66.40	coronavirus.zone	Malicious	65.41
covid19graph.work	Phishing	66.36	coronavirus-map.com	Phishing	65.36
www.covid19ireland.com	Phishing	66.22	coronastats.net	Malicious	63.60
www.covid19maps.info	Phishing	65.83	coronavirusfrance.org	Phishing	1.58

blockpage shown in Fig. 4 (top left) for 74 domains from our COVID-containing list. Interestingly, only domains from the COVID-containing list are resolved to these IPs. Two vantage points in AS3303 and one in AS6830 observed DNS resolutions to an IP address hosting the blockpage shown in Fig. 4 (bottom left), which has previously been identified as one of the blockpages of the web filter Fortinet [44]. The other two IP addresses hosting the blockpage shown in Fig. 4 (right) are observed for nine domains from the COVID-containing list, but these are observed in a large number of vantage points (481 & 108).

What are the Websites that are Blocked? We explore the top websites from our COVID-related test list that are blocked in our probes to DNS resolvers in Switzerland. As shown in Table 3, most of the large-scale blocking in Switzerland seems to be for protecting users from Phishing or Malicious websites (as categorized by Fortiguard's Web Filter service [19]). All of the top 10 websites also fall in our COVID-containing set, primarily contain COVID-19 specific information, and are all categorized as websites containing security threats.

Croatia. Croatia has the second-highest average blocking of COVID-containing domains (2.39%) in Satellite measurements. Similar to Switzerland, Croatia is generally considered as free in the online space, and hence such high levels of filtering of COVID-19 specific content deserve scrutiny. We perform measurements to 12 vantage points in Croatia, spread across six ASes. The vantage point that observes the highest rate of blocking for both COVID-containing (28.66%) and COVID-related (3.49%) domains is located in AS5391 and observes redirection to the Fortinet blockpage shown in Fig. 4 (bottom left) when tested with 43 domains from the *COVID-containing* test list. One other domain from the COVID-related test list is also blocked (`droneinfini.fr`). Similar to our observation in Switzerland, we observe high blocking of Phishing and Malicious websites in Croatia.

Canada. We find significant amounts of application layer keyword filtering in Canada. On average, we see 0.82% and 1.42% blocking of COVID-containing domains in Quack Echo and Quack Discard measurements respectively.

How is the Blocking Spread Out? Quack collected measurements from 201 Echo vantage points distributed across 52 different ASes and 109 Discard vantage

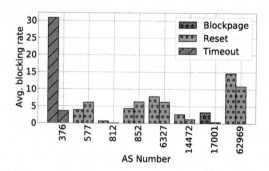

Fig. 5. Blocking distribution in Quack Echo measurements in different ASes in Canada—The left bar shows the average blocking rate of the COVID-containing list and the right bar shows the average blocking rate of the COVID-related list.

points in 34 ASes in Canada. Thirteen Echo vantage points observe blocking of at least one domain from the COVID-related test list, and twelve of these also observe blocking of at least one domain from the COVID-containing test list. Figure 5 shows the amount of blocking across different ASes in our Echo measurements. AS376 observes the highest amount of COVID-containing blocking. Most of the ASes show considerable blocking of both COVID-containing *and* COVID-related domains. Six Discard vantage points observe blocking of at least one domain from the COVID-related and COVID-containing test lists. In our Discard measurements, we observe similar rates of blocking as in Fig. 5 in three ASes: AS376, AS812, and AS17001.

What is the Censored Response? Figure 5 also shows the type of blocking that is performed in the different ASes. While a majority of ASes in Echo measurements inject reset packets, probes to vantage points in AS376 experience connection timeouts, and the vantage point in AS17001 observes a blockpage. The blockpage explicitly mentions that the content has been blocked because it might contain malicious content. We see similar type of blocking in Discard for the ASes performing blocking. Thus, users in Canada observe different censored responses based on the network they connect to.

What Websites are Blocked? Similar to Switzerland and Croatia, a significant proportion of the top blocked websites in Canada may be targeted because they are being perceived to be phishing or malicious (See Table 4). All of the top five blocked domains in Canada (in both Echo and Discard measurements) are COVID-containing domains. Analyzing measurements in the AS that observes the highest amount of COVID-containing blocking, AS376 (RISQ-AS), which consists of 4 vantage points, we see that all of the 48 distinct domains filtered are COVID-containing domains. This AS observes the same blocking pattern in Discard measurements as well. The five distinct domains AS17001 observes to be blocked also belong to our COVID-containing test-list.

Table 4. Top 5 blocked domains in Canada (Application Layer)

Quack Echo			Quack Discard		
domain	category	% of VPs	domain	category	% of VPs
covid-19.uk.com	Phishing	3.93	covid19stats.global	Phishing	5.50
covid19stats.global	Phishing	2.86	coronastats.net	Malicious	4.63
covid-19incanada.com	Business	2.84	covid-19canada.com	Business	4.63
covid19uk.live	Reference	2.82	covid-19ireland.com	Not Rated	4.63
www.covid19-maghreb.live	Phishing	2.81	coronavirus-realtime.com	Malicious	4.63

Other Countries. Countries which typically experience high levels of Internet censorship such as China and Iran also observe high blocking of both *COVID-containing* and *COVID-related* domains (see Table 2). While blocking in these countries may not be strictly related to or caused by the pandemic, it may still hinder users trying to obtain valuable news about the pandemic.

Iran. We performed Quack measurements to 39 Echo vantage points spread across 17 ASes and 11 Discard vantage points spread across 9 ASes in Iran. In both our Echo and Discard measurements, we observe high blocking of popular news websites (e.g., `www.huffpost.com`) and social networking websites (e.g., `www.facebook.com`). In most cases, the blocked response is either a well-known blockpage [44] or a connection timeout. We also performed DNS measurements to 395 vantage points across 61 ASes in Iran, and observe similarly high blocking of popular websites in the COVID-related test list. Some domains in the COVID-containing test list are also blocked (e.g., `coronavirusireland.ie`), indicating filtering policies against websites with pandemic information.

China. Our measurements to 1,417 Echo vantage points (in 70 ASes) and 337 Discard vantage points (in 33 ASes) in China observe large-scale blocking of popular news and media websites and Google services. In China, the majority of blocked responses are connection resets. DNS measurements to 4,279 Satellite vantage points in 60 ASes also show similarly high blocking of COVID-related websites containing news. While the blocking of *COVID-containing* domains forms a smaller proportion of the blocking of *COVID-related* domains, some networks block COVID-specific websites such as `covid19japan.com`.

Kazakhstan and Ecuador. We also observe significant blocking of both *COVID-containing* (2.23%) and *COVID-related* (0.57%) domains in DNS measurements to Kazakhstan. In this case, domains are resolved to state or Internet Service Provider (ISP) blockpages. In Ecuador, we observe significant blocking of both sets of domains using reset injection in application layer measurements (CC 2.5%, CR 2.29%).

4.3 What Categories of COVID-related Websites Are Blocked?

Figure 6 shows the distribution of blocking for different countries in five categories: Business, Government and Legal Organizations, Health and Wellness,

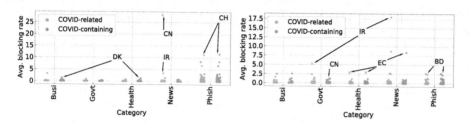

Fig. 6. Blocking distribution across categories—Left: Satellite, right: Quack Echo. The categories were obtained using FortiGuard. Each point on the graph represents a country and the top blocking countries for certain categories have been labeled.

News and Media, and Phishing. As observed in the previous section, Phishing websites observe significant amount of blocking, in both DNS and Application-layer measurements. Since 24.3% of the COVID-containing test list is categorized as Phishing, this blocking appears to be considerably new (since the pandemic started) and COVID-specific. Many news and government websites, which may contain important COVID-19 information, are blocked in our measurements to countries which are known to perform Internet censorship.

4.4   Do COVID-related Websites Perform Phishing?

Throughout our findings, we observe a high blocking rate of many COVID-containing and COVID-related websites that are characterized by the Fortiguard classification service as phishing. Particularly in Switzerland and Croatia, we find the use of the Fortinet web filter (see Fig. 4), which also uses the Fortiguard classification service for blocking dangerous websites.

Given the increased prevalence of phishing during the pandemic [30], such blocking is not surprising. However, it is important that websites containing factual information about COVID-19 without any security threats are not blocked by mistake. To better understand whether the 46 websites blocked by the Fortinet web filter in Switzerland and Croatia are actually security threats, we compare it with three freely available URL classifying services: Checkphish [7] (an online website that checks for signs of phishing in an URL), Palo Alto Networks [29] and WatchGuard [50]; two popular web filters [44].

We report our detailed results in Appendix 2. We observe substantial differences in the categorization. Fortiguard classifies 42 out of the 46 websites tested as security risks with the tags "Phishing" or "Malicious". Palo Alto networks only classifies eight of the 46 as "High risk," "Malware" or "Medium risk." Watchguard classifies 17 of the 46 domains as "Compromised", "Suspicious", "Elevated Exposure" or "Malicious." Six websites are considered risky by both WatchGuard and Palo Alto Networks. Checkphish did not classify any websites as Phishing.

We also manually determine whether each of these websites contain evident security risks. Three of the authors individually visited each of these websites, categorized them, and reached a consensus. Other than `coronavirus`

-`monitor.ru`, which has an insecure looking popup box where card information can be entered, none of the other websites seem to contain visible security threats. Note that the manual classification does not consider the legitimacy of the data. However, many of the websites list their sources (some common ones are Johns Hopkins University dashboard [23] and government websites) and also warn users that there could be inaccuracies in the data. These findings highlight an important issue with web filter-based censorship—the lack of proper auditing and incorrect categorizations of websites may lead to high amounts of unnecessary blocking for thousands of users, given that these web filters are often used by organizations, ISPs, and governments for blocking dangerous websites [35,44].

5   Discussion

Implications and Future Work. Due to the COVID-19 "infodemic", there has been a significant shift in the priorities of many countries throughout the world—the challenge at hand has been achieving a balance between allowing citizens to access important information while also protecting them from harmful misinformation. Our study shows that the large-scale use of URL filtering services may be inadvertently tipping the scale in the wrong direction. While URL classifying and filtering services are known to contain mistakes [33,47], our results indicate that highly searched (and potentially harmless) domains are being blocked in several countries due to these errors. There is a serious lack of transparency surrounding the decisions made by filters and large discrepancies from filter to filter, a concern also echoed by recent work [47]. These issues make detailed auditing of such services necessary. We advocate for further research into the mechanics of filters and their categorization techniques, and for third-parties to monitor and track filtering policies that affect a large number of users, such as ISP and country-level deployments [44].

In cases where COVID-19 related censorship is more intentional, countries could be using genuine reasons supporting the need for information control during the pandemic as a facade for restricting information and continuing censorship in the long run for unrelated reasons [36,52]. Future work should track the overflow of censorship policies enacted during the pandemic over time to prevent unnecessary loss of access. Moreover, more in-depth analyses of the contents of a website will help to determine the reason behind filtering. A recent report [55] highlights that content critical of China's handling of COVID-19 have been reported to be taken down in China, for instance.

Finally, while this study focuses on the filtering of websites related to popular searches of factual COVID-19 information, there is a possibility that misinformation related to COVID-19 is blocked more restrictively. Future work can use our measurement tools to monitor websites that are more likely to contain misinformation. In addition, we do not account for website filtering performed by search engines themselves; whereas top factual results are rarely suppressed by search engines, future work studying misinformation needs to consider whether search engine censorship is a significant contributor to information unavailability. Search results obtained from other search engines such as Yandex or Baidu could also be incorporated in test-lists to allow for more comprehensive findings.

Limitations. When assembling the input lists, we used results from search crawls conducted in nine geo-distributed countries. Our censorship measurements included several countries that were not included in this list and thus, it is possible that there are resources local to these countries that are being filtered. Moreover, by only using the top ten results from each search, we potentially miss measuring the filtering of less popular websites, which we leave for future work.

Even though we run measurements from a large number of vantage points around the globe, our vantage points do not have the granularity required to detect all blocking. Moreover, only a handful of vantage points are available in some countries, and hence our observations may be limited to a specific network or region. Quack sends measurements to port 7 and port 9 and therefore may miss censorship that is only applied to traffic on port 80 or port 443. In addition, the Quack Discard technique cannot detect censorship that only affects outbound traffic. However, studies have shown that such censorship is difficult to perform, so it is unlikely to substantially alter our test results [48]. There is also the possibility that some censors apply mechanisms to evade our detection, although we are not aware of any such measures to-date. Finally, the Maxmind geolocation database we used is known to have inaccuracies [20].

6   Conclusion

In this paper, we have explored the global extent of censorship related to the pandemic using a test list of popular COVID-19 websites and remote censorship measurement techniques. We find generally low levels of blocking related to the pandemic. However, we observe that commercial URL filtering services deployed in countries such as Switzerland and Canada mistakenly consider many COVID-19-related websites as containing phishing threats and block them. When censors engage in blocking of this kind, be it well-intentioned or purely suppressive, it has the potential to cut off this vital flow of information. As an online community, we must advocate for stricter auditing of filtering practices for ensuring that essential information is available to every person that needs it.

Acknowledgements. The authors thank the shepherd Philipp Winter and the reviewers for their constructive feedback. We also thank Prerana Shenoy for her help with data analysis. This work was supported in part by research credits from Google.

Appendix 1

Classifier and Manual Categorizations. Table 5 shows the results of the categorization of the 46 domains blocked by the Fortinet filter in Switzerland and Croatia using different categorization tools.

Table 5. URL Classifier and Manual Categories—NTE stands for Navigation Time Exceeded, E stands for error and NC stands for not categorized.

Website	FortiGuard	CP	PAN	WatchGuard	Manual
canadacovid.ca	Phishing	no	Low	NC	no
co19stats.com	NC	no	Low	NC	no
coronastats.net	Malicious	no	Malware	Malicious Web Sites	no
coronavictimes.net	Phishing	no	Low	Elevated Exposure	no
coronavirus-global.com	Phishing	no	Low	Sports	no
coronavirus-map.com	Phishing	NTE	High	Malicious	no
coronavirus-map.org	Phishing	no	Low	Health	no
coronavirus-monitor.com	Phishing	no	Low	Business and Economy	no
coronavirus-monitor.ru	Malicious	NTE	Medium	Health	yes
coronavirus-realtime.com	Malicious	NTE	Malware	Compromised	no
coronavirus.zone	Malicious	no	Malware	Malicious	no
coronavirusfrance.org	Phishing	no	Low	Elevated Exposure	no
coronavirusireland.ie	Phishing	no	Low	News and Media	no
coronavirusmap.co.uk	Phishing	no	Low	NC	no
coronavirusstatistics.org	Phishing	NTE	Low	NC	no
coronavirusupdate.me	Phishing	no	Low	Shopping	no
coronavirususamap.com	Phishing	no	Low	NC	no
covid-19-fr.fr	Phishing	no	Low	Health	no
covid-19-stats.info	Phishing	no	Malware	Malicious	no
covid-19.uk.com	Phishing	no	Low	NC	no
covid-19ireland.com	NC	E	Low	Elevated Exposure	no
covid-japan.com	Phishing	no	Low	News and Media	no
covid-live.net	Phishing	no	Low	Elevated Exposure	no
covid-stats.net	NC	no	Low	Elevated Exposure	no
covid19-uk.co.uk	Phishing	no	Low	Elevated Exposure	no
covid19dashboard.live	Phishing	no	Low	NC	no
covid19graph.work	Phishing	no	Low	Malicious Web Sites	no
covid19live.org	Phishing	no	Low	Elevated Exposure	no
covid19statistics.org	Phishing	no	Low	Government	no
covid19stats.global	Phishing	no	High	Malicious	no
covid19video.com	Phishing	E	Low	NC	no
droneinfini.fr	Phishing	no	Low	NC	no
koronavirus-today.ru	Phishing	no	Low	NC	no
map-covid-19.com	Phishing	NTE	Low	Reference Materials	no
ru.coronavirus-global.com	Phishing	no	Low	Sports	no
wa-daily-covid-19.com	Phishing	no	Low	Elevated Exposure	no
worldcoronavirus.org	Phishing	no	Low	Elevated Exposure	no
worldometers.cc	NC	E	Low	Suspicious content	no
www.coronalive.info	Phishing	NTE	Low	NC	no
www.coronavictimes.fr	Phishing	no	Low	Business and Economy	no
www.coronavirus-india.net	Phishing	no	Low	NC	no
www.covid19-maghreb.live	Phishing	no	Low	NC	no
www.covid19ireland.com	Phishing	no	Malware	Government	no
www.covid19maps.info	Phishing	NTE	Low	NC	no
www.covidstats.com	Phishing	no	Low	NC	no
www.vaccin-coronavirus.fr	Phishing	no	Low	Health	no

434   A. Vyas et al.

Appendix 2

Search Engine Crawl Keywords. Table 6 shows the list of prefix and suffix combinations used to construct the keywords used for our search engine crawls.

Table 6. Keyword permutations used for search engine crawls—Three terms (corona virus, covid virus, and covid-19 virus) are excluded from the table.

Prefix	Suffix
coronavirus, covid, covid-19	usa, ireland, uk, britain, india, canada, singapore, korea, japan, australia, germany, france, update, news, worldometer, deaths, victims, map, live, infections, stats, toll, death toll, vaccine, dead, \<empty>

References

1. Afroz, S., Fifield, D.: Timeline of Tor censorship (2007). http://www1.icsi.berkeley.edu/~sadia/tor_timeline.pdf
2. Alexa Internet, Inc., Alexa Top 1,000,000 Sites. http://s3.amazonaws.com/alexa-static/top-1m.csv.zip
3. Allcott, H., Gentzkow, M., Yu, C.: Trends in the diffusion of misinformation on social media. Research & Politics (2019)
4. Anonymous. Towards a comprehensive picture of the Great Firewall's DNS censorship. In: Free and Open Communications on the Internet (FOCI) (2014)
5. Aryan, S., Aryan, H., Halderman, J.A.: Internet censorship in Iran: a first look. In: Free and Open Communications on the Internet (FOCI) (2013)
6. Brennen, J.S., Simon, F., Howard, P.N., Nielsen, R.K.: Types, sources, and claims of covid-19 misinformation. Reuters Institute (2020)
7. CheckPhish: Url Scanner to Detect Phishing in Real-time—CheckPhish. https://checkphish.ai/
8. Cheng, C., Barceló, J., Hartnett, A.S., Kubinec, R., Messerschmidt, L.: Covid-19 government response event dataset. Nature Hum. Behav. **4**, 756–768 (2020)
9. Cinelli, M., et al.: The covid-19 social media infodemic. arXiv preprint http://arxiv.org/abs/2003.05004 (2020)
10. Citizen Lab. Block test list. https://github.com/citizenlab/test-lists
11. Coppedge, M., et al.: V-dem codebook v. 10 (2020). https://www.v-dem.net/media/filer_public/28/14/28140582-43d6-4940-948f-a2df84a31893/v-dem_codebook_v10.pdf
12. Crete-Nishihata, M., Dalek, J., Knockel, J., Lawford, N., Wesley, C., Zhou, M.: Censored contagion II: a timeline of information control on Chinese social media during COVID-19 (2020). https://citizenlab.ca/2020/08/censored-contagion-ii-a-timeline-of-information-control-on-chinese-social-media-during-covid-19/
13. Dahir, A.L.: Internet shutdowns are costing African governments more than we thought. https://qz.com/1089749/internet-shutdowns-are-increasingly-taking-a-toll-on-africas-economies/
14. Dainotti, A., et al.: Analysis of country-wide internet outages caused by censorship. In: ACM Internet Measurement Conference (IMC) (2011)

15. Durumeric, Z., Adrian, D., Mirian, A., Bailey, M., Halderman, J.A.: A search engine backed by Internet-wide scanning. In: Proceedings of the 2015 ACM SIGSAC Conference on Computer and Communications Security (2015)
16. Durumeric, Z., Wustrow, E., Halderman, J.A.: ZMap: fast internet-wide scanning and its security applications. In: USENIX Security Symposium (2013)
17. Ensafi, R., Winter, P., Mueen, A., Crandall, J.R.: Analyzing the great firewall of China over space and time. In: Proceedings on Privacy Enhancing Technologies (PETS) (2015)
18. Ferrara, E.: What types of COVID-19 conspiracies are populated by twitter bots? First Monday (2020)
19. FortiNet: Fortiguard labs web filter. https://fortiguard.com/webfilter
20. Gharaibeh, M., Shah, A., Huffaker, B., Zhang, H., Ensafi, R., Papadopoulos, C.: A look at infrastructure geolocation in public and commercial databases. In: ACM Internet Measurement Conference (IMC) (2017)
21. Coronavirus search trends - google trends. https://trends.google.com/trends/story/US_cu_4Rjdh3ABAABMHM_en
22. Jerreat, J.: Coronavirus the new scapegoat for media censorship, rights groups say (2020). https://www.voanews.com/press-freedom/coronavirus-new-scapegoat-media-censorship-rights-groups-say
23. Johns Hopkins University: Coronavirus Resource Center. Covid-19 dashboard by the center for systems science and engineering (csse) at johns hopkins university (jhu). https://coronavirus.jhu.edu/map.html
24. Kyaw, P.P., Xynou, M., Filastò, A.: Myanmar blocks "fake news" websites amid covid-19 pandemic. https://ooni.org/post/2020-myanmar-blocks-websites-amid-covid19/
25. Lachapelle, J., Lührmann, A., Maerz, S.F.: An update on pandemic backsliding: Democracy four months after the beginning of the covid-19 pandemic. Policy Brief, V-Dem Institute (2020)
26. MacKinnon, R.: China's censorship 2.0: how companies censor bloggers. First Monday (2009)
27. MaxMind. https://www.maxmind.com/
28. Ofcom: Half of UK adults exposed to false claims about coronavirus (2020). https://www.ofcom.org.uk/about-ofcom/latest/media/media-releases/2020/half-of-uk-adults-exposed-to-false-claims-about-coronavirus
29. Palo Alto Networks. Test a site. https://urlfiltering.paloaltonetworks.com/
30. PC Magazine: Phishing attacks increase 350 percent amid covid-19 quarantine. https://in.pcmag.com/privacy/135635/phishing-attacks-increase-350-percent-amid-covid-19-quarantine
31. Pearce, P., Ensafi, R., Li, F., Feamster, N., Paxson, V.: Augur: internet-wide detection of connectivity disruptions. In: IEEE Symposium on Security and Privacy (S&P), May 2017
32. Pearce, P., et al.: Global measurement of DNS manipulation. In: USENIX Security Symposium (2017)
33. Peng, P., Yang, L., Song, L., Wang, G.: Opening the blackbox of virustotal: analyzing online phishing scan engines. In: ACM Internet Measurement Conference (IMC) (2019)
34. Radu, R.: Fighting the 'infodemic': legal responses to COVID-19 disinformation. Social Media+Society (2020)
35. Ramesh, R., et al.: Decentralized control: a case study of Russia. In: Proceedings of the Network and Distributed System Security Symposium (NDSS) (2020)

36. Reporters Without Borders: Middle east governments clamp down on coronavirus coverage (2020). https://rsf.org/en/news/middle-east-governments-clamp-down-coronavirus-coverage

37. University of Oregon Route Views Project. www.routeviews.org

38. Ruan, L., Knockel, J., Crete-Nishihata, M.: Censored contagion: how information on the coronavirus is managed on Chinese social media (2020). https://citizenlab.ca/2020/03/censored-contagion-how-information-on-the-coronavirus-is-managed-on-chinese-social-media/

39. Scott, W., Anderson, T., Kohno, T., Krishnamurthy, A.: Satellite: joint analysis of CDNs and network-level interference. In: USENIX Annual Technical Conference (ATC) (2016)

40. SeleniumHQ Browser Automation. www.selenium.dev

41. Singh, L., et al.: A first look at COVID-19 information and misinformation sharing on Twitter (2020)

42. Sundara Raman, R., Evdokimov, L. , Wustrow, E., Halderman, A., Ensafi, R.: Investigating large scale HTTPS interception in Kazakhstan. In: Internet Measurement Conference (IMC). ACM (2020)

43. Sundara Raman, R., Shenoy, P., Kohls, K., Ensafi, R.: Censored planet: an internet-wide, longitudinal censorship observatory. In: ACM SIGSAC Conference on Computer and Communications Security (CCS) (2020)

44. Sundara Raman, R., et al.: Measuring the deployment of network censorship filters at global scale. In: Network and Distributed System Security Symposium (NDSS) (2020)

45. The Tor Project. OONI: Open observatory of network interference. https://ooni.torproject.org/

46. University of Toronto. Citizen Lab. https://citizenlab.ca/

47. Vallina, P., et al.: Mis-shapes, mistakes, misfits: an analysis of domain classification services. In: ACM Internet Measurement Conference (IMC) (2020)

48. VanderSloot, B., McDonald, A., Scott, W., Halderman, J.A., Ensafi, R.: Quack: scalable remote measurement of application-layer censorship. In: USENIX Security Symposium (2018)

49. Vyas, A., Sundara Raman, R., Ceccio, N., Lutscher, P.M., Ensafi, R.: Investigating filtering of COVID-19 websites (2020). https://censoredplanet.org/covid

50. WatchGuard. See a site's content category. https://www.watchguard.com/help/docs/help-center/en-US/Content/en-US/Fireware/services/webblocker/site_categories_see_websense_c.html

51. Winter, P., Lindskog, S.: How the great firewall of china is blocking tor. In: Free and Open Communications on the Internet (FOCI) (2012)

52. Wiseman, J.: European media freedom suffers under COVID-19 response (2020). https://ipi.media/european-media-freedom-suffers-covid-19-response/

53. World Health Organization: Coronavirus disease (COVID-19) pandemic (2020). https://www.who.int/emergencies/diseases/novel-coronavirus-2019

54. Xu, X., Mao, Z.M., Halderman, J.A.: Internet censorship in China: where does the filtering occur? In: International Conference on Passive and Active Network Measurement (PAM) (2011)

55. Zhong, R., Mozur, P., Kao, J., Krolik, A.: No 'Negative' news: how China censored the coronavirus (2020). https://www.nytimes.com/2020/12/19/technology/china-coronavirus-censorship.html

56. Zittrain, J., Edelman, B.: Internet filtering in China. IEEE Internet Comput. 7(2), 70–77 (2003)

Under the Hood of the Ethereum Gossip Protocol

Lucianna Kiffer[1]([✉]), Asad Salman[1], Dave Levin[2], Alan Mislove[1],
and Cristina Nita-Rotaru[1]

[1] Northeastern University, Boston, MA, USA
{lkiffer,amislove}@ccs.neu.edu, {salman.a,c.nitarotaru}@northeastern.edu
[2] University of Maryland, College Park, MD, USA
dml@cs.umd.edu

Abstract. Blockchain protocols' primary security goal is consensus: one version of the global ledger that everyone in the network agrees on. Their proofs of security depend on assumptions on how well their peer-to-peer (P2P) overlay networks operate. Yet, surprisingly, little is understood about what factors influence the P2P network properties. In this work, we extensively study the Ethereum P2P network's connectivity and its block propagation mechanism. We gather data on the Ethereum network by running the official Ethereum client, `geth`, modified to run as a "super peer" with many neighbors. We run this client in North America for over seven months, as well as shorter runs with multiple vantages around the world. Our results expose an incredible amount of churn, and a surprisingly small number of peers who are actually useful (that is, who propagate new blocks). We also find that a node's location has a significant impact on when it hears about blocks, and that the precise behavior of this has changed over time (e.g., nodes in the US have become less likely to hear about new blocks first). Finally, we find prune blocks propagate faster than uncles.

1 Introduction

Ethereum [34] is a cryptocurrency that can also store and execute user-generated programs often called *smart contracts*. Compared to Bitcoin [32], Ethereum is significantly more expressive and can be used to implement decentralized voting protocols, financial contracts, and crowdfunding programs. Today, Ethereum is the second-most-valuable cryptocurrency behind Bitcoin, with a market capitalization of over \$26B [6].

Given its complexity, it may be unsurprising that Ethereum has a number of differences from Bitcoin. For the purposes of this paper, two such differences stand out: *First*, Ethereum is based on a general purpose peer-to-peer (P2P)

We thank the anonymous reviewers and Arthur Gervais for their helpful comments. This research was supported in part by NSF grants CNS-1816802 and CNS-1900879, a Ripple unrestricted gift, and Facebook Fellowship. We also thank the Ethereum Foundation for a gift of AWS credit used toward the collection of our data.

© International Financial Cryptography Association 2021
N. Borisov and C. Diaz (Eds.): FC 2021, LNCS 12675, pp. 437–456, 2021.
https://doi.org/10.1007/978-3-662-64331-0_23

overlay responsible for discovering other nodes and maintaining connectivity. This P2P layer can be used by higher-level protocols other than Ethereum (in fact, we find this is often the case). The Ethereum Network layer sits between the P2P layer and the overlying application layer (the blockchain itself), and is responsible for choosing peers, disseminating new blocks, and reaching network-wide confirmation of transactions. *Second*, Ethereum's 15 s (on average) block interval is dramatically shorter than Bitcoin's 10 *min* (on average). This significantly reduced target block mining interval opens the door to much faster "network confirmation" of accepted transactions.

Thus, the structure of the Ethereum P2P overlay, including aspects such as peer connectivity and block propagation delay, play an important role in achieving the target performance and correct functioning. Most prior measurement work on Ethereum has focused either primarily on the P2P layer [15, 29] or primarily on the application layer (i.e., the blockchain itself [8, 9, 26, 27, 33]), leaving the Ethereum network layer not as well understood.

In this paper, we aim to better understand the network structure of Ethereum, focusing on both how the Ethereum network is formed and evolves over time, as well as how the network is used to propagate new blocks, a crucial part of the consensus mechanism. We do this by integrating information from the P2P layer (e.g., which nodes are available, who nodes choose to connect to), information from the application layer (e.g., which blocks are ultimately accepted), along with information from the Ethereum layer (e.g., which peers nodes exchange block information with, and which peers actually provide the most useful information).

We conduct our study by running a customized version of Ethereum's official Go client, geth, for over seven months, allowing us to observe the evolution of the Ethereum network through multiple protocol changes. We also run multiple nodes in a variety of vantage points across the globe for shorter lengths during this time period, allowing us to study both how our peers interact and how the location in the physical Internet affects the peers' experience in the Ethereum network. The results of our analysis can be summarized as follows:

- **Extensive peer churn:** We observe dramatic levels of churn in the Ethereum network, both in terms of the number of unique peers and connection lengths. Churn can run the risk of disconnecting a network or making it difficult to quickly propagate information throughout it, and challenging to estimate the size of the network. We investigate churn in the Ethereum network and find that 68% of the peer IDs we see in our 200-day scraping period are present only on a single day, and 90% of them are present on fewer than 25 days.
- **Miner centralization:** The top 15 miners are responsible for over 90% of mined blocks. We investigate those miners and find that all but one are well-known mining pools. We also note a difference in the efficiency of miners: the top 3 mining pools have a much greater probability of a block they mine being included in the blockchain (propagating faster and "winning" the block race).

- **Most announcers are long-lived:** Comparing all peers to those who are first to announce a block, we see that those announcing blocks tend to have longer connections, larger average and total connection lengths, and are online more days. Almost 70% of peers are seen only one day, but about 40% of our announcing peers are seen only one day. The latter is still a large percent but there is a set churn in peers who are not participating in block propagation.
- **Announcers are diverse:** Focusing on *which* peers tell our nodes about new blocks first, we find that a large number of peers are responsible for announcing a miner's block first to our node. No one peer announces more than 6% of a miner's blocks to us first.
- **Quick network-wide propagation:** The speed at which new information spreads throughout the Ethereum network is critical in how quickly transactions can complete. We perform a novel analysis of network propagation times by running nodes in three different vantage points (USA, South Korea, and Germany). Despite the diversity of information sources across the three, we find that the difference in time from when the first learns about a block until when the last learns about it is very small: for instance, less than 100 ms for 85% of all new blocks.
- **Location bias:** Although our vantage points in North America, Asia, and Europe did not experience any unfair disadvantages, we observed bias using additional vantages in locations with fewer peers (South America and Oceania). We observe an significant disparity in which locations hear about blocks first, with those two locations being first to hear about blocks only ∼3% of the time.

2   Background

The Ethereum system consists of multiple layers. In this section, we provide an overview of the components we study in this paper, and detail related work.

2.1   Overview

The purpose of Ethereum is to create a *blockchain* via proof-of-work *mining*. Unlike systems that function almost exclusively as a currency, Ethereum is made up of transactions that contain either (a) direct transfers of ETHER (the currency unit of Ethereum) or (b) transactions that create or call *smart contracts*. Transactions of the second type must also pay to run the computation via GAS in extra ETHER sent with the transaction. While much work has examined smart contracts (e.g., [9,27,33]), we are focused on the Ethereum network itself.

Miners are participants in the Ethereum network that listen on the network for transactions and package them into blocks. To successfully create a block, a miner must verify that all transactions included are valid (including code execution and signatures), include the hash from the most recent block in the miner's chain as well as a Proof-of-Work (proof enough computational "work" was done to create this block). Miners do this "work" by creating blocks whose hash[1] has a minimum specified number of leading zeros. The target number of

---

[1] The Ethereum protocol uses their own memory-hard hash function, Ethhash [1].

leading zeros is known as the *difficulty* and is adjusted at every block so that a block will be generated roughly every 15 s. The miner whose block becomes part of the chain is rewarded with 5 ETHER and the GAS of the transactions. Because of the high variance in winning a block, miners often come together to form *mining pools* where block rewards are split among the participants. We observe in (Fig. 1) that the top 15 miners (14 of which are known mining pools) mined over 90% of all blocks.

Mainchain, Uncles, and Prunes are different types of blocks in Ethereum. Blocks that are part of the blockchain containing the history of Ethereum are called mainchain blocks. However, not all valid blocks share this fate. With a target time between blocks of 15 s, it often happens that two or more valid blocks are mined within a short interval of each other by two different miners, contending for the same position in the chain. Both blocks propagate through the network and eventually consensus is reached on which of the two blocks become part of the mainchain.

To still reward mining related to these discarded blocks, miners can also choose to include these valid, but non-mainchain blocks as uncles in the blocks they mine. A miner includes the hash of the discarded block in a special field of the block only if the parent of the uncle (the block the uncle points to) is a block in their own chain up to six blocks prior. Both the miner and the miner of the uncle receive an additional, smaller amount of ETHER.

Finally, some valid blocks may be mined, but never end up in the mainchain or become uncles (e.g. if the announcement of the block is significantly delayed), we refer to such blocks as prunes. Note that because prunes are not on the blockchain at all, we can only observe them by participating in the network and hearing them being announced. On average, we observe roughly 6,000 mainchain blocks, 400 uncle blocks, and 10 prune blocks each day.

2.2 Networking in Ethereum

The Ethereum system is made up of three layers: the *application layer* that contains the blockchain, the *Ethereum layer* that contains peers exchanging information about blocks and transactions, and the *peer-to-peer (P2P) layer* that allows nodes to find others and establish connections (more details in the full version of this paper [28]). We briefly overview these below based on the official documentation [2,4,5], talks [20], and the official client code.

P2P Layer. The P2P layer is divided into two components: a *discovery protocol* that allows nodes to find each other, and *DevP2P* that nodes use to communicate. We detail the Discovery protocol in the full version of this paper [28].

The DevP2P Protocol runs in parallel to the Discovery protocol and is responsible for establishing sessions with other nodes, sending and receiving messages between peers and managing the actual higher-level protocol being run. In Ethereum, DevP2P uses RLPx, which is responsible for encrypting, encoding and transferring messages between peers. Once a peer has been discovered during the execution of the Discovery protocol, the RLPx protocol initiates the TCP handshake and HELLO messages are exchanged. In the HELLO message, both sides send the protocol version, the client software type, the capabilities and version they support, the port they are listening on and their ENODEID. Importantly, the DevP2P protocol checks if the remote node is running the same application-layer protocol (e.g. eth for the Ethereum Wire Protocol), that they support each others' protocol version, and that they agree on the blockchain (i.e., the genesis blocks and any forks). The nodes will disconnect if any of these conditions do not hold, which is surprisingly common: prior work [29] found that over two months in 2018, about 95% of nodes were running the eth protocol, but only 54.5% of those agreed on the blockchain. Otherwise, if the conditions hold, the nodes become *peers* and can exchange messages at the Ethereum layer (we distinguish *nodes* at the P2P layer from *peers* at the Ethereum layer).

Ethereum Layer. The Ethereum Wire Protocol [2] is the application-layer protocol for propagating transactions and blocks, and for requesting block and state data so new clients can sync to the existing state. To be brief, we omit how new clients sync to the blockchain and instead focus on how new messages are propagated.

Transactions are transmitted in full via a TransactionMsg message either by the originator of the transaction or when a node hears about a new transaction.

Blocks are transmitted in a more complicated fashion. When a node hears about a new block, they first verify that the block belongs to their chain and includes the PoW. At this point, the node *propagates* the full block by sending a NewBlockMsg message to a subset of their peers.[2] The node then fully validates the whole block by adding it to their internal state. The node finally sends the hash of the block to its remaining peers who have not heard about the block via a NewBlockHashesMsg message. An overview of this process is provided in the full version of this paper [28].

2.3 Ethereum Implementations

There are several versions of the Ethereum client, the most common are the official Golang implementation called geth and a popular, non-official Rust-based client, Parity. We deploy our measurements using the official geth client, run by a vast majority of the network [7,29]. By default, the geth client used to have the *maxPeer*, a cap of the number of peers the client will maintain, constant set to 50. This cap is enforced by bounding 66% of its *maxPeer* as incoming connections and the remaining connections as outbound. In order to gain visibility into the network, we increased the *maxPeer* cap to 750 during most of our experiments. The geth client will keep on accepting and making connections until its peer cap is met, including looking for additional nodes to connect to via the node discovery protocol.

---

[2] In geth this subset is composed of a square root of their peers who have not heard about the block.

2.4 Related Work

The papers that most closely relate to our work are [15] and [29]. In [15], Gencer et al. run a measurement-based comparative study of the Bitcoin and Ethereum P2P networks with a focus on decentralization properties. For Ethereum they look at peer bandwidth, connection latency (to peers and bounds between nodes), and some amount of efficiency of miners through miner distribution of blocks and uncle counts. In [29], Kim et al. scrape the Ethereum P2P network by connecting to peers just long enough to establish a full DevP2P connection and checking up to the DAO fork (i.e. not a ETC node). They focus their analysis primarily on node client type, "freshness", location/ASes and also connection latency. These two papers ran scrapers collecting quick peer information while we run a long-term full node which is able to collect more temporal node information (i.e. analyze churn in more detail), and connect peer information with the kinds of block data they send us (i.e. block propagation, some miner analysis), as well as capture **prune** blocks which has yet to be observed in Ethereum. We can also distinguish exactly the peers who fully participate in the Ethereum protocol as those who send useful block information, i.e. propagate blocks.

We use ethernodes.org to compare the nodes we see and note that there has been work showing how ethernodes.org data is not representative, e.g. many of the peers it reports are not actually running the mainnet Ethereum protocol [3,29]. They also briefly mention churn, but in no detail. We explore churn in greater detail both in the ethernodes.org data and in our own peer data.

In another Ethereum network measurement study [14], Gao et al. scrape the P2P layer for peers who they make TCP connections with, though similarly to ethernodes.org, a TCP connection does not distinguish mainnet nodes. They enumerate peer tables for those nodes and analyze their topological properties, though peer tables do not represent actual peer connections on the network. Other measurement works in this area include Decker et al. [11], who measure the block propagation delay and fork-rate of Bitcoin[3], work studying peer churn in Bitcoin and other non-blockchain P2P networks [12,25,31], and many works analyzing data extract-able from the blockchain [8,9,26,27,33].

3 Methodology

We now detail our data collection methodology, how we processed the resulting data set, and provide a high-level overview of the data we collected.

3.1 Ethereum Client

We created an instrumented and customized version of the **geth** client [18] that was designed to log detailed information about its network- and application-layer activity. At the P2P layer, our client logs all attempted connections (both inbound and outbound, called *handshakes*) along with remote node information

---

[3] Find a median and mean delay of 6.5 and 12.6 s (from 2013).

including the remote node's ENODEID, IP address, and announced software version. Our client also logs all PING and PONG messages that Ethereum periodically sends as "heartbeats" between nodes (measuring network latency).

At the Ethereum layer, our client logs a number of messages that are exchanged between peers, primarily focused on messages concerning blocks (NewBlockMsg and NewBlockHashesMsg). For each message, our client logs a timestamp and the identity of the remote peer.

To limit any negative impact on the network, our client largely participates in the network in the same manner as a regular full node (e.g., finding peers, exchanging information, etc.). There are two primary modifications we make to enable us to understand the Ethereum network: *First*, we modify our client to *suppress announcing and forwarding one-third of* blocks and transactions (blocks whose hash value is a multiple of three). We do so in order to study how those messages are propagated without our client affecting their dissemination; our client *forwards the other two-thirds* of blocks and transactions as normal.[4] *Second*, we modify our client to allow a much higher *peer cap* (the limit on the number of network-layer peers the client will connect to). We do so in order to study the behavior of many remote peers at once and, as Gencer et al. showed in Bitcoin [17], the more connections we maintain, the earlier we receive block information, meaning we are likely *closer* to their sources.

3.2   Data Collection

We conducted three runs of data collection with different numbers and locations of our clients. We describe these below. In all cases, we use Amazon Web Services' EC2 to host our client, using a r5.2xlarge machine time to ensure the hardware had sufficient capacity. We configured the host operating system to sync with timeservers via the Network Time Protocol service continually to adjust for clock drift. Unless otherwise noted, we set the peer cap in our client to 750 peers (we demonstrate below that we likely connected to the vast majority of other nodes).

We found that the geth client (v1.9.0) appeared to have some memory leaks (that were exacerbated by our modification of the peer cap to a much larger level than normal). As a result, our clients would sometimes crash and be immediately restarted. We found that our client would often take a few hours to build up its peer count (e.g., see Fig. 5), so for our analysis, we ignore any data from before the client reported at least 400 peers.

Peer Cap Experiment. Our choice of a maximum of 750 peers for our long-running measurements was because of a memory leak in the geth client. In order to establish whether our choice of 750 peer cap is representative of the network, we ran three clients in parallel in the us-east-1 Amazon data center (in Virginia, U.S.) with increasing peer limits with peer caps of 500, 1000 and 1,500 peers respectively. We explore this experiment in detail in the full version of this paper [28], and the results suggest that the reachable peers we can connect to at any given time caps at about 1,000 peers.

---

[4] We are unable to avoid forwarding information on *all* blocks/transactions, as doing so would cause other peers to decide to stop peering with our client.

Table 1. Peer and block counts for the *longitudinal experiment, multiple vantage point experiment* and *information propagation experiment*. For the *longitudinal experiment* we look at unique ENODEID and IP, while for the rest we look at ENODEID. We note that useful refers to any peer who announces blocks to us while first refers to peers to who are the first to announce a mainchain block to us.

		Peer counts					Block counts		
runs	location	udp	p2p	peer	useful	first	main	uncle	prune
longitudinal	U.S. ID	1,301,568	194,608	90,265	24,945	12,593			
May-Dec	U.S. IP	339,832	138,107	55,091	22,982	9,359	1,179,883	79,938	2,695
vantage	U.S.	119,892	20,339	8,932	2,822	1,331			
	Seoul	106,397	23,059	9,876	4,865	1,459			
June 6–10,	Frank.	107,559	24,744	10,876	4,695	1,138			
14–16, 2019	All	150,961	31,188	15,644	6,526	2,465	39,345	2,977	113
information	U.S.	299,971	21,257	9,234	5,055	1,214			
	Seoul	295,480	21,024	8,631	5,175	1,822			
propagation	Frank.	289,902	20,708	8,276	5,071	1,349			
May 12-	São P.	290,390	22,112	9,440	5,337	2,152			
23, 2020	Sydney	307,173	23,225	9,643	5,556	1,559			
	All	480,355	30,896	14,613	6,913	3,867	69,199	4779	153

Longitudinal Experiment. Our primary data collection experiment was a long-term longitudinal study of how the Ethereum network behaved over a period of many months. We refer to this experiment as the *longitudinal experiment*, and it consisted of a single client running in the Virginia Amazon data center between May 15th, 2019 and December 13th, 2019.

Multiple Vantage Point Experiment. For a shorter period of time, we also ran a client in the ap-northeast-2 Amazon data center (Seoul, South Korea) as well as a client in the eu-central-1 Amazon data center (Frankfurt, Germany), alongside our Virginia, U.S. client. We refer to this experiment as the *multiple vantage point experiment*, and was run in 2019 between June 6th and June 10th and then again between June 14th and June 16th.

For this experiment, we only consider times where all three nodes were up (with a sufficient peer list, as described above). In total, this experiment resulted in 6 days and 4 h of logged messages.

Information Propagation Experiment. In our multiple vantage point experiment, we observed that our three chosen vantage points tended to be physically close to where most of the blocks were first being announced from (Table 3) and where the majority of our peers are located (Table 2). We finally ran one additional experiment with our three locations in the multiple vantage point experiment, as well as a node in the sa-east-1 Amazon data center (São Paulo, Brazil) and the ap-southeast-2 Amazon data center (Sydney, Australia). We chose these two additional locations as they appeared to be locations where very few (<1%) of blocks are being first announced from, and including them would allow us to better understand how network location affects when information in the Ethereum network is received. We ran this experiment between May 12th and 23rd, 2020, and we refer to it as the *information propagation experiment.*

Limitations. We note that since these are all EC2 instances, running copies of the same machine in different Amazon locations allowed us to maintain location as our only variable (so hardware differences would not affect our results) as well as have the storage and memory capabilities needed. A clear limitation is whether Amazon machines have a biased view of the network, including special links between their centers we cannot control for. We note that a quarter of all peers we connect to in the *longitudinal experiment* are running on EC2 instances, the largest fraction from a single provider. We also weighted this choice with the additional variable of using multiple cloud providers or VPNs which would have added artificial latencies to our connections.

Ethernodes. Ethernodes [7] is a public web site that reports on aggregate statistics for the Ethereum network and is widely cited when reporting statistics about the Ethereum network, including in academic work [13,16,19,23,24]. Between March 30 and October 15th, 2019, we scraped Ethernodes for the Ethereum node information they report from their crawler. In the full version of this paper [28] we use the Ethernodes data as a point of comparison for our data analysis.

4   Analysis

We organize the analysis section by working our way down the different layers involved in the Ethereum protocol. We are interested both in understanding general trends in the network and narrowing in on specifics related to peer behavior. Unless otherwise specified, the bulk of the analysis refers to data from the *longitudinal experiment.*

We start with the **Application layer**, i.e. who is mining blocks. Our main questions are: *How is mining distributed among the top miners, and are the top pools equally efficient? In other words, do some miners appear to have an advantage (e.g., are less likely to mine non-*mainchain* blocks)?*

Next, we move on to the **Ethereum layer** by examining the timestamps of when we hear about different types of blocks. Here we are interested in answering: *How are blocks being propagated in Ethereum and is block propagation correlated to the type of block, block size, or other factors?*

We then examine the **P2P layer**, where we focus on who our nodes connect to/come across. The bulk of the novelty in our work comes from tying peer connectivity behavior with its *usefulness* in block propagation. This is done in the following two layers both in breaking down the behavior of our peers in the *longitudinal experiment* and comparing information received from peers from different vantages. We ask: *What trends can we observe in peer connectivity behavior? How many of the peers that we come across end up being* useful?

Finally, we end our analysis by looking at the **underlying network** and how the position of our nodes in the Internet affects their view of the network. For this we utilize both the *multiple vantage point experiment* and the *information propagation* *experiment* to answer: *Are there advantageous geographic locations from which to run an Ethereum peer and, if so, how large is the disparity between locations?*

4.1 Application Layer

We begin by examining who is mining blocks by looking at the self-advertised `miner id` in the blocks our client hears about. We take data from the seven months of the *longitudinal experiment*, and group blocks by whether they are part of the `mainchain`, `uncles`, or `prunes`.

Figure 1 plots the cumulative distribution of the blocks of different types across miners (note the log scale on the x-axis). We can immediately observe that the fraction of blocks mined is not uniform, and in fact highly skewed towards a very small number of miners. While 90% of all blocks are mined by less than 5% of miners (and the top three miners mine over half of the blocks), over half of the miners mine just a single block. Unsurprisingly, when we examine *when* these blocks are mined, the few miners who mine the majority of the blocks are active for the length of the measurement period, while others who win less frequently come and go more often.

We note that the low number of `miner ids` is not entirely surprising, as miners often group into mining pools and all mine for the same `miner id`. As a result, much of the discrepancy between how many blocks miners win can be explained by dramatic differences in aggregate mining power across pools.

To further explore the discrepancy across miners, we examine each miner's `uncle` to `mainchain` and `uncle` to `prune` ratios in Fig. 1. Recall that `uncles` and `prunes` occur when multiple blocks are mined at once, and eventually one wins. Similar to the analysis of Gencer et al. [15], we say if mining was "fair", we would expect that all miners would typically mine a similar fraction

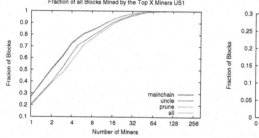
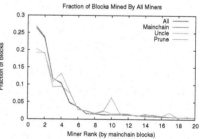

Fig. 1. *Left*: Cumulative distribution of the number of all blocks won by top miners. Note the log scale on the x-axis. *Right*: The fraction of total `mainchain`, `uncle`, and `prune` blocks each miner mines. We see the top 3 miners mine disproportionately more of the `mainchain` blocks than `uncles` or `prunes` and thus have a disproportionate advantage over the other miners.

of uncles and prunes (relative to all blocks they mine)[5]. However, we see that the top mainchain miners tend to have many fewer uncle and prune blocks than mainchain blocks, but that this trend fades as we start to look towards less-powerful miners. This suggests that larger miners appear to have some sort of advantage in the network, as they suffer from uncles and prunes at a much lower rate. Given a block race, having larger mining power increases a miner's odds of winning (as they are more likely to *win* the next block), and network advantages (lower delays) would further increase their odds. It is unclear at which point the former plays a bigger role.

Next, we examine the behavior of the Ethereum protocol layer to better understand how blocks are propagated in the network.

4.2   Ethereum Protocol Layer

We now explore general block trends and how blocks get propagated in the network. In Fig. 2, we examine how our client first hears about blocks (NewBlockMsg or NewBlock HashesMsg) over time. It is clear that new mainchain blocks and uncles are primarily announced to our node first as the full block message, though there are times when some blocks get to it first as hashes. This corresponds to our peers first propagating the full block and then the hashes.[6] Starting in late October, we see the mainchain count starts decreasing. This was due

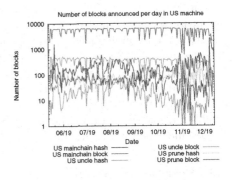

Fig. 2. Count of new blocks by type and by which message we first heard about the new block (NewBlock or NewBlockHash).

to the upcoming *difficulty bomb* which causes the difficulty to gradually increase, speeding up as the deadline approaches; this in turn caused blocks to be mined more slowly.[7]

We next dig deeper into the NewBlockMsg messages to better understand block propagation. Specifically, we look at the incoming NewBlockMsg messages for each block, and measure the difference between the *first* time our client hears about a given block and all subsequent times. Figure 3 presents the cumulative distribution of times for different percentiles for each block, broken down by whether or not it was a block that our client propagated (recall we only propagate 2/3 of blocks at random). We can observe that when we propagate blocks, the lower percentiles tend to be *longer* (compared to when we do not). This may

---

[5] Gencer et al. [15] compared Bitcoin prunes to all blocks mined, but for Ethereum just used uncle counts. They found that at the time Bitcoin had a larger standard deviation in mining fairness than Ethereum.

[6] When prunes are first announced to us via a NewBlockHashesMsg, it generally correspond to times we hear about odd blocks that do not follow the mainchain (i.e. the block number is much smaller or larger than the current height).

[7] The bomb was delayed with the Muir Glacier hardfork in early January 2020.

be surprising, but is likely due to the fact that other nodes will not inform our client if it knows we already know about a block; by propagating a block, we effectively preclude being told. When we propagate a `mainchain` block we receive fewer announcements for it, which is not true for `prunes` or `uncles`.

We further explore the propagation time for different block types in Fig. 3, and note the propagation delay peaks at around 200 ms for all types of blocks. However, `prunes` and `uncles` have a much longer tail, implying their dissemination through the Ethereum network is significantly slower than `mainchain` blocks. We explore whether a block's delay is correlated with any factors about the block. Specifically, we look at the relationship between the median delay of `mainchain` blocks and their `GAS` count and find a very weak correlation coefficient of 0.035. Similarly, we see a similar weak correlation coefficient of 0.031 block size and median delay.

Finally, when we examine the *number* of announcements we receive per block, we notice that we receive between 100 and 300 announcements for most blocks except for `prunes`. The `prune` data is largely skewed by few peers (e.g., 70% of `prunes` are only announced to our client by one peer), and these peers tend to advertise many block hashes with either very low or very high block numbers far from the correct `mainchain`. We note that for these prunes that are both announced primarily as NewBlockHashes (i.e., we do not receive the full block) and in large batches with block numbers that do not correspond to the current height of the `mainchain`, we do not consider them true `prunes` of the `mainchain` and exclude them from the propagation delay analysis of Fig. 3.

4.3   Peer-to-Peer Level

We now turn to examine the P2P protocol layer by looking at trends in our connections to nodes. In Fig. 4 (left), we plot the number of unique nodes our client PING/PONGs, starts a TCP handshake, and fully connects to (i.e. *peers*) in each hour and day. In total in the *longitudinal experiment*, our machine PING/PONGs 1,301,568, starts a TCP connection with 194,608, and fully connects with 90,265 unique ENODEIDs. We see the fluctuation of our client's peer

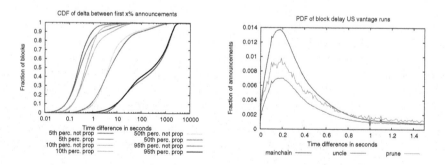

Fig. 3. *Left*: The difference in time for when our *longitudinal experiment* client hears about a block from the first announcement to all subsequent announcements by percentile. *Right*: Probability distribution of the time of subsequent announcements since our client first heard about that block from any peer.

count in Fig. 4(right), where we plot the peer count over time for different runs. We can see the peer count rise steadily during the beginning of a measurement and then fluctuate, often dropping by half before picking up again. We see this significant churn in our full connections in Fig. 5, (left): we compare the average number of peers we have to the number of new connections and connections that end each hour, and see that within an hour we might make up to 3x the number of connections as our average connections. This means each hour, our client makes/ends around 1K–1.5K connections to 300–400 unique ENODEIDs, i.e. reconnecting to the same nodes.

We further explore the trend of re-connecting to the same nodes in Fig. 5, (right), where we plot a breakdown of the length of connections for connected peers based on how long we are connected (*short* is 0–10 s, *medium* is 10–1,000 s, *long* is 1,000 s or more). We can observe that while over 80% of unique peers we connect with in an hour are long connections (>1000 s), we do see around 10% of connections to both short and medium peers.

Peers Who Participate in Block Propagation. Given this high level of churn, looking at *all* connections would be significantly biased by the many short connections. Thus, we focus more narrowly on the peers who actually affect information propagation in the Ethereum network: those peers who propagate blocks to our client, called useful peers.

We plot the count of useful peers in Fig. 6, plotting the number of peers who inform our client of different types of blocks each hour over the course of the run. We can observe around 400 unique peers per hour (and around 1,000–2,000 unique peers per day, not shown) who announce relevant blocks.

We dig deeper into the behavior of different peers by comparing the connection lengths of three groups of peers: all peers, useful peers, and first announcers (those peers who are the first to announce a block to us mined by the top 15 miners). In Fig. 6 we compare connection lengths and number of days we observe these peers. We see a clear distinction between all peers and those announcing blocks to us, where the latter tends to have longer connections and show up more

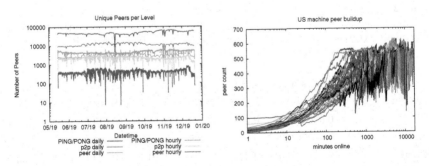

Fig. 4. *Left*: the number of unique peers we PING/PONG, start a TCP connection with, and establish a full connection with per hour and day. *Right*: Peer count per minutes online, a line for each run of the *longitudinal experiment* client, showing significant churn even after we fully join the network.

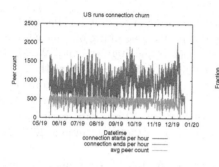
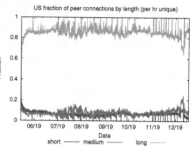

Fig. 5. *Left*: the hourly number of peer connections that we start/end (similar counts), and our average number of peers. *Right*: unique connections per hour by length: short (<10s), medium (10–1000) and long (>1000s). Both figures together show how the majority of the churn (short connections) are due to a minority of our peers.

days. There is an increase around 1,000 s for average peer online times which correspond to many ENODEIDs coming from a few IPs (making up about 30% of the announcing ENODEIDs) who are online only once for about 1,000 s[8]. Finally, the "spike" at 15 s in all connection lengths comes from over 5,000 ENODEIDs mostly from a single IP in China which reconnects many times; it disappears when we normalize by IP in the middle graph.

Peer Location. Next we examine the physical location of peers by using the geolite2 and ip2geotools tools to map IP addresses to continents. In Table 2, we take a closer look at where the peers our client connects to are located. We list all P2P nodes we connect to, all Ethereum peers and all useful peers across the entire run. To observe a snapshot as well, we also include the useful peers from a single 24-hour snapshot in 2019 and another in 2020. Generally the majority of our peers are in Asia, Europe and North America, with useful peers skewing more towards North America and P2P peers coming primarily from Asia.

Table 2. Fraction of peers (by unique IP address) across continents for all P2P connections, all Ethereum peer connections, and all useful peers across the entire *longitudinal experiment*. Also included are the useful peers from two 24 h periods 1 year apart (05/20/2019 and 05/20/2020).

Data set	Fraction of peers in locations							
	Africa	Asia	Europe	N.Amer	Oceania	S.Amer	Unkn	Count
P2P	0.0060	0.472	0.232	0.255	0.0148	0.0144	0.004	138,107
Ethereum	0.0057	0.348	0.283	0.329	0.0173	0.0108	0.006	55,091
useful	0.0014	0.315	0.262	0.398	0.0139	0.0049	0.004	22,982
2019-useful-24 hr	0.0010	0.289	0.286	0.409	0.0093	0.0046	0.0009	1,079
2020-useful-24 hr	0.0037	0.273	0.249	0.459	0.0129	0.0025	0.0006	1,632

---

[8] Mostly Coinbase nodes who appear to be routinely generating a fresh ENODEID.

4.4   Internet Location

Finally, we explore the effect of the network geographical position on how peer connections are made and how blocks are propagated. We discuss the highlights of our findings in Table 3. We first look at the location of the peer who told our *longitudinal experiment* client about each block first. We see that our client primarily first heard blocks from peers in North America, with Europe and Asia closely following. However, it is unclear the extent to which this is due to the fact that our client in the *longitudinal experiment* was located in North America.

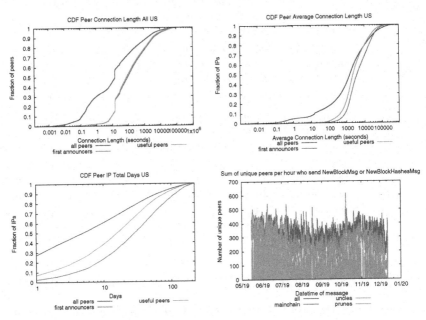

Fig. 6. *Top left*: Cumulative distribution of all connection lengths for peers. *Top right*: Average connection length when grouping peers by IP. *Bottom left*: Total number of days our client observes peers active. *Bottom right*: Number of unique peers who announce blocks to us per hour for each kind of block and total unique per hour.

To explore this, we turn to examine the *multiple vantage point experiment* run, where we also run clients in parallel in Seoul and Frankfurt. We look at the fraction of where the first announcement for *all* blocks are received from by continent, and also filter for just the blocks that machine was the *first* to hear about (i.e. before the other two locations)

We can immediately observe that all three of our clients primarily hear about new blocks from peers on the same continent where they are located, and this effect is particularly strong when they are the first to hear about a block: our U.S. client hears about new blocks for the first time from a North America peer 81% of the time; our Seoul client hears about blocks first from an Asia peer 90% of the time; and our Frankfurt nodes hears about blocks first from a Europe peer 90% of the time. Additionally in the full version of this paper [28] we see some

Table 3. For each experiment and machine, we look at when the node first heard about a block and the location of the peer who told us about the block. For the *multiple vantage point experiment* and *information propagation experiment*, we distinguish when each location was the first to hear about a block.

	Runs	Node	AF	AS	EU	NA	OC	SA	total	fraction
					Peer Location					
All Blocks	*longitudinal*	Virginia	2e−5	0.099	0.158	0.742	9e−4	5e−5	393,276	
	multiple vantage	Virginia	0	0.0679	0.205	0.727	0.000432	5e−5	39,345	
		Seoul	0	0.632	0.101	0.264	4e−3	3e−5	39,345	
		Frankfurt	0	0.0523	0.849	0.0989	3e−5	0	39,345	
	info prop	Virginia	4e−5	0.0469	0.118	0.834	2e−4	0	69,199	
		Seoul	3e−4	0.766	0.048	0.182	0.0038	4e−5	69,199	
		Frankfurt	1e−4	0.103	0.788	0.109	6e−5	3e−5	69,199	
		São Paulo	2e−4	0.153	0.364	0.481	0.001	4e−4	69,199	
		Sydney	9e−5	0.550	0.1006	0.346	0.0045	7e−5	69,199	
First to Hear	*multiple vantage*	Virginia	0	0.0485	0.143	0.808	2e−4	2e−4	12,244	0.311
		Seoul	0	0.897	0.00569	0.0972	2e−4	0	12,474	0.317
		Frankfurt	0	0.0144	0.896	0.0891	0	0	14,627	0.372
	info prop	Virginia	0	0.011	0.0548	0.935	0	0	5,926	0.086
		Seoul	2e−4	0.797	5e−4	0.199	0.0028	0	33,180	0.479
		Frankfurt	4e−5	0.0418	0.905	0.0532	0	0	27,888	0.403
		São Paulo	0	0.465	0.222	0.313	0	0	243	0.003
		Sydney	5e−4	0.808	0	0.188	0.0041	0	1,962	0.028

evidence that the location of our machine effects the duration of it's connection to peers.

To determine which of our thle nodes heard about blocks first *overall* we ensure all of our clients are synced to local timeservers using NTP. All three clients "win" roughly one-third of the time.

The results thus far suggest that the majority of peers are located in North America, Europe, and Asia (this observation is consistent with the peer information posted on ethernodes.org as well) and that may also be where mining is centered (i.e. where blocks are originating from). Thus, we wanted to run an additional run with clients located *far away* from the majority of the network to see how they perceive the network. To do so, we use the *information propagation experiment* runs (which occurred about 1 year after the *multiple vantage point experiment* runs), where we now include additional nodes in Sydney and São Paulo. As before, we observe that the North America, Asia, and European clients all typically hear about blocks first from peers on their continent. However, when we examine the new vantage points, we observe that the São Paulo client receives most of its blocks first from Asia, followed by North America then Europe; the Sydney client receives the vast majority of its blocks first from Asia.

We also examine whether any of our clients are the first to tell one of the other clients about a block. We observe that though it does happen (especially from Frankfurt/US/Seoul to São Paulo and Sydney), it is a small fraction of the 69K blocks mined during these runs. For example, in the *multiple vantage point experiment*, our Seoul client is the first to inform the Virginia client, and Frankfurt is the first to inform the Seoul client about a block first *just once*, while the Virginia client tells the Seoul client about 6 blocks first.

As a final analysis, we examine how "quickly" information in the Ethereum network propagates to our different clients. See the full version of this paper [28] for the plots of propagation time for `mainchain` blocks in both sets of runs. Looking at the *multiple vantage point experiment*, the difference from when the first and second machines hear about a block is less than 100 ms for 85% of the blocks, and about 50 ms for 50% of the blocks. However, looking at the *information propagation experiment*, we can see that the Sydney and São Paulo clients are at a clear disadvantage, with a much longer and fatter tail of incoming messages. We can see this even further in the final column of Table 3, where we see that the São Paulo client and the Sydney client are the first *overall* to hear about blocks only 0.3% and 2.8% of the time, respectively.

5   Discussion

We set out to better understand the structure of the network that powers Ethereum. How this network operates has implications both on the security of the underlying blockchain (e.g. the immutability of the blockchain) and on the experience of users who need access to the blockchain in order to interact with it (e.g. send/hear about transactions). Prior measurement work on Ethereum has focused primarily on information stored on the blockchain or on the peer discovery protocol of Ethereum. The main novelty of this work is on bridging both observations of peer connectivity behavior with the block information the peer provides.

In our *longitudinal experiment* spanning 7 months, we observe a small fraction of the nodes we connect with actually passing all the handshake checks and becoming full peers. We were able to start a TCP connection with 194,608 nodes but only ended up successfully peering with 46% of them (Table 1). Moreover, we found significant churn in the network, with more than 45% of those peers only staying connected for up to 10 s per connection (Fig. 6). Additionally we found that not all of those peers actually tell us about blocks, only about 27% of our peers are `useful`, but they tend to stay connected for much longer time than the non-`useful` ones. Maintaining longer connections with nodes than previous work allowed us to capture propagation behavior of our peers which revealed how few of the nodes we connected to participate in block propagation. Furthermore, while examining the unexpected behavior of peers, we were unable to discover the motivation for the common practice of connecting sporadically for very short periods of time.

In the *longitudinal experiment* we were also able to examine miner behavior. Unsurprisingly we find a small subset of mining ids(primarily big known mining pools) mine the majority of blocks, but at varying efficiencies(i.e. differing ratios of mainchain, uncle and prune blocks). Though only about 14% of our full peers were ever first to announce a block from the top 15 miners to our client, we were unable to find any correlation between which peers are the first announcers for which pools. This is likely by design (of the miners) as tracing blocks back to miners would put them at risk for targeted attacks. Though we do find that first announcers do maintain longer connections than even the useful peers.

In order to connect the behavior of peers to the speed with which information propagates through Ethereum's peer-to-peer network, we looked at how long it takes for our peers to tell us about a block after it is mined (Fig. 3). Though the propagation delay distribution peaks at around 20 ms, prunes and uncles have a longer and heavier tail. This corresponds to mainchain blocks winning block races. Looking deeper into the tail end of the propagation distribution we do find a variety of odd behavior for all blocks. It is often the case that blocks continue to be announced to us by new peers for hours after the first announcement, and even after we have announced the same block to those peers. It is difficult to speculate whether this behavior is malicious or from slow machines/connections. Protocol changes to filter this behavior could thus inadvertently penalize clients with slow connections or hardware who may be trying to honestly participate in the network. We find additional odd behavior with the majority of prune blocks being advertised as having block numbers vastly deviating from the mainchain height, and being advertised by just a handful of peers. As these are sent mostly as new hash announcements (and not the full block), they are likely cheap spamming behavior and should potentially be filtered by the protocol.

Lastly, by running nodes in several parts of the world, we found that the location of the node has an effect on when it hears about blocks first and where it hears them from. Moreover, miners do appear to stand to gain an advantage by operating out of specific locations that hear about blocks sooner. Our work suggests that there may be significant locations at a disadvantage, so the extent of this should be further studied and its implications on the decentralization of the network. A finer appraisal of delay can also be done by observing transaction traffic, as there are significantly more transactions flowing through the network than blocks. Though it is known that transactions can impact consensus [10], actually linking them to miner behavior is significantly more challenging than blocks as blocks must originate from the miner but transactions can generally come from any user in the network. Additionally we believe that understanding the sporadic behavior of peers and the behavior of those peers not involved in block propagation is key to understanding the health of Ethereum's P2P network and should be a focus for future work. Previous work on Eclipsing attacks on both Ethereum and Bitcoin networks have shown how high churn in the network aids an adversary in their attack [21, 22, 30]. Extending connection timeouts to avoid early disconnects is a counter measure they prose, and based on our observations could aid in preventing a portion of our disconnects. Though the experiments we run are resource intensive (e.g. memory and bandwidth to maintain many connections), they can be extended to any P2P network of other cryptocurrencies, changing only the peer cap limit to be sufficient to hit a representative portion of the network. As such, comparing our results to the behavior of other networks would be illuminating.

References

1. Ethash. https://github.com/ethereum/wiki/wiki/Mining#ethash-dag
2. Ethereum wire protocol (eth). https://github.com/ethereum/devp2p/blob/master/caps/eth.md
3. Measuring ethereum nodes. https://medium.com/coinmonks/measuring-ethereum-nodes-530bfff08e9c
4. Node discovery protocol. https://github.com/ethereum/devp2p/blob/master/discv4.md
5. The rlpx transport protocol. https://github.com/ethereum/devp2p/blob/master/rlpx.md
6. Ethereum market capitalization (2020). https://coinmarketcap.com/currencies/ethereum/
7. Ethereum node explorer. ethernodes.org (2020)
8. Anderson, L., Holz, R., Ponomarev, A., Rimba, P., Weber, I.: New kids on the block: an analysis of modern blockchains. arXiv preprint arXiv:1606.06530 (2016)
9. Bartoletti, M., Carta, S., Cimoli, T., Saia, R.: Dissecting Ponzi schemes on ethereum: identification, analysis, and impact. Future Gener. Comput. Syst. **102**, 259–277 (2020)
10. Daian, P., et al.: Flash boys 2.0: frontrunning, transaction reordering, and consensus instability in decentralized exchanges. arXiv preprint arXiv:1904.05234 (2019)
11. Decker, C., Wattenhofer, R.: Information propagation in the bitcoin network. In: IEEE P2P 2013 Proceedings, pp. 1–10. IEEE (2013)
12. Donet Donet, J.A., Pérez-Solà, C., Herrera-Joancomartí, J.: The bitcoin P2P network. In: Böhme, R., Brenner, M., Moore, T., Smith, M. (eds.) FC 2014. LNCS, vol. 8438, pp. 87–102. Springer, Heidelberg (2014). https://doi.org/10.1007/978-3-662-44774-1_7
13. El Ioini, N., Pahl, C., Helmer, S.: A decision framework for blockchain platforms for IoT and edge computing. In: SCITEPRESS (2018)
14. Gao, Y., Shi, J., Wang, X., Tan, Q., Zhao, C., Yin, Z.: Topology measurement and analysis on ethereum P2P network. In: 2019 IEEE Symposium on Computers and Communications (ISCC), pp. 1–7. IEEE (2019)
15. Gencer, A.E., Basu, S., Eyal, I., van Renesse, R., Sirer, E.G.: Decentralization in bitcoin and ethereum networks. In: Meiklejohn, S., Sako, K. (eds.) FC 2018. LNCS, vol. 10957, pp. 439–457. Springer, Heidelberg (2018). https://doi.org/10.1007/978-3-662-58387-6_24
16. Gervais, A., Karame, G.O., Wüst, K., Glykantzis, V., Ritzdorf, H., Capkun, S.: On the security and performance of proof of work blockchains. In: Proceedings of the 2016 ACM SIGSAC Conference on Computer and Communications Security, pp. 3–16. ACM (2016)
17. Gervais, A., Ritzdorf, H., Karame, G.O., Capkun, S.: Tampering with the delivery of blocks and transactions in bitcoin. In: Proceedings of the 22nd ACM SIGSAC Conference on Computer and Communications Security, pp. 692–705 (2015)
18. go-ethereum client. https://github.com/ethereum/go-ethereum

19. Greene, R., Johnstone, M.N.: An investigation into a denial of service attack on an ethereum network. In: Proceedings of the 16th Australian Information Security Management Conference, p. 90 (2018)
20. E. E. Group. Networking: Dev P2P, RPLx, Discovery, and Eth wire protocol: via zoom: https://www.youtube.com/watch?v=hnw59hmk6rk
21. Heilman, E., Kendler, A., Zohar, A., Goldberg, S.: Eclipse attacks on bitcoin's peer-to-peer network. In: 24th {USENIX} Security Symposium ({USENIX} Security 15), pp. 129–144 (2015)
22. Henningsen, S., Teunis, D., Florian, M., Scheuermann, B.: Eclipsing ethereum peers with false friends. In: 2019 IEEE European Symposium on Security and Privacy Workshops (EuroS&PW), pp. 300–309. IEEE (2019)
23. Holotescu, C., et al.: Understanding blockchain opportunities and challenges. In: Conference Proceedings of «eLearning and Software for Education (eLSE)», vol. 4, pp. 275–283 (2018). "Carol I" National Defence University Publishing House
24. Imamura, M., Omote, K.: Difficulty of decentralized structure due to rational user behavior on blockchain. In: Liu, J.K., Huang, X. (eds.) NSS 2019. LNCS, vol. 11928, pp. 504–519. Springer, Cham (2019). https://doi.org/10.1007/978-3-030-36938-5_31
25. Imtiaz, M.A., Starobinski, D., Trachtenberg, A., Younis, N.: Churn in the bitcoin network: characterization and impact. In: 2019 IEEE International Conference on Blockchain and Cryptocurrency (ICBC), pp. 431–439. IEEE (2019)
26. Kiffer, L., Levin, D., Mislove, A.: Stick a fork in it: analyzing the ethereum network partition. In: Proceedings of the 16th ACM Workshop on Hot Topics in Networks, pp. 94–100 (2017)
27. Kiffer, L., Levin, D., Mislove, A.: Analyzing ethereum's contract topology. In: Proceedings of the Internet Measurement Conference, vol. 2018, pp. 494–499 (2018)
28. Kiffer, L., Salman, A., Levin, D., Mislove, A., Nita-Rotaru, C.: Under the hood of the ethereum gossip protocol. https://fc21.ifca.ai/papers/203.pdf
29. Kim, S.K., Ma, Z., Murali, S., Mason, J., Miller, A., Bailey, M.: Measuring ethereum network peers. In: Proceedings of the Internet Measurement Conference, vol. 2018, pp. 91–104 (2018)
30. Marcus, Y., Heilman, E., Goldberg, S.: Low-resource eclipse attacks on ethereum's peer-to-peer network. IACR Cryptol. ePrint Arch. **2018**, 236 (2018)
31. Mariem, S.B., Casas, P., Romiti, M., Donnet, B., Stütz, R., Haslhofer, B.: All that glitters is not bitcoin-unveiling the centralized nature of the BTC (IP) network. In: NOMS 2020–2020 IEEE/IFIP Network Operations and Management Symposium, pp. 1–9. IEEE (2020)
32. Nakamoto, S.: Bitcoin: a peer-to-peer electronic cash system. Technical report (2008)
33. Victor, F., Lüders, B.K.: Measuring ethereum-based ERC20 token networks. In: Goldberg, I., Moore, T. (eds.) FC 2019. LNCS, vol. 11598, pp. 113–129. Springer, Cham (2019). https://doi.org/10.1007/978-3-030-32101-7_8
34. Wood, G., et al.: Ethereum: a secure decentralised generalised transaction ledger. Ethereum Project Yellow Paper **151**(2014), 1–32 (2014)

Liquidations: DeFi on a Knife-Edge

Daniel Perez[1]([✉]), Sam M. Werner[1], Jiahua Xu[2,4], and Benjamin Livshits[1,2,3]

[1] Imperial College London, London, UK
daniel.perez@imperial.ac.uk
[2] University College London, Centre for Blockchain Technologies, London, UK
[3] Brave Software, San Francisco, USA
[4] École polytechnique fédérale de Lausanne, Lausanne, Switzerland

Abstract. The trustless nature of permissionless blockchains renders overcollateralization a key safety component relied upon by decentralized finance (DeFi) protocols. Nonetheless, factors such as price volatility may undermine this mechanism. In order to protect protocols from suffering losses, undercollateralized positions can be *liquidated*. In this paper, we present the first in-depth empirical analysis of liquidations on protocols for loanable funds (PLFs). We examine Compound, one of the most widely used PLFs, for a period starting from its conception to September 2020. We analyze participants' behavior and risk-appetite in particular, to elucidate recent developments in the dynamics of the protocol. Furthermore, we assess how this has changed with a modification in Compound's incentive structure and show that variations of only 3% in an asset's dollar price can result in over 10 m USD becoming liquidable. To further understand the implications of this, we investigate the efficiency of liquidators. We find that liquidators' efficiency has improved significantly over time, with currently over 70% of liquidable positions being immediately liquidated. Lastly, we provide a discussion on how a false sense of security fostered by a misconception of the stability of non-custodial stablecoins, increases the overall liquidation risk faced by Compound participants.

1 Introduction

Decentralized Finance (DeFi) refers to a peer-to-peer, permissionless blockchain-based ecosystem that utilizes the integrity of smart contracts for the advancement and disintermediation of traditional financial primitives [25]. One of the most prominent DeFi applications on the Ethereum blockchain [27] are protocols for loanable funds (PLFs) [13]. On PLFs, markets for loanable funds are established via smart contracts that facilitate borrowing and lending [28]. In the absence of strong identities on Ethereum, creditor protection tends to be ensured through overcollateralization, whereby a borrower must provide collateral worth more than the value of the borrowed amount. In the case where the value of the collateral-to-borrow ratio drops below some liquidation threshold, a borrower defaults on his position and the supplied collateral is sold off at a discount to cover the debt in a process referred to as *liquidation*. However, little is known

© International Financial Cryptography Association 2021
N. Borisov and C. Diaz (Eds.): FC 2021, LNCS 12675, pp. 457–476, 2021.
https://doi.org/10.1007/978-3-662-64331-0_24

about the behavior of agents towards liquidation risk on a PLF. Furthermore, despite liquidators playing a critical role in the DeFi ecosystem, the efficiency with which they liquidate positions has not yet been thoroughly analyzed.

In this paper, we first lay out a framework for quantifying the state of a generic PLF and its markets over time. We subsequently instantiate this framework to all markets on Compound [17], one of the largest PLFs in terms of locked funds. We analyze how liquidation risk has changed over time, specifically after the launch of Compound's governance token. Furthermore, we seek to quantify this liquidation risk through a price sensitivity analysis. In a discussion, we elaborate on how the interdependence of different DeFi protocols can result in agent behavior undermining the assumptions of the protocols' incentive structures.

Contributions. This paper makes the following contributions:

- We present an abstract framework to reason about the state of PLFs.
- We provide an open-source implementation[1] of the proposed framework for Compound, one of the largest PLFs in terms of total locked funds.
- We perform an empirical analysis on the historical data for Compound, from May 7, 2019 to September 6, 2020 and make the following observations: (i) despite increases in the number of suppliers and borrowers, the total funds locked are mostly accounted for by a small subset of participants; (ii) the introduction of Compound's governance token had protocol-wide implications as liquidation risk increased in consequence of higher risk-seeking behavior of participants; (iii) liquidators became significantly more efficient over time, liquidating over 70% of liquidable positions instantly.
- Using our findings, we demonstrate how interaction between protocols' incentive structures can directly result in unexpected risks to participants.

2   Background

In this section we introduce preliminary concepts about blockchains and smart contracts necessary to the understanding of the rest of the paper.

2.1   Blockchain

A blockchain, such as Bitcoin [19] or Ethereum [27], is in essence a decentralized append-only database. Data is added to the blockchain in the form of transactions that are grouped in blocks. Some rules are enforced by the protocols on both transactions and blocks to ensure its correct working. Blockchains need to be able to maintain consensus of which blocks are included. Both Bitcoin and Ethereum use the Proof-of-Work consensus that requires block producers, often called *miners*, to solve a computationally expensive puzzle to produce a new block [21]. An important point to note is that miners are allowed to choose which transactions to include in a block and in which order to include them. This can potentially allow miners to profit from having a transaction included before another one. This is commonly referred to as *miner-extractable value* [8].

---

[1] https://github.com/backdfund/analyzer.

2.2 Smart Contracts

Ethereum Smart Contracts. On Ethereum, smart contracts are programs written in a Turing-complete language, typically Solidity [11], that define a set of rules that may be invoked by any network participant. These programs rely on the Ethereum Virtual Machine (EVM), a low-level stack machine which executes the compiled EVM bytecode of a smart contract [27]. Each instruction has a fee measured in so-called *gas*, and the total gas cost of a transaction is a fixed base fee plus the sum of all instructions' gas [2,20]. The sender of a transaction must then set a gas price, the amount of ETH he is willing to pay per unit of gas consumed for executing the transaction. The transaction fee is thus given by the gas price multiplied with the gas cost [22,26]. Within a transaction, smart contracts can store data in logs, which are metadata specially indexed as part of the transaction. This metadata, commonly referred to as *events*, is typically used to allow users to monitor the activity of a contract externally.

Oracles. One of the major challenges smart contracts face concerns access to off-chain information, i.e. data that does not natively exist on-chain. Oracles are data feeds into smart contracts and provide a mechanism for accessing off-chain information through some third party. In DeFi, oracles are commonly used for price feed data to determine the real-time price of assets. For instance, via the Compound Open Price Feed [6], vetted third party reporters sign off on price data using a known public key, where the resulting feed can be relied upon by smart contracts.

Stablecoins. An alternative to volatile cryptoassets is given by stablecoins, which are priced against a peg and can be either custodial or non-custodial. For custodial stablecoins (e.g. USDC [4]), tokens represent a claim of some off-chain reserve asset, such as fiat currency, which has been entrusted to a custodian. Non-custodial stablecoins (e.g. DAI [18]) seek to establish price stability via economic mechanisms specified by smart contracts. For a thorough discussion on stablecoin design, we direct the reader to [15].

3 Protocols for Loanable Funds (PLF)

In this section, we introduce several concepts of Protocols for Loanable Funds (PLFs) necessary for understanding how liquidations function in DeFi on Ethereum.

3.1 Supplying and Borrowing in DeFi

In DeFi, asset supplying and borrowing is achieved via so-called *protocols for loanable funds* (PLFs) [13], where smart contracts act as trustless intermediaries of loanable funds between suppliers and borrowers in markets of different assets. Unlike traditional peer-to-peer lending, deposits are pooled and instantly available to borrowers. On a DeFi protocol, the aggregate of tokens that the PLF smart contracts hold, which equals the difference between supplied funds and borrowed funds, is termed locked funds [9].

3.2   Interest Model

Borrowers are charged interest on the debt at a floating rate determined by a market's underlying interest rate model. A small fraction of the paid interest is allocated to a pool of reserves, which is set aside in case of market illiquidity, while the remainder is paid out to suppliers of loanable funds. Interest in a given market is generally accrued through market-specific, interest-bearing derivative tokens that appreciate against the underlying asset over time. Hence, a supplier of funds receives derivative tokens in exchange for supplied liquidity, representing his share in the total value of the liquidity pool for the underlying asset. The most prominent PLFs are Compound [5] and Aave [1], with 2.5bn USD and 2.7bn USD in total funds locked respectively, at the time of writing [9].

3.3   Collateralization

Given the pseudonymity of agents in Ethereum, borrow positions need to be overcollateralized to reduce the default risk. Thereby, the borrower of an asset is required to supply collateral, where the total value of the supplied collateral exceeds the total value of the borrowed asset. Each asset is associated with a collateralization ratio, namely the minimum collateral-to-borrow ratio when the asset is used to collateralize a new borrow position. For example, in order to borrow 100 USD worth of DAI with ETH as collateral at a collateralization ratio of 125%, a borrower would have to lock 125 USD worth of ETH to collateralize the borrow position. Thus, the protocol limits monetary risk from defaulted borrow positions, as the underlying collateral of a defaulted position can be sold off to recover the debt. The inverse of the collateralization ratio is referred to as the *collateral factor*, which is the amount of a deposit that may be used as collateral. For example, if the collateralization ratio on a PLF for the market of DAI is 125%, the collateral factor would be 0.8, implying that for each $1 deposit of DAI, the supplier may borrow $0.8 worth of some other asset.

3.4   Liquidation

The process of selling a borrower's collateral to recover the debt value upon default is referred to as *liquidation*. A borrow position can be liquidated once the value of the collateral falls below some pre-determined liquidation threshold, i.e. the minimum acceptable collateral-to-borrow ratio. Any network participant may liquidate these positions by paying the debt asset to acquire the underlying collateral at a discount. Hence, liquidators are incentivized to actively monitor others' collateral-to-borrow ratios. Note that in practice, the amount of liquidable collateral that a single liquidator can purchase may be capped.

3.5   Leveraging

In finance, leverage refers to borrowed funds being used as the funding source for additional, typically more risky capital. In DeFi, leverage is the fundamental component of PLFs, as a borrower is required to first take up the role of a supplier and deposit funds which are to be used as leverage for his borrow positions, as we have just seen. The typical aim of leveraging is to generate higher returns through increased exposure to a particular investment. For example, a borrower wanting to gain increased exposure to ETH may:

1. Supply ETH on a PLF.
2. Leverage the deposited ETH to borrow DAI.
3. Sell the purchased DAI for ETH.
4. Repeat steps 1 to 3 as desired.

This behavior essentially enables users to construct so-called *leveraging spirals*, whereby a user repeatedly re-supplies borrowed funds in order to get increased exposure to some cryptoasset. However, increased exposure comes at the cost of higher downside risk, i.e., the risk of the value of the leveraged asset or borrowed asset to decrease due to changing market conditions.

3.6 Use Cases of PLFs

We present the different incentives[2] an agent may have for borrowing from and/or supplying to a PLF:

Interest Suppliers of funds are incentivized by interest which accrues on a per block basis.

Leveraged long position To take on a long position of an asset refers to purchasing an asset with the expectation that it will appreciate in value. These positions can be taken on a PLF by leveraging the asset on which the long position shall be taken.

Leveraged short position A short position refers to borrowing funds of an asset, which one believes will depreciate in value. Consequently, the taker of a short position sells the borrowed asset, only to repurchase it and pay back the borrower once the price has fallen, while profiting from the price change of the shorted asset. This can be achieved by taking on a leveraged borrow position of a stablecoin, where the locked collateral is the asset to short.

Liquidity mining As a means to attract liquidity, PLFs may distribute governance tokens to their liquidity providers. The way these tokens are distributed depends on the PLF. For instance, on Compound, the governance token COMP[3] is distributed among users across markets proportionally to the total dollar value of funds borrowed and supplied. This directly incentivizes users to mine liquidity in a market through leveraging in order to receive a larger share of governance tokens. For example, a supplier of funds in market A can borrow against his position additional funds of A, at the cost of paying the difference between the earned and paid interest. The incentive for pursuing this

---

[2] Note that leverage on a PLF in DeFi may in part be motivated by tax benefits, as certain jurisdictions may not tax capital gains on borrowed funds. However, a detailed analysis of this lies outside the scope of this paper.

[3] Contract address: 0xc00e94cb662c3520282e6f5717214004a7f26888.

behaviour exists if the reward (i.e. the governance token) exceeds the cost of borrowing.

Token utility An agent may be able to obtain a token from a PLF which has some desired utility. For example, for the case of governance tokens, the desired token utility could be the right to participate in protocol governance or a claim on protocol earnings.

4   Methodology

In this section, we describe our methodology for the different analyses we perform with regard to leveraging on a PLF. To be able to quantify the extent of leveraged positions over time, we first introduce a state transition framework for tracking the supply and borrow positions across all markets on a given PLF. We then describe how we instantiate this framework on the Compound protocol using on-chain events data.

4.1   Definitions

Throughout the paper, we use the following definitions in the context of PLFs:

Market A smart contract acting as the intermediary of loanable funds for a particular cryptoasset, where users supply and borrow funds.

Supply Funds deposited to a market that can be loaned out to other users and used as collateral against depositors' own borrow positions.

Borrow Funds loaned out to users of a market.

Collateral Funds available to back a user's aggregate borrow positions.

Locked funds Funds remaining in the PLF smart contracts, equal to the difference between supplied and borrowed funds.

Supplier A user who deposits funds to a market.

Borrower A user who borrows funds from a market. Since a borrow position must be collateralized by deposited funds, a borrower must also be a supplier.

Liquidator A user who purchases a borrower's supply in a market when the borrower's collateral-to-borrow ratio falls below some threshold.

4.2   States on a PLF

In this section, we provide a formal definition of the state of a PLF. We denote $\mathfrak{P}_t$ as the global state of a PLF at time t. For brevity, in the following definitions, we assume that all the values are at a given time t. We define the global state for the PLF as

$$\mathfrak{P} = (\mathcal{M}, \Gamma, \mathcal{P}, \Lambda)$$

where $\mathcal{M}$ is the set of states of individual markets, Γ is the price the Oracle used, $\mathcal{P}$ is the set of states of individual participants and $\Lambda \in (0, 1)$ is the close factor of the protocol, which specifies the upper bound on the amount of collateral a liquidator may purchase.

We define the state of an individual market $m \in \mathcal{M}$ as

$$m = (\mathcal{I}, \mathcal{B}, \mathcal{S}, \mathcal{C})$$

where $\mathcal{I}$ is the market's interest rate model, $\mathcal{B}$ is the total borrows, $\mathcal{S}$ is the total supply of deposits, and $\mathcal{C}$ is the collateral factor.

$\mathcal{P}^m$ is the state of all participants in market m and the positions of a participant P in this market is defined as

$$P^m = (B^m, S^m)$$

where B^m and S^m are respectively the total borrow positions and total supplied deposits of a market participant in market m.

For a given market m, the total deposits supplied $\mathcal{S}^m$ is thus given by:

$$\mathcal{S}^m = \sum_{P^m \in \mathcal{P}^m} S^m \tag{1}$$

Similarly, the market's total borrows $\mathcal{B}^m$ is given by:

$$\mathcal{B}^m = \sum_{P^m \in \mathcal{P}^m} B^m \tag{2}$$

The state of a participant P is liquidable if the following holds:

$$\frac{\sum_{m \in \mathcal{M}} \left\{ [S^m \cdot \mathcal{C} + \mathcal{I}(S^m)] \cdot \Gamma(m) \cdot \mathcal{K}^m \right\}}{\sum_{m \in \mathcal{M}} \left\{ [B^m + \mathcal{I}(B^m)] \cdot \Gamma(m) \right\}} < 1 \tag{3}$$

where $\Gamma(m)$ returns the price of the underlying asset denominated in a predefined numéraire (e.g. USD), $\mathcal{I}(S^m)$ returns the interest earned with supply S^m, $\mathcal{I}(B^m)$ returns the interest accrued with borrow B^m, and $\mathcal{K}^m \leq 1$ denotes the liquidation threshold of market m. In Compound, liquidation threshold $\mathcal{K}^m$ is set to be constant at 100% protocol-wide, whereas with other protocols such as Aave, $\mathcal{K}^m$ is specific to the collateral asset from market m, and can be dynamically adjusted when the risk level of the asset changes.

The transition from a state of a market m from time t to $t + 1$ is given by some state transition σ, such that $m_t \xrightarrow{\sigma} m_{t+1}$.

4.3   Leveraging Spirals on a PLF

Here we examine the workings of leveraging in DeFi using a PLF. We assume a speculator on some volatile asset B, holds initial capital α in B. In order to increase his exposure to B, the speculator may borrow a stable asset A against his α on a PLF at a collateralization ratio $\delta > 1$. For simplicity, we shall assume in this illustrative example that a speculator will leverage his position on the same PLF. Note that the cost of borrowing is given by some floating interest rate γ for the specific asset market. In return for his collateral, the borrower receives $\frac{\alpha}{\delta}$ in the volatile asset B. As the debt is denominated in units of a stable asset (e.g. DAI), the borrower has an upper limit on his net debt, remaining unaffected by any volatility in the value of asset A. In order to leverage his position, the debt denominated in A may be used to buy[4] additional units of asset B, which can subsequently be used to collateralize a new borrow position. This process is illustrated in Fig. 1 and can be repeated numerous times, by which the total exposure to asset A, the underlying collateral to the total debt in asset A, increases at a decaying rate.

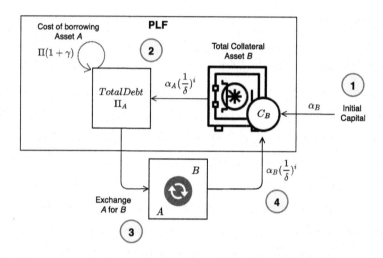

Fig. 1. The steps of leveraging using a PLF. **1.** Initial capital α_B in asset B is deposited as collateral to borrow asset A. **2.** Interest accrues over the debt of the borrow position for asset B. **3.** The borrowed asset A is sold for asset B on the open market. **4.** The newly purchased units of asset B are locked as collateral for a new borrow position of asset A.

The total collateral C a borrower must post through a borrow position with a leverage factor k, a collateralization ratio δ and an initial capital amount α can be expressed as $\sum_{i=0}^{k} \frac{\alpha}{\delta^i}$. Hence, the total debt Π for the corresponding borrow position is:

$$\Pi = \left(\sum_{i=1}^{k} \frac{\alpha}{\delta^i} \right) \cdot (1 + \gamma) \tag{4}$$

where γ is the interest rate. Note that Eq. (4) assumes a borrower uses the same collateralization ratio δ for his positions, as well as that all debt is taken out for the same asset on the same PLF and hence the floating interest rate is shared across all borrow positions.

---

[4] In practice this may be done via automated market makers [29] (e.g. Uniswap [23]) or via decentralized exchanges [10].

Event	Description	State variables affected
Borrow	A new borrow position is created.	$\mathcal{B}$
Mint	cTokens are minted for new deposits.	$\mathcal{S}$
RepayBorrow	A borrow position is partially/fully repaid.	$\mathcal{B}$
LiquidateBorrow	A borrow position is liquidated.	$\mathcal{B}, \mathcal{S}$
Redeem	cTokens are used to redeem deposits of the underlying asset.	$\mathcal{S}$
NewCollateralFactor	The collateral factor for the associated market is updated.	$\mathcal{C}$
AccrueInterest	Interest has accrued for the associated market and its borrow index is updated.	$\mathcal{B}$
NewInterestRateModel	The interest rate model for the associated market is updated.	$\mathcal{I}$
NewInterestParams	The parameters of the interest rate model for the associated market are updated.	$\mathcal{I}$
NewCloseFactor	The close factor is updated.	Λ

Fig. 2. The events emitted by the Compound protocol smart contracts used for initiating state transitions and the states affected by each event.

4.4   States and the Compound PLF

For our analysis, we apply our state transition framework to the Compound PLF. Therefore, we briefly present the workings of Compound in the context of our framework.

State Transitions. We initiate state transitions via events emitted from the Compound protocol smart contracts. We provide an overview of the state variables affected by Compound events in Fig. 2.

Funds Supplied. Every market on Compound has an associated "cToken", a token that continuously appreciates against the underlying asset as interest accrues. For every deposit in a market, a newly-minted amount of the market's associated cToken is transferred to the depositor. Therefore, rather than tracking the total amount of the underlying asset supplied, we account the total deposits of an asset supplied by a market participant in the market's cTokens. Likewise, we account the total supply of deposits in the market in cTokens.

Funds Borrowed. A borrower on Compound must use cTokens as collateral for his borrow position. The borrowing capacity equals the current value of the supply multiplied by the collateral factor for the asset. For example, given an exchange rate of 1 DAI = 50 cDAI, a collateral factor of 0.75 for DAI and a price of 1 DAI = 1 USD, a holder of 500 cDAI (10 DAI) would be permitted to borrow up to 7.5 USD worth of some other asset on Compound. Therefore, as funds are borrowed, an individual's total borrow position, as well as the respective market's total borrows are updated.

Interest. The accrual of interest is tracked per market via a borrow index, which corresponds to the total interest accrued in the market. The borrow index of a market is also used to determine and update the total debt of a borrower in the respective market. When funds are borrowed, the current borrow index for the market is stored with the borrow position. When additional funds are borrowed

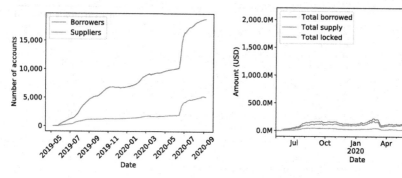

(a) Number of suppliers and borrowers.

(b) Amount of funds supplied, borrowed and locked.

Fig. 3. Number of active accounts and amount of funds on Compound over time.

or repaid, the latest borrow index is used to compute the difference of accrued interest since the last borrow and added to the total debt.

Liquidation. A borrower on Compound is eligible for liquidation should his total supply of collateral, i.e. the value of the sum of the borrower's cToken holdings per market, weighted by each market's collateral factor, be less than the value of the borrower's aggregate debt (Eq. (3)). The maximum amount of debt a liquidator may pay back in exchange for collateral is specified by the close factor of a market.

5   Analysis

In this section, we present the results of the analysis performed with the framework outlined in Sect. 4. We analyze data from the Compound protocol [17] over a period ranging from May 7, 2019—when the first Compound markets were deployed on the Ethereum main network—to September 6, 2020. The full list of contracts considered for our analysis can be found in Appendix A. When analyzing a single market, we choose the market for DAI, as it is the largest by an order of magnitude.

5.1   Borrowers and Suppliers

We first examine the total number of borrowers and suppliers on Compound by considering any Ethereum account that, at any time within the observation period, either exhibited a non-zero cToken balance or borrowed funds for any Compound market. The change in the number of borrowers and suppliers over time is displayed in Fig. 3a.

We see that the total number of suppliers always exceeds the total number of borrowers. This is because on Compound, one can only borrow against funds

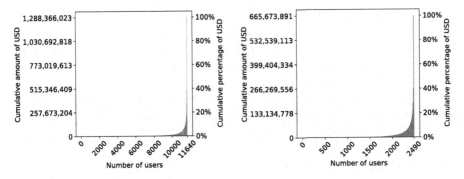

(a) Distribution of supplied funds.   (b) Distribution of borrowed funds.

Fig. 4. Cumulative distribution of funds in USD. Accounts are sorted from least to most wealthy and bucketed in bins of 10, i.e. a single bar represents the sum of 10 accounts.

he supplied as collateral, which automatically makes the borrower also a supplier. Interestingly, the number of suppliers has increased relative to the number of borrowers over time. There is notable sudden jump in both the number of suppliers and borrowers in June 2020.

In terms of total deposits, a very similar trend is observable in Fig. 3b, which shows that at the same time, the total supplied deposits increased, while the total borrows followed shortly after. Furthermore, the total funds borrowed exceeded the total funds locked for the first time in July 2020 and have remained so until the end of the examined period. We discuss the reasons behind this in the next part of this section.

Despite the similarly increasing trend for the number of suppliers/borrowers and amount of supplied/borrowed funds, we can see in Fig. 4 that the majority of funds are borrowed and supplied only by a small number of accounts. For instance, for the suppliers in Fig. 4a, the top user and top 10 users supply 27.4% and 49% of total funds, respectively. For the borrowers shown in Fig. 4b, the top user accounts for 37.1%, while the top 10 users account for 59.9% of total borrows. While one could think that this concentration comes from the fact that top accounts are pools receiving money from several participants, only one of the top 10 suppliers and none of the top 10 borrowers fit in this category. We provide a list of the top suppliers and borrowers with a description of the accounts in Figure 10 of Appendix B.

5.2 Leveraging Spirals

As we have seen in Sect. 3, in PLFs, leveraging can be used either to gain more exposure to a particular currency or to gain some incentive provided by the protocol. To understand how leveraging can affect the total amounts borrowed and supplied on Compound, we use the methodology we defined in Sect. 4.3 to measure the existence of leveraging spirals on Compound.

We find that the top supplier deposited a total of 342 million USD and borrowed 247 million. However, after the inspection of leveraging spirals, we find that the user has provided only 16% of the funds, while the rest of the minted funds have been part of leveraging spirals, which means that the user provided a total of roughly 55 million USD to the protocol.

In total, we find a total of 2,141 accounts using this leveraging spiral technique for a total of over 600 million USD, or roughly half of the total amount of funds supplied to the protocol.

5.3   The COMP Governance Token

The sudden jumps exhibited in Figs. 3a and 3b can be explained by the launch of Compound's governance token, COMP, on June 15, 2020. The COMP governance token allows holders to participate in voting, create proposals, as well as delegate voting rights. In order to empower Compound stakeholders, new COMP is minted every block and distributed among borrowers and suppliers in each market.

Initially, COMP was allocated proportionally to the accrued interest per market. However, the COMP distribution model was modified via a governance vote on July 2, 2020, such that the borrowing interest rate was removed as a weighting mechanism in favor of distributing COMP per market on a borrowing demand basis, i.e. per USD borrowed. The distributed COMP per market is shared equally between a market's borrowers and suppliers, who receive COMP proportionally to their borrowed and supplied amounts, respectively. Hence, a Compound user is incentivized to increase his borrow position as long as the borrowing cost does not exceed the value of his COMP earnings. This presumably explains the drop in the degree of collateralization, as the total amount locked is seen surpassed by the total borrows after the COMP launch (Fig. 3b), leading to elevated liquidation risk of borrow positions.

5.4   Liquidation Risk

Given the high increase in the number of total funds borrowed and supplied, as well as the decrease in liquidity relative to total borrows, we seek to identify and quantify any changes in liquidation risk on Compound since the launch of COMP. Figure 5 shows the total USD value of collateral on Compound and how close collateral amounts are from liquidation. In addition to the substantial increase in the total value of collateral on Compound since the launch of COMP, the risk-seeking behavior of users has also changed. This can be seen by examining collateral to borrow ratios, where since beginning of July, 2020, a total of approximately 350 m to 600 m USD worth of collateral has been within a 5% price range of becoming liquidable. However, it should be noted that the likelihood of the amount of this collateral becoming liquidable highly depends on the price volatility of the collateral asset.

In order to examine how liquidation risk differs across markets, we measure for the largest market on Compound, namely DAI, the sensitivity of collateral becoming liquidable given a decrease in the price of DAI. Figure 6 shows the

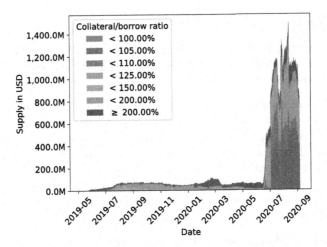

Fig. 5. Collateral locked over time, showing how close the amounts are from being liquidated. Positions can be liquidated when the ratio drops below 100%.

amount of aggregate collateral liquidable at the historic price, as well as at a 3% and 5% decrease relative to the historic price for DAI. We mark the date on which the COMP governance token launched with a dashed line. It can be seen that since the launch of COMP, 3% and 5% price decreases of DAI relative to its peg USD would have resulted in a substantially higher amount of liquidable collateral. In particular, a 3% decrease would have turned collateral worth in excess of 10 million USD liquidable.

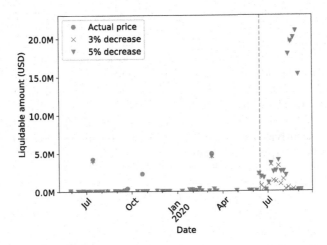

Fig. 6. Sensitivity analysis of the liquidable collateral amount given DAI price movement relative to its peg USD. COMP launch date is marked by the dashed vertical line.

5.5   Liquidations and Liquidators

In order to better understand the implications of the increased liquidation risk since the launch of COMP, we examine historical liquidations on Compound and subsequently measure the efficiency of liquidators.

Historical Liquidations. The increased risk-seeking behavior suggested by the low collateral to borrow ratios presented in the previous section are in accordance with the trend of rising amount of liquidated collateral since the introduction of COMP. The total value of collateral liquidated on Compound over time is shown in Fig. 7. It can be seen that the majority of this collateral was liquidated on a few occasions, perhaps most notably on Black Thursday (March 12, 2020), July 29, 2020 (DAI deviating from its peg significantly), and in early September 2020 (ETH price drop).

Liquidation Efficiency. We measure the efficiency of liquidators as the number of blocks elapsed since a borrow position has become liquidable and the position actually being liquidated. The overall historical efficiency of liquidators is shown as a cumulative distribution function in Fig. 8, from which it can be seen that approximately 60% of the total liquidated collateral (35 million USD) was liquidated within the same block as it became liquidable, suggesting that the majority of liquidations occur via bots in a highly efficient fashion. After 2 blocks have elapsed (on average half a minute), 85% of liquidable collateral has been liquidated, and after 16 blocks this value amounts to 95%.

It is worth noting that liquidation efficiency has been skewed by the more recent liquidation activities which were of a much larger scale than when the protocol was first launched. Specifically, in 2019, only about 26% of the liquidations occurred in the block during which the position became liquidable, compared to 70% in 2020. This resulted in some lost opportunities for liquidators as shown in Fig. 6. The account 0xd062eeb318295a09d4262135ef0092979552afe6, for instance, had more than 3,000,000 USD worth of ETH as collateral exposed at block 8,796,900 for the duration of a single block: the account was roughly 20 USD shy of the liquidation threshold but eventually escaped liquidation. If a liquidator had captured this opportunity, he could have bought half of this collateral (given the close factor of 0.5), at a 10% discount, resulting in a profit of 150,000 USD for a single transaction. It is clear that with such stakes, participants were incentivized to improve liquidation techniques, resulting in a high level of liquidation speed and scale.

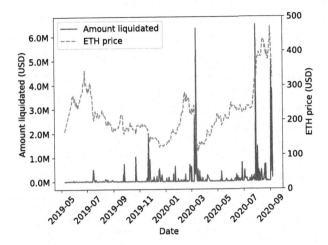

Fig. 7. Amount (in USD) of liquidated collateral from May 2019 to August 2020.

5.6 Summary

In this section, we have analyzed the Compound protocol with a focus on liquidations. We have found that despite the increase in number of suppliers and borrowers over time, the total amount of funds supplied and borrowed remain extremely concentrated among a small set of participants.

We have also seen that the introduction of the COMP governance token has changed how users interact with the protocol and the amount of risk that they are willing to take. Users now borrow vastly more than before, with the total amount borrowed surpassing the total amount locked. Due to excessive borrowing without a sufficiently safe amount of supplied funds, borrow positions now face a higher liquidation risk, such that a crash of 3% in the price of DAI could result in an aggregate liquidation value of over 10 million USD.

Finally, we have shown that the liquidators have become more efficient with time, and are currently able to capture a majority of the liquidable funds instantly.

6 Discussion

In this section, we enumerate several points that we deem important for the future development of PLFs and DeFi protocols. We first discuss the influence of governance tokens, by intention or not, on how users behave within a protocol. Subsequently, we discuss potential risks that lie in the use of governance tokens, and the contagion effect that user behavior in a protocol can have on another protocol. Finally, we discuss how miner-extractable value [8] can potentially affect liquidation incentives in such protocols.

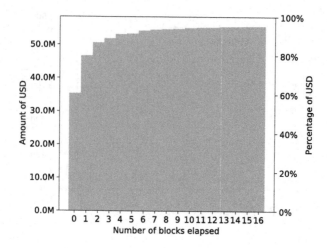

Fig. 8. Number of blocks elapsed from the time a position can be liquidated to actual liquidation on Compound from May 7, 2019 to September 6, 2020, shown as a CDF.

6.1 Governance Token Influence

As analyzed in Sect. 5, the distribution of the COMP token has vastly changed the Compound landscape and user behavior. Until the introduction of the token, borrowing was costly due to the payable interest, which implies a negative cash flow for the borrower. Therefore, a borrower would only borrow if he could justify this negative cash flow with some application external to Compound. With the introduction of this token, borrowing could yield a positive cash flow due to the monetary value of the governance token. This creates a situation where both suppliers and borrowers end up with a positive cash flow, inducing users to maximize both their supply and borrow. This model is, however, only sustainable when the price of the COMP token remains sufficiently high to keep this cash flow positive for borrowers. This directly results in users taking increasingly higher risk in an attempt to gain larger monetary rewards, with liquidators ultimately profiting more from their operations.

6.2 Governance Token Risks

The increased use of governance tokens across DeFi protocols (e.g. YFI on Yearn Finance, AAVE on Aave, UNI on Uniswap) can be seen as a promising step towards achieving a higher degree of decentralization in terms of protocol governance. However, despite the increased usage of governance tokens, to the best of our knowledge there is still a dearth of academic research examining the different governance models and specifically the relation between their security assumptions and the employed governance token. For instance, the option to aggregate governance tokens via flash loans [24] can pose a significant security risk to DeFi protocols should an attacker attempt to propose and execute malicious protocol updates. Furthermore, even in the case of flash loan resistant governance models, the relationship between the financial value of a protocol's governance token and the economically secure regions of the protocol remains unexamined and serves as a further risk that designers of governance models have to take into account. Despite the existence of protective mechanisms against governance attacks on some protocols (e.g. multi-sig approvals or selected "guardians" that are able to halt the governance process), it remains questionable which of such mechanisms are indeed desirable from a decentralized governance perspective and whether there might be more suitable alternatives.

6.3   Contagion Effects

This behavior also indirectly affected other protocols, in particular DAI. The price of DAI is aimed to be pegged to 1 USD resting on an arbitrage mechanism, whereby token holders are incentivized to buy or sell DAI as soon as the price moves below or above 1 USD, respectively. However, a rational user seeking to maximize profit will not sell his DAI if holding it somewhere else would yield higher profits. This was precisely what was happening with Compound, whose users locking their DAI received higher yields in the form of COMP, than from selling DAI at a premium, thereby resulting in upward price pressure [7]. Interestingly, DAI deviating from its peg also has a negative effect for Compound users. Indeed, as we saw in Sect. 5, many Compound users might have been overconfident about the price stability of DAI and thus only collateralize marginally above the threshold when they borrow DAI. This has resulted in large amounts being liquidated due to the actual, higher extent of the volatility in the DAI price.

6.4   Miner-Extractable Value

In the context of PLFs, liquidations can be seen as miner-extractable value. Indeed, it is easy for the miner to check whether a position is liquidable or not after each processed transaction and to add a transaction to liquidate the position immediately after the transaction making it liquidable. In our analysis of the Compound protocol, we have not found any sign of miners participating in liquidations, directly or indirectly. We show the top miners and the top liquidators for each miner in Fig. 11 of Appendix C. Although we found no correlation between miners and liquidators, this is a real risk that could make the role of liquidator, which is essential for the protocol security, less interesting for those who are not collaborating with miners.

7   Related Work

In this section we briefly discuss existing work related to this paper.

A thorough analysis of the Compound protocol with respect to market risks faced by participants was done by [14]. The authors employ agent-based modeling and simulation to perform stress tests in order to show that Compound remains safe under high volatility scenarios and high levels of outstanding debt. Furthermore, the authors demonstrate the potential of Compound to scale to accommodate a larger borrow market while maintaining a low default probability. This differs from our work as we conduct a detailed empirical analysis on Compound, focusing on how agent behavior under different incentive structures on Compound has affected the protocol's state with regard to liquidation risk.

A first in-depth analysis on PLFs is given by [13]. The authors provide a taxonomy on interest rate models employed by PLFs, while also discussing market liquidity, efficiency and interconnectedness across PLFs. As part of their analysis, the authors examine the cumulative percentage of locked funds solely for the Compound markets DAI, ETH, and USDC.

In [3], the authors provide a formal state transition model of PLFs[5] and prove fundamental behavioural properties of PLFs, which had previously only been presented informally in the literature. Additionally, the authors examine attack vectors and risks, such as utilization attacks and interest bearing derivative token risk. This work differs to our work, as the authors of [3] formalize the properties of PLFs through an abstract model, while we provide a thorough empirical analysis with a focus on liquidations and risks brought upon by governance tokens, such as for Compound and the COMP token.

In [16], the authors show how markets for stablecoins are exposed to deleveraging feedback effects, which can cause periods of illiquidity during crisis.

The authors of [12] demonstrate how various DeFi lending protocols are subject to different attack vectors such as governance attacks and undercollateralization. In the context of the proposed governance attack, the lending protocol the authors focus on is Maker [18].

8   Conclusion

In this paper, we presented the first in-depth empirical analysis of liquidations on Compound, one of the largest PLFs in terms of total locked funds, from May 7, 2019 to September 6, 2020. We analyzed agents' behavior and in particular how much risk they are willing to take within the protocol. Furthermore, we assessed how this has changed with the launch of the Compound governance token COMP, where we found that agents take notably higher risks in anticipation of higher earnings. This resulted in variations as little as 3% in an asset's price being able to turn over 10 million USD worth of collateral liquidable. In order to better understand the potential consequences, we then measured the efficiency of liquidators, namely how quickly new liquidation opportunities are captured. Liquidators' efficiency was found to have improved significantly over time, reaching 70% of instant liquidations. Lastly, we demonstrated how overconfidence in the price stability of DAI, increased the overall liquidation risk faced by Compound users. Rather ironically, many users wishing to make the most of the new incentive scheme ended up causing higher volatility in DAI—a dominant

---

[5] Note that in [3], PLFs are referred to as lending pools.

asset of the platform, resulting in liquidation of their own assets. This is not Compound's misdoing, but rather highlights the to date unknown dynamics of incentive structures across different DeFi protocols.

Appendix

Appendix is available online at https://fc21.ifca.ai/papers/144.pdf.

References

1. AAVE: AAVE (2020). https://aave.com/. Accessed 17 Aug 2020
2. Albert, E., Correas, J., Gordillo, P., Román-Díez, G., Rubio, A.: GASOL: gas analysis and optimization for ethereum smart contracts. In: TACAS 2020. LNCS, vol. 12079, pp. 118–125. Springer, Cham (2020). https://doi.org/10.1007/978-3-030-45237-7_7
3. Bartoletti, M., Chiang, J.H.Y., Lluch-Lafuente, A.: SoK: lending pools in decentralized finance. arXiv preprint arXiv:2012.13230 (2020)
4. Circle: USDC (2020). https://www.circle.com/en/usdc
5. Compound: Compound (2019). https://compound.finance/. Accessed 17 Aug 2020
6. Compound: Open price feed (2020). https://compound.finance/prices. Accessed 15 Sept 2020
7. Cyrus: Upcoming comp farming change could impact the dai peg (2020). https://forum.makerdao.com/t/upcoming-comp-farming-change-could-impact-the-dai-peg/2965. Accessed 27 Aug 2020
8. Daian, P., et al.: Flash boys 2.0: frontrunning in decentralized exchanges, miner extractable value, and consensus instability. In: 2020 IEEE Symposium on Security and Privacy (SP), pp. 910–927. IEEE (2020)
9. DeFi Pulse: How do we calculate total value locked (TVL)? (2020). https://defipulse.com/
10. dYdX: dydx (2019). https://dydx.exchange/
11. Solidity v0.8.0 documentation (2020). Accessed 12 Jan 2020
12. Gudgeon, L., Perez, D., Harz, D., Livshits, B., Gervais, A.: The decentralized financial crisis. In: Crypto Valley Conference on Blockchain Technology, pp. 1–15 (2020). https://doi.org/10.1109/CVCBT50464.2020.00005
13. Gudgeon, L., Werner, S.M., Perez, D., Knottenbelt, W.J.: DeFi protocols for loanable funds: interest rates, liquidity and market efficiency (2020)
14. Kao, H.T., Chitra, T., Chiang, R., Morrow, J.: An Analysis of the Market Risk to Participants in the Compound Protocol (2020). https://scfab.github.io/2020/FAB2020_p5.pdf
15. Klages-Mundt, A., Harz, D., Gudgeon, L., Liu, J.Y., Minca, A.: Stablecoins 2.0: economic foundations and risk-based models. In: 2nd ACM Conference on Advances in Financial Technologies (AFT 2020), New York (2020). https://doi.org/10.1145/3419614.3423261
16. Klages-Mundt, A., Minca, A.: (In) stability for the blockchain: Deleveraging spirals and stablecoin attacks. arXiv preprint arXiv:1906.02152 (2019)
17. Leshner, R., Hayes, G.: Compound: The Money Market Protocol. Technical report (2018)

18. Maker: The maker protocol: MakerDAO's multi-collateral Dai (MCD) system. https://makerdao.com/en/whitepaper/. Accessed 08 June 2020
19. Nakamoto, S.: Bitcoin: A Peer-to-Peer Electronic Cash System (2008). www. bitcoin.org
20. Perez, D., Livshits, B.: Broken metre: attacking resource metering in EVM. In: Network and Distributed System Security Symposium. Internet Society, Reston, VA (2020). https://doi.org/10.14722/ndss.2020.24267
21. Perez, D., Xu, J., Livshits, B.: Revisiting transactional statistics of high-scalability blockchains. In: ACM Internet Measurement Conference, vol. 16, pp. 535–550. ACM, New York (2020). https://dl.acm.org/doi/10.1145/3419394.3423628
22. Pierro, G.A., Rocha, H.: The influence factors on ethereum transaction fees. In: 2019 IEEE/ACM 2nd International Workshop on Emerging Trends in Software Engineering for Blockchain (WETSEB), pp. 24–31. IEEE (2019)
23. Uniswap: Uniswap whitepaper (2020). https://hackmd.io/@HaydenAdams/ HJ9jLsfTz#%F0%9F%A6%84-Uniswap-Whitepaper. Accessed 26 Aug 2020
24. Wang, D., et al.: Towards understanding flash loan and its applications in DeFi ecosystem (2020). http://arxiv.org/abs/2010.12252
25. Werner, S.M., Perez, D., Gudgeon, L., Klages-Mundt, A., Harz, D., Knottenbelt, W.J.: SoK: Decentralized Finance (DeFi) (2021). http://arxiv.org/abs/2101.08778
26. Werner, S.M., Pritz, P.J., Perez, D.: Step on the gas? A better approach for recommending the ethereum gas price. In: Pardalos, P., Kotsireas, I., Guo, Y., Knottenbelt, W. (eds.) Mathematical Research for Blockchain Economy. SPBE, pp. 161–177. Springer, Cham (2020). https://doi.org/10.1007/978-3-030-53356-4_10
27. Wood, G., et al.: Ethereum: a secure decentralised generalised transaction ledger. Ethereum Project Yellow Paper **151**(2014), 1–32 (2014)
28. Xu, J., Vadgama, N.: From banks to DeFi: the evolution of the lending market (2021)
29. Xu, J., Vavryk, N., Paruch, K., Cousaert, S.: SoK: Decentralized Exchanges (DEX) with Automated Market Maker (AMM) protocols (2021). http://arxiv.org/abs/ 2103.12732

Cryptography

High-Threshold AVSS with Optimal Communication Complexity

Nicolas AlHaddad[1(✉)], Mayank Varia[1], and Haibin Zhang[2]

[1] Boston University, Boston, USA
{nhaddad,varia}@bu.edu
[2] Shandong Institute of Blockchain, Jinan, China
bchainzhang@aliyun.com

Abstract. Asynchronous verifiable secret sharing (AVSS) protocols protect a secret that is distributed among n parties. Dual-threshold AVSS protocols guarantee consensus in the presence of t Byzantine failures and privacy if fewer than p parties attempt to reconstruct the secret. In this work, we construct a dual-threshold AVSS protocol called HAVEN that is optimal along several dimensions. First, it is a *high-threshold* AVSS scheme, meaning that it is a dual-threshold AVSS with optimal parameters $t < n/3$ and $p < n - t$. Second, it has $O(n^2)$ message complexity, and for large secrets it achieves the optimal $O(n)$ communication overhead, without the need for a public key infrastructure or trusted setup. While these properties have been achieved individually before, to our knowledge this is the first protocol that achieves all of the above simultaneously. The core component of HAVEN is a high-threshold AVSS scheme for small secrets based on polynomial commitments that achieves $O(n^2 \log(n))$ communication overhead, as compared to prior schemes that require $O(n^3)$ overhead with $t < n/4$ Byzantine failures or $O(n^4)$ overhead for the recent high-threshold protocol of Kokoris-Kogias et al. (CCS 2020). Using standard amortization methods based on erasure coding, we can reduce the communication complexity to $O(n|s|)$ for a large secret s.

1 Introduction

Broadcast protocols are a core component in the design of fault-tolerant systems; for example, they enable replica servers to coordinate their actions in state machine replication, and they contribute toward the finality of cryptocurrencies. Reliable broadcast protocols between n servers ensure both that a message is delivered to all servers and that the delivered messages are identical. While there exist many broadcast protocols that assume strict or partial synchrony (i.e., an upper bound on message delivery times), *asynchronous* reliable broadcast protocols do not rely on any timing assumptions and are inherent more robust against denial-of-service and performance attacks. Bracha's asynchronous reliable broadcast protocol has $O(n^2)$ total message complexity and achieves reliability for up to $t < n/3$ Byzantine failures [11], which is optimal for protocols without setup that provide correctness, liveness, and agreement [24].

© International Financial Cryptography Association 2021
N. Borisov and C. Diaz (Eds.): FC 2021, LNCS 12675, pp. 479–498, 2021.
https://doi.org/10.1007/978-3-662-64331-0_25

Asynchronous verifiable secret sharing (AVSS) protocols [19] introduce a fourth guarantee: privacy of the message against any coalition of up to p servers comprising the t Byzantine servers plus $p - t$ honest servers that unintentionally cooperate with the adversary. Combining asynchronous broadcast with a Shamir secret sharing scheme [36] with threshold p, AVSS protocols proceed in two phases: a sharing phase in which the initial holder or *dealer* of a secret message s distributes secret shares of s to all servers, and a reconstruction phase in which any collection of $p + 1$ servers can recover s. This is the asynchronous version of verifiable secret sharing [22] because correct reconstruction is required even against a malicious dealer. While many AVSS protocols consider $p = t$, a subset called *dual-threshold AVSS* protocols consider $p > t$.

In this paper, we explore *high-threshold asynchronous verifiable secret sharing* (HAVSS) protocols, which are a special case of dual-threshold AVSS that can achieve any possible consensus threshold $t < n/3$ and privacy threshold $p < n - t$. These match the known upper bounds for consensus [34] and privacy (the honest servers must be able to reconstruct even if the Byzantine servers refuse to do so). HAVSS enables the generation of an asynchronous fair coin tossing protocol that can be used to remove the trusted dealer assumption needed in many distributed computations, such as efficient asynchronous Byzantine agreement, distributed key generation, threshold signatures, and threshold encryption [14–16,28].

Our Contributions. In this work, we contribute an HAVSS protocol called HAVEN that is optimal along several dimensions:

- HAVEN achieves any consensus threshold of $t < n/3$ and privacy threshold of $p < n - t$.
- HAVEN has $O(n^2)$ message complexity during sharing and reconstruction. Concretely, every server sends 2 messages to each party during sharing (3 for the dealer), and 1 message to each party during reconstruction.
- For a short secret s sampled randomly from a finite field, its communication overhead (i.e., number of field elements sent) is $O(n^2 \log n)$ without trusted setup. If trusted setup is permissible, this can be reduced to $O(n^2)$ in some cases.
- For a long secret s, its communication complexity is $O(n|s|)$.
- HAVEN does not require trusted setup or a public key infrastructure (PKI).

All of these parameters improve upon the recent breakthrough by Kokoris-Kogias et al. [28], the first HAVSS protocol with optimal resilience. Our communication complexity even beats many existing AVSS schemes that were not striving for dual-threshold. Table 1 shows a comparison of our work to several related protocols, which we describe in more detail below.

Why is HAVSS Possible? Suppose there are $n = 3t + 1$ parties, where the dealer is one of the t Byzantine servers, and the honest servers are split into two camps:

- $t + 1$ *informed* servers that always receive valid messages from the Byzantine servers (i.e., what honest servers would have sent), and
- t *clueless* servers that never receive any messages from Byzantine servers.

Table 1. Comparison of our HAVEN protocol with several prior AVSS protocols. Note that HAVEN's communication complexity, computational assumption, and reliance on trusted setup depend on the polynomial commitment scheme used; the contents of this table are predicated on the use of Bulletproofs [13] (cf. Sect. 3.3).

Works	threshold		complexity				avoiding setup		crypto
	dual	high	message	comm.	amortized	rounds	no trust?	no PKI?	assumption
Cachin et al. [15]	✓	✗	$O(n^2)$	$O(\kappa n^3)$	$O(\kappa n^2)$	3	✓	✓	DL
Backes et al. [2]	✗	✗	$O(n^2)$	$O(\kappa n^2)$	$O(\kappa n^2)$	3	✗	✓	t-SDH
Kate et al. [25]	✗	✗	$O(n^2)$	$O(\kappa n^3)$	$O(\kappa n)$	> 4	✗	✗	t-SDH
Kokoris-Kogias et al. [28]	✓	✓	$O(n^2)$	$O(\kappa n^4)$	$O(\kappa n^3)$	4	✓	✗	DL
HAVEN option 1	✓	✓	$O(n^2)$	$O(\kappa n^2)$	$O(\kappa n)$	3	✗	✓	t-SDH
HAVEN option 2	✓	✓	$O(n^2)$	$\tilde{O}(\kappa n^2)$	$O(\kappa n)$	3	✓	✓	DL + ROM

One might wonder: is it even possible to achieve $p = 2t$ privacy? Intuitively, it seems that we run into a paradox. The informed servers can complete the sharing phase because they receive valid messages from $2t+1$ servers (i.e., from their perspective, the clueless servers appear Byzantine). Ergo, the $2t + 1$ informed and clueless servers must collectively be able to recover the secret, even if the Byzantine servers refuse to participate in reconstruction. However, the clueless servers cannot contribute anything meaningful toward the reconstruction because they have only received messages from the informed servers. Hence, if the $t + 1 < p$ informed servers can learn the secret with the clueless servers, then they must have been able to learn the secret without them, breaking privacy.

Fortunately, there is one flaw in the above argument that enables HAVSS (and which schemes like HAVEN must exploit): even if the $t + 1$ informed servers collectively possess enough data to learn the secret, they might not actually transmit this data during reconstruction. Ergo, they might still rely on the clueless servers during the actual reconstruction protocol, even if the clueless servers are relying information that the informed servers collectively know.

Overview of the Construction. The core of HAVEN is a construction for small, randomly chosen secrets. Like other (dual-threshold) AVSS schemes, it broadly follows a "two-layer secret sharing" approach. The dealer begins by constructing a degree p polynomial R that is a Shamir secret sharing with her secret s encoded at location $R(0)$. We call R the *recovery polynomial* because the reconstruction phase consists of each party P_i revealing $R(i)$ so that everyone can interpolate R and learn the secret. Next for $i \in [1, n]$, the dealer constructs the degree t polynomial S_i that is a Shamir secret sharing with the secret encoded at location $R(i) = S_i$. This creates a diagonal pattern as shown on Fig. 1.

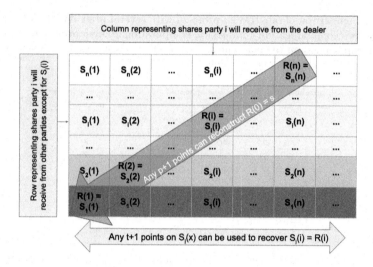

Fig. 1. Overview of the data transmitted during HAVEN. Each party P_i receives column i of this matrix from the dealer; note that this includes $S_i = R(i)$. If P_i never received $R(i)$, then $t + 1$ other parties will send their points on row i, from which P_i can interpolate the polynomial S_i and learn the value $S_i(i) = R(i)$. At the reconstruction stage, any $p + 1$ points on the polynomial (1 per party) suffice to interpolate R and learn the secret $s = R(0)$.

The sharing phase of HAVEN follows a 3-message (send, echo, ready) format, just like Bracha's reliable broadcast. There are two goals that are achieved concurrently:

- Each party P_i must learn S_i, which we call its *share polynomial*. To do this privately, the dealer sends each party one share on everyone else's share polynomial, which they can disperse in the echo stage. Polynomial commitments (and their succinct proofs/arguments) enable each party P_i to verify the integrity of everyone else's claimed point on her share polynomial.
- The parties must collectively reach consensus about which share polynomials to use (against a Byzantine dealer). To do this, the dealer produces a vector commitment of the $n + 1$ polynomial commitments and uses Bracha's reliable broadcast to disseminate this value (which is not sensitive).

Because we provide each server with 1 share on everyone else's S_i, observe that $t + 1$ servers collectively hold enough data to reconstruct all polynomials and recover the secret (as stated above). This is acceptable because HAVSS only aims to protect against t Byzantine adversaries.

Unlike previous (dual-threshold) AVSS constructions, HAVEN does not encompass R and S_i into a (larger) bivariate polynomial. Instead, we directly check for consistency of these univariate polynomials by designing a polynomial commitment scheme that is:

- Homomorphic, in order to construct a succinct proof that the polynomials intersect at the correct point (i.e., that $R(i) - S_i(i) = 0$).
- Degree-revealing, meaning that its proofs demonstrate an upper bound on the degree of the committed polynomial (cf. Definition 4) so that parties can consistently reconstruct it.
- Deterministic, so that once party P_i learns S_i, she can now prove the value at new points. This property allows P_i to prove that she is sending the correct value for $S_i(i) = (R(i))$ during reconstruction.

The communication complexity of HAVEN is dominated by the transmission of a polynomial commitment between each pair of parties. These commitments can be constant-sized with trusted setup, or logarithmic in size otherwise, which leads to the two options shown in Table 1.

Finally, we extend HAVEN into an HAVSS scheme for large, arbitrarily-chosen secrets with linear communication overhead. The idea is simple: choose a short, ephemeral secret key k, and engage in (1) the above HAVSS protocol to share k and (2) an asynchronous verifiable information dispersal protocol [17] to disseminate the ciphertext $Enc_k(s)$ without concern for privacy. The linear overhead to disseminate the ciphertext dominates the cost of HAVSS for secrets of length $|s| = \Omega(n \log n)$ (this can be reduced to $|s| = \Omega(n)$ with trusted setup).

Related Work. Several AVSS protocols were proposed in the 1990s with unconditional security [5,18,19], but at the expense of huge communication complexity. The first practical AVSS was achieved by Cachin et al. [15] using computational assumptions (namely, the discrete logarithm assumption). Their protocol achieves an optimal message complexity of $O(n^2)$ and resilience of $n > 3t$, but their $O(\kappa n^3)$ communication complexity is suboptimal. Cachin et al. [15] also constructed the first dual-threshold AVSS with consensus $t < n/4$ and privacy $p < n/2$, with the same message and communication complexity as above.

Recently, Kokoris-Kogias et al. [28] constructed the first HAVSS protocol. As described above, breaking the privacy barrier from $p < n/2$ to $p < 2n/3$ is a challenging accomplishment. Nevertheless, the improved privacy comes at a price of $O(\kappa n^4)$ communication complexity with 4 rounds of communication, plus the need for a public key infrastructure (PKI) so that any server can pass along digitally-signed messages from other senders to their intended destination. Kokoris-Kogias et al. use their HAVSS in a black-box manner to construct randomness beacons, distributed key generation, threshold signatures, and more; using HAVEN reduces the communication of those constructions too.

Several other works focused on providing linear (amortized) communication overhead of AVSS for large secrets, including Cachin and Tessaro [17] and more recently Basu et al. [4] and Kate et al. [25]. The latter two works use polynomial commitments [26] that require a trusted setup to achieve an optimal communication complexity of $O(\kappa n)$, but for short messages their communication complexity is $O(\kappa n^3)$ in the worst case.

Our construction makes extensive use of polynomial commitments, which were introduced by Kate et al. [26] and subsequently used by Backes et al. [2]

to design an AVSS protocol (with a single threshold). We also leverage recent works that construct polynomial commitments without trusted setup; we use Bulletproofs [13] in our construction, but our techniques are amenable to other polynomial commitment schemes (e.g., [9,10,12]).

Finally, we focus exclusively on worst-case metrics for message and (amortized) communication complexity in this paper. There exist several works that contain a "fast path" and "slow path" approach whose typical communication complexity is comparable to HAVEN and can provide benefits like lower computational cost or higher thresholds for some security properties, even if the worst-case metrics are identical or worse (e.g., [1,3,24,33]).

Organization. The rest of this paper is organized as follows. In Sect. 2, we define (high-threshold) asynchronous verifiable secret sharing as well as many of the building blocks that we need in this work. In Sect. 3, we construct HAVEN for "short" secrets that are approximately equal in length to the security parameter. Finally, in Sect. 4, we amortize HAVEN to achieve lower communication complexity for secrets that are substantially larger than the security parameter.

2 Definitions

In this section, we provide definitions for polynomial and vector commitments that we will use within HAVEN as well as a definition for asynchronous verifiable secret sharing. In the definitions below, κ denotes the security parameter, "negligible" refers to a function vanishing faster than any inverse polynomial, "overwhelming" refers to $1 - \epsilon$ for a negligible function ϵ, and PPT is an abbreviation for probabilistic polynomial time.

2.1 Commitment Schemes

In this work, we consider non-interactive commitment schemes for polynomials and vectors. We begin by defining a polynomial commitment scheme [26]. In this work, we exclusively consider schemes that are homomorphic, and our definition is similar to the notion of "linear combination schemes" from Boneh et al. [8] except that we restrict our attention to *deterministic* schemes.

Definition 1. *A polynomial commitment scheme $\mathcal{P}$ comprises four algorithms* Setup, Com, Eval, Verify *and an optional fifth algorithm* Hom *that act as follows:*

- Setup$(1^\kappa, \mathbb{F}, D) \to$ pp *is given a security parameter κ, a finite field $\mathbb{F}$, and an upper bound D on the degree of any polynomial to be committed. It generates public parameters* pp *that are required for all subsequent operations.*
- Com$(\text{pp}, \phi(x), d) \to \hat{\phi}$ *is given a polynomial $\phi(x) \in \mathbb{F}[x]$ of degree $d \leq D$. It outputs a commitment string $\hat{\phi}$ (throughout this work, we use the hat notation to denote a commitment to a polynomial).*
- Eval$(\text{pp}, \phi, i) \to \langle i, \phi(i), w \rangle$ *is given a polynomial ϕ as well as an index $i \in \mathbb{F}$. It outputs a 3-tuple containing i, the evaluation $\phi(i)$, and witness string w_i.*

- Verify($\mathsf{pp}, \hat{\phi}, y, d$) → *True/False takes as input a commitment $\hat{\phi}$, a 3-tuple $y = \langle i, j, w \rangle$, and a degree d. It outputs a Boolean.*
- Hom($\mathsf{pp}, \hat{\phi}_1, \hat{\phi}_2, a$) → $\widehat{\phi_1 + a\phi_2}$ *takes in commitments to two polynomials ϕ_1 and ϕ_2 of degree at most D, as well as a field element $a \in \mathbb{F}$. Outputs the commitment* Com($\mathsf{pp}, \phi, \max\{d_1, d_2\}$) *to the polynomial $\phi = \phi_1 + a\phi_2$.*

Informally, the Verify method of a polynomial commitment scheme should return True if and only if $\phi(i) = j$, w is a witness previously created by Eval, and the degree of ϕ is at most d. We formalize this guarantee in Definitions 2–5 below.

Definition 1 is mostly similar to prior works that have defined and constructed polynomial commitments [9,10,13,25,26]. There are three differences. First, the verifier learns an upper bound on the degree of the polynomial. Second, we restrict our attention to deterministic Com algorithms, and consequently the witness generation process in Eval is well-specified purely from the polynomial (i.e., without requiring the randomness string used earlier in the Com stage). These changes have consequences for our security definitions (see Definitions 4 and 5) and constructions of polynomial commitments (see Sect. 3.3). Third, we don't include a method to open the entire polynomial ϕ; this is without loss of generality since revealing ϕ is equivalent to revealing enough evaluations to interpolate ϕ.

There are two predominant styles of security definitions for polynomial commitments: game-based definitions that resemble the binding and hiding properties of traditional commitments [25,26], or simulation-based definitions in the vein of zero knowledge proofs of knowledge [9,10,13].

The weaker indistinguishability style suffices for this work, and we use it in the definitions below. Definitions 2, 3, and 5 are nearly identical to their counterparts in [25,26], whereas Definition 4 is a new security guarantee that we require in this work (cf. Sect. 3.3 for constructions). All of these definitions apply equally whether or not the commitment scheme is homomorphic.

Definition 2 (Strong correctness). *Let* $\mathsf{pp} \leftarrow \mathsf{Setup}(1^\kappa, \mathbb{F}, D)$. *For any polynomial $\phi(x) \in \mathbb{F}[x]$ of degree d with associated commitment $\hat{\phi} = \mathsf{Com}(\mathsf{pp}, \phi, d)$:*

- *If $d \leq D$, then for any $i \in \mathbb{F}$ the output $y \leftarrow \mathsf{Eval}(\mathsf{pp}, \hat{\phi}, i)$ of evaluation is successfully verified by* Verify($\mathsf{pp}, \hat{\phi}, y, d$).
- *If $d > D$, then no adversary can succeed with non-negligible probability at creating a commitment $\hat{\phi}$ that is successfully verified at $d + 1$ randomly chosen indices.*

Definition 3 (Evaluation binding). *Let* $\mathsf{pp} \leftarrow \mathsf{Setup}(1^\kappa, \mathbb{F}, D)$. *For any PPT adversary $\mathcal{A}(\mathsf{pp})$ that outputs a commitment $\tilde{\phi}$, a degree d, and two evaluations $y = \langle i, j, w \rangle$ and $y' = \langle i', j', w' \rangle$, there exists a negligible function $\varepsilon(\kappa)$ such that:*

$$\Pr[(\tilde{\phi}, y, y', d) \leftarrow \mathcal{A}(\mathsf{pp}) : i = i' \wedge j \neq j' \wedge \mathsf{Verify}(\mathsf{pp}, \tilde{\phi}, \tilde{y}, d) \wedge \mathsf{Verify}(\mathsf{pp}, \tilde{\phi}, \tilde{y}', d)] < \varepsilon(\kappa).$$

Definition 4 (Degree binding). *Let* $\mathsf{pp} \leftarrow \mathsf{Setup}(1^\kappa, \mathbb{F}, D)$. *For any PPT adversary $\mathcal{A}$ that outputs a polynomial ϕ of degree $\deg(\phi)$, evaluation $\tilde{y}$, and integer d, there exists a negligible function $\varepsilon(\kappa)$ such that:*

$$\Pr[(\phi, \tilde{y}, d) \leftarrow \mathcal{A}(\mathsf{pp}), \hat{\phi} = \mathsf{Com}(\mathsf{pp}, \phi, \deg(\phi)) : \mathsf{Verify}(\mathsf{pp}, \hat{\phi}, \tilde{y}, d) \wedge \deg(\phi) > d] < \varepsilon(\kappa).$$

Definition 5 (Hiding for random polynomials). *Let* pp ← Setup(1^κ, $\mathbb{F}, D$), *d be an arbitrary integer less than D, and $I \subset \mathbb{F}$ be an arbitrary set of indices with $|I| \leq d$. Randomly choose a $\phi \leftarrow \mathbb{F}[x]$ of degree d and construct its commitment $\hat{\phi} = \mathrm{Com}(\mathsf{pp}, \phi, d)$. For all PPT adversaries $\mathcal{A}$, there exists a negligible polynomial $\varepsilon(\kappa)$ such that:*

$$\Pr[(x, y) \leftarrow \mathcal{A}(\mathsf{pp}, \hat{\phi}, \{\mathrm{Eval}(\mathsf{pp}, \phi, i)\}_{i \in I}) : y = \phi(x) \wedge x \notin I] < \varepsilon(\kappa),$$

where the probability is taken over $\mathcal{A}$'s coins and the random choice of ϕ.

In words, the hiding definition states that even given evaluations at the indices in I, no adversary can find a new point on ϕ with non-negligible probability. Note that the hiding property is only achievable for randomly-chosen ϕ because we defined Eval deterministically.

Finally, we provide the syntax for (static) vector commitments, which are succinct encodings of finite, ordered lists in such a way that one can later open a value at a specific location [20,31]. (We use 0-indexing throughout this work.)

Definition 6. *A static vector commitment scheme $\mathcal{V} = $ (vSetup, vCom, vGen, vVerify) comprises four algorithms that operate as follows:*

- *vSetup($1^\kappa, U, L$) → $\bar{\mathsf{pp}}$ is given a security parameter κ, a set U, and a maximum vector length L. It generates public parameters $\bar{\mathsf{pp}}$.*
- *vCom($\bar{\mathsf{pp}}, \boldsymbol{v}$) → C is given a vector $\boldsymbol{v} \in U^\ell$ where $\ell \leq L$. It outputs a commitment string C.*
- *vGen($\bar{\mathsf{pp}}, \boldsymbol{v}, i$) → w_i is given a vector $\boldsymbol{v}$ and an index i. It outputs a witness string w_i.*
- *vVerify($\bar{\mathsf{pp}}, C, u, i, w$) → True/False takes as input a vector commitment C, an element $u \in U$, an index i, and a witness string w_e. It outputs a Boolean value that should only equal True if $u = \boldsymbol{v}[i]$ and w is a witness to this fact.*

This is a special case of a polynomial commitment scheme, and indeed throughout this work we assume that vector commitments are instantiated using our polynomial commitments (see Sect. 3.3) although other instantiations are possible like Merkle trees [32]. Vector commitments also have analogous binding and hiding security guarantees to Definitions 2–5 [20,31]. Without loss of generality, we can consider $U = \{0, 1\}^*$ by hashing strings before running the vector commitment algorithms.

2.2   Dual-Threshold Asynchronous Verifiable Secret Sharing

In this section, we define dual-threshold asynchronous verifiable secret sharing (DAVSS) protocols that are the focus of this work. Our definition is consistent with the works of Cachin et al. [15] and Kokoris-Kogias et al. [28]. Recall that, informally, an AVSS scheme is an interactive protocol between n servers that allows one server (the "dealer") to split a secret among all servers in such a way that they obtain consensus over the shared secret while also protecting the privacy of the secret until reconstruction time, even though some of the servers are adversarial. The term "dual-threshold" means that the number of parties required for reconstruction of the secret may be different than the number of Byzantine failures that can be withstood.

Definition 7. *A* (n, p, t) *dual-threshold asynchronous verifiable secret sharing (DAVSS) protocol involves n servers interacting in two stages.*

- Sharing stage. *This stage begins when a special party, called the "dealer"* P_d, *is activated on an input message of the form* $(ID.d, \mathsf{in}, \mathsf{share}, s)$. *Here, the value* ID.d *is a tag identifying the session, and s is the dealer's secret.* P_d *begins the protocol to share s using ID.d. A server* P_i *has completed the sharing for* ID.d *when it generates a local output of the form* $(ID.d, \mathsf{out}, \mathsf{shared})$.
- Reconstruction stage. *After server* P_i *has completed the sharing stage, it may start reconstruction for* ID.d *when activated on a message* $(ID.d, \mathsf{in}, \mathsf{reconstruct})$. *Eventually, the server halts with output* $(ID.d, \mathsf{out}, \mathsf{reconstructed}, z_i)$. *In this case, we say that* P_i *reconstructs* z_i *for* ID.d.

An (n, p, t)*-DAVSS satisfies the following security guarantees in the presence of an adversary* $\mathcal{A}$ *who can adaptively and maliciously corrupt up to t servers.*

- Liveness. *If* $\mathcal{A}$ *initializes all honest servers on a sharing* ID.d, *delivers all associated messages, and the dealer* P_d *is honest throughout the sharing stage, then with overwhelming probability all honest servers complete the sharing.*
- Privacy. *If an honest dealer shared s using* ID.d *and at most* $p - t$ *honest servers started reconstruction for* ID.d, *then* $\mathcal{A}$ *has no information about s.*
- Agreement. *Provided that* $\mathcal{A}$ *initializes all honest servers on a sharing* ID.d *and delivers all associated messages: (1) if some honest server completes the sharing for* ID.d, *then all honest servers complete the sharing for* ID.d, *and (2) if all honest servers start reconstruction for* ID.d, *then with overwhelming probability every honest server* P_i *reconstructs some* s_i *for* ID.d.
- Correctness. *Once* $p + 1$ *honest servers have completed the sharing for* ID.d, *there exists a fixed value* $z \in \mathbb{F}$ *such that the following holds with overwhelming probability: (1) if the dealer shared s using* ID.d *and is honest throughout the sharing stage, then* $z = s$ *and (2) if an honest server* P_i *reconstructs* z_i *for* ID.d, *then* $z_i = z$.

A high-threshold asynchronous verifiable secret sharing *(HAVSS) protocol is a* (n, p, t)*-DAVSS that supports any choice of* $t < n/3$ *and* $p < n - t$.

3   HAVEN for Short, Uniformly Random Secrets

In this section, we show how to use polynomial commitments to construct an HAVSS protocol called HAVEN for a short secret s that is uniformly sampled from a finite field $\mathbb{F}$. Then, we demonstrate that our construction achieves all the security properties for an HAVSS. Finally, we show how to modify two existing polynomial commitment schemes so that they meet our Definitions 2–5.

3.1   Construction

Like all AVSS protocols, HAVEN proceeds in two phases: a sharing phase in which the dealer distributes shares of her secret s, and a reconstruction phase in which the servers collectively reconstruct the secret. We formally present the two phases of HAVEN in Algorithms 1 and 2, respectively. Here, we present the concepts behind the construction.

Sharing Phase. The sharing phase of HAVEN follows the same communication pattern as Bracha's asynchronous reliable broadcast [11] and the AVSS protocol of Cachin et al. [15]. First, the dealer transmits a $\tilde{O}(n)$-size send message to all parties. Then, everyone sends a $\tilde{O}(1)$-size echo and ready messages to all parties.

Lines 1–14 show the dealer's initial work, culminating in the send message. This is the most complex part of the protocol, and we describe it in detail.

- In lines 2–4, the dealer samples a degree-p *recovery polynomial* R and along with n different degree-t *share polynomials* $S_1, \ldots, S_n$, all in $\mathbb{F}[x]$. They satisfy $R(0) \triangleq s$ and $S_i(i) \triangleq R(i)$, but are otherwise uniformly sampled. Figure 1 pictorially shows the relationships between these polynomials; we stress that they need not be consistent with any low-degree bivariate polynomial.
- In lines 5–6, the dealer computes polynomial commitments of R and all S_i.
- Recall that an evaluation contains one (x, y) coordinate as well as a proof that this coordinate is on the committed polynomial. In line 8, we form a vector $\boldsymbol{y}_i^S$ containing n evaluations, but in a transposed order: this vector contains the evaluation of one point on each share polynomial $S_1, \ldots, S_n$.
- In lines 9–10, we construct the n *test polynomials* $T_i \triangleq R - S_i$ along with evaluations proving that $T_i(i) = 0$ for all i. This proves consistency between the share and recovery polynomials, as shown in Fig. 1. (Interestingly, even though we have committed to R, we never evaluate it directly.)
- In lines 11–12, we build the *root commitment* C; this is a vector commitment to all of the polynomial commitments. Looking ahead, we will run Bracha's reliable broadcast protocol on C, and servers will only believe a polynomial (commitment) if it can be linked back to C. Abusing notation, we assume each polynomial commitment contains the witness to its own inclusion in C (this witness is ignored when running a polynomial Verify check).
- Finally, in lines 13–14, the dealer sends to party P_i the root commitment, all $n + 1$ polynomial commitments, one evaluation on everybody's share polynomial, and all n evaluations of the test polynomial.

When a party P_i receives the send message from the dealer, it performs several checks to ensure that the message is internally consistent (lines 16–18):

- All polynomial evaluations received are verifiably part of S_j and T_j.
- The degrees of the S_j and T_j polynomials are at most t and p, respectively.
- The recovery and share polynomials are equal at $R(i) = S_i(i)$.
- All polynomial commitments link back to the root commitment.

Algorithm 1. Sharing phase of HAVEN, for server P_i and tag ID.d

---

1: UPON RECEIVING (ID.d, in, share, s):   ▷ only if party is the dealer P_d
2:   randomly choose recovery polynomial $R \in \mathbb{F}[x]$ of degree p s.t. $R(0) = s$
3:   **for** $i \in [1, n]$ **do**
4:       randomly choose share polynomial $S_i \in \mathbb{F}[x]$ of degree t s.t. $S_i(i) = R(i)$

5:   compute $\hat{R} = \mathrm{Com}(\mathsf{pp}, R, p)$ ▷ make polynomial commitments
6:   compute each $\hat{S}_i = \mathrm{Com}(\mathsf{pp}, S_i, t)$ and let $\hat{\boldsymbol{S}} = \langle \hat{S}_1, \hat{S}_2, \ldots, \hat{S}_n \rangle$

7:   **for** $i \in [1, n]$ **do**   ▷ evaluate and create witnesses
8:       compute $\boldsymbol{y}_i^S = [\mathrm{Eval}(\mathsf{pp}, S_j, i)$ for $j \in [1, n]]$ ▷ one point on each S_j
9:       compute $\hat{T}_i = \mathrm{Hom}(\hat{R}, \hat{S}_i, -1)$ ▷ $T_i(x) = R(x) - S_i(x)$
10: compute $\boldsymbol{y}^T = [\mathrm{Eval}(\mathsf{pp}, T_i, i)$ for $i \in [1, n]]$ ▷ tests if all $S_i(i) = R(i)$

11: compute $C = \mathrm{vCom}(\bar{\mathsf{pp}}, \langle \hat{R}, \hat{S}_1, \hat{S}_2, \ldots, \hat{S}_n \rangle)$ ▷ root commitment
12: append to $\hat{R}$ and each $\hat{S}_i$ a witness of inclusion in C at the right location

13: **for** $i \in [1, n]$ **do**
14:      send "ID.d, send, set$_i$" to party P_i, where set$_i = \{C, \hat{R}, \hat{\boldsymbol{S}}, \boldsymbol{y}_i^S, \boldsymbol{y}^T\}$

15: UPON RECEIVING (ID.d, send, set$_j$) from P_d for the first time: ▷ echo stage
16:   **if** all Verify$(\mathsf{pp}, \hat{S}_j, \boldsymbol{y}_i^S[j], t)$ and Verify$(\mathsf{pp}, \hat{T}_j, \boldsymbol{y}^T[j], p)$ are true **then**
17:       **if** $\hat{R}$ and all $\hat{\boldsymbol{S}}$ are in C at the expected locations **then**
18:           **if** $T_j(j) = 0$ for all $j \in [1, n]$ **then**   ▷ dealer's message is consistent
19:               **for** $j \in [1, n]$ **do**   ▷ send message to each party P_j
20:                   send "ID.d, echo, info$_{i,j}$" to P_j, where info$_{i,j} = \{C, \hat{S}_j, \boldsymbol{y}_i^S[j]\}$

21: UPON RECEIVING (ID.d, echo, info$_{j,i}$) from P_m for the first time: ▷ ready stage
22:   **if** $\hat{S}_m$ is in C at location m and Verify$(\mathsf{pp}, \hat{S}_m, \boldsymbol{y}_i^S[m], t)$ = True **then**
23:       **if** not yet sent ready and received $2t + 1$ valid echo with this C **then**
24:           send "ID.d, ready, C" to all parties   ▷ Bracha consensus on C

25: UPON RECEIVING (ID.d, ready, C) from P_m for the first time:
26:   **if** not yet sent ready and received $t + 1$ ready with this C **then**
27:       send "ID.d, ready, C" to all parties   ▷ Bracha consensus on C

28:   **if** received $2t + 1$ ready with this C **then**
29:       wait to receive $t + 1$ valid echo with this C ▷ must happen eventually
30:       interpolate S_i from the $t + 1$ valid $\boldsymbol{y}_m^S[i]$ in the received echo
31:       compute $y_i^* = \mathrm{Eval}(\mathsf{pp}, S_i, i)$ ▷ evaluation of $S_i(i)$
32:       output (ID.d, out, shared)   ▷ locally halt

If all checks pass: party P_i sends an echo message to each party P_j containing what it believes to be the root commitment C (as part of Bracha's broadcast) along with two pieces of information about party j's share polynomial: its commitment $\hat{S}_j$ and the evaluation at one point $S_j(i)$ (to help P_j interpolate the polynomial). We stress that when party P_i sends an echo message, she may not yet be able to tell whether her polynomial (commitments) will become the consensus ones, because the Bracha broadcast protocol on C might not be complete.

Algorithm 2. Reconstruction phase of HAVEN, for server P_i and tag ID.d

---

1: UPON RECEIVING (ID.d, in, reconstruct):
2:    **for** j in $[1, n]$ **do**
3:      send (ID.d, reconstruct-share, $\hat{S}_j$, y_j^*)   ▷ to Party P_j

4: UPON RECEIVING (ID.d, reconstruct-share, $\hat{S}_m$, y_m^*):   ▷ from Party P_m
5:    **if** $\hat{S}_m$ in C and Verify(pp, $\hat{S}_m$, y_m^*, t) **then**
6:      **if** received $p + 1$ valid reconstruct-share messages **then**
7:        interpolate R from the $p + 1$ valid points   ▷ assume that $R(j) = S_j(j)$
8:        output (ID.d, out, reconstructed, $R(0)$)

When party P_i receives an echo message from another party, she will disregard the message if either the received polynomial commitment or evaluation cannot link back to the received root commitment (all of which may be different from her local state from the earlier send message). The remainder of the protocol proceeds as in Bracha's broadcast.

Reconstruction Phase. If a party P_i completes the sharing and starts the reconstruction stage, then this party knows the share polynomial S_i and a witness that it links back to the broadcast root commitment. She sends all parties an evaluation of $S_i(i)$ along with the witness linking S_i to the root commitment; observe that P_i can construct this evaluation because the commitment is deterministic. Everyone verifies this evaluation and interprets this point as $R(i)$ instead; this is acceptable because at least $t + 1$ honest parties have verified that $R(j) = S_j(j)$ for all j during the sharing phase (line 18). Given $p + 1$ valid messages from other parties, P_i can interpolate R and recover the secret s.

3.2   Analysis

In this section, we prove that our HAVEN protocol is a high-threshold AVSS.

Theorem 1. *Assuming that the underlying polynomial and vector commitment schemes satisfy Definitions 2–6, then HAVEN protocol is a high threshold AVSS with $O(n^2)$ message complexity and $O(\kappa n^2 c)$ communication complexity, where κ is the security parameter and c is the size of the underlying commitments and evaluations.*

Below, we provide proofs for each of the four security properties in Definition 7 and the efficiency claim.

Proof (Liveness). If the dealer P_d is honest and all messages are delivered, then P_d will send everyone the same root commitment, polynomial commitments. Also, each party receives 1 point on every share polynomial. All of the checks on lines 16–18 pass, so the honest parties can echo these points, from which everyone will be able to send ready messages and interpolate their own share polynomial. If any dishonest party tries to send a malformed commitment or evaluation in their echo message, then evaluation binding (Definition 3) ensures that it will not link back to the root commitment, so honest parties will disregard this message.

Proof (Privacy). We focus first on the reconstruction stage, and we assume without loss of generality that the adversary $\mathcal{A}$ knows her own share polynomials. As a result, she knows t points on the recovery polynomial R and will receive $p - t$ additional points from honest parties. From this information alone, Shamir secret sharing guarantees that $\mathcal{A}$ learns nothing about the secret unless she can distinguish at least 1 more point on R from random.

Next, we consider the information available to the adversary $\mathcal{A}$ during the sharing stage. The dealer's send messages give $\mathcal{A}$ a total of t evaluations on each share polynomial S_i, but the hiding property (Definition 5) guarantees that this is insufficient to distinguish any other point on S_i from random with nonnegligible probability. The subsequent echo and ready messages are of no help because they only contain information about $\mathcal{A}$'s share polynomials, not those of other parties.

Proof (Agreement). Suppose that an honest party P_i has completed the sharing for ID.d. We must show that another (arbitrary) honest P_j will also complete the sharing.

- Since P_i completed the sharing, she heard $2t + 1$ ready messages with the same root commitment C^* and have confirmed that the dealer correctly split the large secret s into proper shares and fingerprinted them correctly in the root commitment C^*. At least $t + 1$ of those senders are honest and will send ready messages to everyone. Due to line 27, this will cause all honest parties to send ready messages if they have not yet done so. Ergo, party P_j will eventually hear $2t + 1$ ready messages with root commitment C^*, thereby satisfying the conditional on line 28.
- Since P_i completed the sharing, she must have sent a ready message in line 24 or line 27 (this is an xor since honest parties only send one ready message).
- The condition for line 27 cannot be satisfied until $t + 1$ parties sent a ready due to line 24, at least one of whom must be honest (say, party P_m). For this to occur, party P_m must have observed $2t + 1$ echo messages that are internally consistent and link to the same root commitment C^*.
- At least $t + 1$ of those echo message senders are honest, so they will also send consistent echo messages to party P_j. Once this happens, P_j can complete the wait step on line 29. Also, the echo messages contain enough information for P_j to compute lines 30–31 and complete the sharing.

Next, suppose all honest servers start reconstruction for ID.d (note that there are at least $p + 1$ honest servers). Because these parties completed the sharing, they each have a share polynomial that can be linked back to the common root commitment C^*. Hence, they can construct an evaluation at $S_i(i)$ that will be accepted by others. Once $p + 1$ such points are received, each honest server can recover a secret.

Proof (Correctness). First, assume that an honest dealer shared a secret s. Then, the share polynomial evaluations at all $\{S_i(i)\}_{i\in[1,n]}$ lie on a degree p polynomial that will recover s. By the Agreement property, once an honest server completes the sharing, the parties will have a common root commitment C^*. Thus, the only way to deviate from a reconstruction of s is to reveal an invalid evaluation of $S_i(i)$, which occurs with negligible probability by evaluation binding (Definition 3).

The second correctness property requires evaluation and degree binding. Even with a dishonest dealer, still the parties reconstruct the secret using $p+1$ of the n points $S_1(1), \ldots, S_n(n)$. This reconstruction is unique if and only if that polynomial is of degree p. Recall that at least $t+1$ honest parties verified during the sharing stage that $R(j) - S_j(j) = 0$ for all j, where this polynomial is of degree p (line 18). Evaluation binding ensures that the $S_i(i)$ evaluations revealed during reconstruction match the values tested earlier, and degree binding ensures that the points lie on a degree p polynomial as desired.

Proof (Efficiency). The protocol achieves a message complexity of $O(n^2)$ because every party sends n echo, ready, and reconstruct-share messages (plus n send messages for the dealer). Also assuming a field size $|\mathbb{F}| = O(\kappa)$, every stage of HAVEN has $O(\kappa n^2 c)$ communication complexity. In the send stage the dealer sends n messages of size $O(\kappa n c)$, and in all other stages each party sends n messages of size $O(\kappa c)$.

3.3   Constructing the Underlying Commitments

To complete our HAVEN construction for short secrets, it remains only to construct deterministic polynomial commitment schemes that satisfy Definitions 2–5 for random polynomials with short commitments and evaluations. In this section, we present two such constructions. The first construction is based on Bulletproofs [13], and it provides constant-size commitments and logarithmic-size evaluations without trusted setup. The second construction is based on the scheme of Kate et al. [26], and its commitments and evaluations are constant-sized at the expense of requiring trusted setup.

Deterministic Bulletproofs. Bulletproofs [13] are constant-sized vector commitments that support logarithmic-sized arguments of the result of an inner product operation applied to two (committed) vectors. One can construct a polynomial commitment from Bulletproofs as follows: $\mathrm{Com}(\mathrm{pp}, \phi, d)$ commits to the vector $\phi = \langle \phi_j \rangle_{j\in[0,d]}$ of coefficients of the polynomial, $\mathrm{Eval}(\mathrm{pp}, \phi, i)$ constructs the vector $\boldsymbol{i} = \langle 1, i, i^2, \ldots, i^d \rangle$ (padding with 0s if needed) and produces an argument to the value of $\phi \cdot \boldsymbol{i} = \phi(i)$, and Verify checks this argument.

The commitment scheme in Bulletproofs is deterministic: $\mathrm{Setup}(1^\kappa, D)$ uniformly samples $D + 1$ group elements $g_0, \ldots, g_D \leftarrow G_\kappa$, and then $\mathrm{Com}(\phi) = \prod_{j=0}^{d} g_j^{\phi_j}$. If the discrete log assumption holds for the family $\mathcal{G} = \{G_\kappa\}_{\kappa\in\mathbb{N}}$, then this commitment scheme is binding, and it is also hiding when the polynomial

ϕ is chosen uniformly at random (even though it is not hiding otherwise) Bulletproofs are also homomorphic, and its argument reveals an upper bound d on the degree of the committed polynomial (it's the number of non-zero entries in the public vector $\boldsymbol{i}$).

The only remaining issue is with Definition 5, since Bulletproof arguments are not hiding. We can resolve the issue of hiding using the blinding technique previously used by [9,12,13,21]. Concretely, because $\mathsf{Eval}(\mathsf{pp}, \phi, i)$ cannot show an argument for the inner product $\boldsymbol{\phi} \cdot \boldsymbol{i}$ directly, instead the evaluator can: sample and commit to a random ephemeral polynomial $\psi \in \mathbb{F}[x]$ of degree d, send this commitment along with the two field elements $\phi(i)$ and $\psi(i)$ to the verifier, query the (public coins) verifier for a challenge $c \in \mathbb{F}$, and use the homomorphic property to construct a non-hiding argument proving that $(\boldsymbol{\psi} + c\boldsymbol{\phi}) \cdot \boldsymbol{i}$ equals $\psi(i) + c\phi(i)$. It is acceptable for this argument to reveal information about $\psi + c\phi$ because the polynomial ψ serves as a one-time pad that hides ϕ from the verifier.

We believe that this construction can be adapted to construct deterministic versions (for random polynomials) of other linear combination schemes [8] such as DARK [12], Dory [30], and the post-quantum polynomial commitment schemes [7,27,37] based on FRI [6]. We leave this as an open question for future work.

Deterministic KZG Commitments. Kate et al. construct two polynomial commitment schemes, the first of which (called $\mathsf{PolyCommit}_{\mathrm{DL}}$ in their work [26, §3.2]) is already deterministic and was shown to meet Definitions 2, 3, and 5 based on the t-bilinear strong Diffie-Hellman assumption. The only discrepancy between our requirements and their construction is Definition 4. We must verify that the commitments of the share polynomials S_i are of degree at most t. However, the $\mathsf{PolyCommit}_{\mathrm{DL}}$ construction is predicated upon using trusted setup to generate powers of a generator element $\mathsf{pp} = \langle g, g^2, \dots, g^D \rangle$, and once this information is public, it is impossible to verify whether a committer has committed to a polynomial of the maximum degree or a smaller one.

If there exist constant integers α and β such that $p = \alpha t + \beta$ (such as the case where $n = 3t + 1$ and $p = 2t$), then there is a simple resolution to this issue: always construct polynomial commitments of maximum degree so that we can rely on strong correctness (Definition 2) instead. Observe that throughout Algorithm 1, there only exist commitments to polynomials of two different degrees: R of degree $p = \alpha t$ (in line 5) and each S_i of degree t (in line 6). In our construction, party P_i must be able to (a) interpolate S_i when given evaluations from $t + 1$ honest parties and (b) verify that the share polynomials are constructed in this fashion. Ergo, we can set the maximum degree $D = p$ during setup, sample S_i as a polynomial of degree D, and adjust line 6 of the Eval method to provide α distinct evaluations of the polynomial to each party (say, party i receives evaluations at the points i, $i + t$, $i + 2t$, ...) as well as β evaluations of the polynomial in common to all parties (say, at points $\alpha t + 1$, $\alpha t + 2$, ..., $\alpha t + \beta$). Each test polynomial T_i is now the difference of two degree-D polynomials, so it is also of degree D with overwhelming probability. Finally, while each party receives α points on each share polynomial S_i, it suffices that only one of those points intersect with R for the test polynomial to guarantee correct reconstruction.

4   Amortizing HAVEN for Long Secrets

In this section, we show how to extend HAVEN to share a large secret s using $O(\kappa n)$ communication complexity such that any $p + 1$ people can reconstruct the secret. Following the techniques used by Krawczyk [29] and Cachin and Tessaro [17], the core idea is to use a communication-efficient protocol for asynchronous reliable broadcast of the ciphertext corresponding to the long secret s, alongside Algorithm 1 to share the ephemeral symmetric key.

Building Blocks. In more detail, our construction uses a (t, n)-information dispersal algorithm IDA [35], a semantically secure symmetric key encryption scheme, and a collision-resistant hash function H. By comparison to Shamir secret sharing, an IDA scheme is similar in that it contains algorithms to split and reconstruct an object to and from shares, respectively, but it differs in two ways:

1. Shares of an IDA might leak information about the original object while Shamir shares do not.
2. Shares of an IDA are smaller in size than the original object while Shamir shares are of the same size.

More formally, an IDA consists of the following two algorithms.

1. split(f, t, n): Splits an object f into n shares such that any t can reconstruct the original object f where each share has size $|f|/t$.
2. reconstruct(s): Takes a vector of t shares and combine them to reconstruct the original object f.

Also, we define an encryption scheme as containing a key generation algorithm, an encryption method Enc : $k, m \mapsto c$, and a decryption method Dec : $k, c \mapsto m$ such that no probabilistic polynomial time adversary can distinguish ciphertexts belonging to two arbitrarily-chosen plaintexts m_0 or m_1 with noticeable probability. A hash function $H : \{0, 1\}^* \to \mathbb{F}$ is called collision resistant if no polynomial time adversary can find two inputs x and $x' \neq x$ such that $H(x) = H(x')$ with non-negligible probability. We refer readers to [23] for formal definitions.

Our New Construction. To support long secrets, our Amortized HAVEN protocol makes the following additions to the sharing phase in Algorithm 1.

– At the start of the protocol, the dealer generates a random key $k \in \mathbb{F}$ and encrypts the large secret s using k by running $c = \text{Enc}_k(s)$. Using split($c, t + 1, n$), the ciphertext is then encoded in n pieces $c_1, \ldots, c_n$ of length $|s|/t$. Additionally, we add $h_i = H(c_i)$ to the vector that forms the root commitment (line 11). Finally, the send message to party P_i also includes the ciphertext c and all witnesses to different hashes of every piece $h_i = H(c_i)$ that is included in the root commitment (line 14).

- Upon receiving (ID.d, send, set$_j$): party P_i adds one more consistency check to the list of requirements for her to produce an echo response. Namely, P_i checks that the every piece c_j is linked back to the root commitment using the witness provided by the dealer. To acquire each piece c_j, P_i runs split$(c, t + 1, n)$ the same way the dealer did. P_i then adds to info$_{i,j}$ the corresponding c_i along with it's witness.
- Upon receiving(ID.d, echo, info$_{j,i}$): party P_i adds one more consistency check to the list of requirements for her to produce a ready response. Namely, P_i checks that every c_m is linked back to the root commitment using the witness provided by P_m. The rest of the protocol proceeds as normal.

At the start of reconstruction, each honest party recovers the large ciphertext by running reconstruct IDA on $t + 1$ pieces that are linked to the root commitment that we have agreement on. The reconstruction phase continues as before and reconstructs the key k. The parties use the symmetric key k to decrypt the ciphertext and recover the original large secret s.

Theorem 2. *Suppose that* $t = O(n)$, *the underlying polynomial and vector commitments satisfy Definitions 2–6,* Enc *is a semantically secure encryption scheme, and* H *is collision resistant hash function. Then, amortized* HAVEN *for a large secret* $s = \Omega(n \log n)$ *is a high threshold AVSS that achieves a message complexity of* $O(n^2)$ *and a communication overhead of* $O(\kappa n)$.

Proof. We first examine communication costs. None of the changes above impact the message complexity: each party still sends $O(n)$ send, echo, ready, and reconstruct-share messages. The communication complexity now has two components: the HAVSS for the short key and the IDA for the long message. These costs sum to $O(\kappa n^2 \log n) + O(((|s|/t) \cdot n) \cdot n) = O(n|s|)$ as desired.

Next, the only two properties of an HAVSS that are directly impacted by the IDA of an encryption of the long secret are privacy and agreement. We argue about each property below in turn. Both properties only require minor adjustments to the arguments made in the proof of Theorem 1.

- Privacy: If the dealer is honest, the privacy argument in Theorem 1 guarantees that the adversary doesn't get hold of the secret key k used to encrypt the large secret s. The only thing that the adversary would get hold of is encrypted shares of the s. By definition of semantic security the attacker will not be able to extract any useful information about s from the ciphertext except with negligible probability.
- Agreement: Since at least $t + 1$ honest parties have to verify that all pieces $\{c_i\}$ are part of the polynomial commitment. Then if agreement is reached over the polynomial commitment, then agreement is reached over the pieces. Availability is also guaranteed, since each honest party has heard $t + 1$ echo messages from honest parties. Hence each honest party would have available $t + 1$ pieces that are consistent with the root commitment, enough to reconstruct the ciphertext c and thus the large secret s.

Acknowledgments. The authors are grateful to Ran Canetti and the anonymous reviewers for their valuable feedback. This material is based upon work supported by the DARPA SIEVE program under Agreement No. HR00112020021 and the National Science Foundation under Grants No. 1414119, 1718135, 1801564, and 1931714.

References

1. Abraham, I., Nayak, K., Ren, L., Shrestha, N.: On the optimality of optimistic responsiveness. IACR Cryptol. ePrint Arch. **2020**, 458 (2020)
2. Backes, M., Datta, A., Kate, A.: Asynchronous computational VSS with reduced communication complexity. In: Dawson, E. (ed.) CT-RSA 2013. LNCS, vol. 7779, pp. 259–276. Springer, Heidelberg (2013). https://doi.org/10.1007/978-3-642-36095-4_17
3. Basu, S., Malkhi, D., Reiter, M., Tomescu, A.: Asynchronous verifiable secret-sharing protocols on a good day. CoRR. abs/1807.03720 (2018)
4. Basu, S., Tomescu, A., Abraham, I., Malkhi, D., Reiter, M.K., Sirer, E.G.: Efficient verifiable secret sharing with share recovery in BFT protocols. In: Proceedings of the 2019 ACM SIGSAC Conference on Computer and Communications Security, CCS 2019, pp. 2387–2402. Association for Computing Machinery, New York (2019)
5. Ben-Or, M., Canetti, R., Goldreich, O.: Asynchronous secure computation. In: Proceedings of the Twenty-Fifth Annual ACM Symposium on Theory of Computing, STOC 1993, pp. 52–61. Association for Computing Machinery, New York (1993)
6. Ben-Sasson, E., Bentov, I., Horesh, Y., Riabzev, M.: Fast reed-solomon interactive oracle proofs of proximity. In: ICALP, vol. 107 of LIPIcs, pp. 14:1–14:17. Schloss Dagstuhl - Leibniz-Zentrum für Informatik (2018)
7. Ben-Sasson, E., Goldberg, L., Kopparty, S., Saraf, S.: DEEP-FRI: sampling outside the box improves soundness. In: ITCS, vol. 151 of LIPIcs, pp. 5:1–5:32. Schloss Dagstuhl - Leibniz-Zentrum für Informatik (2020)
8. Boneh, D., Drake, J., Fisch, B., Gabizon, A.: Halo infinite: recursive zk-SNARKs from any additive polynomial commitment scheme. IACR Cryptol. ePrint Arch. **2020**, 1536 (2020)
9. Bootle, J., Cerulli, A., Chaidos, P., Groth, J., Petit, C.: Efficient zero-knowledge arguments for arithmetic circuits in the discrete log setting. In: Fischlin, M., Coron, J.-S. (eds.) EUROCRYPT 2016, Part II. LNCS, vol. 9666, pp. 327–357. Springer, Heidelberg (2016). https://doi.org/10.1007/978-3-662-49896-5_12
10. Bootle, J., Groth, J.: Efficient batch zero-knowledge arguments for low degree polynomials. In: Abdalla, M., Dahab, R. (eds.) PKC 2018, Part II. LNCS, vol. 10770, pp. 561–588. Springer, Cham (2018). https://doi.org/10.1007/978-3-319-76581-5_19
11. Bracha, G.: Asynchronous byzantine agreement protocols. Inf. Comput. **75**(2), 130–143 (1987)
12. Bünz, B., Fisch, B., Szepieniec, A.: Transparent SNARKs from DARK compilers. In: Canteaut, A., Ishai, Y. (eds.) EUROCRYPT 2020, Part I. LNCS, vol. 12105, pp. 677–706. Springer, Cham (2020). https://doi.org/10.1007/978-3-030-45721-1_24
13. Bünz, B., Bootle, J., Boneh, D., Poelstra, A., Wuille, P., Maxwell, G.: Bulletproofs: short proofs for confidential transactions and more. In: 2018 IEEE Symposium on Security and Privacy (SP), pp. 315–334 (2018)

14. Cachin, C.: An asynchronous protocol for distributed computation of RSA inverses and its applications. In: Proceedings of the Twenty-Second ACM Symposium on Principles of Distributed Computing, PODC 2003, Boston, Massachusetts, USA, July 13–16, 2003, pp. 153–162 (2003)

15. Cachin, C., Kursawe, K., Lysyanskaya, A., Strobl, R.: Asynchronous verifiable secret sharing and proactive cryptosystems. In: ACM Conference on Computer and Communications Security, pp. 88–97. ACM (2002)

16. Cachin, C., Kursawe, K., Shoup, V.: Random oracles in constantipole: practical asynchronous byzantine agreement using cryptography (extended abstract). In: PODC, pp. 123–132. ACM (2000)

17. Cachin, C., Tessaro, S.: Asynchronous verifiable information dispersal. In: Fraigniaud, P. (ed.) DISC 2005. LNCS, vol. 3724, pp. 503–504. Springer, Heidelberg (2005). https://doi.org/10.1007/11561927_42

18. Canetti, R.: Studies in secure multiparty computation and applications. Ph.D. thesis. Citeseer (1996)

19. Canetti, R., Rabin, T.: Fast asynchronous byzantine agreement with optimal resilience. In: STOC, pp. 42–51. ACM (1993)

20. Catalano, D., Fiore, D.: Vector commitments and their applications. In: Kurosawa, K., Hanaoka, G. (eds.) PKC 2013. LNCS, vol. 7778, pp. 55–72. Springer, Heidelberg (2013). https://doi.org/10.1007/978-3-642-36362-7_5

21. Chiesa, A., Forbes, M.A., Spooner, N.: A zero knowledge sumcheck and its applications. Electron. Colloquium Comput. Complex. **24**, 57 (2017)

22. Chor, B., Goldwasser, S., Micali, S., Awerbuch, B.: Verifiable secret sharing and achieving simultaneity in the presence of faults (extended abstract). In: 26th Annual Symposium on Foundations of Computer Science, Portland, Oregon, USA, 21–23 October 1985, pp. 383–395 (1985)

23. Goldreich, O.: A uniform-complexity treatment of encryption and zero-knowledge. J. Cryptol. **6**(1), 21–53 (1993). https://doi.org/10.1007/BF02620230

24. Hirt, M., Kastrati, A., Liu-Zhang, C.-D.: Multi-threshold asynchronous reliable broadcast and consensus. IACR Cryptol. ePrint Arch. **2020**, 958 (2020)

25. Kate, A., Miller, A.K., Yurek, T.: Brief note: asynchronous verifiable secret sharing with optimal resilience and linear amortized overhead. CoRR, abs/1902.06095 (2019)

26. Kate, A., Zaverucha, G.M., Goldberg, I.: Constant-size commitments to polynomials and their applications. In: Abe, M. (ed.) ASIACRYPT 2010. LNCS, vol. 6477, pp. 177–194. Springer, Heidelberg (2010). https://doi.org/10.1007/978-3-642-17373-8_11

27. Kattis, A., Panarin, K., Vlasov, A.: Redshift: transparent SNARKs from list polynomial commitment IOPs. IACR Cryptol. ePrint Arch. **2019**, 1400 (2019)

28. Kokoris-Kogias, E., Spiegelman, A., Malkhi, D.: Asynchronous distributed key generation for computationally-secure randomness, consensus, and threshold signatures. In: Proceedings of the 2020 ACM SIGSAC Conference on Computer and Communications Security (2020)

29. Krawczyk, H.: Secret sharing made short. In: Stinson, D.R. (ed.) CRYPTO 1993. LNCS, vol. 773, pp. 136–146. Springer, Heidelberg (1994). https://doi.org/10.1007/3-540-48329-2_12

30. Lee, J.: Dory: efficient, transparent arguments for generalised inner products and polynomial commitments. IACR Cryptol. ePrint Arch. **2020**, 1274 (2020)

31. Libert, B., Yung, M.: Concise mercurial vector commitments and independent zero-knowledge sets with short proofs. In: Micciancio, D. (ed.) TCC 2010. LNCS, vol. 5978, pp. 499–517. Springer, Heidelberg (2010). https://doi.org/10.1007/978-3-642-11799-2_30

32. Merkle, R.C.: A digital signature based on a conventional encryption function. In: Pomerance, C. (ed.) CRYPTO 1987. LNCS, vol. 293, pp. 369–378. Springer, Heidelberg (1988). https://doi.org/10.1007/3-540-48184-2_32

33. Pass, R., Shi, E.: Hybrid consensus: efficient consensus in the permissionless model. In: DISC, vol. 91 of LIPIcs, pp. 39:1–39:16. Schloss Dagstuhl - Leibniz-Zentrum für Informatik (2017)

34. Pease, M.C., Shostak, R.E., Lamport, L.: Reaching agreement in the presence of faults. J. ACM **27**(2), 228–234 (1980)

35. Rabin, M.O.: Efficient dispersal of information for security, load balancing, and fault tolerance. J. ACM **36**(2), 335–348 (1989)

36. Shamir, A.: How to share a secret. Commun. ACM **22**(11), 612–613 (1979)

37. Vlasov, A., Panarin, K.: Transparent polynomial commitment scheme with polylogarithmic communication complexity. IACR Cryptol. ePrint Arch. **2019**, 1020 (2019)

Fine-Grained Forward Secrecy: Allow-List/Deny-List Encryption and Applications

David Derler[1], Sebastian Ramacher[2], Daniel Slamanig[2],
and Christoph Striecks[2(✉)]

[1] DFINITY, Zurich, Switzerland
david@dfinity.org
[2] AIT Austrian Institute of Technology, Vienna, Austria
{sebastian.ramacher,daniel.slamanig,christoph.striecks}@ait.ac.at

Abstract. Forward secrecy is an important feature for modern cryptographic systems and is widely used in secure messaging such as Signal and WhatsApp as well as in common Internet protocols such as TLS, IPSec, or SSH. The benefit of forward secrecy is that the damage in case of key-leakage is mitigated. Forward-secret encryption schemes provide security of past ciphertexts even if a secret key leaks, which is interesting in settings where cryptographic keys often reside in memory for quite a long time and could be extracted by an adversary, e.g., in cloud computing. The recent concept of puncturable encryption (PE; Green and Miers, IEEE S&P'15) provides a versatile generalization of forward-secret encryption: it allows to puncture secret keys with respect to ciphertexts to prevent the future decryption of these ciphertexts.

We introduce the abstraction of allow-list/deny-list encryption schemes and classify different types of PE schemes using this abstraction. Based on our classification, we identify and close a gap in existing work by introducing a novel variant of PE which we dub *Dual-Form Puncturable Encryption* (DFPE). DFPE significantly enhances and, in particular, generalizes previous variants of PE by allowing an interleaved application of allow- and deny-list operations.

We present a construction of DFPE in prime-order bilinear groups, discuss a direct application of DPFE for enhancing security guarantees within Cloudflare's Geo Key Manager, and show its generic use to construct forward-secret IBE and forward-secret digital signatures.

Keywords: Punturable encryption · Forward secrecy

1 Introduction

Leakage of secret keys is a major security risk in modern systems and cryptographic protocols. For example, key-leakage can be a significant problem in

---

Author list in alphabetical order. See https://www.ams.org/profession/leaders/culture/CultureStatement04.pdf.

N. Borisov and C. Diaz (Eds.): FC 2021, LNCS 12675, pp. 499–519, 2021.
https://doi.org/10.1007/978-3-662-64331-0_26

secure messaging applications such as Signal or WhatsApp, but also in other well-known Internet protocols such as TLS, IPSec, or SSH. Those applications typically address this risk by providing the property of *forward secrecy*. Forward secrecy mitigates the problems associated to the leakage of a long-term secret key in the sense that the confidentiality of the data encrypted in old cipher-texts is still protected after a key is leaked. However, key-leakage is problematic far beyond the aforementioned applications. One of the prime examples of key-leakage being an important risk is when decryption keys are kept in software or trusted execution environments (TEEs) like ARM's TrustZone or the increasingly popular SGX by Intel. Such scenarios are typically found within heavily virtualized environments such as cloud computing. In such settings, it is well known that the shared resources introduce the danger of information leakage, i.e., extracting decryption keys held in shared memory, e.g., via co-located virtual machines controlled by an attacker [34,41,42]. At the same time, microarchitectural attacks such as cache attacks (against TEEs) are getting increasingly sophisticated and more devastating (cf. [35]). While rotating keys frequently helps to reduce the risk, frequently deploying new keys becomes impractical if the frequency gets too high.

Concrete Example. We will illustrate this problem by a concrete practical example. As the use of TLS for securing communication on the Internet grows, content distribution networks (CDNs) such as Cloudflare face a new issue: all of their endpoints terminating TLS connections deployed in colocations all over the world need access to the secret keys associated to the certificate (i.e., public key) to guarantee low latency. As those secret keys belong to the customers, they need to provide the keys to the CDNs or deploy solutions such as Keyless SSL[1], where customers are required to run their own keyserver answering signing requests from the CDN. The latter comes at the cost of higher latency if users are not close to the location of the key server. The former—while providing better latency for users worldwide—faces a different issue: due to various differences in local laws or other regulations surrounding the use of secret keys, customers might not be interested in having their keys exposed to certain locations and areas. Systems like Cloudflare's Geo Key Manager[2] tackle this issue by giving customers the control on the locations their secret keys are stored when shared with Cloudflare. Effectively, customers are able put whole regions on allow-lists, e.g., Europe or the US. At the same time, they are able to put multiple colocations within those regions, e.g., London in Europe, on deny-lists. Finally, they are also able to directly put colocations on the allow-list that are not inside the regions already on allow-lists, e.g., Singapore.

Since the customer's secret keys are highly sensitive, such a system profits from strong security including forward secrecy. The currently deployed solution *does not* provide forward secrecy, a feature that helps to put the distributed keys at a much lower risk. Looking ahead, with our approach, adding areas to

---

[1] https://www.cloudflare.com/ssl/keyless-ssl/.
[2] https://blog.cloudflare.com/introducing-cloudflare-geo-key-manager/.

allow-lists, colocations within these areas on deny-lists, as well as allow-listing single colocations is efficiently possible and adds forward secrecy on top.

Fine-Grained Forward-Secrecy. We will follow the approach of restricting (or customizing) the capabilities of secret keys held in memory via cryptographic means to achieve fine-grained forward secrecy. Arguably, this still does not entirely eliminate the problem of key-leakage. Yet, it helps to significantly reduce the damage if key-leakage happens, and, at the same time, removes the requirement to frequently rotate keys. While forward secrecy can be efficiently obtained in interactive protocols, it is more involved for non-interactive primitives. In the past, forward secrecy has been studied for various non-interactive primitives such as digital signatures [6], identification schemes [1], public-key encryption [10], symmetric cryptography [7], and proxy re-encryption [20]. The basic idea is to discretize time into intervals and to have a fixed public key over a potentially long period of time. However, the secret key "evolves" over time such that a leaked secret key in interval i is no longer useful for any interval $j < i$. In particular, for public-key encryption, this guarantees that all "old" ciphertexts can no longer be decrypted. Obviously, if the switches between intervals happen too frequently, it requires good synchronization, whereas for longer time intervals a looser synchronization (which is desirable) is sufficient. Nevertheless, in any case, the achieved forward-secrecy property is very coarse grained, i.e., switching the interval essentially destroys access to *all* old ciphertexts.

Green and Miers [27] introduced the cryptographic concept of puncturable encryption (PE) as a versatile generalization of forward-secret public-key encryption for asynchronous messaging. The idea here is to provide a more fine-grained forward-secrecy property that allows a secret key to be "punctured" on specific ciphertexts (or tags associated to them) in a way that the resulting decryption key will then no longer be useful to decrypt ciphertexts on which the key has been punctured over time. Following these initial works, a number of alternative PE schemes [14,19,28,37,38] as well as some variations of PE schemes with different puncturing capabilities [21,39] have been proposed.

Allow-List/Deny-List Encryption Schemes. To provide a comprehensive classification of different cryptographic primitives (and mostly PE schemes), we introduce allow-/deny-list (ALDL) encryption. It represents a very simple abstraction of encryption mechanisms maintaining allow and deny lists. Here, ciphertexts and decryption keys are linked to both allow and deny lists in a certain way. Allow lists incorporate positive tags while deny lists have negative tags. A ciphertext can carry two tags—a positive and negative tag—that are determined during the encryption procedure. Decryption keys can be associated to several positive and negative tags. For example, a ciphertext with a positive tag t_+ and negative tag t_- can be decrypted by a secret key that is associated to t_+ but not to t_-. More generally this means that a decryption key that is linked to a positive tag is able to decrypt the ciphertext if that ciphertext has the positive tag attached. On the other hand, a decryption key that is associated to a negative tag is *not* able to decrypt ciphertexts that have those negative tags attached.

On a high level, this has interesting applications and subsumes several cryptographic primitives as shown in Table 1. For example, an identity-based encryption (IBE) [9,15] scheme can be seen as an ALDL encryption scheme where an allow list can contain an identity, i.e., an *id*. Ciphertexts and secret keys are associated to a certain *id* (i.e., a positive tag) from the allow list. If the *id* of the ciphertext matches the secret-key *id*, then decryption works.

Furthermore, a PE scheme can be seen as an ALDL encryption scheme where the deny list contains a set of tags. A ciphertext is associated to a certain negative tag and decryption keys are associated to a deny list of negative tags. Now, when the tag of the ciphertext is on the deny list, then decryption is *not* successful while all other ciphertexts with tags not on the deny list can be successfully decrypted. An interesting application is forward-secret zero round-trip time (0-RTT) key-exchange [19,28].

Recently, Derler et al. [21] and Wei et al. [39] proposed the new forward-secret primitives called fully PE (FuPE) and forward-secret puncturable IBE (fs-PIBE), respectively, that can be abstracted by ALDL encryption in the following sense. Within FuPE, ciphertexts are associated to a positive and negative tag while decryption keys can be first associated to several negative tags in a deny list and a final positive tag in an allow list. In fs-PIBE on the other hand, ciphertexts are also associated to a positive and a negative tag while decryption keys can be first associated to one positive tag in the allow list and afterwards to several negative tags inserted to a deny list. FuPE realized the first forward-secret proxy re-encryption (PRE) scheme while fs-PIBE has been shown to have applications to Cloud e-mails. In these approaches, the order of inserting tags to the allow and deny lists plays a crucial role.

In our work, we want to enhance those capabilities even further. In particular, our work allows to first associate the secret key with several negative tags in a deny list, then with a positive tag in the allow list, and afterwards with several further negative tags again in the deny list, which yields new applications areas not yet covered by existing approaches. Our enhancement gives more flexibility and more fine-grained forward secrecy enhancing techniques from prior works. In Table 1, we compare all discussed approaches.

Our Contribution. We propose a versatile variant of puncturable encryption dubbed dual-form puncturable encryption (DFPE), which extends recent works on PE that are not expressive enough to achieve our goals. We carefully adapt the PE techniques envisioned by Green and Miers [27] and Günther, Hale, Jager, and Lauer [28] to equip PE with *interleaved negative and positive puncturing*. While the concept of Fully PE (FuPE) due to Derler et al. [20,21] is related to our solution, it is not sufficient. In their work, positively punctured keys can no longer be negatively punctured. In contrast to Derler et al.—who can instantiate their FuPE scheme from any Hierarchical Identity-Based Encryption (HIBE) [25] scheme—we require novel tools and in particular the concept of tagged HIBEs (THIBEs), a generalization of HIBEs. Our ideas on THIBEs are related to the work of Abdalla, Kiltz, and Neven [2], but with different goals.

Table 1. Overview of allow-list (AL)/deny-list (DL) encryption variants with actions performed on the allow and deny lists and in which order. We use 1 to denote support for a single tag and ∞ to indicate many tags in arbitrary order. We further list cryptographic primitives and applications abstracted by the ALDL-encryption variants.

ALDL variant	1. action	2. action	3. action	Primitive	applications
1	AL (1)	–	–	IBE	E-mail (e.g., [9])
2	DL (∞)	–	–	PE	Key exchange (e.g., [27,28])
3a	AL (1)	DL (∞)	–	fs-PIBE	Cloud e-mail, weak forward-secret IBE (e.g., [39])
3b	DL (∞)	AL (1)	–	FuPE	Forward-secure PRE (e.g., [21])
4. (this work)	DL (∞)	AL (1)	DL (∞)	DFPE	Enhanced Geo Key Manager, forward-secret IBE and signatures

<u>Dual-Form Puncturable Encryption (DFPE):</u> Loosely speaking, DFPE allows to puncture secret keys on negative tags (like within PE), i.e., a key punctured on a negative tag can no longer decrypt ciphertexts under this tag, but in addition a secret key can be customized to a given positive tag once and then further punctured negatively. Keys customized to a positive tag can only decrypt ciphertexts to this positive tag and whose negative tags are distinct from the ones the key was punctured on. We introduce the concept of DFPE and rigorously model its security requirements. For concrete instantiations of DFPE, we introduce a generalization of HIBEs called tagged HIBEs (THIBEs) along with a suitable security model and which we instantiate using ideas underlying the Boneh-Boyen-Goh (BBG) [8] HIBE. Since it requires some modifications and tweaks to provide the features required by a THIBE scheme, we provide a careful proof of security of our THIBE. A main benefit of starting from the BBG HIBE is that the size of the ciphertexts in our THIBE is constant. Finally, we show how DFPE can be generically constructed from any THIBE and provide a proof-of-concept implementation of our concrete DFPE scheme.

<u>Enhancing Cloudflare's Geo Key Manager:</u> We show how the currently used approach based on a combination of both pairing-based identity-based broadcast encryption (IBBE) [18] and identity-based revocation (IBR) [4], which so far does not provide forward-secrecy, can be instantiated using DFPE as a single primitive. Thereby, it supports the required functionality of adding areas to allow-lists, colocations within these areas on deny-lists, allow-listing single colocations is efficiently possible, and at the same time adds forward secrecy on top while achieving comparable parameter sizes.

<u>Cryptographic Applications:</u> We demonstrate that DFPE is a versatile cryptographic tool by generically instantiating other primitives. This immediately yields (new) constructions thereof. In particular, we show how to generically construct forward-secure IBE [40], thereby—to the best of our knowledge—obtaining the first fs-IBE scheme with compact ciphertexts, as well as forward-secure signatures [1,6,30,31]. Especially, the latter turned out to be an interesting primitive in the context of distributed ledgers [17,17,22,23,26].

We present notation, pairings and the q-wBDHI assumption in Appendix A.

2   Tagged Hierarchical Identity-Based Encryption

Hierarchical identity-based encryption (HIBE) [8, 25, 29] organizes identities in a tree where identities at some level can delegate secret keys to its descendant entities, but cannot decrypt ciphertexts intended for other higher-level identities. A tagged HIBE (THIBE) is a generalization of HIBEs where secret keys can be tagged and ciphertexts are tagged (a concept related to [2] but adapted to different goals in our work). Correctness now ensures that untagged secret keys are capable of decrypting (tagged) ciphertexts if the identities match while tagged secret keys can only decrypt (tagged) ciphertexts correctly if the identities *and* the tag match. The distinguishing feature between HIBEs and THIBEs is that delegated secret keys on any hierarchy can be tagged and, afterwards, even further delegated. In a certain sense, through tagging, secret keys can be further restricted on the same hierarchy level and beyond in their decryption capabilities.

2.1   Definition, Correctness, and Security Notions of THIBEs

Before constructing THIBEs, we first present our THIBE definition and continue with its correctness property as well as its security notions.

Definition 1 (THIBE). *For some hierarchy parameter $\ell \in \mathbb{N}$, a tagged hierarchical identity-based encryption (THIBE) scheme* THIBE *with message space $\mathcal{M}$, tag space $\mathcal{T}$, and identity space $\mathcal{ID}^{\leq \ell}$, consists of the PPT algorithms* (Gen, Del, Tag, Enc, Dec):

Gen($1^\kappa, \ell$) : *output a keypair* (pk, $\mathsf{sk}_\varepsilon^\varepsilon$). *(We assume that* pk *is given as input to* Del, Tag, *and* Dec *implicitly; let $\varepsilon \notin \mathcal{ID} \cup \mathcal{T}$ be a distinguished element associated to non-tagged or non-delegated secret keys.)*

Del($\mathsf{sk}_{id'}^t, id$) : *output a secret key* sk_{id}^t *if $id' \in \mathcal{ID}^{\ell'-1}$ is a prefix of $id \in \mathcal{ID}^{\ell'}$, for some $\ell' \in [\ell]$ else output* $\mathsf{sk}_{id'}^t$.

Tag($\mathsf{sk}_{id}^\varepsilon, t$): *output a secret key* sk_{id}^t *if $t \in \mathcal{T}$, else output* $\mathsf{sk}_{id}^\varepsilon$.

Enc(pk, M, id, t) : *for message $M \in \mathcal{M}$, identity $id \in \mathcal{ID}^{\leq \ell}$, and tag $t \in \mathcal{T}$, output a ciphertext* C_{id}^t.

Dec($\mathsf{sk}_{id'}^{t'}, C_{id}^t$): *output $M \in \mathcal{M} \cup \{\bot\}$.*

Correctness of THIBE. Essentially, correctness follows the HIBE correctness (i.e., a secret key can decrypt a ciphertext if the identity in such key is a prefix of the identity associated to the ciphertext), but we additionally require that the tag in the ciphertext matches the tag in the secret key as well.

More formally, for all $\kappa, \ell \in \mathbb{N}$, all (pk, $\mathsf{sk}_\varepsilon^\varepsilon$) $\leftarrow$ Gen($1^\kappa, \ell$), all $M \in \mathcal{M}$, all $id, id' \in \mathcal{ID}^{\leq \ell} \cup \{\varepsilon\}$ where $id' \in \mathcal{ID}^{\ell'-1}$ is a prefix of $id \in \mathcal{ID}^{\ell'}$, for some $\ell' \in [\ell]$, all $t \in \mathcal{T} \cup \{\varepsilon\}$, all $\mathsf{sk}_{id}^t \leftarrow$ Tag($\mathsf{sk}_{id}^\varepsilon, t$), all $\mathsf{sk}_{id}^t \leftarrow$ Del($\mathsf{sk}_{id'}^\varepsilon, id$), all $t' \in \mathcal{T}$ all $C_{id}^{t'} \leftarrow$ Enc(pk, M, id, t'), we have that Dec($\mathsf{sk}_{id}^t, C_{id}^{t'}$) $= M$ if $t = t'$.

THIBE-IND-CPA and THIBE-IND-CCA Security Notions. A THIBE scheme is THIBE-IND-CPA-secure or THIBE-IND-CCA-secure if and only if any PPT adversary A succeeds in the following experiments only with probability at most negligibly larger than $1/2$.

First, A receives an honestly generated pk. Let $\mathsf{Ext}(\cdot,\cdot,\cdot)$ be a key-extraction oracle that, given $\mathsf{sk}_\varepsilon^\varepsilon$, an identity $id \in \mathcal{ID}^{\leq \ell}$, and a tag $t \in \mathcal{T} \cup \{\varepsilon\}$, outputs a secret key sk_{id}^t via iteratively running Del to compute $\mathsf{sk}_{id}^\varepsilon$ and, afterwards, returning $\mathsf{Tag}(\mathsf{sk}_{id}^\varepsilon, t)$. Furthermore, let Dec' be a decryption oracle that, given $\mathsf{sk}_\varepsilon^\varepsilon$ and a ciphertext C_{id}^t, outputs $\mathsf{Dec}(\mathsf{sk}_{id}^t, C_{id}^t)$, where $\mathsf{sk}_{id}^t \leftarrow \mathsf{Ext}(\mathsf{sk}_\varepsilon^\varepsilon, id, t)$. During the experiment, A may adaptively query the $\mathsf{Ext}(\mathsf{sk}_\varepsilon^\varepsilon, \cdot, \cdot)$-oracle for corresponding secret key $\mathsf{sk}_\varepsilon^\varepsilon$ to pk. Only for THIBE-IND-CCA security, A has access to the decryption oracle Dec'. At some point, A outputs two equal-length messages M_0, M_1 and receives a target ciphertext $C_{id^*}^{t^*} \leftarrow \mathsf{Enc}(\mathsf{pk}, M_b, id^*, t^*)$ in return, for uniform $b \leftarrow \{0,1\}$. Eventually, A outputs a guess b^*. We say that A is valid if and only if A never queried the Ext-oracle on a prefix of id^* for tag $t \in \{t^*, \varepsilon\}$, and only outputs equal-length messages. For THIBE-IND-CCA security, A is only valid if it additionally did not query Dec' on the challenge ciphertext. We say that any valid A succeeds if $b = b^*$. More formally, the experiments are given in Experiment 1.

Experiment $\mathsf{Exp}_{\mathsf{THIBE},A}^{\mathsf{thibe\text{-}ind\text{-}T}}(1^\kappa, \ell)$

$(\mathsf{pk}, \mathsf{sk}_\varepsilon^\varepsilon) \leftarrow \mathsf{Gen}(1^\kappa, \ell)$

$(M_0, M_1, id^*, t^*, ,) \leftarrow A^{\mathsf{Ext}(\mathsf{sk}_\varepsilon^\varepsilon, \cdot, \cdot), \mathsf{Dec}'(\mathsf{sk}_\varepsilon^\varepsilon, \cdot)}(\mathsf{pk})$

$b \xleftarrow{\$} \{0,1\}$

$C^* \leftarrow \mathsf{Enc}(\mathsf{pk}, M_b, id^*, t^*)$

$b^* \leftarrow A^{\mathsf{Ext}(\mathsf{sk}_\varepsilon^\varepsilon, \cdot, \cdot), \mathsf{Dec}'(\mathsf{sk}_\varepsilon^\varepsilon, \cdot)}(, C^*)$

if $b = b^*$ return then 1, else return 0

Experiment 1: THIBE-IND-T-security for THIBE: $\mathsf{T} \in \{\mathsf{CPA}, \mathsf{CCA}\}$.

Definition 2. *For any PPT adversary A, we define the advantage function as*

$$\mathbf{Adv}_{\mathsf{THIBE},A}^{\mathsf{thibe\text{-}ind\text{-}T}}(1^\kappa, \ell) := \left| \Pr\left[\mathsf{Exp}_{\mathsf{THIBE},A}^{\mathsf{thibe\text{-}ind\text{-}T}}(1^\kappa, \ell) = 1\right] - \frac{1}{2} \right|,$$

for integer $\ell \in \mathbb{N}$, for $\mathsf{T} \in \{\mathsf{CPA}, \mathsf{CCA}\}$.

2.2   Constructing Tagged Hierarchical Identity-Based Encryption

We present our construction of a THIBE. The scheme construction closely follows the construction of the Boneh-Boyen-Goh (BBG) HIBE [8], but has one additional distinguished element in the secret keys (used for positive puncturings later in our DFPE construction). This element is not related to any hierarchy

---

$\mathsf{Gen}(1^\kappa, \ell)$:   Generate a bilinear group $\mathsf{BG} := (p, e, G_1, G_2, G_T, g_1, g_2) \leftarrow \mathsf{BGen}(1^\kappa)$,
set $\mathcal{M} := G_T$, set $\mathcal{T} := \{0,1\}^\kappa$, and set $\mathcal{ID} := \mathbb{Z}_p$, sample $g, h, h_0, h_1, \ldots, h_\ell \leftarrow G_1$,
choose $\alpha, r \leftarrow \mathbb{Z}_p$, set $\mathsf{pk} := (\mathsf{BG}, H, g, h, h_0, h_1, \ldots, h_\ell, g_2^\alpha)$, for hash function
$H \colon \mathcal{T} \mapsto \mathbb{Z}_p$ (modelled as RO in the security proof) where $H(\varepsilon) := 0$,
and $\mathsf{sk}_\varepsilon^\varepsilon := (h^\alpha \cdot h_0^r, g_2^r, h_1^r, \ldots, h_\ell^r, g^r)$.

$\mathsf{Del}(\mathsf{sk}_{id'}^t, id)$:   For $id =: (id_1, \ldots, id_{\ell'+1})$ and $\ell' := |id'|$, if $id \neq (id', id_{\ell'+1})$, then
return $\mathsf{sk}_{id'}^t$. Otherwise, if $t = \varepsilon$, parse $\mathsf{sk}_{id'}^t =: (a_0, a_1, K_{\ell'+1}, \ldots, K_\ell, g')$.
Sample $r' \leftarrow \mathbb{Z}_p$ and return

$$\left(a_0 \cdot K_{\ell'+1}^{id_{\ell'+1}} \cdot \left(h_0 \cdot \prod_{i=1}^{|\ell'+1|} h_i^{id_i} \right)^{r'}, a_1 \cdot g_2^{r'}, (K_i \cdot h_i^{r'})_{\ell'+1 < i \leq \ell}, g' \cdot g^{r'} \right).$$

Otherwise, if $t \neq \varepsilon$, parse $\mathsf{sk}_{id'}^t =: (a_0, a_1, K_{\ell'+1}, \ldots, K_\ell)$. Sample $r' \leftarrow \mathbb{Z}_p$ and return

$$\left(a_0 \cdot K_{\ell'+1}^{id_{\ell'+1}} \cdot \left(h_0 \cdot \prod_{i=1}^{\ell'+1} h_i^{id_i} \right)^{r'} \cdot g^{H(t) \cdot r'}, a_1 \cdot g_2^{r'}, (K_i \cdot h_i^{r'})_{\ell'+1 < i \leq \ell} \right).$$

$\mathsf{Tag}(\mathsf{sk}_{id}^\varepsilon, t)$:   If $t = \varepsilon$, return $\mathsf{sk}_{id}^\varepsilon$. Otherwise, set $\ell' := |id|$ and $id =: (id_1, \ldots, id_{\ell'})$.
Parse $\mathsf{sk}_T^\varepsilon =: (a_0, a_1, K_{\ell'+1}, \ldots, K_\ell, g')$. Sample $r' \leftarrow \mathbb{Z}_p$ and return

$$\left(a_0 \cdot g'^{H(t)} \cdot \left(h_0 \cdot \prod_{i=1}^{\ell'} h_i^{id_i} \right)^{r'} \cdot g^{H(t) \cdot r'}, a_1 \cdot g_2^{r'}, (K_i \cdot h_i^{r'})_{\ell' < i \leq \ell} \right).$$

$\mathsf{Enc}(\mathsf{pk}, M, id, t)$:   Set $\ell' := |id|$ and $id =: (id_1, \ldots, id_{\ell'})$. Sample $s \leftarrow \mathbb{Z}_p$, and return

$$(C_1, C_2, C_3) := \left(e(h, g_2^\alpha)^s \cdot M, g_2^s, \left(h_0 \cdot \prod_{i=1}^{\ell'} h_i^{id_i} \right)^s \cdot g^{H(t) \cdot s} \right).$$

$\mathsf{Dec}(\mathsf{sk}_{id'}^{t'}, C_{id}^t)$:   If $id' \neq id$ or $t' \neq t$, return $\bot$. Otherwise, parse $\mathsf{sk}_{id'}^t$ as $(a_0, a_1, \ldots)$
and $(C_1, C_2, C_3) := C_{id}^t$. Return $M' := C_1 \cdot e(C_3, a_1) \cdot e(a_0, C_2)^{-1}$.

Scheme 1: Construction of THIBE.

level and can be embedded into the secret key at any stage. In Scheme 1, we
formally construct our THIBE.

Correctness of THIBE. Correctness essentially follows from the correctness of
the Boneh-Boyen-Goh HIBE [8]; in particular, see that decryption succeeds for
matching secret keys $\mathsf{sk}_{id}^t =: (a_0, a_1, \ldots) = (h^\alpha \cdot (h_0 \cdot \prod_{i=1}^{\ell'} h_i^{id_i} \cdot g^{H(t)})^r, g_2^r)$ and
ciphertexts $C_{id}^t =: (C_1, C_2, C_3) = (e(h, g_2^\alpha)^s \cdot M, g_2^s, (h_0 \cdot \prod_{i=1}^{\ell'} h_i^{id_i} \cdot g^{H(t)})^s)$, for
$id =: (id_1, \ldots, id_{\ell'})$:

$$C_1 \cdot \frac{e(C_3, a_1)}{e(a_0, C_2)} = e(h, g_2^\alpha)^s \cdot M \cdot \frac{e((h_0 \cdot \prod_{i=1}^{\ell'} h_i^{id_i} \cdot g^{H(t)})^s, g_2^r)}{e(h^\alpha \cdot (h_0 \cdot \prod_{i=1}^{\ell'} h_i^{id_i} \cdot g^{H(t)})^r, g_2^s)} = M.$$

Theorem 1. *If the q-wBDHI assumption holds, then* THIBE *defined in Scheme 1 is THIBE-IND-CPA-secure in the random-oracle (RO) model. Concretely, for any valid PPT adversary A with at most $q_k = q_k(\kappa)$ key queries, there is a distinguisher D on q-wBDHI with $q = \ell + 1$, such that*

$$\mathbf{Adv}_{\mathsf{THIBE},A}^{\mathsf{thibe\text{-}sind\text{-}cpa}}(1^\kappa, \ell) \leq q_k \cdot \mathbf{Adv}_{\mathsf{BGen},D}^{\mathsf{q\text{-}wBDHI}}(1^\kappa),$$

for group generator BGen *and number of RO-queries $q_k = q_k(\kappa)$.*

Due to space constraints, we refer the reader to the full version of this work for the proof of Theorem 1.

THIBE-IND-CCA Security. We now discuss how to obtain THIBE-IND-CCA security for our construction THIBE by applying the well-known Fujisaki-Okamoto transform [24]. Basically, the encryption algorithm will encrypt as its message (M, r) with M the original message and r a sufficiently large randomly sampled bit string (this requires an injective encoding (M, r) into the message space of the THIBE scheme). The THIBE-encryption is de-randomized and uses as random coins $H(r)$ where H is a hash function modeled as a random oracle (RO) to obtain the ciphertext C_{id}^t. The decryption algorithm applies the original decryption algorithm from the THIBE-IND-CPA-secure THIBE scheme to receive (M', r'). Then, it re-encrypts (M', r') using random coins $H(r, M')$ to obtain the ciphertext $\overline{C}_{id}^t$. If it holds that $C_{id}^t = \overline{C}_{id}^t$, it outputs M' and otherwise it outputs $\bot$.

Corollary 1. *If the q-wBDHI assumption holds, then* THIBE *defined in Scheme 1 is THIBE-IND-CCA-secure in the RO model. Concretely, for any valid PPT adversary A with at most $q_k = q_k(\kappa)$ key queries, there is a distinguisher D on q-wBDHI with $q = \ell + 1$, such that*

$$\mathbf{Adv}_{\mathsf{THIBE},A}^{\mathsf{thibe\text{-}sind\text{-}cca}}(1^\kappa, \ell) \leq q_k \cdot q_c \cdot \mathbf{Adv}_{\mathsf{BGen},D}^{\mathsf{q\text{-}wBDHI}}(1^\kappa),$$

for group generator BGen *and number of RO-queries $q_k = q_k(\kappa)$ and $q_c = q_c(\kappa)$.*

3 Dual-Form Puncturable Encryption

Puncturable encryption (PE) has been introduced by Green and Miers in [27] and subsequently used and refined in several works, e.g., in [11,16,19,21,28]. We recall, that a PE scheme is a public-key encryption scheme where each ciphertext can be encrypted with respect to one (or more tags). PE features an additional puncturing algorithm that takes a secret key and a tag t as input and produces an updated secret key. This updated secret key is able to decrypt all ciphertexts *except* those tagged with t and (updated) secret keys can be iteratively "punctured" on distinct tags. (In our generalized allow-/deny-list encryption concept, this will correspond to our secret-key manipulation with respect to a deny list.)

Despite being slightly different in their concrete formulation (e.g., some schemes allow single tags, others multiple tags), existing PE schemes all provide the same basic idea in their functionality, i.e., that they allow to puncture secret keys in a way that they can no longer decrypt certain ciphertexts. A notable difference is in the formulation of Fully PE (FuPE) from Derler et al. [20] where secret keys can be punctured with respect to so-called negative tags (resembling the functionality of PE) and in addition to so-called *positive* tags. If a secret key is punctured with respect to a positive tag, then it can *only* decrypt ciphertexts that are tagged with respect to the corresponding positive tag. Although this approach adds more flexibility, it still lacks an important feature, namely, once keys are positively punctured, they can no longer be negatively punctured. Mapped to the application that we have in mind, this means that derived FuPE keys will loose the key-manipulation property (a versatile feature that we want to enable). To mitigate this problem and to make the concepts of PE more comprehensible, we introduce the new notion of Dual-Form PE (DFPE) which enables the negative-puncturing features of keys after those keys have already been positively punctured.

3.1   Definition, Correctness, and Security Notions of DFPE

Before constructing DFPE, we first present our DFPE definition and continue with its correctness property as well as its security notions.

Definition 3 (DFPE). *A Dual-Form Puncturable Encryption (DFPE) scheme* DFPE *with message space* $\mathcal{M}$, *positive and negative tag spaces* $\mathcal{T}_+$ *and* $\mathcal{T}_-$, *respectively, consists of the PPT algorithms* (Gen, NPunc, PPunc, Enc, Dec):

Gen$(1^\kappa, \ell_-)$: *key generation, on input a unary security parameter* $1^\kappa \in \mathbb{N}$ *and maximum number of negative tags* $\ell_- \in \mathbb{N}$, *outputs public and secret keys* $(\mathsf{pk}, \mathsf{sk}_\varepsilon^\varepsilon)$. *(We assume that* pp *implicitly determines* $\mathcal{M}$, $\mathcal{T}_+$, *and* $\mathcal{T}_-$; *we consider* ε *to be not part of the positive and negative tag spaces.)*

NPunc$(\mathsf{sk}_T^{t_+}, t_-)$: *negative puncturing, on input a secret key* $\mathsf{sk}_T^{t_+}$ *with* $T \subset \mathcal{T}_- \cup \{\varepsilon\}$ *and* $t_+ \in \mathcal{T}_+ \cup \{\varepsilon\}$, *and a tag* $t_- \in \mathcal{T}_-$, *outputs* $\mathsf{sk}_{T \cup \{t_-\}}^{t_+}$.

PPunc$(\mathsf{sk}_T^\varepsilon, t_+)$: *positive puncturing, on input a secret key* $\mathsf{sk}_T^\varepsilon$ *and positive tag* $t_+ \in \mathcal{T}_+$, *outputs a key* $\mathsf{sk}_T^{t_+}$.

Enc$(\mathsf{pk}, M, t_-, t_+)$: *encryption, on input a public key* pk, *a message* $M \in \mathcal{M}$, *a negative tag* $t_- \in \mathcal{T}_-$, *and a positive tag* $t_+ \in \mathcal{T}_+$, *outputs a ciphertext* $C_{t_-}^{t_+}$. *(We note that* t_+ *and* t_- *are publicly retrievable given the ciphertext and the public key* pk.)

Dec$(\mathsf{sk}_T^{t'_+}, C_{t_-}^{t_+})$: *on input a secret key* $\mathsf{sk}_T^{t'_+}$ *and a ciphertext* $C_{t_-}^{t_+}$, *outputs* $M \in \mathcal{M}$ *if* $t_- \notin T$ *and* $t'_+ = t_+$; *else output* $\bot$.

Correctness of DFPE. Essentially, correctness ensures that even if a secret key is negatively punctured and afterwards positively punctured, or vice versa, decryption succeeds if the resulting secret key matches the positive tag of the ciphertext and the negative tag of the ciphertext was not already punctured. More formally, for all $\kappa, \ell_- \in \mathbb{N}$, all $(\mathsf{pk}, \mathsf{sk}_\varepsilon^\varepsilon) \leftarrow$ Gen$(1^\kappa, \ell_-)$, all $T \subset \mathcal{T}_- \cup \{\varepsilon\}$, all $t_- \in \mathcal{T}_-$, all $t_+ \in \mathcal{T}_+ \cup \{\varepsilon\}$, all arbitrarily interleaved runs of $\mathsf{sk}_{T \cup \{t_-\}}^{t_+} \leftarrow$

Experiment $\mathsf{Exp}_{\mathsf{DFPE},A}^{\mathsf{dfpe\text{-}ind\text{-}T}}(1^\kappa, \ell_-)$

$(\mathsf{pk}, \mathsf{sk}_\varepsilon^\varepsilon) \leftarrow \mathsf{Gen}(1^\kappa, \ell_-)$

$(M_0, M_1, t_-^*, t_+^*, \mathsf{st}) \leftarrow A^{\mathsf{Ext}(\mathsf{sk}_\varepsilon^\varepsilon, \cdot, \cdot),\, \mathsf{Dec}'(\mathsf{sk}_\varepsilon^\varepsilon, \cdot)}(\mathsf{pk})$

$b \leftarrow \{0, 1\}$

$C^* \leftarrow \mathsf{Enc}(\mathsf{pk}, M_b, t_-^*, t_+^*)$

$b^* \leftarrow A^{\mathsf{Ext}(\mathsf{sk}_\varepsilon^\varepsilon, \cdot, \cdot),\, \mathsf{Dec}'(\mathsf{sk}_\varepsilon^\varepsilon, \cdot)}(\mathsf{st}, \mathsf{pk}, C^*)$

if $b = b^*$ return 1, else return 0

Experiment 2: DFPE-IND-T-security for DFPE: $\mathsf{T} \in \{\mathsf{CPA}, \mathsf{CCA}\}$.

$\mathsf{NPunc}(\mathsf{sk}_T^{t_+}, t_-)$, all $t'_+ \in t_+$ and $\mathsf{sk}_T^{t_+} \leftarrow \mathsf{PPunc}(\mathsf{sk}_T^\varepsilon, t'_+)$, all $M \in \mathcal{M}$, all $C_{t_-}^{t'_+} \leftarrow \mathsf{Enc}(\mathsf{pk}, M, t_-, t'_+)$, we have that $\mathsf{Dec}(\mathsf{sk}_T^{t'_+}, C_{t_-}^{t'_+}) = M$ if $t_- \notin T$.

DFPE-IND-CPA and DFPE-IND-CCA Security Notions. We define security notions for DFPE, dubbed DFPE-IND-CPA and DFPE-IND-CCA. A DFPE scheme is DFPE-IND-CPA-secure or DFPE-IND-CCA-secure if any PPT adversary A succeeds in the following experiment only with probability at most negligibly larger than $1/2$. First, public and secret keys $(\mathsf{pk}, \mathsf{sk}_\varepsilon^\varepsilon)$ are honestly generated. During the experiments, A may adaptively query a $\mathsf{Ext}(\mathsf{sk}_\varepsilon^\varepsilon, \cdot, \cdot)$-oracle, while for the DFPE-IND-CCA experiment, A may adaptively query a $\mathsf{Dec}'(\mathsf{sk}_\varepsilon^\varepsilon, \cdot)$-oracle additionally:

$\mathsf{Ext}(\mathsf{sk}_\varepsilon^\varepsilon, T, t_+)$, on input secret key $\mathsf{sk}_\varepsilon^\varepsilon$, negative-tag set $T \subset \mathcal{T}_-$, and positive tag $t_+ \in \mathcal{T}_+ \cup \{\varepsilon\}$, outputs $\mathsf{sk}_T^{t_+} \leftarrow \mathsf{PPunc}(\mathsf{sk}_{T_\ell}^\varepsilon, t_+)$, for iteratively punctured secret key $\mathsf{sk}_{T_i}^\varepsilon \leftarrow \mathsf{NPunc}(\mathsf{sk}_{T_{i-1}}^\varepsilon, t_{i-1})$, for all pairwise-different tags $(t_0, \ldots, t_{\ell-1}) \in (T)^\ell$ with $\ell := |T|$ and $i \in [\ell]$ in arbitrary order. (It allows the positive tag $t_+ = \varepsilon$ but not the negative-tag set $T = \{\varepsilon\}$ nor the empty set $T = \emptyset$ as input.)

$\mathsf{Dec}'(\mathsf{sk}_\varepsilon^\varepsilon, C_{t_-}^{t_+})$, on input secret key $\mathsf{sk}_\varepsilon^\varepsilon$ and ciphertext $C_{t_-}^{t_+}$, derives $\mathsf{sk}_\varepsilon^{t_+} \leftarrow \mathsf{PPunc}(\mathsf{sk}_\varepsilon^\varepsilon, t_+)$ and outputs $M \leftarrow \mathsf{Dec}(\mathsf{sk}_\varepsilon^{t_+}, C_{t_-}^{t_+})$. (The oracle does not allow a ciphertext input associated to the tags $t_- = \varepsilon$ and $t_+ = \varepsilon$.)

The public key pk is given to A. A outputs equal-length messages (M_0, M_1), a target negative tag $t_-^* \in \mathcal{T}_-$, and a target positive tag $t_+^* \in \mathcal{T}_+$. The target challenge ciphertext $C^* \leftarrow \mathsf{Enc}(\mathsf{pk}, M_b, t_-^*, t_+^*)$, for uniform $b \leftarrow \{0, 1\}$, is given to A. Eventually, A outputs a guess b^*, and succeeds, i.e., the experiment outputs 1, if the equation $b = b^*$ holds.

We say that A is *valid* if and only if A has not queried the Ext-oracle to obtain keys such that the challenge ciphertext can be trivially decrypted; for the DFPE-IND-CCA case, we additionally require that A did not query Dec'-oracle with the challenge ciphertext. More concretely, if any valid PPT A succeeds only with probability at most negligibly larger than $1/2$, then we say an DFPE scheme is DFPE-IND-CPA and DFPE-IND-CCA secure, respectively. In Experiment 2, we formally state the security experiments.

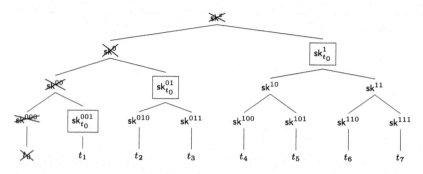

Fig. 1. Example of a DFPE secret key that has been punctured on t_0. The secret key $\mathsf{sk}_{t_0}^{t^+}$ has the $\boxed{\text{boxed}}$ elements $(\mathsf{sk}_{t_0}^{001}, \mathsf{sk}_{t_0}^{01}, \mathsf{sk}_{t_0}^{1})$.

Definition 4. *We define the advantage of an adversary A in the DFPE-IND-T experiment* $\mathsf{Exp}_{\mathsf{DFPE},A}^{\mathsf{dfpe\text{-}ind\text{-}T}}(1^\kappa, \ell_-)$ *as*

$$\mathbf{Adv}_{\mathsf{DFPE},A}^{\mathsf{dfpe\text{-}ind\text{-}T}}(1^\kappa, \ell_-) := \left| \Pr\left[\mathsf{Exp}_{\mathsf{DFPE},A}^{\mathsf{dfpe\text{-}ind\text{-}T}}(1^\kappa, \ell_-) = 1 \right] - \tfrac{1}{2} \right|.$$

We say a DFPE scheme DFPE is DFPE-IND-T-secure for $\mathsf{T} \in \{\mathsf{CPA}, \mathsf{CCA}\}$, *if* $\mathbf{Adv}_{\mathsf{DFPE},A}^{\mathsf{dfpe\text{-}ind\text{-}T}}(1^\kappa, \ell_-)$ *is a negligible function in* κ *for all valid PPT A.*

3.2   Constructing Dual-Form Puncturable Encryption

Subsequently, we present a construction of a DFPE scheme based on pairings. Unfortunately, we cannot instantiate our DFPE scheme directly from HIBEs as done in prior work on PE [28] and Fully PE [20,21]. The reason is that we want to allow puncturings even after secret keys were extracted for a specific positive tag such that those keys can be further restricted with respect to negative tags. Realizing this generically from HIBEs stays unknown, but we use tagged HIBEs (THIBEs) to construct DFPE-IND-CCA-secure DFPE. This allows to fulfill the needs for our applications we have in mind not being achieved before by FuPE. By applying THIBEs, we are able to instantiate our DFPE scheme using Type-3 bilinear groups as they represent the state-of-the-art regarding efficiency and similarity of the security levels of the base and target groups.

To construct a DFPE scheme from THIBEs, we implicitly arrange negative tags of the DFPE scheme associated to secret keys in a complete binary tree, i.e., the nodes represent a prefix bit representation of the negative tag and, hence, the root of the tree is associated with keys $\mathsf{sk}_\varepsilon^{t^+}$ of the DFPE. In Fig. 1, we give an example with a secret key punctured on a negative tag t_0.

We define an additional PPT helper algorithm Trunc to prune the tree to output a punctured secret key that corresponds to a given set of tags. This is reminiscent of prior works, e.g., [10,19,20,28].

Intuition of Trunc. Essentially, Trunc takes the current tree configuration as provided in the secret key (i.e., which tags are already punctured and, hence, how the tree is pruned for such tags). It further receives a negative tag t_- that will be punctured. Trunc first finds all elements from the root to the associated leaf of tag t_-. (Since those elements can be used to derive a secret key for tag t_-.) It delegates the key elements on that path such that no ancestor elements for t_- are available anymore and keeps the other key elements. The result is a pruned tree that excludes secret-key material for t_- for the new set of punctured tags $T \cup \{t_-\}$. The concrete PPT algorithms works as follows (see that the positive tag t_+ is not touched in Trunc).

$\mathsf{Trunc}(\mathsf{sk}_T^{t_+}, t_-)$: on input keys $(\mathsf{sk}_{T,1}, \ldots, \mathsf{sk}_{T,m}) := \mathsf{sk}_T^{t_+}$, for some integer m, output a punctured secret key according to $t_- = (t_1, \ldots, t_\ell)$ as follows:

    1a. let $\mathsf{sk}_{T,i}$ be the secret key part associated to the unique node which is associated to a prefix of t_-. (Such unique element always exists, otherwise t_- would have been punctured already.) Derive delegated secret keys hanging from the path to t_- by iteratively calling Del on all prefixes of t_- starting from the node associated to $\mathsf{sk}_{T,i}$ and set $\mathsf{sk}_T' := (\mathsf{sk}_{T,\leq m}', \mathsf{sk}_{T,m+1}', \mathsf{sk}_{T,m+2}', \ldots)$, where $\mathsf{sk}_{T,\leq m}'$ is the same as $\mathsf{sk}_T^{t_+}$, but without $\mathsf{sk}_{T,i}$, and $\mathsf{sk}_{T,m+1}', \mathsf{sk}_{T,m+2}', \ldots$ are those derived delegated keys via Del hanging from the path to t_-; else,

    1b. if there exist a leaf associated to a t_--secret key $\mathsf{sk}_{T,i}$, for $i \in [m]$, then set $\mathsf{sk}_{T \cup \{t_-\}}^{t_+} := \mathsf{sk}_{T,\leq m}'$, where $\mathsf{sk}_{T,\leq m}'$ is the same as $\mathsf{sk}_T^{t_+}$, but without the leaf-associated secret key $\mathsf{sk}_{T,i}$.

    2. Output $\mathsf{sk}_{T \cup \{t_-\}}^{t_+}$.

Concrete Construction of DFPE. The intuition of the concrete DFPE construction is as follows. Key generation returns the public-secret key pair of the THIBE key generation as its initial public and secret keys. The negative and positive tag spaces are set to $\mathcal{T}_- = |\mathcal{ID}^\ell|$ (i.e., corresponding to a leaf in the tree) and $\mathcal{T}_+ = \mathcal{T}$ (i.e., corresponding to THIBE's tags), respectively. Negative puncturing takes a secret key, runs Trunc to truncate the tree, and returns the punctured secret key (according to the pruned-tree configuration). Positive puncturing takes a secret key and a positive tag t_+, and punctures all part secret keys with t_+ using Tag. Encryption takes the public key, negative and positive tags, and the message to return the output of THIBE's encryption algorithm. Decryption finds the associated secret key part such that the negative tag t_- of the ciphertext is matched (i.e., if t_- was not yet punctured in the secret key, then such key material is available). Furthermore, if the positive tag t_+ of the secret key matches the positive tag of the ciphertext, then decryption returns the output of THIBE's decryption algorithm.

    More formally, let THIBE = (THIBE.Gen, THIBE.Del, THIBE.Tag, THIBE.Enc, THIBE.Dec) with message space $\mathcal{M}_{\mathsf{THIBE}}$, identity space $\mathcal{ID}^{\leq \ell}$, and tag space $\mathcal{T}$ be a THIBE scheme. We present our DFPE scheme DFPE = (Gen, NPunc, PPunc, Enc, Dec) with message space $\mathcal{M} := \mathcal{M}_{\mathsf{THIBE}}$, negative tag space $\mathcal{T}_- := \mathcal{ID}^\ell$, and positive tag space $\mathcal{T}_+ := \mathcal{T}$ in Scheme 2 and further show that it satisfies correctness and the DFPE-IND-CCA security notion.

Gen($1^\kappa, \ell$): Return $(\mathsf{pk}, \mathsf{sk}_\varepsilon^\varepsilon) \leftarrow$ THIBE.Gen($1^\kappa, \ell$). (We assume that the negative tag
  space $\mathcal{T}_-$ is of size $|\mathcal{ID}^\ell|$ for simplicity.)

NPunc(sk_T^{t+}, t_-): Return $\mathsf{sk}_{T \cup \{t_-\}}^{t+} \leftarrow$ Trunc(sk_T^{t+}, t_-).

PPunc($\mathsf{sk}_T^\varepsilon, t_+$): Compute $\mathsf{sk}_{t_i}^{t+} \leftarrow$ THIBE.Tag($\mathsf{sk}_{t_i}^\varepsilon, t_+$), for all $\mathsf{sk}_T^\varepsilon =: (\mathsf{sk}_{t_1}^\varepsilon, \ldots, \mathsf{sk}_{t_m}^\varepsilon)$,
  for some integer m, and output $\mathsf{sk}_T^{t+} := (\mathsf{sk}_{t_i}^{t+})_{i \in [m]}$.

Enc(pk, M, t_-, t_+): Return $C_{t_-}^{t+} \leftarrow$ THIBE.Enc(pk, M, t_-, t_+).

Dec($\mathsf{sk}_T^{t+}, C_{t_-}^{t+}$): Parse $\mathsf{sk}_T^{t+} =: (\ldots, \mathsf{sk}_{t'}^{t+}, \ldots)$ such that t'_- is a prefix of t_-, run $\mathsf{sk}_{t_-}^{t+} \leftarrow$
  THIBE.Del($\mathsf{sk}_{t'}^{t+}, t$), and return $M :=$ THIBE.Dec($\mathsf{sk}_{t_-}^{t+}, C_{t_-}^{t+}$). (Note that if $t_- \notin T$,
  such prefix always exists.)

Scheme 2: DFPE-IND-CCA-secure DFPE scheme DFPE.

Correctness of DFPE. Correctness essentially follows from the correctness of THIBE; in particular, see that if $t_- \notin T$, then there exist a part-secret key that is capable of decrypting the ciphertext. Due to space constraints, for a proof of the following theorem, we refer the reader to the full version of this work.

Theorem 2. *If* THIBE *is a THIBE-IND-CCA-secure THIBE, then* DFPE *defined in Scheme 2 is DFPE-IND-CCA-secure. Concretely, for any valid PPT adversary A, there is an adversary D on the THIBE-IND-CCA-security, such that*

$$\mathbf{Adv}_{\mathsf{DFPE}, A}^{\mathsf{dfpe\text{-}ind\text{-}cca}}(1^\kappa, \ell_-) \leq \mathbf{Adv}_{\mathsf{THIBE}, D}^{\mathsf{thibe\text{-}sind\text{-}cca}}(1^\kappa, \ell_-),$$

for some integer $\ell_- \in \mathbb{N}$.

3.3   Implementation and Evaluation

We have implemented our DFPE-IND-CPA-secure DFPE scheme as presented in Sect. 3.2 in Python 3.8 based on pyrelic[3] using the BN254 curve that yields a security level of around 100 bit [5,33] with the relic pairing library version 0.5.0 [3]. The measurements were performed on a laptop with an Intel Core i7-8650U @ 1.9 GHz running Ubuntu 20.04. In Table 2, we present the average runtime over 100 runs each and sizes of public keys, secret keys and ciphertexts using negative tag spaces of size 2^{48}, 2^{64}, and 2^{80} for a random message, respectively. From Table 2, one can see that the algorithms Gen, Enc, Dec, and PPunc are very efficient. The benchmarks of the Dec algorithm assumes that no additional key extraction is necessary. Thus, the runtime of the decryption is independent of the size of the parameter space. The NPunc algorithm needs less than a second for all levels, but is still the slowest algorithm overall.[4] However,

---

[3] https://github.com/sebastinas/pyrelic, commit 264e6396.
[4] It is a central open issue in the context of PE to make these algorithms more efficient.

Table 2. Performance estimation and evaluation: exponentiations in G_1 and G_2 are denoted as G, pairings as P. Runtime in ms and sizes in bytes.

Tags	Gen	Enc	Dec	PPunc	NPunc	|pk|	$\|sk_\varepsilon^\varepsilon\|$	max $\|sk_T^{id}\|$	$\|C\|$
2^ℓ	G	$\mathcal{O}(\ell)G$	$2P$	$\mathcal{O}(\ell)G$	$\mathcal{O}(\ell^2)G$	G_2	$(\ell+2)G_1, G_2$	$\mathcal{O}(\ell^2)G_1, \mathcal{O}(\ell)G_2$	G_1, G_2
2^{48}	2.0	2.7	0.4	2.3	110.2	64	1664	78336	96
2^{64}	2.6	3.4	0.4	3.0	192.0	64	2176	137216	96
2^{80}	3.1	4.1	0.4	3.7	292.6	64	2688	212480	96

(negative) puncturing is often an offline operation and thus our performance results are perfectly acceptable.

Furthermore, we can observe that the size of ciphertexts do not depend on the size of the negative tag space. In the random oracle model, the basis elements stored in the public key can be derived via the random oracle, so its size can be made independent of the tag space. The size of the secret key depends both on the tag space as well as the performed puncturings. Depending on the exact choice of tags, punctured secret keys can grow up to at most 78 MB, 137 MB and 212 MB, respectively.

4 Applications

4.1 Cloudflare's Geo Key Manager

Let us now continue the discussion on Cloudflare's Geo Key Manager[5] in more detail. The currently used system combines pairing-based constructions of identity-based broadcast encryption (IBBE) [18] as well as identity-based revocation (IBR) [4] schemes with compact ciphertexts in the following way: first, the private key[6] sk is secret shared in two shares sk_1 and sk_2. Using the IBBE scheme, the first share, sk_1 is encrypted with respect to the allowed regions. The second share, sk_2 is encrypted with the IBR scheme revoking access for all denied colocations. Now, if a colocation receives the two ciphertexts, it can recover the encrypted shares only if it is within the allowed region and not one of the denied colocations. Otherwise, it can only recover at most one of the shares. For adding allowed colocations not already contained within one of those allowed areas, sk is additionally encrypted with the IBBE scheme for all allowed colocations. So overall, ciphertexts contain two constant-size IBBE ciphertexts and a constant-size IBR ciphertext. We can obtain the same functionality also from *only* using DFPE. In addition, we also obtain the important property of forward secrecy.

Using DFPE. The idea is to allow the regions using the positive tags and deny colocations by puncturing on unique negative tags assigned to each colocation.

---

[5] https://blog.cloudflare.com/geo-key-manager-how-it-works.
[6] Technically, an encryption key for sk, but that does not make a difference.

Indeed, assume that $(\mathsf{pk}, \mathsf{sk}_\varepsilon^\varepsilon)$ is Cloudflare's DFPE key-pair. Next, Cloudflare would derive keys for each region by using the name of the region as positive tag in the DFPE scheme, e.g., obtaining $\mathsf{sk}_\varepsilon^{\mathrm{EU}}$ for Europe. Each colocation is assigned a unique negative tag and they receive the secret key for the region additionally punctured on that tag, e.g., $\mathsf{sk}_{\mathrm{London}}^{\mathrm{EU}}$ for the European data center in London. If customers now want to store their secret key, they encrypt the key for each allowed region using the region as positive tag and the denied colocations of the corresponding region as negative tags. If a colocation needs to access the key, it can only decrypt if one of the ciphertexts was encrypted for the region and that particular ciphertext was not tagged with one of the positive tags of the colocation. They are unable to decrypt the other ciphertexts, since they do not have access to the positively tagged keys. For denying colocations in allowed regions, we follow the same approach, but encrypt the ciphertext including all negative tags of the region's colocations without the ones being allowed.

Achieving Forward Secrecy. Since DFPE allows to puncture on multiple negative tags, we can additionally obtain forward secrecy as an important new feature: we can partition the tag space into one part containing the colocation tags, and another part identifying time periods by viewing this part as ordered sequence. Thereby, the customers can specify a time epoch as additional negative tag, say $t = 2021\text{-}02$ for ciphertexts decryptable in February 2021. Once the month passed, all colocations puncture the secret keys on the month's tag, and are then no longer able to decrypt those ciphertexts. The time periods can be designed in such a way, that they match the renewal periods of certificates.

We note that when switching to DFPE, each colocation only has to manage one DFPE secret key instead of an IBBE and an IBR secret key and DFPE easily achieves both allowing and denying of areas and colocations with one single primitive, respectively, while at the same time it additionally provides forward-secrecy. The approach of using DFPE, however, comes at the cost of having the size of the ciphertexts depend linearly on the number of allowed areas instead of 3 ciphertexts when using IBBE and IBR. When considering continents, the number of regions is very small (<10), thus our ciphertext size can be considered quasi-constant. Also note that the combined IBBE and IBR ciphertext requires 576 bytes[7] using the same curve, which corresponds to six regions in the DFPE-based approach. Therefore, when considering the continents as regions, we obtain ciphertexts that are at most the same size and, thus, forward secrecy is achieved without additional cost. Additionally, Cloudflare only needs to send the ciphertexts for specific regions to their colocations. Hence, colocations only have to store a single ciphertext. We note that the number of negative tags (denied colocations together with the epoch) does not influence the ciphertext size.

---

[7] https://rwc.iacr.org/2018/Slides/Sullivan.pdf.

4.2   Cryptographic Primitives

Forward-Secret Identity-Based Encryption. Interestingly, although there are some works on forward-secret IBE [12, 32, 36], they all consider a very weak model in which the master secret key stays constant and, hence, the private key generator (PKG) is able to generate user keys for arbitrary time periods and, thus, inherently invalidating an important aspect of forward secrecy. We are only aware of a dedicated construction of a forward-secret hierarchical IBE (HIBE) by Yao et al. [40], which also yields a forward-secret IBE as a special case. This works also considers forward-secrecy for the master secret key. As we will show, DFPE generically yields forward-secret IBE and, thus, offering new instantiations thereof. In particular, to the best of our knowledge, using the concrete DFPE construction, this leads to the first fs-IBE scheme with compact ciphertexts. We recall the definition of an fs-IBE scheme and its security in the full version of the work due to space constraints.

fs-IBE Construction. Having a DFPE scheme allows to construct an fs-IBE scheme by mapping time intervals to negative tags. The only syntactical difference is that the NPunc and PPunc algorithms of DFPE are mapped to the Update and Ext algorithms of fs-IBE. In particular, when we are at a time interval i in the fs-IBE scheme, this corresponds to secret keys that are punctured with respect to tag set $T = \{1, \ldots, i-1\}$ in the DFPE scheme and moving from time interval i to interval $i+1$ corresponds to puncturing the secret key at tag i, i.e., $T := T \cup \{i\}$. It is straightforward to show the following:

Corollary 2. *If the* DFPE *scheme provides DFPE-IND-T-security, then the resulting* fs-IBE *scheme provides fs-IBE-IND-T-security, for* $\mathsf{T} \in \{CPA, CCA\}$.

Forward-Secret Signatures. Forward-secret signatures [1, 6, 30, 31] are a primitive that has recently found interest in distributed ledgers [17, 22, 23, 26].

Having a DFPE scheme and, in particular, a fs-IBE scheme, we can generically construct a forward-secret signature scheme. The idea is simply to adopt the Naor-transform [9], which converts any IBE-IND-CPA secure IBE scheme into an EUF-CMA secure signature scheme. We first briefly recall this transform: We consider an IBE scheme and the master secret key sk acts as the signing key. Let $id = m$, the message to be signed, then sk^m extracted with sk for identity m acts as the signature for m. The signature verification is done by checking if sk^m functions properly as a correct IBE decryption key for identity m by encrypting a random plaintext and checking if decryption yields to the original plaintext.

The basic idea of this transform applied to the forward-secret setting is as follows. We start with the master secret key $\mathsf{sk}_\varepsilon^\varepsilon$ as initial signing key and to develop the signing key over time, we update the secret key to the next time period, i.e., to update the signing key from interval i to interval $i+1$ we run $\mathsf{sk}_{i+1}^\varepsilon \leftarrow \mathsf{Update}(\mathsf{sk}_i^\varepsilon, \varepsilon, i)$. Now, within every time interval i one uses the current signing key with the above Naor-transform. One straightforwardly obtains:

Corollary 3. *If the* fs-IBE *scheme provides fs-IBE-IND-CPA-security, then the signature scheme obtained via the Naor-transform provides EUF-CMA-security.*

Using our DFPE from Sect. 3.2 in the above compiler, this yields forward-secret signatures with the same efficiency as in recent work [22,23,26].

Acknowledgements. This work was supported by the European commission through ECSEL Joint Undertaking (JU) under grant agreement n°783119 (SECREDAS), grant agreement n°826610 (COMP4DRONES), through the Horizon 2020 research and innovation programme under grant agreement n°871743 (KRAKEN), project IoT4CPS funded by the Austrian "ICT of the future" program of the Austrian Research Promotion Agency (FFG) and the Federal Ministry of Austria for Climate Action, Environment, Energy, Mobility, Innovation and Technology (BMK), and by the Austrian Science Fund (FWF) and netidee SCIENCE under grant agreement P31621-N38 (PROFET). The work of the first two authors was partly done while at Graz University of Technology.

A   Notation, Pairings and q-wBDHI Assumption

Notation. For $n \in \mathbb{N}$, let $[n] := \{1, \ldots, n\}$, and let $\kappa \in \mathbb{N}$ be the security parameter. For a finite set S, we denote by $s \leftarrow S$ the process of sampling s uniformly from S. For an algorithm A, let $y \leftarrow A(\kappa, x)$ be the process of running A on input (κ, x) with access to uniformly random coins and assigning the result to y. (If not given explicitly, we assume that κ is implicitly given as input.) To make the random coins r explicit, we write $A(\kappa, x; r)$. We say an algorithm A is probabilistic polynomial time (PPT) if the running time of A is polynomial in κ. A function f is negligible if its absolute value is smaller than the inverse of any polynomial (i.e., if $\forall c \exists k_0 \forall \kappa \geq k_0 : |f(\kappa)| < 1/\kappa^c$). We may write $q = q(\kappa)$ if we mean that the value q depends polynomially on κ.

Pairings. Let G_1, G_2, G_T be cyclic groups of order p. A *pairing* $e : G_1 \times G_2 \to G_T$ is a map that is *bilinear* (i.e., for all $g_1, g_1' \in G_1$ and $g_2, g_2' \in G_2$, we have $e(g_1 \cdot g_1', g_2) = e(g_1, g_2) \cdot e(g_1', g_2)$ and $e(g_1, g_2 \cdot g_2') = e(g_1, g_2) \cdot e(g_1, g_2')$), *non-degenerate* (i.e., for generators $g_1 \in G_1, g_2 \in G_2$, we have that $e(g_1, g_2) \in G_T$ is a generator), and *efficiently computable*. Let BGen be a PPT algorithm that, on input a security parameter κ, outputs $\mathsf{BG} = (p, G_1, G_2, G_T, e, g_1, g_2)$ for generators g_1 and g_2 of G_1 and G_2, respectively, and $\Theta(\kappa)$-bit prime p.

q-wBDHI Assumption. We recall the q-wBDHI [8] assumptions ported to Type-3 groups [13]. We define the advantage of an adversary D with respect to q-wBDHI as

$$\mathbf{Adv}_{\mathsf{BGen}, D}^{q\text{-wBDHI}}(\kappa) := \left| \Pr[D(pp, e(g_1, g_2^r)^{\alpha^{(q+1)}}) = 1] - \Pr[D(pp, e(g_1, g_2^r)^u) = 1] \right|,$$

where $\mathsf{BG} \leftarrow \mathsf{BGen}(1^\kappa)$, and $pp = (\mathsf{BG}, g_1^\alpha, g_1^{\alpha^2}, \ldots, g_1^{\alpha^q}, g_2^\alpha, g_1^r, g_2^r)$, for $\alpha, r, u \leftarrow \mathbb{Z}_p$. We say the q-wBDHI assumption holds if $\mathbf{Adv}_{\mathsf{BGen}, A}^{q\text{-wBDHI}}$ is a negligible function in the security parameter κ for all PPT adversaries A.

References

1. Abdalla, M., An, J.H., Bellare, M., Namprempre, C.: From identification to signatures via the Fiat-Shamir transform: minimizing assumptions for security and forward-security. In: Knudsen, L.R. (ed.) EUROCRYPT 2002. LNCS, vol. 2332, pp. 418–433. Springer, Heidelberg (2002). https://doi.org/10.1007/3-540-46035-7_28
2. Abdalla, M., Kiltz, E., Neven, G.: Generalized key delegation for hierarchical identity-based encryption. In: Biskup, J., López, J. (eds.) ESORICS 2007. LNCS, vol. 4734, pp. 139–154. Springer, Heidelberg (2007). https://doi.org/10.1007/978-3-540-74835-9_10
3. Aranha, D.F., Gouvêa, C.P.L., Markmann, T., Wahby, R.S., Liao, K.: RELIC is an Efficient LIbrary for Cryptography. https://github.com/relic-toolkit/relic
4. Attrapadung, N., Libert, B., de Panafieu, E.: Expressive key-policy attribute-based encryption with constant-size ciphertexts. In: Catalano, D., Fazio, N., Gennaro, R., Nicolosi, A. (eds.) PKC 2011. LNCS, vol. 6571, pp. 90–108. Springer, Heidelberg (2011). https://doi.org/10.1007/978-3-642-19379-8_6
5. Barbulescu, R., Duquesne, S.: Updating key size estimations for pairings. J. Cryptol. 32(4), 1298–1336 (2019)
6. Bellare, M., Miner, S.K.: A forward-secure digital signature scheme. In: Wiener, M. (ed.) CRYPTO 1999. LNCS, vol. 1666, pp. 431–448. Springer, Heidelberg (1999). https://doi.org/10.1007/3-540-48405-1_28
7. Bellare, M., Yee, B.: Forward-security in private-key cryptography. In: Joye, M. (ed.) CT-RSA 2003. LNCS, vol. 2612, pp. 1–18. Springer, Heidelberg (2003). https://doi.org/10.1007/3-540-36563-X_1
8. Boneh, D., Boyen, X., Goh, E.-J.: Hierarchical identity based encryption with constant size ciphertext. In: Cramer, R. (ed.) EUROCRYPT 2005. LNCS, vol. 3494, pp. 440–456. Springer, Heidelberg (2005). https://doi.org/10.1007/11426639_26
9. Boneh, D., Franklin, M.: Identity-based encryption from the Weil pairing. In: Kilian, J. (ed.) CRYPTO 2001. LNCS, vol. 2139, pp. 213–229. Springer, Heidelberg (2001). https://doi.org/10.1007/3-540-44647-8_13
10. Canetti, R., Halevi, S., Katz, J.: A forward-secure public-key encryption scheme. In: Biham, E. (ed.) EUROCRYPT 2003. LNCS, vol. 2656, pp. 255–271. Springer, Heidelberg (2003). https://doi.org/10.1007/3-540-39200-9_16
11. Canetti, R., Raghuraman, S., Richelson, S., Vaikuntanathan, V.: Chosen-ciphertext secure fully homomorphic encryption. In: Fehr, S. (ed.) PKC 2017, Part II. LNCS, vol. 10175, pp. 213–240. Springer, Heidelberg (2017). https://doi.org/10.1007/978-3-662-54388-7_8
12. Catalano, D., Di Raimondo, M., Fiore, D., Gennaro, R., Puglisi, O.: Fully non-interactive onion routing with forward-secrecy. In: Lopez, J., Tsudik, G. (eds.) ACNS 2011. LNCS, vol. 6715, pp. 255–273. Springer, Heidelberg (2011). https://doi.org/10.1007/978-3-642-21554-4_15
13. Chatterjee, S., Menezes, A.: On cryptographic protocols employing asymmetric pairings - the role of Ψ revisited. Discret. Appl. Math. 159(13), 1311–1322 (2011)
14. Cini, V., Ramacher, S., Slamanig, D., Striecks, C.: CCA-secure (puncturable) KEMs from encryption with non-negligible decryption errors. In: Moriai, S., Wang, H. (eds.) ASIACRYPT 2020, Part I. LNCS, vol. 12491, pp. 159–190. Springer, Cham (2020). https://doi.org/10.1007/978-3-030-64837-4_6
15. Cocks, C.: An identity based encryption scheme based on quadratic residues. In: Honary, B. (ed.) Cryptography and Coding 2001. LNCS, vol. 2260, pp. 360–363. Springer, Heidelberg (2001). https://doi.org/10.1007/3-540-45325-3_32

16. Cohen, A., Holmgren, J., Nishimaki, R., Vaikuntanathan, V., Wichs, D.: Watermarking cryptographic capabilities. In: STOC, pp. 1115–1127. ACM (2016)
17. David, B., Gaži, P., Kiayias, A., Russell, A.: Ouroboros Praos: an adaptively-secure, semi-synchronous proof-of-stake blockchain. In: Nielsen, J.B., Rijmen, V. (eds.) EUROCRYPT 2018, Part II. LNCS, vol. 10821, pp. 66–98. Springer, Cham (2018). https://doi.org/10.1007/978-3-319-78375-8_3
18. Delerablée, C.: Identity-based broadcast encryption with constant size ciphertexts and private keys. In: Kurosawa, K. (ed.) ASIACRYPT 2007. LNCS, vol. 4833, pp. 200–215. Springer, Heidelberg (2007). https://doi.org/10.1007/978-3-540-76900-2_12
19. Derler, D., Jager, T., Slamanig, D., Striecks, C.: Bloom filter encryption and applications to efficient forward-secret 0-RTT key exchange. In: Nielsen, J.B., Rijmen, V. (eds.) EUROCRYPT 2018, Part III. LNCS, vol. 10822, pp. 425–455. Springer, Cham (2018). https://doi.org/10.1007/978-3-319-78372-7_14
20. Derler, D., Krenn, S., Lorünser, T., Ramacher, S., Slamanig, D., Striecks, C.: Revisiting proxy re-encryption: forward secrecy, improved security, and applications. In: Abdalla, M., Dahab, R. (eds.) PKC 2018, Part I. LNCS, vol. 10769, pp. 219–250. Springer, Cham (2018). https://doi.org/10.1007/978-3-319-76578-5_8
21. Derler, D., Krenn, S., Lorünser, T., Ramacher, S., Slamanig, D., Striecks, C.: Revisiting proxy re-encryption: forward secrecy, improved security, and applications. IACR ePrint **2018**, 321 (2018)
22. Drijvers, M., Gorbunov, S., Neven, G., Wee, H.: Pixel: multi-signatures for consensus. In: USENIX, pp. 2093–2110. USENIX Association (2020)
23. Drijvers, M., Neven, G.: Forward-secure multi-signatures. IACR Cryptol. ePrint Arch. **2019**, 261 (2019)
24. Fujisaki, E., Okamoto, T.: Secure integration of asymmetric and symmetric encryption schemes. In: Wiener, M. (ed.) CRYPTO 1999. LNCS, vol. 1666, pp. 537–554. Springer, Heidelberg (1999). https://doi.org/10.1007/3-540-48405-1_34
25. Gentry, C., Silverberg, A.: Hierarchical ID-based cryptography. In: Zheng, Y. (ed.) ASIACRYPT 2002. LNCS, vol. 2501, pp. 548–566. Springer, Heidelberg (2002). https://doi.org/10.1007/3-540-36178-2_34
26. Gorbunov, S., Wee, H.: Digital signatures for consensus. Cryptology ePrint Archive, Report 2019/269 (2019)
27. Green, M.D., Miers, I.: Forward secure asynchronous messaging from puncturable encryption. In: IEEE S&P, pp. 305–320. IEEE (2015)
28. Günther, F., Hale, B., Jager, T., Lauer, S.: 0-RTT key exchange with full forward secrecy. In: Coron, J.-S., Nielsen, J.B. (eds.) EUROCRYPT 2017, Part III. LNCS, vol. 10212, pp. 519–548. Springer, Cham (2017). https://doi.org/10.1007/978-3-319-56617-7_18
29. Horwitz, J., Lynn, B.: Toward hierarchical identity-based encryption. In: Knudsen, L.R. (ed.) EUROCRYPT 2002. LNCS, vol. 2332, pp. 466–481. Springer, Heidelberg (2002). https://doi.org/10.1007/3-540-46035-7_31
30. Itkis, G., Reyzin, L.: Forward-secure signatures with optimal signing and verifying. In: Kilian, J. (ed.) CRYPTO 2001. LNCS, vol. 2139, pp. 332–354. Springer, Heidelberg (2001). https://doi.org/10.1007/3-540-44647-8_20
31. Krawczyk, H.: Simple forward-secure signatures from any signature scheme. In: ACM CCS, pp. 108–115. ACM (2000)
32. Lu, Y., Li, J.: Forward-secure identity-based encryption with direct chosen-ciphertext security in the standard model. Adv. Math. Commun. **11**(1), 161–177 (2017)

33. Menezes, A., Sarkar, P., Singh, S.: Challenges with assessing the impact of NFS advances on the security of pairing-based cryptography. In: Phan, R.C.-W., Yung, M. (eds.) Mycrypt 2016. LNCS, vol. 10311, pp. 83–108. Springer, Cham (2017). https://doi.org/10.1007/978-3-319-61273-7_5

34. Ristenpart, T., Tromer, E., Shacham, H., Savage, S.: Hey, you, get off of my cloud: exploring information leakage in third-party compute clouds. In: ACM CCS, pp. 199–212. ACM (2009)

35. Schwarz, M., Gruss, D.: How trusted execution environments fuel research on microarchitectural attacks. IEEE Secur. Priv. **18**(5), 18–27 (2020)

36. Singh, K., Pandurangan, C., Banerjee, A.K.: Lattice based forward-secure identity based encryption scheme with shorter ciphertext. J. Internet Serv. Inf. Secur. **3**(1/2), 5–19 (2013)

37. Sun, S.-F., Sakzad, A., Steinfeld, R., Liu, J.K., Gu, D.: Public-key puncturable encryption: modular and compact constructions. In: Kiayias, A., Kohlweiss, M., Wallden, P., Zikas, V. (eds.) PKC 2020, Part I. LNCS, vol. 12110, pp. 309–338. Springer, Cham (2020). https://doi.org/10.1007/978-3-030-45374-9_11

38. Susilo, W., Duong, D.H., Le, H.Q., Pieprzyk, J.: Puncturable encryption: a generic construction from delegatable fully key-homomorphic encryption. In: Chen, L., Li, N., Liang, K., Schneider, S. (eds.) ESORICS 2020, Part II. LNCS, vol. 12309, pp. 107–127. Springer, Cham (2020). https://doi.org/10.1007/978-3-030-59013-0_6

39. Wei, J., Chen, X., Wang, J., Hu, X., Ma, J.: Forward-secure puncturable identity-based encryption for securing cloud emails. In: Sako, K., Schneider, S., Ryan, P.Y.A. (eds.) ESORICS 2019, Part II. LNCS, vol. 11736, pp. 134–150. Springer, Cham (2019). https://doi.org/10.1007/978-3-030-29962-0_7

40. Yao, D., Fazio, N., Dodis, Y., Lysyanskaya, A.: Id-based encryption for complex hierarchies with applications to forward security and broadcast encryption. In: ACM CCS, pp. 354–363. ACM (2004)

41. Zhang, Y., Juels, A., Reiter, M.K., Ristenpart, T.: Cross-VM side channels and their use to extract private keys. In: ACM CCS, pp. 305–316. ACM (2012)

42. Zhang, Y., Juels, A., Reiter, M.K., Ristenpart, T.: Cross-tenant side-channel attacks in PaaS clouds. In: ACM CCS, pp. 990–1003. ACM (2014)

Faster Homomorphic Encryption over GPGPUs via Hierarchical DGT

Pedro Geraldo M. R. Alves[1]($\boxtimes$)(iD), Jheyne N. Ortiz[1](iD), and Diego F. Aranha[2](iD)

[1] University of Campinas, Campinas, Brazil
{pedro.alves,jheyne.ortiz}@ic.unicamp.br
[2] Aarhus University, Aarhus, Denmark
dfaranha@cs.au.dk

Abstract. Privacy guarantees are still insufficient for outsourced data processing in the cloud. While employing encryption is feasible for data at rest or in transit, it is not for computation without remarkable performance slowdown. Thus, handling data in plaintext during processing is still required, which creates vulnerabilities that can be exploited by malicious entities. Homomorphic encryption schemes enable computation over ciphertexts without knowing the related plaintexts or the decryption key. This work focuses on the challenge of developing an efficient implementation of the BFV scheme on CUDA. This is done by combining and adapting different literature approaches, as the *double*-CRT representation and the Discrete Galois Transform. Moreover, we propose and implement an improved formulation of the DGT inspired by classical algorithms, which computes the transform up to 2.6 times faster than the state-of-the-art. By using these approaches, we obtain up to 3.6 times faster homomorphic multiplication.

Keywords: Fully homomorphic encryption · BFV · CUDA · Polynomial multiplication · Privacy-preserving computing

1 Introduction

With the growing data collection by governments and companies, protecting its secrecy becomes as important as processing and extracting useful information. However, how to efficiently collect and compute user data without undermining their privacy is an open problem. System breaches may happen even when data holders choose the most conservative practices and never share data intentionally.

The Breach Level Index provides distressful statistics about data leakage. It states that most breaches occur by accidental loss on leaving plaintext data exposed inadvertently. Attacks from malicious parties, which explore vulnerabilities to subvert security mechanisms, are also far from negligible [29]. Data can be protected by encryption even in case of leakage. However, encryption-decryption cycles during its lifespan create a weak point in the system's security. Thus, building the system roots attached to mathematical guarantees and dispensable decryption is the only way to achieve a more reliable security.

© International Financial Cryptography Association 2021
N. Borisov and C. Diaz (Eds.): FC 2021, LNCS 12675, pp. 520–540, 2021.
https://doi.org/10.1007/978-3-662-64331-0_27

Homomorphic Encryption (HE) schemes enable data processing while protecting its confidentiality. They allow the evaluation of arithmetic circuits over ciphertexts by a third party without any knowledge of the corresponding plaintexts or the decryption key, preventing the computation's inputs and outcome to be learned. Hence, HE is a natural candidate for solving privacy issues caused by malicious third parties, careless administrators, or other security flaws during the processing, such as side-channel vulnerabilities.

Many of the HE schemes available in the literature rely on the hardness of the Ring-Learning with Errors (RLWE) problem. This assumption offers a strategy for protecting messages, encoded as polynomials in $R_q = \mathbb{Z}_q[x]/(f(x))$, by adding noise in a way that it can only be removed when given a trapdoor. There are several proposals following this approach such as BFV [21], CKKS [13], and TFHE [14]. All depend on polynomial arithmetic as the main building block, so its efficient implementation is critical for adopting HE in the real-world.

CUDA is an important tool for the efficient implementation of polynomial arithmetic. It's a SIMD architecture developed and maintained by NVIDIA for employing the data parallelism potential of a GPU in tasks beyond graphical processing. However, the particularities of CUDA impose challenges for its cryptographic use. Its processing flow demands careful planning to align possible conditional branches with certain thread groups, and its memory paradigm considers several structures with different dimensions and latency characteristics, separated from the machine's main memory. Moreover, at this point, no general-purpose cryptographic library or polynomial arithmetic framework supports CUDA. Hence, these constraints motivate the development of a complete toolkit to work as an arithmetic engine aimed at RLWE-based cryptosystems.

Our Contributions. This work presents mathematical tools and techniques for the efficient implementation of the BFV scheme in CUDA. We follow the literature by employing the Residue Number System (RNS) as the best approach for handling the multiprecision arithmetic required, and the Halevi, Polyakov, and Shoup modification of BFV to solve the division and rounding problem in the RNS domain [9,24]. The main contributions of this study are:

- A novel *hierarchical* formulation of the Discrete Galois Transform (DGT) that offers about two times lower latency on GPUs than the best version available in the literature. Moreover, we collect evidence that suggests it is faster than the commonly used Number Theoretic Transform (NTT). Such formulation is inspired by Bailey's version of the Fast Fourier Transform [7].
- Compatible choice of parameters between the DGT and the RNS representation. We show that the *double*-CRT representation proposed by Gentry et al. is a better implementation design than the usual approach of working with Mersenne or Solinas primes in different rings [10].
- A more efficient, GPU-optimized, state machine which reduces the need for moving data in and out of the DGT domain and between the main memory and the GPU global memory.

These contributions are not limited to the BFV cryptosystem and can be easily applied to other RLWE-based schemes, such as CKKS. Moreover, we provide latency benchmarks from a proof-of-concept implementation named SPOG, which was built based on the methods above. Two relevant works employing the DGT are considered for comparison with our results: Badawi, Polyakov, Aung, Veeravalli, and Rohloff [4]; and Badawi, Veeravalli, Mun, and Aung [6]. When considering homomorphic multiplication as the main performance-critical operation, SPOG offers higher performance against these works, surpassing a 3.6-factor performance improvement against the latter.

2   Mathematical Background

The efficient implementation of an RLWE-based cryptosystem on CUDA requires carefully designed building blocks for adjusting the operations to the architecture's limitations. The BFV cryptosystem, as well as other HE proposals, relies on large parameters for achieving proper security levels. This imposes a challenge in the light of GPGPUs'[1] constraints, for both the size of the coefficients, much larger than the native integer instruction set; and the polynomial arithmetic, that requires highly-optimized algorithms to reduce the computational complexity and improve the scalability of expensive operations, such as polynomial multiplication.

This Section describes the Fan and Vercauteren cryptosystem; presents the Residue Number System (RNS) representation, used to avoid the multiprecision arithmetic; and introduces the Discrete Galois Transform (DGT), a more suitable variant of the Fast Fourier transform (FFT) to GPU implementation.

2.1   The BFV Cryptosystem

Fan and Vercauteren proposed a variant of Brakerski's homomorphic cryptosystem, nowadays referred to as BFV, that relies on the hardness of the Ring-Learning With Errors (RLWE) problem [21]. Classified as a leveled homomorphic encryption scheme (LHE), it is currently one of the most efficient cryptosystems of its class concerning speed and memory consumption and remains untouched by recent advances in cryptanalysis [1,16].

Let $p > 1$ be an integer and n a power-of-2. BFV's basic arithmetic is built upon polynomial rings of the form $R_p = \mathbb{Z}_p[X]/(X^n + 1)$. The scheme defines the following parameter set: a security parameter λ; a decomposition base $\omega > 1$; the modulus $t \geq 2$ that determines the plaintext domain R_t; and the modulus $q \gg t$ that determines the ciphertext domain R_q. Moreover, it makes use of an error distribution χ_{err}, usually a zero-mean discrete Gaussian distribution parameterized by the standard deviation σ.

Let $l = \lfloor \log_\omega q \rfloor$. The main procedures of BFV are the following:

KeyGen(λ, ω): Let sk $\leftarrow R_3$ be the secret key. Sample $a \leftarrow R_q$ uniformly at random and $e \leftarrow \chi_{err}$, and define the public key pk $= (b, a) = ([-(a \cdot \text{sk} + e)]_q, a)$.

---

[1] GPGPU, acronym for General-Purpose Graphics Processing Unit.

Generate the evaluation key evk as: Sample $\mathbf{a}_i \leftarrow R_q$ uniformly at random, $\mathbf{e}_i \leftarrow \chi_{err}$, and compute $\gamma_i = \left([-(\mathbf{a}_i \cdot \mathbf{sk} + \mathbf{e}_i) + \omega^i \cdot \mathbf{sk}^2]_q, \mathbf{a}_i\right)$. Define evk $= \bigcup_{i=0}^{l} \gamma_i$. Output $(\mathbf{sk}, \mathbf{pk}, \mathbf{evk})$.

Encrypt$(m, \mathbf{pk})$: for a plaintext message $m \in R_t$ and a public key $\mathbf{pk} = (b, a)$, sample $u \leftarrow R_2$ uniformly at random and $e_1, e_2 \leftarrow \chi_{err}$, and compute the ciphertext $\mathbf{c} = \left([\Delta m + b \cdot u + e_1]_q, [a \cdot u + e_2]_q\right)$, where $\Delta = \lfloor q/t \rfloor$.

Decrypt$(\mathbf{c}, \mathbf{sk})$: for a ciphertext $\mathbf{c} = (c_0, c_1)$ and the secret key $\mathbf{sk} = s$, recover the plaintext $m = \left[\left\lfloor \frac{t}{q} [c_0 + c_1 \cdot s]_q \right\rceil\right]_t$.

Add$(\mathbf{c}_0, \mathbf{c}_1)$: for ciphertexts $\mathbf{c}_0 = (c_{0,0}, c_{0,1})$ and $\mathbf{c}_1 = (c_{1,0}, c_{1,1})$, compute $\mathbf{c}_{\text{add}} = \left([c_{0,0} + c_{1,0}]_q, [c_{0,1} + c_{1,1}]_q\right)$.

Relin$((c_0, c_1, c_2), \mathbf{evk})$: for $c_0, c_1, c_2 \in R_q$, evk $= (\mathbf{b}, \mathbf{a})$, and a decomposition of c_2 in base w such that $c_2 = \sum_{i=0}^{l} c_2^{(i)} w^i$, return
$$\left(\left[c_0 + \sum_{i=0}^{l} \mathbf{b}_i \cdot c_2^{(i)}\right]_q, \left[c_1 + \sum_{i=0}^{l} \mathbf{a}_i \cdot c_2^{(i)}\right]_q\right).$$

Mul$(\mathbf{c}_0, \mathbf{c}_1, \mathbf{evk})$: for ciphertexts $\mathbf{c}_0 = (c_{0,0}, c_{0,1})$ and $\mathbf{c}_1 = (c_{1,0}, c_{1,1})$, compute
$$c = \left(\left[\left\lfloor \frac{t}{q} \cdot c_{0,0} \cdot c_{1,0} \right\rceil\right]_q, \left[\left\lfloor \frac{t}{q} \cdot (c_{0,0} \cdot c_{1,1} + c_{0,1} \cdot c_{1,0}) \right\rceil\right]_q, \left[\left\lfloor \frac{t}{q} \cdot c_{0,1} \cdot c_{1,1} \right\rceil\right]_q\right)$$
and return $\mathbf{c}_{\text{mul}} = \text{Relin}(c, \mathbf{evk})$.

2.2 Residue Number System

As can be observed in Sect. 2.1, BFV depends upon computationally expensive polynomial operations. Moreover, the literature reveals that big integer arithmetic is required to offer proper security levels [28]. A common strategy in implementations of BFV is to use the Chinese Remainder Theorem (CRT) on the Residue Number System (RNS) to map large integers to a set of smaller residues capable of being evaluated by processor's native instructions [9,19].

Definition 1 (CRT). *Let x be a polynomial in R_q, and $\{p_0, \dots, p_{\ell-1}\}$ a set of pairwise coprimes. The CRT decomposition results in a set X with ℓ residues such that $CRT(x) = \{[x]_{p_0}, \dots, [x]_{p_{\ell-1}}\}$. The inverse $CRT(X)$ is defined as:*
$$\left[\sum_{i=0}^{\ell-1} \frac{M}{p_i} \cdot \left[\left(\frac{M}{p_i}\right)^{-1} X_i\right]_{p_i}\right]_M = x, \text{ where } M = \prod_{i=0}^{\ell-1} p_i.$$

Addition and multiplication in the RNS domain work by applying the operation residue-wise. However, division and modular reduction are more complicated and require a more advanced technique, as described next.

2.3 Division and Rounding Inside the RNS Domain

Some parts of BFV are hardly compatible with RNS, such as the coefficient-wise division and rounding used in decryption and homomorphic multiplication. Motivated by that, two variants of BFV can be found in the literature, BEHZ-BFV and HPS-BFV, which propose modifications to the cryptosystem to support them in the RNS domain [8,24].

Let $Q = \{q_0, q_1, \ldots, q_{\ell-1}\}$ be a RNS basis which we can use to represent any ciphertext, as described in Sect. 2.2. BEHZ-BFV and HPS-BFV claim that the division and rounding can be computed by extending base Q to a new basis $B = \{b_0, b_1, \ldots, b_{k-1}\}$ such that $\prod q_i < \prod b_j$. While BEHZ-BFV looks for an exact rounding, HPS-BFV shows how to build operations to minimize the error and merge it into the natural cryptosystem noise. This allows a much simpler procedure, with a lower computational cost, to be used. HPS-BFV's authors present an analysis that demonstrates that their procedures are simpler and have lower complexity and noise growth than those in BEHZ-BFV.

The HPS-BFV methods are composed by a basis extension procedure, which computes a polynomial representation in a base B from its representation in base Q; and two methods to scale down and round an integer in its RNS representation by t/q, one to be used on decryption, which is a more straightforward scenario that requires the output to be in base $\{t\}$, and one for homomorphic encryption, which is a bit more complicated since the outcome must lie in base B.

Both variants of BFV take the fact that q is not defined as a prime integer. Thus, they represent and work with R_q polynomials in an RNS base composed by a factorization of q, i.e. $q = \prod_{i=0}^{\ell-1} q_i$. One of the advantages of doing this is the automatic merge of the RNS bounds with the ciphertext coefficient domain.

2.4   Discrete Galois Transform

The Fast Fourier Transform (FFT) is a well-known method that offers linear computational cost for polynomial multiplication when the operands lie in its domain and quasi-linear when considering the computation of the transform itself. However, the FFT is defined on $\mathbb{C}$, which makes it harder for its direct applicability in the context of RLWE-based cryptosystems, defined on integer domains. Thus, variations offering the same functionality but built upon integer arithmetic were proposed in the literature, such as the Number Theoretic Transform (NTT) over $GF(p)$, and the Discrete Galois Transform (DGT) over $GF(p^2)$, for some convenient choice of a prime number p [17,26].

The main difference of DGT over NTT is caused by their domains, which results in memory bandwidth savings, as deeply discussed in Sects. 3 and 4. Despite this, they are sufficiently similar so that they share most of the computation data paths and their efficient implementation strategies. Furthermore, as $GF(p^2)$ can be represented in the set of Gaussian integers $\mathbb{Z}_p[i] = \{a + ib \mid a, b \in \mathbb{Z}_p\}$, it uses finite field arithmetic with $\mathbb{Z}_p$ elements as building blocks, which resonates with the representation used by RNS and BFV. In Definition 2 we introduce the base formulation, as done in by Badawi et al. [5].

Definition 2 (Discrete Galois Transform). *Let $p \geq 3$ be a prime number, $x = \{x_0, \ldots, x_{n-1}\}$ be a vector of length n such that $x_k \in GF(p^2)$ for $0 \leq k < n$, and g be an n-th primitive root of unity in $GF(p)$. Then, the DGT and its inverse are defined as: $X_k = \sum_{j=0}^{n-1} x_j g^{-jk} \in GF(p^2)$ and $x_k = n^{-1} \sum_{j=0}^{n-1} X_j g^{jk} \in GF(p^2)$, respectively.*

3   Efficient CUDA Operation on Cyclotomic Rings

An efficient implementation of the arithmetic of cyclotomic polynomial rings requires a convenient approach for polynomial multiplication and a proper data representation, not only with low computational complexity but also that fits well in the processing hardware. This Section provides optimization strategies for implementing polynomial arithmetic on CUDA.

3.1   Fast Polynomial Multiplication

The complexity to compute a polynomial multiplication using a textbook formula is $\Theta\left(n^2\right)$ for n-degree polynomials, which means that performance will be seriously affected with the increase of the degree.

In the context of cryptosystems based on RLWE, as observed by Lindner and Peikert, security is strongly related to the degree of the polynomial ring [25]. Specifically on BFV, Player concludes that a parameter set nowadays considered secure, with an estimated security upper bound close to $\lambda = 128$, requires n between 2^{11} and 2^{15} [28]. Hence, an efficient implementation of polynomial multiplication for operands with a large degree is vital for performance.

FFT-based transforms, such as the NTT, provide a domain in which the polynomial multiplication complexity is reduced to $\Theta\left(n\right)$, and among those, the DGT is a promising variant defined over $GF(p^2)$. As introduced in Sect. 2.4, this field can be represented as the set of Gaussian integers $\mathbb{Z}_p[i] = \{a + ib \mid a, b \in \mathbb{Z}_p\}$, which enables the polynomial folding of inputs and consequently halves their degree. This folding works such that, for a polynomial $P(x) = \sum_{j=0}^{n-1} a_j \cdot x^j$, we have $fold(P(x)) = \sum_{j=0}^{n/2-1}(a_j + i \cdot a_{j+n/2}) \cdot x^j$, for $i = \sqrt{-1}$ and n even.

Considering the use of Gaussian integer arithmetic [3], a first impression may be that the increased cost of the arithmetic nullifies the reduction of the polynomial degree due to the quadratic extension. However, it is important to notice that, by working with half the coefficients, only half the roots, like those in Definition 2, are required compared to the FFT or NTT. In this way, in a memory-constrained scenario, this property implies a speedup caused by fewer memory transactions and enables a more coalesced pattern. In the case of CUDA, such operations may target the GPU's global memory, which is significant in size but has high latency, or even shared or constant memories, which are fast but very small. The resulting increased arithmetic density favors GPU implementations.

Badawi et al. propose Algorithm 1 for polynomial multiplication through the DGT. It first folds both input signals and then applies a twisting by powers of $n/2$-th primitive roots of i, which provides a negacyclic convolution. This equips the algorithm with a free polynomial reduction by a cyclotomic polynomial [17]. Finding these roots is a complex computational task usually performed by brute force when p is sufficiently small. Otherwise, numerical methods may be used. We offer in Appendix B a suggestion for their construction.

There is no need for the bit-reversal procedure in the context of implementing a polynomial multiplication. Thus, an efficient implementation avoids it by

---

Algorithm 1: Polynomial multiplication in $\mathbb{Z}_p[x]/(x^n + 1)$ via DGT

Input: Polynomials $a, b \in \mathbb{Z}_p[x]/(x^n + 1)$, p a prime number, n a power-of-two integer, and h a primitive $\frac{n}{2}$-th root of i modulo p.

Output: $c = a \cdot b \in \mathbb{Z}_p[x]/(x^n + 1)$.

1   **for** $j = 0; j < n/2; j = j + 1$ **do**

2       $a'_j = a_j + ia_{j+n/2}$ // Folding the input polynomials

3       $b'_j = b_j + ib_{j+n/2}$

4   **for** $j = 0; j < n/2; j = j + 1$ **do**

5       $a'_j = h^j \cdot a'_j \pmod{p}$ // Applying the right-angle convolution

6       $b'_j = h^j \cdot b'_j \pmod{p}$

7    $a' = \mathrm{DGT}(a')$ // Computing the DGT of both operands

8    $b' = \mathrm{DGT}(b')$

9   **for** $j = 0; j < n/2; j = j + 1$ **do**

10      $c'_j = a'_j \cdot b'_j \pmod{p}$ // Component-wise multiplying in $\mathbb{Z}_p[i]$

11    $d' = \mathrm{IDGT}(c')$ // Computing the IDGT of the multiplication result

12   **for** $j = 0; j < n/2; j = j + 1$ **do**

13      $u = h^{-j} \cdot d'_j \pmod{p}$ // Removing the twisting factors

14      $c_j = u_{re}$ // Unfolding the result

15      $c_{j+\frac{n}{2}} = u_{im}$

16 **return** c

---

selecting a decimation-in-frequency (DIF) algorithm for the forward transform and a decimation-in-time (DIT) algorithm for the inverse, as defined by Chu and George [15]. In this work, we follow the proposal of Badawi et al. and choose the Gentleman-Sande, a DIF, and the Cooley-Tukey, a DIT, data-paths for the forward and inverse versions of the DGT, respectively [5].

The canonical formulation of these contains a combination of three nested loops, which increases the complexity of its implementation, especially on the CUDA architecture. This structure creates dependencies between the loops and disturbs parallel execution. So, for better compatibility with the programming model, they have to be rewritten by wiping out one layer of nesting and leaving only two loops, an outer loop related to the stride and an inner loop that asserts the access patterns. For each outer loop iteration, the inner one can be completely parallelized. Our proposals have a much weaker dependency between iterations and can be seen in Algorithms 2 and 3.

3.2   An Improved and Hierarchical DGT

The procedures described in Algorithms 2 and 3 require synchronization at the end of each iteration of the outer loop. On CUDA, this enforces a limitation on the polynomial degree at the cost of latency, since the only data structure that provides such synchronicity at the hardware level is a Thread Block, and its dimension is limited to 1024 threads in modern hardware. An alternative implementation involves calling a different CUDA kernel for each iteration, forcing

---

Algorithm 2: Rewritten forward DGT via Gentleman-Sande

Input: A folded vector $x \in \mathbb{Z}[i]^k$, p a prime number, k a power-of-two integer, and g a primitive k-th root of unity modulo p.

Output: $x \leftarrow \mathrm{DGT}(x)$ in bit-reversed ordering.

1 **for** $s = 0; s < \lfloor \log(k) \rfloor; s = s + 1$ **do**

2     $m = \frac{k}{2^{(s+1)}}$

3   **for** $l = 0; l < k/2; l = l + 1$ **do**

4        $j = \frac{2ml}{k}$

5        $i = j + \left(l \mod \frac{k}{2m}\right) \cdot 2m$

6        $a = g^{j \cdot \frac{k}{2^{(\log(k)-s)}}} \pmod{p}$

7        $(u, v) = (x[i], x[i+m])$

8        $(x[i], x[i+m]) = (u + v, a \cdot (u - v)) \pmod{p}$

9 **return** x

Algorithm 3: Rewritten inverse DGT via Cooley-Tukey

Input: A vector $x \in \mathbb{Z}[i]^k$ in bit-reversed order, p a prime number, k a power-of-two integer, and g a primitive k-th root of unity modulo p.

Output: $x \leftarrow k \cdot \mathrm{IDGT}(x)$ in standard ordering.

1 $m = 1$

2 **for** $s = 0; s < \lfloor \log(k) \rfloor; s = s + 1$ **do**

3   **for** $l = 0; l < k/2; l = l + 1$ **do**

4        $j = \frac{2ml}{k}$

5        $i = j + \left(l \mod \frac{k}{2m}\right) \cdot 2m$

6        $a = g^{-j \cdot \frac{k}{2^{s+1}}} \pmod{p}$

7        $(u, v) = (x[i], x[i+m])$

8        $(x[i], x[i+m]) = (u + a \cdot v, u - a \cdot v) \pmod{p}$

9     $m = 2 \cdot m$

10 **return** x

---

a CPU-sided synchronization. This incurs a considerable overhead caused by several kernel calls.

In this scenario, we propose a technique for splitting the DGT transform into smaller blocks that better fit the processing hardware and does not require synchronizing large sets of threads, called hierarchical DGT. It is an adaptation of the four-step FFT algorithm, initially proposed by David H. Bailey and later on revisited by Govindaraju et al. [7,23].

The general idea of the hierarchical DGT and hierarchical inverse DGT, referred to respectively as HDGT and HIDGT, is to split the DGT computation over $\mathbb{Z}_p[x]/(x^n + 1)$ into computations in smaller rings with optimal degree near $\sqrt{n}$. In practice, the vector of coefficients is treated as a matrix and the DGT is performed over the columns and rows of this matrix. The objective of this is to avoid the case in which one is unable to compute the DGT of an entire polynomial in a single CUDA kernel call. We move to a higher granularity approach in which we apply the transform multiple times over arbitrary small polynomials that can perfectly fit in our processing architecture.

The HDGT is described in Algorithm 4. Firstly, the polynomial $a(x)$ is represented by taking its coefficient embedding as $a = (a_0, a_1, \ldots, a_{n-1})$. To be represented in the DGT domain $GF(p^2)$, $a \in \mathbb{Z}_p^n$ is folded as a $(n/2)$-size vector of Gaussian integers $\tilde{a} \in \mathbb{Z}_p[i]^{n/2}$, as described in Sect. 3.1. In the Algorithm, the "right-angle" convolution is given by multiplying the j-th coefficient of $\tilde{a}$ by h^j, for $j \in \mathbb{Z}_{n/2}$, where h is the $(n/2)$-th primitive root of i in $\mathbb{Z}_p[i]$.

After the folding and twisting procedures, the $(n/2)$-length vector of Gaussian integers $\tilde{a}$ is treated as a matrix with dimensions (N_r, N_c). These dimensions shall be chosen so that each coefficient's subset fits in the processing hardware. In our case, the objective is to find a subset that fits in the GPU's shared memory so that the DGT can be performed in a single Thread Block.

Since the bit-reversal is not used in Algorithm 2, the called "step-2" of Bailey's method has to be rewritten. In line 8, the twiddle factors are the powers of g, the $(n/2)$-th root of unity modulo p. Since the output of the DGT is not corrected from the bit-reversed order, the twiddle factors become $g^{\texttt{bit-reversal}(j)\cdot k}$ instead of $g^{j \cdot k}$, which matches the position of the corresponding element in $\tilde{a}$ when it is seen as a matrix.

Algorithm 4: Hierarchical forward DGT

Input: A polynomial $a \in \mathbb{Z}_p[x]/(x^n + 1)$, p a prime number, $n = 2 \cdot N_r \cdot N_c$ a power-of-two integer, h a primitive $n/2$-th root of i modulo p, and g a primitive $n/2$-th root of unity modulo p.

Output: $\tilde{a} = \text{HDGT}(a)$.

1 **for** $j = 0; j < n/2; j = j + 1$ **do**
2      $\tilde{a}_j = a_j + ia_{j+n/2}$ // Fold the input polynomial
3      $\tilde{a}_j = \tilde{a}_j \cdot h^j \pmod{p}$ // Twist the folded polynomial
4 **for** $k = 0; k < N_c; k = k + 1$ **do**
5      $\tilde{a}_{-,k} = \text{DGT}(\tilde{a}_{-,k})$ // Step 1: Apply the DGT through N_c columns
6 **for** $j = 0; j < N_r; j = j + 1$ **do**
7   **for** $k = 0; k < N_c; k = k + 1$ **do**
8          $\tilde{a}_{j,k} = \tilde{a}_{j,k} \cdot g^{\texttt{bit-reversal}(j)\cdot k} \pmod{p}$ // Step 2: Multiplication by the twiddle factors in bit-reversal order
9 **for** $j = 0; j < N_r; j = j + 1$ **do**
10     $\tilde{a}_{j,-} = \text{DGT}(\tilde{a}_{j,-})$ // Step 3: Apply the DGT through the N_r rows
11 **return** $\tilde{a}$

The inverse counterpart of the hierarchical DGT simply executes the inverse steps of the forward transform, and is described in Algorithm 5. It adopts the IDGT transform via Cooley-Tukey, described in Algorithm 3, without bit-reversing the input vector. The algorithm executes the inverse steps of the forward transform by first applying the IDGT over the rows of $\tilde{a}$. The twiddle factors are removed by multiplying $\hat{a}_{j,k}$ by $g^{-\texttt{bit-reversal}(j)\cdot k}$, since the column indexes of the output of the previous step still are in bit-reversed order. Considering that the powers of g can be precomputed, they can be multiplied by N_c^{-1}, avoiding the additional multiplication. Finally, the IDGT is applied over the columns of $\hat{a}$ and the matrix indexes are back to standard ordering. Following the same approach, the powers of h^{-1} can be precomputed already multiplied by the scalar N_r^{-1}. This avoids the multiplication by the scaling factor when applying the IDGT over the columns of $\hat{a}$.

Algorithm 5: Hierarchical inverse DGT

Input: $\tilde{a} = \mathrm{HDGT}(a)$, p a prime number, $n = 2 \cdot N_r \cdot N_c$ a power-of-two integer, h a primitive $n/2$-th root of i modulo p, and g a primitive $n/2$-th root of unity modulo p.

Output: A polynomial $a \in \mathbb{Z}_p[x]/(x^n + 1)$.

1   **for** $j = 0; j < N_r; j = j + 1$ **do**
2     $\hat{a}_{j,\_} = \mathrm{IDGT}(\tilde{a}_{j,\_})$ // Step 3: Apply IDGT to each of N_r rows
3   **for** $j = 0; j < N_r; j = j + 1$ **do**
4   **for** $k = 0; k < N_c; k = k + 1$ **do**
5       $\hat{a}_{j,k} = \hat{a}_{j,k} \cdot g^{-\texttt{bit-reversal}(j) \cdot k} \cdot N_c^{-1} \pmod{p}$ // Step 2: Remove twiddle factors
6   **for** $k = 0; k < N_c; k = k + 1$ **do**
7     $\hat{a}_{\_,k} = \mathrm{IDGT}(\hat{a}_{\_,k})$ // Step 1: Apply IDGT to each of N_c columns
8   **for** $j = 0; j < n/2; j = j + 1$ **do**
9     $\hat{a}_j = \hat{a}_j \cdot h^{-j} \cdot N_r^{-1} \pmod{p}$ // Remove the twisting
10     $a_j = \hat{a}_{j_{re}}$ // Unfold the output polynomial
11     $a_{j+\frac{n}{2}} = \hat{a}_{j_{im}}$
12 **return** a

As in FFT and NTT, the two operands are evaluated using the HDGT for further point-wise multiplication. The polynomial corresponding to $a \cdot b$ in $\mathbb{Z}_p[x]/(x^n + 1)$ is obtained by computing the HIDGT.

3.3 Polynomial Representation and Memory Locality

The usability of an RLWE-based cryptosystem requires the careful selection of a parameter set that satisfies all the security constraints of the application. For instance, with BFV one must select q, t, n, and σ such that a security level λ is achieved. More than that, these parameters together determine the multiplicative depth supported by the scheme. Thus, as discussed by Fan and Vercauteren, the selection of such parameters is too complex to be affected by the particularities of the implementation [21].

A constraint for choosing those is the hardware instruction set. By selecting a big q one may be confronted by the lack of hardware support for native processing of the coefficients. Through RNS, as described in Sect. 2.2, we handle this by splitting big integers in small residues following the limits of the underlying machine.

530   P. G. M. R. Alves et al.

The link between the cryptosystem and RNS must be carefully designed so that data secrecy is provided with suitable performance. For that, Gentry et al. suggested the *double*-CRT representation, which encapsulates data into two layers [22]. The first layer is the RNS representation, as described in Definition 1. After that, a set of polynomial residues with full support for native hardware evaluation of addition and multiplication is obtained. However, we still need a second layer for the latter, since the multiplication of polynomials can achieve a quite high computational complexity without some well-designed algorithm, as discussed in Sect. 3.1. Because of that, the second layer consists of moving each residue, individually, to a different domain with a convenient property for efficient polynomial multiplication. The original proposal of *double*-CRT is the use of the NTT as this transform, but a similar approach using the FFT would also be expected. This work, however, proposes that the second layer of the *double*-CRT should use the DGT instead of the NTT since the former appears to suit much better the cyclotomic ring arithmetic in GPUs and presents more efficient memory access patterns [5].

Another design decision, widespread to HE implementations, is the selection of a single special prime p for the application of the transform over all RNS residues [18,20]. For instance, let x be a polynomial and $\{q_0, \ldots, q_{\ell-1}\}$ a set of ℓ pairwise coprimes, then $\{\mathrm{DGT}_p([x]_{q_0}), \ldots, \mathrm{DGT}_p([x]_{q_{\ell-1}})\}$ is the set of transformed residues. By using such a prime, one is capable of taking advantage of their intrinsic mathematical properties, as in the selection of a Mersenne or Solinas prime, which enables the use of a very efficient modular reduction. Nonetheless, this approach does not interplay well with the RNS layer and requires algorithmic efforts to correct these modular reductions and keep consistency for each residue. In this way, we propose a simpler solution by computing the transform layer using the coprime related to each residue, at the cost of a more expensive modular reduction since, in most cases, there are not enough special primes for the required number of residues. Thus, in this representation, the set of residues becomes $\{\mathrm{DGT}_{q_0}([x]_{q_0}), \ldots, \mathrm{DGT}_{q_{\ell-1}}([x]_{q_{\ell-1}})\}$. Moreover, without the need for those corrections, we become capable of increasing RNS' residues to the biggest supported word size of the target architecture, reducing the number of residues needed. By choosing $q = \prod_{i=0}^{\ell-1} q_i$ we establish a bond between BFV, RNS, and the DGT.

Lastly, our state machine proposal targets the insistent maintenance of data in our version of the *double*-CRT representation in GPU's memory. Data copy between the main memory and the GPU's memory has high latency and must be avoided.

4 Experimental Results

In this Section we present SPOG[2], a proof-of-concept implementation that consolidates the aforementioned techniques by exploring parallel processing on GPGPUs through CUDA.

---

[2] SPOG, acronym for "Secure Processing on GPGPUs".

Designed from scratch, SPOG is a modular implementation in which the arithmetic operations are separated from the cryptosystem. The polynomial operations were implemented on a sister library named CUPOLY, while BFV was implemented separated on SPOG-BFV. Both are based on CUDA and closely follow the sketch provided in Sect. 3, pursuing low-latency methods with a simple API and stretching the size of the residues to the highest supported by modern CUDA-supported GPUs, which is 63-bit residues with 1 bit for storing the sign. By doing this, we guarantee that BFV can be easily replaced by any other scheme based on the RLWE; thus, our work is not restricted to a single scheme. The entire arithmetic implementation can also be replaced without affecting the cryptosystem code. Hence, SPOG is flexible enough to encourage future work to develop and test different setups using the presented libraries.

cuRAND, a NVIDIA probabilistic library, was used for the sampling required by the BFV. This library offers sampling directly to the GPU memory, avoiding the cost of data copy. Sampling uniformly at random from R_x is implemented through its uniform sampler and the result is reduced by x. On the other hand, the discrete Gaussian distribution is not supported by this library. Because of that, an alternative implementation works by truncating a normal distribution, natively supported by cuRAND. The statistical validity of this design still needs to be asserted at the cost of compromising the security. Moreover, to the best of our knowledge, cuRAND lacks sufficient scrutiny by the scientific community so that it can be seen as cryptographic secure. However, this is a common implementation decision in the literature and is also done by the related works cited in Sect. 4.1.

SPOG and CUPOLY source code are available to the community under a *GNU GPLv3* license [2].

4.1 Related Work

We consider Badawi, Polyakov, Aung, Veeravalli, and Rohloff, work, referred as BPAVR, the state-of-the-art implementation in GPUs for BFV [4]. It complements Halevi, Polyakov, and Shoup proposal and provides the first implementation of the HPS-BFV method on a high-end NVIDIA Tesla V100 GPU, demonstrated by the authors to be the fastest and most scalable variant of the scheme when compared to BEHZ-BFV [8,24].

BPAVR do not describe all details regarding their performance results, only presenting latency measurements for decryption and homomorphic multiplication. Because of that, and the fact of their source code is not publicly available, we also consider a similar work of Badawi, Veeravalli, Mun, and Aung, which offers timings for encryption, decryption, homomorphic addition, and homomorphic multiplication for a CUDA-based BFV implementation, denoted by BVMA [6]. The authors compare BVMA with Microsoft SEAL, a reference on the field with support for HPS-BFV [12]; and NFLlib-FV, an equally important work implementing the BEHZ-BFV variant; with impressive speedups on all scenarios [27]. Despite of their efforts for parallel computation, the other libraries presented in that work are CPU-based implementations and thus show a significant slowdown, up to 27 times, when compared to BVMA. Hence, we do not believe that the direct comparison with SPOG is relevant to this paper.

Lastly, both works apply the DGT as the underlying solution to handle polynomial multiplication. So, by comparing SPOG with them, we can collect evidence about the suitability of the HDGT over the DGT for such task.

4.2   Execution Environment, Methodology, and BFV Parameters

The experimental results presented in the next Sections for BPAVR or BVMA are those reported by the authors in their corresponding publications. We do not re-execute the benchmarks provided in the related work. This decision is based on the fact that the implementations and benchmarking tools were not made available to the community. Because of that, we decided to collect our measurements in a similar processing hardware adopted in the related works using the same parameters.

We used Google Cloud's virtual machines (VMs) for emulating the computational environment described in those works. Two instances were considered: *gc.k80* and *gc.v100*, which provide a NVIDIA Tesla K80 GPU, used on BVMA measurements; and a NVIDIA Tesla V100 GPU, used on BPAVR. We precisely followed the execution environment described in each work, running GCC 7.2.1 and CUDA 8.0 at *gc.k80*; and GCC 7.3.1 and CUDA 9.0 at *gc.v100*. CUDA events were used to measure execution time, following the common methodology from the literature.

Our benchmark targets the most relevant primitives for HE. Regarding BFV, implemented in SPOG, we consider encryption, decryption, homomorphic addition, and homomorphic multiplication (including the relinearization cost). On the polynomial arithmetic side, implemented in cuPoly, we focus on the performance gains caused by the replacement of the canonical DGT by the HDGT.

In our measurements, we do not include initialization steps, which are performed only once and have negligible effect on long term runs. Because of that, the latency for generating cryptographic keys is not described in this work. Similarly, sampling is not explicitly considered in the benchmarks, despite of being included in the timings for encryption.

Two different setups are considered for compatibility with each work, both choosing $t = 256$ for the plaintext domain.

BPAVR parameters: Different polynomial ring settings are used identified by the pairs $(\lceil \log(q) \rceil, \log(n)) \in \{(60, 11), (60, 12), (120, 13), (360, 14), (600, 15)\}$ for the ciphertext coefficient domain and the ring degree, respectively. These offer a security level of at least 128 bits [4].

BVMA parameters: Different polynomial ring settings are used identified by the pairs $(\lceil \log(q) \rceil, \log(n)) \in \{(62, 11), (186, 12), (372, 13), (744, 14), (744, 15)\}$ for the ciphertext coefficient domain and the ring degree, respectively. These offer a security level of 80 bits [6].

4.3 Memory Consumption

Let $\hat{q}$ and $\hat{b}$ be the main and auxiliary RNS bases used to represent elements of R_q and used by the HPS-BFV methods described in Sect. 2.3, respectively; and $\mathtt{nres}_{qb}$ the quantity of elements in $\hat{q} \cup \hat{b}$. A BFV ciphertext on SPOG is composed by two N-degree polynomials represented as $\mathtt{nres}_{qb}$ residues with 63-bits coefficients, thus requiring $s(N, \mathtt{nres}_{qb}) := 63 \cdot (2 \cdot N \cdot \mathtt{nres}_{qb})$ bits for storage.

The ciphertext expansion factor, however, depends also on its slot occupancy. Through batching, a single ciphertext can store up to N integer plaintexts [11]. Hence, the expansion factor is given by $\frac{s(N, \mathtt{nres}_{qb})}{63 \cdot \mathtt{batch\_size}}$.

4.4 SPOG Operations

In Table 1 we compare SPOG with BVMA on *gc.k80*, and with BPAVR on *gc.v100*. As mentioned in Sect. 4.1, The authors of BPAVR offer measurements for decryption and homomorphic multiplication only, what inhibits the comparison with SPOG for encryption and homomorphic addition.

One of the major motivations for using a FHE scheme is the applicability of its homomorphic primitives, and because of that, we focus on improving the performance of these. As can be seen, homomorphic multiplication, a critical and known expensive operation, reports speedup between 2.0 and 3.6 times when compared to the BVMA. When compared to the BPAVR these speedups lies between 2 and 2.4. The different characteristics between both setups, considering the processing hardware and the cryptosystem parameters, makes the direct comparison between both data sets impossible, however the performance gains are consistent.

Homomorphic addition, a much simpler operation, presented gains between 2 and 5.2 times when compared to the BVMA. The latter is probably not related to the HDGT, since this procedure is essentially a coefficient-wise addition, but to the better state machine, as described in Sect. 3.3.

Despite our focus in this work does not being on encryption and decryption, the faster polynomial multiplication strategy and the improved state machine offered up to 4.6 times faster encryption and about 2 times faster decryption.

4.5 Efficiency of the HDGT

A major contribution of this work is the HDGT, a novel formulation of the DGT which better explores the parallel capability of GPUs and compensate its memory limitations. However, a carefully evaluation of its quality must be done to understand the performance gains on realistic scenarios. Thus, at this Section, we provide a comparison between the HDGT and the best implementation designs for the canonical DGT.

Table 1. Comparison between SPOG and two state-of-the-art implementations, BVMA and BPAVR. Average running time of 100 independent executions, in milliseconds, for the most relevant BFV operations for the setups described in Sect. 4.2.

		gc.k80				*gc.v100*				
	$\log n$	11	12	13	14	$\log n$	12	13	14	15
Encrypt	SPOG	0.303	0.309	0.575	1.630	–	–	–	–	–
	BVMA	0.541	1.440	2.645	6.657	–	–	–	–	–
	Ratio	**1.785**	**4.660**	**4.600**	**4.084**	–	–	–	–	–
Decrypt	SPOG	0.089	0.098	0.191	0.542	SPOG	0.029	0.031	0.049	0.099
	BVMA	0.151	0.194	0.252	0.610	BPAVR	0.054	0.059	0.087	0.111
	Ratio	**1.697**	**1.980**	**1.319**	**1.125**	Ratio	**1.862**	**1.903**	**1.776**	**1.121**
Hom. Add.	SPOG	0.009	0.010	0.021	0.066	–	–	–	–	–
	BVMA	0.037	0.052	0.068	0.127	–	–	–	–	–
	Ratio	**4.111**	**5.200**	**3.238**	**1.924**	–	–	–	–	–
Hom. Mul.	SPOG	0.926	1.214	3.061	13.914	SPOG	0.423	0.472	0.823	2.325
	BVMA	3.343	3.873	7.700	28.953	BPAVR	0.859	1.012	2.010	4.826
	Ratio	**3.610**	**3.190**	**2.516**	**2.081**	Ratio	**2.031**	**2.144**	**2.442**	**2.076**

As discussed before, the HDGT works by splitting a high-degree polynomial, which does not fit in the processing hardware, and applying the DGT in a divide-and-conquer approach through blocks of arbitrarily small size. To evaluate this design, we implemented the canonical DGT adopting two different strategies, namely DGT-I and DGT-II. The former uses a multi-kernel design which executes the loop synchronization employing a different CUDA kernel for each iteration. This way, the transformation requires $\log \frac{n}{2}$ kernels to process an n-degree polynomial. The latter uses a single-kernel design, which is only compatible with polynomial rings with degree smaller or equal than 4096 since these are the only that fit GPU's shared memory. These strategies are better described in Sect. 3.2. We verified the impact of this change in two important procedures direct affected by the DGT, encryption and homomorphic multiplication.

Table 2 presents the latency measurements. The HDGT is about 2 times faster than the DGT-I, which results in speedups ranging from 1.4 to 2.2 times on BFV's primitives. The DGT-II, though, presents a slowdown in most cases. This relates to the need for serialization within HDGT's steps, which was implemented by splitting the algorithm into 4 sequential kernels. DGT-II is always executed by a single kernel, implying a much smaller overhead. This suggests that the single-kernel design better accommodates smaller instances. Such effect doesn't sustain on *gc.v100* that better handles the high-granularity of the HDGT. Unfortunately, DGT-II is not scalable to bigger rings.

Table 2. Comparison between SPOG running the canonical DGT using a multi-kernel and a single-kernel strategy, called DGT-I and DGT-II, respectively; and the HDGT. The first row group compares the transform alone. Average running time of 100 independent executions, in milliseconds, for the setups described in Sect. 4.2.

		gc.k80					gc.v100				
	$\log n$	11	12	13	14	15	11	12	13	14	15
DGT	HDGT	0.059	0.071	0.146	0.432	0.651	0.018	0.019	0.020	0.031	0.073
	DGT-I	0.114	0.131	0.281	0.711	1.637	0.035	0.034	0.040	0.078	0.188
	Ratio	**1.934**	**1.864**	**1.925**	**1.644**	**2.517**	**1.934**	**1.815**	**2.040**	**2.487**	**2.593**
	DGT-II	0.052	0.091	–	–	–	0.026	0.047	–	–	–
	Ratio	0.881	1.292	–	–	–	1.423	2.492	–	–	–
Encrypt	HDGT	0.303	0.309	0.575	1.630	3.127	0.103	0.098	0.099	0.153	0.315
	DGT-I	0.571	0.499	0.861	2.597	5.835	0.144	0.146	0.159	0.287	0.704
	Ratio	**1.882**	**1.614**	**1.499**	**1.593**	**1.866**	**1.395**	**1.498**	**1.615**	**1.883**	**2.238**
	DGT-II	0.276	0.377	–	–	–	0.120	0.188	–	–	–
	Ratio	0.910	1.220	–	–	–	1.163	1.921	–	–	–
Hom. Mult.	HDGT	0.926	1.214	3.061	13.914	28.990	0.436	0.423	0.472	0.823	2.325
	DGT-I	1.795	2.031	4.231	19.952	42.800	0.795	0.783	0.913	1.609	4.078
	Ratio	**1.938**	**1.673**	**1.382**	**1.434**	**1.476**	**1.825**	**1.850**	**1.934**	**1.956**	**1.754**
	DGT-II	0.642	0.983	–	–	–	0.362	0.466	–	–	–
	Ratio	0.693	0.810	–	–	–	0.830	**1.102**	–	–	–

5   Conclusion

This work investigates strategies to achieve an efficient implementation of the leveled homomorphic encryption scheme BFV on the CUDA architecture. To fulfill this objective, we explored different approaches for the utilization of the DGT in the reduction of the computational complexity of polynomial multiplications. The outcome is an optimized version of the hierarchical DGT, a high granularity implementation of DGT that better fits the GPU processing. Furthermore, the *double*-CRT concept is revisited and an efficient state machine is proposed so we can avoid the costs to alternate between DGT and RNS domains, and between the machine's main memory and GPU's memory.

Our implementation of BFV, named SPOG, is compared with two other works in the literature, BVMA and BPAVR, that represent the state-of-the-art implementations on CUDA. Homomorphic addition, in spite of being a simple and usually fast operation, presented speedups between 2 and 5.2 times over the BVMA. Furthermore, SPOG's homomorphic multiplication showed itself between 2.0 and 3.6 times faster over the BVMA.

As future work, we intend to verify the gains of applying our methods on other relevant RLWE-based cryptosystems such as the CKKS [13], and SPOG as a tool for the acceleration of privacy-focused deep learning algorithms.

Acknowledgements. This work was supported in part by CNPq, grants number 164489/2018-5, 203175/2019-0, and 44265/2019-2; and CAPES grant number 1591123. We specially thank LG for financial support within project *"Privacy-preserving analytics"*, project number 5296; Google for GCP Research Credits Program under number

106101194491; and the Concordium Blockchain Research Center at Aarhus University, Denmark.

A   Properties of Gaussian Integers

This Appendix presents important properties of Gaussian integers and useful results that can be applied on their implementation. In the following, we recall some important properties stated by Wuthrich that are useful to this work [30].

Definition 3 (Norm). *The norm of a Gaussian integer is defined as its product with its conjugate[3]. That is, $N(a+ib) = (a+ib) \cdot (a-ib) = a^2+b^2$, so $N(\alpha) = \alpha \cdot \overline{\alpha}$.*

Proposition 1 (Wuthrich's Proposition 5.7). *For each prime number $p \equiv 1 \mod 4$ there are exactly two Gaussian primes π and $\overline{\pi}$ of norm p.*

Lemma 1 (Wuthrich's Lemma 5.4). *If $\pi \in \mathbb{Z}[i]$ is such that $N(\pi)$ is a prime number, then π is a Gaussian prime.*

Lemma 2 (Wuthrich's Lemma 5.6). *Let p be a prime number with $p \equiv 1 \mod 4$. Then there exists a Gaussian prime π such that $p = \pi \cdot \overline{\pi}$.*

Lemma 3 (Wuthrich's Lemma 5.10). *Any prime $p \equiv 1 \mod 4$ can be written as a sum of two squares. This is a manifestation of Fermat's theorem on sums of two squares.*

From Lemma 2 and Proposition 1, if p is prime such that $p \equiv 1 \mod 4$, then we know that it can be factored as a product of exactly two Gaussian primes that are the conjugate of each other. Lemma 3 is a direct consequence since we know that a prime $p \equiv 1 \mod 4$ can be factored as $p = \pi \cdot \overline{\pi}$ and, assuming that $\pi = a + bi$, we obtain that $\pi \cdot \overline{\pi} = a^2 + b^2$.

B   Generating k-th Primitive Roots of i Modulo p

The use of the DGT for polynomial multiplication in a cyclotomic polynomial ring requires the computation of a k-th root of i modulo a prime p, discussed in Sect. 3.1. This element is used for achieving a cyclotomic polynomial reduction for free when n is a power of two. When p is a Mersenne prime, the literature presents efficient analytic methods; for other choices of p, the best option still is a trial-and-error approach.

Badawi et al. state that a naive implementation of such approach takes 156 hours to find a 2^{14}-th primitive root of i for $p = 2^{64} - 2^{32} + 1$ [5]. Because of that, they propose a more efficient strategy, when $p \equiv 1 \mod 4$, by factoring p in two Gaussian primes, namely f_0 and f_1. This decomposition of p is quite simple and relies on Lemma 2 and Proposition 1.

---

[3] Let $x = a + ib$ be a Gaussian integer. If y is x's conjugate then $y = a - ib$.

Algorithm 6: decompose_in_gaussian_primes: Decomposes a prime.

Input: A prime p
Output: Gaussian integers f_0 and f_1 such that $f_0 \cdot f_1 = p$

1 do
2 $n = \texttt{sample}(\mathbb{Z}_p)$
3 while $n^{(p-1)/2} \not\equiv -1 \mod p$
4 $k = n^{(p-1)/4} \mod p$
5 $u = \texttt{gcd}(p, k + i)$
6 return $(f_0, f_1) = (u, \overline{u})$

Algorithm 6 starts from the Fermat's Little Theorem, which states that if p is a prime then $n^{p-1} \equiv 1 \mod p$ for all $n \in \mathbb{Z}_p$. Hence, the square root of that must be equivalent to either 1 or -1. In the latter case, we can find a number k^2 such that $k \equiv n^{(p-1)/4} \equiv i \mod p$. In other words, if $k^2 \equiv -1 \mod p$ then $k^2 + 1 \equiv 0 \mod p$ and p divides $k^2 + 1$. Since $k^2 + 1$ factors in $(k + i) \cdot (k - i)$, we found a factorization of p.

At this point, there is no guarantee that $k + i$ is a Gaussian prime. By Lemma 4, we find that the greatest common divisor of p and $k + i$ is either $k + i$ or that there exists some u such that $u \mid p$ and $u \mid k + i$. Thus, since $u = \texttt{gcd}(p, k + i)$ results in a Gaussian prime, we take it as the first factor of p. From Lemma 2, $\overline{u}$ is the second factor.

Lemma 4. *Let p be an odd prime such that $p \equiv 1 \mod 4$ and $k \in \mathbb{Z}_p$. The greatest common divisor of p and $k + i$ is $k + i$ or a Gaussian prime u such that $u \mid p$ and $u \mid k + i$.*

Proof. By the Fermat's theorem on sums of two squares, we have that an odd prime p can be expressed as $p = x^2 + y^2$, with $x, y \in \mathbb{Z}$, if, and only if, $p \equiv 1 \mod 4$. Since $x^2 + y^2 = (x + iy)(x - iy)$ and $N(x + iy) = N(x - iy) = p$, then $x + iy$ and $x - iy$ are Gaussian primes and $p = (x + iy)(x - iy)$ is the unique factorization of p in $\mathbb{Z}[i]$, not considering the order of the factors[4].

On the other hand, we have that $(k + i)(k - i) \equiv p \mod p$, by construction. Combining the two facts, we obtain that $p = (x + iy)(x - iy) \equiv (k + i)(k - i)$, which is equivalent to $(k + i)(k - i) = \ell(x + iy)(x - iy)$, for some $\ell \in \mathbb{Z}$.

When $\ell = 1$, we have an equality and we find that $(k + i)$ and $(k - i)$ are indeed the factors of p. When $\ell \neq 1$, $(k+i)$ is not a Gaussian prime and still can be factored in $\mathbb{Z}[i]$; otherwise, it would be a factor of p. We know that p divides $(k + i)(k - i)$ but not $k + i$, or its conjugate, since $k < p$ and $(k + i)/p$ is not a Gaussian integer. Then, $k + i$ and p must share a common factor u that can be found as the greatest common divisor. Since the two factors of p are $x + iy$ and $x + iy$, u must be one of them.

---

[4] Wuthrich proves in Theorem 5.8 that every $0 \neq \alpha \in \mathbb{Z}[i]$ has a unique factorization [30].

Finally, the factors of p can be found by computing the greatest common divisor of p and $k + i$ and then computing its conjugate. Since $p = x^2 + y^2$ and $N(x + iy) = N(x - iy) = x^2 + y^2$, by Lemma 1, the factors are Gaussian primes.

Given a method for factoring a prime number $p \equiv 1 \mod 4$ in $\mathbb{Z}[i]$, Badawi et al. propose Algorithm 7, which makes much faster the step of pre-computing a k-th root of i for a prime $p \equiv 1 \mod 4$ [5]. The method starts by finding the factorization $p = f_0 \cdot f_1 \in \mathbb{Z}_p[i]$ using the Algorithm 6. Thus, we have that each Gaussian prime f_j, with $j = \{0, 1\}$, defines a cyclic group corresponding to the set of Gaussian integers modulo f_j. Then, a k-th root of i modulo p, denoted as h, is constructed via CRT using that $h_j = \zeta_j^{\frac{(p-1)}{4n}} \mod f_j$, with $j = \{0, 1\}$, where ζ_j is a generator for the cyclic group j.

Algorithm 7: Compute the k-th primitive root of $i \mod p$, for a prime number $p \equiv 1 \mod 4$.

Input: An integer k and a prime $p \equiv 1 \mod 4$.
Output: The k-th primitive root of $i \mod p$.

1 $f_0, f_1 = $ decompose_in_gaussian_primes(p)
2 **while** *True* **do**
3   **for** $j = 0; j < 2; j = j + 1$ **do**
4          $\zeta_j = $ sample_generator(f_j); $h_j = \zeta_j^{\lfloor (p-1)/(4k) \rfloor} \mod f_j$
5      $h = f_1 \cdot \left(f_1^{-1} \cdot h_0 \mod f_0 \right) + f_0 \cdot \left(f_0^{-1} \cdot h_1 \mod f_1 \right) \mod p$
6   **if** $h^k \equiv i \mod p$ **then**
7   **return** h

References

1. Albrecht, M., Bai, S., Ducas, L.: A subfield lattice attack on overstretched NTRU assumptions. In: Robshaw, M., Katz, J. (eds.) CRYPTO 2016. LNCS, vol. 9814, pp. 153–178. Springer, Heidelberg (2016). https://doi.org/10.1007/978-3-662-53018-4_6

2. Alves, P.: SPOG: secure processing on GPGPUs (2021). https://github.com/spog-library

3. Alves, P., Ortiz, J.N., Aranha, D.F.: Faster homomorphic encryption over GPGPUs via hierarchical DGT. Cryptology ePrint Archive, Report 2020/861 (2020). https://eprint.iacr.org/2020/861

4. Badawi, A.A., Polyakov, Y., Aung, K.M.M., Veeravalli, B., Rohloff, K.: Implementation and performance evaluation of RNS variants of the BFV homomorphic encryption scheme. IACR Cryptology ePrint Archive **2018**, 589 (2018)

5. Al Badawi, A., Veeravalli, B., Aung, K.M.M.: Efficient polynomial multiplication via modified discrete Galois transform and Negacyclic convolution. In: Arai, K., Kapoor, S., Bhatia, R. (eds.) FICC 2018. AISC, vol. 886, pp. 666–682. Springer, Cham (2019). https://doi.org/10.1007/978-3-030-03402-3_47

6. Badawi, A.Q.A., Veeravalli, B., Mun, C.F., Aung, K.M.M.: High-performance FV somewhat homomorphic encryption on GPUs: an implementation using GPUs. TCHES **1**(2), 70–95 (2018)
7. Bailey, D.H.: FFTs in external or hierarchical memory. J. Supercomput. **4**(1), 23–35 (1990)
8. Bajard, J.-C., Eynard, J., Hasan, M.A., Zucca, V.: A full RNS variant of FV like somewhat homomorphic encryption schemes. In: Avanzi, R., Heys, H. (eds.) SAC 2016. LNCS, vol. 10532, pp. 423–442. Springer, Cham (2017). https://doi.org/10.1007/978-3-319-69453-5_23
9. Bajard, J.C.J., Meloni, N., Plantard, T.: Efficient RNS bases for cryptography. In: IMACS World Congress: Scientific Computation, Applied Mathematics and Simulation (2005)
10. Brakerski, Z., Gentry, C., Vaikuntanathan, V.: (Leveled) fully homomorphic encryption without bootstrapping. ACM Trans. Comput. Theory **6**(3), 13:1–13:36 (2014)
11. Chen, H., Gilad-Bachrach, R., Han, K., Huang, Z., Jalali, A., Laine, K., Lauter, K.E.: Logistic regression over encrypted data from fully homomorphic encryption. IACR Cryptology ePrint Archive **2018**, 462 (2018)
12. Chen, H., Laine, K., Player, R.: Simple encrypted arithmetic library - SEAL v2.1. IACR Cryptology ePrint Archive **2017**, 224 (2017)
13. Cheon, J.H., Kim, A., Kim, M., Song, Y.: Homomorphic encryption for arithmetic of approximate numbers. In: Takagi, T., Peyrin, T. (eds.) ASIACRYPT 2017. LNCS, vol. 10624, pp. 409–437. Springer, Cham (2017). https://doi.org/10.1007/978-3-319-70694-8_15
14. Chillotti, I., Gama, N., Georgieva, M., Izabachène, M.: TFHE: fast fully homomorphic encryption over the torus. J. Cryptol. **33**(1), 34–91 (2020)
15. Chu, E., George, A.: Inside the FFT Black Box: Serial and Parallel Fast Fourier Transform Algorithms. CRC Press (1999)
16. Costache, A., Smart, N.P.: Which ring based somewhat homomorphic encryption scheme is best? In: Sako, K. (ed.) CT-RSA 2016. LNCS, vol. 9610, pp. 325–340. Springer, Cham (2016). https://doi.org/10.1007/978-3-319-29485-8_19
17. Crandall, R.E.: Integer convolution via split-radix fast Galois transform. Center for Advanced Computation Reed College (1999)
18. Dai, W., Sunar, B.: cuHE: a homomorphic encryption accelerator library. In: Pasalic, E., Knudsen, L.R. (eds.) BalkanCryptSec 2015. LNCS, vol. 9540, pp. 169–186. Springer, Cham (2016). https://doi.org/10.1007/978-3-319-29172-7_11
19. Ding, C., Pei, D., Salomaa, A.: Chinese Remainder Theorem: Applications in Computing, Coding, Cryptography. World Scientific (1996)
20. Emmart, N., Weems, C.C.: High precision integer multiplication with a GPU using Strassen's algorithm with multiple FFT sizes. Parallel Process. Lett. **21**(3), 359–375 (2011)
21. Fan, J., Vercauteren, F.: Somewhat practical fully homomorphic encryption. IACR Cryptology ePrint Archive **2012**, 144 (2012)
22. Gentry, C., Halevi, S., Smart, N.P.: Homomorphic evaluation of the AES circuit. In: Safavi-Naini, R., Canetti, R. (eds.) CRYPTO 2012. LNCS, vol. 7417, pp. 850–867. Springer, Heidelberg (2012). https://doi.org/10.1007/978-3-642-32009-5_49
23. Govindaraju, N.K., Lloyd, B., Dotsenko, Y., Smith, B., Manferdelli, J.: High performance discrete Fourier transforms on graphics processors. In: SC, p. 2. IEEE/ACM (2008)

24. Halevi, S., Polyakov, Y., Shoup, V.: An improved RNS variant of the BFV homomorphic encryption scheme. In: Matsui, M. (ed.) CT-RSA 2019. LNCS, vol. 11405, pp. 83–105. Springer, Cham (2019). https://doi.org/10.1007/978-3-030-12612-4_5
25. Lindner, R., Peikert, C.: Better key sizes (and Attacks) for LWE-based encryption. In: Kiayias, A. (ed.) CT-RSA 2011. LNCS, vol. 6558, pp. 319–339. Springer, Heidelberg (2011). https://doi.org/10.1007/978-3-642-19074-2_21
26. Longa, P., Naehrig, M.: Speeding up the number theoretic transform for faster ideal lattice-based cryptography. In: Foresti, S., Persiano, G. (eds.) CANS 2016. LNCS, vol. 10052, pp. 124–139. Springer, Cham (2016). https://doi.org/10.1007/978-3-319-48965-0_8
27. Aguilar-Melchor, C., Barrier, J., Guelton, S., Guinet, A., Killijian, M.-O., Lepoint, T.: NFLLIB: NTT-based fast lattice library. In: Sako, K. (ed.) CT-RSA 2016. LNCS, vol. 9610, pp. 341–356. Springer, Cham (2016). https://doi.org/10.1007/978-3-319-29485-8_20
28. Player, R.: Parameter selection in lattice-based cryptography. Ph.D. thesis, PhD thesis, Royal Holloway, University of London (2018)
29. Thales: 2019 Thales Data Threat Report, USA (2019). https://go.thalesesecurity.com/rs/480-LWA-970/images/2019-DTR-Global-USL-Web.pdf
30. Wuthrich, C.: Further number theory (2011). https://www.maths.nottingham.ac.uk/plp/pmzcw/download/fnt_chap5.pdf. Accessed 18 June 2020

Multi-instance Publicly Verifiable Time-Lock Puzzle and Its Applications

Aydin Abadi[1]([✉]) and Aggelos Kiayias[1,2]

[1] University of Edinburgh, Edinburgh, UK
aydin.abadi@ucl.ac.uk
[2] IOHK, Hong Kong, People's Republic of China
akiayias@inf.ed.ac.uk

Abstract. Time-lock puzzles are elegant protocols that enable a party to lock a message such that no one else can unlock it until a certain time elapses. Nevertheless, existing schemes are not suitable for the case where a server is given *multiple instances* of a puzzle scheme at once and it must unlock them at different points in time. If the schemes are naively used in this setting, then the server has to start solving all puzzles as soon as it receives them, that ultimately imposes significant computation cost and demands a high level of parallelisation. We put forth and formally define a primitive called *"multi-instance time-lock puzzle"* which allows composing a puzzle's instances. We propose a candidate construction: *"chained time-lock puzzle"* (C-TLP). It allows the server, given instances' composition, to solve puzzles sequentially, without having to run parallel computations on them. C-TLP makes black-box use of a standard time-lock puzzle scheme and is accompanied by a lightweight publicly verifiable algorithm. It is the first time-lock puzzle that offers a combination of the above features. We use C-TLP to build the first "outsourced proofs of retrievability" that can support *real-time detection* and *fair payment* while having lower overhead than the state of the art. As another application of C-TLP, we illustrate in certain cases, one can substitute a "verifiable delay function" with C-TLP, to gain much better efficiency.

1 Introduction

Time-lock puzzles are interesting cryptographic primitives that allow sending information to the future. They enable a party to lock a message such that, no one else can unlock it until a certain time has passed[1]. They have a wide range of applications, such as e-voting [12], fair contract signing [8], and sealed-bid auctions [26]. Over the last two decades, a variety of time-lock puzzles have been proposed. Nevertheless, existing puzzle schemes do not offer any efficient remedy for the multi-instance setting, where a server is given multiple instances of a puzzle at once and it should find one puzzle's solution after another. It is a natural generalisation of the single puzzle setting. Application areas include, but not limited to: (a) mass release of confidential documents over time, (b) gradually revealing multiple secret keys, (c) verifying continuous availability of cloud's services, e.g. data storage or secure hardware, or (d) scheduled private

---

[1] There exist protocols that use an assistance of a third party to support time-release of a secret. This protocols' category is not our focus in this paper.

© International Financial Cryptography Association 2021
N. Borisov and C. Diaz (Eds.): FC 2021, LNCS 12675, pp. 541–559, 2021.
https://doi.org/10.1007/978-3-662-64331-0_28

payments, where not only is every payment made after a certain period, but also the payment details remain confidential during the period. If existing puzzle schemes are used directly in the multi-instance setting, then the server has to deal with all puzzle instances, right after it receives them. This results in a significant computation overhead and requires a high level of parallelisation.

In this paper, we propose *"multi-instance time-luck puzzle"*, a primitive that allows composing a puzzle's instances, where given the composition, a server can deal with each instance sequentially. We formally define the primitive and present an instantiation of it, *"chained time-lock puzzle"* (C-TLP). It makes black-box use of a standard time-lock puzzle scheme and is equipped with a *lightweight* verification algorithm that allows anyone to check the correctness of a solution found by the server. Its overall computation complexity of solving z puzzles is equivalent to that of solving only the last puzzle. The same procedure also imposes a communication overhead linear with z, i.e. $O(z)$. C-TLP is the first time-lock puzzle scheme that offers all the above features. Furthermore, we present concrete applications of the primitive and demonstrate its use case in a blockchain-based solution. Specifically, we combine the primitive's instantiation with a smart contract and apply the combination to "outsourced proofs of retrievability" research line, and propose *"smarter outsourced proofs of retrievability"* (SO-PoR) scheme which offers a combination of real-time detection (i.e. a data owner client is notified in almost real-time when a PoR proof is rejected) and fair payment (i.e. in every verification, the storage server is paid only if a PoR proof is accepted) while imposing very low overhead, that makes it particularly suitable for mission-critical data. SO-PoR verification and store phases impose $\frac{1}{4.5}$ and $\frac{1}{46 \times 10^5}$ of computation costs imposed by the same phases in the fastest outsourced PoR. A server-side bandwidth of SO-PoR is much lower too; for instance, for a 1-GB file and 100 verifications, a server in SO-PoR requires 9×10^4 times fewer bits than those required in the state of the art protocol. Also, we show under certain circumstances C-TLP can play the role of a "verifiable delay function" (VDF) but with much lower overhead, i.e. a prover's computation and communication costs will be reduced by factors of 3 and 6.5 respectively.

Summary of Our Contributions. We (a) put forth the notion of multi-instance time-lock puzzle, formally define it, and identify its concrete applications, (b) present a candidate construction, C-TLP, the first multi-instance time-lock puzzle that is built on a standard time-lock puzzle, supports public verifiability, and has low costs, (c) propose the first outsourced PoR that can offer real-time detection and fair payment while maintaining low costs, and (d) show in certain cases, a VDF can be replaced with C-TLP to gain better efficiency.

2 Related Work

In this section, we provide a summary of related work. For a comprehensive survey, we refer readers to the paper's full version [2].

Time-Lock Puzzles. The idea to send information into the *future*, i.e. time-lock puzzle/encryption, was first put forth by Timothy C. May. A time-lock puzzle allows a party to encrypt a message such that it cannot be decrypted until a certain time has passed. In general, a time-lock scheme should allow generating (and verifying) a puzzle to take less time than solving it. The scheme that May proposed relies on a trusted agent. Later, Rivest *et al.* [26] propose an RSA-based puzzle scheme that does not require a trusted agent, and is secure against a receiver who may have access to many computation resources that run in parallel. The latter protocol has been the core of (almost) all later time-lock puzzle schemes that supports the encapsulation of an arbitrary message. Later, [8,15] proposed a scheme which also let a puzzle generator prove (in Zero-knowledge) to a puzzle solver that the correct solution will be recovered after a certain time. Recently, [9,22] propose homomorphic time-lock puzzles, where an arbitrary function can be run over puzzles before they are solved. In the protocols, all puzzles have an identical time parameter, and their solutions are supposed to be discovered at the same time. They are based on the RSA-based puzzle and fully homomorphic encryption, computationally expensive. Very recently, Chvojka *et al.* in [13] propose incremental time-release encryption which lets a server, given a set of encrypted messages, discover messages sequentially over time. It is the closest work to ours. Nevertheless, the scheme uses the RSA time-lock puzzle [26] in a *non-black-box manner*, offers no (public) verification, is based on asymmetric key encryption instead of symmetric key encryption used in the majority of time lock-puzzle schemes, and uses a non-standard (asymmetric) encryption scheme.

Outsourced Proofs of Retrievability. Proofs of retrievability (PoR) schemes, introduced in [18], ensures a client's data on a cloud server is fully accessible. Ever since a variety of PoR's has been proposed. Recently, [3,30] present *outsourced* PoR protocols that let clients outsource the verification to a potentially malicious third-party auditor. The scheme in [3] has the fastest prove and verification algorithms. It uses message authentication code (MAC) based tags, zero-knowledge proofs and error-correcting codes. But, it has several shortcomings, i.e. it offers no real-time detection, provides no efficient way for fair payments and has high costs of setup and auditor onboarding. Xu *et al.* in [30] propose a publicly verifiable outsourced PoR to improve the previous scheme's setup cost. It uses BLS signatures-like tags, polynomial arithmetic and error-correcting codes. It assumes an auditor is fully trusted during each verification whose overhead is higher than [3]. Recently in [5] two protocols are proposed, "basic PoSt" and "compact PoSt". They ensure that a client's data remains available on a server for a period, without the client's involvement in that period. The basic PoSt uses a Merkle tree-based PoR and VDF. It has a high communication cost. Since it requires a verifier to validate VDF's outputs, it imposes a significant computation cost, in practice. The compact PoSt has a lower communication cost than the basic one, as it let the server combine PoR proofs. It is mainly based on a trapdoor delay function (TDF).

Blockchain-Based PoR. There exist distributed PoR schemes that let a client distribute its file among different (tailored) blockchain nodes, e.g. Permacoin [23], Filecoin [21], and KopperCoin [20]. But, they have either a large proof size (e.g. in [21,23]) logarithmic with the file size when a Merkle tree is used, or high concrete verification overhead (e.g. in [20]) due to the use of BLS signatures. There are protocols that use blockchain to verify the retrievability of off-chain data [6,14,17,25,28,31]. Nevertheless, they either impose a high communication/computation cost [6,14,17,25,28], or clients have to be online for each verification [31]. Campanelli *et al.* [10] present a fair exchange mechanism over a blockchain that ensures the server gets paid if it provides an accepting PoR proof. But, this scheme assumes either the client can perform the verification itself or a third-party, acting on the client's behalf, carries out the verification honestly.

3   Preliminaries

In this section we provide the main primitives used in this paper. We also summarise our notations in Table 1.

Table 1. Notation table.

Setting	Symbol	Description	Setting	Symbol	Description
Generic	z	Number of puzzles or delegated verifications	SO-PoR	PRF	Pseudorandom function
	h, h_j	Hash values		$\hat{k}, v_j, l_j$	PRF's keys
	d, d_j	Randomness of commitment		ι	Security parameter, $\iota = 128$-bit
	n	Number of file blocks		p	Large prime number, $|p| = \iota$
	m, m_j	Plaintext messages		w	Blockchain block index
	$\ddot{o}$	Pair representation		g	Blockchain security parameter: chain quality
	$\vec{\sigma}$	Vector representation		λ'	Blockchain generic security parameter
	$\ddot{p} : (m_j, d_j)$	Commitment opening		F	Outsourced encoded file
	$\mathbb{H}$	Hash function		F_j	A file block
C-TLP	λ	TLP security parameter		$|F|$	Number of file blocks, $|F| = n$
	Δ	Time win. message remains hidden		$\|F\|$	File bit-size
	S	Max. squaring done per sec.		σ_i	Permanent tag
	T	$T = S\Delta$		$\sigma_{b,j}$	Disposable tag
	s_j	j-th solution		$\alpha, \alpha_j, r_i, r_{b,j}$	Pseudorandom values
	$\ddot{o}_j$	j-th puzzle, $\ddot{o}_j : (o_{j,1}, o_{j,2})$		c	Number of challenges
	f_j	Time when j-th solution is found		$\mathcal{B}_j$	Blockchain's j-th block
	k, k_j	Sym. key encryption keys		(μ_j, ξ_j)	j-th PoR proof
	pk, sk	Public and secret keys		Δ_1	Time taken to generate a PoR
	q_1, q_2	Large prime numbers		Δ_2	Time taken a contract gets a message
	N	RSA modulus, $N = q_1 q_2$		e	Coins paid for an accepting PoR

3.1   Smart Contract

Cryptocurrencies, such as Bitcoin and Ethereum, in addition to offering a decentralised currency, support computations on transactions. In this setting, often a certain computation logic is encoded in a computer program, called *"smart contract"*. To date, Ethereum is the most predominant cryptocurrency framework that enables users to define arbitrary smart contracts. In this framework, contract code is stored on the blockchain and executed by all parties (i.e. miners) maintaining the cryptocurrency, when the program inputs are provided by transactions. The program execution's correctness is guaranteed by the security of the underlying blockchain components. To prevent a denial of service attack, the framework requires a transaction creator to pay a fee, called *"gas"*, depending on the complexity of the contract running on it.

3.2 Commitment Scheme

A commitment scheme involves two parties: *sender* and *receiver*, and includes two phases: *commit* and *open*. In the commit phase, the sender commits to a message: m as $\text{Com}(m, d) = h$, that involves a secret value: d. At the end of the commit phase, the commitment: h is sent to the receiver. In the open phase, the sender sends the opening: $\ddot{p} = (m, d)$ to the receiver who verifies its correctness: $\text{Ver}(h, \ddot{p}) \stackrel{?}{=} 1$ and accepts if the output is 1. A commitment scheme must satisfy two properties: (a) *hiding*: infeasible for an adversary to learn any information about the committed value: m, until the commitment: h is opened, and (b) *binding*: infeasible for an adversary (i.e. the sender) to open a commitment: h to different values: $\ddot{p}' = (m', d')$ than that used in the commit phase, i.e. infeasible to find $\ddot{p}'$, s.t. $\text{Ver}(h, \ddot{p}) = \text{Ver}(h, \ddot{p}') = 1$, where $\ddot{p} \neq \ddot{p}'$. There exist efficient non-interactive commitment schemes both in (a) the random oracle model using the well-known hash-based scheme that $\text{Com}(m, d)$ involves computing: $\text{H}(m\|d) = h$ and $\text{Ver}(h, \ddot{p})$ requires checking: $\text{H}(m\|d) \stackrel{?}{=} h$, where $\text{H}(.)$ is a collision resistance hash function, and (b) the standard model, e.g. Pedersen scheme [24].

3.3 Pseudorandom Function

Informally, a pseudorandom function (PRF) is a deterministic function that takes a key and an input; and outputs a value indistinguishable from that of a truly random function with the same input. A PRF is formally defined as follows [19].

Definition 1. *Let $W : \{0, 1\}^{\psi} \times \{0, 1\}^{\eta} \to \{0, 1\}^{\iota}$ be an efficient keyed function. It is said W is a pseudorandom function if for all probabilistic polynomial-time distinguishers B, there is a negligible function, $\mu(.)$, such that:*

$$\left| Pr[B^{W_k(\cdot)}(1^{\psi}) = 1] - Pr[B^{\omega(\cdot)}(1^{\psi}) = 1] \right| \leq \mu(\psi)$$

where the key, $k \xleftarrow{\$} \{0, 1\}^{\psi}$, is chosen uniformly at random and ω is chosen uniformly at random from the set of functions mapping η-bit strings to ι-bit strings.

3.4 Time-Lock Puzzle

In this section, we restate the formal definition of a time-lock puzzle as well as RSA-based time-lock puzzle protocol [26]. We consider the RSA-based puzzle because of its simplicity and being the core of (almost) all later time-lock puzzle schemes.

Definition 2 (Time-lock Puzzle). *A time-lock puzzle comprises the following efficient three algorithms, such that the puzzle satisfies completeness and efficiency properties.*

- **Algorithms:**
  - $\texttt{Setup}(1^\lambda, \Delta) \to (pk, sk)$: *a probabilistic algorithm that takes as input security:* 1^λ *and time:* Δ *parameters. It outputs a public-private key pairs:* (pk, sk).
  - $\texttt{GenPuz}(s, pk, sk) \to \ddot{o}$: *a probabilistic algorithm that takes as input a solution:* s *and the public-private key pairs:* (pk, sk). *It outputs a puzzle:* $\ddot{o}$.
  - $\texttt{SolvPuz}(pk, \ddot{o}) \to s$: *a deterministic algorithm that takes as input the public key:* pk *and puzzle:* $\ddot{o}$. *It outputs a solution:* s.
- **Completeness:** *always* $\texttt{SolvPuz}(pk, \texttt{GenPuz}(s, pk, sk)) = s$.
- **Efficiency:** *the run-time of algorithm* $\texttt{SolvPuz}(pk, \ddot{o})$ *is bounded by* $poly(\Delta, \lambda)$, *where* $poly(.)$ *is a polynomial.*

Informally, a time-lock puzzle's security requires that the puzzle solution remain hidden from all adversaries running in parallel within the time period, Δ. It is essential that no adversary can find a solution in time $\delta(\Delta) < \Delta$, using $\pi(\Delta)$ processors running in parallel and after a potentially large amount of pre-computation. So, such factors are explicitly incorporated into the puzzle's definitions [7,16,22].

Definition 3 (Time-lock Puzzle Security). *A time-lock puzzle is secure if for all* λ *and* Δ, *all probabilistic polynomial time adversaries* $\mathcal{A} = (\mathcal{A}_1, \mathcal{A}_2)$ *where* $\mathcal{A}_1$ *runs in total time* $O(poly(\Delta, \lambda))$ *and* $\mathcal{A}_2$ *runs in time* $\delta(\Delta) < \Delta$ *using at most* $\pi(\Delta)$ *parallel processors, there exists a negligible function* $\mu(.)$, *such that:*

$$Pr \left[\mathcal{A}_2(pk, \ddot{o}, state) \to b \; \middle| \; \begin{array}{l} \texttt{Setup}(1^\lambda, \Delta) \to (pk, sk) \\ \mathcal{A}_1(1^\lambda, pk, \Delta) \to (s_0, s_1, state) \\ b \xleftarrow{\$} \{0, 1\} \\ \texttt{GenPuz}(s_b, pk, sk) \to \ddot{o} \end{array} \right] \leq \frac{1}{2} + \mu(\lambda)$$

An RSA-based time-lock puzzle construction that realises the above definitions was proposed in [26]. The construction is as follows.

1. **Setup**: $\texttt{TLP.Setup}(1^\lambda, \Delta)$
   (a) Compute $N = q_1 q_2$, where q_i is a large randomly chosen prime number. Then compute Euler's totient function of N, as: $\phi(N) = (q_1 - 1)(q_2 - 1)$.
   (b) Set $T = S\Delta$ as the total number of squaring needed to decrypt an encrypted message m, where Δ is the period (in seconds) within which the message should remain private and S is the maximum number of squaring modulo N per second that can be performed by a solver.
   (c) Choose a random key: k for a semantically secure symmetric key encryption that has three algorithms: $(\texttt{GenKey}, \texttt{Enc}, \texttt{Dec})$.
   (d) Pick a uniformly random value r from $\mathbb{Z}_N^*$.
   (e) Compute $a = 2^T \bmod \phi(N)$.
   (f) Set $pk = (N, T, r)$ as public key and set $sk = (q_1, q_2, a, k)$ as secret key.
2. **Generate Puzzle**: $\texttt{TLP.GenPuz}(m, pk, sk)$
   (a) Encrypt the message using the symmetric key encryption: $o_1 = \texttt{Enc}(k, m)$.
   (b) Encrypt the key: k, as: $o_2 = k + r^a \bmod N$.
   (c) Sets: $\ddot{o} = (o_1, o_2)$ as ciphertext or puzzle. Next, output $\ddot{o}$.

3. **Solve Puzzle**: TLP.SolvPuz$(pk, \ddot{o})$
   (a) Find b, where $b = r^{2^T} \bmod N$, by using T number of squaring r modulo N.
   (b) Decrypt the key's ciphertext: $k = o_2 - b \bmod N$.
   (c) Decrypt the message's ciphertext: $m = \text{Dec}(k, o_1)$. Output m.

Informally, the time-lock puzzle's security relies on the hardness of factoring problem, the security of the symmetric key encryption, and sequential squaring assumption. We refer readers to the paper's full version [2] for more discussion on the construction and its security.

4   Multi-instance Time-Lock Puzzle

4.1   Strawman Solution

In the following, we elaborate on the problems that would arise if an existing time-lock puzzle is used directly to handle multiple puzzles at once. Without loss of generality, to illustrate the problems, we use the well-known TLP scheme presented in Sect. 3.4.

Consider the case where a client wants a server to learn a vector of messages: $\overrightarrow{m} = [m_1, ..., m_z]$ at times $[f_1, ..., f_z]$ respectively, where the client is available and online only at an earlier time $f_0 < f_1$. For the sake of simplicity, let $\Delta = f_1 - f_0$ and $\Delta = f_{j+1} - f_j$, where $1 \leq j \leq z$. A naive way to address the problem is that the client uses the TLP to encrypt each message m_j separately, such that it can be decrypted at time f_j if all ciphertexts and public keys are passed on to the server at time t_0. For the server to decrypt the messages on time, it needs to start decrypting *all of them* as soon as the ciphertexts and public keys are given to it.

Parallel Composition Problem. The above naive approach yields two serious issues: (a) imposing a high computation cost, as the server has to perform $S\Delta \sum_{j=1}^{z} j$ squaring to decrypt all messages, and (b) demanding a high level of parallelisation, as each puzzle has to be dealt with separately in parallel to the rest. The issues can be cast as *"parallel composition problem"*, where z instances of a puzzle scheme are given at once to a server whose only option, to find solutions on time, is to solve them in parallel.[2] Also, for the client to efficiently compute a_j for each message m_j, where $j > 1$, it has to perform at least one modular multiplication, i.e. $a_j = a_1 a_{j-1} = 2^{jT}$, where $a_1 = 2^T$. In this step, in total $z - 1$ modular multiplications are required to compute all a_j values, for z messages (which is not optimal). Note, we do not see the above issues as previous schemes' flaws, because they were not initially designed for the multi-puzzle setting.

4.2   An Overview of Our Solutions

Our key observation is, in the naive approach, the process of decrypting messages has many overlaps leading to a high computation cost. So, by removing the overlaps, we can considerably lower the overall cost both in *puzzle solving* and *puzzle creating* phases.

---

[2] It should not be confused with the "universally composable" notion put forth in [11].

One of our core ideas is to chain the puzzles. While chaining different puzzles may seem a relatively obvious approach to tackle the issues, designing a secure protocol that also can make black-box use of a standard time-lock puzzle scheme, supports public verifiability, and has low costs is challenging (we refer readers to the paper's full version for a detailed discussion). In our solution, a client first encrypts the message that is supposed to be decrypted after the rest and embeds the information needed for decrypting it into the ciphertext of the message that will be decrypted before that message. In other words, the client integrates the information (i.e. a part of public keys) needed to decrypt message m_j into the ciphertext related to message m_{j-1}. In this case, the server after learning message m_{j-1} at time f_{j-1} learns the public key needed to perform the sequential squaring to decrypt the next message: m_j. This means after fully decrypting m_{j-1}, the server starts squaring sequentially to decrypt m_j.

Addressing Parallel Composition Problem. The above approach solves the parallel composition problem for two main reasons. First, the total number of squaring required to decrypt all z messages is now much lower, i.e. $S \Delta z$, and is equivalent to the number of squaring needed to solve only the last puzzle, i.e. z-th one. Second, it does not call for high parallelisation. Because now the server does not need to deal with all of the puzzles in parallel; instead, it solves them sequentially one after another.

Adding Efficient Publicly Verifiable Algorithm. To let the scheme support efficient public verifiability, we use the following novel trick. The client uses a commitment scheme to commit to every message: m_i and publishes the commitment. Then, it uses the time-lock encryption to encrypt the commitment's opening, i.e. a combination of m_i and a random value. But, unlike the traditional commitment, the client does not open the commitment itself. Instead, the server does that, after it discovers the puzzle's solution. When it finds a solution, it decodes the solution to find the opening and sends it to the public who can check the solution correctness. So, to verify a solution's correctness, a verifier only needs to run the commitment's verification algorithm that is: (a) publicly verifiable, and (b) efficient. It can be built in the random oracle or the standard model.

The approach also allows the client at the setup to compute only a single $a = 2^T$ reusable for all z puzzles, imposing only $O(1)$ cost.

4.3   Multi-instance Time-Lock Puzzle Definition

In this section, we provide a formal definition of a multi-instance time-lock puzzle. Our starting point is the time-lock puzzle definition, i.e. Definition 2, but we extend it from several perspectives, so it can: (a) handle multiple solutions/messages in setup, (b) produce multiple puzzles for the messages, (c) solve the puzzles given the puzzles and public parameters, and (d) support public verifiability. In the following, we provide the formal definition of a multi-instance time-lock puzzle.

Definition 4 (Multi-instance Time-lock Puzzle). *A multi-instance time-lock puzzle has the following five algorithms and satisfies completeness and efficiency properties.*

- *Algorithms:*
  - $\texttt{Setup}(1^\lambda, \Delta, z) \rightarrow (pk, sk, \vec{d})$: *a probabilistic algorithm that takes as input security:* 1^λ *and time:* Δ *parameters and the total number of solutions/puzzles:* z. *Let* $j\Delta$ *be a time period after which* j-*th solution is found. It outputs public-private key pair:* (pk, sk) *and a vector of fixed size secret witnesses:* $\vec{d}$.
  - $\texttt{GenPuz}(\vec{m}, pk, sk, \vec{d}) \rightarrow \ddot{o}$: *a probabilistic algorithm that takes as input a message vector:* $\vec{m} = [m_1, ..., m_z]$, *the public-private key pair:* (pk, sk), *and the witness vector:* $\vec{d}$. *It outputs* $\ddot{o} : (\vec{o}, \vec{h})$, *where* $\vec{o}$ *is a puzzle vector, and* $\vec{h}$ *is a commitment vector. Each* j-*th element in vectors* $\vec{o}$ *and* $\vec{h}$ *corresponds to a solution* s_j *of the form:* $s_j = m_j || d_j$.
  - $\texttt{SolvPuz}(pk, \vec{o}) \rightarrow \vec{s}$: *a deterministic algorithm that takes as input the public key:* pk *and puzzle vector:* $\vec{o}$. *It outputs a solution vector:* $\vec{s}$.
  - $\texttt{Prove}(pk, s_j) \rightarrow \ddot{p}_j$: *a deterministic algorithm that takes the public key:* pk *and a solution:* $s_j \in \vec{s}$. *It outputs a proof,* $\ddot{p}_j : (m_j, d_j)$ *given to the verifier.*
  - $\texttt{Verify}(pk, \ddot{p}_j, h_j) \rightarrow \{0, 1\}$: *a deterministic algorithm that takes public key:* pk, *proof:* $\ddot{p}_j$ *and commitment:* $h_j \in \vec{h}$. *It outputs* 0 *if it rejects, or* 1 *if it accepts.*
- *Completeness: for any honest prover and verifier, it always holds that:*
  - $\texttt{SolvPuz}(pk, [o_1, ..., o_j]) = [s_1, ..., s_j]$, *for every* j, $1 \leq j \leq z$.
  - $\texttt{Verify}(pk, \texttt{Prove}(pk, s_j), h_j) \rightarrow 1$.
- *Efficiency: the run-time of algorithm* $\texttt{SolvPuz}(pk, [o_1, ..., o_j]) = [s_1, ...s_j]$ *is bounded by:* $poly(j\Delta, \lambda)$, *where* $poly(.)$ *is a fixed polynomial and* $1 \leq j \leq z$.

Informally, a multi-instance time-lock puzzle is secure if it satisfies two properties: a solution's *privacy* and *validity*. The former requires its j-th solution to remain hidden from all adversaries running in parallel within time period: $j\Delta$, while the latter one requires that it is infeasible for a PPT adversary to come up with an invalid solution and passes the verification. The two properties are formally defined in Definitions 5 and 6.

Definition 5 (Multi-instance Time-lock Puzzle's Solution-Privacy). *A multi-instance time-lock puzzle is privacy-preserving if for all* λ *and* Δ, *any number of puzzle:* $z \geq 1$, *any* j *(where* $1 \leq j \leq z$), *any pair of randomised algorithm* $\mathcal{A} : (\mathcal{A}_1, \mathcal{A}_2)$, *where* $\mathcal{A}_1$ *runs in time* $O(poly(j\Delta, \lambda))$ *and* $\mathcal{A}_2$ *runs in time* $\delta(j\Delta) < j\Delta$ *using at most* $\pi(\Delta)$ *parallel processors, there exists a negligible function* $\mu(.)$, *such that:*

$$Pr\left[\begin{array}{l}\mathcal{A}_2(pk, \ddot{o}, state) \rightarrow \ddot{a} \\ s.t. \\ \ddot{a} : (b_i, i) \\ m_{b_i, i} = m_{b_j, j}\end{array}\middle|\begin{array}{l}\texttt{Setup}(1^\lambda, \Delta, z) \rightarrow (pk, sk, \vec{d}) \\ \mathcal{A}_1(1^\lambda, pk, z) \rightarrow (\vec{m}, state) \\ \forall j', 1 \leq j' \leq z : b_{j'} \overset{\$}{\leftarrow} \{0, 1\} \\ \texttt{GenPuz}(\vec{m}', pk, sk, \vec{d}) \rightarrow \ddot{o}\end{array}\right] \leq \frac{1}{2} + \mu(\lambda)$$

where $\vec{m} : [(m_{0,1}, m_{1,1}), ..., (m_{0,z}, m_{1,z})]$, $\vec{m}' : (m_{b_1,1}, ..., m_{b_z,z})$, *and* $1 \leq i \leq z$.

The definition above also ensures the solutions to appear after j-th one, remain hidden from the adversary with a high probability, as well. Similar to [7, 16, 22], it captures that even if $\mathcal{A}_1$ computes on the public parameters for a polynomial time, $\mathcal{A}_2$ cannot find j-th solution in time $\delta(j\Delta) < j\Delta$ using $\pi(\Delta)$ parallel processors, with a probability significantly greater than $\frac{1}{2}$. As highlighted in [7], we can set $\delta(\Delta) = (1 - \epsilon)\Delta$ for a small ϵ, where $0 < \epsilon < 1$.

Definition 6 (Multi-instance Time-lock Puzzle's Solution-Validity). *A multi-instance time-lock puzzle preserves a solution validity, if for all λ and Δ, any number of puzzles: $z \geq 1$, all probabilistic polynomial-time adversaries $\mathcal{A} = (\mathcal{A}_1, \mathcal{A}_2)$ that run in time $O(poly(\Delta, \lambda))$ there is negligible function $\mu(.)$, such that:*

$$
Pr \begin{bmatrix}
\mathcal{A}_2(pk, \vec{s}, \ddot{o}, state) \to a \\
s.t. \\
a : (j, \ddot{p}_j, \ddot{p}') \\
\ddot{p}_j : (m_j, d_j), \ddot{p}' : (m', d') \\
m_j \in \vec{m}, d_j \in \vec{d}, m \neq m' \\
\text{Verify}(pk, \ddot{p}, h_j) = 1 \\
\text{Verify}(pk, \ddot{p}', h_j) = 1
\end{bmatrix}
\begin{array}{|l}
\text{Setup}(1^\lambda, \Delta, z) \to (pk, sk, \vec{d}) \\
\mathcal{A}_1(1^\lambda, pk, \Delta, z) \to (\vec{m}, state) \\
\text{GenPuz}(\vec{m}, pk, sk, \vec{d}) \to \ddot{o} \\
\text{SolvPuz}(pk, \vec{o}) \to \vec{s}
\end{array} \leq \mu(\lambda)
$$

where $\vec{m} = [m_1, ..., m_z]$, and $h_j \in \vec{h} \in \ddot{o}$.

Definition 7 (Multi-instance Time-lock Puzzle Security). *A multi-instance time-lock puzzle scheme is secure if it meets solution-privacy and solution-validity properties.*

4.4   Chained Time-Lock Puzzle (C-TLP) Protocol

In this section, we present the chained time-lock puzzle (C-TLP), an instantiation of the multi-instance time lock puzzle. Since we have already presented an outline of C-TLP (in Sect. 4.2), in this section we present C-TLP protocol in detail. Recall, a client wants a server to learn a vector of messages: $\vec{m} = [m_1, ..., m_z]$ at times $[f_1, ..., f_z]$ respectively, where the client is available and online only at an earlier time $f_0 < f_1$. Also, the client wants to ensure that anyone can validate a solution found by the server, i.e. supports public verifiability. For the sake of simplicity, let $\Delta = f_1 - f_0$ and $\Delta = f_{j+1} - f_j$, where $1 \leq j \leq z$ and $T = S\Delta$. Below, we provide C-TLP protocol. We refer readers to the paper's full version [2] for further remarks on the protocol.

1. **Setup**: $\text{Setup}(1^\lambda, \Delta, z)$.
   (a) Call: $\text{TLP.Setup}(1^\lambda, \Delta) \to (\hat{pk}, \hat{sk})$, s.t. $\hat{pk} = (N, T, r_1)$ and $\hat{sk} = (q_1, q_2, a, k_1)$.
   (b) Pick $z - 1$ fixed size random generators: $\vec{r} = [r_2, ..., r_z]$ from $\mathbb{Z}_N^*$.
   (c) Pick $z - 1$ random keys: $[k_2, ..., k_z]$ for a symmetric key encryption. Let $\vec{k} = [k_1, ..., k_z]$, where $k_1 \in \hat{sk}$. Also, pick z fixed size sufficiently large random values: $\vec{d} = [d_1, ..., d_z]$, e.g. $|d_j| = 128$-bit or 1024-bit depending on the choice of a commitment scheme.
   (d) Set $pk = (aux, N, T, r_1)$ as public key. Set $sk = (q_1, q_2, a, \vec{k}, \vec{r}, \vec{d})$ as secret key. Note, aux contains a cryptographic hash function's description and the size of the random values. Also, note that all generators, except r_1 are kept secret. Output pk and sk.
2. **Generate Puzzle**: $\text{GenPuz}(\vec{m}, pk, sk)$
   Encrypt the messages, starting with $j = z$, in descending order. $\forall j, z \geq j \geq 1$:
   (a) Set $pk_j = (N, T, r_j)$ and $sk_j = (q_1, q_2, a, k_j)$. Note, if $j = 1$ then $r_j \in pk$; otherwise (when $j > 1$), $r_j \in \vec{r}$.

(b) Generate a puzzle (or ciphertext pair):
- if $j = z$, then run: TLP.GenPuz$(m_j || d_j, pk_j, sk_j) \rightarrow \ddot{o}_j = (o_{j,1}, o_{j,2})$.
- otherwise, run: TLP.GenPuz$(m_j || d_j || r_{j+1}, pk_j, sk_j) \rightarrow \ddot{o}_j = (o_{j,1}, o_{j,2})$.

(c) Commit to each message, e.g. $\text{H}(m_j || d_j) = h_j$ and output: h_j.

(d) Output: $\ddot{o}_j = (o_{j,1}, o_{j,2})$ as puzzle (or ciphertext pair).

By the end of this phase, vectors of puzzles: $\vec{o} = [\ddot{o}_1, ..., \ddot{o}_z]$ and commitments: $\vec{h} = [h_1, ... h_z]$ are generated. All public parameters and puzzles are given to a server at time $t_0 < t_1$, where $\Delta = f_1 - f_0$.

3. **Solve Puzzle**: SolvPuz$(pk, \vec{o})$

Decrypt the messages, starting with $j = 1$, in ascending order. $\forall j, 1 \le j \le z$:

(a) If $j = 1$, then set $r_j = r_1$, where $r_1 \in pk$; Otherwise, set $r_j = u$.

(b) Set $pk_j = (N, T, r_j)$.

(c) Run: TLP.SolvPuz$(pk_j, \ddot{o}_j) \rightarrow x_j$, where $\ddot{o}_j \in \vec{o}$

(d) Parse x_j. Note that if $j < z$ then $x_j = m_j || d_j || r_{j+1}$; otherwise, we have $x_j = m_j || d_j$. Therefore, x_j is parsed as follows.
- if $j < z$:
  i Parse $m_j || d_j || r_{j+1}$ into $m_j || d_j$ and $u = r_{j+1}$
  ii Output $s_j = m_j || d_j$
- otherwise (when $j = z$), output $s_j = x_j = m_j || d_j$

4. **Prove**: Prove(pk, s_j). Parse s_j into $\ddot{p}_j : (m_j, d_j)$, and send the pair to the verifier.

5. **Verify**: Verify$(pk, \ddot{p}_j, h_j)$. Verifies the commitment, $\text{H}(m_j, d_j) \stackrel{?}{=} h_j$. If passed, accept the solution and output 1; otherwise, reject it and output 0.

Theorem 1 (C-TLP Security). *C-TLP is a secure multi-instance time-lock puzzle.*

Proof (Outline). The proof of Theorem 1 relies on the security of the TLP, symmetric key encryption, and commitment schemes. It is also based on the fact that the probability to find a certain random generator is negligible. It shows both C-TLP's solution privacy (due to security of the above three schemes) and validity (due to the security of the commitment) are satisfied. We refer readers to the paper's full version [2] for detailed proof. □

4.5 Cost Analysis Table

We summarize C-TLP's cost analysis in Table 2. It considers a generic setting where the protocol deals with z puzzles. We refer readers to the paper's full version [2] for detailed analysis.

5 Smarter Outsourced PoR (SO-PoR) Using C-TLP

As discussed in Sect. 2, the existing outsourced PoR's have serious shortcomings, e.g. having high costs, not supporting real-time detection, or suffering from the lack of a fair payment mechanism. In this section, we present SO-PoR to addresses them.

Table 2. C-TLP's detailed cost breakdown

(a) Computation Cost

Protocol	Operation	Protocol Function			Complexity
		GenPuz	SolvPuz	Verify	
C-TLP	Exp.	$z+1$	Tz	—	$O(Tz)$
	Add. or Mul.	z	z	—	
	Commitment	z	—	z	
	Sym. Enc	z	z	—	

(b) Communication Cost (in bit)

Protocol	Model	Client	Server	Complexity
C-TLP	Standard	$3200z$	$1524z$	$O(z)$
	R.O.	$2432z$	$628z$	

5.1 SO-PoR Overview

SO-PoR uses a unique combination of (a) homomorphic MAC-based PoR [27], (b) C-TLP, (c) a smart contract, (d) a pre-computation technique, and (e) blockchain-based random extraction beacon [1,3]. It uses the MAC-based PoR, due to its high efficiency. Since the MACs are privately verifiable and secret verification keys are needed to check PoR proofs, SO-PoR also uses C-TLP to efficiently make them publicly verifiable. In this case, C-TLP encapsulates the verification keys and reveals each of them to verifiers only after a certain time. SO-PoR also uses a smart contract which acts as a public verifier on the client's behalf to verify proofs and pay an honest server. The pre-computation technique allows the client at setup to generate a constant number of *disposable* homomorphic MACs for each verification. The combination of disposable homomorphic MACs and C-TLP makes it possible to (a) use a smart contract and (b) take advantage of MACs efficiency in the setting where public verifiability is needed. This combination has applications beyond PoR. A blockchain-based random extraction beacon allows the server to independently derive a set of unpredictable random values from the blockchain such that the values' correctness is publicly verifiable.

At a high-level SO-PoR works as follows. The client encodes its file using an error-correcting code and for each j-th verification it does the following. It picks two random keys: (v_j, l_j) of a PRF. It uses v_j to generate c random blocks' indices, i.e. challenged blocks. It uses l_j to generate a disposable MAC on each challenged block. It also uses C-TLP to make two puzzles, one that encapsulates v_j, and another that encapsulates l_j. It deposits enough coins to cover z successful PoR verifications in a smart contract. The client sends the encoded file, tags and the puzzles to the server. When j-th PoR proof is needed, the server manages to discover key v_j that lets it determine which file blocks are challenges. The server also uses the beacon to extract a set of random values from the blockchain. Using the MACs, challenged blocks, and beacon's outputs, the server generates a compact PoR proof. The server sends the proof to the contract. After that, it can delete the related disposable MACs. For the same verification, after a fixed time, it manages to find the related MACs verification key: l_j. It sends the key to the server who checks the correctness of l_j and PoR proof. If the contract accepts all proofs, then it pays the server for j-th verification; otherwise, it notifies the client.

5.2 SO-PoR Model Overview

SO-PoR model is built upon the traditional PoR paradigm [27] which is a challenge-response protocol where a server proves to an honest client that its file is retrievable (see the paper's full version [2] for a formal definition of the PoR). In SO-PoR, however, a client may not be available for verification. So, it wants to delegate a set of verifications that it cannot carry out. Informally, in this setting, it (in addition to file retrievability) must have three guarantees: (a) *verification correctness*: every verification is performed honestly, so the client can trust the verification's result without redoing it, (b) *real-time detection*: the client is notified in almost real-time when a proof is rejected, and (c) *fair payment*: in every verification, the server is paid only if a proof is accepted. In SO-PoR, three parties are involved: an honest client, potentially malicious server and a standard smart contract. SO-PoR also, analogous to [27], allows a client to perform the verification itself, when it is available. We present our formal definition of SO-PoR in the paper's full version [2].

5.3 SO-PoR Protocol

This section presents SO-PoR protocol in detail, followed by the rationale behind it.

1. **Client-side Setup**.
    (a) **Gen. Public and Private Keys**: Picks a fresh key: $\hat{k}$ and two vectors of keys: $\vec{v}$ and $\vec{l}$, where each vector contains z fresh keys. It picks a large prime number: p whose size is determined by a security parameter, (i.e. its bit-length is equal to the bit-length of $\text{PRF}(.)$'s output, $|p| = \iota$). Moreover, it runs $\texttt{Setup}(.)$ in C-TLP scheme to generate a key pair: (pk, sk).
    (b) **Gen. Other Public Parameters**: Sets c to the total number of blocks challenged in each verification. It defines parameters: w and g, where w is an index of a future block: $\mathcal{B}_w$ in a blockchain that will be added to the blockchain (permanent state) at about the time first delegated verification will be done, and g is a security parameter referring to the number of blocks (in a row) starting from w. It sets z: the total number of verifications, $||F||$: file bit size, Δ_1: the maximum time is taken by the server to generate a proof, Δ_2: time window in which a message is (sent by the server and) received by the contract, and e amount of coins paid to the server for each successful verification. Sets $\hat{pk} : (pk, e, g, w, p, c, z, \Delta_1, \Delta_2)$.
    (c) **Sign and Deploy Smart Contract**: Signs and deploys a smart contract: $\mathcal{SC}$ to a blockchain. It stores public parameters: $(z, ||F||, \Delta_1, \Delta_2, c, g, p, w)$, on the contract. It deposits ez coins to the contract. Then, it asks the server to sign the contract. The server signs if it agrees on all parameters.
2. **Client-side Store**.
    (a) **Encode File**: Splits an error-corrected file, e.g. under Reed-Solomon codes, into n blocks; $F : [F_1, ..., F_n]$, where $F_i \in \mathbb{F}_p$.
    (b) **Gen. Permanent Tags**: Using the key: $\hat{k}$, it computes n pseudorandom values: r_i and single value: α, as follows.

$$\alpha = \mathrm{PRF}(\hat{k}, n+1) \bmod p, \qquad \forall i, 1 \le i \le n : r_i = \mathrm{PRF}(\hat{k}, i) \bmod p$$

It uses the pseudorandom values to compute tags for the file blocks.

$$\forall i, 1 \le i \le n : \sigma_i = r_i + \alpha \cdot F_i \bmod p$$

So, at the end of this step, a set of tags are generated, $\sigma : \{\sigma_1, ..., \sigma_n\}$.

(c) **Gen. Disposable Tags**: For j-th verification ($1 \le j \le z$):

   i chooses the related key: $v_j \in \vec{v}$ and computes c pseudorandom indices.

$$\forall b, 1 \le b \le c : x_{b,j} = \mathrm{PRF}(v_j, b) \bmod n$$

   ii picks the corresponding key: $l_j \in \vec{l}$ and computes c pseudorandom values: $r_{b,j}$ and single value: α_j, as follows.

$$\alpha_j = \mathrm{PRF}(l_j, c+1) \bmod p, \qquad \forall b, 1 \le b \le c : r_{b,j} = \mathrm{PRF}(l_j, b) \bmod p$$

   iii generates c disposable tags.

$$\forall b, 1 \le b \le c : \sigma_{b,j} = r_{b,j} + \alpha_j \cdot F_y \bmod p$$

where $y = x_{b,j}$. At the end of this step, a set σ_j of c tags are computed, $\sigma_j : \{\sigma_{1,j}, ..., \sigma_{c,j}\}$.

(d) **Gen. Puzzles**: Sets $\vec{m} = [v_1, l_1, ..., v_z, l_z]$ and then encrypts the vector's elements, by running: $\mathrm{GenPuz}(\vec{m}, pk, sk)$ in C-TLP scheme. This yields a puzzle vector: $[(V_1, L_1), ..., (V_z, L_z)]$ and a commitment vector: $\vec{h}$. The encryption is done in such a way that in each j-th pair, V_j will be fully decrypted at times t_j and L_j will be decrypted at time t'_j, where $t_j + \Delta_1 + \Delta_2 \le t'_j < t_{j+1}$.

(e) **Outsource File**: Stores $F, n, \hat{pk}, \{\sigma, \sigma_1, ..., \sigma_z, (V_1, L_1), ..., (V_z, L_z)\}$ on the server. Also, it stores $\vec{h}$ on the smart contract.

3. **Cloud-Side Proof Generation**. For j-th verification ($1 \le j \le z$), the cloud:

(a) **Solve Puzzle and Regen. Indices**: Receives and parses the output of $\mathrm{SolvPuz}(.)$ in C-TLP, to extract v_j, at time t_j. Using v_j, it regenerates c pseudorandom indices.

$$\forall b, 1 \le b \le c : x_{b,j} = \mathrm{PRF}(v_j, b) \bmod n$$

(b) **Extract Key**: Extracts a seed: u_j, from the blockchain as follows: $u_j = \mathrm{H}(\mathcal{B}_\gamma || ... || \mathcal{B}_\zeta)$, where $\gamma = w + (j-1) \cdot g$ and $\zeta = w + j \cdot g$.

(c) **Gen. PoR**: Generates a PoR proof.

$$\mu_j = \sum_{b=1}^{c} \mathrm{PRF}(u_j, b) \cdot F_y \bmod p, \qquad \xi_j = \sum_{b=1}^{c} \mathrm{PRF}(u_j, b) \cdot \sigma_{b,j} \bmod p$$

where y is a pseudorandom index: $y = x_{b,j}$

(d) **Register Proofs**: Sends the PoR proof: (μ_j, ξ_j) to the smart contract within Δ_1.

(e) *Solve Puzzle and Regen. Verification Key*: Receives and parses the output of algorithm SolvPuz(.) in C-TLP to extract l_j, at time t'_j. Also, it runs Prove(.) in C-TLP, to generate a proof: $\ddot{p}_j$, of l_j's correctness. It sends $\ddot{p}_j$ (containing l_j) to the contract, so it can be received by the contract within Δ_2.

4. *Smart Contract-Side Verification.* For j-th verification ($1 \leq j \leq z$), the contract:

(a) *Check Arrival Time*: checks the arrival time of the decrypted values sent by the server. In particular, it checks, if (μ_j, ξ_j) was received in the time window: $(t_j, t_j + \Delta_1 + \Delta_2]$ and whether l_j was received in the time window: $(t'_j, t'_j + \Delta_2]$.

(b) *Verify Puzzle Solution*: runs Verify(.) in C-TLP to verify $\ddot{p}_j$ (i.e. checks the correctness of $l_j \in \ddot{p}_j$). If approved, then it regenerates the seed: $u_j = H(\mathcal{B}_\gamma || ... || \mathcal{B}_\zeta)$, where $\gamma = w + (j-1) \cdot g$ and $\zeta = w + j \cdot g$.

(c) *Verify PoR*: regenerates the pseudorandom values and verifies the PoR proof.

$$\xi_j \overset{?}{=} \mu_j \cdot \text{PRF}(l_j, c+1) + \sum_{b=1}^{c} (\text{PRF}(u_j, b) \cdot \text{PRF}(l_j, b)) \bmod p \qquad (1)$$

(d) *Pay*: if Eq. 1 holds, pays and asks the server to delete all disposable tags for this verification, i.e. σ_j.

If either check fails, it aborts and notifies the client.

5. *Client-server PoR*: When the client is online, it can interact with the server to check its data availability too. In particular, it sends c random challenges and random indices to the server who computes POR using only: (a) the messages sent by the client in this step, (b) the file: F, and (c) the tags: $\sigma_i \in \sigma$, generated in step 2b. The proof generation and verification are similar to the MAC-based schemes, e.g. [27].

Theorem 2. *SO-PoR protocol is secure if the MACs are unforgeable,* PRF(.) *is a secure pseudorandom function, the blockchain and C-TLP protocol are secure, and* $H(\mathcal{B}_\gamma || ... || \mathcal{B}_\zeta)$ *outputs an unpredictable random value (where $\zeta - \gamma$ is a security parameter).*

Proof (Outline). Let $\mathcal{M}_i$ be a blockchain miners and β be the maximum number of miners which can be corrupted in a secure blockchain. We first argue that the adversary who corrupts either $C \subseteq \{\mathcal{M}_1, ..., \mathcal{M}_\beta\}$ or $C' \subseteq \{\mathcal{S}, \mathcal{M}_1, ..., \mathcal{M}_{\beta-1}\}$ with a high probability, cannot influence the output of Verify(.) performed by a smart contract in a blockchain (i.e. the verification correctness holds) due to the security of the underlying blockchain. Then, we argue that if a proof produced by an adversary who corrupts $C' \subseteq \{\mathcal{S}, \mathcal{M}_1, ..., \mathcal{M}_{\beta-1}\}$ is accepted by Verify(.) with probability at least ϵ, then the file can be extracted by a means of an extraction algorithm, due to the security of the underlying MACs, PRF(.) and C-TLP as well as the unpredictability of random extractor beacon's output, i.e. $H(\mathcal{B}_\gamma || ... || \mathcal{B}_\zeta)$. Next, we argue that after the server broadcasts a proof at a certain time to the network, the client can get a correct output of Verify(.) at most after time period Υ, by a means of reading the blockchain, due to the correctness of Verify(.) and the maximum delay on the client's view of the output (i.e. Υ-real-time detection). Also, we argue that fair payment is held due to the security of blockchain and correctness of Pay(.). We refer readers to the paper's full version [2] for detailed proof. □

5.4   Evaluation

In this section, we provide a summary of comparisons between SO-PoR and outsourced PoRs [3,5,30]. Among the two protocols in [5] we only consider "basic PoSt" as it supports public verifiability. Briefly, in terms of property, only SO-PoR offers an explicit solution for real-time detection and fair payment. In terms of computation cost, the verification algorithm in SO-PoR is much faster than the other three protocols; Specifically, when $c = 460$, SO-PoR verification[3] needs about 4.5 times fewer computation than the verification required in the fastest outsourced PoR [3]. Also, [3] has the worst store cost, that is much higher than that of SO-PoR; e.g. for a 1-GB file, SO-PoR requires over 46×10^5 times fewer exponentiations than [3] needs in the same phase. SO-PoR and [5] require a server to solve puzzles (and the imposed cost has to be compensated by the client) but the other two protocols do not need that. Also, I/O cost and proof complexity of all protocols are $O(1)$ except [5] whose I/O cost and proof complexity are $O(\log n)$. The server-side bandwidth of SO-PoR is much lower than the rest; e.g., for 1-GB file and $z = 100$ verifications, a server in SO-PoR requires 9×10^4, 7 and 1729 times fewer bits than those required in [3,30] and [5] respectively. A client in SO-PoR has a higher bandwidth than the rest (but this cost is one-off). Thus, SO-PoR offers additional properties, it has lower verification cost and lower server-side bandwidth than the rest while its other costs remain reasonable. Table 3 outlines the cost comparison results. For a full analysis, we refer readers to the paper's full version [2] where we also compare SO-PoR costs with that of the most efficient traditional PoR [27].

Table 3. Outsourced PoR's cost comparison. z: total verifications, c: number of challenges for each verification, n: total number of file blocks, $c' = (0.1)c$, and $||F||$: file bit size.

Protocols	Operation	Computation Cost				Communication Cost			
		Store	SolvPuz	Prove	Verify	Client	Server	Verifier	Proof Size
SO-PoR	Exp.	$z+1$	Tz	–	–	$128(n+$	$884z$	–	$O(1)$
	Add. or Mul.	$2(n+cz)$	z	$4cz$	$2z(1+c)$	$cz+19z)$			
[3]	Exp.	$9n$	–	–	–	$128n$	$256z+$	$4672n+$	$O(1)$
	Add. or Mul.	$10n$	–	$4z(c+c')$	$z(9c+3)$		$||F||$	$256z$	
[30]	Exp.	–	–	$z(3+c)$	$6z$	$2048n$	$6144z$	–	$O(1)$
	Add. or Mul.	$4n$	–	$2z(3c+4)$	$2cz$				
	Pairing	–	–	$7z$	–				
[5]	Exp.	–	$3Tz$	–	$3z$	128	$128cz\log n+$	–	$O(\log n)$
	Add. or Mul.	–	Tz	–	–		$4096z$		

---

[3] As shown in [4], to ensure 99% of file blocks is retrievable, it suffices to set $c = 460$.

6 C-TLP as Efficient Variant of VDF

There are cases where a client wants a server to learn distinct random challenges, at different points in time within a certain period, without the client's involvement in that period. Such challenges can let the server generate certain proofs that include but are not limited to the *continuous availability of services*, such as data storage or secure hardware. The obvious candidates that can meet the above needs are VDF (if public verifiability is desirable) and TDF (if private verifiability suffices). PoSt protocols in [5] are two examples of the above cases. We observed that in these cases, VDF/TDF can be replaced with C-TLP to gain better efficiency. The idea is that the client computes random challenges, encodes them into C-TLP puzzles and sends them to the server who can eventually solve each puzzle, extract a subset of challenges and use them for the related proof scheme while letting the public efficiently verify the solutions' correctness. To illustrate the efficiency gain, we compare C-TLP performance with the two current VDF functions [7,29]. Table 4 summarises the result. The cost analysis considers the generic setting where z outputs are generated. Among several VDF schemes proposed in [7], we focus on the one that uses sequential squaring, as it is more efficient than the other schemes in [7]. As the table indicates, the overall cost of [7] in each of the three phases is much higher than C-TLP and [29]. Now, we compare the computation cost of C-TLP with [29]. At setup, a client in C-TLP performs at most $3z + 1$ more exponentiations than it does in [29]. But, at both prove and verify phases, C-TLP outperforms [7], especially when they are in the same model. In particular, at the prove phase, C-TLP, in both models, requires Tz fewer multiplications than [29] does. Also, in the same phase, it requires 3 times fewer exponentiations than [29]. In the verify phase, when C-TLP is in the standard model, it has a slightly lower cost than [29] has in the random oracle model. However, when both of them are in the random oracle model, C-TLP has a much lower cost, as it requires no exponentiations whereas [29] needs $3z$ exponentiations. Hence, C-TLP supports both standard and random oracle models and in both paradigms, it outperforms the fasted VDF, i.e. [29], designed in the random oracle model. Furthermore, the proof size in C-TLP is 3.2 and 6.5 times shorter than [7] and [29] respectively, when they are in the same model. In the paper's full version [2], we also show how C-TLP can be employed in the PoSt protocols [5] to reduce costs.

Table 4. VDF's cost comparison

Protocols	Model	Operation	Computation Cost			Proof size (bit)
			Setup	Prove	Verify	
C-TLP	Standard	Exp.	$3z + 1$	Tz	$2z$	$1524z$
		Mul.	z	—	z	
	R.O.	Exp.	$z + 1$	Tz	—	$628z$
		Mul.	—	—	—	
[7]	R.O.	Exp.	2^{30}	Tz	z	$2048z$
		Mul.	—	$2z \cdot 2^{30}$	$2z \cdot 2^{30}$	
[29]	R.O.	Exp.	—	$3Tz$	$3z$	$4096z$
		Mul.	—	Tz	—	

7 Conclusion

Time-lock puzzles are important cryptographic protocols with various applications. But, existing puzzle schemes are not suitable to deal with multiple puzzles at once. In this work, we put forth the concept of composing multiple puzzles, where given puzzles composition at once, a server can find one puzzle's solution after another. This process does not require the server to deal with all of them in parallel which reliefs the server from having numerous parallel processors and allows it to save considerable computation overhead. We proposed a candidate construction: chained time-lock puzzle (C-TLP) that possesses the aforementioned features. Furthermore, C-TLP is equipped with an efficient verification algorithm publicly executable. We also illustrated how to use C-TLP to construct an efficient outsourced proofs of retrievability scheme that supports *real-time detection* and *fair payment* while keeping its costs considerably lower than the state of the art protocols. Moreover, we showed how VDFs in certain settings can be replaced with C-TLP to gain considerable cost improvement.

Acknowledgment. Aydin Abadi is supported in part by EPSRC under "OxChain" project with grant number EP/N028198/1 and by the European Union's Horizon 2020 Research and Innovation Programme under "FENTEC" project with grant number 780108.

References

1. Abadi, A., Ciampi, M., Kiayias, A., Zikas, V.: Timed signatures and zero-knowledge proofs-timestamping in the blockchain era-. IACR Cryptol. ePrint Arch. **2019**, 644 (2019)
2. Abadi, A., Kiayias, A.: Multi-instance publicly verifiable time-lock puzzle and its applications (full version). Financial cryptography repository (2021). https://fc21.ifca.ai/papers/115.pdf
3. Armknecht, F., Bohli, J.M., Karame, G.O., Liu, Z., Reuter, C.A.: Outsourced proofs of retrievability. In: CCS 2014 (2014)
4. Ateniese, G., et al.: Provable data possession at untrusted stores. In: CCS 2007 (2007)
5. Ateniese, G., Chen, L., Etemad, M., Tang, Q.: Proof of storage-time: efficiently checking continuous data availability. In: NDSS 2020 (2020)
6. Banerjee, P., Nikam, N., Ruj, S.: Blockchain enabled privacy preserving data audit. CoRR abs/1904.12362 (2019)
7. Boneh, D., Bonneau, J., Bünz, B., Fisch, B.: Verifiable delay functions. In: Shacham, H., Boldyreva, A. (eds.) CRYPTO 2018, Part I. LNCS, vol. 10991, pp. 757–788. Springer, Cham (2018). https://doi.org/10.1007/978-3-319-96884-1_25
8. Boneh, D., Naor, M.: Timed commitments. In: Bellare, M. (ed.) CRYPTO 2000. LNCS, vol. 1880, pp. 236–254. Springer, Heidelberg (2000). https://doi.org/10.1007/3-540-44598-6_15
9. Brakerski, Z., Döttling, N., Garg, S., Malavolta, G.: Leveraging linear decryption: rate-1 fully-homomorphic encryption and time-lock puzzles. In: Hofheinz, D., Rosen, A. (eds.) TCC 2019, Part II. LNCS, vol. 11892, pp. 407–437. Springer, Cham (2019). https://doi.org/10.1007/978-3-030-36033-7_16
10. Campanelli, M., Gennaro, R., Goldfeder, S., Nizzardo, L.: Zero-knowledge contingent payments revisited: attacks and payments for services. In: CCS 2017 (2017)
11. Canetti, R.: Universally composable security: a new paradigm for cryptographic protocols. In: 42nd Annual Symposium on Foundations of Computer Science, FOCS 2001, 14–17 October 2001, Las Vegas, Nevada, USA, pp. 136–145. IEEE Computer Society (2001)

12. Chen, H., Deviani, R.: A secure e-voting system based on RSA time-lock puzzle mechanism. In: BWCCA 2012 (2012)
13. Chvojka, P., Jager, T., Slamanig, D., Striecks, C.: Generic constructions of incremental and homomorphic timed-release encryption. IACR Cryptol. ePrint Arch. **2020**, 739 (2020)
14. Francati, D., et al.: Audita: a blockchain-based auditing framework for off-chain storage. CoRR 2019 (2019)
15. Garay, J.A., Jakobsson, M.: Timed release of standard digital signatures. In: Blaze, M. (ed.) FC 2002. LNCS, vol. 2357, pp. 168–182. Springer, Heidelberg (2003). https://doi.org/10.1007/3-540-36504-4_13
16. Garay, J.A., Kiayias, A., Panagiotakos, G.: Iterated search problems and blockchain security under falsifiable assumptions. IACR Cryptol. ePrint Arch. **2019**, 315 (2019)
17. Hao, K., Xin, J., Wang, Z., Jiang, Z., Wang, G.: Decentralized data integrity verification model in untrusted environment. In: Cai, Y., Ishikawa, Y., Xu, J. (eds.) APWeb-WAIM 2018, Part II. LNCS, vol. 10988, pp. 410–424. Springer, Cham (2018). https://doi.org/10.1007/978-3-319-96893-3_31
18. Juels, A., Kaliski Jr., B.S.: PORs: proofs of retrievability for large files. In: CCS 2007 (2007)
19. Katz, J., Lindell, Y.: Introduction to Modern Cryptography. Chapman and Hall/CRC Press, Boca Raton (2007)
20. Kopp, H., Bösch, C., Kargl, F.: KopperCoin – a distributed file storage with financial incentives. In: Bao, F., Chen, L., Deng, R.H., Wang, G. (eds.) ISPEC 2016. LNCS, vol. 10060, pp. 79–93. Springer, Cham (2016). https://doi.org/10.1007/978-3-319-49151-6_6
21. Labs, P.: Filecoin: a decentralized storage network (2017). https://filecoin.io/filecoin.pdf
22. Malavolta, G., Thyagarajan, S.A.K.: Homomorphic time-lock puzzles and applications. In: Boldyreva, A., Micciancio, D. (eds.) CRYPTO 2019, Part I. LNCS, vol. 11692, pp. 620–649. Springer, Cham (2019). https://doi.org/10.1007/978-3-030-26948-7_22
23. Miller, A., Juels, A., Shi, E., Parno, B., Katz, J.: Permacoin: repurposing bitcoin work for data preservation. In: S&P 2014 (2014)
24. Pedersen, T.P.: Non-interactive and information-theoretic secure verifiable secret sharing. In: Feigenbaum, J. (ed.) CRYPTO 1991. LNCS, vol. 576, pp. 129–140. Springer, Heidelberg (1992). https://doi.org/10.1007/3-540-46766-1_9
25. Renner, T., Müller, J., Kao, O.: Endolith: a blockchain-based framework to enhance data retention in cloud storages. In: PDP 2018 (2018)
26. Rivest, R.L., Shamir, A., Wagner, D.A.: Time-lock puzzles and timed-release crypto. Tech. rep. (1996)
27. Shacham, H., Waters, B.: Compact proofs of retrievability. In: Pieprzyk, J. (ed.) ASIACRYPT 2008. LNCS, vol. 5350, pp. 90–107. Springer, Heidelberg (2008). https://doi.org/10.1007/978-3-540-89255-7_7
28. Vorick, D., Champine, L.: Sia: simple decentralized storage. Nebulous Inc. (2014)
29. Wesolowski, B.: Efficient verifiable delay functions. In: Ishai, Y., Rijmen, V. (eds.) EUROCRYPT 2019, Part III. LNCS, vol. 11478, pp. 379–407. Springer, Cham (2019). https://doi.org/10.1007/978-3-030-17659-4_13
30. Xu, J., Yang, A., Zhou, J., Wong, D.S.: Lightweight delegatable proofs of storage. In: Askoxylakis, I., Ioannidis, S., Katsikas, S., Meadows, C. (eds.) ESORICS 2016, Part I. LNCS, vol. 9878, pp. 324–343. Springer, Cham (2016). https://doi.org/10.1007/978-3-319-45744-4_16
31. Zhang, Y., Deng, R.H., Liu, X., Zheng, D.: Blockchain based efficient and robust fair payment for outsourcing services in cloud computing. Inf. Sci. **462**, 262–277 (2018)

Practical Post-quantum Few-Time Verifiable Random Function with Applications to Algorand

Muhammed F. Esgin[1,2(✉)], Veronika Kuchta[3], Amin Sakzad[1], Ron Steinfeld[1], Zhenfei Zhang[4], Shifeng Sun[1], and Shumo Chu[5]

[1] Monash University, Melbourne, Australia
muhammed.esgin@monash.edu
[2] CSIRO's Data61, Melbourne, Australia
[3] The University of Queensland, Brisbane, Australia
[4] Manta Network, Boston, USA
[5] University of California, Santa Barbara, USA

Abstract. In this work, we introduce the *first practical post-quantum* verifiable random function (VRF) that relies on well-known (module) lattice problems, namely Module-SIS and Module-LWE. Our construction, named LB-VRF, results in a VRF value of only 84 bytes and a proof of around only 5 KB (in comparison to several MBs in earlier works), and runs in about 3 ms for evaluation and about 1 ms for verification.

In order to design a practical scheme, we need to restrict the number of VRF outputs per key pair, which makes our construction *few-time*. Despite this restriction, we show how our few-time LB-VRF can be used in practice and, in particular, we estimate the performance of Algorand using LB-VRF. We find that, due to the significant increase in the communication size in comparison to classical constructions, which is inherent in all existing lattice-based schemes, the throughput in LB-VRF-based consensus protocol is reduced, but remains practical. In particular, in a medium-sized network with 100 nodes, our platform records a 1.14× to 3.4× reduction in throughput, depending on the accompanying signature used. In the case of a large network with 500 nodes, we can still maintain at least 24 transactions per second. This is still much better than Bitcoin, which processes only about 5 transactions per second.

Keywords: Post-quantum · Verifiable random function · Blockchain · Lattice · Algorand

1 Introduction

The notion of verifiable random function (VRF) was put forth by Micali, Rabin and Vadhan [35]. It allows a user to generate a random value that is both authenticated and publicly verifiable. VRFs have been used in practice, for example, in

Z. Zhang—Work was done while with Algorand.

N. Borisov and C. Diaz (Eds.): FC 2021, LNCS 12675, pp. 560–578, 2021.
https://doi.org/10.1007/978-3-662-64331-0_29

DNSSEC protocol [22], and in blockchain consensus protocols [12,21] to establish Proof-of-Stake. In both cases, a VRF serves as a fundamental building block to provide verifiable random inputs to the protocol. There are currently two main VRF constructions namely, ECVRF [38] (based on elliptic curves), and BLS-VRF [8,9] (based on pairings). Specifically, ECVRF over curve25519 is currently in the standardization process by CRFG [23] and is deployed by Algorand [12,21], while BLS-VRF is adopted by Dfinity [26].

The main drawback of the above-mentioned VRF constructions is that they are vulnerable to quantum attacks. This is a significant concern especially in the blockchain setting since attackers may "rewrite history" if they are able to forge the VRF (with a quantum computer). Let us explain why this is a major concern even today. In a blockchain use case as in Algorand, VRF is used to ensure that the committee members are selected honestly for all the blocks that are already committed on the chain. A new user, who has no record of the previous blocks, can be assured of the validity of the blocks by looking at the votes that has been recorded as long as VRF remains secure. In such protocols, since a block is agreed by the majority of the committee members, there will never be a fork of the blockchain. However, when the VRF security is compromised, one can "rewrite history" by corrupting selected committee members for any given round (including rounds in the past), and then can create a fork to the blockchain subsequent to that round. As a result, a potential future security threat against the integrity of VRFs is important even today. To circumvent such a threat, in this paper we introduce the *first post-quantum* VRF construction that does not rely on heavy machinery and meets practical efficiency levels. We emphasize that our focus in this paper is realization of *practical* constructions.

Technical Challenges in the Lattice Setting. Construction of an *efficient* lattice-based VRF is quite challenging as realizing long-term pseudorandomness and uniqueness properties together (while maintaining practicality) does not go well in the lattice setting. To understand why that is the case, let us first briefly explain how ECVRF works.

In ECVRF, the secret key is a field element x and the corresponding public key is a group element xG for some public generator G. The ECVRF output is then a group element xP, where $P = H(xG, \mu)$ is computed deterministically from the VRF input μ and a public key xG for some publicly computable function H. Then, a sigma protocol (with Fiat-Shamir transformation) is applied to prove that both the VRF output xP and the public key xG have the same discrete logarithm with respect to P and G, respectively (i.e., $x = \log_G(xG) = \log_P(xP)$). In essence, pseudorandomness follows from DDH assumption and the uniqueness comes from the fact that, for a fixed input μ and a fixed public key xG, there is a unique xP such that $x = \log_G(xG)$ and $P = H(xG, \mu)$.

Issue with Long-Term Pseudorandomness in the Lattice Setting. The main technique to hide a secret key $\mathbf{s}$ in lattice-based cryptography is to disturb a lattice point by computing $t = \langle \mathbf{b}, \mathbf{s} \rangle + e$, where $\mathbf{b}$ is a public vector, $\mathbf{s}$ is the secret vector and e is a *small* (secret) error sampled from some error distribution. Assuming that computations are done over a ring $\mathfrak{R}$, t is precisely a Module-LWE (MLWE) sample in $\mathfrak{R}$ and is indistinguishable from a uniformly random element in $\mathfrak{R}$ based on MLWE.

Now, let's see the difficulty in constructing an MLWE-based lattice analogue of the above DDH-based VRF. In this lattice-based VRF, for a fixed user secret key $\mathbf{s}$, one can map an input message μ together with the user public key to a vector $\mathbf{b} = H(pk, \mu)$ using a deterministic function H (modelled as a random oracle). From here, with the hope of hiding the secret $\mathbf{s}$, one may attempt to compute the corresponding VRF value as $v = \langle \mathbf{b}, \mathbf{s} \rangle + e$ for some error e sampled from an error set of many elements. However, unlike the DDH-based setting above, this approach violates the uniqueness property as there are multiple small e values that can be used, and thus multiple possible VRF values for a given (pk, μ).

An alternative approach could be to choose the error in a *deterministic* way. In particular, one may compute $v = \mathtt{Round}(\langle \mathbf{b}, \mathbf{s} \rangle)$ for some rounding function $\mathtt{Round}(\cdot)$, which simply chops off some least significant bits, and rely for pseudorandomness on the learning with rounding (LWR) problem [5]. In fact, this approach has been used to construct lattice-based pseudorandom functions (PRFs) [31,41]. The issue here is that currently, there is no known *efficient* zero-knowledge proof to prove that the VRF evaluator indeed computed v in this fashion. For example, the recent results from [41] yield such a proof of size in the order of several MBs. Therefore, this approach does not address our practical goals.

Issue with Uniqueness in the Lattice Setting. Another orthogonal issue is in relation to uniqueness. Efficient lattice-based signature schemes are nondeterministic and therefore standard transformation from a unique signature to a VRF (as given in [35]) does not trivially work. Moreover, the approach taken in [38] to prove uniqueness of the ECVRF construction also does not apply in the lattice setting. In particular, the authors in [38] show that for any given VRF output that is not generated honestly and any valid proof, there exists a *single* random oracle output c that can make the proof verify. As the chance of hitting that challenge is negligibly small, the uniqueness follows. However, the same idea does not work in the lattice setting.

1.1   Our Contribution

We propose the *first practical* verifiable random function, named LB-VRF, based on standard post-quantum hardness assumptions, namely Module-SIS (MSIS) and Module-LWE (MLWE). A single LB-VRF proof costs around 5KB and runs in about 3 ms for evaluation and 1 ms for verification. To show the practicality of our results, we implemented LB-VRF and tested it in practice. We discuss the implementation and evaluation further below.

The main drawback of our construction is that a single key pair can only be used to generate a limited number k of VRF outputs. Therefore, we say that our LB-VRF construction is 'k-time'. However, we show that this aspect is not a significant disadvantage in the blockchain setting as the users can frequently update their keys. In fact, some privacy-enhanced blockchain applications such as Monero and Zcash employ one-time public keys per transaction (see, for example, [6,18,36,37,39,40,42]). For instance, as detailed in Sect. 4.1.6 of Zcash specification [28], a fresh signature key pair is generated for each transaction.

We also note that the aspect of being k-time is only required to satisfy *pseudorandomness* (i.e., to prevent the user secret key from being leaked), and is not related to the soundness (i.e., uniqueness). That is, it is infeasible for a cheating prover, even by violating the k-time property, to produce incorrect VRF outputs that pass the verification algorithm.

Main Idea. A user secret key in LB-VRF is a short vector $\mathbf{s}$, and the public key becomes $\mathbf{t} = \mathbf{A}\mathbf{s}$ for a public matrix $\mathbf{A}$. Then, we use the so-called "Fiat-Shamir with Aborts" technique [33] to prove knowledge of the secret key. However, this proof is *relaxed* in the sense that it only proves knowledge of $\mathbf{s}'$ such that $\bar{c}\mathbf{t} = \mathbf{A}\mathbf{s}'$ for some secret relaxation factor $\bar{c}$ (i.e., the proof has a *knowledge gap*). This relaxation complicates the uniqueness proof. If we would want to prove an *exact* relation, then such a proof alone would require about 50 KBs [17], which we consider too costly for our target blockchain application.

From the discussion about the pseudorandomness in the introduction, the option that remains at hand, and the one we employ in LB-VRF for the computation of the VRF value v, is to use no error at all, i.e. set $v = \langle \mathbf{b}, \mathbf{s} \rangle$. This method only leaks a limited amount information on $\mathbf{s}$ for a relatively small number k of VRF outputs, but fortunately it suffices for our application of VRF to blockchain protocols. This method does, however, leak too much information on the secret $\mathbf{s}$ when *many* VRF outputs are computed with the same key. In particular, one cannot output, say, 2^{64} VRF values $v_i = \langle \mathbf{b}_i, \mathbf{s} \rangle$ where $\mathbf{b}_i = H(pk, \mu_i)$ (at least while still preserving practicality). This issue with long-term pseudorandomness does not seem to be efficiently addressable with the existing lattice-based tools.

More concretely, we map the VRF input μ and the user public key $\mathbf{t}$ to a vector $\mathbf{b}$ using a random oracle. We then prove in zero-knowledge that the VRF value computed as $v = \langle \mathbf{b}, \mathbf{s} \rangle$ is well-formed. However, again due to the *relaxed* nature of the underlying zero-knowledge proof that we use to achieve short proofs, the uniqueness does not immediately follow. To handle this, we show via a "double rewinding" argument that as long as the MSIS problem is hard (with certain parameters), any two VRF outputs computed by an *efficient* uniqueness attack algorithm under the same public key and input must be the same (see the proof of Theorem 31). Therefore, we can only achieve *computational* uniqueness, based on the standard MSIS hardness assumption. In regards to pseudorandomness, we show that it follows from MLWE as long as at most k VRF outputs are produced under a single key pair.

To further reduce the VRF value size and increase computational efficiency, we introduce an additional optimization technique which performs the VRF value computation in a *subring* of a commonly-used cyclotomic ring. We show that the uniqueness security property is still preserved even when using this optimisation technique. This technique results in $\approx 8\times$ smaller VRF values for typical parameters compared to outputting the full ring element as the VRF output, and approximately doubles the evaluation and verification speed.

Implementation and Deployment. We present an efficient implementation of our k-time LB-VRF. In particular, we implement the "worst-case" (in terms of performance) setting where a single key pair is used only once (i.e., $k = 1$) and show that even that case is practical. Our code is open-sourced[1]. We compare the performance of our scheme against ECVRF over curve25519 and BLS-VRF over BLS12-381 curve. The implementation details are provided in Sect. 4.

Table 1. Comparison of our scheme and classical VRFs.

	ECVRF [4]	BLS-VRF [3]	LB-VRF
PK size	32 bytes	96 bytes	3.32 KB
Proof size	80 bytes	48 bytes	4.94 KB
Prove time	0.2 ms	0.6 ms	3.1 ms
Verification time	0.2 ms	2.0 ms	1.3 ms

Since our construction increases sizes significantly, it is important to understand how practical our scheme can really be in real world protocols. For a fair comparison, we also investigate the impact of integrating our scheme to the Algorand protocol. With both ECVRF and Ed25519 signatures, Algorand blockchain is able to transmit 5 MB of data per block, with a block generation time of less than 5 s. This allows Algorand to achieve 1000 transactions per second (TPS), with over 1000 nodes, as of today. We report the performance estimation of our LB-VRF with four different signatures, Ed25519 (used by Algorand), and 3 NIST PQC third round candidates. The data is presented in Table 2, and more details are provided in Sect. 4.

Table 2. Performance comparison in terms of TPS (the numbers are approximate). TPS (transactions per second) is a generic metric used by multiple blockchain platforms. In comparison, Bitcoin achieves about 5 TPS.

| VRF Type | ECVRF | LB-VRF | LB-VRF | LB-VRF | LB-VRF |
Sign. Type	+ Ed25519	+ Ed25519	+ Dilithium	+ Falcon	+ Rainbow
10 nodes	1000	1000	353	624	997
100 nodes	1000	862	292	532	860
500 nodes	1000	250	24	120	250
Assumption	ECC	lattice + ECC	lattice	lattice	lattice + MQ

---

[1] https://github.com/zhenfeizhang/lb-vrf

1.2 Related Work

Originally introduced by Micali, Rabin and Vadhan [35], VRFs have become an important cryptographic primitive in several applications. In [35], the authors show a relation between VRFs and unique signatures by combining the unpredictability property of a unique signature with the verifiability by extending the Goldreich-Goldwasser-Micali construction of a pseudorandom function [24]. The concept of a VRF has been investigated further in [32] and [15]. In [32] the authors provide a construction of a verifiable unpredictable function (VUF) from a unique signature scheme and turn it into a VRF using the original transform from [35]. The aforementioned VRFs are constructed from number-theoretic assumptions. More number-theoretic constructions are given in [1,7,14,27,29]. In [10] the authors introduced the notion of weak VRF where pseudorandomness is required to hold only for randomly selected inputs. Further VRF-related primitives such as simulatable VRF, constrained VRF have been introduced in [11,19].

On the side of quantum-safe proposals, feasibility of a lattice-based VRF was given in [25,41]. The construction in [25] relies on heavy machinery such as constrained PRFs and there is no practical efficiency evaluation provided. In the latter work, the authors in [41] briefly mention in a remark (without a rigorous security or performance analysis) that their zero-knowledge proofs give rise to a lattice-based VRF construction. However, the authors claim that this construction satisfies only *trusted* uniqueness, which is not sufficient for blockchain applications. Moreover, this construction is expected to be far from practical as even more basic proofs in [41] require MBs of communication.

2 Preliminaries

We use λ and to denote the security parameter a function negligible in λ. We define the polynomial rings $\mathcal{R} := \mathbb{Z}[x]/(x^d + 1)$ and $\mathcal{R}_q := \mathbb{Z}_q[x]/(x^d + 1)$ for d a power of 2. We denote by bold, capital letters (e.g. $\mathbf{M}$) matrices whose elements are in $\mathcal{R}$ and denote by bold, lower case letters (e.g. $\mathbf{v}$), vectors whose elements are in $\mathcal{R}$. $\mathbb{S}_c$ denotes the set of polynomials in $\mathcal{R}$ with infinity norm at most $c \in \mathbb{Z}^+$. We write 0^n to denote the n-dimensional zero vector and $\mathbf{I}_n$ for the n-dimensional identity matrix.

Let $\mathcal{R}_p \cong \mathcal{R}_p^{(1)} \times \cdots \times \mathcal{R}_p^{(s)}$ for some $s \geq 1$. That is, $\mathcal{R}_p^{(i)} = \mathbb{Z}_p[x]/(f_i(x))$ such that f_i with $\deg(f_i) = d/s$ is an irreducible factor of $x^d + 1 \bmod p$ for each $i = 1, \ldots, s$. In our LB-VRF construction, a set of operations will be performed in $\mathcal{R}_p^{(1)}$ for better efficiency. We will denote this ring by $\bar{\mathcal{R}}_p = \mathbb{Z}_p[x]/(f(x))$ (see Table 3 for the concrete ring $\bar{\mathcal{R}}_p$). The other subrings $\mathcal{R}_p^{(2)}, \ldots, \mathcal{R}_p^{(s)}$ of $\mathcal{R}_p$ will not be of concern for our construction.

Definition 2.1 (MSIS$_{q,n,m,\beta}$ [30]). *Let $\mathcal{R}$ be some ring and $\mathcal{K}$ a uniform distribution over $\mathcal{R}_q^{n \times m}$. Given a random matrix $\mathbf{A} \in \mathcal{R}_q^{n \times m}$ sampled from $\mathcal{K}$, find a non-zero vector $\mathbf{v} \in \mathcal{R}_q^m$ such that $\mathbf{A} \cdot \mathbf{v} = 0$ and $\|\mathbf{v}\| \leq \beta$.*

566   M. F. Esgin et al.

Definition 2.2 (MLWE$_{q,n,m,\chi}$ *[30]*)**.** *Let χ be a distribution over $\mathcal{R}_q$, $\mathbf{s} \xleftarrow{\$} \chi^m$ be a secret key. The MLWE$_{q,\mathbf{s}}$ distribution is obtained by sampling $\mathbf{A} \xleftarrow{\$} \mathcal{R}_q^{n \times m}$ and error $\mathbf{e} \xleftarrow{\$} \chi^n$ and outputting $(\mathbf{A}, \mathbf{A} \cdot \mathbf{s} + \mathbf{e})$. The goal is to distinguish the MLWE$_{q,\mathbf{s}}$ output from the uniform distribution $\mathcal{U}(\mathcal{R}_q^{n \times m}, \mathcal{R}_q^n)$.*

In our analysis, we use the following result that helps us argue the invertibility of challenge differences.

Lemma 2.3 (*[34]*)**.** *Let $n \geq k > 1$ be powers of 2 and $p \equiv 2k+1 \pmod{4k}$ be a prime. Any f in $\mathbb{Z}_p[X]/(X^n + 1)$ is invertible if one of the following is satisfied*

$$0 < \|f\|_\infty < p^{1/k}/\sqrt{k} \quad or \quad 0 < \|f\| < p^{1/k}.$$

2.1 Verifiable Random Function

Definition 2.4 (Verifiable Random Function *[35]*)**.** *Let* ParamGen, KeyGen, VRFEval, Verify *be polynomial-time algorithms where:*

ParamGen(1^λ): *On input a security parameter 1^λ, this probabilistic algorithm outputs some global, public parameter pp.*

KeyGen(pp): *On input public parameter pp this probabilistic algorithm outputs two binary stings, a secret key sk and a public key pk.*

VRFEval(sk, x): *On input a secret key sk and an input $x \in \{0,1\}^{\ell(\lambda)}$, this algorithm outputs (v, π) for the VRF value $v \in \{0,1\}^{m(\lambda)}$ and the corresponding proof π proving the correctness of v.*

Verify$_{pk}(v, x, \pi)$: *On input (pk, v, x, π), this probabilistic algorithm outputs either 1 or 0.*

A VRF is required to have the following security properties [35]:

Provability: *If (v, π) is the output of* VRFEval(sk, x)*, then* Verify$_{pk}(v, x, \pi)$ *outputs 1.*

Pseudorandomness: *Let $\mathcal{A} = (\mathcal{A}_1, \mathcal{A}_2)$ be a polynomial-time adversary playing the following experiment* Exp-PRand*:*

  1. $pp \leftarrow$ ParamGen(1^λ)
  2. $(pk, sk) \leftarrow$ KeyGen(pp)
  3. $(x, st) \leftarrow \mathcal{A}_1^{\mathcal{O}_{\mathsf{VRFEval}}(\cdot)}(pk)$
  4. $(v_0, \pi_0) \leftarrow$ VRFEval(sk, x)
  5. $v_1 \xleftarrow{\$} \{0,1\}^{m(\lambda)}$
  6. $b \xleftarrow{\$} \{0,1\}$
  7. $b' \leftarrow \mathcal{A}_2^{\mathcal{O}_{\mathsf{VRFEval}}(\cdot)}(v_b, st)$

where $\mathcal{O}_{\mathsf{VRFEval}}(\cdot)$ is an oracle that on input a value x outputs the VRF value v and the corresponding proof of correctness $\pi(sk, x)$.

The adversary $\mathcal{A}$ that did not issue any queries to $\mathcal{O}_{\mathsf{VRFEval}}$ on the value x, wins the above game with probability:

$$\Pr[b = b' \mid \mathcal{A} \text{ runs Exp-PRand}] \leq \frac{1}{2} + \text{negl}(\lambda).$$

Unconditional Full Uniqueness: *No values* $(pk, v_1, v_2, x, \pi_1, \pi_2)$ *can satisfy* $\mathsf{Verify}_{pk}(v_1, x, \pi_1) = \mathsf{Verify}_{pk}(v_2, x, \pi_2) = 1$ *when* $v_1 \neq v_2$.

In our work, we make two modifications to the above standard VRF security model. First, we use a k-time variant of the pseudorandomness property, where the $\mathcal{O}_{\mathsf{VRFEval}}(\cdot)$ oracle can be queried at most $k - 1$ times by the adversary (together with the challenge query to $\mathsf{VRFEval}(\cdot)$ in the pseudorandomness experiment, this gives a total of k $\mathsf{VRFEval}(\cdot)$ queries in the experiment). We also define the VRF output space to be $\bar{\mathcal{R}}_p$ (which is determined by our scheme's public parameters pp), rather than $\{0,1\}^{m(\lambda)}$ used in the original definition. The latter change does not introduce any difficulties since a pseudorandom output in $\bar{\mathcal{R}}_p$ can be easily mapped into a pseudorandom binary string with a cryptographic hash function or a randomness extractor.

Second, we slightly modify the "Unconditional Full Uniqueness" property of a VRF to a weaker "Computational Full Uniqueness", where the adversary is assumed to run in polynomial time. In particular, we define it as follows.

Definition 2.5 (Computational Full Uniqueness). *Let* $pp \leftarrow$ $\mathsf{ParamGen}(1^\lambda)$. *A VRF is said to satisfy computational full uniqueness, if, on input* pp, *a polynomial-time adversary* $\mathcal{A}$ *outputs* $(x, pk, v_1, \pi_1, v_2, \pi_2) \leftarrow \mathcal{A}(pp)$ *such that* $\mathsf{Verify}_{pk}(v_1, x, \pi_1) = \mathsf{Verify}_{pk}(v_2, x, \pi_2) = 1$ *and* $v_1 \neq v_2$ *with at most* $\mathsf{negl}(\lambda)$ *probability.*

Remark 2.6 The notion of computational uniqueness has been first introduced in [20]. However, it is defined w.r.t. VRF without parameter generation algorithm $\mathsf{ParamGen}(1^\lambda)$, implying that public parameters can also be set maliciously. Such a notion was actually defined in the context of anonymous VRF, which is an extension of a standard VRF.

Remark 2.7 There is also a notion of computational *trusted* uniqueness [38] in the literature, in which one roughly requires that, given the VRF public key pk, each VRF input corresponds to a unique VRF output. The word "trusted" is basically used to indicate that the key generation process is trusted. Hence, in such a model, uniqueness with respect to untrusted key generation process is not a concern.

In the application of VRF to the blockchain consensus protocols [12,21], it was observed in [13] that pseudorandomness is not sufficient, and in fact an additional security property is needed, which is called the *unpredictability under malicious key generation* in [13, Section 3.2]. Informally, it means that an attacker that can maliciously choose the VRF key cannot bias the VRF output on a randomly chosen input, as long as the attacker has no information on the random input when choosing its VRF key. Accordingly, we formally define below an *unbiasability* property that captures this requirement in the same spirit with [13]. However, for consistency with the rest of our game-based security notions, we provide a game-based definition, whereas the one in [13] is in the universal composability (UC) framework.

Unbiasability: Let $\mathcal{A} = (\mathcal{A}_1, \mathcal{A}_2)$ be a polynomial-time adversary playing the following experiment Exp-Bias:

1. $pp \leftarrow \mathsf{ParamGen}(1^\lambda)$
2. $(st, pk, v^*) \leftarrow \mathcal{A}_1(pp)$
3. $x \xleftarrow{\$} \{0,1\}^{\ell(\lambda)}$
4. $(\pi, v) \leftarrow \mathcal{A}_2(x, st)$
5. $b \leftarrow \mathsf{Verify}_{pk}(v, x, \pi)$

$\mathcal{A}$ wins if $b = 1$ and $v = v^*$. We say that a VRF is *unbiasable* if

$$\Pr[\mathcal{A} \text{ wins Exp-Bias}] \leq 2^{-m(\lambda)} + \mathsf{negl}(\lambda).$$

3 Lattice-Based Few-Time Verifiable Random Function

3.1 k-time LB-VRF Construction

We use the parameter $k \in \mathbb{Z}^+$ to denote that a particular public-secret key pair output by KeyGen below is used to generate at most k VRF outputs. We further define the following challenge set:

$$\mathcal{C} = \{ c \in \mathcal{R} : \|c\|_\infty \leq 1 \wedge \|c\|_1 \leq \kappa \}. \tag{1}$$

When performing operations over $\bar{\mathcal{R}}_p$, if a term $\mathbf{x}$ is initially defined over $\mathcal{R}$, then we first compute $\bar{\mathbf{x}} = \mathbf{x} \bmod (p, f(x))$ and then perform the remaining operations over $\bar{\mathcal{R}}_p$. For example, given $\mathbf{x} \in \mathcal{R}^s$ and $\mathbf{y} \in \bar{\mathcal{R}}_p^s$ for $s \geq 1$, $\langle \mathbf{x}, \mathbf{y} \rangle \in \bar{\mathcal{R}}_p$ indicates that $\langle \bar{\mathbf{x}}, \mathbf{y} \rangle$ is computed over $\bar{\mathcal{R}}_p$, where $\bar{\mathbf{x}} = \mathbf{x} \bmod (p, f(x))$.

$\mathsf{ParamGen}(1^\lambda)$: On input a security parameter λ, it outputs a public parameter $pp = (\mathbf{A}, G, H)$, where $G : \{0,1\}^* \to \bar{\mathcal{R}}_p^{n+\ell+k}$ and $H : \{0,1\}^* \to \mathcal{C}$ are two hash functions, and $\mathbf{A} \xleftarrow{\$} \mathcal{R}_q^{n \times (n+\ell+k)}$.

$\mathsf{KeyGen}(pp)$: On input the public parameters pp, it randomly samples $\mathbf{s} \xleftarrow{\$} \mathbb{S}_1^{n+\ell+k}$, computes $\mathbf{t} = \mathbf{A} \cdot \mathbf{s} \in \mathcal{R}_q^n$ and outputs $pk = \mathbf{t}$ and $sk = \mathbf{s}$.

$\mathsf{VRFEval}(\mathbf{A}, \mathbf{t}, \mathbf{s}, \mu)$: On input public parameters pp, a public key $\mathbf{t}$, a secret key $\mathbf{s}$, and a message $\mu \in \{0,1\}^*$, perform the following.

1. Compute $\mathbf{b} = G(\mathbf{A}, \mathbf{t}, \mu) \in \bar{\mathcal{R}}_p^{n+\ell+k}$.
2. Compute $v = \langle \mathbf{b}, \mathbf{s} \rangle \in \bar{\mathcal{R}}_p$.
3. Pick $\mathbf{y} \xleftarrow{\$} \mathbb{S}_\beta^{n+\ell+k}$.
4. Compute $\mathbf{w}_1 = \mathbf{A} \cdot \mathbf{y} \in \mathcal{R}_q^n$.
5. Compute $w_2 = \langle \mathbf{b}, \mathbf{y} \rangle \in \bar{\mathcal{R}}_p$.
6. Compute $c = H(\mathbf{A}, \mathbf{t}, \mu, \mathbf{w}_1, w_2, v)$.
7. Compute $\mathbf{z} = \mathbf{y} + c \cdot \mathbf{s} \in \mathcal{R}^{n+\ell+k}$; if $\|\mathbf{z}\|_\infty > \beta - \kappa$ goto step 3.

The algorithm outputs the VRF proof $\pi := (\mathbf{z}, c)$ and the VRF value v.

$\mathsf{Verify}_{pk}(\pi, v, \mathbf{A}, \mu)$: On input VRF public key $pk = \mathbf{t}$, the VRF proof $\pi = (\mathbf{z}, c)$, the VRF value v, public parameter $\mathbf{A}$ and a message μ the algorithm computes:

1. Check $\|\mathbf{z}\|_\infty \overset{?}{\leq} \beta - \kappa$.

2. Compute $\mathbf{w}_1' := \mathbf{A} \cdot \mathbf{z} - c \cdot \mathbf{t}$ over $\mathcal{R}_q$.
3. Compute $w_2' := \langle \mathbf{b}, \mathbf{z} \rangle - c \cdot v$ over $\bar{\mathcal{R}}_p$ for $\mathbf{b} = G(\mathbf{A}, \mathbf{t}, \mu) \in \bar{\mathcal{R}}_p^{n+\ell+k}$.
4. Check $c \stackrel{?}{=} H(\mathbf{A}, \mathbf{t}, \mu, \mathbf{w}_1', w_2', v)$.

Table 3 summarizes the 3 different concrete parameter settings. For a detailed rationale behind these settings, please refer to the full version of this paper[2].

Table 3. Summary of identifiers and results of the parameter setting.

Param.	Explanation	Set I	Set II	Set III
k	# of VRF outputs per key pair	1	3	5
d	$d = \dim(\mathcal{R}_q)$	256	256	256
q	prime $q \equiv 1 \bmod 2d$	100679681	$\sim 2^{26.8}$	$\sim 2^{27.1}$
p	prime $p \equiv 17 \bmod 32$	2097169	$\sim 2^{20}$	$\sim 2^{20}$
$\mathcal{R}_q$	polynomial ring $\mathbb{Z}_q[x]/(x^d + 1)$			
$f(x)$	a factor of $x^d + 1 \bmod p$	$x^{32} + 852368$		
$\bar{\mathcal{R}}_p$	polynomial ring $\mathbb{Z}_p[x]/(f(x))$			
n	MSIS rank	4	4	4
ℓ	MLWE rank	4	4	4
κ	Hamming weight of a challenge	39	39	39
β	max. coeff of masking randomness	89856	109824	129792
	average number of restarts	< 3	< 3	< 3
RHF	MSIS/MLWE root-Hermite factor	≈ 1.0045	≈ 1.0046	≈ 1.0047
Proof size	size of a proof $(c, \mathbf{z})$	4.94 KB	6.13 KB	7.34 KB
VRF size	size of a VRF evaluation v	84 Bytes	84 Bytes	84 Bytes
PK size	size of a public key $\mathbf{t}$	3.32 KB	3.34 KB	3.39 KB

3.2   Security Analysis

The provability of our k-time LB-VRF construction follows via straightforward investigation. The pseudorandomness and unbiasability properties are also discussed and proved in the full version of the paper. We now focus on computational full uniqueness of our scheme.

Computational Full Uniqueness. For the computational full uniqueness property, the following are the two main requirements:

- hardness of $\mathsf{MSIS}_{q,n,n+\ell+k,\gamma}$ for $\gamma = 8\kappa\beta\sqrt{n+\ell+k}$,
  - Looking ahead, this implies that (13) below holds without mod q and therefore also over $\bar{\mathcal{R}}_p$.
- any challenge difference is invertible in $\bar{\mathcal{R}}_p$.

---

[2] https://eprint.iacr.org/2020/1222.pdf.

Theorem 31 (Uniqueness). *Let* $\gamma = 8\kappa\beta\sqrt{n+\ell+k}$ *for the parameters* $\kappa, \beta, n, \ell, k$ *defined in Table 3 and assume that* $\mathsf{MSIS}_{q,n,n+\ell+k,\gamma}$ *is hard with* $q > \gamma/2$. *Further, let* $p > 2^{20}$ *be a prime such that* $p \equiv 17 \bmod 32$. *Then, k-time LB-VRF construction satisfies computational full uniqueness in the random oracle model.*

Proof. Let $\mathcal{A}$ be a PPT adversary against computational full uniqueness of k-time LB-VRF construction. We will show that two valid VRF evaluations produced by $\mathcal{A}$ on the same input must be the same, or else the $\mathsf{MSIS}_{q,n,n+\ell+k,\gamma}$ problem is solved, which occurs with negligible probability by the assumed hardness of the latter problem.

Let $\mathbf{A} \xleftarrow{\$} \mathcal{R}_q^{n\times(n+\ell+k)}$, and G and H be two random oracles. Denote $pp = (\mathbf{A}, G, H)$ as the public parameters output by ParamGen. Then, $\mathcal{A}(pp)$ outputs two valid VRF proof-evaluation pairs (π_0, v_0) with $\pi_0 = (\mathbf{z}_0, c_0)$ and (π_0', v_0') with $\pi_0' = (\mathbf{z}_0', c_0')$.

Rewind 1: Using a standard forking argument, we rewind $\mathcal{A}$ to the point $c_0 = H(\mathbf{A}, \mathbf{t}, \mu, \mathbf{A}\mathbf{z}_0 - c_0\mathbf{t}, \langle \mathbf{b}, \mathbf{z}_0 \rangle - c_0 v_0, v_0)$ was queried, and return another challenge c_1 for the same input. With non-negligible probability, $\mathcal{A}$ produces another valid VRF output using c_1 such that $(\pi_1 = (\mathbf{z}_1, c_1), v_1)$ is a valid VRF proof-evaluation pair. Here, $\mathcal{A}$ may output a second valid pair, but we simply discard it.

Rewind 2: In a similar fashion as above, we rewind $\mathcal{A}$ to the point $c_0' = H(\mathbf{A}, \mathbf{t}, \mu, \mathbf{A}\mathbf{z}_0' - c_0'\mathbf{t}, \langle \mathbf{b}, \mathbf{z}_0' \rangle - c_0' v_0', v_0')$ was queried, and return another challenge c_1' for the same input. With non-negligible probability, $\mathcal{A}$ produces another valid VRF output using c_1' such that $(\pi_1' = (\mathbf{z}_1', c_1'), v_1')$ is a valid proof-evaluation pair. Again, $\mathcal{A}$ may output a second valid pair, but we simply discard it.

Overall, we have the following satisfied for $(\pi_0 = (\mathbf{z}_0, c_0), v_0), (\pi_1 = (\mathbf{z}_1, c_1), v_1), (\pi_0' = (\mathbf{z}_0', c_0'), v_0'), (\pi_1' = (\mathbf{z}_1', c_1'), v_1')$

$$
\begin{aligned}
&(\mathbf{A}, \mathbf{t}, \mu, \mathbf{A}\mathbf{z}_0 - c_0\mathbf{t}, \langle \mathbf{b}, \mathbf{z}_0 \rangle - c_0 v_0, v_0) \\
={}&(\mathbf{A}, \mathbf{t}, \mu, \mathbf{A}\mathbf{z}_1 - c_1\mathbf{t}, \langle \mathbf{b}, \mathbf{z}_1 \rangle - c_1 v_1, v_1),
\end{aligned}
\tag{2}
$$

$$
\begin{aligned}
&(\mathbf{A}, \mathbf{t}, \mu, \mathbf{A}\mathbf{z}_0' - c_0'\mathbf{t}, \langle \mathbf{b}, \mathbf{z}_0' \rangle - c_0' v_0', v_0') \\
={}&(\mathbf{A}, \mathbf{t}, \mu, \mathbf{A}\mathbf{z}_1' - c_1'\mathbf{t}, \langle \mathbf{b}, \mathbf{z}_1' \rangle - c_1' v_1', v_1').
\end{aligned}
\tag{3}
$$

The above two equalities implies the following

$$v_0 = v_1 =: v, \tag{4}$$

$$v_0' = v_1' =: v', \tag{5}$$

$$\mathbf{A}\mathbf{z}_0 - c_0\mathbf{t} = \mathbf{A}\mathbf{z}_1 - c_1\mathbf{t} \quad \text{over } \mathcal{R}_q, \tag{6}$$

$$\mathbf{A}\mathbf{z}_0' - c_0'\mathbf{t} = \mathbf{A}\mathbf{z}_1' - c_1'\mathbf{t} \quad \text{over } \mathcal{R}_q, \tag{7}$$

$$\langle \mathbf{b}, \mathbf{z}_0 \rangle - c_0 v_0 = \langle \mathbf{b}, \mathbf{z}_1 \rangle - c_1 v_1 \quad \text{over } \bar{\mathcal{R}}_p, \tag{8}$$

$$\langle \mathbf{b}, \mathbf{z}_0' \rangle - c_0' v_0' = \langle \mathbf{b}, \mathbf{z}_1' \rangle - c_1' v_1' \quad \text{over } \bar{\mathcal{R}}_p. \tag{9}$$

From now on, we stick to the notations v and v' due to (4) and (5). Rewriting (6) and (7), we get

$$\mathbf{A}(\mathbf{z}_0 - \mathbf{z}_1) = (c_0 - c_1)\mathbf{t}, \tag{10}$$
$$\mathbf{A}(\mathbf{z}'_0 - \mathbf{z}'_1) = (c'_0 - c'_1)\mathbf{t}, \tag{11}$$

Define $\bar{\mathbf{z}} := \mathbf{z}_0 - \mathbf{z}_1$, $\bar{\mathbf{z}}' := \mathbf{z}'_0 - \mathbf{z}'_1$, $\bar{c} := c_0 - c_1$ and $\bar{c}' := c'_0 - c'_1$. Multiplying (10) by $\bar{c}'$ and (11) by $\bar{c}$ and subtracting off the results, we get

$$\mathbf{A}\left(\bar{c}'\bar{\mathbf{z}} - \bar{c}\bar{\mathbf{z}}'\right) = \mathbf{0}. \tag{12}$$

Note that the following holds

$$\|\bar{c}'\bar{\mathbf{z}} - \bar{c}\bar{\mathbf{z}}'\| \le \|\bar{c}'\bar{\mathbf{z}} - \bar{c}\bar{\mathbf{z}}'\|_\infty \cdot \sqrt{n+\ell+k} \le 2 \cdot \|\bar{c}'\|_1 \|\bar{\mathbf{z}}\|_\infty \cdot \sqrt{n+\ell+k}$$
$$\le 2 \cdot 2\kappa \cdot 2\beta \cdot \sqrt{n+\ell+k} = 8\kappa\beta\sqrt{n+\ell+k}.$$

By the assumption that $\mathsf{MSIS}_{q,n,n+\ell+k,\gamma}$ for $\gamma = 8\kappa\beta\sqrt{n+\ell+k}$ is hard, we conclude from (12) that, except for negligible probability,

$$\bar{c}'\bar{\mathbf{z}} = \bar{c}\bar{\mathbf{z}}' \quad \text{over } \mathcal{R}. \tag{13}$$

The fact that there is no $\bmod q$ reduction comes from the following: $\|\bar{c}'\bar{\mathbf{z}}\|_\infty, \|\bar{c}\bar{\mathbf{z}}'\|_\infty < \gamma < q/2$.

Next, from (8), we get (replacing v_0 and v_1 with v)

$$\langle \mathbf{b}, \mathbf{z}_0 \rangle - c_0 v = \langle \mathbf{b}, \mathbf{z}_1 \rangle - c_1 v \quad \text{over } \bar{\mathcal{R}}_p,$$
$$\Longleftrightarrow \quad \langle \mathbf{b}, \bar{\mathbf{z}} \rangle = \bar{c}v \quad \text{over } \bar{\mathcal{R}}_p. \tag{14}$$

Similarly, from (9), we get

$$\langle \mathbf{b}, \bar{\mathbf{z}}' \rangle = \bar{c}'v' \quad \text{over } \bar{\mathcal{R}}_p. \tag{15}$$

Multiplying (14) by $\bar{c}'$ and (15) by $\bar{c}$, and then subtracting off the results, we get

$$\langle \mathbf{b}, \bar{c}'\bar{\mathbf{z}} - \bar{c}\bar{\mathbf{z}}' \rangle = \bar{c}\bar{c}'\left(v - v'\right) \quad \text{over } \bar{\mathcal{R}}_p. \tag{16}$$

Now since (13) holds over $\mathcal{R}$, by reducing $\bmod p$, it also holds over $\mathcal{R}_p$, and by further reducing $\bmod f$ it also holds over $\bar{\mathcal{R}}_p$. Therefore, the left-hand side of (16) is equal to 0. By the assumption on p and Lemma 2.3, any challenge difference is invertible in $\mathcal{R}_p$ and thus also in $\bar{\mathcal{R}}_p$. This implies that $v = v'$. $\quad\square$

4   Implementation

4.1   Implementation of LB-VRF

We implemented Set I parameters (see Table 3) of our LB-VRF using Rust language. The source code of our implementation is available on GitHub[3]. The

---

[3] https://github.com/zhenfeizhang/lb-vrf.

core operations are ring arithmetic over $\mathcal{R}_q$ and $\bar{\mathcal{R}}_p$, hash functions, and extendable output functions. We use SHA512 as our hash function, and ChaCha20 to extend hash digests into vector $\mathbf{b}$ and challenge c. For ring multiplications, we use index based method for polynomial multiplications involving secret keys or challenges (both are ternary polynomials); school book multiplication for $\bar{\mathcal{R}}_p$; and NTT multiplications for $\mathcal{R}_q$. We also hand-picked p, q and $f(x)$ for efficient mod reduction. We leave architecture-dependent optimizations, such as AVX2, to future work.

Our tests were conducted over a MacBookPro 2018, with an Intel(R) Core(TM) i7-8559U CPU @ 2.70 GHz. The benchmark was conducted with Rust's benchmark tool known as *criterion*. The benchmark data is shown in Table 1. One may see that although the speed of LB-VRF is on par with classical VRFs, the size is significantly increased. This is unfortunately an inherit drawback from the current state of post-quantum cryptography.

4.2   Integration into Algorand Blockchain

Algorand's TPS Model. To illustrate our benchmark results better, it is important to understand the bottleneck of the current Algorand protocol. Algorand's mainnet currently employs over 1000 nodes. A node is a whale holder of tokens and is likely to self-elect as a voter. Algorand allows for roughly 5.4 MB of "payload" transmission per round as a result of their efficient consensus protocol. To break up this data, 1000 nodes implies 1000 ECVRF proofs, which is 80 KB of data. It is straightforward to see that the majority of the data is reserved for transactions. If we assume that a transaction is 1 KB on average, with an additional 64 bytes of data for authentications, then Algorand allows for 5K transactions per block, or, roughly 1K transaction per second (TPS). Therefore, we estimate the Algorand TPS throughput as follows:

$$\mathrm{TPS}_1 = \frac{\text{payload size} - (\text{total VRF cost}) \times \#\text{nodes}}{(\text{transaction size} + \text{signature size}) \times \text{blocktime}}.$$

It is also important to distinguish two notions

- Blocksize: a block is a set of data that is agreed by all the participants. Typically, it consists of transactions.
- Payload: the data that is transmitted through the network, during a block time. Typically, it consists of transactions and VRF data.

Note that the VRF data are not included in a block. This is because, during the voting, different committee member may have different views of the (subset of) voters, and there does not need to be a global view. Alternatively speaking, the committee does not need to agree on all votes, as long as each committee member has seen enough votes.

Our Model. We envision that our k-time VRF may be deployed as follows. A user commits to a k-time VRF public key, pk_1, at round n via publishing a hash digest, along with a signature, of the public key. This allows her to use this VRF key at any round after $n+t$ (for a suitable parameter $t \geq 0$) via transmitting both the VRF public key and the VRF output to the other voters. Additionally, she similarly commits to $\lceil t/k \rceil - 1$ more public keys at rounds $n+1, \ldots, n+\lceil t/k \rceil - 1$ (i.e., $s := \lceil t/k \rceil$ public keys $\mathsf{pk}_1, \ldots, \mathsf{pk}_s$ are committed in total). This additional step is to make sure that the user can still participate in consensus right after the first public key pk_1 is consumed (without having to wait for t rounds).

Now at some round $n + t + i$ for $i \geq 0$, the VRF output is accepted if it is verified under the public key which hashes to the committed digest at round n. If the user has used k time of the VRF already, it needs to commit to a new public key and start using pk_2 in the next round(s). On the other hand, if the VRF output does not result into a winning ticket, the user does not publish anything, and thus, retains its ability to use the VRF key in future rounds. Overall, the user always has exactly s "usable" public keys committed on blockchain and uses the earliest committed key in creating the VRF output. The verifier therefore needs to scan the blocks starting from n to make sure that the user is using the first of s VRF public keys committed. This step prevents the users from choosing between committed public keys.

We remark that for a given round n_1, the user may choose not to publish its public key even if it wins the lottery, and therefore retains its current public key for a later round n_2. This also happens for ECVRF where the user can forfeit a winning ticket. This does not harm the security as long as the user cannot predict the VRF output for n_2. Our VRF protocol requires the user to commit to a VRF public key at least t blocks prior to using it.

Since our VRF data becomes non-negligible compared to the whole payload, for a fair comparison, we set the network payload size as an invariant in our estimation, rather than the blocksize. In addition, we also alter the content in a block. For a k-time VRF, the user needs to commit to the VRF public key several rounds prior to using it. This commitment must be recorded in a block.

Concretely, in our model, we further set $k = 1$ to minimize VRF cost, and have the following estimation:

$$\mathrm{TPS}_2 = \frac{\text{payload size} - (\text{total VRF cost} + \text{digest} + \text{signature}) \times \#\text{nodes}}{(\text{transaction size} + \text{signature size}) \times \text{blocktime}}.$$

Our Estimation. It is easy to see that our LB-VRF cannot scale to 1K nodes as 1K nodes already imply 8 MB of LB-VRF data (see below). We therefore compare our scheme with a maximum of 500 nodes. We note that although this number is smaller than the current status of Algorand, it is already sufficient for large blockchain platforms, and already exceeds the number of nodes of Algorand when it was launched.

Using the above formula, we computed estimates for the TPS of Algorand using our LB-VRF in combination with a variety of post-quantum signature schemes, in Table 2. In this computation, we make the following assumptions. We assume a payload size of 5.4 MB. Since our LB-VRF is a one-time VRF, we assume that in the Algorand consensus protocol, a node publishes both the

VRF output, as well as the next VRF public key the node is committed to use. Therefore, in the TPS estimation formula above, we take the total VRF cost to be the sum of LB-VRF's VRF size (84 bytes), proof size (4.94 KB), and public-key length (3.32 KB), which is around 8 KB, using parameter set I in Table 3. In addition, we also require 32 bytes hash digest for the next VRF public key, and a signature of various bytes (see below) to authenticate that VRF public key. As done for Algorand, we assume 1 KB data for a transaction size. As Algorand generates a block in about 5 s, we take blocktime as 5 s[4]. The last moving part in the equation is the signature size, which we set as 64 bytes for Ed25519, 700 bytes for Falcon[5], 2 KB for Dilithium [16], and 66 bytes for Rainbow[6].

Note that the post-quantum security of the signature scheme used in the consensus protocol is not of as a big concern as the VRF because the adversary cannot affect the consensus steps in the past by breaking the signature scheme. Therefore, until the quantum threat is imminent, one may opt to keep using Ed25519 as the signature in the hybrid "LB-VRF + Ed25519" mode, and switch to a post-quantum signature only when large-scale quantum computers are expected very soon.

Our Result. We test our LB-VRF with a modified version of Algorand's reference implementation [2]. Our tests were conducted over a testnet with a maximum of 8 nodes, due to the limitation of resources. We use pingpong package from [2] to initiate transactions with increasing rates till the network saturates. We deploy the test over ARDC Nectar Research Cloud. Each node is a m3.small instance with 2 vCPU, 30GB Disk and 4GB RAM. The results are summarised in Table 4.

We remark that the main purpose of this test is not to show how TPS progresses with increasing number of nodes, which will be largely dominated by the network topology. Indeed, the current behaviour is inconclusive in that respect. Instead, we want to observe the impact of replacing an ECVRF with an LB-VRF, for a same network setting. As expected, both the TPS and Tx per block is reduced slightly, for both local setting and cloud setting. The block generation time is slightly slower for the cloud setting due to the network latency. On the other hand, we only see marginal differences for block generation time between the ECVRF version and the LB-VRF version. For small networks, when the blockchain network cannot fully utilize the TPS, we argue that a LB-VRF based consensus is practical.

---

[4] This is a rough estimation in September 2020. Since then, Algorand has upgraded its consensus for faster block generation time.
[5] https://falcon-sign.info/.
[6] https://www.pqcrainbow.org/.

Table 4. Cloud experiment with variable number of nodes

Setting	Metrics	Algorand with ECVRF	Algorand with LB-VRF
2 Nodes	TPS	771	746
	Tx per block	3322	3251
	Block time	4.30 s	4.35 s
4 Nodes	TPS	941	836
	Tx per block	4255	3648
	Block time	4.52 s	4.36 s
8 Nodes	TPS	821	811
	Tx per block	3637	3525
	Block time	4.42 s	4.34 s

Acknowledgment. This work was supported in part by Australian Research Council Discovery Grant DP180102199 and also by use of the Nectar Research Cloud, a collaborative Australian research platform supported by the National Collaborative Research Infrastructure Strategy (NCRIS).

References

1. Abdalla, M., Catalano, D., Fiore, D.: Verifiable random functions from identity-based key encapsulation. In: Joux, A. (ed.) EUROCRYPT 2009. LNCS, vol. 5479, pp. 554–571. Springer, Heidelberg (2009). https://doi.org/10.1007/978-3-642-01001-9_32

2. Algorand: Goal: a reference implementation of Algorand. https://github.com/algorand/go-algorand

3. Algorand: Reference implementation of BLS signature. https://github.com/algorand/bls_sigs_ref

4. Algorand: Source code of ECVRF. https://github.com/algorand/libsodium

5. Banerjee, A., Peikert, C., Rosen, A.: Pseudorandom functions and lattices. In: Pointcheval, D., Johansson, T. (eds.) EUROCRYPT 2012. LNCS, vol. 7237, pp. 719–737. Springer, Heidelberg (2012). https://doi.org/10.1007/978-3-642-29011-4_42

6. Ben-Sasson, E., et al.: Zerocash: decentralized anonymous payments from bitcoin. In: IEEE Symposium on Security and Privacy, S&P, pp. 459–474. IEEE Computer Society (2014)

7. Bitansky, N.: Verifiable random functions from non-interactive witness-indistinguishable proofs. In: Kalai, Y., Reyzin, L. (eds.) TCC 2017. LNCS, vol. 10678, pp. 567–594. Springer, Cham (2017). https://doi.org/10.1007/978-3-319-70503-3_19

8. Boneh, D., Gentry, C., Lynn, B., Shacham, H.: Aggregate and verifiably encrypted signatures from bilinear maps. In: Biham, E. (ed.) EUROCRYPT 2003. LNCS, vol. 2656, pp. 416–432. Springer, Heidelberg (2003). https://doi.org/10.1007/3-540-39200-9_26

9. Boneh, D., Lynn, B., Shacham, H.: Short signatures from the Weil pairing. In: Boyd, C. (ed.) ASIACRYPT 2001. LNCS, vol. 2248, pp. 514–532. Springer, Heidelberg (2001). https://doi.org/10.1007/3-540-45682-1_30

10. Brakerski, Z., Goldwasser, S., Rothblum, G.N., Vaikuntanathan, V.: Weak verifiable random functions. In: Reingold, O. (ed.) TCC 2009. LNCS, vol. 5444, pp. 558–576. Springer, Heidelberg (2009). https://doi.org/10.1007/978-3-642-00457-5_33

11. Chase, M., Lysyanskaya, A.: Simulatable VRFs with applications to multi-theorem NIZK. In: Menezes, A. (ed.) CRYPTO 2007. LNCS, vol. 4622, pp. 303–322. Springer, Heidelberg (2007). https://doi.org/10.1007/978-3-540-74143-5_17

12. Chen, J., Gorbunov, S., Micali, S., Vlachos, G.: ALGORAND AGREEMENT: super fast and partition resilient byzantine agreement. IACR Cryptology ePrint Archive **2018**, 377 (2018)

13. David, B., Gaži, P., Kiayias, A., Russell, A.: Ouroboros Praos: an adaptively-secure, semi-synchronous proof-of-stake blockchain. In: Nielsen, J.B., Rijmen, V. (eds.) EUROCRYPT 2018. LNCS, vol. 10821, pp. 66–98. Springer, Cham (2018). https://doi.org/10.1007/978-3-319-78375-8_3

14. Dodis, Y.: Efficient construction of (distributed) verifiable random functions. In: Desmedt, Y.G. (ed.) PKC 2003. LNCS, vol. 2567, pp. 1–17. Springer, Heidelberg (2003). https://doi.org/10.1007/3-540-36288-6_1

15. Dodis, Y., Yampolskiy, A.: A verifiable random function with short proofs and keys. In: Vaudenay, S. (ed.) PKC 2005. LNCS, vol. 3386, pp. 416–431. Springer, Heidelberg (2005). https://doi.org/10.1007/978-3-540-30580-4_28

16. Ducas, L., et al.: CRYSTALS-Dilithium: a lattice-based digital signature scheme. IACR Trans. Cryptogr. Hardw. Embed. Syst. **2018**(1), 238–268 (2018)

17. Esgin, M.F., Nguyen, N.K., Seiler, G.: Practical exact proofs from lattices: new techniques to exploit fully-splitting rings. In: Moriai, S., Wang, H. (eds.) ASIACRYPT 2020. LNCS, vol. 12492, pp. 259–288. Springer, Cham (2020). https://doi.org/10.1007/978-3-030-64834-3_9

18. Esgin, M.F., Zhao, R.K., Steinfeld, R., Liu, J.K., Liu, D.: MatRiCT: efficient, scalable and post-quantum blockchain confidential transactions protocol. In: ACM Conference on Computer and Communications Security, pp. 567–584. ACM (2019). https://eprint.iacr.org/2019/1287

19. Fuchsbauer, G.: Constrained verifiable random functions. In: Abdalla, M., De Prisco, R. (eds.) SCN 2014. LNCS, vol. 8642, pp. 95–114. Springer, Cham (2014). https://doi.org/10.1007/978-3-319-10879-7_7

20. Ganesh, C., Orlandi, C., Tschudi, D.: Proof-of-stake protocols for privacy-aware blockchains. In: Ishai, Y., Rijmen, V. (eds.) EUROCRYPT 2019. LNCS, vol. 11476, pp. 690–719. Springer, Cham (2019). https://doi.org/10.1007/978-3-030-17653-2_23

21. Gilad, Y., Hemo, R., Micali, S., Vlachos, G., Zeldovich, N.: Algorand: scaling byzantine agreements for cryptocurrencies. In: Proceedings of the 26th Symposium on Operating Systems Principles, Shanghai, China, 28–31 October 2017, pp. 51–68. ACM (2017)

22. Goldberg, S., Naor, M., Papadopoulos, D., Reyzin, L., Vasant, S., Ziv, A.: NSEC5: provably preventing DNSSEC zone enumeration. In: NDSS 2015 (2015)

23. Goldberg, S., Reyzin, L., Papadopoulos, D., Včelák, J.: Verifiable random functions (VRFs). Internet Engineering Task Force, June 2020. https://tools.ietf.org/html/draft-irtf-cfrg-vrf-07

24. Goldreich, O., Goldwasser, S., Micali, S.: How to construct random functions (extended abstract). In: 25th Annual Symposium on Foundations of Computer Science, West Palm Beach, Florida, USA, 24–26 October 1984, pp. 464–479. IEEE Computer Society (1984)

25. Goyal, R., Hohenberger, S., Koppula, V., Waters, B.: A generic approach to constructing and proving verifiable random functions. In: Kalai, Y., Reyzin, L. (eds.) TCC 2017. LNCS, vol. 10678, pp. 537–566. Springer, Cham (2017). https://doi.org/10.1007/978-3-319-70503-3_18

26. Hanke, T., Movahedi, M., Williams, D.: Dfinity technology overview series, consensus system. arXiv preprint arXiv:1805.04548 (2018)

27. Hohenberger, S., Waters, B.: Constructing verifiable random functions with large input spaces. In: Gilbert, H. (ed.) EUROCRYPT 2010. LNCS, vol. 6110, pp. 656–672. Springer, Heidelberg (2010). https://doi.org/10.1007/978-3-642-13190-5_33

28. Hopwood, D., Bowe, S., Hornby, T., Wilcox, N.: Zcash protocol specification. Version 2020.1.14 [Overwinter+Sapling+Blossom+Heartwood+Canopy] (2020). https://github.com/zcash/zips/blob/master/protocol/protocol.pdf

29. Jager, T.: Verifiable random functions from weaker assumptions. In: Dodis, Y., Nielsen, J.B. (eds.) TCC 2015. LNCS, vol. 9015, pp. 121–143. Springer, Heidelberg (2015). https://doi.org/10.1007/978-3-662-46497-7_5

30. Langlois, A., Stehlé, D.: Worst-case to average-case reductions for module lattices. Des. Codes Cryptogr. 75(3), 565–599 (2015)

31. Libert, B., Ling, S., Nguyen, K., Wang, H.: Zero-knowledge arguments for lattice-based PRFs and applications to E-Cash. In: Takagi, T., Peyrin, T. (eds.) ASIACRYPT 2017. LNCS, vol. 10626, pp. 304–335. Springer, Cham (2017). https://doi.org/10.1007/978-3-319-70700-6_11

32. Lysyanskaya, A.: Unique signatures and verifiable random functions from the DH-DDH separation. In: Yung, M. (ed.) CRYPTO 2002. LNCS, vol. 2442, pp. 597–612. Springer, Heidelberg (2002). https://doi.org/10.1007/3-540-45708-9_38

33. Lyubashevsky, V.: Fiat-Shamir with aborts: applications to lattice and factoring-based signatures. In: Matsui, M. (ed.) ASIACRYPT 2009. LNCS, vol. 5912, pp. 598–616. Springer, Heidelberg (2009). https://doi.org/10.1007/978-3-642-10366-7_35

34. Lyubashevsky, V., Seiler, G.: Short, invertible elements in partially splitting cyclotomic rings and applications to lattice-based zero-knowledge proofs. In: Nielsen, J.B., Rijmen, V. (eds.) EUROCRYPT 2018. LNCS, vol. 10820, pp. 204–224. Springer, Cham (2018). https://doi.org/10.1007/978-3-319-78381-9_8

35. Micali, S., Rabin, M.O., Vadhan, S.P.: Verifiable random functions. In: 40th Annual Symposium on Foundations of Computer Science, FOCS 1999, 17–18 October 1999, New York, NY, USA, pp. 120–130. IEEE Computer Society (1999)

36. Miers, I., Garman, C., Green, M., Rubin, A.D.: Zerocoin: anonymous distributed E-Cash from bitcoin. In: 2013 IEEE SP 2013, pp. 397–411. IEEE Computer Society (2013)

37. Noether, S., Mackenzie, A.: Ring confidential transactions. Ledger 1, 1–18 (2016)

38. Papadopoulos, D., et al.: Making NSEC5 practical for DNSSEC. Cryptology ePrint Archive, Report 2017/099 (2017). https://eprint.iacr.org/2017/099

39. Sun, S.-F., Au, M.H., Liu, J.K., Yuen, T.H.: RingCT 2.0: a compact accumulator-based (linkable ring signature) protocol for blockchain cryptocurrency Monero. In: Foley, S.N., Gollmann, D., Snekkenes, E. (eds.) ESORICS 2017. LNCS, vol. 10493, pp. 456–474. Springer, Cham (2017). https://doi.org/10.1007/978-3-319-66399-9_25

40. van Saberhagen, N.: Cryptonote v 1.0 (2012). https://cryptonote.org/whitepaper_v1.pdf
41. Yang, R., Au, M.H., Zhang, Z., Xu, Q., Yu, Z., Whyte, W.: Efficient lattice-based zero-knowledge arguments with standard soundness: construction and applications. In: Boldyreva, A., Micciancio, D. (eds.) CRYPTO 2019. LNCS, vol. 11692, pp. 147–175. Springer, Cham (2019). https://doi.org/10.1007/978-3-030-26948-7_6
42. Yuen, T.H., et al.: RingCT 3.0 for blockchain confidential transaction: shorter size and stronger security. In: Bonneau, J., Heninger, N. (eds.) FC 2020. LNCS, vol. 12059, pp. 464–483. Springer, Cham (2020). https://doi.org/10.1007/978-3-030-51280-4_25

Practical Witness-Key-Agreement for Blockchain-Based Dark Pools Financial Trading

Chan Nam Ngo[1]([⊠])([iD]), Fabio Massacci[1,2]([iD]), Florian Kerschbaum[3],
and Julian Williams[4]([iD])

[1] University of Trento, Trento, Italy
channam.ngo@unitn.it, fabio.massacci@ieee.org
[2] Vrije Universiteit Amsterdam, Amsterdam, The Netherlands
[3] University of Waterloo, Waterloo, Canada
florian.kerschbaum@uwaterloo.ca
[4] Durham Business School, Durham, UK
julian.williams@durham.ac.uk

Abstract. We introduce a new cryptographic scheme, Witness Key Agreement (WKA), that allows a party to securely agree on a secret key with a counter party holding publicly committed information only if the counter party also owns a secret witness in a desired (arithmetic) relation with the committed information.

Our motivating applications are over-the-counter (OTC) markets and dark pools, popular trading mechanisms. In such pools investors wish to communicate only to trading partners whose transaction conditions and asset holdings satisfy some constraints. The investor must establish a secure, authenticated channel with eligible traders where the latter committed information matches a desired relation. At the same time traders should be able to show eligibility while keeping their financial information secret.

We construct a WKA scheme for languages of statements proven in the designated-verifier Succinct Zero-Knowledge Non-Interactive Argument of Knowledge Proof System (zk-SNARK). We illustrate the practical feasibility of our construction with some arithmetic circuits of practical interest by using data from US\$ denominated corporate securities traded on Bloomberg Tradebook.

Keywords: Blockchain-based dark pool · Witness-key-agreement · zk-SNARK · Quadratic Arithmetic Program · Designated-verifier

1 Introduction

Existing Blockchain-Based Financial Systems. Financial intermediation is traditionally based on trusted third party solutions, such as exchanges (e.g.

This research was conducted during the author's visit to the University of Waterloo.

N. Borisov and C. Diaz (Eds.): FC 2021, LNCS 12675, pp. 579–598, 2021.
https://doi.org/10.1007/978-3-662-64331-0_30

NASDAQ or CME) or clearing mechanisms (e.g. EU's TARGET2-Securities and US's Depository Trust & Clearing Corporation).

New technologies have been recently proposed to replace these intermediaries with distributed protocols on blockchain. See for example ZeroCash [36], a cryptocurrency, or FuturesMEX [33], a crypto-based distributed futures exchange, or the dark pool exchange with three parties [11]. In those systems, the users commit financial information (e.g. accounts, bids and quotes) to a blockchain and use zero-knowledge proofs to show that their committed information satisfy a certain relation to preserve the integrity of the market and the solvency of the users. Noticeably, anonymity in those systems is as critical as confidentiality, e.g. the linkage of one's transactions can lead to strategic attacks against them [32].

New Dark Pools Requirements. Private markets, i.e. dark pools, further reduce public information to protect large investors. The investor in a dark pool, who wants to sell at least v shares at price p, wants to disclose v and p only to traders who committed to have cash $c \geq pv$. Alternatively she might be willing to buy from somebody who has at least v' shares (an iceberg quote) or accept a price pegged within an interval, etc. For the very same reasons, the trader might not want to make his information fully public, but just to reassure the investor that he meets the constraints.

To make distributed dark pools possible, we propose *Witness Key Agreement* (WKA). In presence of a public blockchain holding parties' publicly committed information, WKA allows a party (the Verifier) to post a problem relation (e.g. a desired arithmetic or boolean combination of secret information) and securely agree on a secret key with another party (the Prover) holding a secret witness that *both* corresponds to the publicly committed information *and* satisfies the desired relation (i.e. the implicitly defined problem instance of the relation between the commits and the secret witness).

Witness Key Agreement. Given n parties each having committed their private information ω and published the respective commitments ϕ anonymously on a public bulletin board, we consider the problem that a party wants to securely and anonymously agree on a secret key k with each counterparty based on their committed information ω. The initiating party wants to make sure that (and the key agreement is only successful if) the counterparty's committed information ω satisfies a public relation R (given by the initiating party), i.e. $R(\phi, \omega) = 1$, while each counterparty does not want to disclose their ω.

With our problem we push further the envelope of Non-Interactive Zero Knowledge (NIZK) [22]. In both cases, given an instance and an NP-relation R, a party (the Prover) can convince another party (the Verifier) that there exists a witness ω of the instance ϕ such that $R(\phi, \omega) = 1$, without leaking information about it. The successful outcome of NIZK is the binary verification result 1 while our desired outcome is a shared secret key.

Anonymity-Preserving Communication Model. In our problem, we consider the anonymity of each party as critical as other WKA security properties. Therefore, our communication model assumes an anonymous network to hide the

Table 1. Dark pool example relations

In each relation we denote $[\![x]\!] = \mathsf{SHA256}(x; r_x)$ the public SHA256 commitment of the secret business variable x using randomness r_x. For a dark pool transaction we denote by c the cash capacity of a trader, c' the threshold given by the investor. For a bid we denote (p, v) as the bid price and the bid volume.

Sufficient Capacity (SC)	
Public $\phi = ([\![c]\!], c')$	Secret $\omega = (c, r_c)$
Conditions: $[\![c]\!] = \mathsf{SHA256}(c; r_c) \wedge c \geq c'$	
Price Range (PR)	
Public $\phi = ([\![p]\!], p'_+, p'_-)$	Secret $\omega = (p, r_p)$
Conditions: $[\![p]\!] = \mathsf{SHA256}(p; r_p) \wedge p'_- \leq p \leq p'_+$	
Matchable Bid (MB)	
Public $\phi = ([\![p]\!], [\![v]\!], p'_+, p'_-, c')$	Secret $\omega = (p, v, r_p, r_v)$
Conditions: $[\![p]\!] = \mathsf{SHA256}(p; r_p),\ p'_- \leq p \leq p'_+ \wedge [\![v]\!] = \mathsf{SHA256}(v; r_v),\ c' \geq pv$	

parties' identities (e.g., IP address) and all WKA communication must utilize the public bulletin board (e.g. a blockchain), i.e. to publish a message, a party sends it through the anonymous network to the public bulletin board which is readable by all parties.[1]

Practical WKA Construction. We base our WKA construction on the concrete efficient construction of zk-SNARK from Non-Interactive Linear Proof (NILP) [24] for Quadratic Arithmetic Programs (QAP) [19] given by Groth [24] and we utilize Linear-Only Encryption (LE) [6] to compile such NILP to a WKA scheme. We provide the *first practical Witness Key Agreement under designated-verifier zk-SNARK proof for QAP*. In our WKA scheme construction a designated verifier can first broadcast a common reference string as a challenge for the relation R of interest. A prover can then publish a partial zk-SNARK proof as a response for the committed instance that satisfies R. Using the partial proof, the verifier can derive a shared secret key with the prover.

Non-goals. The focus of our protocol design is to protect against *digital* attacks on integrity, anonymity and confidentiality. *Physical, economic and social* attacks are, and always will be, possible similarly to centralized systems (e.g. insider trading, cartels manipulating the underlying assets or the availability glitches such as the NASDAQ ones [38]) and they are typically dealt with by ex-post law enforcement [31].

2 Dark Pools as a Motivating Application for WKA

From a security perspective the constraints from the investor are easily captured by an NP-relation R as in Table 1 where the instance ϕ is the public information (i.e. the trader's commitment and the investor's constraints) and the witness

---

[1] WKA does not intend to hide whether the Prover/Verifier established communication as they are completely anonymous.

ω is the private information (the trader's committed information). An investor may look for traders with enough capacity and use the Sufficient Capacity (SC) relation in Table 1. A trader may ask the investor to show interest in some price ranges, e.g. from p'_- to p'_+ using the Price Range (PR) relation and in addition check the consistency of the challenged threshold using Matchable Bid (MB), if the investor has previously committed to desired bid price p and volume v, where $c' \geq pv$. Thus, the investor can simply post the relation R and use WKA to securely agree on a secret key with each interested and eligible trader holding a secret witness ω (to their committed instance ϕ) that satisfies the desired relation, i.e. $R(\phi, \omega) = 1$. Each agreed key can then be used for the negotiation (usually a conversation, not just a single message) of the offer between the investor and each eligible trader.

Our WKA construction also aims for succinct communication which is important when using a distributed ledger. The committed information (the instance) is also frequently updated, while the relation R of interest may be persistent. WKA is advantageous in this case as it works efficiently with different instances of the same relation. Additionally, WKA allows the trader to send a message encrypted using the key along with the public response (that will be used by the verifier to reconstruct the key and decrypt the message). This may save one round and is key when executing over a blockchain.[2]

3   Related Work and Alternative Candidate Schemes

We summarize a comparison of WKA in terms of usability and efficiency against applicable alternative candidate schemes in Table 2. (We refer the reader to the Appendix A of the full version of the paper [34] for more details).

A *trivial (but wrong)* solution is to ask each prover to couple a public key pk with a zk-SNARK proof π for the satisfaction of the arithmetic relation R. The verifier can then encrypt the private offer with pk after verifying the proof π. Only the prover with the corresponding private key sk can decrypt. Since the decryption condition above says nothing about the validity of π, one cannot guarantee that pk is actually from the prover that produced π. Signature of Knowledge [25] (SoK), can be used to sign the public key pk. However, SoK delivers only pk of the prover thus allows only a one-way communication from the verifier to the prover. Further, the prover cannot make sure that the upcoming message encrypted with pk is from the verifier: as pk is public, anyone can see it

---

[2] One can argue that there could be DDOS attacks where an attacker can post either malformed offers, or correctly formed ones but they have no intention of filling, to the blockchain. In the first case, as the Verifier only needs to forge the last proof element F (1) while the Prover has to compute the full proof $(4(m-1+3n))$ as shown in Table 3, such an attack will require tremendous effort from the Prover but not so much from the Verifier. In the second case, unfortunately we cannot solve this as it exists even in the centralized system. A trader/investor can post an offer, and cancel it before it is filled or immediately in the next round. However, at the point the offer was posted, the exchange cannot know whether the offer will be canceled or not.

Table 2. Comparison of solutions

n is the number of parties. The comparison criteria include: (i) **A**: is anonymous communication supported? (ii) **PB**: does the solution satisfies proportional burdern, i.e. only the involved parties perform the computation? (iii) **DL**: does the solution considers the information bound on a distributed ledger? (iv) **AC**: are arithmetic circuits supported? (v) **BR**: blockchain-round complexity, i.e. the number of rounds happen on the blockchain; (vi) **BC**: blockchain-communication complexity, i.e. the size of the data communicated through the blockchain; and (vii) **C**: computational complexity.

Solution	A	PB	DL	AC	BR	BC	C
Full MPC [27]	y		y	y	13	$O(n^2)$	$O(n^2)$
2-3 Servers MPC [11]		y		y	N/A	N/A	$O(1)$
Paired 2PC [27]	y		y	y	2	$O(n)$	$O(n)$
Practical WE [18]	y	y	y		1	$O(1)$	$O(1)$
Practical AKE [26]	y	y	y		2	$O(1)$	$O(1)$
WKA (ours)	y	y	y	y	2	$O(1)$	$O(1)$

Full MPC fails proportional burden, yields an unacceptable 13 rounds of blockchain communication and have a high communication and computational complexity ($O(n^2)$). Using 2-3 servers MPC, one obtains better efficiency (no communication over blockchain; communication and computational complexity stay constant w.r.t n). Yet, it does not leverage existing ledgers; and anonymity, which is critical, is not guaranteed. Paired 2PC yields a desirable 2 rounds of blockchain communication. However, in order to guarantee anonymity, it fails proportional burden; the communication and computational complexity also become unacceptable ($O(n)$). Practical WE and AKE only supports algebraic relations. WKA is practical and satisfies all requirements.

and send a message to the prover using pk. Other similar generic constructions are generally based on the modification of R to include a transformation of k_r. Our WKA scheme uses directly R which yields a lower bound of circuit complexity. Besides, those approaches usually require full proof verification (that involves pairings, e.g. 5 as in [24]), which is more costly than our construction, where the Verifier directly forges the last proof element (only computation in the field F) and it even stops 1 step early.

Secure Multiparty Computation (MPC) [12] can be a general solution but is with either usability and efficiency issues. Firstly, setting up an MPC using existing distributed ledgers is not trivial as every party must be known in advanced or a PKI must be available in the setup phase for securing the communication over the ledger, e.g. as in [8]. Additionally, general Full MPC (where n parties join the computation, e.g. [27]) yields an unacceptable 13 rounds of blockchain communication; while the 2–3 Servers MPC (where n parties secret share their private inputs to the servers and let them perform the computation, e.g. [11]) and Paired 2PC (where the verifier contacts and perform a 2PC with each other party, e.g. [27]) fail to guarantee anonymity which can be critical [32].

Authenticated key exchanges (AKE) [5,9] only support relations on credentials. Here we have other relations among values not related to credentials as they can change dynamically. Language-AKE [26] is more flexible but it does not support non-algebraic relations such as SHA-256 employed by ZeroCash [36]. One can also use Witness Encryption [18] (WE) with the desired arithmetic relation R, and only the provers who possess the witness ω for that instance ϕ such that $R(\phi, \omega) = 1$ could decrypt. However, general WE constructions [3,16,17,20] are impractical while practical WE under a GS proof [13] cannot support arithmetic relation of depth greater than 1, e.g. SHA-256 as employed by ZeroCash [36]).

4   Witness Key Agreement

Notations. A multivariate polynomial $t : \mathbb{F}^m \to \mathbb{F}$ over a finite field $\mathbb{F}$ has a degree d if the degree of each monomial in t is at most d and a monomial has degree d. A multivalued multivariate polynomial $\mathbf{t} : \mathbb{F}^m \to \mathbb{F}^\mu$ is a vector of polynomials $(t_1, \ldots, t_\mu)$ where each $t_i : \mathbb{F}^m \to \mathbb{F}$ is a multivariate polynomial. We denote a scalar by x and a vector by $\mathbf{x}$. We write $x \leftarrow \mathbb{X}$ when picking an element x uniformly from a finite set $\mathbb{X}$. We write $y \leftarrow \mathsf{A}(x)$ when picking the randomness r and returning $y = \mathsf{A}(x; r)$. $\Pr[\epsilon | \Omega]$ denotes the probability of an event ϵ over the probability space Ω. We denote the security parameter by 1^λ in the unary form and the negligible function as $\mathsf{negl}(\cdot)$. Given two probability functions $f, g : \mathbb{N} \to [0,1]$ we write $f(\lambda) \approx g(\lambda)$ when $|f(\lambda) - g(\lambda)| = O(\lambda^{-c})$ for every constant $c > 0$. We say that f is *negligible* when $f(\lambda) \approx 0$.

Remark 1 (Generation of the relation R). We follow the notation of Groth [24] so that a relation generator $\mathcal{R}$ receives a security parameter 1^λ and returns a polynomial-time decidable binary relation R, i.e. $R \leftarrow \mathcal{R}(1^\lambda)$. Hence for notational simplicity we can assume 1^λ can be deduced from R.

Definition 1 (Witness Key Agreement). *Let L be an NP-language with the witness relation $R(\phi, \omega)$. We call ϕ an instance of L and ω a witness for ϕ. A Witness Key Agreement (WKA) scheme Ω for L is a tuple of polynomial-time algorithms (*KChallenge, KResponse, KDerive*):*

$(\mathsf{p}_c, \mathsf{s}_c) \leftarrow \mathsf{KChallenge}(R)$ *is run by the verifier and takes as input the relation R (from which the security parameter 1^λ can be deduced), outputs a public and a secret challenge parameter $(\mathsf{p}_c, \mathsf{s}_c)$.*

$(\mathsf{p}_r, \mathsf{k}_r) \leftarrow \mathsf{KResponse}(R, \mathsf{p}_c, \phi, \omega)$ *is run by the prover with inputs the relation R, the public challenge parameter p_c, the instance ϕ, and the corresponding witness ω, outputs a public response parameter p_r and a secret key k_r.*

$\{\mathsf{k}_c, \perp\} \leftarrow \mathsf{KDerive}(R, \mathsf{s}_c, \phi, \mathsf{p}_r)$ *is run by the verifier and takes as input the relation R, the secret challenge parameter s_c, the instance ϕ and the public response parameter p_r, outputs a key k_c or $\perp$ (Fig. 1).*

Security Properties. WKA is closely related to Non-Interactive Zero-Knowledge (NIZK) Proof System. The key difference is the outcome of NIZK is only a binary verification result while WKA's outcome is a key upon success. Hence the security properties of WKA are also very similar to those of NIZK. Furthermore, we require WKA to be secure against MITM attack. (See

Perfect Correctness Given a true instance, the key agreement is successful, i.e.

$$\Pr\left[k_c = k_r \,\middle|\, \begin{matrix} R \leftarrow \mathcal{R}(1^\lambda) \\ R(\phi,\omega) = 1 \end{matrix} \,\middle|\, \begin{matrix} (\mathsf{p}_c, \mathsf{s}_c) \leftarrow \mathsf{KChallenge}(R) \\ (\mathsf{p}_r, k_r) \leftarrow \mathsf{KResponse}(R, \mathsf{p}_c, \phi, \omega) \\ k_c \leftarrow \mathsf{KDerive}(R, \mathsf{s}_c, \phi, \mathsf{p}_r) \end{matrix}\right] = 1 \qquad (1)$$

Computational Adaptive Knowledge Soundness The key agreement is successful only with negligible probability if the prover knows no witness for the instance, i.e. for any PPT $\hat{\mathcal{A}}$, there exists a poly-time extractor $\epsilon_{\hat{\mathcal{A}}}$

$$\Pr\left[\begin{matrix} R(\phi,\omega) \neq 1 \\ k_c = k_r \end{matrix} \,\middle|\, \begin{matrix} R \leftarrow \mathcal{R}(1^\lambda) \\ (\mathsf{p}_c, \mathsf{s}_c) \leftarrow \mathsf{KChallenge}(R) \\ (\phi, \mathsf{p}_r, k_r) \leftarrow \hat{\mathcal{A}}(R, \mathsf{p}_c) \\ k_c \leftarrow \mathsf{KDerive}(R, \mathsf{s}_c, \phi, \mathsf{p}_r) \\ \omega \leftarrow \epsilon_{\hat{\mathcal{A}}}(R, \phi, \mathsf{p}_r, k_c) \end{matrix}\right] < \mathsf{negl}(\lambda) \qquad (2)$$

Perfect Honest Verifier Zero-knowledge The response leaks nothing about the witness in the honest setup, i.e. there is a simulator $\mathcal{S}_{ZK}$ that outputs a simulated response (p_r, k_r) and key k_c. Formally, for all $\lambda \in \mathbb{N}$, $R \leftarrow \mathcal{R}(1^\lambda)$, $R(\phi,\omega) = 1$ and any PPT $\hat{\mathcal{A}}$:

$$\Pr\left[\hat{\mathcal{A}}(R, \mathsf{p}_c, \mathsf{s}_c, \phi, \mathsf{p}_r, k_c) = 1 \,\middle|\, \begin{matrix} (\mathsf{p}_c, \mathsf{s}_c) \leftarrow \mathsf{KChallenge}(R) \\ (\mathsf{p}_r, k_r) \leftarrow \mathsf{KResponse}(R, \mathsf{p}_c, \phi, \omega) \\ k_c \leftarrow \mathsf{KDerive}(R, \mathsf{s}_c, \phi, \mathsf{p}_r) \end{matrix}\right] \qquad (3)$$

$$= \Pr\left[\hat{\mathcal{A}}(R, \mathsf{p}_c, \mathsf{s}_c, \phi, \mathsf{p}_r, k_c) = 1 \,\middle|\, \begin{matrix} (\mathsf{p}_c, \mathsf{s}_c) \leftarrow \mathsf{KChallenge}(R) \\ (\mathsf{p}_r, k_r, k_c) \leftarrow \mathcal{S}_{ZK}(R, \mathsf{p}_c, \mathsf{s}_c, \phi) \end{matrix}\right]$$

Perfect Response and Key Indistinguishability The public response and the agreed key can be simulated without knowledge of a witness, i.e. for all $\lambda \in \mathbb{N}$, $R \leftarrow \mathcal{R}(1^\lambda)$, $R(\phi,\omega) = 1$ there is a simulator $\mathcal{S}_{RKI}$ s.t. for any PPT $\hat{\mathcal{A}}$:

$$\Pr\left[\hat{\mathcal{A}}(R, \mathsf{p}_c, \phi, \mathsf{p}_r, k_r) = 1 \,\middle|\, \begin{matrix} (\mathsf{p}_c, \mathsf{s}_c) \leftarrow \mathsf{KChallenge}(R) \\ (\mathsf{p}_r, k_r) \leftarrow \mathsf{KResponse}(R, \mathsf{p}_c, \phi, \omega) \end{matrix}\right]$$
$$= \Pr\left[\hat{\mathcal{A}}(R, \mathsf{p}_c, \phi, \mathsf{p}_r, k_r) = 1 \,\middle|\, \begin{matrix} (\mathsf{p}_c, \mathsf{s}_c) \leftarrow \mathsf{KChallenge}(R) \\ (\mathsf{p}_r, k_r) \leftarrow \mathcal{S}_{RKI}(R, \mathsf{p}_c, \phi) \end{matrix}\right] \qquad (4)$$

Security against Man-In-The-Middle Attack The key agreement is successful only with negligible probability under Man-In-The-Middle Attack, i.e. for any PPT $\hat{\mathcal{A}}$:

$$\Pr\left[k_c = k_r' \,\middle|\, \begin{matrix} R \leftarrow \mathcal{R}(1^\lambda) \\ R(\phi,\omega) = 1 \end{matrix} \,\middle|\, \begin{matrix} (\mathsf{p}_c, \mathsf{s}_c) \leftarrow \mathsf{KChallenge}(R) \\ (\mathsf{p}_c', \mathsf{s}_c') \leftarrow \mathsf{KChallenge}(R) \\ (\mathsf{p}_r, k_r) \leftarrow \mathsf{KResponse}(R, \mathsf{p}_c', \phi, \omega) \\ (\mathsf{p}_r', k_r') \leftarrow \hat{\mathcal{A}}(R, \mathsf{p}_c, \mathsf{p}_c', \mathsf{s}_c', \mathsf{p}_r, \phi) \\ k_c \leftarrow \mathsf{KDerive}(R, \mathsf{s}_c, \phi, \mathsf{p}_r') \end{matrix}\right] < \mathsf{negl}(\lambda) \quad (5)$$

Fig. 1. Security of witness key agreement scheme

Appendix B of [34] for a trivial WKA generic construction that is insecure under MITM attack.)

WKA Construction Roadmap. We base our WKA construction on the efficient construction of zk-SNARK from Non-Interactive Linear Proof (NILP) [24] for Quadratic Arithmetic Programs (QAP) [19] given by Groth [24] and we utilize Linear-Only Encryption (LE) [6] to compile such NILP to a WKA scheme.

Linear Interactive Proofs (LIP) [6] is an extension of interactive proofs [23] in which each prover's message is an *affine combination* of the previous messages sent by the verifier.

Groth renamed the input-oblivious two-message LIPs into NILP [24] to clarify the connection between LIP and NIZK. NILP considers only *adversaries using affine prover strategies*, i.e. a strategy which can be described by a tuple $(\boldsymbol{\Pi}, \boldsymbol{\pi}_0)$ where $\boldsymbol{\Pi} \in \mathbb{F}^{k \times y}$ represents a linear function and $\boldsymbol{\pi}_0 \in \mathbb{F}^k$ represents an affine shift. Then, on input a query vector $\boldsymbol{\sigma} \in \mathbb{F}^y$, the response vector $\boldsymbol{\pi} \in \mathbb{F}^k$ is constructed by evaluating the affine relation $\boldsymbol{\pi} = \boldsymbol{\Pi}\boldsymbol{\sigma} + \boldsymbol{\pi}_0$.

Key Observation. The proof $\boldsymbol{\pi}$ obtained with NILP consists of k elements (by evaluating k linear functions[3] corresponding to the proof matrix $\boldsymbol{\Pi}$), in which the k-th element can be obtained in two ways given the first $k-1$ elements [24]: (1) On the prover's side, if $\boldsymbol{\pi}$ is valid then the first $k-1$ elements fully determine the last one; (2) On the verifier's side, the first $k-1$ elements can be used in a proof forging formula to obtain the last one. By the prover computing $\boldsymbol{\pi}$ and publishing the first $k-1$ elements of $\boldsymbol{\pi}$, both parties can agree on the last element to use as a shared secret key for secure communication.[4] With this observation we construct WKA from a new NILP notion: *split designated verifier NILP* (Sect. 5).

Succinct zero-knowledge non-interactive argument of knowledge (zk-SNARK) follows the relaxation from Perfect Soundness to Computational Soundness [21]. Bitansky et al. [6] also showed that NILP can be compiled into both publicly verifiable (verifier degree 2, using bilinear maps) and designated-verifier (using linear-only encryption scheme) zk-SNARK. Intuitively the prover computes the proof $\boldsymbol{\pi}$ as linear combinations of the CRS $\boldsymbol{\sigma}$ and the verifier checks the argument by checking the quadratic equations corresponding to the relation R.

Linear-Only Encryption (LE) scheme Σ (Bitansky et al. [6]), e.g. a two-ciphertexts variant of Paillier [35], is a tuple of polynomial-time algorithms (KeyGen, Enc, ImgVer, Dec, Add) where the ImgVer (image verification) prevents oblivious ciphertext samplings in the image of Enc using pk, i.e. this property prevents the adversary from encrypting plaintexts from scratch (see appendix E of [34] for further details), and Add is for evaluating linear combi-

---

[3] In the concrete construction by Groth [24] (see also Fig. 3), $k = 3$ and the proof matrix $\boldsymbol{\Pi}$ is represented as the coefficients of the linear functions.

[4] The concrete example of this observation can be seen in Fig. 3 in Sect. 6. The first two elements A and B (Eq. (7) and (8)) uniquely define C (Eq. (9)) and they can be fed into the proof forging formula (Eq. (11)) to get the 3rd element C which should be the same for either party.

nations of valid ciphertexts. An LE scheme satisfies *correctness, additive homomorphism, indistinguishability under chosen plaintext attack* (IND-CPA) and in addition *linear-only homomorphism* which essentially says that it is infeasible to generate a new valid ciphertext except by evaluating an affine combination of valid ciphertexts (via Add)[5]. Such LE scheme can be instantiated using existing encryption schemes. The security of an LE scheme relies on the assumptions of q-power Diffie-Hellman, q-power Knowledge of Exponent and q-power Knowledge of Equality [6].

For relation functionality and efficiency in WKA we leverage on *Quadratic Arithmetic Programs* (QAP) by Gennaro et al. [19]: an arithmetic circuit can be transformed into a system of equations that check the consistency of a set of instance variables ϕ and witness variables ω in a relation R. The consistency checker is compiled into zk-SNARK. Thus zk-SNARK for QAP covers applications that employ arithmetic relations of multiplicative depth larger than one such as SHA256. In our WKA construction the partial proof size is also succinct, as it has at most 3 elements regardless of R. Response computation and key derivation are efficient, i.e. only linear in QAP size.

Limitations of Our WKA Construction. Our WKA scheme, as any scheme, inherits the limitations of its components:, i.e. the designated-verifier zk-SNARK that is compiled from an NILP for QAP by Groth [24]. Firstly zk-SNARKs are not known to satisfy composability and therefore cannot be run out of the box in parallel in the design of larger protocols [30].[6] In a basic dark pool scenario we only consider sequential composition where each execution of WKA concludes before the next execution begins [10]. For extended scenario one might need to use other instruments to identify parallel runs as described in Principle 10 of security protocol design by Abadi and Needham [1]. However, note that we still consider security against MITM attack, which is important for key agreement protocols. Secondly our WKA scheme makes use of QAP [19] hence it is only as efficient as the circuit expressing the constraints. Finally, we opted for simplicity rather than making the WKA scheme subversion-resistant as this which would require the zero-knowledge property be maintained even when the CRS is maliciously generated (see Bellare *et al.* [4]). Abdolmaleki *et al.* [2] and Fuchsbauer [15] constructed subversion-resistant NIZK based on Groth's zk-SNARK construction [24]. However, both works consider only the publicly verifiable zk-SNARK construction based on bilinear groups. Our WKA construction requires

---

[5] This property formally guarantees that given a valid ciphertext π by an adversary, it is possible to *efficiently* extract the corresponding affine function (Π, π_0) that explains π. Such property is important for Knowledge Soundness of WKA.

[6] Users are advised to run the shared secret through a hash function modelled as a random oracle before using it as a key for any other cryptosystem.

designated-verifier zk-SNARK, and therefore those constructions are not applicable to our scheme. Hence, we consider only honest setups.[7]

5   WKA from NILP

We first define our *split designated verifier NILP* based on Groth's definition [24]. The CRS is first split into two parts (σ_P, σ_V) where σ_V is only available to the verifier. Subsequently, in proof computation we split the proof matrix $\Pi \in \mathbb{F}^{k \times y}$ into two parts: $\Pi_1 \in \mathbb{F}^{k-1 \times y}$ and $\Pi_2 \in \mathbb{F}^{1 \times y}$. The proof π is also split into $\pi_1 = \Pi_1 \sigma_P$ that consists of $k-1$ elements and $\pi_2 = \Pi_2 \sigma_P$ consists of the last element. This split of Π and π is not necessary in a zk-SNARK proof system but it is essential in our WKA scheme as we need to split the proof into two parts (See our key observation in Sect. 4).

Definition 2 (Split designated-verifier NILP). *Let L be an NP-language with the witness relation $R(\phi, \omega)$. We call ϕ an instance of L and ω a witness for ϕ. A split designated-verifier (split DV) NILP for L consists of the tuple of polynomial-time algorithms (*Setup, Prove, Verify, Simulate*):*

$(\sigma_P, \sigma_V) \leftarrow$ Setup(R): *output $\sigma_P \in \mathbb{F}^y$ and $\sigma_V \in \mathbb{F}^x$.*

$(\pi_1, \pi_2) \leftarrow$ Prove(R, σ, ϕ, ω): *obtain $(\Pi_1, \Pi_2) \leftarrow$ ProofMatrix(R, ϕ, ω) where $\Pi_1 \in \mathbb{F}^{k-1 \times y}$ and $\Pi_2 \in \mathbb{F}^{1 \times y}$ and output $\pi_1 = \Pi_1 \sigma_P$ and $\pi_2 = \Pi_2 \sigma_P$*

$\{0, 1\} \leftarrow$ Verify($R, \sigma_V, \phi, \pi_1, \pi_2$): *obtain $\mathbf{t} \leftarrow$ Test(R, ϕ) where $\mathbf{t} : \mathbb{F}^{y+k} \to \mathbb{F}^\eta$ is an arithmetic circuit corresponding to the evaluation of multivariate polynomials such that $\mathbf{t}(\sigma_V, \pi_1, \pi_2) = 0$ if π is valid..*

$(\pi_1, \pi_2) \leftarrow$ Simulate(R, σ_V, ϕ): *obtain $\mathbf{t} \leftarrow$ Test(R, ϕ) and solve $\mathbf{t}(\sigma_V, \pi_1, \pi_2) = 0$ for the output (π_1, π_2).*

where y, x, k, η and d are constants or polynomials in 1^λ (deduced from R [24]).

A tuple of PPT algorithms (Setup, Prove, Verify, Simulate) is a split DV NILP if it has perfect completeness, perfect zero-knowledge and statistical soundness against affine prover strategies.

Construction of Witness Key Agreement. We construct WKA from Split DV NILP as shown in Fig. 2. Below we describe the construction at a high level.

We first modify the LE scheme's encryption algorithm interface for explicit used randomness. We omit the randomness r and write only $[m] \leftarrow$ Enc(pk, m) in case r is not necessary in subsequent computation. We write $[m] =$ Enc(pk, m, r)

---

[7] Such an assumption can be relaxed by asking a TTP to generate the CRS (such as Bloomberg itself). Using a TTP for bootstrapping security protocols have been considered in literature, see for example HAWK [29]. This is a much weaker trust assumption than managing orders themselves because the generation of the CRS requires only the relation R and the public key for the encryption. Therefore such a TTP is only trusted to do the computation correctly. Without the private key, the TTP cannot learn additional information.

to incorporate the randomness directly into the encryption algorithm. Secondly we require that the additive homomorphism of LE applies to both the message and the randomness used, i.e. $\mathsf{Add}(\mathsf{pk}, \langle[m_i, r_i]\rangle, \langle\alpha_i\rangle)$ evaluates $[\sum \alpha_i m_i, \sum \alpha_i r_i]$.

The Challenge Phase. In KChallenge, the verifier generates a CRS $(\boldsymbol{\sigma}_P, \boldsymbol{\sigma}_V)$ from R (using a split DV NILP). The verifier then encrypts each elements $\{\sigma_{P,i}\}_{i=1}^{y}$ of the $\boldsymbol{\sigma}_P$ with an LE scheme (with key pair pk, sk). Additionally, we require the verifier to encrypt the randomnesses $\{r_{P,i}\}_{i=1}^{y}$ that are used for the encryption of the CRS $\{\sigma_{P,i}\}_{i=1}^{y}$ in KChallenge into $\{[r_{P,i}]\}_{i=1}^{y}$. Finally s/he publishes a challenge that consists of pk and the encrypted elements. The verifier keeps private sk of the LE scheme and the plain CRS $\boldsymbol{\sigma}_V$.

The Response Phase. Upon seeing the challenge, in KResponse, the prover computes a response by generating a valid proof $\boldsymbol{\pi}$ for the desired tuple (ϕ, ω) (using the proof matrix of the split DV NILP and the additive homomorphic operation Add of the LE scheme). When the prover evaluates the last encrypted element $[\pi_2, r_2]$ using the proof matrix $\boldsymbol{\Pi}_2$ and the encrypted CRS $\{[\sigma_{P,i}]\}_{i=1}^{y}$, by the additively homomorphic property of the LE scheme, s/he can also evaluate the ciphertext $[r_2]$ of the randomness r_2 of the encrypted $[\pi_2, r_2]$ using the same $\boldsymbol{\Pi}_2$ and $\{[r_{P,i}]\}$. The prover publishes the first encrypted $k-1$ elements $\{[\pi_{1,j}, r_{1,j}]\}_{j=1}^{k-1}$ and the encrypted randomness $[r_2]$ as a public response and keeps secret the last encrypted element $[\pi_2, r_2]$.

Following Groth [24] we assume 1^λ can be deduced from R.

$(\mathsf{p}_c, \mathsf{s}_c) \leftarrow \mathsf{KChallenge}(R)$ runs as follows.
1. Fix a linear-only encryption scheme Σ;
2. Run $(\mathsf{pk}, \mathsf{sk}) \leftarrow \Sigma.\mathsf{KeyGen}(1^\lambda)$ where 1^λ is the security parameter deduced from R (see Remark 1); and $(\boldsymbol{\sigma}_P, \boldsymbol{\sigma}_V) \leftarrow \mathsf{Setup}(R)$;
3. Encrypt $[\sigma_{P,i}, r_{P,i}] \leftarrow \Sigma.\mathsf{Enc}(\mathsf{pk}, \sigma_{P,i})$ for each $\sigma_{P,i} \in \boldsymbol{\sigma}_P$;
4. Encrypt $[r_{P,i}] \leftarrow \Sigma.\mathsf{Enc}(\mathsf{pk}, r_{P,i})$ for each $r_{P,i}$ above;
5. Return $\mathsf{p}_c = (\mathsf{pk}, \{[\sigma_{P,i}, r_{P,i}]\}_{i=1}^{y}, \{[r_{P,i}]\}_{i=1}^{y})$ and $\mathsf{s}_c = (\mathsf{sk}, \boldsymbol{\sigma}_V)$.

$(\mathsf{p}_r, \mathsf{k}_r) \leftarrow \mathsf{KResponse}(R, \mathsf{p}_c, \phi, \omega)$: Upon receiving the challenge p_c,
1. Run $(\boldsymbol{\Pi}_1, \boldsymbol{\Pi}_2) \leftarrow \mathsf{ProofMatrix}(\phi, \omega | R)$;
2. Compute $\{[\pi_{1,j}, r_{1,j}]\}_{j=1}^{k-1} = \boldsymbol{\Pi}_1(\{[\sigma_{P,i}, r_{P,i}]\}_{i=1}^{y})$ (with $\Sigma.\mathsf{Add}$);
3. Compute $[\pi_2, r_2] = \boldsymbol{\Pi}_2(\{[\sigma_{P,i}, r_{P,i}]\}_{i=1}^{y})$ (with $\Sigma.\mathsf{Add}$);
4. Compute $[r_2] = \boldsymbol{\Pi}_2(\{[r_{P,i}]\}_{i=1}^{y})$ (with $\Sigma.\mathsf{Add}$);
5. Return $\mathsf{p}_r = (\{[\pi_{1,j}, r_{1,j}]\}_{j=1}^{k}, [r_2])$ and $\mathsf{k}_r = [\pi_2, r_2]$.

$\{\mathsf{k}_c, \perp\} \leftarrow \mathsf{KDerive}(R, \mathsf{s}_c, \phi, \mathsf{p}_r)$ Output $\perp$ if any verification fails:
1. Verify $\mathsf{ImgVer}(\mathsf{sk}, [\pi_{1,j}, r_{1,j}]) = 1$ for $1 \le j \le k-1$; and $\mathsf{ImgVer}(\mathsf{sk}, [r_2]) = 1$;
2. Decrypt $\pi_{1,j} = \Sigma.\mathsf{Dec}(\mathsf{sk}, [\pi_{1,j}, r_{1,j}])$ for $1 \le j \le k-1$;
3. Obtain $\mathbf{t} \leftarrow \mathsf{Test}(R, \phi)$; use $\{\pi_{1,j}\}_{j=1}^{k-1}$ to solve $\mathbf{t}(\boldsymbol{\sigma}_V, \{\pi_{1,j}\}_{j=1}^{k}, \pi_2) = 0$ for π_2;
4. Decrypt $r_2 = \Sigma.\mathsf{Dec}(\mathsf{sk}, [r_2])$
5. Return $\mathsf{k}_r = \Sigma.\mathsf{Enc}(\mathsf{pk}, \pi_2, r_2)$ (r_2 as randomness).

Fig. 2. Construction of witness key agreement

The Key Derive Phase. When the verifier sees the instance ϕ and the corresponding response, in KDerive, s/he can decrypt the encrypted elements using sk to get $\{\pi_{1,j}\}_{j=1}^{k-1}$ and forge the last element π_2 using the plain CRS σ_V. The verifier then uses the evaluated $[r_2]$ to reconstruct the correct ciphertext $[\pi_2, r_2]$ of the last element, i.e. the verifier decrypts $[r_2]$ to get r_2 to use as the randomness in the final encryption of π_2 to get $[\pi_2]$. After that, both parties agree on the same $[\pi_2, r_2]$.

We refer the reader to Appendix C of [34] for the proof sketch of our main theorem as follows.

Theorem 1 (Security of WKA). *If Σ satisfies correctness, additive homomorphism, IND-CPA and linear-only homomorphism, and the underlying split DV NILP satisfies perfect completeness, perfect zero-knowledge and statistical knowledge soundness against affine prover strategies, then Ω satisfies correctness, adaptive knowledge soundness, honest verifier zero-knowledge, response and key indistinguishability, and security against man-in-the-middle attack.*

6   WKA from NILP Based on QAP

We recall the formal definition of Quadratic Arithmetic Programs (QAP) [19] and how to construct a NILP for QAP [24].

Definition 3 (QAP). *A quadratic arithmetic program $\mathbb{Q}$ over a field $\mathbb{F}$ for a relation $R(\phi, \omega)$ consists of three sets of polynomial $\{u_i(X), v_i(X), w_i(X)\}_{i=0}^{m}$ and a target polynomial $t(X) = \Pi_{q=1}^{n}(X - r_q)$ such that with $a_0 = 1$, $\phi = \{a_i\}_{i=1}^{l}$, and $\omega = \{a_i\}_{i=l+1}^{m}$, the following Eq. (12) holds.*

$$\sum_{i=0}^{m} a_i u_i(X) \sum_{i=0}^{m} a_i v_i(X) = \sum_{i=0}^{m} a_i w_i(X) + h(X)t(X) \tag{12}$$

where $u_i(X), v_i(X), w_i(X)$ are of degree $n-1$ and $h(X)$ is of degree $n-2$.

Remark 2 (QAP description). For convenience we follow the QAP description of Groth [24], we consider the QAP
   R, i.e.

$$(\mathbb{F}, aux, l, \{u_i(X), v_i(X), w_i(X)\}_{i=0}^{m}, t(X))$$

where $\mathbb{F}$ is a finite field; aux is some auxiliary information; $1 \leq l \leq m$; $u_i(X)$, $v_i(X)$, $w_i(X)$, $t(X) \in \mathbb{F}[X]$, $u_i(X)$, $v_i(X)$, $w_i(X)$ are of at most degree $n-1$. Such QAP defines a binary relation

$$R = \left\{ (\phi, \omega) \left| \begin{array}{l} a_0 = 1, \phi = \{a_i\}_{i=1}^{l}, \omega = \{a_i\}_{i=l+1}^{m} \\ \sum_{i=0}^{m} a_i u_i(X) \sum_{i=0}^{m} a_i v_i(X) \\ = \sum_{i=0}^{m} a_i w_i(X) + h(X)t(X) \end{array} \right. \right\}$$

We consider the QAP that defines a binary relation R as described in Remark 2. NILP for such QAP is defined as a tuple of polynomial-time algorithms (Setup, Prove, Verify, Simulate):

$(\sigma, \tau) \leftarrow$ Setup(R): Pick $\alpha, \beta, \gamma, \delta, x \leftarrow \mathbb{F}^*$. Set $\tau = (\alpha, \beta, \gamma, \delta, x)$ and σ:

$$\sigma = \alpha, \beta, \gamma, \delta, \{x^i\}_{i=0}^{n-1}, \left\{ \frac{\beta u_i(x) + \alpha v_i(x) + w_i(x)}{\gamma} \right\}_{i=0}^{l},$$

$$\left\{ \frac{\beta u_i(x) + \alpha v_i(x) + w_i(x)}{\delta} \right\}_{i=l+1}^{m}, \left\{ \frac{x^i t(x)}{\delta} \right\}_{i=0}^{n-2} \tag{6}$$

$\pi \leftarrow$ Prove$(R, \sigma, a_1, \ldots, a_m)$: Pick $r, s \leftarrow \mathbb{F}$ and compute

$$A = \alpha + \sum_{i=0}^{m} a_i u_i(x) + r\delta \tag{7}$$

$$B = \beta + \sum_{i=0}^{m} a_i v_i(x) + s\delta \tag{8}$$

$$C = \sum_{i=l+1}^{m} a_i \frac{\beta u_i(x) + \alpha v_i(x) + w_i(x)}{\delta} + \frac{h(x)t(x)}{\delta} + sA + rB - rs\delta \tag{9}$$

In NILP [24], $\pi = (A, B, C)$. In Split DV NILP, $\pi_1 = (A, B)$ and $\pi_2 = (C)$.
$\{0, 1\} \leftarrow$ Verify$(R, \sigma, a_1, \ldots, a_l, \pi)$: Output 1 iff:

$$AB = \alpha\beta + \sum_{i=0}^{l} a_i \frac{\beta u_i(x) + \alpha v_i(x) + w_i(x)}{\gamma} \gamma + C\delta \tag{10}$$

$\pi \leftarrow$ Simulate$(\tau | R, a_1, \ldots, a_l)$: Pick $A, B \leftarrow \mathbb{F}$, and output $\pi = (A, B, C)$ where:

$$C = \frac{AB}{\delta} - \frac{\alpha\beta}{\delta} - \frac{\sum_{i=0}^{l} a_i(\beta u_i(x) + \alpha v_i(x) + w_i(x))}{\delta} \tag{11}$$

Fig. 3. Split NILP for QAP based on Groth [24]

A split DV NILP for QAP can be directly reformulated as in Fig. 3 by modifying the Prove algorithm. We simply split the proof matrices into two matrices Π_1 and Π_2 where $\Pi_1 \in \mathbb{F}^{2 \times y}$ corresponds to the matrix used in Eq. (7) and (8) while $\Pi_2 \in \mathbb{F}^{1 \times y}$ corresponds to the matrix used in Eq. (9). Since the NILP in Fig. 3 is secure (see Groth's security proof [24, Theorem 1]), our split DV NILP is also secure (see Appendix D of [34]). We show in Fig. 4 how to construct Ω using a split DV NILP obtained from the NILP in Fig. 3.

We assume 1^λ can be deduced from R. Comparing to the original NILP in Fig. 3, our NILP does not make use of γ. As we only need Eq (7), (8), (9) and (11) that do not contains γ (γ is only needed in the verification equation Eq. (10)).

$(\mathsf{p}_c, \mathsf{s}_c) \leftarrow \mathsf{KChallenge}(R)$: Fix an LE scheme Σ (with key pair $(\mathsf{pk}, \mathsf{sk}) \leftarrow \Sigma.\mathsf{KeyGen}(1^\lambda)$), run $(\sigma_P, \sigma_V) \leftarrow \mathsf{Setup}(R)$ to obtain $\sigma_V = (\alpha, \beta, \delta, x)$ and generate $\{[\sigma_{P,i}, r_{P,i}] \leftarrow \Sigma.\mathsf{Enc}(\mathsf{pk}, \sigma_{P,i})\}$ and $[r_{P,i}] \leftarrow \Sigma.\mathsf{Enc}(\mathsf{pk}, r_{P,i})$ for each $\sigma_{P,i} \in \sigma_P$ where

$$\sigma_P = \alpha, \beta, \delta, \{x^i\}_{i=0}^{n-1}, \left\{ \frac{\beta u_i(x) + \alpha v_i(x) + w_i(x)}{\delta} \right\}_{i=l+1}^{m}, \left\{ \frac{x^i t(x)}{\delta} \right\}_{i=0}^{n-2}; \quad (13)$$

Return $\mathsf{p}_c = (\mathsf{pk}, \{[\sigma_{P,i}, r_{P,i}]_{i=1}^{y}\}, \{[r_{P,i}]_{i=1}^{y}\})$ and $\mathsf{s}_c = (\mathsf{sk}, \sigma_V)$.

$(\mathsf{p}_r, \mathsf{k}_r) \leftarrow \mathsf{KResponse}(\phi = \{a_i\}_{i=0}^{l}, \omega = \{a_i\}_{i=l+1}^{m}, R, \mathsf{p}_c)$: Upon receiving the challenge p_c,

1. Pick $r, s \leftarrow \mathbb{F}$;
2. Compute $[A]$, $[B]$, and $[C]$ (as well as $[r_2]$) using the affine functions in Fig. 3 (Eq. (7), (8) and (9)) on $\{[\sigma_{P,i}, r_{P,i}]_{i=1}^{y}\}$ (and $\{[r_{P,i}]_{i=1}^{y}\}$) with $\Sigma.\mathsf{Add}$;
3. Set $[\pi_{1,1}] = [A]$, $[\pi_{1,2}] = [B]$ and $[\pi_2, r_2] = [C]$;
4. Return $\mathsf{p}_r = ([\pi_{1,1}], [\pi_{1,2}], [r_2])$ and $\mathsf{k}_r = [\pi_2, r_2]$.

$\{\mathsf{k}_c, \perp\} \leftarrow \mathsf{KDerive}(R, \mathsf{s}_c, \phi, \mathsf{p}_r)$ outputs $\perp$ if any verification fails:

1. Verify $\mathsf{ImgVer}(\mathsf{pk}, [\pi_{1,j}]) = 1$ for $j = \{1, 2\}$;
2. Verify $\mathsf{ImgVer}(\mathsf{pk}, [r_2]) = 1$;
3. Decrypt $A = \Sigma.\mathsf{Dec}(\mathsf{sk}, [\pi_{1,1}])$; and $B = \Sigma.\mathsf{Dec}(\mathsf{sk}, [\pi_{1,2}])$;
4. Decrypt $r_2 = \Sigma.\mathsf{Dec}(\mathsf{sk}, [r_2])$;
5. Compute C as in Eq. (11) with A and B;
6. Return $\mathsf{k}_r = \Sigma.\mathsf{Enc}(\mathsf{pk}, C, r_2)$ (using r_2 as randomness).

Fig. 4. Witness key agreement for QAP

Table 3. Theoretical performance evaluation

Alg.	#Enc	#Dec	#Mult
KChallenge	$4(m - l + 2n)$	–	–
KResponse	–	–	$4(m - l + 3n)$
KDerive	1	k	–

m is the number of variables in a QAP, l is the number of instance variables, and $n - 1$ is the degree of polynomials in the QAP. The number of decryption k is construction dependent. In our case we have $k = 3$.

Theorem 2. *If the LE scheme Σ satisfies correctness, additive homomorphism, IND-CPA and linear-only homomorphism, then the construction in Fig. 4 yields a WKA scheme Ω that satisfies correctness, adaptive knowledge soundness, honest verifier zero-knowledge, response and key indistinguishability, and security against man-in-the-middle attack.*

7   Instantiation and Performance Evaluation

Instantiation. We choose to instantiate the linear-only encryption scheme Σ with a variant of the Paillier cryptosystem [35] similarly to Gennaro *et al.* [19] and Bitansky *et al.* [6] (see Appendix E of [34]).

Theoretical WKA Performance Evaluation. We can then estimate the theoretical performance of our WKA scheme Ω based on the number of encryptions, decryptions, and scalar multiplications for computing $\boldsymbol{\Pi}_1(\{[\sigma_{P,i}]\})$ and $\boldsymbol{\Pi}_2(\{[\sigma_{P,i}]\})$ (Table 3). Let m be the number of variables of a QAP, l be the number of instance variables, and $n-1$ be the degree of polynomials of the QAP. The KChallenge algorithm requires the generation of $\{[\sigma_{P,i}]\}$ hence $m - l + 2n$ encryptions on the investor's side. The KResponse algorithm requires only the proof computation on the trader's side which yields $m - l + 3n$ scalar multiplications. The above numbers are doubled to fix the malleability of the scheme (see Appendix E of [34]). It is then doubled again for computing the ciphertexts of the randomnesses. Finally the KDerive algorithm only requires k decryptions and one encryption on the investor's side. The proof size is also only 6 Paillier ciphertexts.

Baseline Performance. Paillier [35] is the main ingredient in our construction and its performance is well-studied in literature. Several optimization techniques were already present in the original paper [35], and Jost *et al.* [28] took a step further to improve the performance by orders of magnitude faster compared to a naïve implementation.

For the timing of the Paillier encryption scheme we use the data from Table 4 by Jost *et al.* [28] *as an upper bound*[8] for the encryption time. The numbers were obtained on an Intel i7-4600U CPU at 2.10 GHz with 4 cores running Ubuntu 64-bit v14.04. In particular, the reported result shows that, at 2048-bit key length, the encryption rate for 32-bit messages can reach 56 K/s at the cost of 5.7 s pre-computation time.

Table 4. Specific circuit evaluation

Relation R	m	$n-1$	$\mathcal{T}_C$ (s)	$\mathcal{T}_R$ (s)
SC	25821	28312	5.8	7.8
PR	26080	28572	5.8	7.9
PR'	26598	29094	6	8
MB	51382	56361	11.6	15.6

We support 2048-bit key length and provide 112-bit security. Recall m is the number of variables and $n - 1$ is the degree of polynomials of the QAP. SC and PR are used for our dark pool simulation.

---

[8] Benchmarked in 2015. As such, it provides a lower bound to our WKA performance.

Circuit Evaluation. We implement the relations SC, PR, MB and a new relation PR' which is the same as PR but with added check, e.g. $(p_1 < p < p_2) \vee (p_3 < p < p_4)$, in Table 1 as arithmetic circuits with the libsnark library [37] and measure the number of required variables m and the corresponding degree of the polynomials $(n-1)$. Finally the runtime of KChallenge and KResponse, the most costly for 138-bit security for guessing r [28], 2048-bit key length, using the 32-bit messages and the encryption rate as in Scheme 3 from Jost et al. [28]. The evaluation of the new PR' relation and the MB relation illustrates the scalability of WKA. PR' consists of 1 consistency check for 1 commitment (1 private variable) and 4 arithmetic conditions with public variables, while MB consists of 2 consistency checks for 2 commitments (2 private variables). MB is in fact a building block for more general relation: $c' > p_1 \cdot v_1 + p_2 \cdot v_2 + p_3 \cdot p_3 + \ldots p_h \cdot v_h$. This is usable for both Multi-bids Auction and Biometrics Sharing (Hamming distance between two extracted features). This will require $2h$ commitments as it scales linearly with the number of private variables.

As shown in Table 4, the performances of SC, PR and PR' are close as their circuit complexity are similar to each other, as SC, PR and PR' require only one commitment consistency check while MB requires two of them. Hence, the runtime of MB is approximately double that of the others. KChallenge ($\mathcal{T}_C$) requires only 5.8 s for the SC while PI takes only 5.9 s. After the KChallenge, the key-agreement with KResponse ($\mathcal{T}_R$) takes only 7.8 s for SC and 7.9 s for PR. Even if we add 1 s of one-way network latency into each message as we are employing an anonymous network (e.g. Tor) [14, Fig. 2]. The overhead of each WKA operation is lower than any known permission-less blockchain's block generation time (with Ethereum being the fastest at around 15 s).[9] Hence each step can be fit within a single block generation time.[10]

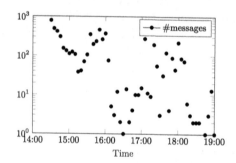

For an actual trade it requires multiple messages. For a high day, the number of messages can reach 14103 (with 55 trades). For a low day, the number of messages is only 4514 (with 53 trades).

Fig. 5. Example of Tradebook messages and trades (May 1st, 2019)

---

[9] https://ethstats.net/.

[10] In our protocol, the blockchain is the actual bottleneck. Looking at Table 4, the runtime of each step (including setups) is less than the block time of the fastest permissionless blockchain (Ethereum roughly generates a block every 15 s). Hence evaluating the interfaces of our scheme with the blockchain is equivalent to evaluating the blockchain itself. We should add that the current blockchain technologies is not adequate yet for high speed dark pools. Our major concern and main evaluation focus therefore is our scheme's crypto overhead.

Dark Pools Simulation. For our simulation we make use of the Bloomberg Tradebook [7] for the period 13/03–1/5/2019 (35 trading days).

The Tradebook only contains the number of messages and the number of trades per day (see Fig. 5). Using WKA, an investor can setup a secure conversation including multiple messages which eventually lead to a trade. This means that the number of conversations (i.e. the truly necessary WKA executions) can be much smaller than the number of messages in Fig. 5. These conversations can also happen in parallel if they belong to different trades (or traders). From the available data we cannot know exactly *which messages belong to the same conversation*, or *how many conversations there are* and *the point of time at which they happened* as this is the whole point of a Dark Pool. We therefore considered the *worst possible case* where each message is a conversation by itself (almost always ending nowhere) and they are executed sequentially one after another by a single trader. We also considered a more plausible scenario *one trade-one trader* where each trade is done by a different trader and all messages of the day eventually belong to some trade.

We can combine the number of messages and trades from the extracted market data (examples shown in Fig. 5) and Table 4 to estimate the corresponding execution overhead throughout a day of trading. The final results are reported in Fig. 6. Performance is evaluated in terms of execution overhead to the expected processing time (1 day) as in a realistic setting using actual trading data is at least comparable on a day by day basis: if we were to run a day of trading messages, we would expect it to not take more than a day to actually exchange those messages.

We combine the relations SC with PR and we consider the execution time of a message as the running time of SC's KChallenge (5.8 s). For trades execution time we consider the sequential execution of KResponse from SC and the whole challenge and response time of PR (21.6 s), adding the one-way delay of Tor (1 s) per message. As shown in Fig. 6, even under worst possible assumption, only 7 days out of 35 days require more than 1 day of execution in our simulation. With a less extreme approach (solid line) the overhead is smaller than 10%.

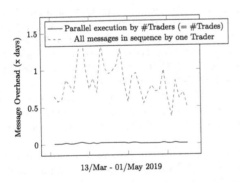

13/Mar - 01/May 2019

Assuming all computation done sequentially by 1 trader and messages are sent through Tor, only 7 out of 35 days of trading exhibits overheads greater than 1x in our simulation. With a more plausible scenario (each trade is done by a different trader) the overhead is at most 2%.

Fig. 6. WKA evaluation on bloomberg tradebook

8 Conclusion

We introduced the notion of witness-key-agreement. Specifically we defined split designated-verifier non-interactive linear proof following Groth's definition of NILP [24]. We then compiled the obtained split DV NILP into a Witness Key Agreement scheme using Linear-Only Encryption. Our obtained construction is efficient. After a one-time setup that yields a common challenge for a relation R of interest, a party can agree on a secret key with another party given that the latter knows a witness of a committed instance.

Finally, our concrete WKA scheme for quadratic arithmetic programs yields both succinct communication complexity, i.e. the response to the common challenge consists of only 3 encrypted elements (6 Paillier ciphertexts), and efficient response computation and key derivation, i.e. only linear to the QAP size.

Our scheme is particularly suitable for private auctions in financial intermediation in which one party wants to privately communicate with another party about committed financial information which satisfies a relation R of interest. It is also usable in other applications such as biometric-data sharing.

Our new notions, i.e. Witness-Key-Agreement and Split Designated Verifier NILP may be of independent research interest as well as interesting application of NILP.

Acknowledgements. We thank Ian Goldberg, Ivan Visconti, and the anonymous reviewers for their many insightful comments and suggestions. Chan Nam Ngo and Fabio Massacci were partly supported by the European Commission under the H2020 Programme Grant Agreement No. 830929 (CyberSec4Europe). Florian Kerschbaum was supported by NSERC grants RGPIN-05849, CRDPJ-531191, IRC537591, and the Royal Bank of Canada.

References

1. Abadi, M., Needham, R.: Prudent engineering practice for cryptographic protocols. IEEE Trans. Software Eng. **22**(1), 6–15 (1996)
2. Abdolmaleki, B., Baghery, K., Lipmaa, H., Zając, M.: A subversion-resistant SNARK. In: Takagi, T., Peyrin, T. (eds.) ASIACRYPT 2017. LNCS, vol. 10626, pp. 3–33. Springer, Cham (2017). https://doi.org/10.1007/978-3-319-70700-6_1
3. Abusalah, H., Fuchsbauer, G., Pietrzak, K.: Offline witness encryption. In: Manulis, M., Sadeghi, A.-R., Schneider, S. (eds.) ACNS 2016. LNCS, vol. 9696, pp. 285–303. Springer, Cham (2016). https://doi.org/10.1007/978-3-319-39555-5_16
4. Bellare, M., Fuchsbauer, G., Scafuro, A.: NIZKs with an untrusted CRS: security in the face of parameter subversion. In: Cheon, J.H., Takagi, T. (eds.) ASIACRYPT 2016. LNCS, vol. 10032, pp. 777–804. Springer, Heidelberg (2016). https://doi.org/10.1007/978-3-662-53890-6_26
5. Bellovin, S.M., Merritt, M.: Encrypted key exchange: password-based protocols secure against dictionary attacks. In: 1992 IEEE Computer Society Symposium on Research in Security and Privacy, pp. 72–84. IEEE (1992)

6. Bitansky, N., Chiesa, A., Ishai, Y., Paneth, O., Ostrovsky, R.: Succinct non-interactive arguments via linear interactive proofs. In: Sahai, A. (ed.) TCC 2013. LNCS, vol. 7785, pp. 315–333. Springer, Heidelberg (2013). https://doi.org/10.1007/978-3-642-36594-2_18

7. Bloomberg: Tradebook Bloomberg Professional Services (2019). https://www.bloomberg.com/professional/solution/tradebook/. Accessed 01 May 2019

8. Bonawitz, K., et al.: Practical secure aggregation for privacy-preserving machine learning. In: Proceedings of the 2017 ACM SIGSAC Conference on Computer and Communications Security, pp. 1175–1191. ACM (2017)

9. Camenisch, J., Casati, N., Gross, T., Shoup, V.: Credential authenticated identification and key exchange. In: Rabin, T. (ed.) CRYPTO 2010. LNCS, vol. 6223, pp. 255–276. Springer, Heidelberg (2010). https://doi.org/10.1007/978-3-642-14623-7_14

10. Canetti, R.: Universally composable security: a new paradigm for cryptographic protocols. In: 2001 IEEE International Conference on Cluster Computing, pp. 136–145. IEEE (2001)

11. Cartlidge, J., Smart, N.P., Talibi Alaoui, Y.: MPC joins the dark side. In: Proceedings of the 2019 ACM Asia Conference on Computer and Communications Security, pp. 148–159 (2019)

12. Chaum, D., Crépeau, C., Damgard, I.: Multiparty unconditionally secure protocols. In: The Twentieth ACM Symposium on Theory of Computing, pp. 11–19. ACM (1988)

13. Derler, D., Slamanig, D.: Practical witness encryption for algebraic languages or how to encrypt under Groth-Sahai proofs. Des. Codes Crypt. **86**(11), 2525–2547 (2018)

14. Dhungel, P., Steiner, M., Rimac, I., Hilt, V., Ross, K.W.: Waiting for anonymity: Understanding delays in the tor overlay. In: 2010 IEEE Tenth International Conference on Peer-to-Peer Computing (P2P), pp. 1–4. IEEE (2010)

15. Fuchsbauer, G.: Subversion-zero-knowledge SNARKs. In: Abdalla, M., Dahab, R. (eds.) PKC 2018. LNCS, vol. 10769, pp. 315–347. Springer, Cham (2018). https://doi.org/10.1007/978-3-319-76578-5_11

16. Garg, S., Gentry, C., Halevi, S.: Candidate multilinear maps from ideal lattices. In: Johansson, T., Nguyen, P.Q. (eds.) EUROCRYPT 2013. LNCS, vol. 7881, pp. 1–17. Springer, Heidelberg (2013). https://doi.org/10.1007/978-3-642-38348-9_1

17. Garg, S., Gentry, C., Halevi, S., Raykova, M., Sahai, A., Waters, B.: Candidate indistinguishability obfuscation and functional encryption for all circuits. SIAM J. Comput. **45**(3), 882–929 (2016)

18. Garg, S., Gentry, C., Sahai, A., Waters, B.: Witness encryption and its applications. In: 45th ACM Symposium on Theory of Computing, pp. 467–476. ACM (2013)

19. Gennaro, R., Gentry, C., Parno, B., Raykova, M.: Quadratic span programs and succinct NIZKs without PCPs. In: Johansson, T., Nguyen, P.Q. (eds.) EUROCRYPT 2013. LNCS, vol. 7881, pp. 626–645. Springer, Heidelberg (2013). https://doi.org/10.1007/978-3-642-38348-9_37

20. Gentry, C., Lewko, A., Waters, B.: Witness encryption from instance independent assumptions. In: Garay, J.A., Gennaro, R. (eds.) CRYPTO 2014. LNCS, vol. 8616, pp. 426–443. Springer, Heidelberg (2014). https://doi.org/10.1007/978-3-662-44371-2_24

21. Gentry, C., Wichs, D.: Separating succinct non-interactive arguments from all falsifiable assumptions. In: 43rd ACM Symposium on Theory of Computing, pp. 99–108. ACM (2011)

22. Goldreich, O., Micali, S., Wigderson, A.: Proofs that yield nothing but their validity or all languages in NP have zero-knowledge proof systems. J. ACM **38**(3), 690–728 (1991)
23. Goldwasser, S., Micali, S., Rackoff, C.: The knowledge complexity of interactive proof systems. SIAM J. Comput. **18**(1), 186–208 (1989)
24. Groth, J.: On the size of pairing-based non-interactive arguments. In: Fischlin, M., Coron, J.-S. (eds.) EUROCRYPT 2016. LNCS, vol. 9666, pp. 305–326. Springer, Heidelberg (2016). https://doi.org/10.1007/978-3-662-49896-5_11
25. Groth, J., Maller, M.: Snarky signatures: minimal signatures of knowledge from simulation-extractable SNARKs. In: Katz, J., Shacham, H. (eds.) CRYPTO 2017. LNCS, vol. 10402, pp. 581–612. Springer, Cham (2017). https://doi.org/10.1007/978-3-319-63715-0_20
26. Ben Hamouda, F., Blazy, O., Chevalier, C., Pointcheval, D., Vergnaud, D.: Efficient UC-secure authenticated key-exchange for algebraic languages. In: Kurosawa, K., Hanaoka, G. (eds.) PKC 2013. LNCS, vol. 7778, pp. 272–291. Springer, Heidelberg (2013). https://doi.org/10.1007/978-3-642-36362-7_18
27. Hazay, C., Scholl, P., Soria-Vazquez, E.: Low cost constant round MPC combining BMR and oblivious transfer. In: Takagi, T., Peyrin, T. (eds.) ASIACRYPT 2017. LNCS, vol. 10624, pp. 598–628. Springer, Cham (2017). https://doi.org/10.1007/978-3-319-70694-8_21
28. Jost, C., Lam, H., Maximov, A., Smeets, B.J.: Encryption Performance Improvements of the Paillier Cryptosystem. IACR Cryptology ePrint Archive **2015**, 864 (2015)
29. Kosba, A., Miller, A., Shi, E., Wen, Z., Papamanthou, C.: Hawk: the blockchain model of cryptography and privacy-preserving smart contracts. In: 2016 IEEE Symposium on Security and Privacy, pp. 839–858. IEEE (2016)
30. Kosba, A.E., et al.: How to Use SNARKs in Universally Composable Protocols. IACR Cryptology ePrint Archive **2015**, 1093 (2015)
31. Markham, J.W.: Manipulation of commodity futures prices-the unprosecutable crime. Yale J. Regul. **8**, 281 (1991)
32. Massacci, F., Ngo, C.N., Nie, J., Venturi, D., Williams, J.: The seconomics (security-economics) vulnerabilities of decentralized autonomous organizations. In: Stajano, F., Anderson, J., Christianson, B., Matyáš, V. (eds.) Security Protocols 2017. LNCS, vol. 10476, pp. 171–179. Springer, Cham (2017). https://doi.org/10.1007/978-3-319-71075-4_19
33. Massacci, F., Ngo, C.N., Nie, J., Venturi, D., Williams, J.: FuturesMEX: secure, distributed futures market exchange. In: 2018 IEEE Symposium on Security and Privacy, pp. 335–353. IEEE (2018)
34. Ngo, C.N., Massacci, F., Kerschbaum, F., Williams, J.: Practical Witness-Key-Agreement for Blockchain-based Dark Pools Financial Trading. IFCA Archive, 2021 (2021). https://fc21.ifca.ai/papers/113.pdf. Accessed 26 Mar 2021
35. Paillier, P.: Public-key cryptosystems based on composite degree residuosity classes. In: Stern, J. (ed.) EUROCRYPT 1999. LNCS, vol. 1592, pp. 223–238. Springer, Heidelberg (1999). https://doi.org/10.1007/3-540-48910-X_16
36. Sasson, E.B., et al.: ZeroCash: decentralized anonymous payments from bitcoin. In: 2014 IEEE Symposium on Security and Privacy, pp. 459–474. IEEE (2014)
37. SCIPR Lab: libsnark: a C++ library for zkSNARK proofs (2019). https://github.com/scipr-lab/libsnark. Accessed 01 May 2019
38. TheVerge: Data glitch sets tech company stock prices at USD 123.47. https://www.theverge.com/2017/7/3/15917950/nasdaq-nyse-stock-market-data-error. Accessed 01 May 2019

Author Index